Beneath the Mask

An Introduction to Theories of Personality

Eighth Edition

Beneath the Mask
An Introduction to Theories of Personality

Eighth Edition

Robert N. Sollod
Cleveland State University

John P. Wilson
Cleveland State University

Christopher F. Monte
Manhattanville College

WILEY

John Wiley & Sons, Inc.

Publisher	*Jay O'Callaghan*
Executive Editor	*Chris Johnson*
Assistant Editor	*Eileen McKeever*
Marketing Manager	*Jeffrey Ruckert*
Production Editor	*Barbara Russiello*
Senior Designer	*Kevin Murphy*
Illustration Editor	*Anna Melhorn*
Senior Media Editor	*Lynn Pearlman*
Photo Editor	*Sheena Goldstein*
Cover Design	*Kevin Murphy*
Cover Photo	*Infinity Limited*

This book was set in 10/12 Times Roman by Laserwords Private Limited, Chennai, India and printed and bound by Hamilton Printing Company. The cover was printed by Phoenix Color.

The book is printed on acid-free paper. ∞

To order books or for customer service, please call 1-800-CALL WILEY (225-5945).

Library of Congress Cataloging-in-Publication Data

Sollod, Robert N.
  Beneath the mask : an introduction to theories of personality / Robert
N. Sollod, John P. Wilson, Christopher F. Monte.—8th ed.
      p. cm.
  Includes bibliographical references and index.
  ISBN 978-0-471-72412-4 (cloth : alk. paper)
  1. Personality—Textbooks. I. Wilson, John P. (John Preston) II.
Monte, Christopher F. III. Title.
  BF698.M64 2008
  155.2—dc22

                                                    2007047634

Printed in the United States of America

10 9 8 7 6 5 4 3 2 1

Only connect

E. M. Forster, *Howard's End*

I have striven
Not to ridicule,
Not to decry,
Nor to scorn
Human actions,
But to understand them.

Baruch Spinoza

DEDICATION

To my wife,
Silvana Turkovic,
and my sons,
Matthew C. Wilson
and Michael J. Wilson

About the Authors

Christopher F. Monte, Ph.D., died in December 1998. He had long been a Professor of Psychology at Manhattanville College in Purchase, New York. Dr. Monte was known for his thorough and thoughtful scholarship, which is well represented in *Beneath the Mask*. His other books include *Psychology's Scientific Endeavor, Still Life: Clinical Portraits in Psychopathology* and *Merlin: The Sorcerer's Guide to Survival in College*.

Dr. Monte received master degrees from Fairfield University in Counseling and The New School for Social Research in Psychology, and his doctorate in Clinical Psychology from St. John's University. Dr. Monte was selected to write the section on "Theories of Personality" for the American Psychological Association's *Encyclopedia of American Psychology*, which was published posthumously in 2000.

Robert N. Sollod, Ph.D., was a Professor of Psychology at Cleveland State University. He received his B.A. in Social Relations from Harvard University, an M.A. from Duquesne University in their psychology program emphasizing existential phenomenology, and a Ph.D. in Clinical Psychology from Teachers College, Columbia University. Dr. Sollod studied with and interviewed many of the leading personality theorists about whom he has written in *Beneath the Mask* and elsewhere. Prior to moving to Ohio, Dr. Sollod taught at New York University and Yeshiva University.

Teaching at the college and graduate level, Dr. Sollod had been involved in wide-ranging scholarly activities and maintained a professional practice since 1974. Areas in which he published include the origins of personality theories and psychotherapeutic approaches, psychotherapy integration, spirituality and psychotherapy, and religion and higher education. He contributed the section on "Religious Experience: Religious and Spiritual Practices" in the American Psychological Association's *Encyclopedia of American Psychology*. He was a longtime member of the Society for the Exploration of Psychotherapy Integration (SEPI).

John P. Wilson, Ph.D., is a professor of Psychology at Cleveland State University. He received his B.A. in psychology at Baldwin-Wallace Collee, M.A. an Ph.D. at Michigan State University in personality and social psychology. Dr. Wilson is a coauthor with Joel Aronoff of *Personality in the Social Process*.

Dr. Wilson is an internationally recognized expert in posttraumatic stress disorder (PTSD) and cofounder of the International Society for Traumatic Stress Studies (ISTSS). He is the author and editor of more than 12 books on trauma and PTSD, including *The Posttraumatic Self: Restoring Meaning and Wholeness to Personality* and *Cross-Cultural Assessment of Psychological Trauma and PTSD* with Catherine C. So-Kum Tang.

IN MEMORIAM

Professor Robert Sollod passed away in 2005, after a long and courageous battle with kidney and heart failure. Dr. Sollod's creativity, brilliance, and concern for psychology and the spiritual life were sustained throughout the course of his illness until the end. Despite pain and suffering, he continued his research interests and became an advocate for those suffering from kidney failure and other diseases. He truly loved working on this book, *Beneath the Mask*, and regularly consulted with me as his colleague, asking for my input on specific theories and chapters which I discussed with him. Most of those revisions are reflected in Chapters 1–8, 13, and elsewhere. It was a joyful and intellectually engaging process for both of us. We had conversations in my office over coffee until the sad day came when he became critically ill. His wife, Ms. Jeanine Low-Beer, remained by his side until his last moments. It is an honor for me to serve as the transitional caretaker of this very fine textbook on personality theories.

John P. Wilson

Preface

Human nature has long been a matter of curiosity and great interest. People have always wanted to be able to understand and predict the behavior of others. The award-winning biologist and Pulitzer Prize recipient writer Edward O. Wilson coined the term *biophilia*, to indicate the human love for and fascination with the life around us. How much greater is our caring for and interest in other people and their lives.

Until the 1900s, accumulating and conveying the understanding of human nature was left to philosophers, writers, and historians. Educated people tried to fathom human nature not only through personal experience but also by studying Plutarch, Plato, Baruch Spinoza, and Arthur Schopenhauer, reading William Shakespeare and Charles Dickens, and studying the lives of historical figures. For all its depth and comprehensiveness, such knowledge did not provide any type of systematic or testable way of looking at human nature.

With the advent of modern psychology, new ways of trying to understand human nature came to center stage. The great personality theories we are studying here are the result of the endeavors in the past century to discover and formulate new understandings of personality. These "grand theories" represent humanity's relatively recent flowering of inquiry into personality and human nature. They provide fascinating insights that have affected the ways in which we experience life as well as our thinking and our behavior.

ABOUT *BENEATH THE MASK*

Theories of personality are psychological models of human nature that, with surprising frequency, reflect the nature of their creators. *Beneath the Mask* presents classical theories of human nature, much as each theorist might if the theorist were to teach his or her ideas to people encountering them for the first time. Prominence is given to the theorist's progression of ideas, for often the sequence of the theorist's thinking and the changes embodied in the stream of ideas over time are more engaging and valuable than the final product. We intend to make it possible for the reader to go directly from an account of a theory in *Beneath the Mask* to the theorist's own works without the disorientation that comes from learning ideas in predigested textbook form.

A sympathetic approach to theories of personality is not new. What makes the eight editions of *Beneath the Mask* unique is this continuing emphasis on presenting the ideas of personality theorists *developmentally*. A developmental account of a personality theory necessarily incorporates the *personal origins of ideas* to illuminate the links between the psychology of each theorist and that theorist's own psychology of persons.

To be complete and consistent, a developmental approach to theories of personality requires some exploration of how the personal histories, conflicts, and intentions of the theorist entered that thinker's portrait of people. *Beneath the Mask* has emphasized the importance of understanding these personal sources from its first edition. Experience in the classroom with this approach is that it not only leads to a fuller understanding of the theories, but that it makes them memorable by scaling them to human proportions. Put another way, *Beneath the Mask* demonstrates how the thinking that led to the major theories is nested in the life experience of the theorists within the context of the surrounding culture. In many cases, we find that the theories represent creative solutions to problems experienced by the theorist.

One consequence of a developmental approach for teaching about theories of personality is that the efficiency of reducing complex theories to concise summaries of a few basic principles is lost. Gained is the more time-consuming, but also more interesting and exciting task of following the theorist's creative process, with many of its false starts, puzzling personal questions, and, one hopes, eventual solutions. There is an important advantage in this approach. Observing the thinking processes of idea-makers is an apprenticeship in cognition: Sometimes totally unaware that they are doing so, readers find themselves inductively reasoning to the solution of a problem as the theorist that they are reading about has done, or they deduce questions, see anomalies, or discover exceptions to a new theory in the way that a previously studied theorist might have done. Attention to thinking about psychological issues, along with its errors and sequential changes, teaches psychological thinking.

PEDAGOGICAL CHANGES

- Glossaries of terms and concepts have been included for each chapter. These should facilitate reviewing the important concepts that are covered. Glossary terms are indicated in boldface type within the text. Please note that we define terms as used by the theorist or theorists emphasized in each chapter.
- The dates and places of the major theorists' births and deaths are listed at the beginning of each chapter.
- We have included "Only Connect" boxes in most chapters. These boxes point out connections between the ideas of one theorist and other ideas, usually of other theorists.
- The "For Further Reading" sections have been updated.

SPECIFIC CHANGES BY CHAPTER

Chapter 1 further explores foundations of personality research.

Chapter 2 now includes information on the lesser known parts of the Oedipus complex, the inverted negative complex, and the complete complex.

Chapter 3 presents an overview of Freud's dynamic model of the mind and discusses its significant import.

Chapter 4 (previously Chapter 5) presents a new view of Adler as a person and how his life influenced his theory.

Changes to Chapter 5 (previously Chapter 4) include a new discussion of Jung and his personal struggles as they relate to his analytic psychology.

Chapter 6 is now exclusively about Anna Freud; information about Margaret S. Mahler has been deleted.

Chapter 7 information about Heinz Kohut has been deleted.

Chapter 8 contains greater emphasis on the importance of identity in Erik Erikson's life and in his theorizing as well as some comments regarding a more flexible application of his theories. A new figure illustrates epigenetic development to highlight how identity changes over the life cycle.

Chapter 9 expands the perspective of Sullivan as a person to his views as a practitioner.

Chapter 10 includes a perspective of Horney as a pioneering analyst with similarities to Anna Freud in the understanding of basic anxiety and personality style.

Chapter 11 on Gordon Allport discusses Allport's life and the development of his theories. The connection of his thinking with later cognitive theorists is indicated.

Chapter 12 on Rollo May includes concepts from phenomenology as well as the existential tradition. May is portrayed as an *existential phenomenologist* rather than as a pure existentialist.

Chapter 13 includes new material on Abraham Maslow's life and a more complete understanding of some intellectual and philosophical roots of Carl Rogers' thinking. What some consider the fourth force, transpersonal psychology, is briefly introduced. Additional critical views of Maslow's approach are presented for the first time in order to achieve greater balance and compliance. The section on peak experiences has been greatly expanded.

Chapter 14 (previously Chapter 15) on George Kelly includes more about the impact of American culture on his inventive approach and also further material on the connection of his work with other theories and some developments in personal construct psychology. [*Note:* Chapter 14 on John B. Watson and B. F. Skinner from the seventh edition has been deleted from this edition.]

Chapter 15 (previously Chapter 16), is now devoted to Albert Bandura, emphasizing his contributions as a social cognitive theorist with material on his life history and the development of his theories. [*Note:* The Dollard and Miller sections from the seventh edition have been deleted.]

Chapter 16 (previously Chapter 17) on Hans Eysenck discusses his early life and iconoclastic personality as well as additional material on his many later contributions, including the "Big Five" theory in personality, based on factor analysis.

Chapter 17 (previously Chapter 18) deals with Edward O. Wilson and evolutionary psychology and the development of major concepts of this theory.

The previous Chapter 19 on an overview of Personality Theories has been deleted from this edition.

A suggestion for students and professors: *Beneath the Mask: An Introduction to Theories of Personality* is a text rich in material. A good deal of this material is biographical and concerns details and important incidents in the theorists' lives. Much of this material can be read in a relaxed manner, as if it were a novel or short story, rather than a textbook every sentence of which has to be studied and memorized. It is suggested that professors encourage students to absorb, think about, and discuss the material related to the life history of the theorists and study, learn from, and dialogue with the important concepts, theories, and findings of each theory. We have included glossaries of important terms and concepts to assist in such learning. Attempts to study the life history material in a too-detailed way or to attempt to memorize it can result in frustration and the retention of relatively unimportant details, often at the expense of learning central concepts. The biographical material, when read with interest and curiosity, can lead to deeper understanding and greater retention of conceptual material.

Thanks is extended to all those who helped with this edition. Included are Robert Denton, Barbara Durfey, Adriana Faur, Patrick McElfresh, Craig Madden, Irene Mathews, Brad Potthoff, Diane Rethinger, Rosalind Sackoff, and Rebecca Smolak. Susan Pantle further developed the Instructor's Manual and Test Bank. I have learned much over the years from many of my undergraduate and graduate students. Also members of my department and university offered support, information, feedback, and encouragement.

Quite a few people offered extensive critical reviews and frank suggestions, many of which I accepted. Some also freely provided resource and autobiographical material. These included Albert Bandura of Stanford University, Cheryl Bluestone of Queensboro Community College, S. R. Coleman of Cleveland State University, Peter Ebersole of California State University-Fullerton, Kevin Keating of Broward Community College, Alan Lipman of Georgetown University, Donald McBurney of the University of Pittsburgh, Kathy Horton of Harvard University, Christine Osgood of Bethel College, Jackson Rainer of Gardner-Webb University, Paul Vitz and David Wolitzky of New York University, and Edward O. Wilson of Harvard University.

John P. Wilson
Cleveland State University
September 2007

Contents

4. Alfred Adler / *Individual Psychology*   121

5. Carl Gustav Jung / *Analytical Psychology*   147

6. Anna Freud / *Widening the Scope of Psychoanalysis: Ego Psychology*   179

16. Hans Eysenck /
Biologically Based Typology   **496**

17. Edward O. Wilson /
Evolutionary Psychology   **534**

Chapter 1

Basic Issues: How to
Approach the Study
of Personality Theories

*... neither the whole of truth nor the whole of good is revealed to any single observer,
although each observer gains a partial superiority of insight from the peculiar position in
which he stands.*

William James

*It will happen for a time, that the pupil will find his intellectual power has grown by the study
of his master's mind. But in all unbalanced minds, the classification is idolized, passes for the
end, and not for a speedily exhaustible means, so that the walls of the system blend to their
eye in the remote horizon with the walls of the universe.*

Ralph Waldo Emerson

Nothing is real 'til it's local.

Anonymous

A USEFUL METAPHOR: THE MASK AND THE PERSON BENEATH

"The terms **personality** in English, *personalité* in French, and *personlichkeit* in German
closely resemble the *personalitas* of medieval Latin. In classical Latin *persona* alone
was used. All scholars agree that this word originally meant 'mask.'" These words
were written by the American psychologist, Gordon Allport (Allport, 1961, p. 25).

Allport further traced the meaning of the term *persona* to an even earlier phrase in
Latin: *per sonare*, meaning "to sound through." The phrase "per sonare" or, literally, "to
make sound through" referred to the mouthpiece of the theatrical mask through which
an actor's voice was projected. Subsequent meanings as cited by Allport demonstrate
that the meaning of the term *persona* slowly evolved to a more abstract designation indicating the appearance—the mask—and referring also to the person beneath it
(Allport, 1961). The **mask metaphor** frequently occurs in personality theories and is
a major theme in this text.

Allport has noted the difference between his approach to personality and that of
Freud: Allport was one of the founders of academic personality theory. He did his
graduate dissertation in the area of personality theory and developed the first college
course on the subject of personality, which he taught with a great sense of mission
from the 1930s through the 1960s at Harvard University.

In 1962, Allport recounted the courage and emerging sense of self-direction that had been necessary for him as a young graduate student to pursue the field of personality as a subject for his dissertation:

> ... each graduate student was allowed to say in two or three minutes what he was working on for his Ph.D. thesis. It came around to my turn and I said I was trying to make an experimental study of the traits of the human personality. Titchener [a leading experimental psychologist] glared at me. ... [t]he silence seemed like an hour but probably it was a minute. ... It was a cruel cut for a young graduate student! (Allport, 1962, p. 3)

Allport continued that his more supportive mentor, who had seen the event, later took him aside and said,

> "Oh, you *don't* care what Titchener thinks." And it suddenly occurred to me I didn't care—it was irrelevant. I think that event probably was a benign trauma because over the succeeding years, I have not cared what my colleagues thought and that's been fortunate. I have definitely been a maverick, a minority deviant in modern psychology. But, I couldn't care less. It doesn't trouble me and I think this early experience has something to do with it. (Allport, 1962, p. 3)

BEGINNING THE STUDY OF PERSONALITY: A PERSONAL NOTE

I remember that, as an undergraduate science major taking a personality psychology course[1] for the first time, I thought it would be a course about only the superficial, surface aspect of people. One of my quickly corrected misconceptions was that it would be a course about popularity, charisma, or personal attractiveness. Some people, I thought, had a "lot of personality" and others did not. I wondered if it was plausible to teach a whole course around this subject.

When I first entered the course, I found that the professor often spoke about the surface of a person—the observable behaviors. It turned out that only some of these behaviors had to do with popularity. I shortly discovered that the personality course also looked beneath the surface to probe the depths of human nature. At times, it went far beneath the surface—*beneath the mask*.

And the adventure I began then in learning to look beneath the surface, to understand or "stand under" the surface, has continued throughout my life and in my work. This adventure has enriched my life and the lives of many other students of personality. Christopher Monte was certainly fascinated and gained much insight over the years by endeavoring to understand the topic of personality and to explore in some depth the personalities of the theorists themselves.

One concept that intrigued me even as a science major entering a personality course was that the human personality is a fundamental unit and level of organization. Knowing a lot about atoms and molecules did not seem to lead directly to much knowledge about personality. Furthermore, personality seemed to be a vital level to study as it was somewhere between the microscopic on one hand and the great dimensions of culture, society, and history on the other. In addition, persons are sentient and conscious beings. I did not think it possible to attribute these qualities to molecules, to nations, or to galaxies.

Around this time I discovered the philosophy of *personalism*, which recognized the inherent value and dignity of the human person. It questioned any type of subordination of the individual to political or economic structures or even to cultural trends. Some spiritual teachings indicated that saving the life of a person was equivalent to rescuing

---

[1]Professor Gordon Allport taught this course.

a whole world from destruction. At any rate, personality seemed a topic well worthy of study—even to my mind so steeped in a scientific subculture.

In addition, there was the sense of mystery and unknowability about personality. *How many people fully understand themselves? How many of us can describe our own personalities accurately?* Most of us are, at best, knowledgeable about a few other people and ourselves. New acquaintances may appear mysterious and unpredictable to us until we construct a theory that is more or less adequate to explain and predict their behavior. I was hoping that the Theories of Personality course might provide tools for me to gain greater insight into the people around me, and into myself as well.

As you encounter the theories in this text, it will be interesting to notice if and how the person-mask dichotomy is handled. A theorist may be concerned with peripheral variables that are easily observable—mask, or with central variables that touch upon the very core—the inner person. Some psychologists see no reason to look for "an inner person" when overt behavior is adequate for scientific study or prediction and control of specific behaviors. These psychologists think that theories of personality should attend only to observable behavior with no inferences or assumptions about an inner core of experience. And a few theorists do not make the distinction between the outer and the inner.

Those theorists who tried to integrate the inner and outer perspectives hoped personality psychology would be able to reconstruct the whole person and weld together the elements of person and mask into a unified framework. Sigmund Freud emphasized the distinction between the surface and what was beneath it and included aspects of both in his model of the psyche. Carl Gustav Jung considered the persona to be the image presented to others, the social role, as contrasted with the sum total of the person's conscious and unconscious psychic life. He viewed it as one part of a more inclusive whole, which he termed the *psyche*.

ONE TRUTH OR MANY PERSPECTIVES?

When you start to explore the different theories of personality, you will discover many ways of looking at and making sense of personality. The theories are different in their assumptions, the data or evidence they consider, and their conclusions. Some seem diametrically opposed. It is helpful to realize that, if all psychologists agreed on only one way of looking at personality, then there would be no need for a text about "theories" of personality. We could proceed with a single theory that is accepted by all. There is, particularly in academic settings, a tendency for some specialists to advocate a single theory. Perhaps you have had a professor who is such an adherent. Advocating a single theory is useful for focus and for networking, but the subject of personality is so complex that it is difficult to imagine how one single theory would suffice to explain all that we need to know about human behavior.

A Latin phrase is relevant: *Cave hominem unius libri*. Translated literally, it means "Beware the man of one book." It means that people who have a single slant or perspective do not have a balanced or reliable view. This is true of psychology. The well-educated psychologist has a broad background and is familiar with many views and theories even though he or she may prefer and be committed to a specific approach. Every theory has some strengths and some weaknesses, and we should be honest enough, even when we prefer a given approach, to be aware of its shortcomings.

Another concept that may be helpful to students of personality is the limitation of **reductionism**, or what could be termed "nothing-but-ism." A biologist, considering the cell to be the building block of life, may conclude that life is *nothing but* the

---

BOX 1.1   *Personal Experience: My Reductionistic College Roommate*

As an undergraduate, I once had a roommate who could appropriately be labeled a *reductionist*. His name was Fred, and he was a bio-chem major. At the time he was my roommate, he was dating a biology major. Let's call her Joyce. One day, I was chatting with Fred about their relationship. "Are you in love?" I asked. His answer astounded me. "Love?" he responded. "There is no such thing. What there is is biologically based bonding." He also indicated that he and his partner shared this non-romantic and reductionistic view of relationships. After some reflection, I surmised that, as self-styled biological reductionists, they must at least be intellectually compatible.

---

behavior of cells. A Freudian may notice *nothing but* psychodynamics. A behaviorist who has studied patterns of reinforcement and extinction, may conclude that behavior is *nothing but* those patterns. A cognitive theorist may conclude that personality is *nothing but* the result of cognitive structures or schemas.

Some personality theorists themselves were passionately involved in trying to prove or argue that their theories were true and that others were false. Some of the theorists were inspired by the idea that their predecessors' ideas—particularly in the case of Freud—were in some way limited or wrong. Allport, for example, is known to have repeated the unattributed quote that, as far as the unconscious was concerned, "Freud went down deeper, stayed longer and came up dirtier than anyone else." [I suspect that this was one of Allport's own favorite sayings.] Freud, for his part, pushed Alfred Adler out of being the editor of a psychoanalytic journal. He wrote, "I have finally got rid of Adler. ...The damage is not great." (Freud, in Freud & Jung, 1974, p. 376)

Such feuding is unprofessional and often seems silly, but we need to acknowledge that it is a consequence of the commitment the theorists had to their own particular vision of reality. Sigmund Freud wanted people to acknowledge and understand that their real motives were often not as lofty and idealistic as they thought—to acknowledge that they were often hypocrites regarding sex and aggression. He wanted humankind to be elevated by a small group of psychoanalyzed people with a high degree of self-knowledge, insight and rationality. Gordon Allport was concerned about the loss of individuality that was accompanying the rise of psychological science. Carl Jung had a deep commitment to understanding the spiritual dimension of human existence, and Carl Rogers wanted psychologists and people in general to view personal freedom as a fundamental goal. The descriptions and theories of personality by these individuals are not mere neutral descriptions. Their visions of what life is and what life should be are as distinctive and different as the visions of artists such as a Vincent Van Gogh, Norman Rockwell, or Thomas Eakins.

Students of personality thus have a problem. How can we come to grips with various theories with differing concepts when each proclaims itself to be uniquely true? One answer comes from the philosophy of **pluralism**—the notion that there are many realities and that more than one perspective may be correct. Regarding the theories of Freud and Rogers, for example, it could be that their life experiences and thinking revealed to each of them a different aspect of personality. A phenomenological psychologist would say that each was attuned, or open, to different realities.

It is an intellectual and emotional challenge for both the beginning and advanced student of personality theory to understand the differences between the theorists without siding immediately with one or a few and against the others. Cognitive developmental theorists would see the steps in addressing this challenge as first one of seeing some value in all theories, and then finally adopting a specific point of view to which one may become committed (Perry, 1970). This process is parallel on a higher level to the ability to take different visual perspectives—to imagine, for example, what a group of objects might look like when seen from the side or from the back, and then choosing a preferred perspective.

The theorists themselves occasionally tried to understand why they disagreed with their colleagues. Jung was perplexed by the differences between Freud and those around him, including Adler and Jung himself. He said that he developed the theory of psychological types to explain these huge differences. In other words, their conceptions of personality were different because they were temperamentally different.

In this text, we point out that these theorists had different life experiences—especially different childhood experiences. They spent their formative years under a variety of historical, social, and cultural influences, took different paths in life, and had different values. We will see how many theories of personality arose as a creative response on the part of a theorist to the difficult circumstances and challenges of his or her life. Furthermore, each of their life histories occurred within a specific context. In brief, we find that each of the major personality theorists was aware of different aspects of experience and of personality.

What approach do we take in presenting most of the actual theories of personality in this text? We follow the history of each theory's development and demonstrate its progression through the "changes of mind" that its creator may have experienced. We seek to illuminate each theorist's own struggle to understand human nature.

PERSONALITY THEORIES AS CREATIVE SOLUTIONS TO PERSONAL PROBLEMS

One question often arises when students think about a career in psychology or in one of the other mental health professions: If I have difficult psychological problems, does this necessarily make me less qualified to help others? The answer is demonstrated in the troubled lives of some of the major personality theorists. Personal problems *may* provide a source of understanding and of personal growth, but having such problems, however, is neither a necessary nor sufficient background for a person to become a creative theorist. Psychological problems often have the silver lining of drawing a person's attention to the realm of personality and to the necessity of developing self-knowledge and the knowledge of others. This is true of many people who intend to make helping others psychologically a career focus. Once a person's attention is focused on their problems, they should work toward a successful resolution of them.

A theory of personality and of psychotherapy is often a theorist's means of passing on his or her personal approach or solution to life's difficulties to others. For example, we will find in the case of Sigmund Freud an intense and unwavering introspection, with Carl Jung an ability to merge visions and fantastic inner experiences, with Carl Rogers a focus on an optimistic approach to the challenges of the present, and with Erik Erikson an attempt to develop a unique identity. We take the position in this book that we want to understand the personality theories deeply and unforgettably by trying to understand something about the lives of the theorists and how and why they developed the theories for which they are known.

This approach has the advantage that we will see some theories in terms of the life experiences of the personality theorists and in the social-historical contexts from which the theories emerged. It will become clear, for example, how Freud's theory was a response to many of the difficulties of his own life as well as a response to

---

BOX 1.2   *Only Connect...*

Ellenberger's concept of creative illness is similar to the mythic theme of the "wounded healer"
found in many cultures and literatures throughout history. The insights and healing abilities of
the "wounded healer" emerge from his or her
struggles with pain, suffering, illness and injury.
As we will see in Chapter 5, Carl Jung labeled
such universal themes *archetypes* and believed
they were part of the collective unconscious of all
humans. In Jung's view, the personality theorists
that we consider to have a creative illness would
be considered to be *wounded healers*. Jung's own
life experience can be understood within this
framework.

---

upper-middle-class European morality at the end of the nineteenth century. Decades
later, Carl Rogers' more optimistic theory of personality was deeply connected to and
reflective of his own approach to life and affected by trends in American culture and
society in the middle of the twentieth century.

Henri Ellenberger (1970) has advanced the notion that a wide range of influential
psychological theories have their origins in what he termed the creative illnesses of
their creators. A *creative illness*, or a psychological malady deeply intertwined with a
creative process and perhaps contributing to it, can take a variety of forms, ranging in
intensity from mild anxiety through neurotic maladjustment to psychotic separations
from reality (Ellenberger, 1970, p. 447). The dominating preoccupation in a creative illness is absorption with some intellectual-creative problem involving attempts to make
social reality intelligible. The stricken, creatively ill persons become intensely preoccupied with a search for the truth; they become absorbed with self, suffering intense
feelings of isolation until, suddenly, the suffering ends abruptly. The termination period
is often marked by feelings of exhilaration: "The subject emerges from his ordeal with
a permanent transformation in his personality and the conviction that he has discovered
a great truth or a new spiritual world" (Ellenberger, 1970, p. 48). Ellenberger regards
such major figures as Sigmund Freud and Carl Jung as illustrative cases. He believes
they had each resolved their creative illness through the creation of a generalized theory
of human nature.

Ellenberger's concept of creative illness is a valuable one. Dramatic and acute
personal disturbances are involved in the origination of many theories. In addition to
Sigmund Freud and Carl Jung, the clearest cases for creative illness in the theorists
we review in *Beneath the Mask* can be made for Alfred Adler, Erik Erikson, and
Rollo May. There is less certainty regarding Karen Horney and Carl Rogers. In other
instances, such as that of Bandura's social cognitive approach, the creative illness
hypothesis does not appear relevant.

WHAT ABOUT ABNORMAL PSYCHOLOGY?

Most personality theory textbooks do not focus on the specific topic of abnormal
psychology. That is another discipline and is centered on the causes, descriptions,
diagnoses, and treatments of pathological conditions. Such a project is outside the
scope of this text. Much of the formal field of abnormal psychology falls within the
medical model of mental disorder. Yet, there is a good deal of overlap between the two
fields even though their emphases are very different. Within each chapter of the present
text, we will thus consider how each theorist approaches—if at all—the question of
psychopathology.

From their onset, many theories of personality were constructed with close attention to the abnormal. Psychopathology was seen as an extreme example. By deciphering what had gone wrong in atypical cases, principles could be derived that would explain the typical. With some exceptions, theorists peered into the depths of their own and others' psychopathology to construct their vision of general personality functioning. Sigmund Freud began the trend as early as 1895 with his first model of personality that he described as a "general psychology" with equal importance for normal and abnormal functioning (Freud, 1895, pp. 283–284). But, in truth, his neurologically-based theory of personality was derived largely from the treatment of hysterical conversion and other "neurotic" disorders.

Other personality theories had little basis in psychopathology and were based on studying normal or exceptionally healthy or creative people. Gordon Allport's trait theory and Abraham Maslow's concept of self-actualization are two such theories, as is George Kelly's idea that each person is a theory-builder, which is an example of a theory having to do with normal, active coping. Maslow's study of "self-actualization" is parallel to medicine's consideration of "wellness" as more than the simple absence of disease.

It is important to consider that our points of view and values are sometimes involved in the judgment of what is pathological and what is not. One example is that in totalitarian societies with great pressure for conformity, holding certain political opinions may be taken as evidence of psychopathology. In the 1980s, to take a much-noted example, many Soviet dissidents were hospitalized with the diagnosis of "creeping schizophrenia." This diagnosis was based largely on their opinions, social activism, and, in some cases, a judgment reinforced by their belief in God. One of the authors of the present book was acquainted with a street person hospitalized in one of our local medical centers. The street person viewed his mania as a valuable mental state. As expected, he quit taking his medications after discharge. Many children who are currently diagnosed with attention deficit disorder (ADD) and hyperactivity might have not been so diagnosed only a few years ago. We might ask whether more children are now suffering from this condition or whether our criteria have changed as a result of different expectations. A person with a pattern of changing jobs and partners may be viewed as self-actualizing, narcissistic, or unstable depending on one's perspective. There are many reasons to believe that diagnostic criteria are highly context-dependent.

In addition, as we explore the different personality theories, we will find different explanations for pathology, such as inadequate defenses (Freud), blockage of personal growth (Rogers), responses to hypercompetitive upbringing (Horney), or lack of balance in psychological development (Jung). For example, let us examine the case of a college student who is showing signs of clinical depression and may receive a corresponding diagnosis. Different theories of personality would often lead to varying ways of conceptualizing and understanding the phenomenon of depression. A Freudian psychoanalyst may suspect that the depression is caused by vulnerabilities stemming from the person's childhood experiences. But a Jungian or a practitioner informed by the theories of Erik Erikson may see the depression in terms of having unfulfilled potential for adventure or for involved and caring behavior. Adlerians might see it as resulting from a lifestyle of avoiding challenges, and psychologists in the tradition of Karen Horney might analyze it as a reaction to unloving parenting involving an emphasis on hypercompetitive behavior. A behaviorist may see the depression as a response to a reduced amount of positive reinforcement in this student's environment. A cognitive theorist might consider the depression a consequence of the student's negative views or self-talk. And a psychopharmacologically-oriented practitioner may view the depression in terms of serotonin depletion. These varying explanations have different implications for our attitude toward, and treatment of, depression. What is confusing is that these explanations are not necessarily mutually exclusive.

Psychology does not have as many elaborately defined categories for normal or healthy behavior as for the pathological. This gap reflects a century of emphasizing disorders and deficiencies. In the study of personality we want to try to understand and use theories that explain not only pathological behavior but also normal, healthy, creative, inspiring, achieving, or courageous behavior. The rapidly developing positive psychology movement, which addresses the question of optimal psychological functioning, is currently a very active area of psychological research and theorizing. Some personality theories welcome the study of the whole range of human behavior—from the difficult-to-understand mutterings of people in the dreariest mental hospitals to the daily life of the so-called average person to the achievements of the greatest scientists and artists. Many theories may focus only on health or illness, but it is possible for theoreticians to cover the whole gamut.

PERSONOLOGY OR PERSONALITY THEORY?

One issue in the field of personality is the distinction between personologists and other investigators of personality. Personologists have had distinctively different research traditions and conceptual strategies from that of psychologists who have traditionally been known as personality theorists. Henry A. Murray, an early pioneer of **personology**, defined the concept this way:

> The branch of psychology that principally concerns itself with the study of human lives and the factors that influence their course, which investigates individual differences and types of personality, may be termed "personology" instead of "the psychology of personality". . . . (1938, p. 4)

As Robert White, one of Murray's students and himself an eminent **personologist** explained, Henry Murray came from a tradition of medical research where multiple sources of information, detailed diagnostic interviews, and complete histories were routine procedure. What was not routine was Murray's incorporation of these detailed, clinical methods into personality psychology. At Harvard, in the 1930s, Murray set up a Diagnostic Council of clinical psychologists and graduate students in clinical psychology. Members of the council included students and faculty who would later go on to shape the field of personality, among them Gordon Allport, Erik Erikson, Robert White, and Murray himself. The goal was to examine in detail individual life histories using every method they could devise or borrow: experimentation, observation, interviewing, personality testing, life history analysis, and direct contact of every member of the council with every subject in the research program. The work led eventually to Murray (1938) and his collaborators' classic book *Explorations in Personality*. As White has pointed out, there has been a dearth of efforts in psychology to study the individual personality in all of its complexity and richness (see Sanford, 1985). We prefer sometimes to give two personality tests to a group of people and simply correlate the results as if that were somehow indicative of this intricate and elaborate system called personality.

> Of course there are many elaborations upon this design, introducing experimental situations, different treatments, and highly sophisticated statistical procedures. But none of these entail any real personal contact with the subjects or any attempt to think of them as more than

momentarily living people. For some time I have described this type of research as *studying personality without actually looking at it*. (White, 1981, p. 15; italics in original)

Most of the theories we examine have a long historical development. And some of the theories reflect, sometimes to a surprising degree, the richness of the human personality in the tradition of personology. But something is lost for what is gained in detail and complexity. As we shall see, many of the theories are more literary and less scientific than we would like. Striking a balance between study of the individual and obtaining generalizable results is a very difficult art.

IMPACT OF CULTURE AND SOCIETY

Students of personality are becoming increasingly aware of the influence of culture and society on the makeup of personality. The study of *multicultural dimensions* of personality is only at its beginning, and we have only a beginning understanding of how personality may differ across cultures. It appears quite likely that certain givens in our Western psychological view, such as the existence of an "identity crisis," are far from universal. One European scholar, J.H. Van Den Berg (1961), argued that the assumption of a fixed human nature was not well taken. Many areas we considered to be part of human nature, he asserted, were actually culturally determined. For example, the stage of adolescence might be viewed as a historical development or invention. Teenagers in the 1800s were considered capable of doing adult work and starting their own families. They did not go through the modern experience of adolescence, which includes a major emphasis on identity issues. Furthermore, the sheltered innocence and naïveté taken as a hallmark of childhood in the 1950s is no longer the case. Many of the theories of personality we are considering do not take into account the makeup of the culture or of the society in which they were formed, even though it is evident that cultural factors had a strong influence on the theories.

Some theorists have taken the position that there are numerous commonalities through time and cross-culturally. These theorists draw from various sources. Carl Jung looked at many cultures to find similar themes. Behaviorists sometimes focus on similarities between humans, all primates and, at times, among all vertebrates, or even invertebrates and other organisms. **Evolutionary psychologists** (Chapter 16), making new and, at times, controversial contributions to personality theory, see human behavior in light of underlying commonalities that have come to exist through evolutionary processes.

So, in some way, it appears that both those who argue for the variability of human behavior and the constancy of human nature have some convincing arguments and much evidence on their side. One possible answer is to see the possibility of constancy of human nature and, at the same time, differences and changes that are occurring. Behaviorists understand that conditioning is a given for everyone, but the specific behaviors that might be learned are infinitely variable. In Freud's theory, for example, the formation of a superego is a developmental given, but the contents of a person's superego vary according to upbringing.

It is thus possible for personality to be seen as having structural or relatively unchangeable elements as well as content elements that change. For each theory that we will examine, we may inquire how much the theory sees human nature as immutable and how much it views personality as a protean phenomenon, that is, able to take on many forms. Often this fixed-flexible dimension is seen as a polarity, but, as indicated, some theories represent both fixed and changeable aspects to personality.

The same holds true for the apparent nature-nurture dichotomy. Regardless of how extreme an advocate of nature or nurture we might be, we have to admit the vital importance of the other side. Theories emphasizing the importance of the family environment nevertheless take for granted certain aspects of genetics and the physical environment. Those emphasizing the importance of biological variation assume that the environment is within certain limits. So, we may consider within each theoretical framework the relative impact of nature and nurture. One way of classifying theories is to consider to what extent they emphasize either nature or nurture. We may consider what aspects of nature or nurture are emphasized.

Sometimes personality theories contain within themselves contradictory elements or paradoxes that make evaluating and classifying them quite difficult. This is particularly true of theories that involve psychotherapy. That aspect of the theory used to describe the patient or client is often different from the implicit or explicit view that the theory has of the therapist. For example, psychoanalytic theory views people as largely reactive and driven by unconscious dynamics. However, it is precisely the trained psychoanalyst who has transcended this condition. Rogers' therapist is a person who has learned to be focused on the "other," whereas the Rogerian client is focused on his or her own feelings.

THREE MAJOR TOOLS FOR EVALUATING PERSONALITY THEORIES

To evaluate a theory of personality is not simple, and the job demands complex tools. There are so many dimensions on which to compare and to rate theories of personality that the task can be daunting. For someone coming to the field for the first time, the wealth of qualities that can be assessed may obstruct the opportunity of discovering common elements or important strengths and weaknesses.

In this book our strategy is to emphasize three fundamental dimensions to evaluate the personality theories presented. At the end of each chapter, you will find an evaluation section in which we discuss the theory at hand in terms of three qualities that give substantial information about the theory's empirical usefulness, validity, and model of human nature. The three qualities we will emphasize as tools of analysis are:

1. **Refutability:** Does a theory state what it would take to prove itself wrong? Scientific theories are refutable or testable, and unscientific ones are not. In general, refutability assures some measurable degree of accuracy, usefulness, and predictive power. The most refutable theories are sometimes less helpful in understanding the complexities of individual experience and behavior. Some aspects of a theory may be testable while others are not.

2. **Active human agency** or **passive human agency:** Does the theory picture people as passive receptacles of reality? Or are they active agents who shape their own inner and outer realities? Does a theory embody a combination of both views?

3. **Idiographic focus** or **nomothetic focus:** Does the theory emphasize the uniqueness or pattern of particular qualities that an individual embodies? Or does it instead explore the general universal aspects of human behavior? Does a theory embody some interactive combination of idiographic and nomothetic focus?

Tool One: Refutability

Refutability (testability) relates to whether there is an empirical basis to the theory and to whether a given theory of personality leads to any specific predictions about behavior. Prediction and control are the usual criteria for scientific theories. A theory may be plausible and have internal consistency and a good deal of comprehensiveness and yet not be helpful in predicting and controlling behavior.

According to the philosopher of science, Karl Popper (1959, 1963), a refutable theory must state not only what is expected to happen in certain experimental conditions, but also what is expected not to occur. In effect, the adequate scientific theory must include a statement of what observations it would take to disprove it. If such disconfirming observations can be made, the theory is refuted. This criterion of refutability guarantees that scientific theories will be stated in empirical, testable terms. The "good" theory specifies what it takes to falsify itself. The "poor" theory not only fails to specify falsification procedures, but it may be so vaguely stated that it can be compatible with any and all observations.

There is a difference between a theory having the desirable property of refutability and the actual refutation of the theory. A theory that is not refutable cannot be proven either right *or* wrong, whereas a theory that has been refuted is considered disproved. When a philosopher of science says that a theory is refutable, there is no implication that the theory has been or will be refuted. The only necessary quality of a refutable theory is that it be potentially refutable, that is, testable.

There is a continuing tension between the goal of refutability in personality theory and the desire to account comprehensively for the whole range of experience, thought and behavior. No theory has both comprehensively and refutably accounted for the wholeness, for the uniqueness, for the universality of human propensities, foibles, drives, abilities, and desires. Sometimes, the goal of empathy or understanding differs from the scientific emphases on refutability, prediction, and control.

Tool Two: Active or Passive Human Agency

Buss (1978) contends that each major psychological tradition attempts to solve this fundamental scientific puzzle: Does the theory have a view of *active human agency* or one of *passive human agency*? Does the person construct reality, or does reality construct the person? Put another way, each school, depending on the history to which it is reacting, asserts either that human beings are active, creative, relatively free constructors of their lives, or that people are passive, uninventive, determined receptacles of reality. In essence, each theory asserts that people are subjects or objects (Buss, 1978, p. 60; Fischer, 1977). Many theories, we will find, combine the two views, even while emphasizing one or the other. This is logical as people may be viewed as both subjects and objects, active creators and passive recipients of stimulation.

Tool Three: Idiographic or Nomothetic Focus

Gordon Allport (1937) introduced into psychology a basic distinction and a fundamental dilemma with which philosophers had struggled for decades. He borrowed the terms *idiographic* and *nomothetic* from the philosopher Wilhelm Windelband (1894) to describe the apparent conflict between two basic interests of the psychologist. As a scientist, the psychologist is interested in obtaining data and results that apply to specific groupings of people or generally to all people. Concerns such as these that focus on generalizability or even universality are called *nomothetic*.

The clinician proceeds to use this understanding therapeutically for his or her particular client. Such a clinician's concerns for the individual or for the unique case are termed *idiographic*. The same thing holds for the psychologist helping to choose a chief executive officer for a large firm. He or she wants to help discover if one particular individual is suited for the role. Intelligence agency psychologists work under a cover of secrecy to understand the personalities and to predict the behaviors of powerful foreign leaders. They rely on life history data, analysis of expressive behaviors, content analyses, and the accounts of many people familiar with the subject. Very little of this confidential work is published in journals.

In many cases, the idiographic and the nomothetic can be complementary, so that information derived from the study of one person may very well have aspects that are shared by other, similar people. Conversely, nomothetic "laws" that purport to be universal may be found to apply to a particular individual in a particular way. It is sometimes possible to appreciate and integrate both the nomothetic and idiographic elements in a given theory. The psychotherapy integration movement has been active in considering the possibility of actually integrating theories that are generally viewed as incompatible. The classic and contemporary theories that we consider fall at various points between the two extremes.

Allport (1961, 1968) later developed the concept of a **morphogenic approach** to emphasize that uniqueness sometimes results from the pattern of general traits that an individual embodies rather than from strictly and absolutely unique qualities. The morphogenic concept is somewhere between a nomothetic approach and the idea of a total focus on individuality.

A quotation of Allport refers to the nomothetic, the morphogenic and the idiographic aspects of personality:

> "In some ways, each of us is like every other human being, in some ways we are like some other human beings, and in some ways each of us is unique."

ADDITIONAL DIMENSIONS OF PERSONALITY THEORIES

We have already explored some questions that may be asked of any theory of personality. We will be specifically using the three tools of analysis discussed previously: **active** or **passive human agency**, **refutability**, **idiographic** or **nomothetic focus**. These questions, as we have seen, need not always be answered yes or no. Many "in-betweens" are known and some theories contain contradictory elements. Honest and informed scholars may arrive at different answers regarding these questions.

In this text, there is enough information for students to make some informed responses regarding additional dimensions of personality theories. (You may arrive at different conclusions than we do regarding human agency, refutability, and idiographic or nomothetic focus.) We encourage students of personality theory to think about these questions and engage in an active dialogue with the text, with other students, and with the professor in regard to the theory you are studying.

Some additional considerations: To what degree does the theory have *heuristic* value, in other words, how useful is the theory in enabling us to come up with new or productive ways of thinking about or dealing with a problem or topic?

- Does the theory stem from the theorist's effort to make sense of her or his own life experience?
- Does the theory seem culturally embedded or is it generally applicable? A more refined version of this question is, "What aspects of a given theory are culturally embedded and which are more universal?"

- How does the theorist's experience as a person of male or female gender affect the theory? To what extent does the theory lead to understanding the role of women at different times in Western culture?
- To what extent is the theory derived from study of pathology, the "normal" person, or of the exceptional individual? A related question is, "To what extent does the theory attempt to explain pathological, normal, or exceptional behavior?" Does the theory have a comprehensive view, one that includes psychopathology, normal behavior, and exceptional behavior, or does it focus only on one area?
- Does the theory help us to understand specific individuals? Does the theory help us fathom what a specific person is thinking and feeling and what his or her underlying goals and motives are? Does it lead to an understanding of how a person is experiencing reality?
- A somewhat different emphasis is the traditional nature-nurture question. Although we take the position that both are necessary factors, it is interesting to see how much weight each theory gives to each side of this debate. Does it recognize an interaction between nature and nurture?
- What, if any, life events have led the theorists themselves to view people as shaped by external forces and inner urges? What life events have led them to interpret people as largely or potentially independent steersmen of reality?
- Does the personality theory include a theory of development? What ages are covered as significant in the process? Is a stage theory included within the theory?
- A historically interesting question is to categorize the theory in one of three ways: (a) directly in the line of Freudian thinking (e.g., Anna Freud's theory), (b) a response against major dimensions of Freudian thinking (e.g., Adler's or Jung's theory), or (c) entirely removed from the Freudian tradition (e.g., radical behaviorism).
- Is there a form of psychotherapy associated with the theory? If so, has the theory led to the development of a psychotherapeutic tradition, with associated institutes, organizations, journals, etc.?
- Evaluate each theory in terms of its values: Does it promote individuality, altruism, religiosity, or communal spirit? Does it seem more consistent with a liberal, conservative, socialistic, or other political philosophy?
- Is the theorist European or American? How does their relation to European or American culture and history influence the personality theory?
- What is the approach of each theory toward spirituality and religion? Does it consider these areas at all? If so, indicate how much, and whether in a positive, neutral, or negative way.
- To what extent does the theorist's religious background and identification have an impact on the theory? What, if any, appears to be the impact?
- Does the theory focus on overt behavior, thinking, emotions, or on the individual's experience of reality?
- A more personal question: To what extent does a given theory overlap or help you understand your own life experience or the experience of those you know? Does it help you understand contemporary or historical personalities or even fictional characters?

We encourage you to add additional questions or dimensions to consider.

SOME WELCOMING WORDS

We are pleased to welcome you to the study of personality, the study of personality theories, and an introduction to the theorists themselves. We trust that this text will lead to a deep understanding of the topic that will stay with you. By knowing about the biographical and cultural framework in which the theories were developed as well as the thinking that went into developing the theories, we hope that you will develop a deeper than average understanding of the major personality theories. We hope that you will be able, perhaps tentatively at first, to see how these theories may help you understand your own life experience a bit better. We trust that you will become able to see your life and the lives of others from different perspectives. For some students, such understanding has led to considerable insight and personal growth. We hope it brings you the sense of satisfaction that comes from understanding life a little better.

FOR FURTHER READING

In each chapter, we will indicate a few of the most relevant and accessible resources for further study. In addition, the Wiley web site for *Beneath the Mask* has a more complete summary of additional reading that is relevant for the topics covered in each chapter.

For this chapter, we encourage students to access the student portion of the web site for this text and to review the various sections there.

The url for this text's web site is www.wiley.com/college/sollod

You might also try checking out some of the links there for the various theorists and their personality theories.

GLOSSARY

Active human agency: The concept that a person is actively in charge of his/her behaviors, thoughts, and feelings. In this view, the individual shapes his or her own inner and outer realities.

Evolutionary psychologists: Those who study the approach to understanding human psychology—including all of its basic areas such as learning, cognition, perception, personality and psychopathology—from the point of view of evolutionary theory.

Idiographic focus: An approach concerned with identifying the unique combination of traits and other characteristics that best accounts for the personality of a single individual. It is an in-depth analysis of one individual and the dimensions relevant to that person's personality.

Mask metaphor: The dichotomy between appearance (the mask) and the actor (inner person). It deals with an important distinction between superficial and fundamental characteristics.

Morphogenic approach: An approach that classifies people according to the patterns of traits they display. It is midway between an idiographic and a nomothetic approach.

Nomothetic focus: An approach that seeks to establish general laws of human functioning, that is, to understand the behavior and experience of people in general or groups of people.

Passive human agency: The individual is seen as a passive recipient of environmental forces or inner urges. The person is viewed as shaped by inner or outer forces beyond his or her control.

Personality: A pattern of relatively permanent traits, dispositions, or propensities that lend consistency to a person's behavior and thought processes.

Personologist: A psychologist who is concerned with the life history and the coherent stream of feelings, events, traits, and situations that characterize individual personalities.

Personology: The branch of psychology that principally concerns itself with the study of individual human lives.

Pluralism: A philosophical approach that takes into account the validity of many different points of view and theoretical explanations.

Reductionism: Any theoretical approach that attempts to explain all human behavior according to a single theory.

Refutability: The idea that a theory is formulated in such a way that leads to tests either supporting or contradicting its tenets. Refutability leads to a measurable degree of accuracy and predictive power.

Chapter 2

Sigmund Freud

Psychoanalysis: The Clinical Evidence

The past is never dead. It's not even past.

William Faulkner

"The hysteric suffers mostly from reminiscences."

Sigmund Freud

Go, now, and do heart-work
On all the images imprisoned within you,
For you overpower them,
But you know them not.

Ranier Marla Rilke, "Turning Point"

Sigmund Freud   Born: 1856   Freiberg, Moravia,
Austro-Hungarian Empire
Died: 1939   London, England

About Freud's Clinical Psychoanalysis

Freud's theories are the result of his persistent quest to understand the complexity of the human psyche. It was his lifework to understand and to help others understand the convoluted ways that the rational and the irrational clash within each of us.

This chapter explores Freud's development of the following central concepts:

- Many disorders previously considered to be physical in origin are really psychological in origin. They are determined by the experiences and/or the needs and desires of people.
- The mind is compartmentalized. Part of the mind is unconscious and often, outside of the person's awareness, determines behavior.
- Neurotic symptoms both partly express and partly shield hidden impulses or taboo memories.

- Just as real or imagined experience may underlie the development of symptoms, so psychoanalysis, a form of therapy involving talking about the experiences, may lead to their resolution.
- A process involving successive psychosexual stages characterizes normal human development; regression or fixation may occur in instances of psychopathology.

Freud's classic theory remains a powerful though controversial influence on other theorists and clinicians more than 65 years after his death. Even many of those who do not think they are following in his footsteps nonetheless agree with many of his ideas and continue many of his practices.

A PERSONAL ASIDE: WHY STUDY FREUD'S IDEAS?

Over the years that I have been studying and teaching the subject of theories of personality, psychology students and even academic and professional colleagues have frequently questioned the relevance of Freud's ideas for their lives or for the field of psychology. Among the numerous criticisms have been vehement, often personal, attacks. Those familiar with the Freudian intellectual legacy know that this type of reaction is nothing new. People began to express their disagreements about Freud and his ideas throughout his career. When he was only twenty-nine years old and first presented his ideas about hypnosis and hysteria to his medical peers in Vienna, he was hissed, booed, and shouted at. The idea that hidden thoughts could cause physical bodily symptoms seemed ridiculous to them.

Freud sometimes took the role of being an objective critic of the way people saw themselves, and as a challenger of their sense of being truly civilized and self-directed. His iconoclastic ambitions included overthrowing the more conventional and comfortable notions that people had about human nature. Intellectual historians—and Freud himself—have noted that, in the progress to a modern scientific outlook, there have been three major "de-centering jolts" that have influenced our thinking. One was the Copernican revolution, which removed the earth from the center of the cosmos, the second was the Darwinian revolution, which placed humans within the context of biological evolution, and the third was the Freudian revolution, which indicated that humans were sometimes acting for reasons outside of their conscious awareness or control.

Freud's last recorded statement not long before his death included the following proud and somewhat bitter reminiscence (in English):

> People did not believe in my facts and thought my theories unsavory. Resistance was strong and unrelenting. In the end, I succeeded in acquiring pupils and building up an international psychoanalytic association. But the struggle is not yet over. (Freud, S., 1938. BBC recording in London—transcript and audio clip from Library of Congress http://www.loc.gov).

Given the controversies surrounding Freud and his ideas, it is difficult to form an accurate view of what he actually thought and, even harder, a sensible appraisal of the value of his contributions. The Freud scholar, Barry Silverstein, has offered the observations that:

> ... contemporary psychology textbook portrayals of Freud, and popular introductory books on Freud characteristically fail to offer an historically accurate account of Freud and his work. ... [These sources] also suffer from agenda driven attempts to write history to defend or demolish contemporary psychoanalytic practice and polemical attempts to present the author's own version of Freud as the "real Freud." (Silverstein, 2003, p. 2)

But Silverstein concludes that the effort to understand Freud accurately is worthwhile because of Freud's profound influence on contemporary culture and on American psychology and psychotherapy. He points to Freud's status as the most cited author in American introductory psychology textbooks and his leadership in the number of citations in psychology literature. (Silverstein, 2003, p. 2)

Some examples of Freud's impact were noted in the introductory section to this chapter, *About Freud's Clinical Psychoanalysis*. Even the fifty-minute hour, used by practically all therapists—from behaviorists to those of a humanistic orientation—goes right back to Freud—as does the idea of talk therapy itself, not to mention such fundamental concepts as the *ego*, the *superego*, and *defense mechanisms* such as *projection* and *repression*. The list of Freudian concepts and therapeutic methods that are still important in psychology is very long. Silverstein also observed that many Freudian ideas were first rejected in American psychology, but later were *co-opted* from Freud, sometimes in new terminology (Silverstein, 2003, p. xx).

While writing about different theories in *Beneath the Mask*, I have frequently noted how a theorist has engaged in one strategy or another regarding Freudian approaches: The first and simplest strategy is to take a Freudian concept and change its meaning to something very different or even the opposite of the original meaning. So, for example, Alfred Adler (Chapter 4) saw the unconscious as assisting the ego in its goals and planning, whereas Freud had viewed the ego as serving the id. Cognitively-oriented theorists emphasize the importance of conscious ideas and thoughts rather than Freud's emphasis on the unconscious. Freud's **penis envy** is replaced by *womb envy* in some theories. Freud had a deterministic view of personality, whereas Jung and Adler repudiated determinism in favor of a view of personality as a purposeful, goal-directed system. A second strategy is to take a Freudian idea and translate it into another, as it were, dialect. For example, it is easy to find versions of Freudian *defense mechanisms* in many of the theories we will be studying. But what they are called, what is defended and what is defended against may all be different. As you study the theories in this text, for example, consider concepts such as *safeguarding mechanisms, auxiliary conflict solutions, ideal self-image, selective activation of internal control*, and *mechanisms of moral disengagement*.

In all of these examples is a tendency toward what can be labeled *successionism*, that is, seeing an approach that comes after another as superior to the traditional approach, even though it may contain many of the same elements as the predecessor. The most classic examples are religious—of Judaism looking down on pagan religions and in many New Testament passages in which Christianity is viewed as a successor of Judaism. Is this so different from the way that humanism, behaviorism, and cognitive theorists view their Freudian predecessors?

Let us now go from the abstract to a specific place, culture, and time. We find ourselves in an affluent area of a powerful and cosmopolitan Vienna toward the end of the nineteenth century. World War I, the Great Depression, and World War II have not yet occurred, nor has the rise of communism. There is a prevalent belief in the development of science and technology, the ongoing progress of civilization and in human rationality.

THE HYSTERICAL NEUROSIS OF BERTHA PAPPENHEIM

It was 1882 in Vienna, the capital of the Austro-Hungarian Empire. A prominent Viennese physician, Dr. Josef Breuer, had a perplexing case that would eventually lead to a theory of hysterical neurosis, a method of psychological treatment, and the

BOX 2.1   *Will We Ever Know the Real Freud? Probably Not*

In this text, we are drawing for the most part on Freud's own narratives of clinical work, which comprise what is termed the "official" or "traditional" version of Freud's thinking. All we know for sure about such material is that it represents the way that Freud *wanted* people to think about the development of his ideas. His accounts of case histories proceed logically to the development of his ideas and theories in a stepwise fashion. It is a little too neat to be fully credible.

In fact, Freud destroyed his papers more than once to make it harder if not impossible to trace the source and development of his ideas. In 1885, he actually wrote a letter to his fiancée that included the following remarkable passage:

I have destroyed all my notes of the past fourteen years, as well as letters, scientific excerpts, and the manuscripts of my papers.... As for the biographers, let them worry, we have no desire to make it too

easy for then... and I am already looking forward to seeing them go astray (Freud, E.I., 1960, pp. 152–153)

In addition, there are "made up" aspects of the narratives and parts that have been changed or omitted. For example, there is strong evidence that some of this material—including the rather widely disseminated idea that Anna O. had a false pregnancy—was invented by Freud. Bertha Pappenheim's treatment with Breuer was presented by Freud as a cure. In fact, she had a major remission shortly afterwards and had a subsequent hospitalization with many debilitating symptoms before her actual recovery somewhat later. (Borch-Jacobsen, M. 1996; Ellenberger, 1972; Silverstein, 2003, pp. 12–14)

Freud himself thus appeared to use some of the same ego defenses that he discovered in his patients. Such defenses involved distorting reality in order to make it more palatable.

germ of a comprehensive theory of personality and psychotherapy that would have a major impact on our thinking about human nature. At the time, Breuer was a mentor and friend of Sigmund Freud, an intense, brilliant and ambitious young doctor. The story of the case that Breuer treated is the version presented in Freud's first book, co-authored with Breuer, titled *Studies in Hysteria* (Breuer, J. & Freud, S., 1895). As indicated in Box 2.1, all we can be sure of in the fascinating Sherlock Holmes-like story that follows is that it is the "official version" of the case and of Bertha's ostensible "cure."

Fraülein Bertha Pappenheim, who was to be called "Anna O" in later writings by Breuer and Freud, (Jones, 1953, p. 223n.), was a charming, attractive, intelligent, and witty young woman who had developed a series of disorders. The name *Anna O* stood for the *alpha* and *omega* of neurosis, or as an author might write today, "Neurosis from A to Z." Her disorders included paralysis of limbs and disturbed vision—each without any apparent physical basis. At one point, she seemed to have a dual personality. These symptoms apparently emerged after the onset of her father's long, terminal illness. Though many physicians were consulted, no physical basis had been found for her bewildering maladies. Breuer diagnosed Bertha's collection of symptoms as a case of **hysterical neurosis**.

Although long recognized as a disorder, the causes of hysterical neurosis had thus far not been accurately understood. The affliction received its name from the Greek word *uterus*. It was the opinion of the ancient Greeks that hysteria was "for women only" because the disease was thought to be the result of what they termed a "wandering womb." The traveling womb was thought to be responsible for an array of symptoms in various parts of the body such as the temporary paralysis of limbs or the dysfunction of sense organs. Josef Breuer did not share such archaic and unscientific views about the nature of hysteria. But he still did not have an adequate explanation for Bertha Pappenheim's symptoms.

Breuer described two markedly different ways that Bertha behaved:

> Two entirely distinct states of consciousness were present, which alternated very frequently and without warning and which became more and more differentiated in the course of the illness. In one of these states she recognized her surroundings; she was melancholy and anxious, but relatively normal. In the other state she hallucinated and was "naughty"—that is to say, she was abusive, used to throw the cushions at people, so far as the contractures [in her limbs] at various times allowed, tore buttons off her bedclothes and linen with those of her fingers which she could move, and so on. . . . There were extremely rapid changes of mood leading to excessive but quite temporary high spirits, and at other times severe anxiety, stubborn opposition to every therapeutic effort and frightening hallucinations of black snakes, which was how she saw her hair ribbons and similar things. . . . (Breuer, in Breuer & Freud, 1893–1895, p. 24)[1]

In addition, Bertha began to exhibit other forms of disturbance. She occasionally left out words from her spoken language. She gradually increased these omissions until her speech was rendered largely nonsensical, illogical, and ungrammatical. She even displayed self-willed or **elective mutism** for a period of two weeks. At this time, Breuer speculated that something must have recently annoyed and offended her, which resulted in her deciding not to speak about it. Breuer's tactic of insisting that they discuss the problem was apparently effective, and Bertha began to speak again (Breuer, in Breuer & Freud, 1893–1895, p. 25).

Bertha, whose native tongue was German, now displayed a new symptom: At times, she switched into speaking only English. Nothing could convince Bertha, who seemed to be unaware of her change in language, that the German-speaking people to whom she spoke English could not understand her.

"CLOUDS": SELF-INDUCED HYPNOSIS

Bertha's father died in April, nine months after her speech disturbances developed. According to Breuer, "This [her father's death] was the most severe physical trauma that she could possibly have experienced. A violent outburst of excitement was succeeded by profound stupor which lasted about two days and from which she emerged in a greatly changed state." (Breuer, in Breuer & Freud, 1893–1895, p. 26)

Bertha's loss of feeling in her hands and feet as well as her paralysis returned, along with what would now be called **tunnel vision**. Her field of vision was greatly narrowed as when one looks through a keyhole. For example, " . . . in a bunch of flowers which gave her much pleasure she could only see one flower at a time."

> She complained of not being able to recognize people. Normally, she said, she had been able to recognize faces without having to make any deliberate effort; now she was obliged to do laborious "recognizing work" [she used this phrase in English] and had to say to herself "this person's nose is such-and-such, his hair is such-and-such, so he must be so-and-so." (Breuer, in Breuer & Freud, 1893–1895, p. 26)

Bertha's behavior varied with some regularity. She was usually upset during the early part of the day; she then presented a dismal picture. She hallucinated, talked incoherently, and experienced severe anxiety. Bertha usually became calm, quiet and

---

[1]Reference citations throughout this chapter and the next that indicate the writings of Sigmund Freud (or, in this case of Josef Breuer) refer to the volumes of the *Standard Edition of the Complete Psychological Works of Sigmund Freud*, translated under the general editorship of James Strachey, with the collaboration of Anna Freud, and published by the Hogarth Press, London. Citations to the *Standard Edition* employ only the original publication date of the work, so that you may follow the chronology of Freud's thought.

sleepy during the course of the day and sank into a deep, semi-sleep by sunset. She used the English word **"clouds"** to capture the intangible, drifting quality of these semi-sleep periods. Today we would term this waking-sleeping or sleeping-waking state a **hypnagogic state**.

Bertha's family had noticed that the content of Bertha's daytime hallucinations seemed to resemble an actual book of fairy tales with similar themes. Bertha's fantasies were sad, yet at first they had charming and poetic aspects. However after her father's death, their tone became more somber. At this time, Bertha's daytime hallucinations came to center around an anxious young girl sitting near the bedside of a sick patient.

During Bertha's evening hypnagogic states, Breuer found he was able to elicit the content of Bertha's stories simply by repeating several words or phrases from her fantasies. After Bertha recounted her daytime hallucinations and stories to Breuer, she became quieter, more lucid, and cheerful. As a result, she became almost symptom-free for the rest of the night. Little by little, through a combination of accident and intent, doctor and patient together shaped a method to relieve Bertha of her anxiety and her symptoms, at least temporarily. They had thus made an important discovery, a **"talking cure"** that involved a kind of verbal **catharsis** (literally, a cleansing or purifying). The term *catharsis* was derived from the Greek philosopher Aristotle, who had used it to describe the emotional release and purification engendered in the audience during their viewing of a tragic drama. Bertha called the emotional release produced by her semi-hypnotic conversations with Breuer **"chimney sweeping."**

Breuer was particularly struck by the details of how a long-standing symptom went away during an unplanned conversation with her. Breuer noted the connection between the hysterical symptom Bertha experienced and her blocking of an emotion from expression as well as the alleviation of the symptom after the expression of the emotion. Breuer recounted this event:

> It was in the summer during a period of extreme heat, and the patient was suffering very badly from thirst; for, *without being able to account for it in any way*, she suddenly found it impossible to drink. She would take up the glass of water she longed for, but as soon as it touched her lips she would push it away like someone suffering from hydrophobia. As she did this, she was obviously in an absence [self-induced hypnotic state] for a couple of seconds. ... This [condition] had lasted for some six weeks, when one day during hypnosis she grumbled about her English lady-companion whom she did not care for, and went on to describe, *with every sign of disgust*, how she had once gone into that lady's room and how her [the lady-companion's] little dog—horrid creature!—had drunk out of a glass there. The patient [Bertha] had said nothing, as she had wanted to be polite. After giving further *energetic expression to the anger she had held back*, she asked for something to drink, drank a large quantity of water without any difficulty and woke from her hypnosis with the glass at her lips; and thereupon the disturbance vanished, never to return. (Breuer, in Breuer & Freud, 1893–1895, pp. 34–35)

Here, Breuer thought, the secret of the *origin* and the *form* of hysterical symptoms was finally revealed. Bertha had experienced emotions of disgust and anger intensely, but they had been blocked from expression. However, even though the emotions of disgust and anger were not expressed, Breuer reasoned that they were not eradicated. Indeed, the **strangulated affect**, as Breuer (and Freud) would later call these dammed-up emotions, remained to haunt Bertha. Bertha's suppressed disgust and anger surfaced in her symptom of disgust for water and a refusal to drink it. When the incident that had precipitated the original feelings was recalled in hypnosis, Bertha's pent-up emotions were finally released and this symptom receded.

After this success, Breuer systematically explored with Bertha the possibility that other no longer remembered incidents lay at the root of her remaining symptoms. Breuer adopted the procedure of asking Bertha during hypnosis to tell him her thoughts about a particular symptom. This exploration was often difficult, and it required great concentration. On some occasions, the whole process ground to a halt because the memory of the initiating cause of a symptom would not surface.

Most dramatically, under hypnosis, Bertha recounted the story of a particularly long and frightening night vigil she had spent at her sick father's bedside. This apparent memory with expression of associated affect led to the removal or alleviation of many symptoms including visual disturbances, language problems, hallucinations, and the paralysis of Bertha's right arm.

> She fell into a waking dream and saw a black snake coming towards the sick man from the wall to bite him. ... Her right arm, over the back of the chair, had gone to sleep and had become anesthetic and paretic; and when she looked at it the fingers turned into little snakes with death's heads (the nails). (It seems probable that she had tried to use her paralyzed right arm to drive off the snake and its anesthesia and paralysis had consequently become associated with the hallucination of the snake.) When the snake vanished, in her terror she tried to pray. But language failed her: *she could find no tongue in which to speak, till at last she thought of some children's verses in English, and then found herself able to think and pray in that language*. (Breuer, in Breuer & Freud, 1893–1895, pp. 38–39; italics added)

Bertha's Treatment Ends: The "Official Version"

Symptom by symptom, feeling-event by feeling-event, the thread of Bertha's hysteria was unraveled with the assistance of Breuer and the **cathartic method**. During the course of the treatment, a period lasting almost two years, an intense relationship developed between Breuer and Bertha. Fraülein Pappenheim found herself in the hands of a caring, humane, and fatherly physician, who was clearly interested in her suffering in ways that transcended the typical doctor-patient relationship.

Breuer's wife became jealous of her husband's involvement with this fascinating patient, and she provoked in Breuer a strong reaction of guilt. He decided precipitously to end his treatment of Bertha, a decision strengthened by her improvement and apparent cure, and he announced this intention to her. Ernest Jones, Freud's official biographer, provides an account, based on a conversation with Freud years later, of what followed Breuer's announcement of his intent to terminate treatment:

> ... that evening ... [Breuer] was fetched back to find ... [Bertha] in a greatly excited state, apparently as ill as ever. The patient, who according to him had appeared to be an asexual being and had never made any allusion to such a forbidden topic throughout the treatment, was now in the throes of an hysterical childbirth (pseudocyesis), the logical termination of a phantom pregnancy that had been invisibly developing in response to Breuer's ministrations. Though profoundly shocked, he managed to calm her down by hypnotizing her, and then fled the house in a cold sweat. The next day he and his wife left for Venice to spend a second honeymoon. ... (Jones, 1953, p. 224. Freud himself hinted at this story in *An Autobiographical Study*, 1925a, p. 26.)

Breuer felt tremendously threatened by Bertha's **pseudocyesis**. He also, for the time being, lost almost all professional interest in hysterical neurosis.

The Posttreatment Bertha: When is a Cure Not a Cure?

This account of Bertha's illness and treatment by Breuer, and the historical additions provided by Jones (1953), appears to be inaccurate, incomplete and embellished.

Figure 2.1 Fraülein Bertha Pappenheim (Anna O). Bertha was an attractive and intelligent, though deeply troubled, patient of Dr. Josef Breuer, Freud's mentor. She contributed to the development of the "talking cure" and went on to have a significant career in her own right.

Breuer's hitherto unknown case history, although substantially different from the published version in *Studies on Hysteria* (with Freud, 1895), nevertheless matched the published case *in lacking all reference to the hysterical childbirth*. As indicated in Box 2.1, it was probably a story fabricated by Freud, perhaps to explain Breuer's sudden termination of the case.

Ellenberger (1970, 1972) interviewed surviving relatives and acquaintances of Bertha Pappenheim and engaged in some clever detective work to find the sanitorium in which the patient sought refuge after the final episode with Breuer. In 1882 Bertha was *far from cured*, and the severity of her illness suggests that she did not suffer from hysterical neurosis but was likely a patient who had a borderline personality disorder with some psychotic features. The case history of Bertha that Breuer wrote in 1882 for the sanatorium doctors was published in Hirschmuller (1978, pp. 276–292).

The Bellevue Sanitorium doctors' follow-up report indicates that during her stay, Bertha became habituated to large doses of chloral and morphine, administered to relieve severe facial neuralgia. Among other comments, the report cites the patient's "unpleasant irritation against her family," and her "disparaging judgments against the ineffectiveness of science in regard to her sufferings." In the evenings, she again lost ability to speak in German, substituting English phrases for sentences begun in her

The Contributions of Bertha Pappenheim

Eventually, Bertha Pappenheim recovered from her illness to become an active feminist and supporter of Jewish causes, a writer of over thirty books, and a leading figure in developing the field of social work in Germany. She campaigned against the oppression of women, coercive slavery of prostitutes, and for the betterment of conditions for poor and orphaned children. In her later years, she experienced a complete turnabout from her early antireligious attitudes to deeply religious and altruistic traits. (Ellenberger, 1970, p. 481)

One can speculate that her eventual cure was a two-step process. The first step was the therapy with Breuer, which *may* have freed her of some disabling symptoms. The second step consisted of her own actions, which she took to remedy the conditions around her. In trying to make the world a better place, she was remedying the very conditions that had led her—and other women—into a sense of uselessness and helplessness, if not actual paralysis and disability. Perhaps her illness was an expression of the thwarted role of a talented woman in late nineteenth century Vienna.

By the end of World War II, Bertha Pappenheim was revered as a founder of the field of social work and as a brave opponent of Nazism. In 1954, the West German government issued a postage stamp bearing her picture (Ellenberger, 1970, p. 481). The full story of Bertha Pappenheim's subsequent life is beyond the scope of our present purposes (see biographies by Freeman, 1972, and Guttmann, 2001).

As we have seen, at least according to the "official version", Bertha Pappenheim also played a major role in the early developments that led to psychoanalysis. Her ability to recover material hidden from conscious awareness and to access and express hidden emotions—the process she discribed as "chimney sweeping"—was a crucial first step that eventually led to Freud's model of the psyche and development of psychoanalysis.

failing native tongue. Last, the report mentions that the patient would sit for hours under a picture of her father, and she would speak of visiting his tomb.

Breuer's Contributions to the Development of Psychoanalytic Thought

The young Sigmund Freud, a doctor in training at the University of Vienna, had been befriended and mentored by the older and more experienced Dr. Josef Breuer. In 1882, shortly after Breuer had terminated his treatment of Bertha Pappenheim, Freud heard the fascinating details of the important case. He was greatly interested and repeatedly asked Breuer to tell him the details of the story (Jones, 1953, p. 226).

It was upon the contributions of Breuer that the young Sigmund Freud built the foundations of the structure of what would eventually develop into psychoanalytic theory and practice. Breuer's rendition of the case of Bertha illustrated that:

- Hysterical symptoms were meaningful and possessed a certain underlying logic.
- The origin of the hysterical symptom was an intense, emotionally abrasive experience. Though no longer remembered, the past experience *actively operated unconsciously*, pressing for release and goading the patient to find symbolic means of expressing the discomfort.
- Symptoms could be removed (at least temporarily) by promoting the expression of the strangulated emotion dating from the past traumatic experience. This was termed the **cathartic method**. In the terminology of the *Studies on Hysteria*, the goal of the cathartic method was to enable the patient to "abreact" the painful feelings, that is, to literally "react away" the trapped energy. Any effectiveness of the cathartic method supported the theory that symptoms were the result of dammed-up emotional (affective) energy.

BOX 2.3   *Author's First Person Account—"Nothing's real 'til it's local"*

As a graduate student, I was not too impressed with Breuer's and Freud's early work having to do with accessing traumatic events, catharsis and the alleviation of symptoms. That is, until many years later, when I myself ran into this sequence in my own experience. Some nights, while falling asleep, in a sleeping-waking state or hypnagogic state very much like what Bertha termed "clouds," I had the imagery—in my mind's eye—of being suspended or hanging upside down.

Over a period of a few nights, I tried to explore this imagery when I was in the process of falling asleep. The imagery I "saw" presented itself in a tunnel vision, like looking through a keyhole. I tried to enlarge the view. What I eventually saw was that I was hanging from the stirrup of a pony that was dragging me by one foot which was caught in the stirrup!

I remembered that this event had actually occurred when I was three years old. There was a pony ride near our apartment in Atlantic City. I was riding a formerly friendly pony, which threw me and dragged me in the sand under the famous Boardwalk. My head came dangerously close to smashing against the pillars supporting the walkway. I remember that my mother was screaming. As a brave little boy, I did not allow myself to cry or scream. I must have stifled any expression of fear or terror. After the incident, I had to be taken to a doctor's office for treatment of minor injuries.

What I accessed over the next few nights was the fact that I still had a lot of fear associated with this memory. I reviewed it again and again in imagery until I got most of the anxiety about it "out of my system." I noted that after this process, there was some chronic muscle tension in my shoulders and neck that went away. Could the muscle tension have been a symptom, a somatic expression of the unexpressed anxiety associated with this event? I wondered.

I remember thinking, at the time, that there might possibly be something to Breuer's and Freud's theorizing and cathartic method after all.

It is not easy to determine how much Sigmund Freud contributed to this interpretation of hysterical symptoms. Freud was always generous in giving most of the credit to Breuer for the early theory of hysteria that they proposed in their joint publications, the "Preliminary Communication" of 1893 and their full monograph, *Studies on Hysteria* of 1895.

It was also Breuer's conviction that the essential precondition for the occurrence of hysterical symptoms was the presence of a tendency to self-induced hypnotic states of consciousness. Thus, for Breuer, any intensely experienced emotion that occurred during one of these hypnoid states that was prevented from immediate expression could serve as the origin of a hysterical symptom. It was this idea that Freud modified to a theory involving, not hypnotic states, but conflict and defense. In fact, by the time Freud co-authored *Studies on Hysteria*, in which the hypnotic-state origin of hysterical symptoms was published, he had already shifted to a model involving conflict and defense against unacceptable memories. (Silverstein, 2003, p. 11)

HYPNOSIS AND HYSTERIA: FROM PATHOLOGY TO CURE

Freud began to engage in a series of studies that involved his own clinical work as well as travels to France and direct contact with leading figures who were exploring the nature of hypnosis and the relation of hypnosis to the development and cure of hysterical symptomatology.

Figure 2.2 Franz Brentano.
The influential philosopher provided a counter-balance to Freud's heavily scientific education.
Freud had taken five philosophy courses from Professor Brentano while a student at the
University of Vienna (Merlan, 1949). Brentano was an early phenomenologist, who
emphasized the impact of the *ideas* that people held. This was at variance with the
conventional materialistic emphasis in much of Freud's pre-medical education. The effect of
Brentano's ideas on Freud's thinking is profound. Freud saw human behavior as a result both
of the physical or material structure of the human organism and *also* of the ideas that people
held about reality. Partly as a result of having been steeped in Brentano's philosophical views,
Freud would later be open to Charcot's emphasis on the importance of the specific *ideas*
hysterics held in the development of their symptoms. (McIntosh, D.I. 1977, pp. 207–227;
Silverstein, 2003, pp. 26–35)

The Influence of Jean-Martin Charcot

Freud's early reliance on the technique of **hypnotism**—a necessary adjunct to catharsis—
had other roots besides Breuer's successful treatment of Bertha. In 1885, Freud was
awarded a traveling grant to attend the lecture-demonstrations of the famous neuropathol-
ogist Jean-Martin Charcot (1825–1893) in Paris, at the equally renowned Salpêtrière
Hospital (Freud, 1925a, pp. 12–16).

Charcot investigated the symptoms and causes of hysteria. He repeatedly demonstrated that the behaviors associated with the disease could be removed temporarily and
then restored under hypnosis at the suggestion of the physician. This famous French
clinician had also demonstrated that hysterical symptoms parallel the hysteric's understanding of any given physical disorder. Thus, for example, the patient who has recently
been involved in a frightening accident, but who emerges unscathed, may nevertheless
exhibit all the symptoms he or she expects to have. He or she might experience **glove
anesthesia**, for example. In this disorder, it is as if all of the hand that could fit into
an imaginary glove were anesthetized or without sensation. This disorder does not
fit the distribution of nerves in the hand, even though it may fit the patient's notion
of a disorder. As this type of numbness was not caused by any discernable organic
or structural deficit, it was considered a functional disorder, a form of **functional**

Figure 2.3 Professor Jean-Martin Charcot in Paris.
In this representation, Charcot is demonstrating hypnosis and hypnotic anesthesia. Note the expressions of astonishment and wonder on the faces of the physicians in the audience.

anesthesia. Thus, in Charcot's view, the specific *ideas* held by the subject played a major role in the development of hysterical symptoms.

Vulnerability to hypnotic trances, Charcot believed, was also required for hysterical disorders to develop. Such vulnerability was the necessary biological precondition—related to abnormal brain physiology—for the emergence of hysterical symptomatology. (It was, incidentally, from Charcot that Breuer had adopted the idea that hysteria required a "hypnoid state" in order for the damming up of feelings to take place.) Charcot believed hysterical symptoms originated in *auto-suggested ideas* that took root when a biologically vulnerable person was in a *hypnotic-like state of consciousness* that occurred as a reaction to some trauma or emotional shock. Charcot believed that both traumatically-caused, hypnotic-like states of consciousness as well as analogous induced hypnotic trance states were based on abnormal brain physiology. In Charcot's view, a person's pathological vulnerability to trance or hypnotic states of consciousness led both to the development of hysterical symptoms and also to the impossibility of permanent cure through hypnosis. The reason for the individual's inability to be permanently cured was that Charcot saw ongoing susceptibility to hypnosis as a fundamental part of hysterical pathology.

Freud was exposed to the following set of major ideas concerning hypnosis as a result of his contact with Charcot. These ideas formed a foundation upon which Freud could continue his further investigations.

1. A patient's *ideas* in the form of presuppositions, or unconscious autosuggestions about a given disorder directed the specific symptoms. e.g., glove anesthesia

Figure 2.4 Fanny Moser (Frau Emmy von N) with her daughters.
The formidable Madame Moser was Freud's first catharsis patient. "Keep still—Don't say anything!—Don't touch me!" she sporadically repeated as a magically protective phrase.

2. These suggestions could take root only in the presence of abnormal brain physiology that Charcot thought was characteristic of hysterics.

3. Males as well as females could develop hysteria. This contradicted the older
notions that hysteria was caused by a "wandering womb" or that it was based
on female physiology.

4. Symptoms could be removed, modified, or reinstated by hypnotism and in the
very people who were susceptible to developing hysteric symptomatology.

Freud would shortly discover however, that the medical establishment in Vienna
viewed the hypnotic approach to remedying the hysteric's suffering with incredulity.
In his *Autobiographical Study*, Freud recounted his formal presentation of Charcot's
findings to the Viennese Society of Physicians and the unpleasant rejection it engendered. He was shouted at, hissed and booed by the audience (Freud, 1925a,
pp. 15ff.).

The Influence of Liebeault and Bernheim

Meanwhile, in another part of France, two physicians, Ambroise-Auguste Liebeault
(1823–1904) and Hippolyte Bernheim (1837–1919), founded a clinic at Nancy that
used hypnotism in the treatment of hysteria (cf. Watson, 1963, pp. 303–304; and Zilboorg, 1941, pp. 361–378). The physicians associated with the Nancy School, as it

came to be known, emphasized the purely pragmatic use of hypnotism as a cure for their hysteric patients. Liebeault and Bernheim held a view opposite to Charcot's theory of the close relation of hypnosis to hysteria. They asserted that hysteria and hypnotism were not necessarily related and that hypnotic states in themselves could not be the biological cause of hysterical disorder (Murphy & Kovach, 1972, p. 156). In 1889, Freud traveled back to France, this time to visit the Liebeault-Bernheim clinic at Nancy in an attempt to refine his hypnotic technique (Freud, 1925a, p. 17).

The rivalry between Charcot and Bernheim concerned the nature of hypnosis. Charcot believed that hypnosis required a unique, abnormal mental "trance" state, but Bernheim thought that hypnosis resulted from the willingness of a subject, in an ordinary state of consciousness, to be influenced by the hypnotist's suggestions. Eventually, by 1889, Freud found himself in agreement with Bernheim's position that hypnosis was a result of the "power of suggestion."

Freud nonetheless found that not all patients could be hypnotized. Even though, as Bernheim believed, trance induction was not necessary, some people still would not or could not accept the hypnotist's suggestion and thus were resistant to hypnosis. Clinically, Freud began to observe that, even in cases where hypnotism was successful, the success depended deeply on the personal relationship between the physician and the patient. Hypnosis, Freud found, was an unreliable technique for accessing the hidden memories of hysterics. His search for a new technique received its first important, if altogether unintentional guidance from a new patient, "Frau Emmy von N."

FRAU EMMY VON N.

"Keep still—Don't say anything!—Don't touch me!" These words greeted Freud on an afternoon in May 1889 when he first visited his new patient with the pseudonym, "Frau Emmy von N." Frau Emmy was lying on a couch when Freud entered, and she greeted her new physician. Interposed between perfectly coherent and logical, softly spoken amenities, came the striking utterance, "Keep still—Don't say anything!—Don't touch me!" She also evidenced several tic-like facial twitches, punctuated by grimaces of disgust and fear that contorted her pleasant face every time she repeated: "Keep still!—Don't say anything!—Don't touch me!" Frau Emmy had a tendency to stutter, and her speech was often accompanied by a smacking sound that Freud tried to convey to the reader by describing it as comparable to the call of a forest bird (Freud, in Breuer & Freud, 1893–1895, p. 49). Freud first suspected that Frau Emmy's behaviors involved some form of protective ritual to ward off a repetitive hallucination.

The Real Frau Emmy von N.: Fanny Moser

"Frau Emmy von N." was actually the 41-year-old Fanny Sulzer-Wart Moser, born in 1848 to a large aristocratic Swiss family (Appignanesi & Forrester, 1992, pp. 91ff.). Fanny was a middle child in the family with 13 brothers and sisters, the youngest born six years after her. Five of her siblings died when she was a child, including a brother addicted to morphine. At age 19, Fanny found her mother dead, probably of a stroke.

At age 22, Fanny Sulzer-Wart married Heinrich Moser, a wealthy manufacturer who was 40 years her senior. When Heinrich died of a heart attack two days after the birth of their second daughter—Fanny was then 26 years old—her husband's children by a prior marriage accused Fanny of having poisoned him to take possession of his considerable estate and deprive them of their inheritance. The body was exhumed but no evidence of foul play was found. Fanny Moser became one of the wealthiest women in Europe.

Fanny Moser was seen as a scandalous woman in the upper-class social circles of European society. Rumors of her alleged complicity in the death of her husband persisted for many years. Nevertheless, Fanny Moser became a salon hostess. She entertained celebrity artists and intellectuals on a large estate in Switzerland and earned a reputation for colorful extravagance. By 1889, she was depressed; she suffered from tics, hallucinations, insomnia, and pain (Appignanesi & Forrester, 1992, p. 91ff.). Indeed, she had been ill since the death of her husband. Accompanied by her daughters, ages 15 and 17, she traveled to Vienna for medical treatment. The prominent physician, Dr. Josef Breuer, recommended that she see Freud. For the rest of the story, we return to the case history of "Frau Emmy von N."

Tracing Symptoms to Their Origins

Freud suggested that Frau Emmy (i.e., Fanny Moser) enter a sanitarium, where he would visit her daily. Fortunately, Frau Emmy, unlike some of his later patients, proved to be an admirable hypnotic subject. As the therapeutic relationship progressed, Freud attempted to trace each of Frau Emmy's symptoms to its root by asking her, under hypnosis, to explain its meaning. For example, Freud asked her to explain the meaning of her persistent phrase, "Keep still!—Don't say anything—Don't touch me!"

> She explained that when she had frightening thoughts she was afraid of their being interrupted in their course, because then everything would get confused and things would be even worse. The "Keep still!" related to the fact that the animal shapes [hallucinations] which appeared to her when she was in a bad state started moving and began to attack her if anyone made a movement in her presence. The final injunction "Don't touch me!" was derived from the following experiences. She told me how, when her brother had been so ill from taking a lot of morphine—she was 19 at the time—he used often to seize hold of her; and how, another time, an acquaintance had suddenly gone mad in the house and had caught her by the arm; and lastly, how, when she was 28 and her daughter was very ill, the child had caught hold of her so forcibly in its delirium that she was almost choked. Though these four instances were so widely separated in time, she told them in a single sentence and in such rapid succession that they might have been a single episode in four acts. (Freud, in Breuer & Freud, 1893–1895, pp. 56–57)

Thus far, as Freud's account clearly indicates, he held to the conception of hysteria that Breuer had developed in working with Bertha Pappenheim. The patient's unconscious memory had to be searched through hypnotism for hidden emotional experiences that had not been fully expressed when they occurred. By allowing Frau Emmy to reexperience the strangulated affect of those events, catharsis was achieved. But Frau Emmy's list of traumatic experiences was endless.

Although Freud used hypnotic suggestion to remove her fears and the power of her memories to instill terror, Frau Emmy experienced relapses. She sometimes succumbed to new fears and hallucinations. Freud realized that his hypnotic suggestions and emotional catharsis were only partially successful. Tracing the symptom to its origin and freeing the choked emotional energy could not of themselves explain why a particular event had been traumatic or permanently cure the symptoms. It is worth noting again, in this regard, that Bertha Pappenheim herself had not been completely cured by Breuer's similar work.

FIRST CLUE IN THE DISCOVERY OF FREE ASSOCIATION: FREUD LEARNS TO LISTEN

Frau Emmy von N., the first patient with whom Freud employed the cathartic method, would also be the person who provided the first clue to the discovery of a new technique of conducting therapy, free association. That clue assumed great significance in later years, when Freud would have trouble with the hypnotic method.

Frau Emmy, despite Freud's hypnotic suggestions to the contrary, continued to recall frightening experiences with animals and terrifying hallucinations based on animal content. Freud, quite willing to accept the fact that each new instance of anxiety had to be removed separately, took to quizzing Frau Emmy closely on each occasion. She had reported intense stomachaches, and Freud noticed that reports of stomach pains coincided with each new animal terror. He questioned her under hypnosis on the possible origin of the stomachaches, but she seemed reluctant to continue examining each symptom with such exactness.

> Her answer, which she gave rather grudgingly, was that she did not know. I requested her to remember by tomorrow. She then said in a definitely grumbling tone that I was not to keep on asking her where this and that came from, but to let her tell me what she had to say.
> (Freud, in Breuer & Freud, 1893–1895, p. 63)

Frau Emmy's offhand and somewhat petulant remark was a momentous occasion in Freud's intellectual history. Jones, Freud's biographer, remarks with understatement worthy of Freud himself, that "he took the hint" and thus approached one step closer to a substitute for hypnosis (1953, p. 244).

In more concrete and immediate terms, Freud's acceptance of Frau Emmy's "suggestion" meant that he would allow more free rein in the handling of his patient. He would permit her feelings and strivings to direct the flow and content of their therapeutic conversation. He was moving away from hypnosis, in which the physician directs everything, to the pressure or concentration technique and eventually to free association. Each step increasingly relied on the autonomy of the patient.

False Connections: Deceptions of Memory

Freud had already begun to suspect that certain of the contents of mental processes revealed during hypnosis might be forms of self-deception designed to screen deeper and more threatening material. Thus he believed that one form of this self-protective deception involved an attempt by the unconscious mind to *falsely connect* one memory with another to obscure the real connections between thoughts. Such real connections, left undisturbed, might lead to the eventual recall of a threatening memory.

On one occasion, for example, Frau Emmy had a restless morning because she was worried that the hotel where her children and their governess were staying had a faulty elevator. She had recommended that the children use the elevator, and was now anxious over the thought that the elevator might fail. But a strange thing happened when Freud questioned Frau Emmy under hypnosis about the reason for her anxiety. Fully expecting to hear again the story of her concern for her children's safety, Freud was puzzled when Frau Emmy related instead a worry that her massage treatments would have to stop because her menstrual period might begin. The explanation for this hypnotic non sequitur, Freud reasoned, might be found in the self-protective tendency of the mind to distort and to obscure connections between anxiety-arousing ideas. Ideas can be rearranged into sequences that block conscious recognition of the correct sequence of ideas, the sequence that is connected to some anxiety-provoking thought.

Freud was able to decipher the meaning of Frau Emmy's jumbled thought train. Her real concern was for her oldest daughter, who was having some difficulty walking because of a severe attack of ovarian neuralgia. Frau Emmy had just that morning solicitously inquired of the children's governess if the girl, in her pain, had used the elevator to descend from the upper floor of the hotel instead of walking down. Then, blotting out the true source of her anxiety, her daughter's illness, Frau Emmy recalled only its oblique connection with the elevator. By displacing the anxiety to the least threatening component of the sequence, the elevator, the thought sequence became transformed:

> Not afraid of consequences of daughter's illness, but afraid that elevator might fail.

The perceptive Freud noticed that the anxious impulse was not only displaced to another thought, but that the displacement had occurred along meaningful associative lines.

> Daughter's menstrual problem → her own menstrual problem → elevator fear.

Consequently, during hypnosis only the topmost displacement, fear of the elevator, had given way to the next item in the sequence, Frau Emmy's own menstrual problem. Even though hypnotic exploration with her physician had enabled penetration one layer down through the sequence, the fundamental layer—anxiety over the daughter's menstrual problem—was left untouched.

Relapse: Intensification of Symptoms

Within seven weeks of the beginning of treatment, Frau Emmy's condition was sufficiently improved to warrant her dismissal from the sanitarium. It appeared that the cathartic method had once again worked its miracle. This happy outcome, however, did not last long.

Seven months later, Breuer received word from Frau Emmy that her oldest daughter had suffered a recurrence of her ovarian difficulties, and this time the daughter had succumbed to a "severe nervous illness" as well. The girl had visited a gynecologist for her difficulty. During the treatment, she had manifested all the signs of a severe emotional disturbance. Frau Emmy had concluded that Freud was responsible for the daughter's condition because he had treated the subject so lightly during his therapy with her. Thus, Frau Emmy relapsed into the state in which Freud had first encountered her. After much coaxing, Breuer persuaded Frau Emmy that Freud was not at fault, and one year elapsed before she again visited her old physician.

Overdetermination of Symptoms

Frau Emmy now began a period of self-inflicted semi-starvation (anorexia). She refused to eat complete meals, and she drank very little. Freud ordered her to increase her intake of food and liquid, and there followed a somewhat uncharacteristic argument between patient and physician.

Two days passed and Frau Emmy mellowed a little. Freud put her into hypnosis and asked why she could not eat and drink normally.

> "I'm thinking how, when I was a child [Frau Emmy began], it often happened that out of naughtiness I refused to eat my meat at dinner. My mother was very severe about this and

under the threat of . . . punishment I was obliged two hours later to eat the meat, which had been left standing on the same plate. The meat was quite cold by then and the fat was set so hard" (she showed her disgust) " . . . I can still see the fork in front of me . . . one of its prongs was a little bent. Whenever I sit down to a meal I see the plates before me with the cold meat and fat on them. And how, many years later, I lived with my brother who was an officer and who had that horrible disease [venereal disease]. I knew that it was contagious and was terribly afraid of making a mistake and picking up his knife and fork" (she shuddered) " . . . and in spite of that I ate my meals with him so that no one should know that he was ill. And how, soon after that, I nursed my other brother when he had consumption so badly. We ate by the side of his bed and the spittoon always stood on the table, open" (she shuddered again) " . . . and he had a habit of spitting across the plates into the spittoon. This always made me feel so sick, but I couldn't show it, for fear of hurting his feelings." (Freud, in Breuer & Freud, 1893–1895, p. 82)

We can discern in Frau Emmy's reminiscences a phenomenon that Freud called *overdetermination*. Each symptom, Freud discovered, had not one cause, not one root, but multiple determinants that had become associatively bonded together in the patient's thoughts. Consequently, one overt symptom represented many emotional threads woven to a single pattern. Conversely, a branching network of emotionally related ideas, impulses, and meanings supported each symptom. In Frau Emmy's case, the unitary symptom of refusing to eat capped a latent amalgam of previous experiences that centered on the arousal of disgust for the act of eating; cold meat and fat; fear of contracting a "foul" disease through shared eating implements; and revulsion at the act of spitting into a spittoon over dinner.

Freud again helped his patient to *abreact* or express these repressed emotions. From that time on, Frau Emmy was able to eat relatively normally, and she began to recover her composure in most other respects as well.

THE THEORETICAL YIELD FROM FRAU EMMY'S THERAPY

The case of Frau Emmy von N. is important for a firm understanding of psychoanalytic theory because it provides a vivid illustration of the clinical data on which Freud exercised his powers of observation, imagination, and reason. There are at least five important features of the case that deserve consideration:

1. A doctor using a new method of treatment for the first time might rigidly adhere to the technique to gain facility with its use. In so doing, he or she would be concerned with maintaining the correct form and be temporarily blind to the method's shortcomings and limitations. This was not the case with Freud's use of Breuer and Bertha's cathartic method. Freud was sensitive to the limitations of hypnosis and to the shortcoming of catharsis in achieving an understanding of the network of strangled emotions.

2. We must not forget that it was Frau Emmy who provided for Freud a service similar to the one provided for Breuer by Bertha, namely, a timely hint about how to proceed. Frau Emmy's irritation with Freud's incessant probing, questioning, ordering, and badgering led her to modify her physician's technique. She wished to be allowed to speak her mind without interruption. This hint was to stand Freud in good stead several years later as he searched about for a way to modify his procedure with patients not susceptible to hypnotic suggestion.

3. Freud had been led to hypothesize that the workings of the mind could be directed toward defending the person's conscious self or ego from the recognition of unpleasant, frightening, or unacceptable thoughts. Frau Emmy's concern

over her daughter's illness had been obscured by a conscious, but associatively related, concern for the safety of her children in the hotel elevator. The conscious shield-memories (elevator fear, menstrual-interference-with-massage) served to distract her thinking from the more threatening idea of her daughter's illness. Defense, not confusion, was responsible for the displacements.

4. We can see evidence from this early case that Freud's attention was directed to the importance of childhood incidents, childhood emotions, and childhood conflicts in establishing the basis of an intricate associative chain of ideas that influences adult behavior. Frau Emmy's childhood dinnertime experiences with cold meat and fat and her terrifying experiences with death and disease had certainly not passed from her memory with time.

5. Freud puzzled over the recurrence of Frau Emmy's symptoms after a temporary remission. To account for the return of some symptoms in the face of massive hypnotic suggestion to abandon them, Freud found it necessary to hypothesize that the fundamental cause of the symptom had not been reached (cf. Freud, 1896c). Such symptoms, he discovered, were *overdetermined* by multiple contributing causes and complex chains of experiences. Therefore, deeper probing was often necessary.

THE EVOLUTION OF METHOD: FRAÜLEIN VON R.

In 1892, Freud faced an intensification of his difficulties with the cathartic method: Fraülein Elisabeth von R., a pseudonym for Fraülein Ilona Weiss, his latest patient, could not be hypnotized.

Hypnotism had been an invaluable adjunct in applying the cathartic method, widening the scope of the patient's consciousness and "putting within ... [the patient's] reach knowledge which he did not possess in his waking life" (Freud, 1925a, p. 27). Freud had experienced the same difficulty with some of his other patients. In fact, some patients were not even willing to try to submit to hypnosis. Freud suspected that unwillingness to be hypnotized, whether verbally expressed or mutely evident in uncooperative behavior, formed the basis for all such failures (Freud, in Breuer & Freud, 1893–1895, p. 268).

Fraülein Weiss, therefore, posed a formidable problem because she was either unable or unwilling to achieve the customary somnambulistic state. Freud suspected that her hysterical symptoms of intense pain in her legs and her inability to stand or to walk for long periods were connected with some experience that she could recall if only she felt free enough. The greatest difficulty confronting Freud in the treatment of Fraülein Weiss was to devise a way to enable her to discuss her symptoms freely and without reservation in the absence of hypnosis.

The Real Elisabeth von R.: Ilona Weiss

Elisabeth von R. was actually Fraülein Ilona Weiss, the youngest of three daughters of a well-to-do Hungarian family (Appignanesi & Forrester, 1992, pp. 108ff.). She was an intelligent, ambitious, and independent young woman who wanted to pursue her education rather than the traditional role of wife and mother. Ilona had a close relationship with her father, who, by all accounts, treated her as the son he had wanted. Ilona nursed him until his death after he developed a heart condition. Her leg pains began at that time, but a full paralysis did not occur until about two years after his death.

BOX 2.4 *Only Connect...*

Over the course of his career, Freud would develop his thinking and modify his methods in response to difficulties he would experience with other patients just as he had in his treatment of Frau Emmy von N. and Fraülein Elisabeth von R. We will find that other creative personality theorists, ranging from Carl Jung to Erik Erikson, Harry Stack Sullivan, Carl Rogers and Albert Bandura would learn from and change their ideas in response to what to them were surprising reactions or responses from their patients or research subjects. It is when things went *not as predicted* that they had the greatest opportunity for new discoveries.

Freud learned from Fraülein Ilona Weiss that she had nursed her father after his heart attack for a period of one-and-a-half years. She slept in her father's room, attended to his needs morning and night, and forced herself to remain cheerful and encouraging. Taking care of a sick person is often more stressful than being ill oneself. Ilona experienced an attack of severe pain in her legs during this period, an attack so intense that she had to take to her bed and become a patient herself. Two years after her father's death, her leg pains returned. They were unbearable, and Ilona was unable to walk at all.

Furthermore, because of the death of her father, family members were very unhappy. Ilona's eldest sister married a talented and ambitious man, who unfortunately did not respect their mother; Ilona was resentful both toward her new brother-in-law and toward her sister for deserting the family. Her other sister also married in this period. The married couple remained close to the family. This sister then became pregnant and died in childbirth. The widowed brother-in-law was overcome with grief, and he withdrew from Ilona's family. In the space of a few years, Ilona had lost by death or by alienation those most important to her. She now began a period of almost total social isolation.

For Freud, the case history as thus far related was hard to understand. It contained no overt indication of the cause of Ilona's hysterical symptoms. Freud was stymied. In the past, such obstacles had been overcome by the judicious use of hypnotism. His frustration was not helped much by Ilona's often biting remarks about his treatment's lack of effectiveness.

With candor and lack of defensiveness, Freud conceded, "I was obliged to admit that she was in the right" (Freud, in Breuer & Freud, 1893–1895, p. 145).

SECOND CLUE TO THE FREE ASSOCIATION METHOD: THE PRESSURE OR CONCENTRATION TECHNIQUE

Freud drew on his experiences with Bernheim at the Nancy Clinic. He remembered an unusual demonstration during which Bernheim had suggested to one of his patients under hypnosis that he, Bernheim, was no longer present in the room. Bernheim further encouraged the patient in the belief that she would not see him no matter what he might do. Bernheim followed this hypnotic suggestion with a variety of threatening gestures directly in front of the subject's face, but she behaved in every way as if Bernheim no longer existed. Bernheim then added to his previous instructions the command to remember nothing of what had transpired, a typical **posthypnotic amnesia** command.

Bringing the patient back to wakefulness, he proceeded to demonstrate that the patient could recall what had transpired, despite the hypnotic amnesia. All that the hypnotist had to do was to insist strongly, urgently, and convincingly enough that the subject do so. To aid the process of recall, Bernheim placed his hand on the forehead of the subject, who was awake, and pressed firmly, while insisting that the memory of the previous events return. Much to Freud's surprise, the subject could recall the events of the hypnotic session. Thus, Bernheim had shown Freud that the patient actually does have a memory of the events but does not know that she or he remembers until a strong suggestion to that effect was made. This was Freud's clue to finding his way out of his lack of therapeutic progress with the hypnotism-resistant Fraülein von R. (hereafter referred to as Ilona).

Willful concentration thus became the basis of Freud's new approach to therapy and the investigation of unconscious processes. It is worth noting that the new **pressure or concentration technique** was no less dependent than hypnotism had been on the quality of the relationship between doctor and patient. The new method, in fact, was really another form of using the patient's suggestibility to achieve therapeutic progress. Freud described his new strategy as follows:

> I decided to start from the assumption that my patients knew everything that was of any pathogenic [disease-causing] significance and that it was only a question of obliging them to communicate it. Thus when I reached a point at which, after asking a patient some question such as "How long have you had this symptom?" or: "What was its origin?" I was met with the answer: "I really don't know," I proceeded as follows: I placed my hand on the patient's forehead or took her head between my hands and said: "You will think of it under the pressure of my hand. At the moment at which I relax my pressure you will see something in front of you or something will come into your head. Catch hold of it. It will be what we are looking for.—Well, what have you seen or what has occurred to you?" (Freud, in Breuer & Freud, 1893–1895, p. 110)

Using the new pressure or concentration technique with Ilona brought immediate results. After a long silence, she admitted that the pressure of Freud's hand had brought forth an important recollection. She remembered an evening in which a young man had romantically escorted her home from the social affair they had attended, the pleasure of their intimate conversation during the walk, and her feelings of distress on returning home to nurse her father.

Freud found that approach had been as successful in obtaining results as had Bernheim's technique, which he was imitating. Apparently, even the reluctant Ilona could recall events that seemed meaningful in context without hypnotism. Freud thought that whatever ideas were evoked by the pressure or concentration technique *had to* be related to the symptoms at hand. He still had not discovered the actual relationship between these newly recalled incidents and the ongoing process of Ilona's neurotic symptoms.

Conflict, Symbol, Conversion

Freud observed that Ilona's memories were conflicted. She had known the young man for a short time, and because he could not yet support a wife, and because Ilona was dutifully bound to her ailing father, she had resolved to wait until she and her young man were independent before marrying. But, at the same time, she felt that her feelings for the young man were somehow incompatible with her equally worthy resolve to care for her father. She recalled that the night of the social gathering, after which she had walked home with the man, marked the height of her awareness of the conflict between her affection for the young man and her responsibility to her father.

BOX 2.5   *Update—The Current Status of Theories about Hypnosis:*
Continuing Controversy

It is clear that researchers and theorists have still not resolved the questions Freud had about the necessity of trance induction vs. non-trance views of the process of hypnotic suggestion. My colleague, Professor Benjamin Wallace, a contemporary expert in the area of research on hypnosis, has contributed the following summary of current theories of hypnosis:

> The *trance theory* (Hilgard, 1973) postulates that hypnosis is a process that involves an altered state of consciousness, or a trance, during which the subject is in a heightened state of susceptibility or responsiveness to suggestions or commands. Therefore, in hypnosis, an individual must either be temporarily dissociated from the normal waking state of awareness or consciousness, or be minimally capable of performing some tasks with hypnosis which are not as easily accomplished or even possible to accomplish at all without hypnosis. (Wallace, B., e-mail communication to author, January 21, 2005)

> A second theory by Sarbin and Coe (1972) focuses on the social context in which hypnosis takes place. Unlike the trance theory, the *sociological theory* does not propose that hypnotized individuals behave as they do because they have undergone a change in the state of consciousness. Rather, it proposes that hypnotized subjects behave as they do because they are striving to enact the role of a hypnotized subject as it is defined by the hypnotist and society in general.

> Barber (1969) has suggested that hypnosis does not require a trance or a trance state in order for the phenomenon to be demonstrated. According to this *task-motivation theory*, hypnosis is not an altered state of consciousness. Rather, it is a predisposition in a normal state of awareness to attend to commands and suggestions from a hypnotist. Barber believes that most of the phenomena purported to come about as a result of hypnosis can be demonstrated in a non-hypnotic, wakeful situation. A subject who has positive attitudes about hypnosis, who is sufficiently motivated to perform a given task, and who expects that a given task is possible with hypnosis, can perform hypnotic feats without being in an altered state of consciousness. (All excerpted from Wallace, B., & Fisher, L. E. (1999). *Consciousness and Behavior* (4th ed.). Boston: Allyn and Bacon.)

Current state of affairs: There has not been a clear resolution concerning which theory is correct. Each theory still has its proponents and opponents.

When Ilona returned home late that night, she found her father's condition worsened, and she reproached herself for having sacrificed her father's care to her own pleasure. Ilona never again left her father for a whole evening. As a result, she saw her young man only rarely thereafter.

At the death of Ilona's father, the young man withdrew from her. Eventually, he moved far away and contact between the two was not maintained. Not only was the loss of her first love a painful experience for Ilona but she had not resolved the conflict between her feelings for the young man and her sense of duty to her father. The emotional quality of Ilona's incompatible feelings remained untouched.

On the basis of these revelations developed through the pressure or concentration technique, Freud reasoned that Ilona's symptoms were a technique of defense by which she had unconsciously converted her painful conflicting emotions into a bodily manifestation. Ilona confirmed Freud's interpretation by informing him that she now knew why her leg pains always began at the same point on her thigh: This was the exact place upon which her father rested his leg every morning while she changed the bandages on his swollen leg. Clearly, the pain in her own legs had arisen through association and symbolization with her father's painful leg. Furthermore, as Freud and Ilona discussed this interpretation, the pain in her legs intensified, or as Freud put it: "her painful legs began to 'join in the conversation' ..." (Freud, in Breuer & Freud, 1893–1895, p. 148).

Freud followed up her several symptoms using the new pressure or concentration technique. When asked, for instance, why other areas of her legs were painful, Ilona produced a series of recollections of other emotionally painful events. Moreover, each of these events was connected by association or by symbolization with her legs or with the act of walking. For the pain she felt while standing, she produced a memory of standing at the door when her father was brought home after his heart attack. In her fright on that occasion, she had been frozen in place. When Freud asked her what else the notion of "standing" meant to her, she reproduced a memory of standing "as though spellbound" by her sister's deathbed.

Yet, despite the insights that had been attained, there seemed to be some hesitation, some difficulty in recalling certain feelings, desires, or events. It was as if Ilona, though cooperating with Freud in the removal of her symptoms, was nonetheless resisting the recollection of some important ideas. Freud wondered whether the new pressure or concentration technique was already proving to be a failure. Perhaps, he reasoned, there might be yet another psychological process at work here?

Resistance: Defensive Barrier to Psychological Pain

On those occasions when Freud applied the pressure or concentration technique and Ilona reported that nothing had occurred to her, Freud detected behind her tense and preoccupied facial expression a hint that ideas had come to her. For some reason, Freud suspected, Ilona did not want to communicate her thoughts to him:

> I could think of two motives for this concealment. Either she was applying criticism to the idea, which she had no right to do, on the ground of its not being important enough or of its being an irrelevant reply to the question she had been asked: or she hesitated to produce it because—she found it too disagreeable to tell. (Freud, in Breuer & Freud, 1893–1895, p. 153)

Freud therefore decided to proceed as if he had the greatest confidence in his technique. He informed his patient that he knew full well that she had thought of something under the pressure of his hand, and that if she continued to conceal it, she would never be rid of her pains.

Freud had correctly surmised that the cause of her recalcitrance was emotional resistance. Ilona reluctantly complied:

> ELIZABETH [ILONA]: "I could have said it to you the first time."
> FREUD: "And why didn't you?"
> ELIZABETH [ILONA]: "I thought I could avoid it, but it came back each time," or
> "I thought it wasn't what you wanted." (Freud, in Breuer & Freud, 1893–1895, p. 154)

It was at this point, using the concept of resistance that Freud was able to gather the several threads of evidence he had been collecting from his patients into a new series of insights:

1. **Resistance** to recalling significant emotional events is another form of defensive maneuver that the conscious mind employs to ward off threatening thoughts and feelings.

2. But such thoughts, though consciously resisted, may nevertheless continue to exert unconscious pressure in their striving for expression, if not in their original form, then in disguised form.

3. Thus, Ilona's *symptoms* were not only the result of strangulated emotion; they were, indeed, the *unconsciously symbolic expression* of an unresolved **conflict**.

4. Her symptoms were substitute expressions of the conflicted emotions.

5. Ilona's conflict was pushed from conscious awareness because it had never been adequately resolved.

6. It continued to be a source of painful and unacceptable self-perceptions for Ilona.

Ilona's conflict over her duty to her father and her incompatible desire for the companionship of her young man certainly fit this mold. Yet, Freud discovered, there had to be more to it because the expression of her emotions had not completely removed Ilona's symptoms. A still unresolved conflict had to be continuing to operate behind some formidable resistance to its recall.

Symptoms as Self-Punishment

Covering old territory, again from his new perspective, Freud began to question Ilona again about the origins of her pains. Her thoughts turned back to the summer resort where she had stayed just before her sister's death in childbirth, her worries over her father's illness, and her feelings of despair and loneliness at having been unable to accomplish anything in life. Particularly strong at this period had been her desire for love, a desire that, contrary to her previous resolve to do without men after her unhappy love affair, had begun to soften her "frozen nature."

With these feelings uppermost in mind, the marriage of her sister to a man who cared lovingly and tenderly for her made a profound impression on Ilona. She knew that her sister regretted becoming pregnant again so soon after her first child's birth. However, Ilona also knew and marveled at the way her sister bore the discomfort of the illness resulting from her pregnancy with absolute calm.

Ilona went on a walk with this brother-in-law at a summer resort. He had wanted to remain with his sick wife, but even she urged him to accompany Ilona, and he relented. Ilona enjoyed the afternoon she spent with her sister's husband tremendously because they talked freely and intimately, and, for the first time, she had the feeling that someone really understood her. In consequence, she became overwhelmed with the desire to possess a man with the qualities of her brother-in-law. In fact, so strong was this desire that, a few days after their walk, Ilona returned to the place in the woods where they had been together and, in a reverie, dreamed of a man like him who might make her as happy as her sister. She arose from the reverie with her legs in pain.

The nature of her hidden conflict had become crystal clear to Freud: Ilona desired her brother-in-law, but she felt guilty over such feelings, particularly so because his wife—her own sister—was now ill and helpless. As clear as the conflict was to Freud, it was obscure to Ilona. Because she had, apparently, never admitted the existence of these feelings, her guilty wish had remained utterly alien to her conscious personality. Ironically, several months after that fateful walk in the woods, Ilona's wish almost came true. She was called to her sister's sickbed but, by the time she arrived, her sister was dead.

At that moment of dreadful certainty that her beloved sister was dead without bidding them farewell and without having eased her last days with her care—at that very moment another thought had shot through Elisabeth's mind, and now forced itself irresistibly upon her once more, like a flash of lightning in the dark: "Now he is free again and I can be his wife." (Freud, in Breuer & Freud, 1893–1895, p. 156)

Here was the confirmation of Freud's burgeoning speculations about conflict and emotional resistance. Ilona had converted a series of painful ideas into bodily symptoms to exact a kind of self-punishment. She had an illicit wish for her brother-in-law and was guilty for the feeling of gladness at the thought that her sister's death had freed him to marry her. By the time she had come to treatment with Freud, the memory of her love and guilt had already been defensively isolated from her awareness.

Ilona was devastated at the eventual realization of her own feelings. Freud was kind to point out, however, that, strictly speaking, she was not responsible for her feelings and, more important, her symptoms and suffering were proof enough of her sound moral sense.

THE THEORETICAL YIELD FROM FRAÜLEIN ILONA WEISS'S THERAPY

Freud had progressed sufficiently in his use of the cathartic method with Fraülein Ilona Weiss to consolidate his observations into important theoretical concepts.

Developing the Pressure or Concentration Technique

Fraülein Weiss's lack of susceptibility to hypnotism had initially prodded Freud into the search for a new therapeutic technique. Ilona thus provided the occasion for Freud's incorporation of a second clue in the process of developing his ultimate psychoanalytic method of free association. Freud recalled that Bernheim had demonstrated at the clinic in Nancy that a posthypnotic patient could willfully remember her previous hypnotic experiences if she was authoritatively pressured to do so. This had been the prototype for Freud's development of the pressure or concentration technique using hand pressure with the recalcitrant Ilona. (Freud's first clue was Frau Emmy's acid remark that he should allow her to speak her mind without interruption.)

Defense and Resistance

Freud discovered, through use of the pressure or concentration technique, that active **resistance** to unacceptable ideas directed Ilona's thought processes. Ironically, only through the loss of hypnotism as a therapeutic tool could the significance, cause, and direction of the process of resistance be uncovered. Because the patient in the hypnotic state is largely freed from active avoidance of unacceptable impulses and ideas, the defensive nature of this "forgetting" in the conscious state could not be discerned.

Freud's discovery clearly had brought about a drastic change not only in the way therapy was conducted, but also in the theoretical conception by which its effects were to be understood. Breuer's cathartic method focused on the problem of breaching the patient's conscious amnesia through hypnosis to reach dammed-up emotions. Once reached, these feelings could finally be spent in a therapeutic reenactment of the traumatic moment. Then, hypnotic suggestion was employed to help the patient forget the unpleasantness of his or her experiences and to conduct his or her life without the troublesome symptom. Freud, in contrast, was reshaping therapy by zeroing in, not on the symptom and its backlog of unexpressed emotion, but on the patient's unwillingness to recall painful or unacceptable thoughts.

The goal of psychotherapy for Freud became the examination and interpretation of the patient's resistances in an attempt to enable the patient to deal with conflicts that had festered, defensively protected from real resolution. Thus, by working with, rather than by circumventing, emotional resistance, Freud discovered that hysterical symptoms were a form of psychological defense against threatening ideas and wishes. The symptoms of the neurosis were symbolic and associative replacements for the pain of unresolved, "forgotten" conflicts.

Repression and Conflict

Fraülein Weiss could not willingly recall her desire for her sister's husband or her guilt feelings, and she vigorously resisted the thought when pressured. Therefore a psychological factor that actively keeps the memory out of consciousness must have been operating. Furthermore, this same counterforce must have been responsible for originally removing the memory from awareness. Freud labeled this hypothetical force *repression*.

Repression is a kind of motivated amnesia for certain impulses, ideas, or events. Resistance to recall is evidence of motivated forgetting or repression. Not just any unpleasant thought or any painful memory is repressed. Only memories, thoughts, and ideas that are somehow connected to impulses or wishes that are unacceptable to the individual's conscious ethical standards are capable of causing the intense anxiety needed to trigger repression (Freud, 1910b, p. 24).

Repression is characterized by the unconscious, automatic nature of the "forgetting" that it accomplishes. When repression operates, the individual is not aware of avoiding certain thoughts or impulses. It is like forgetting that you have forgotten and what you have forgotten. Another way of thinking of repression is that the forgetting is somehow in advance of any overt awareness of the thought or impulse itself.

The thought that Ilona was glad that her sister was dead because her sister's death freed her husband to marry again was a totally unacceptable idea to Ilona's ethical self. If the problem had been only a momentary or less threatening desire for her sister's husband, Ilona would probably have only *suppressed* (not repressed) the thought. **Suppression** involves the conscious or deliberate avoidance of certain ideas with the individual's full awareness that he or she refuses to entertain them.

Here is one way of keeping repression and suppression distinct: A person is not consciously aware, *does not know*, what content(s) he or she is repressing, but *is aware* of what he or she suppresses.

A Dynamic Unconscious

Though removed from consciousness by repression, emotions continue to operate unconsciously, thus comprising what Freud termed the **dynamic unconscious**. Freud concluded that an emotion might produce symptoms that symbolically, or through association with other ideas, replace the expression of the emotion. Repression of wishes or impulses is not always an adequate response to conflict or strong enough to keep symptoms from emerging. A symptom, Freud discovered, could express the emotion in distorted form. In Fraülein Weiss's case, the symptoms of pain in her legs and the inability to walk or stand were shaped by a series of symbolic ("standing alone") and associative links:

- standing in shock by her dead sister's bed;
- walking with her brother-in-law;
- walking with her first love while she should have been caring for her father; and
- allowing her father to place his leg on her thigh to be bandaged.

Breuer had been right: The energy of the strangulated emotion had to be expressed somehow. But the cause of the neurotic's symptoms was not simply the damming up of emotional energy. First, Freud realized, there had to be a wish or an impulse that was incompatible with an individual's conscious self-perception. Such a wish would be at odds with his or her everyday ethical principles. Only this incompatibility could carry the conflict to an ego-threatening intensity. Then the conflict's associated emotions could be dammed up by repression. **Conflict** of a wish with a conscious ethical principle is the essence of defense by repression. It is an active, dynamic process giving painful, if mute, evidence of the power of unconscious forces.

It is interesting to note that some early attempts at experimental testing of the Freudian hypothesis of repression sorely missed the point. In their enthusiasm to design experiments, some of the experimenters naively assumed that any anxiety-provoking idea could trigger repression. This unsophisticated version of the theory often led to the creation of mild forms of anxiety or unpleasantness as experimental analogs of Freud's ideas. In a great number of cases, these attempts did not come close to the kind and the quality of anguish that Freud conceptualized as the basis of repression. The mechanism of repression remains a difficult phenomenon to study in the laboratory (see Monte, 1975, Chapter 3).

A FINAL CLUE TO THE FREE ASSOCIATION METHOD

For his final modification of his developing therapeutic procedures, Freud followed yet another clue, a recollection from his own youth. One of his favorite authors, Ludwig Borne, had offered the following advice to those who wish to write creatively:

> Take a few sheets of paper and for three days on end write down, without fabrication or hypocrisy, everything that comes into your head. Write down what you think of yourself, of your wife, of the Turkish War, of Goethe, of Fonk's trial, of the Last Judgment, of your superiors—and when three days have passed you will be quite out of your senses with astonishment at the new and unheard-of-thoughts you have had. (Quoted in Freud, 1920b, p. 265. See also Jones, 1953, p. 246)

Borne's proposal to stimulate playful creativity apparently left a lasting impression on Freud. He now began to follow Borne's advice, not for writing, but for allowing his patients free play for their thoughts during therapy. Freud developed a technique of therapeutic communication designed to permit patients to roam freely through their fleeting thoughts, verbalizing each idea as it occurred. He permitted his patients to omit nothing. Freud instructed each of his patients in the new technique of **free association** in the following way:

> You will notice that as you relate things various thoughts will occur to you which you would like to put aside on the ground of certain criticisms and objections. You will be tempted to say to yourself that this or that is irrelevant here, or is quite unimportant, or

nonsensical, so that there is no need to say it. *You must never give in to these criticisms, but must say it in spite of them—indeed, you must say it precisely because you have an aversion to doing so. . . .* Finally, never forget that you have promised to be absolutely honest, and never leave anything out because, for some reason or other, it is unpleasant to tell it. (1913a, pp. 134–135; italics added)

Freud's **fundamental rule of psychoanalysis** was for the patient to say everything that came to mind without editing or censoring the stream of thought. Sometimes patients had great difficulty following the fundamental rule. They would engage Freud in conversation about the decorations in his office, or in a discussion about the state of the weather, or they would pursue some abstract and irrelevant topic on which they considered themselves expert—anything rather than abandon logical and emotional censorship over their thoughts.

With careful prodding, urging, with constant reminders and corrections, Freud helped his patients see the importance of allowing the mind to take its own path. The associations that emerged did not prove to be random or accidental. Freud discovered that the sequence, content, and speed of the flow of ideas revealed an underlying logic.

FREUD'S CONTINUING THEORIZING ABOUT HYPNOSIS

Freud eventually gave up the use of hypnosis as well as the pressure or concentration technique when he developed free association. Nonetheless, he had an ongoing concern with developing an explanation for why hypnotic suggestion could produce powerful effects, at least in some subjects. Silverstein and Silverstein (1990) have explored and presented Freud's evolving explanations of the power of hypnosis.

As early as 1890, Freud speculated that a hypnotized person adopted a relationship to a hypnotist as shown only by a child to a parent. By 1905, with his later adoption of the concept of childhood sexual desire for the parent, Freud asserted that transference was the determining factor in hypnotic suggestion. In this explanation, a subject unconsciously fixated his/her libido or sexual desire on the hypnotist as if the hypnotist were the parent. Then the subject would behave in a compliant manner so as to win the hypnotist's (the transferential parent's) love.

In 1921, Freud invoked his understanding of human evolution to help explain the power of hypnosis. He asserted that the submissive posture adopted by a hypnotized person was not only a re-enactment of a child's attitude toward its parents but also the activation of a universally inherited predisposition to re-enact a submissive stance toward the primal father. As Freud had hypothesized in *Totem and Taboo* (1913b) this primal father (what today we might term the ultimate "alpha male") demanded absolute obedience within the original human social group (Silverstein and Silverstein, 1990).

COMPROMISE FORMATION: THE MEANING OF SYMPTOMS

Consider the following description of disordered behavior:

An 11-year-old boy would not sleep each night until he had performed the following compulsive ceremony. He recounted to his mother every minute detail of the day; all scraps of paper, lint, or rubbish on the carpet in his bedroom had to be picked up; the bed had to be pushed up against the wall; three chairs, no more, no fewer, must stand by the bed; the pillows must be placed in a particular pattern on the bed. Finally, just before sleeping, the boy had to kick out with his legs a certain specified number of times and then lie on his side. Only then would sleep come. (Based on Freud, 1896b, p. 172)

The young boy's sleep ritual is evidence of a disorder known as **obsessional neurosis**. Obsessional neurotics practice a variety of ritualistic behaviors to avoid the experience of anxiety. When the obsessive is prevented from carrying out the behavior in question, he or she succumbs to an intense anxiety attack. The obsessive patient suffers from ostensibly unwanted, but continually intrusive, ideas that threaten to flood consciousness. Performance of a ritual-like series of behaviors temporarily alleviates the discomfort produced by the constant succession of the obsessive ideas. How could Freud make sense of the connection between the obsessive ideas and the compulsive anxiety-reducing ritualistic behaviors? Utilizing his new conception of **defense**, Freud sought to unlock the mystery of the obsessive person's behavior by attempting to understand the personal meaning of symptoms.

> The nature of obsessional neurosis can be expressed in a simple formula. Obsessional ideas are invariably transformed self-reproaches which have reemerged from repression and which always relate to some sexual act that was performed with pleasure in childhood. (1896b, p. 169)

Unable to sleep until his ceremonial acts involving chairs, pillows, bed, and rug had been accomplished, along with a detailed explanation to his mother of the day's events, the 11 year-old boy was able to reveal in analysis the defensive nature of these compulsive behaviors. Some years earlier, a servant girl had abused him sexually at bedtime. She had lain on top of him in the bed, and this memory was forgotten until a recent similar experience revived it. The defensive meaning of the ceremony became clear:

> The chairs were placed in front of the bed and the bed pushed against the wall in order that nobody else should be able to get at the bed; the pillows were arranged in a particular way so that they should be differently arranged from how they were on that evening; the movements with his legs were to kick away the person who was lying on him; sleeping on his side was because in the scene [with the servant girl] he had been lying on his back; his circumstantial confession to his mother was because, in obedience to a prohibition by his seductress, he had been silent to his mother about this and other sexual experiences; and, finally, the reason for his keeping his bedroom floor clean was that neglect to do so had been the chief reproach that he had so far had to hear from his mother. (Freud, 1896b, pp. 172n.–173n.)

Each of these compulsive behaviors served a double purpose. First, they served as a means of self-initiated, self-inflicted punishment for having engaged in behavior that was pleasurable but "bad." Second, performance of the ritual allowed the boy no time to think about the guilt-provoking memory or about possible future seductions. Thus, distraction as a type of avoidance as well as self-imposed penance formed the basis of his symptoms.

Paradoxically, the obsessive ideas and the compulsive acts were also a means of gratifying the pleasurable (yet anxiety-triggering) impulse involved in the taboo sexual activity. Each night, through the symptomatic ritual, the original seduction was recalled or relived. Freud therefore termed these symptoms **"compromise formations"**: they balanced the anxiety and the guilt of the conscious personality against the pleasurable gratifications sought by the unconscious.

Only by assuming the defensively altered form of the ritual acts could the repressed memory of the seduction take a place in consciousness. In effect, the symptoms symbolically substituted for the sexual gratification that the boy would not allow himself in reality (Freud, 1916, p. 368). The patient reproached himself for "bad wishes" and guilt-provoking experiences, expiating the guilt by ritual, while his symptoms achieved partial gratification of the very same wish that he sought to repudiate. In performing his defensive ritual against seduction, the young boy reenacted, not any the less completely, the very experience he struggled to escape. It was a way of "having one's cake" and "not having it" at the same time.

SEXUAL MOTIVES AS THE BASIS OF CONFLICT: ORIGINS OF THE HYPOTHESIS

In 1895, the common denominator that Freud believed he had discovered among his patients was the presence of frustrated or guilt-laden erotic impulses; such impulses he believed were disturbing because they activated repressed memories of original traumas in the form of early childhood sexual experiences (Silverstein, 2003, pp. 46–53). Thus, to take but two examples, Fraülein Weiss suffered the pain of unacceptable desire for her brother-in-law because this desire clashed with her sense of moral responsibility; the 11-year-old boy's sleep ritual involved the stress produced by a pleasurable, yet anxiety-laden, seduction. In each such case, from 1895 through 1896, Freud believed that he was able to trace the sexual themes back to actual sexual incidents and experiences in his patients' childhoods. At this time, Freud believed that children's capacity for sexual excitation normally was undeveloped or nonexistent. Nevertheless, he believed that repressed memories of childhood sexual abuse could cause sexual excitation and emotional conflict in adult hysterical patients that lay at the root of their symptoms (Silverstein, 2003, pp. 46–53).

Freud recalled some years later in writing the "History of the Psychoanalytic Movement" (1914b) that offhand comments of Breuer, Charcot, and a gynecologist named Chrobak about the sexual nature of neurotic disorders in women had shown that the idea of the sexual basis of hysteria had fleetingly passed through the minds of other workers in the field. Chrobak and Breuer later denied any knowledge of such comments, and Freud concluded that Charcot, too, would have joined them in denial had he had the opportunity (Jones, 1953, p. 248).

In thinking about the relationship between sexuality and neuroses, Freud developed a theory that stressed physiological as well as psychological aspects of sexuality. In 1895, he reasoned that the level of sexual hormones in the bloodstream affected the level of excitation in the nervous system. In adults, *too high a level of sexual hormones* could overexcite the nervous system and lead to a physically caused neurosis called **anxiety neurosis**. On the other hand, *too low a level of sexual hormones* could lead to a weakened, fatigue-prone, physically caused neurosis called **neurasthenia**. Freud conceptualized hysteria, obsessive ideas, and phobias as **defense neuroses**, the products of the ego's attempts to defend against threatening sexual thoughts. Although Freud's therapy for psychoneuroses was purely psychological, a "talking cure," his theory to explain neuroses anchored the strength of sexual thoughts and feelings to an organic base in sexual physiology (see Silverstein, 1985, 2003). Freud eventually also included a constitutional factor in his theory, as some people were capable of strong sexual drives without feeling threatened or overwhelmed by them, whereas others developed neuroses even though they had weaker sexual drives.

Freud's Development of the Seduction Hypothesis

Intrigued by the direction his clinical investigations were taking, Freud asked the logical question: Why should sexual experiences and sexual motives be the common denominator in the cases he had observed? The answer, he suspected, could be found only by examining the neurotic's fundamental defensive response: repression.

Only emotional content intense enough to overwhelm the ego was ever subject to repression in the patients Freud had treated. One would, therefore, logically expect—if sexual motives were the common denominator—that any emotion connected with the sexual experience of patients would have been correspondingly intense. But there is a problem with this supposition. Most of Freud's patients were able through analysis to trace the critical sexual experiences to their childhood years when, presumably, their physical capacity for sexual stimulation had been undeveloped or nonexistent. Hence, the seduction by an adult in childhood could not have led to full understanding or to full sexual arousal with its normal accompaniment of emotional excitation. How, then, could these relatively mild childhood feelings ever have been intense enough to trigger repression? The time sequence was wrong. Logically, the sequence should have been, first, some sexual experience like a forceful seduction by an adult; then, repression of the experience because of the intensity of the conflict between feelings of pleasurable arousal and feelings of guilt or anxiety; and, finally, the outbreak of neurotic symptoms in behalf of the repressed impulses. However, if the traumatic seduction had taken place in childhood, as many of his patients reported, this sequence was impossible. There could not have been sufficient sexual arousal or pleasure in a child to establish an intense enough conflict to trigger repression at that time. In order for repression to have occurred, a new, inverted sequence had to be postulated, placing repression at the end of the process.

Freud developed the following formulation of the **seduction hypothesis** to explain all cases of hysterical neurosis: The sexual experience (seduction) occurs first; then amnesia for it until some stimulus or situation triggers by its similarity recall of the incident at maturity; then, finally, repression and symptom formation after maturity has been reached. In other words, neurosis was not a product of childhood, but a process begun in those early years and brought to fruition in maturity (Freud, 1896b, 1896c, and 1898, pp. 279–285). Freud examined the new hypothesis carefully. Ordinarily, he knew, when sexual fantasies or thoughts with sexual content are entertained, an adult becomes sexually aroused. This actual physical arousal is always more intense than any later, secondary memory of the experience. But if his reasoning up to this point was correct, a sexual seduction experienced before physical maturity (that is, before eight to ten years) would be experienced only as a somewhat faded recollection years later in maturity. It becomes necessary, therefore, to assume that the memory is intensified from some other source of energy (cf. Freud, 1954, Letter No. 52, p. 174).

Freud supposed that the source of energy was the bodily arousal associated with sexual excitation. Furthermore, he supposed that physical sexual arousal could be rechanneled into psychological emotional arousal. The result would be a conversion of physical, biological energy into mental, psychological energy. If such a process were possible, then the memory of the earlier experience (that is, the seduction) would initiate the deferred bodily arousal some years after the experience, when the individual had developed the biological capacity for appropriate somatic response. In this delayed version, it is the memory of the experience that leads to the kind of intense physical arousal that would be stronger than the original passive-seduction experience itself.

Proportionate adult anxiety and guilt would accompany and augment the memory image—intensifying it—to bring about the conflicting psychological state of affairs that was not possible during the actual experience in childhood (cf. Freud, 1896b, pp. 172–175 and pp. 166n.–167n; see also 1916, Lecture XXIII, pp. 361–371).

Abandonment of the Seduction Hypothesis

The seduction hypothesis was an elegant one, for it accounted in one stroke for two observations:

- reports of childhood seductions by Freud's patients;
- the fact that his patients had been mentally healthy throughout childhood, succumbing to neurotic disorder only in adulthood.

However, new questions arose:

- What accounts for the period of childhood amnesia during which the seduction experience remains dormant?
- What stimulates the recollection of these early seductions in adulthood?

In supplying answers to these questions, Freud realized that he had made a major error.

Reviewing the evidence on which the seduction hypothesis had been based, Freud discovered that he had been a victim of his own naïveté. In a letter written to his friend Wilhelm Fliess on September 21, 1897, Freud revealed how some critical rethinking had caused the collapse of his seduction theory (1954, pp. 215–217). He enumerated the reasons:

- the high improbability of universal sexual abuse of children by their fathers, even though for a time it had seemed credible;
- the failure of his patients' revelations of such seductions to accomplish any lasting therapeutic effect;
- the hard-won insight that the unconscious cannot distinguish between reality and fantasy, an insight that had forced the conclusion that the reports of childhood seduction were not of real events but of imagined happenings;
- the discovery that, even in the severe psychoses, when the unconscious contents flood consciousness, no infantile sexual seductions are revealed.

Freud could only comment, years later:

> ... If the reader feels inclined to shake his head at my credulity, I cannot altogether blame him. ... When, however, I was at last obliged to recognize that these scenes were only phantasies which my patients had made up or which I myself forced on them, I was for a time completely at a loss. (1925a, p. 34)

From the Seduction Hypothesis to a Theory of Childhood Sexuality

Freud did not long remain in this bewildered state. He began to revise his thinking in the light of the new evidence that seduction tales were fantasies, products of the imagination.

> If hysterical subjects trace back their symptoms to traumas that are fictitious, then the new fact that emerges is precisely that *they create such scenes in phantasy*, and this psychical reality requires to be taken into account alongside practical reality. This reflection was soon followed by the discovery that these phantasies were intended to cover up the autoerotic activity of the first years of childhood, to embellish it and raise it to a higher plane. And now, from behind the phantasies, the whole range of a child's sexual life came to light. (1914b, pp. 17–18; italics added)

Freud was gradually coming to the view that children are not passive participants in erotic activities imposed on them, as the seduction hypothesis had it, but they are, instead, active initiators of autoerotic behaviors. He would thus replace the seduction theory with the idea of **childhood sexuality**. Moreover, Freud had begun to understand the importance of fantasy in the mental economy of his patients. Imaginary events, he realized, occupied the same status as real events in the unconscious.

FREUD'S INTEGRITY QUESTIONED—
AND THE QUESTIONER QUESTIONED

Freud's own account of his reasons for abandoning the seduction hypothesis has been challenged by Jeffrey Masson (1984a, 1984b). Masson charged that Freud needed to abandon the seduction hypothesis to protect his professional standing and the professional image of his friend Dr. Wilhelm Fliess, a Viennese eye, ear, nose, and throat doctor.

Masson (1984b) marshaled evidence from his access to Freud's letters to Fliess, many of which were then unpublished. A complete edition of Freud's letters to Fliess, edited by Masson, was published in 1985. The bulk of the evidence cannot be reviewed here, but we can briefly summarize the main features of Masson's argument in this section.

Freud's experiences in Paris with Charcot exposed him to an eminent pathologist, Paul Brouardel, who taught fellow physicians about the brutal effects of child rape. Freud also had read several clinical texts on sexual abuse of children. Masson concludes that Freud was keenly aware of the reality of sexual seduction and assault.

Also, Masson considered the case of Emma Eckstein significant. One of Freud's earliest patients was Emma Eckstein, a 27-year-old woman who suffered a variety of hysteric symptoms and menstrual complaints. Freud referred Emma Eckstein to his friend Fliess for nasal surgery in an effort to control her menstrual difficulties. Fliess had developed an odd and eccentric theory relating nasal difficulties with sexual functioning. His theory was that the functioning of the nasal mucous membranes was somehow causally connected to the activity of the mucous membranes of the vulva.

Fliess botched the surgery by leaving a piece of surgical gauze in Emma's nasal cavity, and during the weeks that followed, Emma hemorrhaged profusely to a point of near death. Freud eventually consulted another nasal surgeon and Emma's life was saved, but she remained badly disfigured for the remainder of her life. When the second surgeon began removing the gauze, Freud actually became sickened and dizzy and had to retreat to the next room. Freud reported that another member of the household gave him a small glass of brandy, which restored his composure. He wrote to Fliess that when he returned still somewhat shaky to the room where Emma and the surgeon were working, "She greeted me with the condescending remark, 'So this is the strong sex'" (Freud, 1985, p. 117).

Masson concludes that Freud needed to avoid blaming Fliess both for the strangeness of his treatment of Emma Eckstein's problems and for his lack of surgical skill. One way to defend Fliess and himself was to blame the victim. That is to say, Freud assumed initially that her continued nasal bleeding was another of her hysterical symptoms, not the result of Fliess's interventions. In this way, Freud abandoned the reality of sexual seduction as the cause of hysterical symptoms in favor of the patient's own fantasies and wishes. The stage was set to drop the seduction hypothesis in favor of seduction fantasies created by the patients themselves.

Masson argues that Freud abandoned the seduction hypothesis for these reasons:

- his realistic concern that the professional community would not look kindly on a psychiatrist who employed such data as the basis for his theories;
- his involvement in the Emma Eckstein case, and his consequent guilt and shame; and
- possible indirect pressure from Fliess to abandon the theory because of Fliess's advocacy of the idea of child sexuality. Masson asserted that Fliess was a possible child abuser/seducer, a pedophile, himself.

According to Masson's critique, Freud had to abandon the seduction hypothesis in favor of a theory that emphasized fantasy rather than the harsh facts of reality. Masson stated what he thought was the main consequence for psychoanalysis:

> ... by shifting the emphasis from an actual world of sadness, misery, and cruelty to an internal stage on which actors performed invented dramas for an invisible audience of their own creation, Freud began a trend away from the real world that, it seems to me, is at the root of the present-day sterility of psychoanalysis. (1984b, p. 144)

Thus, Masson (1984a & b) indicates that he thinks that Freud's early patients truly recovered repressed memories of actual early childhood sexual abuse while in treatment with Freud, and that Freud's error was in not granting validity to the stories of such abuse that his patients freely recounted.

However, as Silverstein points out, Freud (1896c) tells us that before he applied his treatment, his patients claimed no memories of childhood sexual abuse. This lack of reported memories persisted *in spite of* Freud's forceful instructions to produce accounts of early repressed sexual experiences. Silverstein argues that, by 1897, Freud must have finally realized that most early childhood sexual abuse narratives he had extracted from his patients were the products of his suggestions while he utilized the pressure or concentration technique. Silverstein further asserts that, faced with the dilemma of accepting the likelihood that he was putting thoughts into his patients' minds, versus the proposition that he had succeeded in recovering actual repressed thoughts that were the products of his patients' unconscious minds, Freud opted for the second assertion. (Silverstein, 2003, pp. 46–53)

To protect his theory of repression, by 1897, Freud argued that his patients did remember childhood sexual manipulation of their genitals; and these memories really were the products of the patients' unconscious minds, not the result of his suggestions. However, in Freud's new view, the patients' memories of early childhood sexual abuse were **false memories**. They did not reflect actual childhood events. These false memories were actually instances of **compromise formations**—they were symbolic expressions of what was truly repressed, early childhood sexual fantasies concerning the parents, and memories of early childhood masturbatory activities. (Silverstein, pp. 46–53)

It is noteworthy that, even today, the issue of the veracity of adult "memories" of having been sexually abused as children is still controversial. Even the testimony of children who state that they have recently been sexually abused is often false or questionable. Obviously, some such memories and accounts are valid. But some are not. A century after Freud's efforts, the problem of how to distinguish between those that are valid and those that are false memories or reports remains unsolved. Knowing the difficulty of this issue and our contemporary lack of resolution of the issues in this area, it is hard to blame Freud for the approach that he took.

PERSONAL SOURCES OF THE HYPOTHESIS:
FREUD'S SELF-ANALYSIS

In the months before he announced to Fliess his not-quite-fatal error of the seduction hypothesis, Freud had begun to subject his own dreams and thoughts to careful scrutiny through the method of free association (Jones, 1953, pp. 319–323; Kris, 1954, p. 30). Beginning in the summer of 1897, Freud embarked on a process of self-exploration that was to occupy him for the rest of his life. Although we cannot trace the entire progress of his self-analysis here, several crucial discoveries deserve our consideration both for what they reveal about Freud and for the light they throw on the origins of some of his ideas. For, much to his own amazement, Freud uncovered a more-or-less erotic love for his mother and an equally disturbing hostility toward his father. These discoveries were later to be incorporated into psychoanalytic theory as central tenets (Freud, 1900, pp. 318, 583).

The triggering incident for Freud's application of the psychoanalytic method to himself seems to have been the emotional aftermath of his father's death in October 1896. Though Freud did not at this time begin his "official" self-analysis, the emotional upheaval of the loss and some resulting family discord over proper funeral rites occasioned a dream about his father that provoked in him some residue of unexpected guilt. The dream led Freud to suspect that he was not as sorry for the loss of his father as he should have been. Yet, as he wrote to Fliess, he experienced a feeling of "being torn up by the roots," and he continued to be troubled in this way for some months (1954, Letter No. 50, p. 170). Some years later, in *The Interpretation of Dreams* (1900, p. xxvi), Freud acknowledged that his father's death was "the most poignant loss of a man's life" and had played a significant part in both his self-analysis and in the writing of that book. We take up the matters of Freud's ambivalent relationship to his father and the effect of that relationship on his theory in Chapter 3.

Another motive for Freud's undertaking the task of self-analysis was his discovery in himself of several neurotic symptoms (Schur, 1972, esp. Chapter 4). He had a disproportionate concern with the prospect of an early death, which was prompted by some cardiac symptoms. Freud also evidenced a phobia regarding travel. His concern for his health and the fear that he was developing severe heart disease may have included an element of neurotic anxiety even though his physical symptoms were certainly real enough (Jones, 1953; Schur, 1972). Freud also developed what, today, we would consider an addiction to nicotine. He continued smoking his cigars even when faced with painful surgery operations for cancerous lesions in his mouth.

A somewhat different neurotic symptom involved Freud's behavior when setting out on the journeys he professed to love so much. Throughout his life, he would frequently turn up at a railway station hours before his train was scheduled to depart, apparently in a compulsive attempt not to miss his train. But he would just as often enter the wrong rail station or board the wrong train. Freud recognized that these were symptomatic acts suggestive of anxiety and an unconscious fear of embarking on a journey.

Freud was motivated by his awareness of some of his neurotic patterns to try to face and accept whatever truths he could discover within himself. Freud wanted to have insight into the depths of his personality and to become master of his fate. He thus applied to himself methods of self-exploration that were similar to the approaches he was so carefully shaping with his patients.

Self-Recognition of Oedipal Feelings: Freud's Two Mothers

During his self-analysis Freud discovered within himself several components of what he would later call the "Oedipus complex." As his self-analysis progressed, he was able to reconstruct and, with his mother's help, corroborate several memories from childhood. These reconstructions allowed him to piece together a fairly accurate account of his own emotional life in childhood. One such memory fragment concerned the recollection of the elderly woman who had been the infant Freud's nanny along with the memory of a seemingly unconnected, but especially important, train ride with his mother:

> ... the "prime originator" [of my troubles] was a woman, ugly, elderly, but clever, who told me a great deal about God Almighty and Hell and who gave me a high opinion of my own capacities; and that later (between the ages of two and two-and-a-half) my libido [sexual interest] was stirred up towards *matrem*, namely on the occasion of a journey with her from Leipzig to Vienna, during which we must have spent the night together and I must have had an opportunity of seeing her *nudam*.... (1897, Letter No. 70, p. 262)

This passage from Freud's correspondence with Fliess is notable for a number of reasons:

1. It is a clear indication of the importance of an idea that Freud had begun to toy with: namely, that the child experiences sexual impulses toward his mother. By "sexual", Freud meant to include all pleasurable and affectionate interactions, commonly called love, between mother and child (see, for example, Freud, 1925a, p. 38). In this same letter, Freud hinted that his anxiety over traveling could be dated to the train ride with his mother and the residue of guilt that remained from his feelings toward her.

2. The second important aspect of this memory fragment is Freud's admission of such feelings himself. Notice, however, that both the word for "mother" (*matrem*) and the word for "nude" (*nudam*) are in Latin, as though writing them in his native German would have made them more threatening. Freud must have experienced firsthand the kind of emotional resistance that his patients often exhibited.

3. Freud evidenced another characteristic typical of a patient undergoing psychoanalysis, an erring sense of time. Freud could not have been only two or two-and-a-half years old, as he states. Ernest Jones, after careful research, places the date of the train ride somewhat later, at around the age of four (1953, p. 13). Max Schur, Freud's more recent biographer, concurs with Jones's estimate (1972, p. 120). Indeed, Schur suggests that it is probable that the infant Freud had often observed some intimate scenes between his mother and father in the crowded conditions of their home.

4. The "prime originator" mentioned in the letter was the nursemaid who had cared for Freud as an infant and for several years of his childhood. This enigmatic old woman had popped in and out of Freud's memories for years. During his self-analysis, the memory finally yielded its secret. To substantiate his analysis, Freud asked his mother, now in her old age, to confirm the facts of his recollection. She confirmed that he had indeed had a nurse who was elderly but clever, and that she had been arrested for stealing his silver coins and toys. At the time of the incident, Freud's mother had relinquished his care to the nursemaid because she was in the last stages of pregnancy with Freud's youngest sister, Anna. Freud's self-analysis revealed that this nanny had a profound impact on

his conception of himself, and that she had taught him a good deal about her religion. Paul Vitz has speculated that she even secretly baptized the baby Freud, who developed a "Christian unconscious" (Vitz, 1988). Moreover, this nanny was "my instructress in sexual matters, and chided me for being clumsy and not being able to do anything. . . ." (Freud, 1954, p. 220)

Thus, this "elderly but clever woman" was in charge of the young Freud, associated with sexuality in his memory, and most important, equated with his mother (Grigg, 1973; see also Gedo, 1976, pp. 298ff.). The identification in memory of the nanny and his mother had other determinants as well. Freud's older half brother, Philipp, had become a father substitute during the time of Freud's mother's pregnancy; and it was Philipp who had gone to fetch a policeman to arrest the nanny for her thefts. Freud's mother, helping her son to recollect these events, told Freud that Philipp's action had resulted in the nanny's imprisonment for 10 months. Thus, in the young Freud's mind, Philipp was responsible for the disappearance of one of his "mothers." Or, to put it another way, one of Freud's "fathers" enforced a separation between young Sigmund and one of his "mothers." With these facts in hand, Freud could focus his self-analysis on even more probing questions.

The Theme of Disappearing Persons

How had the equation between his nanny and his mother come about? Why was the nanny's disappearance so acutely felt? Freud's self-analysis provided the answers:

> I said to myself if the old woman disappeared so suddenly [on account of her imprisonment], it must be possible to point to the impression this made on me. Where is that impression, then? A scene then occurred to me, which for the last 29 years has occasionally emerged in my conscious memory without my understanding it. My mother was nowhere to be found: I was screaming my head off. My brother, Philipp, 20 years older than me, was holding open a cupboard for me, and when I found that my mother was not inside it either, I began crying still more, till, looking slim and beautiful, she came in by the door. What can this mean? Why was my brother opening the cupboard, though he knew that my mother was not in it, so that this could not pacify me? And then suddenly I understood. I had asked him to do it. When I missed my mother, I had been afraid she had vanished from me just as the old woman had a short time before [i.e., the maid's imprisonment]. Now I must have heard that the old woman had been locked up and consequently I must have thought that my mother had been too—or rather had been "boxed up"; for my brother Philipp, who is 63 now, is fond to this very day of talking in this punning fashion. The fact that it was to him in particular that I turned proves that I knew quite well of his share in the nurse's disappearance. (1897, Letter No. 7, pp. 264–265)

Freud's memory had condensed the account of the maid's disappearance with the memory of his mother's pregnancy. Analysis of the reconstructed memory was revealing. There was the implied accusation against Philipp to the effect that he had made Freud's mother vanish. Philipp was represented as a rival who controlled the whereabouts of Freud's mother—a rival, that is, who possessed adult authority. From other details of Freud's life it was clear that Philipp also represented a specific father substitute. Note, too, that Freud's mother appeared in the memory as "slim and beautiful," emphasizing that her pregnancy was over.

Three elements, then, required interpretation:

- concern over Freud's mother's pregnancy;
- the demand that Freud's half brother open the cupboard; and

• an implied connection between Philipp causing the maid's disappearance and the disappearance of Freud's own mother.

Freud's self-analysis allowed him to clarify the relations among these three elements, as he reported some years later in *The Psychopathology of Everyday Life*:

> Anyone who is interested in the mental life of these years of childhood will find it easy to guess the deeper determinant of the demand made on the big brother [i.e., the request to open the cupboard]. The child of not yet three [i.e., Freud himself] had understood that the little sister [Bertha] who had recently arrived had grown inside his mother. He was very far from approving of this addition to the family, and was full of mistrust and anxiety that his mother's inside might conceal still more children. The wardrobe or cupboard was a symbol for him of his mother's inside. So he insisted on looking into this cupboard and turned for this to his big brother, who [as is clear from other material] had taken his father's place as the child's rival. Besides the well-founded suspicion that this brother had had the lost nurse "boxed up," there was a further suspicion against him—namely that he had in some way introduced the recently born baby into his mother's inside. (1901, p. 51n.)

The young Freud's disappointment when the cupboard was opened and his mother was not to be found inside was assuaged only by his relief when she reappeared "slim and beautiful," that is, without any other unwanted children. Key emotions contained in these disturbing memories involved the desperate fear of losing his mother to an adult rival, the vague understanding that men somehow put babies inside women, and the defensive telescoping of the maid's having been "boxed up" at the hands of the same adult rival with the memory of his mother's disappearance. Freud had thus discovered within himself the essential elements of the emotional constellation to be known later as the Oedipus complex.

Freud was singularly and passionately attached to his mother. He idealized her, and she, in turn, idolized him (Bernstein, 1976; Fromm, 1959; Gedo, 1976; Grigg, 1973; Jones, 1953; Stolorow & Atwood, 1978). A good portion of his self-analysis had shown Freud, that, as a child, he wished to share his mother with no one, and that he had viewed every potential rival for her attentions with enormous hostility. His enforced separation from his real mother by virtue of her pregnancy, and his experience of a similarly imposed separation from his surrogate mother by a surrogate father figure helped Freud to comprehend the strength of a child's attachment to his mother and the child's desire for her exclusive attentions (Stolorow & Atwood, 1978). Freud was even able to face the enormity of his own aggression against rivals for his mother's love in his reconstruction of his death wishes against one such competitor, his younger brother Julius.

Julius did in fact die when Sigmund was 23 months old, and to the young, wishful Freud this death must have seemed like the magical fulfillment of desire. As he was to theorize years later in works such as *Totem and Taboo* (1913b), the neurotic personality behaves as though thoughts were omnipotent. He had wished for the death of Julius, and it must have seemed the thought itself was sufficient to bring reality into line with desire. During his self-analysis, Freud reported this discovery to Fliess:

> ... I welcomed my one-year-younger brother (who died within a few months) with ill wishes and real infantile jealousy, and that his death left the germ of guilt in me. (Freud, 1954, p. 219)

It is no wonder that the theme of disappearing persons held such significance for Freud. In his lifetime he had been exposed to the possibility of a "disappearing" previous wife of his father, to a disappearing mother substitute, to a disappearing mother, and to a disappearing younger rival for his mother's attentions. Thus, in short

Figure 2.5 Sigmund Freud and his mother, Amalie Nathanson Freud, in 1872.
Freud was 16 years old at the time this photograph was taken. The conventional pose with the distance between mother and son belies the deep attachment Freud felt for his mother.

Source: Jones, E. (1953) by permission of Sigmund Freud Copyrights Ltd.

succession, through what must have been a painful self-exploration, Freud discovered in his own mental economy hostile wishes toward his father and toward his siblings; erotic wishes toward his mother; and a tangled series of anxieties and guilt that had forced these experiences out of consciousness.

Freud never ceased his self-analysis, reserving the last half hour of his day throughout his life for such self-exploration (Jones, 1953, p. 327). It was from the earliest self-analytic attempts that Freud derived his most fertile ideas, those which he sought to corroborate further with his patients. The implication of these early disturbing self-insights was clear: Children are capable of diffuse sexual feelings, and the first objects of their erotic endeavors and resulting jealous aggression are their parents, the people with whom they have had the most intimate contact.

It becomes necessary at this point to break off this essentially chronological treatment of psychoanalytic theory to gather together the several threads of Freud's continually evolving views of sexual development.

PSYCHOSEXUAL DEVELOPMENT: OEDIPUS AND ELECTRA

Human infants are born essentially helpless and vulnerable to all manner of painful and potentially lethal stimulation. It is only through the efforts of their caretakers that infants survive the first several years of life.

Erotogenic Bodily Zones

Consider the situation of the well-cared-for infant. When it experiences hunger, its cries bring its mother or caretaker with nourishment in the form of breast or bottle. The sucking response, with which it meets the nipple or bottle, though reflex at first, not only provides the needed nourishment to terminate the hunger pains, but also becomes a pleasurable source of stimulation. Gentle stimulation of the lips and mouth is quite satisfying and sensually pleasing. Even a thumb may become an object of sensual pleasure. The infant is finding satisfaction through the stimulation of its own body; it is, in Freud's terms, behaving *autoerotically* (1905, pp. 181–182).

The pleasurable activity of the mouth may be thought of as the prototype for various other potentially pleasurable zones of the body that yield satisfaction to rhythmic stimulation. Primary of such **erotogenic zones**, as they are called, are those areas of the body characterized by the presence of a mucous membrane, for example, the anus. But the infant's body pleasures are not restricted to mucous membrane areas. With time, these mucous membrane prototypes yield their dominance so that almost any part of the body may become an erotogenic zone. Thus the skin, when tickled or stroked, leads to great delight; the anus during elimination provides a sense of satisfaction at the pleasure of discharging tension, and so on.

Freud emphasized that children explore their own bodies, seeking sensations of pleasure. Consequently, Freud concluded, the infant's chief aim is the attainment of bodily or "organ pleasure" based on its experiences with the world, its body, and its caretakers. Food and the breast or bottle provided the first such experience and the mother or caretaker was the medium through which that learning took place. In Freud's day, the mother was directly connected with almost every other important—pleasurable and unpleasurable—activity of the infant's life. Freud therefore concluded that the mother would become the object of the child's constantly developing modes of seeking new pleasures.

The Widened Meaning of "Sexual"

The biological force underlying the child's pleasure-seeking activity is the sexual drive or **libido** (cf. Freud, 1905, p. 135; and 1916, p. 313). (Libido is a concept we give much more detailed consideration in the context of Freud's theory of instincts in Chapter 3.) The term "sexual" cannot be confined to the adult sense in which it is customarily used to indicate genital, procreative activity. Genital primacy, one component of the generalized sexual instinct, or libido, is a relatively late, postpubertal development. Genital sexuality has origins far more diffuse and deeply rooted in infantile pleasure-seeking activity than is ordinarily realized. Adult genital sexuality is only the final step in a long apprenticeship to pleasure.

The Oedipus Complex

The **Oedipus complex** occurs as a kind of emotionally climactic midpoint in the developmental sequence of the male child's ever-increasing interest in pleasurable sexual activity. In the first **psychosexual stages**, the child's dominant erotogenic zones are the oral and the anal areas. Eventually, however, through exploration of his own body, he discovers the pleasure to be derived from manipulation of a new zone, the genital area. It is at this point, when the mother first discovers the child's errant hand seeking out that taboo part of his body, that she is likely to take measures to prevent such "perversity." Her admonitions may take the form of direct or veiled threats to remove the tempting organ, or, more typically, she may delegate the responsibility to father (Freud, 1940, p. 189). Parental practices like these may have been widespread in Freud's post-Victorian age, but it is doubtful that a contemporary mother or father would resort to such extreme threats.

Even if such a threat is at first unbelievable, it easily becomes more real when it is reinforced by the sight, however accidental, of the female genitals. The young boy becomes convinced that castration is not only possible, but, in fact, has already been accomplished in some individuals. The distinction between the sexes is still obscure to the frightened and chastened boy.

In some diffuse and vaguely understood way, the pleasurable sensation produced by self-manipulation of the sexual organs is perceived by the child as connected with his relationship to his mother, displacing his earlier oral and anal interests.

> At this point in the developmental sequence, the child senses that his mother's attention and her warmly soothing ministrations are not exclusively his. Besides troublesome siblings, mother must be shared with father, and the child soon comes to resent and to be jealous of this interloper. Freud assumed that with increasing sophistication the child develops a belief that his father knows, or at least suspects, how much he would like to be rid of him. Anxiety-stricken and guilty, the young boy feels certain that his intense anger and avid pleasure-seeking are impossible to conceal. His submissive and overtly loving behavior, he feels, is but a transparent facade to an all-knowing, all-powerful father. What more appropriate retribution could father plan to exact than the removal of that organ that provides the most pleasure at this stage? Castration by the father becomes the overwhelming fear of the child's burgeoning ego, and this imagined outrage must be dealt with by the mechanisms of defense. Most notable of these is the mechanism of repression. (Monte, 1975, p. 100)

The period during which this emotional constellation of love, jealousy, and castration fear occurs is called the phallic stage of psychosexual development. Emotional ambivalence is the hallmark of the phallic stage, for the young boy not only must learn to give up his chosen love object, he must also reconcile his contradictory feelings of love for and anger at his father.

The Electra Complex

In the boy, it seemed clear that the Oedipus complex was dissolved by the real or fantasized threat of castration. However, since the girl, by virtue of her anatomical development, does not fear the loss of a penis, she must assume that its absence indicates that she has already been deprived. Consequently, for her the realization that she has been castrated initiates the Oedipus complex in the female or, as commonly labeled, the **Electra complex**. Freud alternately rejected and then accepted the term *Electra complex* for the distinctly different feminine version of this emotional constellation (cf. Freud, 1931, p. 229 for his arguments against the use of the term; and 1940, p. 194, for his apparent acceptance). Regardless of the term employed, the Electra complex in the female involves several highly distinctive processes that differentiate her from the male.

Attachment to the Mother: "Penis Envy"

Just as the little boy takes his mother as the first love object, the little girl likewise attaches herself intimately to her mother. Thus, like the little boy, she will also eventually have to relinquish her first love object. More significantly, however, she will also have to relinquish her first erotogenic zone of pleasurable genital stimulation, the

BOX 2.6   *Only Connect...*

Ruth Munroe's example of penis envy does not prove either the universality of penis envy in our own culture or the Freudian assertion that penis envy is a consequence only of anatomy rather than of cultural factors. The psychoanalytical theorist, Karen Horney, as indicated in Chapter 10, takes the point of view that penis envy occurs only if women are treated as infe-

riors. The anatomical differences between the sexes, in her view, are imbued with culturally defined meanings. Horney asserted that men are prone to womb envy, which parallels penis envy in women. Penis envy involves a sense of relative powerlessness, whereas womb envy represents a feeling of lack of connectedness with nature or of genuine creativity.

clitoris. When she first discovers that her clitoris is not a penis: "... she envies boys its possession; her whole development may be said to take place under the colors of envy for the penis" (Freud, 1940, p. 193).

An example of **penis envy** in a young child was provided by Ruth Munroe. Dr. Munroe, a psychologist, was skeptical about Freud's theory until:

> ... she observed her four year-old daughter in a bathtub with her brother. The daughter suddenly exclaimed, "My weewee (penis) is all gone,"—apparently comparing herself with her brother for the first time. Munroe tried to reassure her, but nothing worked, and for some weeks she objected violently even to being called a girl. (1955, pp. 217–218, as quoted in Crain, 1992, p. 233)

This example, however, by no means *proves* the universality of the experience of penis envy in little girls.

With the discovery that she lacks what, in her view, is an essential anatomical item, the girl at first tries to convince herself that her perception is wrong. She has seized on the clitoris as the nearest proximity to the external male genitalia, but the choice has not been successful. Maturation forces her to abandon even more fully any notion of a comparable external genital to that of boys. Ultimately, the girl is forced to the realization that she is lacking not only the penis, but also all the virtues of maleness that possession of such an organ implies.

> A variety of negative outcomes is possible: The girl, as she grows up, may develop a masculinity complex, in which she devoutly protests the injustice she perceives and comes to assume all the essential male personality characteristics in defiance of her alleged inferiority. On the other hand, she may eventually abandon sexual activity altogether in her attempt to avoid any reminder of her inferiority. (Freud, 1931, p. 230)

Devaluation of the Mother

In the light of her discovery that lack of a penis is a universal attribute of girls, devaluation of the mother and abandonment of her as a love object occurs (Freud, 1931, p. 233). Hostility accompanies this breaking off of the attachment for a variety of reasons. Some of these may include the real or fantasized idea that her mother deprived her of pleasures rightfully hers, or that her mother shortchanged her in affection, or, most important, that it was mother who deprived her of the envied organ. The hostility can reach a peak when a sibling is born:

> ... what the child grudges the unwanted intruder and rival is not only the suckling but also all the other signs of maternal care. It feels that it has been dethroned, despoiled, prejudiced

in its rights; it casts a jealous hatred upon the new baby and develops a grievance against the faithless mother.... (Freud, 1933, p. 123)

Consequently, it is to the father that the young girl now turns in her effort to obtain that which she "knows" her mother cannot provide.

Search for a Penis Substitute

Freud's earlier work with neurotic female patients had revealed the almost universal presence of a seduction-by-an-adult fantasy. In most of his published writings of the period he alluded to seduction, but Freud barely hinted that the seduction was accomplished by the patient's own father. He had, however, made the role of the father in the seduction tales of his patients known to his friend, Wilhelm Fliess, during the course of their correspondence (1897, p. 259; also in 1954, Letter No. 69, p. 215). In later published writings, Freud indicated that indeed it was the father who had been reported to have seduced his own child early in the child's life (1925a, p. 34). It was not until 1931, however, almost 35 years after his ideas on the role of childhood sexuality had replaced the original seduction hypothesis, that Freud revealed, in a paper on female sexuality, that mothers, too, had been indicted in the seduction fantasies (1931, p. 238; see also 1933, pp. 120–121).

Of course, both types of seduction fantasy now made sense: In Freud's mind, they were products not of a perverse whimsy of hysterical patients, but of the female Oedipal stage of development. In the pre-Oedipal phase, the object of the seduction fantasy is the mother for both boys and girls. During the Oedipal period proper, the father becomes the focus of the girl's fantasy. She wishes for a penis from her father or a symbolic penis substitute, a baby. She cannot obtain a penis from her mother, who likewise lacks this vital equipment. With the wish for a "penis-baby," the girl fully enters the Oedipal phase (Freud, 1925b, p. 256).

Resolution of the Oedipus Complex and the Electra Complex

Freud summarized the dissolution of the boy's Oedipus complex:

> In boys... the complex is not simply repressed, it is literally smashed to pieces by the shock of threatened castration. Its libidinal cathexes are abandoned [i.e., the attachment to mother], desexualized and in part sublimated.... (1925b, p. 257)

In his final model of the mind, Freud extended this line of reasoning to show that the dissolution of the Oedipus complex results in the identification of the boy with his father and in the establishment of a "superego" or special agency of morality incorporated from the parents.

For the girl, however, the Electra complex has no such clear-cut, final outcome. Because the threat of castration, the motive for its dissolution in the boy, has affected the beginning of the Electra complex, the same fear cannot be the basis for its resolution. Instead, the female complex may undergo slow fading with time, or, in some cases, may meet its end through massive repression (Freud, 1925b, p. 257). Freud's view of the male Oedipus complex and the corresponding female Electra complex is summarized in Table 2.1.

Freud drew several conclusions that today would rightly be considered antifeminist or male supremacist. Among these was the notion that women do not develop as strong a conscience (superego) as men. In Freud's view, only the fear of castration makes possible the development of a strong conscience. In future chapters, we will see how

Table 2.1   Successive Stages of the Oedipus and Electra Complexes Contrasted

Oedipus complex (boy)

Motive	Consequence	Outcome
1. Attachment to mother (feeding, bodily care)	Jealousy of rivals, particularly of father	Feelings of hostility toward father
2. Castration fear (sight of female genitals; possible threats)	Fear of punishment by father for his desires to possess mother	Intensification of rivalry with father; development of need to camouflage hostility
3. Need to appease father and prevent imagined attack	Creation of facade of meekness and love for father	Repression of hostility and fear; relinquishment of mother; identification with father

"A mother is only brought unlimited satisfaction by her relation to a son; this is altogether the most perfect, the most free from ambivalence of all human relationships" (Freud, 1933, p. 133).

Electra complex (girl)

Motive	Consequence	Outcome
1. Attachment to mother (feeding, bodily care)	Jealousy of rivals	General feelings of inferiority; discovery of genital differences from males
2. Penis envy (sight of male genitals)	Jealousy of male organ and of male privileges	Devaluation of mother and of female role; adoption of male behaviors
3. Attachment to father as more powerful than mother	Seeking from father a penis substitute—a baby	Identification with female behaviors to appeal to father; slow fading of penis envy and mother devaluation

" . . . girls hold their mother responsible for their lack of a penis and do not forgive her for their being thus put at a disadvantage" (Freud, 1933, p. 124)

prominent female psychoanalysts were first concerned about Freud's view of male superiority and then endeavored to correct Freud's male bias.

THE COMPLETE OEDIPAL COMPLEX

In one of his last major works, *The Ego and the Id* (1923), Freud presented a more complex analysis and explanation of the Oedipus complex in psychosexual development. He described three subtypes of the triangular nature of relationships between the child and his or her parents: (1) the normal positive Oedipus complex; (2) the inverted negative Oedipus complex; and (3) the complete Oedipus complex. The normal positive Oedipus complex has been described in the preceding section. However, the inverted negative and complete complex are less well represented in textbooks on theories of personality and yet are crucial to understand the way Freud conceptualized the evolution of the Oedipus complex in psychosexual development. To establish the "bigger picture," Freud delineated that the complete Oedipus complex was determined by several interacting processes: (1) the constitutional bisexuality of the child and the parents which he referred to as the "masculine and feminine sexual dispositions" (1923a, p. 28); (2) the nature of early attachment relationships to the mother or nurturant care providers; and (3) the fusion of parent identifications in the child which creates modifications in the ego to form "a precipitate in the ego" that results in a superego and early structure of gender identification. (1923a, p. 30) Let us take a more detailed look at these determinants of the complete Oedipus complex.

Genetic Bisexual Dispositions

It was Freud's view that all persons have genetically determined "constitutional dispositions" in terms of possessing masculine and feminine hormones. As such, he proposed that the degree of genetically determined masculinity or femininity reflected constitutional bisexuality that then subsequently influenced how the child attached (i.e., identified and connected) to the bisexual characteristics of masculine or feminine personality characteristics of his or her parental figures or care providers.

> The whole subject, however, is so complicated that it will be necessary to go into it in greater detail. The intricacy of the problem is due to two factors: the triangular character of the Oedipus situation and the constitutional bisexuality of each individual. In its simplified form the case of a male child may be described as follows. At a very early age the little boy develops an object-cathexis for his mother, which originally related to the mother's breast and is the prototype of an object-choice on the anaclitic model; the boy deals with his father by identifying himself with him. For a time these two relationships proceed side by side, until the boy's sexual wishes in regard to his mother become more intense and his father is perceived as an obstacle to them; from this time the Oedipus complex originates. His identification with his father then takes on a hostile coloring and changes into a wish to get rid of his father in order to take his place with his mother. Henceforward his relation to his father is ambivalent; it seems as if the ambivalence inherent in the identification from the beginning had become manifest. An ambivalent attitude to his father and an **object-relations** of a solely affectionate kind to his mother make up the content of the simple positive Oedipus complex in a boy. (1923a, pp. 26–27)

Thus, it may be seen that the simple Oedipus complex is one in which the boy's increased affection for his mother is reduced in its intensity and a stronger identification with the father occurs in the male child. This defines the simple positive Oedipal complex as gender identification with the father for the male child, or mother identification for the female child, which preserves the anaclitic attachments so critical to the earliest stages of psychological attachment and trust in the world. However, according to Freud, the nature of the Oedipal situation is complex with resulting consequences for ego development and modification.

> Along with the demolition of the Oedipus complex, the boy's object-cathexis of his mother must be given up. Its place may be filled with one of two things: either an identification with his mother or an intensification of his identification with his father. We are accustomed to regard the latter outcome as the more normal; it permits the affectionate relation to the mother to be in a measure retained. In this way the dissolution of the Oedipus complex would consolidate the masculinity in a boy's character. In a precisely analogous way, the outcome of the Oedipus attitude in a little girl may be an intensification of her identification with her mother (or the setting up of such an identification for the first time—a result which will fix the child's feminine character. (1923a, p. 29)

This quote illustrates Freud's point that gender identity is, in part, shaped by the resolution of the Oedipus complex through the processes of identification with the parents.

But the situation is not so elegantly simple because of the constitutional bisexuality in the child. Freud provides further insight by saying:

> These identifications are not what we should have expected [from the previous account (p. 24)], since they do not introduce the abandoned object into the ego; but this alternative outcome may also occur, and is easier to observe in girls than in boys. Analysis very often shows that a little girl, after she has had to relinquish her father as a love-object, will bring her masculinity into prominence and identify herself with her father (that is, with the object which has been lost), instead of with her mother. This will clearly depend on whether the masculinity in her disposition—whatever that may consist in—is strong enough. (1923a, p. 28)

This passage illustrates what Freud meant by the constitutional bisexuality in the child, as both masculine and feminine personality characteristics may emerge from identification with the parents' personal attributes and dimensions of personality. Moreover, he goes on to state that the simple positive Oedipus complex is *not* the most common form or subtype in the triangular relationship between the child and care providers.

The Complete Oedipal Dynamics

To further illustrate the complex nature of the Oedipal process in childhood, Freud states:

> It would appear, therefore, that in both sexes the relative strength of the masculine and feminine sexual dispositions is what determines whether the outcome of the Oedipus situation shall be an identification with the father or with the mother. This is one of the ways in which bisexuality takes a hand in the subsequent vicissitudes of the Oedipus complex. The other way is even more important. *For one gets an impression that the simple Oedipus complex is by no means its commonest form, but rather represents a simplification or schematization which, to be sure, is often enough justified for practical purposes. Closer study usually discloses the more complete Oedipus complex, which is twofold, positive and negative, and is due to the bisexuality originally present in children: that is to say, a boy has not merely an ambivalent attitude towards his father and an affectionate object-choice towards his mother, but at the same time he also behaves like a girl and displays an affectionate feminine attitude to his father and a corresponding jealousy and hostility towards his mother*. It is this complicating element introduced by bisexuality that makes it so difficult to obtain a clear view of the facts in connection with the earliest object-choices and identifications, and still more difficult to describe them intelligibly. It may even be that the ambivalence displayed in the relations to the parents should be attributed entirely to bisexuality and that it is not, as I have represented above, developed out of identification in consequence of rivalry. (1923a, p. 29)

This passage illustrates the emergent structure of the complete Oedipus complex and, logically, creates the subtypes, simple positive (boy to father; girl to mother) and the inverted simple negative (boy to mother; girl to father), as determined by the genetic or constitutional factors of masculinity and femininity. So, what then comprises the complete Oedipus complex, the most common form of childhood identification by the child with his or her parents or care providers? Here is what Freud says:

> In my opinion it is advisable in general, and quite especially where neurotics are concerned, to assume the existence of the complete Oedipus complex. Analytic experience then shows that in a number of cases one or the other constituent disappears, except for barely distinguishable traces; so that the result is a series with the normal positive Oedipus complex at one end and the inverted negative one at the other, while its intermediate members exhibit the complete form with one or other of its two components preponderating. *At the dissolution of the Oedipus complex the four trends of which it consists will group*

themselves in such a way as to produce a father-identification and a mother-identification. The father-identification will preserve the object-relation to the mother which belonged to the positive-complex and will at the same time replace the object-relation to the father which belonged to the inverted complex: and the same will be true, *mutatis mutandis*, of the mother-identification. The relative intensity of the two identifications in any individual will reflect the preponderance in him of one or other of the two sexual dispositions. (1923a, p. 30)

Thus, we can see from this passage that there are many possible "combinations" of identifications by the child with his or her parents or care providers. This can be illustrated as follows:

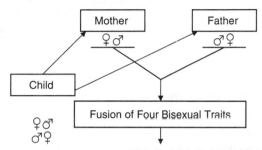

• Gender identification with both parents
• Formation of the ego ideal and super-ego

The critical phrase here is the grammatical conjunction, "and," meaning that there is a dual identification with both parents and their respective masculine and feminine personality attributes which subsequently produces "a precipitate in the ego." This precipitate, like a chemical reaction in a laboratory experiment with fluids, produces a change in ego functioning and in the developing child. Thus, the most accurate characterization of the Oedipus complex is that of the complete Oedipus analysis which culminates in gender identity and the birth of the ego ideal or superego, the basis of interjecting morality, ethics, and the rules of cultural propriety regarding need satisfaction. Freud writes:

The broad general outcome of the sexual phase dominated by the Oedipus complex may, therefore, be taken to be the forming of a precipitate in the ego, consisting of these two identifications in some way united with each other. This modification of the ego retains its special position; it confronts the other contents of the ego as an ego ideal or super-ego. The super-ego is, however, not simply a residue of the earliest object-choices of the id; it also represents an energetic reaction-formation against those choices. Its relation to the ego is not exhausted by the precept: 'You *ought to be* like this (like your father).' It also comprises the prohibition: 'You *may not be* like this (like your father)—that is, you may not do all that he does; some things are his prerogative.' This double aspect of the ego ideal derives from the fact that the ego ideal had the task of repressing the Oedipus complex; indeed, it is to that revolutionary event that it owes its existence. Clearly the repression of the Oedipus complex was no easy task. The child's parents, and especially his father, were perceived as the obstacle to a realization of his Oedipus wishes; so his infantile ego fortified itself for the carrying out of the repression by erecting this same obstacle within itself. It borrowed strength to do this, so to speak, from the father, and this loan was an extraordinarily momentous act. The super-ego retains the character of the father, while the more powerful the Oedipus complex was and the more rapidly it succumbed to repression (under the influence of authority, religious teaching, schooling and reading), the stricter will be the domination of the super-ego over the ego later on—in the form of conscience or perhaps of an unconscious sense of guilt. (1923a, p. 30, italics retained)

The Complete Oedipus Complex and Attachment Processes

To add another critical component to understanding the complete Oedipus complex, it is essential to note that the phase of psychosexual development dominated by the Oedipal complex had its origins in those that preceded it developmentally, starting with the oral stage. The early attachment of the infant to the biological mother or care provider set up an attachment and bonding process based on nurturant care which serves to help the dependent infant have a sense of trust and reliability in others and the world, in general. This attachment and bonding process is not only natural, but critical for ego development and the foundations of identity which will differentiate in epigenetic life-span development throughout childhood, adolescence and early adulthood.

What is the relevance of early attachment to the complete Oedipus complex? In essence, Freud saw attachment and psychosexual development as a continual process of libidinal (need) satisfaction in which the child relied on nurturant care providers for love, emotional and social support to gradually learn to master life's challenges. By the time and age of the Oedipal complex (approximately ages 4–7), these affiliative bonds intensify in depth and intensity due to cognitive development (i.e., imagination, fantasy, language, play, future-orientation, etc.). Freud states:

> At the very beginning, in the individual's primitive oral phase, object-cathexis and identification are no doubt indistinguishable from each other. We can only suppose that later on object-cathexes proceed from the id, which feels erotic trends as needs. The ego, which to begin with is still feeble, becomes aware of the object-cathexes, and either acquiesces in them or tries to fend them off by the process of repression.
>
> When it happens that a person has to give up a sexual object, there quite often ensues an alteration of his ego which can only be described as a setting up of the object inside the ego, as it occurs in melancholia; the exact nature of this substitution is as yet unknown to us. It may be that this introjection, which is a kind of regression to the mechanism of the oral phase, the ego makes it easier for the object to be given up or renders that process possible. It may be that this identification is the sole condition under which the id can give up its objects. At any rate the process, especially in the early phases of development, is a very frequent one, and it makes it possible to suppose that the character of the ego is a precipitate of abandoned object-cathexes and that it contains the history of those object-choices. (1923a, p. 24)

We can see from this quote that Freud is emphasizing the importance of early attachment processes to the capacity to identify with "objects" cathected (i.e., invested with psychic energy) in the service of need satisfaction. This entire process continues and grows in intensity and complexity as the child proceeds through the neurobiological (i.e., genetic) stages of development, a natural and expectable pattern of progression based on the foundations of personality. Therefore, by the age of the complete Oedipal complex, the preceding attachments and modes of emotional gratification reach a crest which subsequently defines the Oedipus complex itself.

Freud clearly saw that the earliest origins of the complete Oedipus complex were in the oral stage, in which the infant was dependent on the mother or care provider for essential need gratifications. As noted earlier, Freud used psychoanalytic language to describe "object-choice on the analytic model." This language refers to the critical early bonding of the newborn infant to the mother, through breastfeeding or other forms of nurturant care at the beginning of life. However, as development progresses in all of its naturally occurring forms, these primordial attachment relationships not only grow and change but begin to crystallize around age four, thus setting the stage for the Oedipal complex in all of its possible variations and complexities, depending on the quality of care and love given by the parents at this stage of life.

PSYCHOSEXUAL STAGES: LIBIDINAL ORGANIZATION

Along with the discovery that sexuality is wider in scope than adult genital activities imply, Freud was able to discern a sequence in the development of the expression of libido or sexual energy. Characteristic patterns of sexual instinct organization prevail at each stage; each pattern centers on an erotogenic zone that dominates the given age.

Pregenital Organizations: Oral and Anal Periods

Libido is organized, in the first year of life, around the pleasurable activities of the mouth. Thus the attachment to the breast is a prototype of pleasurable behavior for the infant, a behavior that is, incidentally, clearly pregenital in character (Freud, 1916, p. 328).

The oral phase is marked, first, by the pleasure obtained from feeding, then by the development of purely sensual sucking in which the infant obtains oral pleasure by sucking nonnutritive objects like the thumb. In this way, the infant's own body provides sensual pleasure, justly characterizing this part of the oral period as autoerotic (Freud, 1905, pp. 179–181). Further development tends toward the decreasing importance of autoerotic activity and a search for an external love object. The dominant erotogenic zone during the oral phase is not genital. Freud noted that its flow of pleasure seemed analogous to sexual satisfaction:

> No one who has seen a baby sinking back satiated from the breast and falling asleep with flushed cheeks and a blissful smile can escape the reflection that this picture persists as a prototype of the expression of sexual satisfaction in later life. (Freud, 1905, p. 182)

With the development of the first teeth and with the possibility of chewing rather than simply swallowing food, children enter a phase of development characterized by a shift from a passive to an active orientation to their environment. From now on, the central concern for the infant is the attainment of self-mastery. From around the age of 18 months through the second year of life, children are subject to increased manipulation and discipline by the mother as she attempts to toilet train them. They discover that retention and expulsion of feces set a rhythmic pattern of tension and relief that is associated not only with pleasure but with social approval and motherly love. When they stubbornly retain their feces, or expel them in inappropriate places, they incur their mothers' wrath. When, on the other hand, they accomplish fecal elimination in a suitable place, at the appropriate time, each receives approval and other loving communications. The pleasures derived from retention and expulsion of feces are clearly pregenital (1905, pp. 186–187).

Transient Genital Organization: The Phallic Period

Sometime at the end of the third year or in the beginning of the fourth year of the child's life and extending into the sixth year, a phase of libidinal organization is entered in which the genital organs play a brief, but not yet, adult role. Through their bodily self-explorations and through the attentions of their mothers to their physical care and cleanliness, children discover that manipulation of the genital region produces pleasurable sensations. There ensues a period of infantile masturbation. Because children do not yet know shame, they express an unabashed curiosity about the genitals of others, along with a guiltless exhibitionism of their own (Freud, 1905, p. 194). As an example, the five-year-old nephew of one of the authors was playing in his bath. He stuck his penis into a small plastic container and proudly said, "Look, Uncle Bob, my 'pee-er' fits right in!" Such a vivid example, however, does not necessarily indicate or prove the universality of the type of behavior Freud had proposed for the phallic period.

It is during this period of "sexual researches" that the Oedipus complex arises (Freud, 1908a). Freud called this period the phallic stage of psychosexual development because for both the boy and the girl, in their own ways, it is the male organ that dominates their thinking and inquiry.

The Latency Period

In Freud's theory, the sexual forces dating from infancy become subject to mounting repression that require the sexual impulses to be rechanneled into nonsexual outlets. In the sixth year of life, the child's sexual activities, along with the Oedipus complex, are temporarily dethroned from their status as major elements of the child's developmental history, but the sexual drive does not cease to exist. Instead, libidinal impulses become latent, obscured by the overlay of learned shame, disgust, and morality. Freud, however, was of the opinion that the sexual impulses would become dormant at this stage even without cultural pressures because the phenomenon of latency is biologically determined (1905, pp. 177–178). In any event, the period of latency extends from the sixth to about the eleventh year of life, or roughly from the resolution of the Oedipus complex to the onset of puberty. At puberty, truly adult, primarily genital, sexuality emerges.

The Genital Period

Biologically capable of procreating because their hormonal and anatomical development permit the production of viable sperm and eggs, the pubescent child's sexuality is no longer dominated by its earlier infantile aim of the attainment of pleasure to the exclusion of all else. The adult sexual aim is the discharge of sexual products. This adult sexual aim also provides individual pleasure in addition to its essentially reproductive goal (Freud, 1905, p. 207).

The lengthy periods of development leading up to the adult's sexual status had as their ultimate goal the establishment of *genital primacy*. Genital arousal and the production of sexual tension is an early step toward the species-preserving goal of procreation. Three sources of sexual arousal are now possible for the adult. They include but are not limited to:

1. memories and impulses from the pregenital periods;
2. direct manipulation and stimulation of the genitalia and other erotogenic zones;
3. stimulation from the chemical hormonal discharges from within the interior of the body (Freud, 1905, p. 208).

Thus the genital period is the culmination of all those trends in the development of the libido, begun in infancy, and played out through the biological development of the mature organism.

We summarize the psychosexual stages with their chief developmental issues and love objects in Table 2.2.

Fixation

Fixation (of libido) may occur at any of the stages, thereby stunting and distorting the sequence of development that follows.

Table 2.2   The Psychosexual Stages

Psychosexual stage	Libidinal zone	Chief developmental issue	Libidinal object
1. Oral [birth to 1 year]	Mouth, skin, thumb	Passive incorporation of all good through mouth; autoerotic sensuality.	Mother's breast; own body
2. Anal [2 to 3 years]	Anus, bowels	Active seeking for tension reduction; self-mastery; passive submission.	Own body
3. Phallic [4 to 6 years]	Genitals, skin	Oedipus and Electra conflicts; possession of mother; identification with same-sexed parent; ambivalence of love relationships.	Mother for boy; father for girl
4. Latency [6 to 11 years]	None	Repression of pregenital forms of libido; learning culturally appropriate shame and disgust for inappropriate love objects	Repressed previous objects.
5. Genital [adolescence onward]	Genital primacy	Reproduction; sexual intimacy.	Heterosexual partner

Based on Freud, 1905 and 1916.

Fixation involves lagging behind or being stuck in the development of one of the components of the maturing sexual drive. One of the child's pregenital modes of attaining pleasure may cease its progression toward adult expression. It then becomes a dominant means of attaining satisfaction. For example, the pleasure of the anal phase, smearing and playing with feces, may be so great that the renunciation required by the child's toilet training program is very difficult for the child to accept. Though children eventually submit to the toilet training routine, their final socialization may be fixated on behaviors going back to the anal stage. As an adult, compulsively defensive traits like stinginess ("not letting go") and compulsive concern about filth make their appearance as a result of fixation regarding the struggles and issues of the toilet training period.

An Illustrative Type: "Anal-Erotic Personality"

One kind of fixated personality is the anal-erotic character. In adulthood, this person is characterized by the presence of a triad of related traits: orderliness, thriftiness, and obstinacy. Freud pointed out that he thought a common pattern of experiences occurred during the anal stage of their psychosexual development in all adults who exhibit a high degree of these traits. It is important to note that Freud did not actually systematically observe such toilet training but based his theory from the accounts of adult patients as well as personal observations and perusal of literature.

The anal-erotic types recalled more than the usual difficulty with toilet training as children, and they exasperated their parents by refusing to empty their bowels when, as Freud put it, "they were placed on the pot." Thus, these children expressed their

Decades after Freud formulated the concept of regression, the ego psychologist Anna Freud (Chapter 6) further elaborated his insights with empirical observations when she worked with children who had suffered loss and dislocation during World War II. Many had regressed to earlier levels of functioning but recovered quickly when she helped provide a secure and loving environment. Her observations and studies led to an elaborate model of child development.

defiance and self-mastery in an anal way, forcing their parents' use of increasingly extreme measures to accomplish this necessary act of socialization.

In Freud's view, anal-erotic children knew no shame or disgust at this early age, and therefore they found pleasure in examining or playing with feces and pleasure in retaining them until release of tension produces the greatest satisfaction. Eventually they succumb to parental pressures for rigid orderliness and cleanliness and to a learned disgust for unclean products of the body. By adulthood, therefore, anal-erotic children have had to develop defensive measures to guard against reemergence of the taboo pleasures. The result is a personality overladen with defensive reactions against its own impulses to obtain pleasure in anal, that is, "dirty," ways. The anal-erotic adult, consequently, becomes a model of cleanliness and orderliness, but a model who bears the hallmark of exaggeration in the pursuit of these desirable goals. Excessive, even compulsive, desire for order, neatness, and antiseptic spotlessness develops to ensure that the earlier and opposite traits remain submerged.

The trait of obstinacy is clearly related to children's attempts at self-mastery as indicated by their refusal to "go on demand." Instead, they prefer to "let go" only when they decide to experience the pleasure of tension reduction, and anal-erotic children prolong this release until an optimal amount of satisfaction can be obtained.

Thriftiness is also related to early developments in the anal period, as can be seen from the similar tendency of the stingy adult who "never lets go" of anything. Tightness with money may unconsciously represent earlier attempts to control fecal elimination against the demands by others to "let go." Stingy persons may even express unwillingness to part with their money by saying, "Who would want the filthy stuff," or, "Money only brings ruin."

Tongue in cheek, Freud remarked in a letter to Fliess that, because he was immersed in working out the details of the anal period of libidinal development and because he had begun to see its wide significance for adult behavior, he considered himself to be the "new Midas," for everything he now touched turned to shit (1954, Letter No. 79, p. 240; Freud, 1985, p. 288; see also Freud, 1908b for a more detailed account of anal character types).

Regression

Another difficulty in psychosexual development may occur when there is cause for a return to an earlier stage's mode of response. Such a return is called **regression (of libido)**, and it usually implies a primitivization of behavior in the service of the personality's defense against stress. For example, the six-year-old who, for one reason or another, finds their school experiences anxiety-provoking and intolerable may return to an infantile mode of attaining peace and tranquility by narrowing attention to pleasurable oral stimulation. He or she consequently regresses to thumb sucking, much to the dismay of parents and teacher.

Fixation and *regression* bear an important relationship to each other. The more intense the fixation of libido at early stages of development, the more susceptible that individual will be to regression (Freud, 1916, pp. 339–341).

EVALUATING CLINICAL PSYCHOANALYSIS

Much like the intimate relationships of the conflicted people he described so lucidly, Freud's theory has sustained a love-hate conflict with the rest of psychology. In 1934, the psychologist Saul Rosenzweig sent Freud reprints of some experimental studies that purported to support psychoanalysis. Freud responded in a brief postcard to Rosenzweig that psychoanalysis rested on so many reliable observations that it was independent of experimental verification. "Still," Freud added, "it can do no harm." This widely quoted anecdote has been taken as emblematic of Freud's ambivalent attitudes toward both the theory he created and the science he seemed to revere (e.g., Eysenck and Wilson, 1973, p. xi; Gay, 1988, p. 523n.; Postman, 1962, p. 702).

In fact, given the scope, breadth, and grand goals of psychoanalysis, it seems that Freud's attitude about the relevance of scientific verification to his theory was less a product of arrogance than it was a result of intellectual overload. By his own account, from the very beginning of his work, Freud wanted psychoanalysis to be a general psychology. Psychoanalysis was designed to encompass all of human action and thought. Normal and "abnormal" would yield to psychoanalytic principles. The net effect of this bigger-than-life ambition was a theory that "explained" virtually every human behavior or motive of which we can conceive.

We can admire Freud's ambition, but we have to temper our admiration with a dose of antigrandiosity. One of Christopher Monte's college professors, John M. Egan, had a memorable way of describing this tension between the intellectual attractiveness of Freud's majestic ideas and the rude requirement that such ideas be accurate. Egan used to say that it would take a hundred psychologists a hundred years just to devise experimental tests of one page of Freud's writing. One could say that Freud "bit off more than anyone would be able to chew."

In Chapter 1, we introduced three main qualitative dimensions by which to analyze and compare theories of personality: refutability, human agency, and idiographic-nomothetic focus. Freud's theory is presented in two large parts, the early clinical observations discussed in this chapter and the later structural theoretical formulations discussed in Chapter 3. Our analysis that follows in this chapter will concern only Freud's clinical observations as developed by "early Freud." Freud's later formulations will be evaluated separately in Chapter 3.

Refutability of Psychoanalysis

Freud's basic propositions are stated in terms that are most often not testable or refutable. It is hard to identify any Freudian variables that are directly observable. For example, consider the proposition of repression and the Oedipus complex. By definition, a repressed wish or thought is absent from awareness. And by definition, all boys have experienced an erotic attachment to mother and ambivalent feelings of love and hate toward father. But, again by psychoanalytic definition, all conscious memory of the Oedipal events is repressed. What evidence could count against the proposition that boys have Oedipus complexes if the very behaviors and memory that constitute this "universal" emotional conflict are unavailable for examination by the person or by an outside observer? If an emotion or thought is unconscious, this means it is not conscious, not in a person's awareness.

Imagine telling the mythical "man on the street" that sometime between ages three and six years, he lusted after his mother, hated his father, and was terrified that his father would remove his penis. If our man on the street protests that this is nonsense or berates us for being offensive, we must point out to him that he is incredulous or offended precisely because he is repressing these experiences! And, indeed, the more he protests, the more we are prone to assume that he is threatened by these ideas precisely because he, like all males, has repressed his Oedipal strivings. What possible evidence could the man produce that would disconfirm our theoretical assertion that he was Oedipal as a child? By our psychoanalytic definition, both the hypothetical phenomenon and its evidence are not directly observable.

The problem is not that the psychoanalytic constructs of repression or of the Oedipus complex are fantastic, bizarre, or untrue. The real problem is that they are not readily testable in the form in which Freud proposed them. Someone, perhaps soon, may find a creative and scientifically acceptable way to do so. But for each failure of a concept to provide the possibility of disconfirmation, the theory is weakened as an acceptable scientific account of human action and thought.

On the whole, with exceptions, the history of classical psychoanalytic theory is a story of profoundly interesting and engaging ideas that are colossal monuments to untestability. But that is not the whole story. For there are also ideas in Freudian theory that are testable and that have received both experimental and observational tests. Even allowing for those few Freudian concepts that lend themselves to test and for those potentially testable ideas that some creative psychologists will fashion from Freud's work, psychoanalysis has to be rated low in scientific testability.

Freud's Conception of Human Agency

Freud painted a portrait of his early patients as shaped by reality. His neurological model conceptualized the human nervous system as a tension-reduction machine whose evolutionary history designed it for quick discharge of tension in response to mounting needs. Left to its own devices, the human nervous system is a passive discharger of tension. It strives to quell irritations such as hunger, thirst, and sexual desire. Seen in this way, drives are irritants, and the nervous system responds only when an itch must be scratched. "Reality makes much of us," Freud wrote, but he failed to see how much we make of reality.

The person who emerges from Freud's early clinical work is one who "defends" against threatening wishes, one who tolerates conflict until tolerance fails and then is "forced" to repress it. People "involuntarily" disavow their own frightening wishes only to find disguised or "compromised" ways to satisfy them in neurotic "symptoms." Human psychosexual development proceeds, in Freud's earliest conception, as a halting process of advance and retreat, development and fixation.

Balancing this picture to a certain extent, paradoxically, is Freud's development of psychoanalysis. This treatment was intended to help people become more aware of their psychodynamics and come to grips with the more frightening contents of their psyche. A psychoanalytic patient had to be highly motivated, persistent, and willing to be open to very uncomfortable and often unsettling insights. The analyst, in order to be effective, could not be at the mercy of unconscious dynamics but had to be aware of them. Goethe's insight that by recognizing limitations a person can become free applies here.

So, even though Freud saw humans as fundamentally reactive, he believed that some small portion of humanity could replace unknowing instinctually determined reactivity with clear insight and more rational behavior.

Freud's Balance of Nomothetic and Idiographic

Freud's intention was to create a theory that was universally applicable, a theory with a strong nomothetic emphasis. But he also intended a theory that could deal with the specifics of a given patient. As an example, he wanted to understand hysterical neurosis as a phenomenon and also the behavior of a given patient with hysterical conversion symptoms.

Many of his later concepts, such as the *ego*, the *id*, and the *superego*, as well as *defense mechanisms*, **transference**, and **countertransference** are generally applicable. His writings refer to the application of such general or nomothetic concepts to specific individuals. Transference, for example, is considered a general phenomenon, but the specifics of any individual's transference are unique and tied in to his or her own experience. People may use many general defenses such as repression or denial, but the content of what is repressed or denied is often idiosyncratic.

Freud often demonstrated the value of theory by alluding to specific case histories. He also modified his theories based on his experience with cases. Thus, there was a dialogue between individual cases and Freud's more general theory. From Freud's point of view, such a case-by-case strategy facilitated his belief that what the analyst infers from his or her patient's behavior is generally of value.

We conclude, therefore, that Freud's theory combines the nomothetic with the idiographic. Early Freud was more idiographic and later Freud, as we shall see in Chapter 3, somewhat more nomothetic in emphasis.

SUMMARY

Fraülein Bertha Pappenheim's long array of hysterical symptoms was eventually viewed by her physician, Dr. Josef Breuer, as coherent, meaningful, and reflective of an underlying emotional logic. This was far from the conventional approach, which did not attribute any particular meaning to such symptoms. Breuer soon discovered in an unusual collaboration with his patient that the coherence and logic of her symptoms had its origins in strangulated emotions.

Dr. Sigmund Freud, Breuer's young colleague, was greatly interested in the case of Bertha, especially after his visit with Professor Charcot in Paris, during which he observed this renowned physician produce and remove hysterical symptoms through hypnosis. Applying Breuer and Bertha's method of *catharsis*, the "talking cure," Freud soon found that hypnosis could be achieved only with few of his patients.

Freud examined and sometimes modified his therapeutic techniques and refined his thinking based on the difficulties he experienced trying to help his patients. The limitations of the applicability of hypnotic induction led to Freud's use of a method he learned from Bernheim, the *pressure or concentration technique*. Finally, Freud developed the technique of free association. With the method of free association in hand, Freud soon discovered the emotional resistances that had been hidden by hypnosis. Examining and removing these resistances revealed to Freud one of the fundamental notions of his psychology, the mechanism of *repression*. Freud concluded that repressed ideas and impulses require a continual outlay of energy to prevent their return to consciousness. He viewed the symptoms of neurotic disorder as the return of the repudiated material in compromise form, a form acceptable to the ego. Symptoms allow the simultaneous satisfaction and rejection of the unacceptable impulse or idea in symbolic form.

Much to his own amazement, Freud found that sexual impulses were the common denominator for classifying unacceptable thoughts. Freud thought that, in practically every case, adults with hysterical symptoms had repressed often incestuous memories of sexual trauma that they had presumably experienced as infants and children. The theory based on this observation is termed the *seduction hypothesis*. Soon, however, Freud saw how untenable the idea of universal childhood seduction was, and simultaneously he faced a momentous conclusion: children are not merely passive recipients of sexual attentions by adults, but, rather, they are active sexual creatures who seek pleasure in a variety of diffuse ways before the onset of purely genital sexuality at puberty.

For the infant, pleasure seeking is connected with developing erotogenic zones in a sequence of psychosexual maturation that shows the sexual instinct to be very much broader than adult notions of genital sexuality ordinarily admit. An emotional climax in sexual development is the Oedipal phase, in which the male child focuses his pleasure-seeking activities on the mother, and he views siblings and father as hostile rivals. The girl, on the other hand, who also initially takes her mother as the first love object, relinquishes mother for father when she realizes that girls, including mother, do not possess a penis. The Electra and Oedipus complexes are only one part of Freud's scheme of psychosexual development, a scheme that involves five phases:

1. the *oral stage*, in which pleasurable activities center on the activities of the mouth;
2. the *anal stage*, in which the critical developments involve retention and expulsion of feces, as well as learning generalized self-mastery;
3. the *phallic stage*, the time period of the Oedipus and Electra complexes;

4. the *latency stage*, during which time the child's sexual interests and impulses lie dormant until puberty; and
5. the *genital stage* of adult sexuality and interest in the opposite sex.

Sometimes development does not proceed smoothly through the five stages because anxiety, threat, or frustration block further maturation. Such blocking is termed *fixation* in the Freudian scheme. It is intimately related to another phenomenon of development called *regression*. Regression is a partial return to an earlier form of impulse gratification when current stresses frustrate the normal progression of the sex drive's development.

When we examine Freud's early formulations on the dimensions of refutability, human agency, and idiographic versus nomothetic focus, we find:

- The theory is structured from many assumptions that are, for the most part, not testable because they do not have readily observable referents.
- The person in psychoanalytic theory is pictured as a passive receptacle rather than as an active agent. The process of psychoanalysis, however, enables the person to become aware of the workings of the psyche and reach a certain degree of self-understanding, if not mastery.
- Much of early psychoanalysis is focused on the unique characteristics and life events of individuals. However, it also refers to structures and processes that are general and universal, such as the *id*, the *ego*, the *superego*, and *repression*. Thus, one finds in psychoanalysis a balance between the idiographic and the nomothetic.

In the next chapter, we take up the matters of Freud's dream theory, his changing views of the instincts, and his final model of the mind.

FOR FURTHER READING

Freud's writings in psychology span over 43 years of theorizing and fill 23 volumes in the definitive translation of *The Standard Edition of the Complete Psychological Works of Sigmund Freud* edited by James Strachey (New York: Norton, 2000). Perhaps the single best overview of Freud's early ideas is contained in his *Introductory Lectures on Psychoanalysis* (New York: Norton, 1965). Another excellent introduction to Freud's ideas, written by Freud himself,

can be found in *The Ego and the Id* (New York: Norton, 1990). *The Interpretation of Dreams* (New York: Avon, 1983) remains the most popular book Freud wrote; this early work of Freud's is still a fascinating book to read and shows Freud as a sleuth on the track of the unconscious workings of the mind.

The Freud scholar, Barry Silverstein has contributed a knowledgeable and balanced summary of

Freud's development of his sometimes controversial ideas in *What Was Freud Thinking? A Short Historical Introduction to Freud's Theories and Therapies* (Dubuque, IA: Kendall/Hunt, 2003). In addition, he has contributed a series of articles on different aspects of Freud's thought. Among the most relevant are:

- Silverstein, B. (1985). Freud's psychology and its organic foundation: sexuality and mind-body interactionism. *The Psychoanalytic Review*, 72, 203–228.
- Silverstein, B. (1989a). Freud's dualistic mind-body interactionism: implications for the development of his psychology. *Psychological Reports*, 64, 1091–1097.

- Silverstein, B. (1989b). Oedipal politics and scientific creativity: Freud's 1915 phylogenetic fantasy. *The Psychoanalytic Review*, 76, 403–424.
- Silverstein, S.M. & Silverstein, B.R. (1990). Freud and hypnosis: the development of an interactionist perspective. *The Annual of Psychoanalysis*, 18, 175–194.

Biographies and other books about Freud are plentiful. Two of the more interesting and well received in recent years are Paul Ferris's *Dr Freud: A Life* (Washington, DC: Counterpoint, 1997) and Louis Breger's *Freud: Darkness in the Midst of Vision—An Analytical Biography* (New York: Wiley, 2000).

Additional bibliographic sources and relevant Internet sites are listed on the web pages associated with this text at www.wiley.com/college/sollod

GLOSSARY

Anxiety neurosis: A neurosis whose main symptom is anxiety; thought by Freud to be caused by too high a level of sexual excitation.

Catharsis: A release of emotions by expressing them.

Cathartic method: The therapeutic use of inducing a catharis to release conflicted emotional states.

Childhood sexuality: Freud's idea that children are active initiators of autoerotic behaviors designed to bring sensual pleasure; Freud replaced the seduction theory with the idea of childhood sexuality.

"Chimney sweeping": Bertha Pappenheim's term for her recollection of emotionally-charged memories and subsequent verbal catharsis in a semi-hypnotic state.

"Clouds": The term that Bertha Pappenheim used to describe her hypnagogic states. She often felt as if she were floating on a cloud.

Compromise formations: Symptoms that balance the anxiety and guilt of the conscious personality against the pleasurable gratifications sought by the unconscious.

Conflict: In Freud's theory, conflict occurs when an unconscious wish or an impulse is incompatible with the individual's conscious views and principles.

Countertransference: The process of a therapist inappropriately projecting feelings or emotions from previous relationships onto a patient.

Defense: Any one of a number of psychological means used to keep anxiety-provoking material out of awareness in order to reduce or avoid anxiety.

Defense neuroses: Neuroses that Freud conceptualized as arising from the ego's attempts to defend against threatening sexual thoughts.

Dynamic unconscious: A part of the mind in which thoughts and emotions removed from consciousness by repression continue to operate unconsciously; Freud concluded that they might produce symptoms that replace direct expression of the thoughts or emotions.

Elective mutism: An inability to speak that has no organic basis. It is either consciously willed or caused by unconscious motives.

Electra complex: The psychological process during the phallic stage in which a female child detaches from her mother upon discovering that she too has no penis; she then devalues the mother and turns to her father; she starts identifying with female behaviors to appeal to her father and get a penis substitute from him—a baby.

Erotogenic zones: Pleasurable zones of the body that are a source of sensual pleasure.

False memories: Fantasies or mental fabrications that a person thinks or alleges are memories of actual occurrences.

Fixation (of libido): In the course of psychosexual development, an individual lags behind or becomes fixated in development at a specific stage. It may lead to oral, anal, or phallic personality types.

Free association: A therapeutic technique devised by Freud to encourage patients to report spontaneously any thoughts or fantasies that occur to them.

Functional anesthesia: Numbness of a part of the body, usually in one's hands or feet, without discernable physical cause.

Fundamental rule of psychoanalysis: Patients were to say everything that came to mind without editing or censoring the stream of thought.

Glove anesthesia: A disorder in which it is as if all of the hand that could fit into an imaginary glove were anesthetized or without sensation. This disorder does not fit the distribution of nerves in the hand, and was thus thought by Charcot to be caused by a person's ideas.

Hypnagogic state: A state between waking and sleeping. A person often has greater access to unconscious thoughts and is more open to suggestion in this state.

Hypnotism: A technique that Freud used to produce a state of consciousness that allows the patient to bring to the surface feelings or emotions that would otherwise be repressed.

Hysterical neurosis: A disorder involving various physical ailments such as paralysis and blindness without an apparent physical cause. Originally thought to be caused by a "wandering womb" in women and subsequently considered psychological in origin.

Libido: The biological force underlying the individual's pleasure-seeking activity.

Neurasthenia: A diagnostic category used in Freud's day that referred to a general lack of energy or vigor. Freud believed that this was caused by a lack of or a depletion of sexual energy.

Object-Relations: An approach, exemplified by Melanie Klein and D. W. Winnicott, that focuses on the nature and quality of how the person structures and deals with interpersonal relations or what they term "object relations."

Obsessional neurosis: A disorder in which individuals engage in ritualistic acts to keep from feeling anxiety.

Oedipus complex: The psychological process during the phallic stage in which a male child becomes sexually attracted to his mother and competes with his father for her attention; this stage is resolved when the boy identifies with his father due to fear of castration.

Penis envy: The envy that a girl presumably experiences toward boys when she discovers that she has no penis. Freud considered penis envy to be biologically based.

Posthypnotic amnesia: The induced forgetting of the material brought to the surface during hypnosis.

Pressure or concentration technique: Method first used by Bernheim to aid the patient in remembering hidden thoughts; the therapist placed his hand on the forehead of the subject and pressed firmly, while insisting that the memory of the previous events return.

Pseudocyesis: A hysterical false pregnancy that evidences most of the usual signs of advanced pregnancy, but with no fetus in the womb.

Psychosexual stages: Stages of development in which a specific area of the body is sexualized and determines how a person interacts with others socially.

Regression (of libido): The return to an earlier stage of psychosexual development.

Repression: Motivated forgetting or amnesia characterized by its unconscious, automatic nature; repression serves to keep painful, undesirable, or anxiety-provoking thoughts out of consciousness.

Resistance: Defensive process to ward off threatening thoughts or feelings. Such threatening contents may continue to exert unconscious "pressure" in their striving for expression.

Seduction hypothesis: Freud's theory that all women who experienced hysterical symptoms had been sexually molested or seduced as children; Freud had found that all of his hysterical patients recalled an early sexual encounter under hypnosis.

Strangulated affect: Unexpressed or "dammed up" feelings or emotions, which are often the cause of hysterical symptoms.

Suppression: The conscious or deliberate avoidance of threatening ideas.

"Talking cure": The process of talking activity with a therapist, using free association, to address emotional conflicts.

Transference: The process of a patient inappropriately projecting feelings or emotions from previous relationships onto a therapist.

Tunnel vision: A narrowing of the field of vision as though one were looking through a circular hole or cylinder.

Chapter 3

Sigmund Freud

Psychoanalysis:
The Dynamic Model of the Mind

But these two discoveries—that the life of our sexual instincts cannot be wholly tamed, and that mental processes are in themselves unconscious . . . amount to a statement that the ego is not master in its own house.

Sigmund Freud (1917a, p. 143)

A man on horseback rode through a town at breakneck speed. A passer-by saw him and called out, "Where are you going in such a hurry?" He answered, "I don't know. Ask the horse!"

Anonymous as cited in Sigmund Freud (1923, pp. 25; 1933, p.77)

About Freud's Model of the Mind

Central to Freud's early clinical work was the concept that observable behavior is a disguised derivative of unconscious wishes. The derivatives included neurotic symptoms, slips of the tongue, and many self-defeating behaviors. Freud's story of exploration continues in this chapter with his study of dreams as disguised ways to satisfy taboo wishes.

Freud's struggle to understand the war between instinct and reason led to his model of a divided mind. He moved away from directly reporting clinical experiences with patients toward an increasingly complex intellectual representation of human self-division.

Some major aspects of Freud's model of the mind in his mature theorizing include:

- a picture of the means by which the conscious part of the mind allows the unconscious part to satisfy its urges in relatively non-threatening ways;
- a step-wise model of childhood psycho-sexual development—with implications for understanding adult personality and psychopathology as well;
- a structural model of the mind that pictures the war between reason and instinct as a conflict of mental agencies each obeying its own rules of operation;

- an approach to psychotherapy which emphasized the goals of attaining insight into one's patterns of emotion, thinking and behavior as well as the possibility of reworking these patterns. The way the mind handles the processes within it is thus susceptible to therapeutic modification.

DREAMS AS WISH FULFILLMENT

Consider the following dream of Freud's daughter, Anna:

> My youngest daughter, then 19 months old, had had an attack of vomiting one morning and had consequently been kept without food all day. During the night after this day of starvation she was heard calling out excitedly in her sleep: "Anna Fweud, stwawbewwies, wild stwawbewwies, omblet, pudden!" At that time she was in the habit of using her own name to express the idea of taking possession of something. The menu included pretty well everything that must have seemed to her to make up a desirable meal. (Freud, 1900, p. 130)

Clearly, as can be discerned in Anna's menu, children's dreams are relatively transparent embodiments of wishes come true. There is no disguise here to obscure Anna's craving for goodies. Anna's dream was of an undisguised wish receiving undisguised fulfillment.

Freud had already come to the conclusion that dreams are mental states designed for **wish fulfillment**. The dream, he reasoned in the "Project for a Scientific Psychology" (1895), is a hallucinatory state that serves to structure dream events, not as they are in the external world, but as we would like them to be. Sometimes, however, unconscious desires come up against conscious restraint, so the dream processes have to pursue devious or indirect paths to wish fulfillment. Freud stated the fundamental implication of this insight in the dictum "The interpretation of dreams is the royal road to a knowledge of the unconscious mind" (1900, p. 608). In other words, through examining and interpreting dreams, we can find out what desires and wishes are hidden in the unconscious.

By examining a dreamer's nighttime productions, the skilled observer can detect those motives and wishes that are hidden from view during waking life, motives and wishes that the dreamer can entertain only in the disguised, compromise form that dream imagery represents. Compared with the dreams of children, adult productions usually do not evidence the simplicity and directness of Anna's "stwawbewwies-and-pudden" fancy.

Disguised Wish Fulfillment

Compare the following adult dream with Anna's innocently lucid construction:

> The patient, who was a young girl, began thus: "As you will remember, my sister has only one boy left now—Karl; she lost his elder brother, Otto, while I was still living with her. Otto was my favorite; I more or less brought him up. I'm fond of the little one too, but of course, not nearly so fond as I was of the one who died. Last night, then, I dreamt that *I saw Karl lying before me dead. He was lying in his little coffin with his hands folded and with candles all round—in fact just like little Otto, whose death was such a blow to me*." (Freud, 1900, p. 152)

If it is true that dreams are the fulfillment of wishes, then surely this dream by one of Freud's patients must embody the wish that little Karl had died instead of little Otto.

Assured from his knowledge of his patient that she was not cruel, Freud considered the dream carefully. He asked her to tell him everything that came to mind when she thought of the separate elements of the dream. It is important to note that the interpretation of this particular dream is possible only when the analyst knows the past history of the dreamer, as well as the context provided by the dreamer's personality. In Freud's view, dreams usually fit into the unique experiences and circumstances of a dreamer's life.

Freud knew that, after his patient had been orphaned, she had been raised in the house of an elder sister. A particular male visitor to the sister's home, nicknamed "the professor" by virtue of his occupation as a professional lecturer, had made quite a romantic impression on Freud's patient. They made marriage plans, which were disrupted. He ceased to visit the sister's home. Freud's patient nonetheless secretly longed to see and to be with him. On the other hand, through hurt pride, she tried to convince herself to relinquish any romantic attachment to him. Her resolve was not an easy one to keep. Whenever she learned that he was to appear in a public lecture, she quietly became a part of the audience. Yet she would observe him only at a discreet distance, and she never allowed herself to confront him directly. In fact, she seized upon every opportunity, however trivial, to see this professor. She had even experienced a moment of happiness at the funeral of little Otto when her professor had made an appearance to express his condolences. It was this continual vacillation between approach and withdrawal that chiefly characterized the patient's behavior.

Here, of course, was the key to her dream. If little Karl was to die, his funeral would provide another opportunity to see her professor without any direct attempt on her part to bring about the meeting. Her wish, therefore, was not directly for Karl's death, but only for a meeting with her professor. The dream had created from her past history of associations a perfectly logical pretext for furthering the satisfaction of her ambivalent desire. Thus the lucidity and directness of Anna's "stwawbewwy dream" is not to be found here.

We can view adult processes and hysterical symptoms as similar if we make the assumption, as Freud did, that both dreams and symptoms conceal ideas that are not acceptable to the conscious personality. Freud found evidence in several of his own dreams that particularly threatening desires were frequently the kernels from which nighttime fantasies grew.

PERSONAL SOURCES: FREUD'S FATHER AND MOTHER DREAMS

We saw in Chapter 2 that Freud had begun a self-analysis in the summer of 1897, and that the precipitating incident for the task was his emotional distress over the death of his father. Throughout *The Interpretation of Dreams*, and in one or two of his other works, Freud employed his own dreams, elucidated by self-analysis, as examples of his concepts. Like his patient's Karl and Otto dream, Freud's own dreams also revealed how important it was for the analyst to understand the dreamer's personal symbols and meanings.

Immediately following his father's funeral, Freud had a dream about a sign hanging in a barbershop that he visited every day. The analysis given in *The Interpretation of Dreams* provides a detailed account:

> During the night before my father's funeral I had a dream of a printed notice, placard or poster [in a barbershop]—rather like the notices forbidding one to smoke in a railway waiting room—on which appeared either
>
> "You are requested to close the eyes"
OR
"You are requested to close an eye"....

Each of these two versions had a meaning of its own, and led in a different direction when the dream was interpreted. I had chosen the simplest possible ritual for the funeral, for I knew my father's own views on such ceremonies. But some other members of the family were not sympathetic to such puritanical simplicity and thought we should be disgraced in the eyes of those who attended the funeral. Hence one of the versions: "You are requested to close an eye," i.e., to "wink" or "overlook" [the simplicity of the services]. Here it is particularly easy to see the meaning of the vagueness expressed by the "either-or." (Freud, 1900, p. 318)

The dream was, upon analysis, clearly a form of self-reproach for not providing the "proper" full-fledged funeral that members of the family expected and desired. Simultaneously, the dream represented the ultimate act of a son's duty toward his father; namely, the closing of his father's eyes at death. It was as though the dream condensed the idea of "failing to do your duty" with the idea of "filial duty" in a clever word picture.

Freud suspected that the dream was in some way connected with ever deeper feelings of guilt. Perhaps he did not love his father as much as he thought? There was evidence for this because on the day of the funeral Freud was actually late in arriving. He said he had been detained in *a barbershop*. The seemingly inexcusable lateness, coupled with his desire for relatively austere last rites for his father, must have seemed to members of Freud's family indications of supreme lack of respect. The important point is that to Freud, too, such behavior indicated some negativity toward his father.

Personal Sources of Freud's Ambivalent Love for His Father

During his extensive self-analysis, Freud uncovered some roots of his hostility toward his father and accompanying guilt pangs. The barbershop dream just discussed had emphasized the theme of filial duty—the duty of a son for a father. Instead of respect for his father, Freud had been neglectful. Freud's father died in October 1896; by 1899 Freud had included in *The Interpretation of Dreams* several pieces of his self-therapeutic efforts to cope with the complex emotions triggered by the loss and by Freud's concerns over his own neglectful behavior. By 1904, on a vacation to Greece with his brother Alexander, Freud's guilt over his father's death reached a crisis. Eight years after the event, Freud was still experiencing the painful reverberations of this experience.

The Acropolis Episode

In 1936, only three years before his own death, suffering terminal cancer of the jaw and mouth, Freud published an account of a crisis experience in Greece. Standing upon the Acropolis, surveying the majesty of the landscape and ruminating on the impressive history of the site, Freud was abruptly thrust outside of himself, as though he were suddenly two people. His own later description of the experience was that he endured a "splitting of consciousness." One part of himself was astonished to find that the fabled city of Athens existed! Freud thought, "So all this really *does* exist, just as we learnt at school!" (1936, p. 241). The other, more reality-oriented aspect of Freud's personality was astonished, too, as though unaware that Athens and its landscape had ever been the subject of doubt. Freud interpreted his splitting of awareness as a form of *derealization*, a kind of defensive disbelief in the reality of things in an effort to ward off a segment of threatening experiences. He was able to analyze the experience to uncover the chain of associations that underlay his defensive maneuver; the chain led straight back to his guilt and hostility associated with his father. Schur (1972) has provided additional details that Freud was apparently unwilling to publish as part of his analysis.

From Freud's own account, we learn that as a child he harbored doubts, not of the existence of Athens, but of the possibility that he would ever see it with his own eyes. To see Athens had the personal meaning of "going such a long way," that is, becoming successful enough to make the dream of distant travel possible. Because his youth was one of poverty, the wish to travel to distant places was a desire to escape the privations of his real existence. Freud vividly expressed his sentiments, "When first one catches sight of the sea, crosses the ocean and experiences as realities cities and land which for so long had been distant, unattainable things of desire—one feels like a hero who has performed deeds of improbable greatness" (1936, p. 247). The symbolic meaning of travel to fabled cities, especially to the city of Rome, was, for Freud, intricately connected with a host of guilt-laden and aggressive feelings toward his father (for details of Freud's "Rome neurosis" see Grigg, 1973 and Schorske, 1975).

In the present instance, the visit to the Acropolis brought to Freud's mind the further association of Napoleon, during his coronation as emperor, turning to his *brother* to remark how pleasant it would be if their father could be present this day. But herein lay the crux of the defensive disbelief in Athens' reality. To "have come so far" was equivalent to success, the special success of having gone further than one's own father:

> The very theme of Athens and the Acropolis in itself contained evidence of the son's superiority. Our father had been in business, he had had no secondary education, and Athens could not have meant much to him. Thus what interfered with our enjoyment of the journey to Athens was a feeling of *filial piety*. (Freud, 1936, pp. 247–248)

Just as the barbershop dream after the funeral had contained an allusion to filial duty, the experience of derealization on the Acropolis embodied the sense of filial piety or reverence for his father. It was as though the trip to Athens had been not merely a surpassing of his father but a betrayal of him as well. Such intolerable guilt and its implied hostility had to be defended against. As Freud put it, he was overcome with the unsettling sense that *"What I see here is not real."*

Suffering from terminal cancer, with thoughts of death nearly always in his mind, Freud concluded the Acropolis account with this sentence: "And now you will no longer wonder that the recollection of this incident on the Acropolis should have troubled me so often since I myself have grown old and stand in need of forbearance and can travel no more" (1936, p. 248). It is possible that at one level of his understanding, Freud was accepting his imminent end as fitting punishment for having surpassed his father; certainly, this last statement suggests his identification with the fate of his father.

Freud's Death Fear

Schur (1972, pp. 225ff.) has shown that there were other important determinants of the Acropolis episode that involved Freud's relationship with Wilhelm Fliess. An eccentric Berlin physician, Fliess played the role of mentor and confidant during Freud's self-analysis in an extensive interchange of letters and a series of personal meetings, or "congresses," as Freud termed them. Through a complex system of biological numerology and critical-period theory, Fliess had predicted the year of Freud's death—completely wrongly, as it turned out—and in so doing fed directly Freud's already superstitious concern with the prospects of his own demise. Fliess's critical period calculations had set Freud's death near the age of 51; but Freud's superstitious turn of mind, after the death of his father, had its own chosen date. Freud was

---

BOX 3.1   *Only Connect . . .*

Freud's preoccupation with his mortality is consistent with some of the existential approaches to personality (see Chapter 12). The existential writers, philosophers and psychologists emphasized the fact that each person is responsible for the meanings that he or she expresses and the choices that he or she makes. Given the emphasis on choosing within a finite framework, a person who has an existential point of view might be very concerned with mortality and the limited time that is available for defining the meaning of his or her life and contributions. Chapters 2 and 3 indicated the degree to which Freud was concerned with his role in intellectual history and with his reputation. His obsession with the date of his death is of a piece with these existential concerns.

---

convinced that the year of his death would be between the ages of 61 and 62. A productive consequence also resulted from Freud's preoccupation with his mortality: Freud's superstitious belief that he would die between 1917 and 1918 significantly motivated him to write the clarifying metapsychological papers he published in 1915 and 1917. He thought that these papers would serve as his theoretical last testament, in the event that he did die at his predicted time (Silverstein, 1986, p.10).

Freud's Relationship to His Mother: The Birds'-Beaked-People Dream

Another of Freud's dreams indicates the complexity of the verbal linkages that may be employed defensively to obscure threatening wishes. In his seventh or eighth year, Freud's self-analysis revealed, he had dreamt of his mother with a "peculiarly peaceful, sleeping expression on her features." In the dream, he saw her being carried into a room by two or three people with birds' beaks. Then they laid her on a bed (Freud, 1900, p.583). The bizarre creatures with birds' beaks brought to Freud's mind the association of the illustrations of bird-masked people in a particular edition of the Bible called the *Phillippson's* Bible.

Further analysis revealed an association to the name "Phillippson" in the form of a memory of an "ill-mannered boy" named Phillipp, who was the first person to reveal to the young Freud the vulgar word for sexual intercourse. In German, the word *vogeln* is slang for copulation, and it is derived from the proper form of the word *Vogel*, which means "bird." Hence, the associative chain from people with *birds'* beaks to the *Phillippson* Bible to the boy named *Phillipp* had revealed a sexual connotation to the dream images.

The expression of his mother's face in the dream reminds Freud of his dying grandfather, whom he had observed in a coma a few days before the grandfather's death. However, when the young Freud awoke from the dream, he had rushed into his parents' room to wake his mother and was quite relieved to discover that she was indeed alive.

Why, then, had the dream depicted her in a state similar to death—a state, that is, similar to his grandfather's coma? Surely the dream could not have been the representation of a wish that his mother die? On the contrary, Freud's anxiety at the thought of her death had forced him, upon awakening, to rush into her room to confirm that she was still alive. Perhaps, he thought, his anxiety over her death was a form of disguise to prevent recognition of the sexual longing the dream had really depicted, a sexual longing for his mother.

Another interpretation of this dream is that the anxiety Freud experienced was due to a death wish directed toward his mother. This interpretation proceeds from the well-established fact that Freud's relationship to his mother was an especially close one. Freud consciously held a very idealized conception of the relationship between a mother and a son, suggesting at one point in his writings that it was altogether the most perfect and free from ambivalence of all human relationships (Freud, 1933, p. 133). Robert Stolorow and George Atwood (1978) suggest that Freud had an intense need to preserve an entirely positive image of his mother, an idealistic vision of her that had to be defended at all costs. When, as a child, he experienced resentment and rage toward her for having more children and for deserting him to do so, his only means of dealing with his hatred toward a figure he so dearly loved was **repression**, followed by "splitting" his image of her into a good mother and a hateful mother. In his interpretation of the birds'-beaked-people dream, Freud avoided the obvious meaning of hostility toward his mother, and displaced the death wish interpretation onto his father.

Stolorow and Atwood (1978) pointed out that Freud's theory of psychosexual development views the origin of personal conflicts as lying in the child's own internalized, but universal, biological urges. Actual parental influences on the child were minimized:

> In Freud's theoretical view of infantile development, the sources of evil were located not in the parents (mother), but rather in the child himself, in his own sexual and aggressive drives.... Specifically, through the relocation of the sources of badness into the child, Freud absolved his mother from blame for her betrayals of him and safeguarded her idealized image from invasions by his unconscious ambivalence. Freud's wish to banish (destroy) the treacherous mother ["treacherous" because she disappeared and gave birth to rivals] was thus replaced in his theory with the child's need to repress his own evil wishes. (Stolorow & Atwood, 1978, p. 232; see also Stolorow & Atwood, 1979, p. 67)

Stolorow and Atwood are probably correct in their assumption that Freud needed to locate the "sources of badness" in his own internalized biological states. They are probably also correct in assuming that, in so doing, Freud exonerated his mother from the taint of his rageful impulses and defensive distortions. However, it seems clear that Freud also exonerated himself from guilt for these unacceptable impulses. By proposing that erotic attachment to mother and murderous rivalry with both father and siblings are biological and fixed universals (with a phylogenetic history, no less), Freud, in effect, absolved himself of personal responsibility.

It is also necessary to consider the fact that, even if Freud had angry feelings toward his mother, the depth of his displaced rage toward his father matched or surpassed them. In principle, consequently, we would have to assume that, whether defensively displaced or genuinely, Freud harbored hostile wishes toward nearly every significant member of his family. In either case, the evidence supports the view that Freud distanced himself from his conflicting feelings by conceptualizing them as human inevitables.

Freud's ambitious goal in the analysis of his dreams was not only self-therapy, but also the attempt to unmask the secrets of unconscious mental life. Freud's own dreams point up the difficult nature of the task. For Freud sought no less an accomplishment than the explanation of how dreams are structured to conceal significant but unacceptable motives from consciousness—how dreams can both satisfy real desires and, at the same time, keep them hidden from conscious awareness.

MANIFEST AND LATENT DREAM CONTENT: THE MASK

In light of the disguised nature of wish fulfillment in adult dreams, even the most elementary description of dream processes must include a distinction between the readily accessible disguise and the less accessible ideas that lie behind the distortion. Freud referred to the dream's facade or mask as consisting of all those recalled sights, images, ideas, sounds, and smells that compose the story of the dream. Behind the facade, *beneath the mask* of recallable elements, lie the "perverse," unacceptable impulses that, like "masked criminals," are far commoner in mental life than straightforward, undisguised urges (Freud, 1925c, p. 132).

Freud's use of the mask metaphor is an apt analogy for his more technical distinction between the manifest and **latent content** of the dream. The manifest or surface content corresponds to the mask, whereas the impulses, thus disguised like "masked criminals," are properly termed latent content or hidden content. The dreamer generally easily recalls **manifest content**. By contrast, the latent content can be arrived at only by careful interpretation of the manifest content.

The mental processes that convert strivings, wishes, and needs into the disguised images of the manifest content are collectively called dream work. In a sense, the analyst's interpretation of a dream is an attempt to undo the dream work, to unmask the manifest content, and reveal the more fundamental latent content from which the dream was constructed.

The Dream Work

Once distortion or disguise is recognized as a general phenomenon of dream imagery, it becomes necessary to search for a cause of the distortion. Freud postulated that the wishes or needs that initiate the dream are unacceptable to a special part of the conscious mind called the "censorship system." The censorship system is actually on the frontier of consciousness, a border guard, so to speak, between the unconscious and conscious systems of the mind.

The censorship system is very selective about the wishes and needs it allows the dreamer to entertain or remember consciously. Wishes that are morally unacceptable to the dreamer who is awake are also unacceptable to the sleeping dreamer's censor. In consequence, this ethical arm of the mental apparatus heavily censors wishes or urges that arise from the unconscious during sleep. Thus the distortion in those wishes as they appear in the manifest dream is a direct result of the efforts of the ever-watchful preconscious dream censor.

The two systems of the mind, the *unconscious system* from which the wishes emerge and the **preconscious censorship system** that prevents those wishes from freely entering consciousness, constitute the mechanism of **dream work** or dream formation (Freud, 1900, pp. 144–145). Unacceptable wishes can be prevented from gaining access to consciousness in only one way. The censorship system must selectively distort the wish, transforming it into an alternate form that does not clash with the conscious ethical standards of the personality. Conversely, the only way the unconscious can achieve satisfaction for its pressing urges is to evade the censor by masquerading the unacceptability of its wishes behind a facade of related but more neutral ideas. Hence the distortion in dreams is a joint product of two architects: the unconscious system and the censor.

FOUR PROCESSES OF DREAM WORK

Freud was able to isolate four separate processes in the dream work of these two architects that account for the form of the manifest dream:

1. condensation,
2. displacement,

3. visual representation, and

4. secondary revision.

The Work of Condensation

One of the mundane facts about the *interpretation* of a dream, but a fact that contains a significant clue about dream distortion, is that a remembered dream (i.e., the manifest content) can be recounted in relatively few words. In contrast, the *interpretation* of the manifest dream, penetrating to the latent content, may produce as much as 12 times the amount of information (Freud, 1900, p. 279). Freud concluded, therefore, that the manifest content is an unsurpassed model of compression, or **condensation** as it was called in Freud's technical vocabulary.

It might be possible to conclude hastily that the work of condensation is merely a one-way editing process whereby only a select few elements of the mass of unconscious material are chosen for representation in the manifest content. In this simplistic view, condensation is accomplished by a process of omission. But free association to the few manifest elements of a dream usually reveals that each manifest element has multiple, two-way relationships with every other element, and each component is, therefore, at least partially redundant.

Borrowing a concept from the study of hysterical symptoms, it can be said that the manifest dream content is **overdetermined**. Several unconscious ideas band together to contribute to one common manifest element. Simultaneously, each manifest element has connections to several other manifest elements, which, of course, have their own connections to other groups of unconscious, latent ideas that have similarly banded together. The picture that Freud paints of condensation is more like an associative web than it is like a chain.

Condensation, consequently, is not a process of simple omission. It is a technique of creative compression. Each segment of the manifest content is a nodal point upon which a great number of latent ideas converge (Freud, 1900, p. 283). The latent dream thoughts are thus condensed into the manifest dream content much as a composite photograph of a single person is constructed from the characteristics of several individuals: It may "look like A perhaps, but may be dressed like B, may do something that we remember C doing, and at the same time we may know that he is D" (Freud, 1916, p. 171). Freud's description sounds very much like the constructing of a "Mr. Potato Head" toy, building a composite from several elements.

The Work of Displacement

Displacement is a technique the censorship agency of the mind employs to replace a latent dream element in consciousness by a more remote idea, or to accomplish a shifting of the dream's recalled emphasis away from an important idea and toward an unimportant one. Thus displacement may proceed by two paths: replacement of one idea with a remote associate, or the shifting emotional accent from one thought to another. The dreamer is left with the impression of having dreamed a very strangely connected sequence of thoughts, or of having very absurdly made "much ado about nothing."

Freud employed an amusing anecdote in his *Introductory Lectures* to illustrate the concept of displacement:

There was a blacksmith in the village, who had committed a capital offence. The Court decided that the crime must be punished; but as the blacksmith was the only one in the village and was indispensable, and as on the other hand there were three tailors living there, one of *them* was hanged instead. (1916, pp. 174–175)

Whereas condensation was responsible for compressing the latent thoughts into the abbreviated form of the manifest content, displacement is responsible for the mind's selection of elements from which the manifest dream is constructed.

Beginning with the latent, unacceptable wish at the center, the dream work of displacement spins outward from this nucleus a web of increasingly remote associations. Each strand of this associative web is connected both to the central latent wish and to every other associated idea in the network. Hence, manifest elements are redundant in the sense that the unacceptable wish is dispersed simultaneously into many interconnected and mutually excitatory strands of the web. Because each of these strands shares a common origin, the nuclear wish, recollection of the ideas along any other strand excites recollection of nearby, connected strands of ideas.

One way to view the manifest dream, therefore, is to conceive of it as an associative "beating around the bush," whereby the unacceptable nucleus wish of the latent content is dispersed into any available channel of the web except one that leads directly back to the origin. The pattern of associatively connected, overlapping, and redundant ideas evoked by the dreamer during free association to a manifest element is evidence of this delicately tangled skein. Displacement robs the latent content of its normal sequence of ideas, substituting the sequence of the associative web, and it likewise rechannels the latent content's original focus of emotional intensity into the diffuse lattice of the web.

The Work of Visual Representation

Abstract ideas, wishes, and urges that form the latent thoughts of the dream are by themselves colorless and ephemeral. Within the scope of the dream, these abstract thoughts must be converted into concrete visual images with the kind of primitive pictorial quality that readily lends itself to the manipulations of condensation and displacement (Freud, 1900, p. 339). Although not all the elements of the latent content are converted into visual images, on the whole the translation of abstract thoughts into concrete pictures constitutes the essence of a dream (Freud, 1916, p. 175).

The translation of abstract thoughts into visual imagery typically follows the path of converting the symbolic labels representing the idea into a physical and concrete act or **visual representation**. For example, the abstract idea of "possession" can be converted into the visually concrete act of "sitting on the object." Children often employ this strategy to protect a treasured possession from the grasp of an overwhelming playmate (Freud, 1916, p. 176n.).

To take another illustration, Freud reported the recollections of Herbert Silberer, who, in a sleepy, twilight state, often converted some abstract intellectual task into visual imagery. On one occasion, Silberer thought of having to revise an uneven or rough passage in an essay he was writing. He then pictured himself planing a piece of wood (Freud, 1900, p. 344). In another episode, Silberer had the experience of losing his train of thought so that he had to return to the beginning to pick up the thread of logic. Silberer subsequently had the visual image of a printer's typesetting form for a page with the last lines of type fallen away (Freud, 1900, p. 345).

Thus, one can see that the translation of abstract thoughts into visual imagery represents a process of personal, individualized symbolization. The dreamer creates concrete pictures to represent abstract thoughts. This process is opposite to the process often found in literature, that of transforming concrete acts into abstract symbols.

The Work of Secondary Revision

All the mechanisms of the dream work discussed thus far have as their common goal getting around or appeasing of dream censorship. The dream work can condense, displace, and represent in visual form the latent dream thoughts in its attempt to disguise them. For the most part, these three mechanisms distort and break apart the latent elements' form and organization. Thus, these dream mechanisms often produce an absurd or difficult to understand dream. When the dreamer tries to recall and make sense of the dream, however, the gaps, distortions, and substitutions seem lacking in harmony and logic.

The dreamer's waking need is for logical coherence and consistency in mental activities. Consequently, to bring order to what otherwise would be experienced as chaos, that part of the mind between unconsciousness and consciousness exerts an organizing, sense-making influence on the confused and bizarre stories that might emerge. In those twilight moments just before waking from a dream, it is the *preconscious mind* that struggles to mold the dreamer's creations into a form comprehensible to waking intelligence.

The preconscious mind thus attempts to patch together, into an understandable, coherent whole, the scattered and apparently nonsensical elements of the latent dream. In so doing, the preconscious is, in effect, subjecting the dream to an interpretation before the dreamer is fully awake. Whatever that interpretation is, the elements of the dream will be fitted to its outlines until what was scattered and diffuse becomes organized and reasonable.

It is this preinterpretation that introduces further distortion into the recalled manifest content. Freud called this process of constructing a coherent whole from the scattered dream elements **secondary revision**. In a sense, the preconscious treats the dream elements to a kind of further elaboration designed to mold what is patently unconnected and absurd into a logically consistent structure.

Sometimes the secondary revision occurs during the dream itself. For instance, a particular dream may be so laden with unpleasant emotional intensity that the various patterns of distortion introduced by the mechanisms of condensation and displacement are not sufficient to satisfy all the demands of the dream censorship. If the ever-watchful dream censor were to be aroused to action, the dreamer's sleep would surely be disturbed or disrupted in an effort to halt the dream. To lessen the impact of such a dream without recourse to interrupting the dreamer's sleep, there occurs instead a kind of judgmental interpretation on the part of the dreamer that, after all, *"It's only a dream"* (Freud, 1900, p. 489).

STUDY OF THE DREAM: THEORETICAL YIELD

Psychoanalytic dream interpretation is a careful labor of elucidating the apparent absurdities of the recalled dream by viewing such productions as evidence of the dreamer's nonconscious mental processes and contents. Accurate interpretation of the dream, therefore, lifts the disguise, makes intelligible the distortions, and replaces absurdity with understanding. The long hidden logic of the unconscious is made accessible. Freud considered the study of the dream one of his most fundamental and lasting achievements. A brief survey of the theoretical yield is in order.

Regressive and Archaic Nature of Dreams

The medium of dreams is visual imagery. It was Freud's opinion that visual imagery represents an earlier and more primitive mode of mental operation than verbal thought. Thus the dream is an archaic production—a return to a mode of thought characteristic of the early years of childhood before language achieves its prominence in our relations to the world. Each individual initially begins mental life, Freud asserted, with sensory impressions and memory images of such impressions. Words are attached to these images only later in development, so that, at the outset, the child does not code mental activities into language labels (Freud, 1916, pp. 180–181; see also Freud, 1900, pp. 189ff.).

Dreams are a return to this archaic mode of mental functioning, and often, "to our surprise, we find the child and child's impulses still living on in the dream" (Freud, 1900, p. 191). Dream processes, then, are a regression to the earlier years of the dreamer's mental life. Correctly translated, a dream's latent content may contain a wish that dates from childhood.

Sexual and Aggressive Motives of Childhood

On the whole, adults retain very few memories of the first five or six years of life. With rare exception, most of us can recall but one or two incidents that we now presume, precisely because they are remembered, to have been overwhelmingly important at the time. But key memories and feelings are conspicuously absent from adult consciousness. Recollection of our Oedipal sexual and aggressive strivings remains inaccessible to consciousness because **infantile amnesia** obscures them in addition to a great wealth of experiences of the childhood epoch.

However, it was Freud's discovery that these memories are not lost. Instead, they are only inaccessible or latent. Having become part of the unconscious, these childhood memories, strivings, and wishes may emerge during dreams when triggered by some current, thematically similar, incident.

The "Hellish" Unconscious

Consider the necessity of censorship in dreams. Dreamers entertain wishes and desires that would seem so perverse and unethical to them if awake that the dream work must disguise these thoughts beyond conscious recognition. What is the source of these monumentally "evil" inclinations? Obviously, since dreams are a product of the unconscious, the unconscious must be the source of the impulses that the conscious personality, the ego, finds objectionable. But during sleep, the censorship agency is less stringent, more easily pacified by partial disguise, and it allows the ego to be flooded with material that is customarily held in check.

> The ego, freed from all ethical bonds, also finds itself at one with all the demands of sexual desire, even those that have long been condemned by our aesthetic upbringing and those, which contradict all the requirements of moral restraint. The desire of pleasure—the "libido," as we call it—chooses its objects without inhibition, and by preference, indeed, the forbidden ones: not only other men's wives, but above all incestuous objects, objects sanctified by the common agreement of mankind, a man's mother and sister, a woman's father and brother.... Lusts which we think of as remote from human nature show themselves strong enough to provoke dreams. Hatred, too, rages without restraint. Wishes for revenge and death directed against those who are nearest and dearest in waking life, against the dreamer's parents, brothers, and sisters, husband or wife, and his own children

are nothing unusual. These censored wishes appear to rise up out of a positive Hell; after they have been interpreted when we are awake, no censorship of them seems to us too severe. (Freud, 1916, pp. 142–143)

Are we to conclude, on the basis of the seemingly reprehensible content of adult dreams, that dreams simply expose the inherently evil character of humanity? On the contrary, Freud protested. It is not that dreams expose evil, hellish strivings of adults, but that adults interpret such feelings in themselves as evil when they become aware of them. Actually, the egoistic, unrestrained sexual and aggressive urges found in dreams date from childhood, when ethical and realistic standards of conduct, which we attribute to adult understanding, were yet undeveloped.

Against the standards of adult ethics, such wishes as sexual desire for a parent and murderous intent directed toward rivals are absolutely wrong, shocking, and condemnable. But for *infants* such reactions are understandable, given that they are at once helpless, yet dominated by urgent needs for immediate gratification of their wishes. That gratification can come only from those persons who are in charge of their care, and who, therefore, are in intimate contact with them. For infants it is not morally outrageous to desire the exclusive possession of their mothers; it is not shocking that they expect this accustomed fulfiller of every pleasure also to be the object of their sexual explorations and curiosity; it is not a condemnable quality of infants that they harbor wishes for the annihilation of brothers, sisters, and father, along with anyone else who rivals their insistent and pressing commitment to mother, the satisfier. To the infant, unschooled in shame, disgust, or morality, such presumed desires would be the merely ordinary parts of daily existence. To the adult, recollecting these feelings in dreams, guilt and horror seem the only appropriate responses.

It is with these memories, wishes, and strivings that the ethical and realistic demands of later socialization will clash. The forces of repression will thrust them into the unconscious: "...what is unconscious in mental life is also what is infantile" (Freud, 1916, p. 210). Adult dreams regress to the archaic and amoral level of infancy, and they deceptively appear to shed light on the vileness of the adult unconscious.

The obvious question arises: "What triggers the reemergence of these latent, infantile strivings in adult dreams?" Freud suggested that something in the dreamer's current waking life—it could be an incident, a frustrated desire, the emotionally abrasive happenings of the day—connects by association with memories stored in the unconscious and, together with them, initiates a dream. Archaic wishes in the unconscious link up with these "day's residues," as Freud called them, to produce the dream thoughts. Dream thoughts are thus dominated by events that have given us pause for reflection during the day and which bear some associative similarity to the archaic wishes in the unconscious. The explanation, of course, may apply the other way round: Events that give us pause during the day do so because they are connected with repressed wishes in the unconscious (Freud, 1900, pp. 169, 174). Indeed, in either case, dreams are the royal road to an understanding of the unconscious mind.

Counterwishes: Anxiety Dreams

If dreams are indeed wish fulfillments, then why do we sometimes dream dreams that apparently run counter to our most cherished desires? Indeed, why do our dreams sometimes contain elements of our most dreaded fears? To answer these questions, and to account for the apparent contradiction, we must ask a further question: "Whose wish is fulfilled by a dream?"

No doubt a wish-fulfillment must bring pleasure; but the question then arises "To whom?" To the person who has the wish of course. But as we know, a dreamer's relation to his wishes is a quite peculiar one. He repudiates them and censors them—he has no liking for them, in short. So that their fulfillment will give him no pleasure, but just the opposite; and experience shows that this opposite appears in the form of anxiety.... Thus a dreamer in his relation to his dream-wishes can only be compared to an amalgamation of two separate people who are linked by some important common element. (Freud, 1900, pp. 580–581; this passage was added as a footnote in 1919; the same paragraph is included in Freud, 1916, pp. 215–216)

The amalgamated personage referred to in this passage describes, of course, the conflicting relationship between the dreamers unconscious, the source of the wish, and the preconscious censorship agency, the source of the repudiation. Thus although the wish fulfillment embodied in the dream brings pleasure to the unconscious, the anxiety element introduced by the distortion of the dream work is meant to satisfy the ever-watchful censor.

If we conceive of the mind as divided between the two agencies—the unconscious pleasure-seeking system, and the preconscious censorship system—the compromise nature of anxiety dreams becomes apparent. On the one hand, the unconscious is allowed some expression and some satisfaction of its repressed urges in the dream. On the other hand, the ethical arm of personality is allowed some control over the unacceptability of the wishes (Freud, 1900, p. 581). Dreams, just like neurotic symptoms, are compromise formations that allow both an outlet for the discharge of the wish's tension and a censorship mechanism to repudiate the now gratified, but still unacceptable, wish.

Repression and the Unpleasure Principle

Consider once again the state of human infants. Striving to obtain satisfaction for their needs and to avoid mounting somatic tension, infants soon learn the distinction between a fantasized and a real satisfier. Frustration and unpleasure are the tutors in a curriculum that includes the lessons that imagined food cannot be eaten, hallucinatory milk cannot be drunk, and an ephemeral mother cannot be cuddled. In order to survive, the infant must learn that the wish fulfillments embodied in dream states and fantasies have to be pursued in reality.

When *real* satisfactions for its desires are not forthcoming, the infant experiences psychological and sometimes bodily pain that Freud termed *unpleasure*. Conversely, when the unconscious obtains gratification of its desires, the result is the physical and mental state of *pleasure*.

A further set of lessons, however, must be mastered to ensure a comfortable and safe existence. This "unpleasure principle" is a two-edged sword. It motivates infants to avoid the discomfort of hallucinatory need satisfaction. It also emphasizes the importance of actively avoiding painful or noxious stimulation as well. Hence, the newly developed preconscious reality-scanning system may operate to promote escape or flight from certain forms of excitation when, on the basis of past experience, it recognizes some stimuli as potentially threatening. This class of unpleasure-producing stimuli might include, for example, as the child matures, lighted matches, hot radiators, and an angry mother.

Furthermore, even the internal, mental representations of such stimuli would trigger avoidance responses in the mental apparatus. But in the case of internal stimulation, the mental apparatus cannot engage in the physical act of flight. Instead, mental withdrawal occurs that takes the form of an *anticathexis*, the removal of **cathexes**,[1] charges of mental energy, or the diversion of attention from the memory image of the noxious stimulus.

THE REALITY PRINCIPLE

The infant's newest mental attainment under the influence of the unpleasure principle is its ability to delay the motor activity that is normally employed in obtaining gratification. The infant will now wait until there is a clear indication of the existence of reality from its preconscious perceptual system. It is the reality-testing orientation to the world that provides the infant with a reliable income of pleasure. We might, therefore, redefine a wish in these terms: A wish is a quantity of unpleasurable excitation resulting from a need that can be completely satisfied only by a real object or by specific and instrumental activity in the external world.

Thus infants' intercourse with the world is governed not only by the pleasure-unpleasure principle, but by the **reality principle** as well. With the adoption of this more sophisticated mental strategy, external reality increases in importance in infants' mental lives. Infants will increasingly use their senses to scan the environment for appropriate objects of satisfaction demanded by the reality principle (Freud, 1911, p. 220).

Primary and Secondary Process Thought

Our description of the unpleasure and reality principles is incomplete because their joint functioning is more complicated than a simple picture might suggest. The unconscious system, for example, apparently knows no bounds to its wishfulness, and it is well satisfied with only hallucinatory wish satisfaction. Behaving as if reality did not exist, the unconscious does not by itself discriminate between real and imaginary objects. Its only interest is in the distinction between pleasure and unpleasure.

Moreover, as revealed in manifest dreams and in neurotic symptoms, the unconscious system's sum total of mental energy is highly mobile and capable of all sorts of shifts, condensations, and displacements. All of these mental acrobatics are, of course, directed to the attainment of satisfaction at all cost. Freud characterized this state of affairs in the unconscious as **primary process thinking.** The chief characteristics of primary process thinking are the urgency with which tension reduction is sought, the plasticity or mobility of its energy, and its disregard for reality.

In contrast to the primary process functioning of the unconscious system, the preconscious system operates in accord with the reality principle by delaying gratification.

---

[1]The term **cathexes** is a translation of a German term Freud had first used in his "Project for a Scientific Psychology" (1895). The project was a detailed neurological model of the mind in which Freud postulated coordinated systems of neurons with the brain as the basis of various psychological processes, including repression and dreams. Certain of the neurons in this model become permeable to the flow of energy (electrochemical discharges) within the nervous system and they "fill up" with quantities of it. Freud used the German word *Besetzung*, which roughly means "to fill up," or "to occupy," in describing the flow of energy in and out of the neurons. His translators converted the German word to the more technical sounding *cathexis* from a Greek root meaning "to hold on to." Freud abandoned the neurological model but not the analogous idea of psychic energy systems that could fill up and discharge their quantities of energy, that is, their cathexis of excitation.

This kind of mental functioning, characterized by an interest in the demands of reality and an ability to delay gratification, Freud termed **secondary process thinking**. Because secondary process mental functioning develops later than primary process thinking, and because such reality-oriented mental activity is characteristic of truly adult thought, Freud considered secondary process thought to be a clear developmental advance over primary process functioning.

THE MEANINGS OF THE *UNCONSCIOUS* IN PSYCHOANALYSIS

The way in which Freud had used the term, **unconscious**, in his early writings led to some confusion about the reasons for which an idea might be removed from consciousness. Freud, therefore, distinguished three ways in which the term unconscious was used in psychoanalysis.

The first meaning, indicating the existence of ideas that are not *now*—at this precise moment—in consciousness, is a purely *descriptive* one. Thus, for example, although few of us keep our own phone number in the forefront of our minds at every minute of the day, we can nevertheless recall that item when necessary. Our phone number is only temporarily out of immediate awareness. There is no a priori reason why it cannot be brought into consciousness at will. Such items that can easily be made conscious are conceptualized as residing in the preconscious system (Freud, 1912, p. 262). Hence, this first meaning of *unconscious* is descriptive of those occasions when the limitations of consciousness and the human attention span necessitate the simple omission of some content.

In contrast with this purely descriptive sense, there are memories of early childhood incidents, impulses, and desires that are unacceptable or threatening to the conscious ego and cannot be recalled. Such memories are repressed from consciousness. Hysterical symptoms owe their existence to such unconscious ideas that, despite their intensity and their activity, remain separate from conscious awareness. Repressed memories are never admitted to consciousness so long as repression operates successfully. There is a continual expenditure of energy required to keep threatening memories out of awareness. This type of unconscious, full of threatening desires and memories, is called the *dynamic* unconscious (Freud, 1912, pp. 263–264).

The unconscious is thus characterized by the high mobility of its cathexes of energy as evidenced in its ability to condense, displace, and distort ideas. Furthermore, the unconscious responds to the demands of the **pleasure principle** by its continual press for immediate gratification of wishes, in contrast with the delayed, inhibitory, reality-testing orientation of the preconscious. In consequence, the unconscious must be conceptualized as a unique system operating in accordance with its own local rules of conduct side by side with the other systems of the mind that, likewise, operate in conformity with their intrinsic standards of conduct. This usage of the word *unconscious* conveys the systematic meaning of the term, indicating the independent status of the unconscious as a system among systems.

In summary, Freud distinguished among three meanings of the term *unconscious*: the *descriptive*, the *dynamic*, and the *systematic*. Each of these usages might be thought of as corresponding to a question:

- What is unconscious? (descriptive)
- Why is it unconscious? (dynamic)
- Where is the unconscious idea? (systematic)

The Concept of "Metapsychology"

The complexity of the term *unconscious* led Freud to the useful strategy of distinguishing among its separate but interrelated meanings. Using a similar approach, Freud now began to distinguish among the various facets of any psychological event. He resurrected a term from his earlier work to describe the process of conceptualizing mental processes from multiple viewpoints simultaneously. **Metapsychology** (meaning "above" or "beyond" psychology) was the technical term to be used whenever a psychological process was understood from its descriptive, systematic, and dynamic aspects. Unfortunately, Freud introduced some confusion into the concept by changing his vocabulary each time he wrote about metapsychology (cf. Freud, 1915c, p. 181; 1933, pp. 70ff.).

The *systematic* meaning was sometimes identified as the **topographic** viewpoint, indicating not only Freud's conception of different systems but also that he viewed the systems as spatially arrayed. At this point in his career, Freud pictured the unconscious, preconscious, and conscious systems as three adjacent compartments (see 1900, Chapter 7). Hence, the topographic viewpoint referred not only to the unique properties of a particular system of the mind but also to its particular location with respect to the other systems and the paths of its access to consciousness at any moment in time.

In a similar way, Freud enlarged the meaning of the term dynamic by suggesting that not only are there competing and conflicting forces behind psychological processes but also that their relative magnitudes or quantities of energy may be measurable. Hence, the term *economic* was coined to indicate the differing degrees of intensity with which dynamic interactions take place (1915c, p. 180).

Other psychoanalysts have pointed to another component of metapsychology inherent in Freud's way of understanding behavior. Any symptom, dream, or act has a psychological history within the life history of the individual. By reconstructing the many events (or memories of them) that coalesced into one mental process, the

Table 3.1   Components of Freud's Metapsychology

Metapsychological viewpoint	Clinical referent
1. Descriptive	Momentary absence from awareness of particular ideas or feelings that can easily be made conscious at will.
2. Systematic (or topographic)	Special quality of a mental event due to the unique characteristics of the psychological system in which it originates, presently occupies, or to which it has access by virtue of its location.
3. Dynamic	Energetic mobility of the competing, conflicting forces that prevent an idea or feeling from becoming conscious or allow it to enter awareness only in disguised form.
4. Economic	Relative intensities or quantities of the competing dynamic forces, and their changes in strength over time.
5. Genetic	Reconstruction of the multiple origins of any psychological event in the life history of the person.
6. Adaptive	Degree to which a psychological process or act functions in resolving unconscious conflicts and in the healthy management of life events.

origins of symptoms, ideas, beliefs, resistances, feelings, and so on are reached. This life history viewpoint is what Freud called the genetic approach, and it constitutes another facet of metapsychology (A. Freud, 1969, p. 153).

Finally, analysts who followed Freud have also stressed the non-conflictive aspects of some psychological events. Thus Hartmann (1939, 1964) emphasized the adaptive quality of psychological processes that function not only to resolve individuals' personal conflicts but also serve them in a healthy way to fit comfortably into the life they and their environment create. Hence, the **adaptive viewpoint** is added alongside the others as a component of metapsychology.

It is clear that the Freudian way of viewing any human event requires attention to the complex interplay of a host of determinants. Metapsychology requires that each person be regarded as an intricate, but understandable, organism. The various facets of metapsychology are summarized in Table 3.1.

METAPSYCHOLOGY OF REPRESSION

Repression, you may recall, is the way in which the mental apparatus deals with wishful impulses from which physical flight is impossible. Instead, these inescapable and unacceptable impulses are not admitted to awareness. Consider the paradox involved in proposing a mechanism like repression. Wishful impulses demand satisfaction and, when it is forthcoming, pleasure is the usual result. But in the case of a repressed impulse, something has happened to a wishful idea that makes satisfaction so unpleasurable that denial of its existence is the only means of dealing with it. Yet the impulse continues to press for release.

It thus seems that one of the preconditions for an impulse to be subject to repression is that satisfaction of the impulse be simultaneously pleasurable and unpleasurable. The only way to account for this disparity of aims is to assume that the reason a repressed impulse has been denied release into consciousness is because its satisfaction would create pleasure for one mental system at the expense of the even more grave unpleasure evoked in a competing system. This is the conflict between unconscious wishful demands and conscious restraint.

A Balance of Pleasure and Unpleasure

Freud clearly conceived of repression as the expression of a balance between these two motives: the seeking after pleasure and the avoidance of unpleasure. In the case of a repressed impulse, however, the motive force of unpleasure is more intense than the pleasure to be obtained from satisfaction of the impulse. Repression occurs, consequently, when the balance between pleasure and unpleasure is tipped in the direction of unpleasure.

The process of **repression** requires that the preconscious system prevent the emergence of the unconscious impulse into awareness by withdrawing a sum of mental energy (cathexis) from the offending impulse. However, having lost the cathexis of the preconscious, the unacceptable impulse may still retain the cathexis of energy from the unconscious, where it originated. Consequently, the repressed impulse can continue to make assaults on the preconscious system indefinitely, drawing on its reserve of energy in the unconscious. The simple expedient of withdrawing preconscious energy from the impulse is not sufficient to prevent the impulse from unendingly repeating its attempts at entry into consciousness (Freud, 1915c, p. 180).

BOX 3.2   *More on the Term Cathexis*

Cathexis is a translation of a German term Freud had first used in his "Project for a Scientific Psychology" (1895). The project was a detailed **neurological model** of the mind in which Freud postulated coordinated systems of neurons with the brain as the basis of various psychological processes, including repression and dreams. Certain of the neurons in this model become permeable to the flow of energy (electrochemical discharges) within the nervous system and they "fill up" with quantities of it. Freud used the German word *Besetzung*, which roughly means "to fill up," or "to occupy," in describing the flow of energy in and out of the neurons. His translators converted the German word to the more technical sounding

cathexis from a Greek root meaning "to hold on to." Freud eventually abandoned the neurological model, but not the analogous idea of psychic energy systems that could fill up and discharge their quantities of energy, that is, their cathexis of excitation.

The concept of cathexis is also related to the idea of an "intentional" idea, which was proposed by the philosopher Franz Brentano, one of Freud's most prominent college professors. An intentional idea is one that *intends* or points to an outer object. Chapter 7 explores the concept of cathexis in object relations theory, and Chapter 12 explores the concept of intentionality in existential phenomenology.

What is needed to accomplish the subjugation of the impulse is another, opposing quantity of energy, strong enough to resist the unconsciously endowed impulse's cathexis of energy. Such an opposing supply of energy would, in effect, serve as a barrier against the reemergence of the rejected impulse. Freud called this barrier that is set up by the preconscious an **anticathexis**. Anticathexis is the primary mode of dealing with unacceptable unconscious content. Clearly, to enable repression to remain effective, an anticathexis requires a continual expenditure of energy by the preconscious.

Primal Repression and Repression Proper

With the development of the theoretical concept of anticathexis, Freud could account for the creation and presence of repressed derivatives in consciousness, like symptoms and seduction fantasies. He now conceived of repression as a two-stage process to effect this theoretical advance.

In the first stage, the ideational representative of the unacceptable impulse is denied access to consciousness by the preconscious setting up an anticathexis as a barrier. The first stage is called **primal repression**. The immediate result of primal repression is that the repressed idea or impulse is fixated or frozen in development. No further modification or maturation of the repressed content can occur (Freud, 1915b, p. 148). Significant acts of primal repression occur during the first six or eight years of life, and in their role of immobilized, unconscious memories they become important sensitizing or predisposing factors for later acts of adult repression.

The second stage of repression is called **repression proper**, and it is directed against any derivatives or associates of the originally repressed impulses that may enter consciousness. Repression proper is rather like an "after pressure," to use Freud's descriptive phrase, whereby ideas, trains of thought, or perceptions that are associatively linked to the primally repressed impulse are also denied access to consciousness. Repression proper consists of the preconscious system's withdrawing its cathexis (energy) from the derivative. Repression proper thus cooperates with primal repression to ensure that unacceptable impulses and associated ideas remain out of consciousness awareness.

Thus repression is not a unitary act. Or, more precisely, repressions of primal derivatives that occur after infancy depend on the mass of primarily repressed impulses already present in the unconscious. An idea or an impulse cannot be removed from awareness by repression proper unless there has already been an act of predisposing primal repression to exert a "pulling effect" on subsequent derivatives. At the same time, the preconscious system actively strives from its vantage point on the threshold of awareness to eject these offending ideas by pushing them away from consciousness (cf. Freud, 1900, p. 547n.).

INSTINCTS OF THE UNCONSCIOUS

Terms like *excitation*, *impulse*, *wish*, and *tension*, dating almost from the very beginning of Freud's psychological writing, were replaced in his later work by the term *instinct*. In his 1915 metapsychological paper, "Instincts and Their Vicissitudes," Freud carefully delineated two distinctions between stimuli and instincts:

- Freud pointed out that physical stimuli impinge on the organism from the external environment, whereas instinctual urges develop from within the organism. Although the organism, through the use of reflexes, may escape or even terminate external stimulation, internal instinctual demand cannot be escaped by flight. An organism cannot flee the demands of its own body.
- A second distinguishing feature is that stimulation originating in the environment is only temporary in its impact on the organism. Instinctual, internal excitation terminates only when the tissue need that gives rise to the instinct is satisfied. Thus instincts may be thought of as needs seeking appropriate satisfactions (Freud, 1915a, p. 119).

Freud returned in his discussion of instinct to his earlier idea of the nervous system as an apparatus that functions to reduce stimulation and excitation to the lowest possible level. In Freud's view, the nervous system is assigned the task of "mastering stimuli" by discharging excitation almost as soon as it builds up (1915a, p. 120). Called the principle of constancy by Breuer and Freud, this idea of the nervous system repeatedly returning to some optimal state of minimum arousal is similar to the modern biologist's concept of **homeostasis**. It follows, in consequence, that this essential task is complicated in the case of an instinct because the nervous system cannot master instinctual demands by the expedient of flight. Furthermore, because the nervous system is governed by the **pleasure principle**—the seeking after pleasure by the discharge of unpleasurable mounting tension—instincts must not be dealt with in a way that merely avoids their demand; the nervous system must find a way to reduce the biological deficit (or to satisfy the urge) that the demand represents.

For Freud, then, the concept of instinct was both a psychological and a biological one, on the border between bodily and mental phenomena. An instinct is a mental representation of a physical or bodily need (1915a, p. 122).

CHARACTERISTICS OF INSTINCTS

Freud distinguished four characteristics of an instinct:

1. **Pressure:** The amount of force or strength of the demand made by the instinct on the mind is described as pressure. Thus, for example, deprivation of food for 24 hours produces greater instinctual pressure (hunger) than deprivation for only four hours.

2. **Aim:** Instinctual impulses all strive toward one goal or aim: satisfaction or tension reduction. Whereas satisfaction is clearly the universal aim of an instinct, a given instinct may operate to achieve its aim in differing ways. Freud distinguishes, therefore, between *ultimate aim*, the immediate gratification of demand, and *intermediate aim*, the substitute forms of satisfaction for which an instinct may strive when blocked from a directly suitable goal. The sexual instinct is particularly prone to this widening of its aims. For example, the aim of the sexual instincts is "organ pleasure," a pleasing sensation attached to a particular part of the body when stimulated. With maturation, the sexual instincts become focused on the aim of reproduction (Freud, 1915a, p. 126).

3. **Object:** To obtain its ultimate aim of satisfaction, the instinct must seek some concrete, usually external, object that has the power to reduce its tension. For example, an infant's hunger drive is directed toward the object of food. The object of an instinct is its most variable characteristic. Thus displacement from one satisfying object to another, a process so characteristic of the wish fulfillments in dreams, is possible. Some prisoners, for example, confined with members of their own sex, might resort to homosexual gratification as a substitute for heterosexual satisfaction, only to return to exclusive heterosexual gratification upon release.

4. **Source:** The source of instincts reside in the physical-chemical processes of the body. The sexual instincts, for example, have their physiological sources in hormonal secretions, central nervous system activity, and genital arousal; the hunger instinct originates in the viscera (and also in some parts of the central nervous system).

DUALISTIC DIVISION OF THE INSTINCTS: HUNGER VERSUS LOVE

It is clear that Freud viewed the instincts, though biologically based, as essentially malleable and plastic in the course of an organism's life history. During their collision with life's circumstances, the instincts may undergo modifications or reversals of expression. These vicissitudes, to use Freud's translators' term, share the common motive of avoiding the psychological or biological discomfort that would result from free, undisguised expression of an instinctual urge. Repression, as we have seen, is one of the vicissitudes that an instinct may undergo.

Although instincts may be expressed and satisfied in diverse ways, Freud was hesitant to catalog a seemingly infinite list of biological demands and their mental representatives. Instead, he proposed a concise, bipolar division of all instincts into two great classes: instincts in the service of the preservation of the individual's life, and instincts directed toward the attainment of pleasure. *Life maintenance* and *pleasure* are the two poles around which the operations of the mental apparatus are organized.

According to this dualistic scheme, Freud asserted that the ego was the seat of the organism's instincts for self-preservation, whereas striving for pleasure was a function of the child's developing sexual equipment. Though Freud did not provide a name for the energy of the ego instincts, he employed the term **libido** to denote the energy of the sexual or pleasure instincts (e.g., 1916, p. 313). Libido was broadly conceived as general pleasurable stimulation rather than as restricted to genital, sexual pleasure. Thus Freud's original dualistic classification of the instincts pitted the ego instincts against the sexual (pleasure) instincts: survival versus libido.

The ego instincts have as their main goal the preservation and continuance of the safety and bodily integrity of the individual. Sexual (pleasure) instincts, on the other hand, are directed to the preservation of the species. Consequently, in Freud's original dualism, the ego instincts are individual-centered and the sexual instincts are, ultimately, species-centered. This dichotomy, Freud pointed out, is roughly similar to the division between *hunger* (individual self-preservation) and *love* (other-centered pleasure).

Freud introduced this division of the instincts in a paper in 1910 (1910b, p. 214; see editor's footnote), and he maintained the dualism of which he was so fond for a number of years. The bulk of his writing in subsequent years, however, was focused on the sexual instincts with the effect of obscuring by neglect the role of the ego instincts. But the ego instincts were to come into their own in psychoanalysis as Freud's clinical practice revealed some disconcerting anomalies and violations of the dualistic hunger-love scheme.

An Exception to the Hunger-Love Model: Narcissism

In the dualistic conception of the instincts, libido, the energy of the sexual or pleasure instincts, should be a separate quantity from that of the ego instincts. Freud noted a disconcerting exception to this separation hypothesis in the case of some psychotic patients.

One of the main characteristics of some forms of schizophrenia is the withdrawal of the patient's interest from the external world. They behave as if reality no longer existed and in every way as though only their own ideas, feelings, or urges mattered. Freud's instinct theory would characterize such withdrawal as the retraction of libido from external objects and persons. Simultaneously with this retraction of libido, however, there occurs what seems to be an expansion of ego instinctual energy, an increase in the ego's self-interest. In short, psychotics overvalue their own ideas, their own bodies, and their own person. Why should this reciprocal increase in ego instinct occur at the same time as outwardly directed libido is diminished—unless the two forms of energy are not separate? Freud had to conclude that libido could be turned back on the ego and that libido could donate to the ego's disposal some of the energy normally expended outwardly:

> The libido that has been withdrawn from the external world has been directed to the ego and thus gives rise to an attitude that may be called **narcissism.** (1914a, p. 75)

Clearly the energies of the ego and sexual instincts are not separate. They commingle, one drawing on the reserves of the other at various times. Freud had thus introduced a new distinction into his theory of instincts. He postulated that in the earliest stages of life there is a supply of libidinal energy in the ego that produces a primary state of narcissism or self-love. It is from this pool of primary **ego libido** that the later, external **object libido** emerges. But the original pool of ego libido remains in the ego, and it is this supply that is expanded or contracted in the narcissism of psychosis. In consequence, ego instinctual energy and sexual instinctual energy are not completely independent, but initially emerge from a common pool. Thus in the beginning all instinctual energy was one libido. Later developments cause the differentiation into ego libido and object libido.

Freud had thus revised his dualistic notion of the instincts, altering the nature of the conflict from that of a clash between ego instincts and sexual instincts to that of a clash between two forms of libido: ego libido conflicts with object libido. Freud was fond of dualistic, bipolar explanations of events and certainly ego and object libido fit the favored pattern.

Another Exception: The Death "Instinct"

By considering the narcissistic pool of ego libido the primal source of all significant interactions with the world, Freud had virtually erected libido as the unitary scheme of explanation. He was not, as some of his critics accused, attempting to sexualize all human behavior. His distinction between the self-preservation nature of ego libido and the pleasure-seeking orientation of object libido had maintained and paralleled his original division between ego and sexual instincts. But the problem for Freud was that his clinical experience had uncovered the essentially conflict-ridden nature of human behavior and neurosis. A unitary scheme of instinctual dynamics based solely on libido deprived psychoanalytic theory of the ability to specify the elements of the conflict precisely. What was needed was a new dualistic scheme in which libido (both object and ego libido) could be contrasted against some other, independent pool of instinctual energy.

In 1920, Freud solved the problem. He published a startlingly speculative account of a profoundly revised instinct theory whereby libido was contrasted with a newly discerned instinctual energy, the *death instinct*. Thus Freud returned to a dualistic conception of mental energy. At the same time, he traveled beyond his earlier model of the mind by transcending even the seemingly secure dominance of the pleasure principle. For in revising his instinct theory, Freud replaced the pleasure principle as the fundamental mental rule with an even more basic "law," the *repetition compulsion*. It is no wonder that Freud entitled the book in which he made these radical, and for some psychoanalysts, disturbing revelations *Beyond the Pleasure Principle*. Consequently, we turn now to a survey of the evidence on which Freud predicated his final, most radical revision. It may be of some help to refer to Figure 3.1 to obtain an overview of the sequence of changes in Freud's three revisions of his instinct theory.

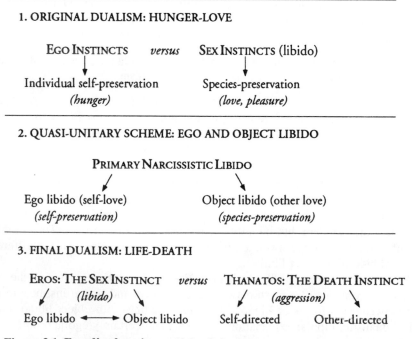

Figure 3.1 Freud's changing models of the instincts.

BEHAVIORS BEYOND THE PLEASURE PRINCIPLE: THE CLINICAL EVIDENCE

Ernst's "Gone" Game

At one-and-a-half years, Freud's eldest grandson, Ernst, played a strangely symbolic game. He would momentarily take hold of any available small object, throw it into a corner of the room or under the bed, and croon loudly the German word for "gone" (*fort*) with a peculiarly long, drawn-out "o-o-o-o" pronunciation. Immediately upon throwing his toys away from himself, Ernst would retrieve them only long enough, it seemed to Freud, to begin the dispersal again. Freud soon realized that the sole use Ernst made of his toys was to play this strangely compelling game of "gone."

Ernst was singularly attached to his mother and especially sensitive to periods of her absence. Not that Ernst ever cried or showed any other obvious form of protest to separation from his mother. In all respects, Ernst was a "good" child. In September 1915, while Freud was spending several weeks with his daughter Sophie at her home in Hamburg, he had the opportunity to observe Ernst's extraordinary game (Jones, 1957, p. 267). Freud found himself peculiarly moved by Ernst's pastime.

As if to confirm his growing apprehension that the "game" was somehow strangely symbolic of Ernst's sense of loss at his mother's absence, Freud was able to make the following further observation: Ernst had as one of his toys a wooden reel (probably similar to a thread spool) with a piece of string firmly attached.

> It never occurred to [Ernst] to pull it along the floor behind him, for instance, and play at its being a carriage. What he did was to hold the reel by the string and very skillfully throw it over the edge of his curtained cot, so that it disappeared into it, at the same time uttering his expressive "o-o-o-o." He then pulled the reel out of the cot again by the string and hailed its reappearance with a joyful "da" ["there"]. This, then, was the complete game—disappearance and return. (1920a, p. 15)

On another occasion, when Ernst's mother had been away for several hours, her return was greeted by her son's exclamation, "Baby o-o-o-o!" In the light of Freud's earlier observations, such an utterance could only be meant to communicate: "Ernst (baby) was gone!"—an interpretation that was confirmed when it was discovered that Ernst had tried a variation of his "gone" game with a full-length mirror. Not quite reaching the floor, the mirror had provided the inventive Ernst with the opportunity to make himself "gone" each time he crouched below its bottom edge (Freud, 1920a, p. 15n.).

"Gone" was more than a game. It was a form of self-discipline by which Ernst had sought to master the unpleasurable prospect of his mother's periodic absences. He could not, however, symbolically act out the pleasurable return of a missing love object until he had first staged its unpleasurable disappearance. In his "game," Ernst was particularly successful because the disappearance and return of his toys were directly under his control, as contrasted with the absences of his mother, which he could experience only as a circumstance imposed from without.

Ernst had developed a technique of symbolically repeating an unpleasurable experience. In its original form, the experience had to be endured passively. By his re-creations, Ernst could *actively* control the event, and he could express a kind of defiance: "All right, go away—I don't need you!" Sadly, when Ernst was almost six years old, his mother died of pneumonia; in his terms, she was permanently "gone."

On the theoretical level, Freud offered Ernst's game as one example of a violation of the pleasure principle. It showed clearly that unpleasurable events could be reworked, repeated, and relived, despite their painful quality, until they were mastered. Yet, Ernst's game was not a definite example. Freud pointed out that such cases could be interpreted as consistent with, rather than beyond, the pleasure principle because the eventual outcome was pleasurable. He searched about for another example of a behavior beyond the pleasure principle.

Recurring Posttraumatic Dreams

In the dreams of patients suffering from hysterialike paralysis and apparent physical illness following upon some life-threatening accident like a railway collision or exposure to stress on the battlefield, Freud found another illustration of an urge to repeat unpleasant experiences. Traumatic neurosis resembles hysterical symptomatology in that the afflicted individual shows no organic basis or demonstrable physical cause for the symptoms. But, more important, in many such cases the individual experiences recurring dreams that each night recreate the traumatic situation of the accident or battlefield. By contrast, such patients in their waking state are usually more concerned with forgetting the trauma than with reliving it. The dream, however, instead of pleasurably fulfilling some wish, returns the patient to the situation and to the fright that was once helplessly endured.

Reliving Painful Memories

As a last example of an apparent violation of the dominance of the pleasure principle, Freud cited an observation from the realm of psychotherapy. Often, during psychoanalysis, patients treat analysts as if they were particular authority figures from the patients' own past. They thrust onto their therapist attitudes and desires that would be appropriate only to the real figures of their past lives. In effect, the patients relive significant experiences and attitudes of their life histories with the therapist as their present target.

> ... [The patient] is obliged to repeat the repressed material as a contemporary experience instead of, as the physician would prefer to see, remembering it as something belonging to the past (Freud, 1920a, p. 18).

Transference is the name that Freud gave to this tendency of patients to react to their therapists with emotions reproduced from childhood. Because the material that is thus repeated originates in the unconscious, and because the conscious ego is occupied with the repression of that material, Freud concluded that the compulsion to repeat must also originate in the unconscious. Therefore, in the conflict between the ego and the unconscious, reexperience of the repressed material must figure as a potent source of unpleasure for the beleaguered ego.

For every instance cited—Ernst's game, traumatic dreams, transference in therapy—the common denominator is individuals are acting under the compulsion endlessly to repeat unpleasurable experiences.

REDUCTION OF THE PLEASURE PRINCIPLE TO A PLEASURE "TENDENCY"

Freud had in mind cases like Ernst's game, transference, and traumatic dreams when he modified his conception of the pleasure principle from a dominating influence to that of a trend in mental life:

> If such a dominance [of pleasure] existed, the immense majority of our mental processes would have to be accompanied by pleasure or to lead to pleasure, whereas universal

experience completely contradicts any such conclusion. The most that can be said, therefore, is that there exists in the mind a strong *tendency* toward the pleasure principle, but the tendency is opposed by certain other forces or circumstances, so that the final outcome cannot always be in harmony with the tendency towards pleasure. (1920a, pp. 9–10)

The opposing forces were, of course, those underlying the compulsion to repeat unpleasurable experiences until, like Ernst's, they are mastered. Freud was now prepared to embark on a speculative reexamination of his previous accounts of the mental apparatus. His intention was to bring his discrepant findings about violations of the pleasure principle into harmony with the rest of psychoanalytic theory.

The Nirvana Principle

The overwhelming necessity governing the operation of the mental apparatus is the reduction of excitation, tension, or drive, and the need to maintain a relatively stable state of stimulation-free existence. Freud, following Breuer, had originally adopted the term "constancy principle" to describe the tension reduction efforts of the nervous system. Breuer had borrowed the term from the psychophysicist Gustav Fechner.

In *Beyond the Pleasure Principle*, Freud incorporated some new terminology from Barbara Low to replace the constancy principle. Freud now employed the **nirvana principle** to indicate the homeostatic trend of nervous system functioning whereby it attempts to divest itself of disturbing tensions and excess stimulation. In fact, Freud had thought that the Nirvana principle and the pleasure principle were essentially intimately related so that the nervous system's adherence to the Nirvana principle was guaranteed by the operation of the pleasure principle. That is, reduction of tension and the maintenance of an almost stimulation-free state implied by the Nirvana principle are pleasurable. However, in a paper written in 1924, Freud changed his mind and distinguished between the two principles.

The distinction was necessary, Freud thought, because certain states of pleasure require increases in excitation rather than the reduction of excitation. One state, for example, that would violate the Nirvana principle, but accord with the pleasure principle, is sexual excitation, in which rising amounts of bodily tension in the genitals produce pleasurable sensation (Freud, 1924, p. 160). Therefore, the Nirvana principle and the pleasure principle were distinguishable as separate, but complementary, trends in mental life.

Conservative Nature of Instincts

As Ernst played his evocative game of "gone," and as traumatic neurotic patients relive their frightful experiences in nightly dreams, so too the instincts, when viewed from the perspective of the nervous system's ultimate goal of tension reduction, seem to function to repeat the past. Instincts operate to return to an earlier state—to the excitation-free state prior to stimulation.

> It seems, then, that an instinct is an urge inherent in organic life to restore an earlier state of things which the living entity has been obliged to abandon under the pressure of external disturbing forces . . . or, to put it another way, instincts are the expression of the inertia inherent in organic life. (Freud, 1920a, p. 36; italics added)

Freud was postulating that mental life is essentially conservative in quality. The mental apparatus is periodically disturbed by outside stimulation and internal needs but, on the whole, strives to maintain itself in the state of quietude that characterizes its functioning prior to such disturbances. A "Nirvanalike" state of peaceful freedom from need is the principal goal of the mental apparatus, for it is this satiety that conforms faultlessly to the pleasure principle.

As primitive organisms evolved, however, their trend toward maintaining a constant state and inertial resistance to change would have been overcome by the continuous flux of external conditions, the constant change of environmental pressures, which make their demands on living things. Thus the instincts developed in unison with the increasing biological complexity of the evolving primitive organisms in order to maintain the capacity of the organism perpetually to restore an internal state of harmony in the face of a changing environment. The hunger instinct is a good example. When hunger tension mounts, we seek food and achieve satisfaction, but within a few hours, food again must be sought to return to the state of satisfaction, and so on.

Such striving is always returning to or repeating the earlier state of quietude before the world or internal needs made their demands. In its most fundamental form, the compulsion to repeat is the ultimate conservative trend: an urge to gain complete quietude, total freedom from stimulation and need, and absolute independence of the world. In short, the aim is death. In Freud's exposition:

> It would be in contradiction to the conservative nature of the instincts if the goal of life were a state of things that had never been attained. On the contrary, it must be an *old* state of things, an initial state from which the living entity has at one time or other departed and to which it is striving to return by the circuitous paths along which its development leads. If we are to take it as a truth that knows no exception that everything living dies for internal reasons—becomes inorganic once again—then we shall be compelled to say "*the aim of all life is death*" and, looking backwards, that "*inanimate things existed before living ones*." (Freud, 1920a, p. 38)

In Freud's view, accidental death arising from external causes would cheat the organism of the completion of its cycle by merely terminating organic life. The organism would be deprived of achieving a return to the earlier state of inorganic existence that is an intrinsic part of its cellular structure. In consequence, accidental death, illness, and injury merely short-circuit the process and circumvent the aim of life. The organism must gain death in its own way—the gradual burning out of the life energies.

REVISION OF INSTINCT THEORY: EROS AND DEATH

Freud's bold proposal of a death instinct brings the new theory into direct conflict with his original dualistic model of the instincts whereby one-half of the dichotomy was asserted to be constituted of self-preservation ego instincts. Of what use to the organism are self-preservation instincts if the ultimate aim of life is death? Freud ingeniously answered this question by placing the ego instincts in the service of the death instincts as their agent of successful discharge:

> [Self-preservative instincts] . . . are component instincts whose function it is to assure that the organism shall follow its own path to death, and to ward off any possible ways of returning to inorganic existence other than those which are immanent in the organism itself. . . . What we are left with is the fact that the organism wishes to die only in its own fashion. Thus these guardians of life [i.e., self-preservative instincts] too, were originally the myrmidons of death. (Freud, 1920a, p. 39)

Although Freud himself never, except in conversation with colleagues, used the term **Thanatos** to refer to the death instinct, his followers have almost universally adopted the term as the official name (Jones, 1957, p. 273). (*Thanatos*, incidentally, is the name of the Greek god of death and was first used to refer to the death instinct by Freud's pupil Paul Federn.)

The other half of the original dualistic classification of the instincts, the sexual instincts, presented yet another problem to the hypothesis of a death instinct. How could instincts that serve the continuity of life, the longevity of a species, be brought into line with the penultimate conservatism of the death instinct in its striving toward the dissolution of life? The answer is that these two forces conflict.

Eros and Immortality

The instincts that guard the development of the germ cells, sperm, and egg, that provide them with safety during their time of generativity, and that motivate the union of male and female are the sexual instincts, collectively termed *libido*. Clearly the sexual instincts are the true-life instincts since they operate against the forces of death and dissolution by attempting to immortalize the organism through its progeny. Paradoxically, the other class of instincts, ego instincts, subserve death by striving to promote the self-preservation of the organism until it dies in its own way, of its own immanent causes. Thus, in *Beyond the Pleasure Principle*, the ego instincts presented Freud with a problem of classification. In which group, life or death, should the ego instincts be included? Freud eventually combined the ego instincts with the sexual instincts and considered them to be part of the libido's press for the continuity of life while they nevertheless serve the inexorable aims of death.

Freud had retained much of his desired dualistic classification by opposing the death instincts to be combined life instincts (ego and object libido) (1920a, p. 41). In honor of the changed scheme, Freud assigned to the unified sexual and ego instincts the term **Eros**, the name of the god of love and passion. Consequently, the dichotomy in Freud's theory was changed from the conflict between love and hunger to the opposition between life and death. All organisms die. If they bear the spark of immortality, it is evidenced only in their ability to confer equally transient life.

Eros and Bisexuality: Return to Unity

Freud had one further problem that had to be solved before his life-death dualism could be brought into the main body of psychoanalytic theory. How is Eros governed by the compulsion to repeat, a compulsion that is basic to all instincts? The death instinct operates to return the organism to the prior evolutionary state of inorganic existence. But what is Eros attempting to repeat; to what does it seek to return?

The answer, Freud speculated, lies in the origin of the two sexes. He suggested, hesitantly at first, that Plato's myth of the origin of the human race might be a poetic representation of a fundamental truth. In the *Symposium*, Plato, speaking through the character of Aristophanes, recounts a myth in which the original human sexes existed in three varieties: male, female, and the union of the two. Those bisexual humans had

BOX 3.3   *Only Connect...*

Carl Jung (see Chapter 5) also concluded that personality contained bisexual elements. His concepts of *animus* and *anima* indicated the male and female aspects of the *psyche* in both genders, at least according to cultural norms of the time. Jung said that in males the animus was conscious and the anima unconscious, whereas in females, the reverse was true.

BOX 3.4 *Sequel*

In a conversation between Anna Freud and Christopher Monte in July 1974, Anna Freud insisted that contemporary presentations of psychoanalysis, like this one, should exclude the neurological model from consideration because psychoanalysis is a *psychological theory*, not a modified form of neurological science. She conceded that her father's early training in neurology had been influential in shaping his thinking and that his habit of framing his thoughts in biological terms was not easily overcome.

When Professor Monte suggested that, were her father alive today, he might adopt for his use some of the recent advances in biology and neurology, she stated that her father had created a psychology—not merely a type of neurology that had been translated into psychological language. Anna Freud reemphasized that her father would not have returned to neurological ideas under any circumstances.

Given the many advances in neuropsychology in the past three decades and Freud's ongoing awareness of developments in the field of science, openness to a modified neurological model would seem true to the spirit of Freudian investigation and theorizing.

double sets of hands, feet, and sexual organs, but, because they offended the gods, Zeus decided to cut them into two. After the division, each half human, desiring its missing component, sought out its mate. They threw their arms about each other, eager to merge again into unity. Freud commented,

> Shall we follow the hint given us by the poet-philosopher, and venture on the hypothesis that living substance at that time of its coming to life was torn apart into small particles, which have ever since endeavored to reunify through the sexual instincts? That these instincts, in which the chemical affinity of inanimate matter persisted, gradually succeeded, as they developed through the kingdom of protista, in overcoming the difficulties put in the way of that endeavor by an environment charged with dangerous stimuli—stimuli which compelled them to form a protective cortical layer? That these splintered fragments of living substance in this way attained a multicellular condition and finally transferred the instinct for reuniting, in the most highly concentrated form, to the germ cells? (1920a, p. 58)

Freud had returned to the concept of the inherently bisexual nature of the human constitution as the basis of the compulsion to repeat in Eros. Humans are striving in their sexual activity to attain the wholeness of sexuality that once was the hallmark of the earliest organisms. The compulsion to repeat is evidenced by Eros in the active striving of males and females to consummate sexual union—that is, in their striving to repeat evolutionary history.[2]

Death Derivatives: Aggression and Hate

Operating silently and invisibly, the death instinct is rarely observable in pure form. The existence of the death instinct can only be inferred from the operation of its more observable derivatives: namely, a tendency in humans to behave aggressively and their capacity to harbor destructive intent. These more observable derivatives of the death instinct emerge when the life instinct, Eros, succeeds in preventing the full

---

[2]It is interesting that Freud later rejected this formula of the *compulsion to repeat* in Eros. In one of his last considerations of the subject, "An Outline of Psychoanalysis" (1940), Freud came to the conclusion that the hypothesis that living substance was once a unity that, having been separated, now struggles toward reunion could not be supported by biological fact (1940, p. 149n.). He did not, however, offer an alternative basis for Eros's repetition compulsion, and by his omission, he left himself open to the criticism that Eros no longer fits his own definition of an instinct (cf. Fromm, 1973, Appendix).

self-destructive expression of Thanatos. Thus when Thanatos is deprived of expression within the individual, it emerges as other-directed, displaced aggression. Eros succeeds in preventing the death instinct from achieving the destruction of the individual by diverting the death instinct's energy to other individuals. The price of Eros's success is high.

Yet it was Freud's opinion that the death instinct and Eros are generally mingled throughout life. He believed that Eros generally succeeds in preventing Thanatos from attaining the organism's dissolution at the cost of creating outwardly directed human hate and aggression. Where Eros succeeds in constructive unification of humans, the death instinct wins a victory for human misery (Freud, 1930, p. 119).[3]

Freud's changing views of how the instincts were organized, from the original hunger-love dualism to the final Eros-Thanatos dichotomy, are summarized in Figure 3.1.

THE FINAL STRUCTURAL MODEL OF THE MIND

In 1923, in a book entitled *The Ego and the Id*, Freud again embarked on a major theoretical adventure. During the course of his career, he had constructed two major models of the mind. The first was a neurological model (1895), which he soon abandoned. The second, proposed in Chapter 7 of the *Interpretation of Dreams* (1900), was a distinctly psychological theory based on a spatial or topographical analogy. It was from this topographical model that terms like *unconscious* and *preconscious* originated. Both of these previous models, however, had serious flaws and ambiguities, chief of which was their inability to depict unambiguously the interplay of combining and competing forces within the personality.

In *The Ego and the Id* (1923), Freud created a final **structural model** of the mind that no longer represented mental functioning as divided among sharply separated and rigidly compartmentalized subsystems. One can think of the personality that results as a *composite*. The different parts operate, to some degree as separate psychic entities, sometimes functioning autonomously, even while interacting. Three newly named agencies, the *id*, the *ego*, and the *superego*, subsumed all of the mental functions previously assigned to the unconscious and the preconscious.

Id, Ego, Superego Terminology

Because the unconscious could no longer be restricted to a distinct region of the mind, and because it could not be employed solely as a description of momentarily latent thoughts, the term **id** would from now on indicate that part of selfhood that is alien to or

---

[3]The concept of a death instinct aroused enormous controversy and criticism from sources within and outside psychoanalysis. Ernest Jones, Freud's biographer and himself a psychoanalyst, found very little support in biology or in medicine for the death instinct. He suggested that Freud's proposal of the concept could be understood only in terms of Freud's personal reaction to the prospect of death. That eventually was periodically impressed on Freud's mind by the loss of members of his own family, some early recurring cardiac problems, and by his ultimately fatal protracted illness of cancer of the jaw and mouth (Jones, 1957, p. 278; see also Wallace, 1976). Max Schur, Freud's personal physician during the latter part of his life, also criticized the death instinct along much the same lines as Jones in his insistence that the concept of the death instinct served an important role in Freud's personal mental economy (1972, Chapter 12). Erich Fromm, a leading psychoanalytic thinker, argued that the concept of the death instinct was not consistent with Freud's definition of an instinct, which emphasized the achievement of bodily satisfaction through tension reduction. The death instinct strives not for tension reduction within the organism, but for the *actual dissolution* of the organism's life integrity (Fromm, 1973, p. 366).

isolated from the conscious self, or **ego**. Freud adopted the Latinized term id (originally, the simple German pronoun *das es*, meaning "it"—referring to the impersonal nature of this part of the psyche) from Georg Groddeck (1922), a physician who had become interested in psychoanalysis. Freud's translators converted the terminology to Latin equivalents to preserve in English translation the technical flavor of the terms.

In a similar way, Freud's translators converted his other plain German pronouns to Latin equivalents, so that the simple German for "I" (*Ich*) became the Latin *ego*, and the German for "over-I" became **superego**.

THE ID

Developmentally, the id is the oldest portion of personality. The existence of the id dates from birth. "Originally, to be sure, everything was id..." (Freud, 1940, p. 163). Because the id is the most archaic portion of personality, already operative before the infant has had much in the way of transactions with the world, it must contain all of the unlearned, innate strivings that we have come to know "psychoanalytically" as the instincts. Thus Freud characterized the id as a "cauldron full of seething excitations," fueled by the energies of the organic processes of the instincts and striving toward one goal: immediate satisfaction of its wishes.

The id is to be regarded as the pool of mental representatives of the biological processes underlying bodily needs, a pool populated, therefore, by Eros and the death instinct: "... but it has no organization, produces no collective will, but only a striving to bring about the satisfaction of the instinctual needs subject to the observance of the pleasure principle" (Freud, 1933, p. 73).

Like its precursor, the unconscious, the id is an untrammeled, primeval chaos free of the laws governing logical thought. Contrary impulses exist side by side without canceling each other; the passage of time exerts no influence on the id; and wishful impulses, after the passage of decades, behave as if they had just occurred (Freud, 1933, p. 74). Freud summarized the characteristics of the id in much the same way as he had previously spoken of the unconscious:

> The id of course knows no judgments of value: no good and evil, no morality. The economic or, if you prefer, the quantitative factor, which is intimately linked to the pleasure principle, dominates all its processes. Instinctual cathexes seeking discharge—that, in our view, is all there is in the id. It even seems that the energy of these instinctual impulses is in a state different from that in the other regions of the mind, far more mobile and capable of discharge. ... (1933, p. 74)

Because it is ruled by primary process thinking, condensations and displacements of its energy are not only possible for the id, they are an inevitable result of the id's striving for satisfaction without due regard for the goodness, evilness, realness, or appropriateness of its objects. In many ways, the id operates on the principle that whatever brings satisfaction to a want, desire, or wishful impulse is good; whatever hinders or frustrates such satisfaction is bad. "The id obeys the inexorable pleasure principle" (Freud, 1940, p. 198).

THE EGO

Left to itself, the id's unbridled striving would bring about the destruction of the organism. The id's lack of organization, its diffuseness and disregard for reality must be tamed in the service of survival. It is to the ego that the task of self-preservation falls.

The ego develops out of the id. In fact, the ego is a differentiated part of the id that has become specialized and organized in response to its constant exposure to external stimulation. Thus the ego is conceived as having an intimate relationship with the outermost layer of the organism, the perceptual and conscious systems that are localized in the cortical layer of the brain.

Clearly, Freud pictured the ego as developing from the id in response to the organism's need for a mediator between its internal needs and the demands of reality. The ego is thus the reality-oriented arm of the mental apparatus, though it is simultaneously responsive to internal conditions as well.

With reference to the external environment, the ego's functions are familiar ones: to become aware of stimuli and their location; to avoid excessively strong stimulation; and to learn to bring about changes in the external world that would be to its own advantage in pursuing survival. For this last activity, the ego must govern the muscular apparatus of the organism (Freud, 1933, p. 75).

Correspondingly, with reference to the internal environment, including the id, the ego functions to gain control over the expression of the instincts. The ego must decide whether the instincts are to be immediately satisfied as the id demands, or if their satisfaction is to be postponed to later times more favorable to wish fulfillment, or, finally, whether the instinctual demand should be totally denied expression, that is, whether the instinct should be repressed.

With the development of the ego as a specialized and efficiently organized portion of the id, the organism correspondingly increases in the degree of sophistication with which it approaches the tasks of life. For one thing, the pleasure principle is "dethroned" by the **reality principle** as the ego seeks to provide safe and realistically appropriate pleasures for the id. "To adopt a popular mode of speaking, we might say that the ego stands for reason and good sense while the id stands for the untamed passions" (Freud, 1933, p. 76).

Metaphorically, the ego is fighting a battle on two fronts: It must not only protect the organism from excessively strong demands from within, it must also seek to satisfy these demands in an external world fraught with danger. Such external dangers can be dealt with by flight, that is, by the removal of the organism from the dangerous situations. Internal threats to the integrity of the organism, that is, impulses whose satisfaction would bring the organism into contact with external dangers, are dealt with by the ego in an analogous way, namely, by mental flight or repression.

Thus there is a portion of the id-ego amalgam that becomes separated from the conscious functioning of the ego. That separated part, the repressed, then behaves in every way as if it were part of the unconscious. This zone of alien content is nevertheless part of the ego, though functionally, dynamically separated from it.

It is important in this context of defense by repression to note that it is the id that is the great reservoir of libido or sexual energy. In his previous writings, Freud had characterized the ego, in his then broad usage of the term, as the reservoir of libido. But actually there is no contradiction, for the ego is a specialized aspect of the id, and while it is only the very tip of a deep iceberg, the ego is nonetheless an integral part of that mass (Freud, 1923, pp. 30, 38).

In the original state of being at birth, the total energy of Eros, libido, is available to the undifferentiated id-ego amalgam. Eros's presence serves to neutralize the death instinct (Freud, 1940, p. 149). The ego is, therefore, primarily narcissistic at this stage, and it cathects itself with libido. Only when the ego becomes differentiated from the id will it direct its cathexes of libido to external objects. Once a quality of its libido is externalized as object libido, the ego's remaining store of libido comes into opposition with the death instinct. Ego libido, as contrasted with the externalized object libido, thus works in the service of the organism's own preservation, and ego libido operates to keep the organism from premature harm that might cheat the death instinct of its opportunity to bring the organism to its immanent destiny. Thus it is the particular developmental stage that determines whether it is the undifferentiated id-ego unity or the id alone that occupies the focus of attention as the reservoir of libido.

While the ego is fighting a two-front battle with the internal and external worlds, there is yet a third front that the ego is compelled to consider during its intercourse with life and death. This third front is the superego.

THE SUPEREGO

When the id is forced by circumstances beyond its control to give up its love objects, as for example, in the boy's renunciation of the mother at the resolution of the Oedipus complex, it is compensated for the loss by the ego (Freud, 1916, p. 249; 1923, p. 23ff.). The ego undergoes an alteration by which it takes on the characteristics of the lost love object. An analogous process can be seen more clearly in adulthood when one marriage partner is widowed. The surviving spouse may then unconsciously adopt the habits or the speech patterns of the deceased, or an item of the deceased's apparel, as if to compensate for the loss by reinstating at least a part of that person's identity in the survivor's own behavior.

> When the ego assumes the features of the [lost] object, it is forcing itself, so to speak, upon the id as a love-object and is trying to make good the id's loss by saying: "Look, you can love me too—I am so like the object." (Freud, 1923, p. 30)

This process of modeling itself on the lost love object, as the ego attempts to pacify the id, is called **identification**. Identification is an important part of the processes by which the superego is formed. Freud emphasized the importance of the process of renunciation of a love object for the process of identification with a parent and subsequent development of the superego. Freud de-emphasized the importance of simple imitation learning and role-modeling in the identification process (see Chapter 16).

Freud was clearer in his elucidation of the development of the superego in boys than in girls. As indicated in Chapter 2, Freud thought that a less painful process of renunciation occurred in girls than in boys, one that led to a weaker superego or conscience. This process was less painful and marked in girls than in boys for two reasons. First, girls, unlike boys, did not have to renounce their close relationship with the mother. The Electra complex involved desire for the father and competition with the mother, but repressing these desires did not mean giving up an already close relationship with the mother. In addition, the little girl did not have the fear of castration by the parent of the opposite sex.

In Freud's model, during the phallic stage of libidinal development, the young boy seeks his mother as a desirable love object and begins to perceive his father as a competitor. Without recapitulating the entire progress of the Oedipal situation (Chapter 2), you may recall that the boy relinquishes his mother as love object, identifies with his father in order to be like him because father possesses desirable objects, and the child represses his libidinal cathexes toward mother.

Freud's formulation of identification is self-contradictory, as Roger Brown (1965, p. 379) pointed out. According to Freud's account, since the boy must relinquish his mother as a love object, he should identify with her, not with his father. Likewise, the girl, having relinquished her father, should identify with him. Obviously this sequence will not do since boys usually assume a masculine sexual identity and girls similarly identify with their mothers. Freud noted the discrepancy between his proposed mechanism of identification and the actual outcome (1923, p. 32). As a result, he returned to one of his long-standing ideas, the inherent bisexuality of human nature. In this view, because most boys are more male than female, they thus identify only partially with mother but largely with father. The converse is true for girls. Such bisexual identification is not necessarily hidden or unconscious. Many people are aware of traits they have that are like their father and other traits that are like those of their mother. Commenting on Freud's theory of inherent bisexuality, Brown stated, "if that assumption is acceptable to Freud he does not need all the rest of his theoretical apparatus . . ." (1965, p. 379).

Undaunted by his own discovery of the inconsistency of his theory and relying on the concept of bisexuality, Freud proposed that the Oedipus complex is comprised of both positive and negative aspects. It is positive in the sense that the boy actively strives to be like his father and to identify with him. But the Oedipus complex may also have negative properties because of a boy's inherent feminine components. The boy may behave passively or "girlishly" toward the father because he has partially identified with mother when he was forced to renounce her as love object. In this way, the boy may also attempt to appease his father by an overtly submissive attitude. For girls, of course, the opposite set of behaviors dominates, for the girl has partially identified with father and so behaves in subtle masculine ways (Freud, 1923, p. 33). The final outcome, however, is as expected: Boys identify with their fathers, and girls model themselves on their mothers.

Sometime around the age of five, a child goes through a process of **internalization** in becoming like the father or mother. Children thus internalize the standards of adult authority, but more important they also internalize (identify with) the parental standards of rightness, morality, and goodness. A new internal agency continues from within to exercise these judgmental functions autonomously, without parental input. In terms of psychoanalytic theory, a superego has been formed. Through the process of identification with the parent of the same sex, the development of the superego represents the resolution of the Oedipal complex in the boy and the Electra complex in the girl.

Freud elaborated the dynamics of resolving the Oedipal complex in some detail. The boy's ego not only must strive to be like the all-powerful father who possesses the all-desirable mother, it must also establish the boundaries that limit the degree to which he acts the role of the father (Freud, 1923, p. 34). Out of fear of his competitor, the boy must not carry the identification as far as actual possession of the mother. Hence, the boy internalizes the prohibitions that he imagines his father might enforce. As a direct result, the superego is formed. The development of the superego in a boy is a combination of the active striving to be like the father and the anxiety-motivated attempts to anticipate the father's proscriptions.

The next step in the sequence is the repression of his Oedipal strivings. Repression of desire for mother and hostility toward father is not an easy undertaking for the boy's ego and must occur outside of any conscious awareness. The force that such repression requires is a measure of the strength of the internalized superego. For it is the superego that embodies the anxiety and resultant identification with authority that remain after the Oedipal strivings are repressed. To say it another way, the superego replaces the strength of the Oedipal wishes in the mental economy with the equal or stronger energy of the father identification. Or, as Freud repeatedly stated it, "The superego is the heir of the Oedipal complex." (Freud, 1923, p. 48).

Superego as Conscience

An important quantitative relationship may be inferred from the fact that the superego becomes the repository of the quantity of energy that was required to master and to repress the incestuous desires (Freud, 1923, pp. 34–35; 1930, p. 123). The greater the instinctual gratification that is renounced in both the girl and the boy, the more severe the superego grows in its judgments of the ego (Freud, 1923, p. 54; 1930, p. 129).

In effect, the intensity of the impulse or desire that is mastered is assimilated by the superego, increasing its supply of energy for future moral judgments. In less technical language, the greater the temptation to which persons fail to yield, the greater will be the pangs of their consciences in future temptations. In short, the superego is fed by the energy of the renounced id impulse, and it grows more scrupulous with each moral triumph.

The paradox is clear: The more aggression you virtuously renounce, the more your conscience reproaches you. Common sense, contrary to psychoanalytic theory, suggests that the stronger a person's conscience, the more virtuous he or she will be. Freud reversed the temporal sequence in this apparent truism, and he suggested that

...the more virtuous a man is, the more severe and distrustful is...[the behavior of his conscience], so that ultimately it is precisely those people who have carried saintliness furthest who reproach themselves with the worst sinfulness. (1930, pp. 125–126)

Clearly, Freud meant to emphasize that once the superego was established within the personality to be fed by the energy of renounced id impulses, it could be as harsh and unyielding in its demands as the id in its relationship to the ego. "From the point of view of instinctual control, or morality, it may be said of the id that it is totally non-moral, of the ego that it strives to be moral, and of the superego that it can be super-moral and then become as cruel as only the id can be" (Freud, 1923, p. 540).

ID, EGO, SUPEREGO INTERACTIONS

Because the superego was formed at a stage in developmental history when children usually idealized their parents and saw in them every kind of perfection, it follows that the standards of the superego will likewise have the character of the parents' idealized image (Freud, 1933, p. 64). Conscience is thus a standard of perfection, an ideal, rather than a realistic appraisal of behavior. Consequently, in their rearing of children, parents exemplify not so much a standard of experience tempered by a realistic appraisal of life, but rather the idealistic standard of their own superegos (Freud, 1933, p. 67).

Freud employed a diagrammatic summary of his new structural model that, reproduced here as Figure 3.2, is helpful in recapitulating the essential points.

Figure 3.2 shows the location of the three mental structures: id, ego, and superego. It also indicates the important relationships that bind them.

The ego is situated near, and oriented toward, the perceptual-conscious end of the organism, and it is thus in direct contact with the external world. But the diagram also clearly indicates a segment of the ego that functions *dynamically* like the unconscious system.

In Figure 3.2, this ego-alien segment is illustrated in its separation from conscious ego activity by two diagonal lines that define the boundary of repressed content. The ego is thus both conscious in its orientation toward the perceptual end of the apparatus and dynamically unconscious by virtue of its repressions.

Although Freud did not include the superego in the diagram that he used in *The Ego and the Id* (1923, p. 24), by the time he had written his *New Introductory Lectures*, almost ten years later, he found a way to include the superego in such diagrammatic summaries. Lying along the left-hand margin of the drawing in Figure 3.2, the superego clearly merges into the unconscious id, for, as "the heir of the Oedipus complex it has intimate relations with the id; it is more remote than the ego from the perceptual system" (Freud, 1933, p. 79).

The superego, therefore, is structured of both conscious and unconscious components, and, as a moral or ethical agency, functions both consciously and unconsciously. That is to say, the superego has relations with both the unconscious id and the unconscious portion of the ego, and some of the superego's moral demands are accessible to the conscious ego.

Figure 3.2 The dynamic model of the mind. Note that the diagram depicts the three agencies of the mind with no sharp boundaries between them. In Freud's last model, the mind was represented as an amalgam of blending, combining, and competing forces. See text for explanation. Based on Freud, 1933, p. 78.

In thinking of this division of the personality into an ego, superego, and an id, you will not, of course, have pictured sharp frontiers like the artificial ones drawn in political geography. We cannot do justice to the characteristics of the mind by linear outlines like those in a drawing or in a primitive painting, but rather by areas of color melting into one another as they are presented by modern artists. After making the separation we must allow what we have separated to merge together once more. (Freud, 1933, p. 79)

The ego's task is to balance the instincts of the id against the censure of the superego while it simultaneously appraises reality and its exigencies. In Freud's words, for the ego *"Life is not easy!"* When the ego is compelled to recognize its own weaknesses in carrying out successfully its often overwhelming tasks, anxiety results. There are three forms of such **anxiety**:

1. *Realistic anxiety*—the result of fear of the *external world*.
2. *Neurotic anxiety*—fear of being overwhelmed by the *id's instincts*.
3. *Moral anxiety*—fear of the *superego's censure*.

FREUD'S CHANGING CONCEPTIONS OF ANXIETY

In the earliest days of Freud's theorizing, he came to view anxiety as the result of unexpressed or dammed-up libido. The neurotic's badly distorted relations with the world and its people, he found, are often expressed in sexual difficulty. Normal, satisfying sexual relations are frequently foregone as a welter of neurotic symptoms and other defensive measures sap the individual's capacity for joyous living. Unexpressed libido, the dammed-up energy of the sexual impulses that have thus succumbed to repression, is then explosively released in a transformed state, the state of anxiety. In short, in Freud's early thinking, repression of sexual impulses is the cause of anxiety (cf. Freud, 1894; 1896a; 1896b; 1896c; and 1898).

According to this early view, anxiety was instinctual, arising from repressed unconscious sexual urges. But if it were true that such feelings were restricted to unconscious origin, the conscious ego as depicted in the new structural model with its separation from the repressed would never experience the unpleasant affect of anxiety. Furthermore, if the ego did not experience the anxiety, it would never trigger repressive counter-forces to cast the unacceptable, anxiety-producing impulses from consciousness in the first place (Freud, 1926, pp. 140, 161). Freud's new structural model demanded that the ego be the seat of anxiety, and so Freud was required to rethink the problem.

Birth Trauma as the Prototype of Adult Anxiety

Through a slow return to and development of his neurological ideas, Freud renounced the view of anxiety as transformed libido. In his early neurological model of the "Project for a Scientific Psychology," Freud had experimented with the idea that anxiety originates from a sense of overwhelming helplessness (1895). The ego experiences the perception of being overpowered or flooded with too much stimulation. In infancy, the first of such experiences is the act of birth. *The newborn infant has been thrust from its warm, dark, safe existence in the mother's body into the confusing, demanding, changing, and irritating external environment* (Freud, 1926). In successive stages of life, other situations will evoke the same emotional response of helplessness, stimulus flooding, and the experience of being overpowered. Separation from the mother (recall

Ernst's "gone" game) provokes distress in most infants. Such separation is an example of a later life situation that harbors the threat of helplessness.

The common denominator in all such cases of anxiety is the sense of abandonment and the concern that life's demands will overwhelm the isolated, helpless ego. When anxiety mounts to a frightening level, neurotic symptoms may be formed as attempts to stifle the tide of mental confusion and emotional pain. Adult neurotics develop symptoms to control their anxiety over threats that they perceive as truly life threatening, just as life threatening as early abandonment by the mother. Overt symptoms thus unconsciously replace what they can no longer consciously bear (Freud, 1933, p. 85). The question of significance thus changed for Freud from how libido could be transformed into anxiety to how anxiety was produced from the ego's perceptions.

As early as 1909, in a footnote to *The Interpretation of Dreams*, Freud pointed out that "...the act of birth is the first experience of anxiety, and thus the source and prototype of the affect of anxiety" (1900, pp. 400–401). In effect, Freud was postulating that the birth situation and the ensuing **birth trauma** is every individual's first experience with the unpleasurable state of anxiety, and that it is the first experience that serves as the model against which the ego compares future situations in making its responses to reality and to the demands of the id and superego.

A colleague of Freud's, Otto Rank, broadened the concept of birth trauma beyond its status as the prototype for anxiety. Rank established the birth trauma as the central event in all psychological development (Rank, 1929; 1932). In emphasizing its significance for neurotic symptomatology, Rank dethroned the main psychoanalytic concepts of the Oedipus complex and sexual strivings from their central role. For Rank, the birth trauma was the nucleus from which all human development, neurotic and normal, proceeds. Freud subsequently repudiated Rank's heretical ideas.

Figure 3.3 A 1937 photograph of Freud in his study with his prized dog, Lun Yug.
Nineteen thirty-seven was a difficult time for Freud. Suffering from cancer of the jaw, he would shortly be forced by Nazi persecution to leave Vienna. He would die in London in 1939.

Freud's Chronology of Danger and Possibly Traumatic Situations

As the child's ego develops, Freud reasoned, anxiety becomes less and less an experience of flooding helplessness and more and more a signal to avoid such danger and potential trauma. See Table 3.2. The prototype for the danger situation and trauma of ego disruption is birth. If an ego were present at birth, it would be helpless. Only through the care of the mother does the infant survive, feel comforted, and become eventually tension-free. But at base, the danger situation of birth is the fear of death.

Throughout infancy, the child learns that survival depends on this "love object," the mother, being present to minister to its needs. When she is absent—loss of the object—the burgeoning ego experiences potential danger, and senses that mounting needs will go unsatisfied to the point of annihilation.

Later, after the first year of life during the anal period of two to three years, the toddler recognizes that absence of mother does not mean abandonment. Instead, what now counts for survival is getting the mother's love. For it is only by her loving anticipations of its needs that the child receives gratifications that assure safety and survival. An angry or aloof mother does not care. The danger situation for the ego is now transformed into a fear of the loss of the mother's love.

At the phallic phase, the time of the Oedipus complex around ages three to five, the male child learns that father can retaliate for his secret wishes to possess mother exclusively. Furthermore, beginning sexual interest has become vaguely attached to the person of the mother, and this interest becomes a source of additional fear should father detect these taboo wishes.

The fear that assails the child's ego now is a fear of castration, for what more appropriate punishment could father exact than removal of the offending organ? In more general terms, the child experiences this new danger situation not only as an

Table 3.2   Freud's Chronology of Danger and Possibly Traumatic Situations

Development period	Danger situation	Ego experience of anxiety
Birth	Global feelings of flooding, distress, helplessness	No awareness of outside world, but survival is threatened.
First year (Oral phase)	Fear of loss of the love object (mother)	Feelings of helplessness occur when mother is out of sight, understanding that she is needed for survival.
Two to three years (Anal phase)	Fear of loss of the object's love	Learns that survival and need satisfaction depend on mother's loving and caring.
Four to six years (Phallic phase)	Castration fear and anxiety over injury	Oedipal dynamics result in castration fear because of desire to possess love object exclusively, attack anticipated.
Post-Oedipal through adulthood	Fear of superego censure: fear of negative self-judgments	After internalization of parental standards, superego judges ego's efforts to satisfy id, and may condemn some wishes or ideas. Fear of self-evaluation.

Based on Freud, 1926 and 1933. *Evaluating Theoretical Psychoanalysis*

Oedipal fear but also as a broader fear of injury and physical insult to the body. What the analogous process for girls may be, Freud did not say. But the implication from his writing is that girls experience similar danger signals because they interpret their discovery that they do not have a penis as meaning that they have already been injured.

Finally, in the post-Oedipal period persisting until adulthood, the ego responds to ever more sophisticated danger signals. Having internalized the moral standards of the parents in the form of the superego, the ego responds with anxiety to judgments of the superego that a particular id impulse is dangerous. Thus the final danger situation is fear of one's own self-evaluations.

Three common features are shared by all the danger situations.

1. The experience of helplessness is the central core of anxiety: feeling helpless to manage internal needs, helpless to cope with external threats and signals of disintegration, and feeling helpless to maintain survival.

2. Second, each danger situation is a derivative or a representation of the experience of loss. In order, these losses are loss of complete dependence (birth), loss of the love object, loss of the object's love, loss of a body part, and loss of self-esteem or self-love.

3. Danger situations are potentially traumatic.

We should mention that this final experience of loss contained in the fear of one's own self-judgments is strikingly similar to Freud's earliest theory of repression discussed in Chapter 2: Namely, wishes that clash with one's self-image are very threatening.

EVALUATING THEORETICAL PSYCHOANALYSIS

In Chapter 2, clinical psychoanalysis was evaluated in terms of its scientific testability, conception of human agency as passive, except for the very existence of psychoanalysis itself, and its acknowledgement of both nomothetic and idiographic aspects of the human personality. These conclusions are relevant for the psychoanalytic model of the mind.

In this section, we focus on the question of whether testable propositions can be drawn from the more *theoretical* psychoanalytic psychology.

While considering some of the limitations of psychoanalytic theory and practice, we should also indicate some of the lasting contributions of Freud's work:

1. He established that many disorders that had previously been considered organically caused actually had psychological causation, that is, they had to do with an individual's personal *experiences*.

2. He demonstrated that verbal psychotherapy or a *talking cure* might be a means of treatment, rather than physical measures.

3. His work indicated that, in addition to conscious thought, unconscious mental processes could also occur.

4. His work indicated the importance of drives, especially the sexual drive, in the human makeup.

5. He emphasized insight and patients' own activity in finding answers to their problems.

6. His many useful concepts including transference, countertransference, defense mechanisms, and many others have relevance far beyond the confines of psychoanalysis per se. Even down to the institution of the 50-minute psychotherapeutic hour, with its roots in Freud's work, the helping professions have been affected by Freud's foundational innovations.

What Did Freud Leave Undone?

Freud thought that his own greatest accomplishment had been the exploration of the drives of the unconscious id. Freud's focus had been on conflict, with the powerful id drives seen as the foundation of all human endeavors. The ego was, for the most part, conceptualized as the rider of the spirited horse, directing the horse where the horse wants to go. If we ask the inevitable question, "What did Freud leave undone?" we can provide at least three answers:

He neglected the individual's direct relationships to interpersonal reality, especially to the reality of the mother in her role as the nurturing, shaping, esteem-building, trust-building influence in development.

Freud failed to complete his picture of the ego as the executive of the personality, capable of more than safe and reliable id satisfactions. Although Freud implied that the ego could function relatively autonomously, his theory sorely lacked a coherent account of how persons adapt to the reality that they themselves helped to create. Without the id pulling the strings in the background, there is no way in classical Freudian theory to explain logically and convincingly the various ways that persons master obstacles beyond instinctual conflict or derive satisfactions from enterprises other than conflict resolution.

Freudian structural, dynamic theory runs the risk of losing sight of the whole person, the overall synthesizing, integrating, coordinating function. In Freud's theory, the ego was to be the seat of an overall integrating and coordinating function, but he failed to develop this idea beyond simple and scattered statements of its existence.

What did Freud leave undone? He left the picture of the ego's own functions incomplete—particularly how it was able to deal with external reality. And Freud omitted from consideration the fact that most riders can and do control and direct their mounts.

We shall see in subsequent chapters that Anna Freud, Erik Erikson and many other psychoanalytically-oriented personality theorists who followed Freud stressed the autonomy and self-sufficiency of the ego. They built on Freud's achievements with increasing sophistication and heightened concern for whole persons, who could be proactive as well as re-active. In contemporary ego psychology, humans are viewed as neither completely drive-bound nor fully free of their instinctive desires.

Refutability of Psychoanalysis

As Freud built increasingly complex abstractions to represent his clinical observations, psychoanalysis grew more distant from clinical experience. Freud thought of his theoretical abstractions from about 1914 onward as a "metapsychology" ("beyond psychology") in the sense that the theoretical concepts evolved out of, but surpassed, the psychological observations on which they were based.

Freud sometimes regarded his metapsychological creations as metaphors for unmapped brain processes and structures, not as "internal agents" in a literal sense. Rather, he seems to have hoped that his structural metaphors would someday be anchored to brain function and location when the sciences of neuroanatomy and neurophysiology had progressed. He was open to the medical and physiological knowledge of his day. In fact, the hypothalamus and structures of the limbic system have—subsequent to Freud's theorizing—been found to be associated with the desires Freud attributed to the id, such as hunger, sexual desire, and aggression. The frontal lobe is associated with a sense of reality, an ego function. Higher cortical functions also relate to activities that Freud attributed to the ego (Miller L., 1991).

Yet there are lengthy theoretical discussions in some of Freud's major books where he intellectually manipulates metapsychological concepts as if they were real, as if they were to be understood as reality. In his popular lectures and essays, for example, he treats his model of the mind quite dramatically so that ego, id, and superego are described in terms of war metaphors, battle strategies, and advances and retreats, having motives and expectations of their own as if they were individual people inside the person. (Freud, 1910a, 1916, 1933, 1940).

But in his more professional writings Freud expresses the idea that these "structures" are metaphors (e.g., 1923, 1926). The puzzle for scholars and scientists is to discover the nature of what underlies the metaphors (see the answers proposed by Parisi, 1987, 1988; Silverstein, 1985, 1988, 1989a, 1989b; Sulloway, 1979). The phenomenologically-oriented psychoanalyst Roy Schafer (1976, 1983) has indicated that many Freudians have taken his metaphors as literally true and as replacements for the *actual experiences* that they represent. The id, for example is seen as a stand-in for a whole array of sexual desires and experiences. The term *reification*, in this context, refers to turning human experience into an object or a thing.

So we are left with a continuing intellectual conversation continuing long after Freud's death. Freudian concepts such as id, ego, superego, and the various defense mechanisms are drawn from human experience and, in a sense, can be seen as representing nothing more than different aspects of such experience. At the same time findings in neuroanatomy and neurophysiology correspond to many Freudian concepts. So it looks as if they are not *merely metaphors*. They might also represent underlying physiological realities, at a different level from personal experience. Our evolving view is that many of Freud's terms are both metaphorical expressions originally derived from human experience and that they also have turned out to point to underlying brain structures, processes and experience.

The testability of Freud's theory is another area deserving mention. Large parts of his theory have to do with the presumed experiential life and perceptions of infants and children who are at a preverbal level and who have a very limited means of expressing their feelings and perceptions other than in a very global way. Numerous inferences about the specifics of their inner life are made from Freud's own adult recollections, and his work with clients. Whether Freud's ideas about the workings of the infant's mind (for example, the apprehensions and emotional life of the infant), are more than the result of the imagination of adults is difficult to determine.

There is one more major limitation regarding the refutability of Freud's ideas. His observations were all made within the particular social and cultural framework of his times. His clients were largely upper class Europeans. His findings about personality may not reflect universal content or processes but simply aspects of human nature manifest in a particular culture, place, and historical epoch. Certainly, ideas regarding sexuality and the roles of men and women have changed since his day. Some of Freud's ideas could very well turn out not to be valid or at least not relevant in twenty-first century North America. Such results would not necessarily indicate that his concepts would not have been valid in the Europe of the early 1900s.

Seymour Fisher and Roger Greenberg (1996) arrived at what seems to be a balanced assessment of the scientific status of Freud's ideas. They indicated that some of Freud's ideas have been empirically validated whereas others have not stood the test of further appraisal. Still other aspects of his theory have not yet been empirically tested. Here are a few of Fisher and Greenberg's conclusions:

- On depression: Freud's notion that the experience of loss is the trigger for depression receives little support from the scientific literature. There is some evidence that accumulated early and late losses over a lifetime are linked to depression, but the evidence is weak. Freud's related idea that non-nurturing or disapproving parents make a child vulnerable to depression receives moderate support. The strongest support was for Freud's notion that depression is linked to a passive orientation marked by feelings of oral dependency and fixation to the oral stage of psychosexual development.

- On the Oral Personality: Freud's concept of the existence of an orally dependent personality type prone to the use of repression and denial was supported by factor analytic research that demonstrated meaningful clustering of the personality traits described in Freud's theory.

- On the Anal Personality Types: Freud's "anal-retentive" and "anal-erotic" personality types likewise received substantial support from factor-analytic studies that demonstrate a clustering of the relevant traits.

- On the Oedipus Complex and Penis Envy: The Oedipus theory advanced by Freud, including his hypotheses about the origins of homosexuality and the severity of individual moral self-judgment, had *no support* in the scientific literature. However, derivations of Oedipal theory based on the concept of "penis envy" received some support in Fisher and Greenberg's view.

- On the Significance of Dreams: Freudian dream theory, especially his notion that dreams were disguised fulfillment of taboo wishes, was largely contradicted by current dream research.

Greenberg and Fisher (1996, p. 267) point out that they did not review what seem to be supportive studies of Freud's concepts of repression and the unconscious. On the whole, they conclude that many aspects of Freud's theory have received scientific support, but much of the theory still either could be tested but have not yet been evaluated, defies scientific testing, or has failed the tests made. We expect that additional aspects of Freud's theory will continue to be tested and either validated or contradicted by empirical findings. Gosling (1999) has provided documentation that a good deal of empirical research in the area of psychoanalysis has been conducted, only to be largely ignored by the current cognitive psychological mainstream. Partly in response to accountability concerns from those agencies funding psychotherapy, contemporary psychoanalysts have stepped up their development of collaborative empirical studies to gauge the effectiveness of psychoanalysis.

SUMMARY

Anna Freud's "stwawbewwies" dream reveals the essential nature of dream processes: the fantasized fulfillment of wishes. As Freud investigated dream processes of adults, however, he soon learned that their productions differed from the lucid creations of children. Distortion and disguise are introduced into the story of the dream by the mechanisms of dream work, including displacement, condensation, visual representation, and secondary revision. Thus, Freud found dreams have both a latent and a manifest content.

Freud next embarked on a revision and a tightening of his psychological theory in a series of important "metapsychological" papers. Freud now saw repression as a two-stage process: primal repression against early unacceptable impulses and repression proper against later adult derivatives.

Because of the basic conflict underlying the neurotic behavior of the patients he observed, Freud contrasted the self-preservative instincts (e.g., hunger) with the instincts of pleasure (sex, libido). The dualistic classification of hunger versus love eventually had to be revised when Freud's speculations revealed the presence of an even more fundamental dichotomy in instinctual life: life versus death.

In *Beyond the Pleasure Principle* (1920a), Freud created a new picture of the workings of the mind. This altered view included Freud's argument that the nervous system had evolved in such a way as to minimize the excitatory level of the organism by directing the organism's efforts to satisfy needs immediately. The ultimate aim of an instinct is to return the organism to the unresponsive state of inorganic matter, namely, to the state of death. Since the death instinct cannot be directly observed, its derivatives of hate, anger, and aggression are the only overt evidence of its existence. When the life instincts, or *Eros* as Freud now called the combined ego and sexual instincts, oppose the death instinct, the energy of destruction is turned outward from the individual and displaced onto other individuals.

Freud proceeded to a total revision of his conception of the mind. He created a structural model that depicted the mind as a blending, merging amal-gam of forces. The structural model had three divisions: id, ego, and superego.

1. The id, formerly the unconscious, is the seat of the instincts, and is a cauldron of fury, striving to gain immediate satisfaction of its urges.

2. To accommodate the id's desires and needs, a specialized portion, the ego, emerges from the id to steer a safe course through reality and to maintain satisfactory relations with the world.

3. By the age of five or six, another agency, the superego, is internalized within the child. The superego is the "heir of the Oedipal complex," for it is based on the child's identification with the parents, and assimilates the energy of the renounced Oedipal desires. The superego is the moral or ethical arm of personality, and it has final say in matters of ego-id relations.

Freud's conception of anxiety changed over the years from the early view that anxiety is the result of dammed-up sexual impulses to the concept that the ego responds to a variety of danger and potentially traumatic situations with signals of unpleasure. Freud experimented with the idea that the prototype of anxiety is the trauma of birth and, more generally, that anxiety is an ego reaction to perceptions of being overwhelmed or flooded by intense stimulation.

As we saw in Chapter 2, research has validated some Freudian concepts and disproven others. Many more Freudian hypotheses have not been adequately tested—partly because Freud did not promulgate them in easily testable form.

FOR FURTHER READING

The best overviews in Freud's own writings of his later theory are to be found in two complementary sets of lectures. The first of these dates from his prestructural model of the mind and is entitled *Introductory Lectures on Psychoanalysis*, Vol. XV and XVI of *The Standard Edition* or in paperback under the title *A General Introduction to Psychoanalysis* (New York: Washington Square Press, 1960). The second set of lectures dates from his development of the id-ego-superego model and can be found in Vol. XXII of *The Standard Edition* under the title *New Introductory Lectures on Psychoanalysis*. This is also available in paperback (New York: W.W. Norton, 1968).

A straightforward introduction to psychoanalysis is Anna Freud's, *The Harvard Lectures* (New York: International Universities Press, 1992).

A scholarly, balanced contemporary exposition of the development of Freud's later ideas is Barry Silverstein's *What Was Freud Thinking? A Short Historical Introduction to Freud's Theories and Therapies* (Dubuque, IA: Kendall/Hunt, 2003).

Additional suggestions For Further Reading are listed and described on the *Beneath the Mask* web site: www.wiley.com/college/sollod

GLOSSARY

Adaptive viewpoint: Point of view that some psychological processes have the purpose of healthy adaptation.

Aim: Instinctual impulses strive toward satisfaction or tension reduction. An *ultimate aim* is the immediate gratification of an instinctual demand, and an *intermediate aim* is the substitute form of satisfaction when an instinct is blocked from obtaining a suitable goal.

Anticathexis: The barrier that is set up by the preconscious to deal with unacceptable unconscious content through repression. Also, the removal of charges of mental energy (cathexes), or the diversion of attention from the *memory image* of a noxious stimulus; a form of mental withdrawal from threatening stimuli.

Anxiety: Feelings arising from the ego's sense of being overwhelmed and helpless. Freud defined three types: *Realistic anxiety* is triggered by real and objective sources of danger in the *external world*. *Neurotic anxiety* is caused when *id's instinctual impulses* threaten the ego. *Moral anxiety* is felt when the individual disregards moral and ethical concerns and fears the *superego's censure*.

Birth trauma: The anxiety the infant experiences when leaving the safety of the womb and being flooded with too much stimulation upon birth. The birth trauma is an individual's first experience, which serves as the model against which the ego compares future situations.

Cathexis: (from a Greek root, meaning "to hold on to") A term used to describe the attachment of mental energy to a variety of thoughts, feelings, or objects. One example is the attachment of libido to external objects. The plural is **cathexes**.

Condensation: In dream interpretation, the idea that manifest content is a model of compression, or condensation. Many latent meanings of a dream are hidden in one manifest image.

Displacement: A technique the censorship agency of the mind uses to replace a latent dream element in consciousness by a more remote idea, or to accomplish a shifting of the dream's recalled emphasis away from an important idea and toward an unimportant one.

Dream work: Dream formation; the various mechanisms or mental processes used to transform latent strivings, wishes, or impulses into more acceptable forms by distorting or disguising their true meaning in manifest content.

Ego: Arising from the id, it is that part of the personality that is in contact with reality. It acts as a mediator between the urges of the id and the demands of the superego. It uses reason and problem-solving strategies to solve the often-incompatible demands of the id and superego.

Ego libido: That portion of the original pool of libido remaining in the ego.

Eros: (a term derived from *Eros*, the Greek god of love and passion) The combined sexual and ego instinct. Preservation of the self and of the species are involved in this instinct.

Homeostasis: A state of balance or equilibrium. Applied to the nervous system, it indicates an optimal state of minimal arousal and physiological equilibrium.

Id: The unconscious and the oldest component of the personality. It contains mental representations of the instincts and leads to urges to satisfy instinctual needs. It operates according to the pleasure principle.

Identification: The process of modeling itself on the lost love object, as the ego attempts to pacify the id. Identification is an important part of the processes by which the superego is formed as part of resolution of the Oedipal complex. More generally, identification refers to taking on the characteristics of another in order to soothe anxieties and alleviate internal conflicts.

Infantile amnesia: A type of amnesia or blanket forgetting that prevents recollection of any Oedipal sexual and aggressive strivings of childhood as well as other memories. These memories are not really lost but remain in the unconscious.

Internalization: The process by which children identify with the standards of rightness, morality, and goodness originally enforced by their parents. A new internal agency, the superego, functions autonomously and continues from within to exercise moral judgments.

Latent content: Repressed or disguised thoughts or wishes expressed in a dream; the hidden meaning behind the storyline of a dream.

Libido: In Freudian theory, the energy of the sexual or pleasure instincts. Later theorists such as Carl Jung and Alfred Adler would develop alternative definitions of *libido*.

Manifest content: The surface meaning of a dream, that is, images, storylines, and symbols as observed and remembered by the dreamer as they appear to be.

Metapsychology: Literally, "beyond psychology"; metapsychology is the term used by Freud whenever a psychological process is understood from its descriptive, systematic, and dynamic aspects. One must look at the complex interplay of multiple determinants.

Narcissism: The process in which some libidinal energy is directed toward a person's own ego.

Neurological model: Freud's model of psychological processes as determined by the electrochemical activities of systems of neurons within the brain. Freud ultimately abandoned this theory, and many Freudians consider it only a metaphor for human experience.

Nirvana principle: The homeostatic trend of the nervous system to divest itself of disturbing tensions and excess stimulation. The associated mental processes also strive to reduce excitation and tension, and maintain stability. It is an urge to gain or retain complete quietude.

Object: A concrete, usually external, object that has the power to reduce or to satisfy an instinctual need. Appropriate objects may be changed many times to satisfy a specific instinct.

Object libido: That portion of the original pool of libido used to bond to a variety of external objects.

Overdetermined: In dream interpretation, the idea that several unconscious ideas band together to contribute to one common manifest element.

Pleasure principle: The seeking after pleasure by the discharge of unpleasurable mounting tension. The nervous system must find a way to reduce the biological deficit (or to satisfy the urge) that an instinctual demand represents.

Preconscious censorship system: The mental system that prevents those wishes that are morally unacceptable to an individual from entering waking, post-dream consciousness. It also attempts to patch together the scattered and apparently nonsensical elements of a latent dream into an understandable, coherent, and acceptable whole.

Pressure: The amount of force or strength of the demand made by the instinctual need on the mind.

Primal repression: The fixating or freezing of unacceptable ideas or impulses. Significant acts of primal repression occur during the first six or eight years of life.

Primary process thinking: The id satisfies bodily needs in two ways: Through reflexive action, it reduces tension and through wish fulfillment, it imagines the object to satisfy the need. The imagery or fantasy temporarily reduces the tension linked to the need. The unconscious knows no bound to its wishfulness and fantasized objects. Primary process thinking does not take reality into account.

Reality principle: The principle that directs the ego's activities. It causes the ego to interact realistically with the environment to satisfy the id's sensual appetites and also the superego's moral concerns.

Repression: The processes by which unconscious impulses and memories are kept out of awareness. Unlike *suppression, repression* occurs outside of conscious awareness. There are two types of repression: *primal repression* and *repression proper.*

Repression proper: The process whereby ideas, trains of thought, or perceptions that are associatively linked to the primarily repressed impulse are also denied access to consciousness. Repression proper thus cooperates with primal repression to ensure that unacceptable impulses and associated ideas remain buried.

Secondary process thinking: Deals with the ego's efforts to bring about genuine biological satisfaction. The ego takes the demands of reality into consideration and delays gratification of the need until an appropriate object is found. It tries to match the object to the person's need.

Secondary revision: The process by which a dream is reconstructed or reshaped into a coherent whole from fragmented and chaotic elements.

Source: The origin of all instincts is located in the physical-chemical processes of the body.

Structural model: The model of the mind that divides it into three agencies—the id, ego, and superego. It subsumes all of the mental functions previously assigned to the unconscious and the preconscious.

Superego: An internal agency, formed in the resolution of the Oedipal complex, which internalizes the values of society and the standards originally enforced by parents. The superego criticizes the ego for acting against its injunctions.

Thanatos: (a term derived from *Thanatos*, the Greek god of death) The death instinct. It is a desire to return to a state of inorganic existence in which there are no biological demands to be met. Two derivatives of this instinct are aggression and destruction—desire to destroy others or destroy the self.

Transference: A term Freud gave to patients' tendencies to react to their therapists with emotions reproduced from childhood. Patients *transferred* feelings that often originated with their parents to their therapists.

Topographic/systematic model: The model of the mind that divides it into the unconscious, the preconscious, and conscious systems.

Unconscious: A term Freud used to describe that part of the mind containing instincts, thoughts, and emotions that were not part of or acceptable to the conscious mind. Freud attached three different meanings to the term *unconscious*: the *descriptive unconscious*, the *dynamic unconscious*, and the *systematic unconscious*.

Visual representation: Within dreamwork, the conversion of the abstract thought of a dream into a concrete visual image.

Wish fulfillment: Freud's concept that dreams bring about the fulfillment of often, but not always, unacceptable wishes or desires.

Chapter 4

Alfred Adler

Individual Psychology

The most important question of the healthy and the diseased mental life is not whence? but, whither?

Alfred Adler

If life gives you lemons, make lemonade.

Anonymous

To see with the eyes of another, to hear with the ears of another, to feel with the heart of another

Alfred Adler

Alfred Adler   Born: 1870 Penzing, Austria
Died: 1937 Aberdeen, Scotland
(while on a speaking tour)

Adler's Individual Psychology

Alfred Adler began as an adherent of Freud's theory. After almost a decade, as a result of major disagreements, the two men ended their collaboration. Subsequently, Adler devoted himself to the development of his own theoretical and therapeutic approach, which he called individual psychology to distinguish it from other approaches. Some ideas central to Adler's theory are:

- Each person strives for superiority or personal competence.
- Each person develops a style of life that is partly deliberate and partly unconscious. A person's style of life indicates a consistent approach to many situations.

121

For example, one person might be typified as avoidant, another enthusiastically collaborative, a third combative or aggressive.

- The most important qualities of a healthy personality are an acquired capacity for "fellow feeling" (what Adler called *Gemeinschaftsgefuhl*), and accompanying concern to foster the well-being of others or what Adler termed, social interest.
- The ego is that part of the psyche that is creative. It creates new realities through the process of setting goals and bringing them into fruition. This is called *fictional finalism*.

ADLER'S BOYHOOD DIFFICULTIES: ILLNESS, REJECTION, AND THE FEAR OF DEATH

Adler's childhood was fraught with major difficulties and challenges. He was a chronically sick and weak child who suffered from rickets, a nutritional deficiency that results in softening of the bones. He was thus unable to compete well in many areas with his older brother or with peers (Bottome, 1957; Orgler, 1963). One of Adler's childhood recollections drawn from the age of two indicates his special sensitivity to feelings of inferiority:

> I remember sitting on a bench bandaged up on account of rickets, with my healthy elder brother sitting opposite me. He could run, jump, and move about quite effortlessly, while for me, movement of any sort was a strain and an effort. Everyone went to great pains to help me, and my mother and father did all that was in their power to do. (Quoted in Bottome, 1957, pp. 30–31)

Also, Adler was resentful toward his mother over the birth of his younger brother, for this child "dethroned" him and became his mother's favorite (Mosak & Kopp, 1973, p. 158).

As a child, Adler had a series of actual brushes with death. As a young boy, he had twice been run over by a car and recalled regaining consciousness on the living room sofa (Orgler, 1963, p. 2). Also, Adler's younger brother died in a bed beside his when he was only three. At the age of five, Adler became so profoundly ill with pneumonia that the family physician gave him up for lost. However, he beat the odds and eventually recovered.

As child of five through the age of 35, Adler had what we would today term a "false memory" (Adler, 1959, pp. 179–180). This false memory was of Adler as a child mastering the fear of death.

> I remember that the path to the school led over a cemetery. I was frightened every time and was exceedingly put out at beholding the other children pass the cemetery without paying the least attention to it, while every step I took was accompanied by a feeling of fear and horror. Apart from the extreme discomfort occasioned by this fear I was also annoyed at the idea of being less courageous than the others. One day I made up my mind to put an end to this fear of death. Again, I decided upon a treatment of hardening. I stayed at some distance behind the others, placed my schoolbag on the ground near the wall of the cemetery and ran across it a dozen times, until I felt that I had mastered the fear. (Adler, 1959)

Only at the age of 35, in conversation with a childhood school chum, did Adler finally learn that *there had never been* a cemetery on the way to their school. Adler's unconscious mind had woven the story of his boyhood mastery of the fear of the cemetery as well as the cemetery itself (Adler, 1959, p. 180; Orgler, 1963, p. 37).

Adler recounted that his fearful pre-*occupation* with the possibility of death led to his choice of physician as his adult *occupation*:

> From that time on I recall always thinking of myself in the future as a physician. This means that I had set a goal from which I could expect an end to my childlike distress, my fear of death. . . . I came to choose the occupation of physician in order to overcome death and the fear of death. (Adler, in Ansbacher & Ansbacher, 1956, p. 199)

In 1929, Adler indicated his preoccupation with the topic of death and his awareness of the importance of death for personality development. He showed how a person's confrontation with death could underlie the subsequent direction of his or her life. Some people may seek a type of immortality through their descendants. Others may seek to defy death through the attainment of personal greatness in art or science or seek immortality of the soul through religion or spirituality. Adler himself chose to become a physician to be able to struggle directly against death.

It turns out that, as an adult physician, Adler was still beleaguered by the powerful reality of death. Hertha Orgler (1963), Adler's biographer and friend, reports that Adler actually gave up his general medical practice after the death of several of his diabetic patients. Practicing before insulin was discovered, Adler found himself powerless to prevent these patients' deaths.

FREUD AND ADLER: DISSENT
OVER THE FUNDAMENTAL HUMAN MOTIVE

Adler disagreed energetically with Freud over the issue of the central motive in human personality. He was convinced that human motivation could not be subsumed under the category of pleasure or sexuality. He thought that a model of personality was needed that accorded more weight to other fundamental human strivings. As he developed his own point of view, Adler considered the striving to compensate for a sense of helplessness and perceived inferiorities as the primary motivating factor in shaping personality.

In 1902, Adler wrote a defense of Freud's *Interpretation of Dreams* that was published in one of Vienna's foremost newspapers. Freud subsequently invited Adler and several others to meet with him for a series of informal seminars (cf. Ansbacher & Ansbacher, 1973, p. 336n.; Furtmüller, 1973; Jones, 1955). Adler did join the select group of intellectuals surrounding Freud, but he never became as completely committed to the Freudian viewpoint as most of the others.

Some of Freud's correspondence with Carl Gustav Jung reveals the growing depth of intellectual disdain that Freud had toward Adler. Freud was convinced that Adler's psychology was too superficial, too concerned with conscious functioning, and too neglectful of the most fundamental tenet of psychoanalytic motivation theory, the importance of unconscious determinants of behavior. Shortly before Adler's resignation in 1911, Freud wrote to Jung, expressing his disappointment at the direction he believed Adler's theorizing was taking:

> I see now that Adler's seeming decisiveness concealed a good deal of confusion. I would never have expected a psychoanalyst to be so taken in by the ego. In reality the ego is like the clown in the circus, who is always putting in his oar to make the audience think that whatever happens is his doing (Freud, in Freud & Jung, 1974, p. 400).

Ironically, Freud and Jung would have their own bitter and upsetting falling-out within a few years.

Widening personal and theoretical differences between Freud and Adler were becoming obvious. The group of psychoanalysts, called the Vienna Psychoanalytic Society, a seminar group, decided to clear the air by having a formal debate on the differences between Freud and Adler. Adler was therefore invited to give a systematic presentation of his ideas beginning on January 4, 1911, and extending over the course of the next several sessions. On February 22, after the members of the group had discussed Adler's ideas and Freud himself commented on the differences between their two viewpoints, Adler resigned from the presidency of the Vienna Psychoanalytic Society. By May 24, he terminated all contact with the group and, at Freud's suggestion, withdrew as coeditor of the *Zentralblatt*, an important psychoanalytic journal.

For Adler, the society's meetings devoted to the differences between his views and those of Freud allowed him to formulate and crystallize the essential tenets of his own developing viewpoint. His break from Freud eventually enabled him to develop his own views and to train other therapists in his new approach. Before undertaking a study of Adler's theory, we briefly explore Adler's own presentation of his divergence from orthodox psychoanalysis.

ADLER'S DIFFERENCES WITH FREUD

There were a number of areas in which Adler emphasized his differences with Freud's approach to understanding personality. Six of the major areas of disagreement are: the ego as creative rather than reactive, the Oedipus complex as striving for superiority not love or sex, social interest vs. narcissism, motivation through goals or drives, personality as unified rather than fragmented, dreams as aides to action and not windows to the unconscious.

The Ego: Creative Not Reactive

Adler viewed the **ego** not as the servant of the id's desires but as an independent aspect of the psyche. Adler believed that creative activity, bringing ideas into fruition, was the primary function of mankind. He viewed the ego as that part of the personality responsible for such creativity. Adler viewed the ego as the seat of the individual's sense of wholeness, of the person's identity (1931, in 1973, p. 206). On the other hand, Freud emphasized the ego's relationship to the unconscious. Freud also believed that the ego had to adapt to external demands. Thus, to Freud, the ego's main functions were psychological survival and adjustment—not creativity. (Cf. Maslow's concept of *hierarchy of needs*, Chapter 10)

The Oedipus Complex: Striving for Superiority not Love or Sex

In Adler's view, the **Oedipus complex** was not a purely sexual phenomenon in which the male child vainly attempts to possess the mother. Rather, Adler thought that equal, if not greater, weight should be attached to the child's striving to overcome his sense of weakness and inferiority. This leads to competition with the father in order to secure equal or greater strength and power. Adler affirmed "that the boy wants to grow beyond himself, wants to attain a superiority over his father" (Adler, 1931, in 1973, p. 207).

Social Interest vs. Narcissism

When Freud developed the concept of narcissistic ego libido, he had in mind a protective channeling of energy into the self—a healthy self-interest or self-love. Adler, however, thought that the Freudian notion of narcissism indicated a personality turned in on itself. It was the opposite of a genuine concern for the well-being of others, or what Adler termed a healthy *social interest*. Adler believed that the narcissistic attitude, contrary to Freudian theory, is neither innate nor instinctual, but learned or acquired. In Adler's view, narcissistic people fear that they are essentially too weak and too powerless to survive, and they try to control this fear by avoiding any sense of obligation to others (1931, in 1973, p. 208). Adler viewed such an approach as a pathological style of life.

Motivation Toward Goals or Satisfying Drives?

For Adler, human motivation cannot be understood in terms of attempts to reduce the discomfort of mounting biological tensions like sex, hunger, and fatigue. Rather, persons strive toward goals they have chosen. Adler put the matter this way:

> The main problem of psychology is not to comprehend the causal factors as in physiology, but the direction-giving, pulling forces, and goals which guide all other psychological movements. (1931, in 1973, p. 216)

Personality: Unity versus Fragmentation

Adler thought that Freudian theory had fragmented personality into competing parts rather than a complete functioning unity. Adler emphasized that personality has a fundamental, innate, evolutionary tendency to grow and to become whole.

Dreams: Aides to Action Not Windows on the Unconscious

In Freud's theory, the dream itself is a focus of attention and a source of insights into the unconscious depths of one's personality. Freud saw dreams as the "royal road" to the unconscious, but Adler viewed them as helping the ego to take action. For Adler, dreams were not to be interpreted as disguised unacceptable wishes. Instead, they represent attempts to resolve problems that dreamers have not mastered with their conscious powers of reason (Adler, 1973, p. 214).

Like Freud, Adler believed that the dream was disguised. In contrast to Freud, however, he was convinced that the purpose of a dream had to do with the mood that it evoked. This mood would enable the dreamer to take an action that he or she might otherwise have been reluctant to attempt. For example, a person may wake up from a dream with the energy and enthusiasm to tackle a new project or to take a new direction in life.

ON HUMAN NATURE—ADLER, THE NAÏVE OPTIMIST, OR FREUD, THE REALISTIC PESSIMIST?

Adler's view that people are basically good and capable of genuine altruistic social concern was opposite to Freud's growing pessimism and fatalism about human nature. Depending on where one stands oneself, one might view Adler as expressing a healthy optimism and Freud as darkly pessimistic; or Freud as realistic and Adler as naïve. Adler seems to be expressing how people are at their best and Freud as how people unfortunately often behave. Given two bloody world wars and the associated killing of civilians, ethnic cleansing, and genocide, Freud's attitude should not be dismissed out of hand. In fact, he did have to flee as a refugee from Nazi Germany. Adler died in 1937 in Scotland, before the horrors of World War II took place.

In 1930, Freud expressed his pessimism and negative view of human nature in a passage in *Civilization and Its Discontents*, in which he wrote about the age-old precept: "Thou shalt love thy neighbor as thyself":

> ...[people] are, on the contrary, creatures among whose instinctual endowments is to be reckoned a powerful share of aggressiveness. As a result, their neighbor is for them not only a potential helper or sexual object, but also someone who tempts them to satisfy their aggressiveness on him, to exploit his capacity for work without compensation, to use him sexually without his consent, to seize his possessions, to humiliate him, to cause him pain, to torture and to kill him. *Homo homini lupus* [*Man is a wolf to man*]. (Freud, 1930, pp. 110–111)

Adler was genuinely shocked by this statement (Orgler, 1963). To him, it was contrary to all reasonable views of human nature to assume that humans were inherently evil. He attributed Freud's outlook to his personality makeup. In Adler's view, Freud's psychology was indicative of his having been a *pampered child*, with the effect such a role would have had on his degree of selfishness and self-centeredness:

> And, indeed, if we look closely we shall find that the Freudian theory is the consistent psychology of the pampered child, who feels that his instincts must never be denied, who looks on it as unfair that other people should exist, who asks always, "Why should I love my neighbor? Does my neighbor love me?" (Adler, 1931, p. 97)

FROM MINUS TO PLUS SELF-ESTIMATES

In light of Adler's childhood infirmities and his experiences of helplessness in the face of death, it is not surprising that he developed the concept of the **inferiority complex** (1927, 1929a, 1931, 1964). Adler was acutely aware that a sense of powerlessness in the face of death is not the only way that an inferiority complex may arise. Physical inferiorities in the form of damaged or diseased organs may also be contributing factors. These defects may impede or prevent successful competition. Adler presumed that *all children*, merely by virtue of their small size, limited knowledge and ability, and lesser strength than adults often feel weak, helpless, and inferior.

Adler continually refined his concept of inferiority. First, he began with the view that the sense of inferiority was rooted in physical organ defects or illnesses. Adler gradually moved toward a *psychological*, or more precisely, a *phenomenological* (see Chapter 4) emphasis on a person's *perception* of his or her own physical inferiorities. By focusing on individual's subjective perceptions of their inferiorities, cultural and social factors such as group membership, occupation, ethnicity, religious affiliation and class could be seen as relevant to a person's feelings of inferiority. Finally, Adler added to his theory a new element, that of strivings to compensate for the sense of inferiority. He developed concepts such as the *masculine protest, superiority strivings*, and *perfection strivings*, which rapidly took their respective places in Adler's maturing personality theory.

Organ Inferiority: Compensatory Strivings

Adler's first medical office was located in a working-class neighborhood of Vienna. His patients were markedly different from Freud's largely well-heeled clients. Situated near the famous Prater amusement park, Adler's practice also included entertainers and artists. One can imagine that strongmen, acrobats, and contortionists of the Prater filled his waiting room!

Furtmüller (1973) has suggested in his biographical essay on Adler that, early on, these patients directed Adler's attention to the relevance of physical weakness and strength for patterns of adaptation.

> All these people [i.e., Prater entertainers], who earned their living by exhibiting their extraordinary bodily strength and skills, showed to Adler their physical weaknesses and ailments. It was partly the observation of such patients as these that led to his conception of overcompensation [for perceived inferiority]. (p. 334)

Adler had fought his own childhood battles with **organ inferiority** in struggling to compete with his brother and other children in physical activities. In 1907, Adler published his essay "Study of Organ Inferiority and Its Psychical Compensation," in which he asserted that all persons at first succumb to disease in whichever of their organs is least well developed, less successfully functioning, and generally "inferior" from birth. Adler theorized that the organism as a whole is governed by the principle of equilibrium or balance. As a result, the initially inferior organ would compensate for any defect, damage or lack of development that it might have. Undergoing increased growth and functioning power, the initially inferior organ or related organs might *overcompensate* for the previous deficit. For example, individuals with a speech defect may become so involved in learning how to master it that they transform the inferiority into the basis for a career. By becoming a speech therapist, an orator, or an actor the individual can overcompensate for what had been a perceived inferiority (1907, p. 29).

Adler did not yet include his characteristic later emphasis on the individual's subjective perception of inferiority. At this stage of his theorizing, Adler thought of **compensation** and **overcompensation** as biological processes.

The Aggression Drive

Adler's next step, taken in 1908, was to assert the existence of an inherent **aggression drive**. Still working from a generally psychoanalytic framework, Adler wanted to maintain some of the importance of Freud's basic pleasure principle. Thus Adler proposed that *both* the drives of sexuality and of aggression were both fundamental (though, as we shall see, not equal). Along with these two primary biological urges, a number of diverse secondary drives associated with sensory processes like seeing, smelling, and hearing also had to be included in any account of motivated behavior. Adler's unique contribution was the idea that no drive stands alone, that there is a **confluence of drives** that enter into an **integrative amalgam** in which each separate component drive is subordinated to the whole (Adler, 1908, p. 30).

It was clear, however, that Adler saw the aggression drive as *the* dominant and governing force shaping the confluence of drives:

> From early childhood, we can say from the first day (first cry) we find a stand of the child toward the environment which cannot be called anything but hostile. If one looks for the cause of this position, one finds it determined by the difficulty of affording satisfaction for the organ [i.e., the sites of drive; e.g., hunger]. This circumstance as well as the further relationships of the hostile, belligerent position of the individual toward the environment indicates a drive toward fighting for satisfaction which I shall call "aggression drive." (Adler, 1908, p. 34)

Furthermore, Adler thought that drives could be displaced from their original form and goals and transformed into new types of expression. Some changes that were possible in his model of personality included:

- *Transformation of a drive into its opposite:* the unconscious drive to eat, for example, becomes the conscious refusal to eat.
- *Displacement of a drive to another goal:* the unconscious love for father becomes a conscious love for a teacher or other authority figure.
- *Redirection of a drive to one's own person:* the unconscious repressed drive to see becomes the conscious drive to be looked at; in other words, exhibitionism.
- *Displacement onto a second strong drive:* the repression of one drive may enhance the expression of another. Thus, blocking of the sex drive's direct expression may increase the drive to "look" at sexual objects. (Adler, 1908, pp. 32–33).

In his paper "Instincts and Their Vicissitudes" (1915a), Freud elaborated the first two of these transformations, for which he gave Adler some credit.

Balancing his emphasis on aggression, Adler also pointed out the importance of love and affection in the development of the child's personality. Parts of the drives to look, to touch, and to listen, join in a unique *confluence of drives* that Adler called the **need for affection**:

> Children want to be fondled [i.e., to be touched], loved, and praised [i.e., to be looked at]. They have a tendency to cuddle up, always to remain close to loved persons, and to want to be taken into the bed with them. (Adler, 1908, p. 40)

Adler found the striving for affection in some areas in which Freud perceived only sexual drives.

MASCULINE PROTEST: NOT FOR MEN ONLY

Adler's theorizing began with an emphasis on the biological nature of the organism and its defects: organ inferiority and the confluence of drives. In 1910, Adler shifted his focus to the psychological level. He became interested in the *experience* and *perceived significance* of organ inferiorities. Adler first connected the biological fact of organ inferiority to its psychological impact of marked feeling of inferiority. Thus children with marked defects like stuttering, clumsiness, deafness, visual deficits, or disfigurement develop a feeling of inferiority in relation to others.

Adler identified such inferiority feelings with femininity, and superiority strivings as masculine. Today, we view identification of inferiority with femininity and masculinity with superiority as biased, inaccurate, and poorly chosen terms. In early twentieth-century Western culture, however, they were common, though not universal, metaphors.

> ...any form of uninhibited aggression, activity, potency, power, and the traits of being brave, free, rich, aggressive or sadistic can be considered [stereotypically] masculine. All inhibitions and deficiencies, as well as cowardliness, obedience, poverty, and similar traits, can be considered as [stereotypically] feminine. (Adler, 1910, p. 47)

Even in spite of the dated and conventional meanings of *feminine* and *masculine*, Adler did not equate such concepts with biological gender. Neither boys nor girls, according to Adler, wish to be locked into the "minus" role then assigned to the traditional concept of the female. All persons, girls as well as boys, therefore, may engage in what Adler termed **masculine protest**. He defined this concept as a compensatory **striving for superiority** in *both* males and females. The masculine protest overlays a defensive network of compensatory traits, as illustrated in Table 4.1.

Table 4.1   Traits of Superiority Striving

Inferiority character traits	*Masculine protest compensatory traits*
timidity indecision insecurity shyness cowardliness increased need for support submissive obedience fantasies of smallness masochism	impudence stubbornness rebelliousness impertinence courage defiance fantasy of hero, warrior, grandeur

Based on Adler, 1910, p. 53

Striving for superiority is a two-phase process. In the first phase, children's sense of inferiority in relation to the adults around them fosters a timid, passive, and insecure feeling of smallness. In the second phase, a superordinate striving for superiority, for autonomy, and for assertive expression of "masculinity" compensates for these inferiority feelings.

SOCIAL INTEREST AND ADLER'S RELIGIOUS VALUES

Adler's emphasis on altruism is a secularized expression of Judeo-Christian values. Adler was brought up as a Jew and converted to Protestantism in adulthood. His ideal of an altruistic and creative role for human beings is consistent with Jewish ethical teachings. The Adlerian therapeutic goal of making the world a better place, whether it be in the area of one's occupation, impact on society, or influence on family and friends, is almost identical to the Hebrew dictate, *tikun olum*, "making the world a better place." Adler's view of human creativity can be considered a more outward version of mystical Judaism's concept that humanity's most important role is to assist God in His creative purposes. In addition, Adler's concept of social interest is in accord with Christian teachings emphasizing the fundamental importance of helping one's fellow human beings.

INDIVIDUALITY, SOCIAL INTEREST AND STYLE OF LIFE: VAIHINGER'S IDEA OF FICTIONAL FINALISM

The philosopher Hans Vaihinger (1911) published a book devoted to explaining the ways in which people create and live by the process of hypothetical or "as if" thinking. He termed this process **fictional finalism**. Entitled *The Philosophy of "As If,"* Vaihinger's book so impressed Adler that he modified and adopted several of its concepts for his theory.

In Vaihinger's **Philosophy of "As If,"** fictions were working hypotheses—useful theories and interpretations of reality that are valuable in making sense of life and guiding one's actions. Thus, although Vaihinger was skeptical regarding religion, he acknowledged that behaving "as if" there were a God lent meaning to people's lives. Similarly, the legal profession must operate "as if" corporations were persons.

Physicists sometimes proceed "as if" electricity were a fluid or "as if" light consisted of discrete packets of energy. In his book, Vaihinger indicated that both science and ordinary life proceeded by inventing and testing "as ifs" or hypotheses to see if they are of value (1911).

The fiction or hypothesis may or may not coincide with the objective fact it seeks to represent, but it may prove to be useful to the thinker. For Vaihinger, "truth is merely the most expedient degree of error, and error the last expedient degree of ideation"; but all such ideation is nevertheless fictional—hypothetical, invented, or made-up. An accepted theory is therefore subject to being replaced by a more useful, effective or applicable one.

How would Vaihinger's concept of fictional finalism be applied to a person's life? Let us say that a college student, let's call her Sally, would like to become a practicing attorney. She imagines a future in which she is a lawyer, and decides to take pre-law courses. She develops her academic skills and takes care to prepare for the LSAT in her junior year. In short, she acts *as if* her goal were to become a reality. Finally, after many years of purposive effort, she enters the bar and begins the practice of law. Her dream has become a reality. How did this happen? It was through the planning and goal-directed activities of the ego, through the *process of fictional finalism*. For Vaihinger as well as for Adler, this is the creative process of humanity. The concepts of fictional finalism and the ego as creative apply to practically everything—the course of study you are taking, this textbook, the college or university you attend. All of these realities are the results of the dreams, goals, and ego activities of many people.

Adler found Vaihinger's views consistent with his own thinking. He agreed with Vaihinger's emphasis on subjective perceptions and views and the active individual nature of the process of creating fictions. In Vaihinger's formulation, all individuals create fictions that are unique to them, that result from their personal inventiveness. (Cf. George Kelly's personal construct theory in Chapter 14). Vaihinger also made it clear that the creation of fictions was sometimes "carried on in the darkness of the unconscious," a proposition for which Adler's psychoanalytic experience readied him to accept (cf. Ansbacher & Ansbacher, 1956, p. 88).

Vaihinger's concept of fictions became for Adler the means to understanding the goal-directedness of personality and the creative process of the ego. He adopted the notion of a fictional final goal in the sense of an ultimate ambition at the center of a person's existence. Although Adler eventually dropped the term *fictional* from his designation of this ultimate goal, three meanings of the concept derived from Vaihinger remained in his theoretical formulations (Ansbacher & Ansbacher, 1956, p. 90):

- The goal is subjective and personally meaningful.
- The individual creates the goal to deal with the challenges of life.
- The goal is unconscious.

Adler developed his theory by synthesizing Vaihinger's concept of a fictional goal with his already existing theories having to do with the importance of a person's sense of inferiority and compensatory strivings.

COMBINING VAIHINGER'S IDEAS WITH HIS OWN THEORY

In combining Vaihinger's ideas with his own thinking, Adler theorized that the motive underlying the creation of a fictional goal is the need to overcome a sense of inferiority

---

Vaihinger's ideas are also similar to those of the psychologist George Kelly (Chapter 14). Kelly was a cognitive personality theorist, who also saw people as inventing, developing, and testing models of reality. Vaihinger's "as ifs" are equivalent to Kelly's "constructs." Both are hypotheses or theories that can be tested through application or experimentation. Vaihinger was an early proponent of the view that people are proactive constructors of reality.

---

and to develop a sense of superiority. In Adler's own words, the creativity of the personality is "that power which expresses itself in the desire to develop, to strive, and to achieve—and even to compensate for defeats in one direction by striving for success in another" (1929a, p. 1):

> In each mind, there is the conception of a goal or ideal to get beyond the present state, and to overcome the present deficiencies and difficulties by postulating a concrete aim for the future. By means of this concrete aim or goal the individual can think and feel himself superior to the difficulties of the present because he has in mind his success of the future. (Adler, 1929a, p. 2)

In Adler's theory, an individual's life takes shape and direction in accordance with an unconscious plan to overcome sensed inferior traits. Each person creates a fictional goal, that is, a subjective guiding ideal in order to master their sense of inferiority. This ideal of mastery shapes the person's role and character [note the *mask metaphor* in the quotation below]:

> The fictional, abstract ideal is the point of origin for the formation and differentiation of the given psychological resources [of the individual] into preparatory attitudes, readiness, and character traits. The individual then wears the character traits demanded by his fictional goal, just as the character mask (persona) of the ancient actor had to fit the finale of the tragedy. . . . The self-ideal [i.e., fictional goal] . . . carries within itself all abilities and gifts of which the so-disposed child considers himself deprived. (Adler, in 1956, pp. 94–95)

Adler pictured the creation of a superordinate goal through the process of fictional finalism (invented goal-directed activity) as beginning in early childhood. The child, from the base of his early **feelings of inferiority**, formulates a "prototype" of his later mature personality. This prototype is based on imitation of one or more of the "strongest" person or persons in his childhood environment. This prototype is the model for what Adler termed the "guiding self-ideal." The child's maturing personality becomes unified around such a guiding self-ideal (Adler, 1929a, pp. 3–4).

THE NEUROTIC PERSONALITY: OVERDOING THE SEARCH FOR PERFECTION

In Adler's view, the dominant goal of the neurotic is an attempt to acquire self-security through developing a sense of personal superiority. In their efforts to win security, neurotics are very self-centered and have an inflated perception of self. A healthy interest in the being of others, in their welfare, in their commonality with the self, is excluded from the neurotic's personality development and style of life. In spite of such efforts, the neurotic is still plagued with doubts and feelings of inferiority.

Neurotic Self-Absorption

Adler portrayed the neurotic person as self-involved and self-absorbed.[1] Feelings of inferiority are intensified in the neurotic person because real or imagined threats to self-esteem abound in every interaction with another, in every task attempted, and in every memory recalled. The neurotic becomes focused on self-protection:

> When scrutinized, the neurotic will be found to be an individual placed in a test situation who is attempting to solve his problems in the interest of his own personal ambition rather than in the interest of the common welfare. This holds true of all neuroses. All neuroses grow out of the psychic tensions of an individual who is not socially well prepared when he is confronted with a task which demands for its solution more social interest than he is capable of. (Adler, 1932, p. 91)

Neurotic Safeguarding Strategies

In order to protect his or her vulnerable self-esteem, the neurotic person develops a "far-flung net of safeguards" (Adler, 1913, p. 264). **Safeguarding strategies** are the defense mechanisms of Adlerian personality theory. Unlike the Freudian version of defense mechanisms, which are focused most on protecting the ego from *internal*, instinctual dangers, Adler's safeguards are aimed more at protecting self-esteem from *external*, usually interpersonal, threats. Table 4.2 summarizes Adler's safeguards and provides a listing of comparable Freudian mechanisms. The similarities between safeguards and defense mechanisms range from substantial to superficial, and it might be helpful to consult Chapter 6 for a more complete account of Anna Freud's classic defense mechanisms.

Adler enumerated three classes of safeguarding strategies, each with its own subtypes:

1. **Excuses or rationalizing strategies**
2. **Aggressive strategies**
3. **Distancing strategies**

Excuses or Rationalizing Strategies

The neurotic develops symptoms that inhibit or impede some kinds of interpersonal functioning. He or she feels secure because a certain freedom to do less, achieve less, and demand less of self develops. It is as if the neurotic were excusing self from the usual demands of life by saying, "See, I have this illness or this symptom, so I cannot be expected to perform at my best." In Freudian theory, neurotic symptoms not only solve the neurotic conflict, but also provide *secondary gains* in the form of sympathy from people and a lessening of demands. Adler's concept of "excuses" is akin to the Freudian concept of secondary gain.

Aggressive Strategies

In order to safeguard self-esteem, a neurotic person can express either open or disguised hostility to others and to self. Adler distinguishes three main categories of aggressive safeguarding:

---

[1] It must be remembered that the term *neurosis* was used by Adler, and by most clinicians of the period, as a generalized term for a broad range of psychological dysfunction. Today, *neurosis* is not a currently acceptable official diagnostic label for treatment or for insurance purposes.

Table 4.2   Safeguards and Comparable Defense Mechanisms

Adlerian "safeguard"	Description	Comparable Freudian defense mechanism
Excuses	Neurotic symptoms used as reasons to escape life's demands, cannot perform at one's best.	• Rationalization • Secondary gain
Aggression	1. *Depreciation:* strategies for feeling superior by making others feel inferior, or overvaluing self relative to others or being overly solicitous of others' welfare as a way to control them.	• Reaction formation • Altruistic surrender • Reversal
	2. *Accusation:* unconscious feelings of deprivation lead to blaming others for one's own feelings of inferiority and frustration. Sometimes person blames fate.	• Displacement • Rationalization • Projection
	3. *Self-accusation* (guilt): blaming self, "cursing" self, and suicidal thoughts and acts sometimes to gain attention, sometimes as a displaced intention to really hurt someone else. Or sometimes self-blame is a way of punishing others by making them feel guilty.	• Turning against self • Reversal • Asceticism
Distancing	Reflects the basic neurotic conflict between feelings of inferiority and strivings for superiority.	
	1. *Moving backward* by using symptoms to avoid social obligations, being helpless, "can't do anything."	• Fixation • Regression
	2. *Standing still* by refusing to do anything or participate in life, especially when demands are made.	• Inhibition • Regression
	3. *Hesitation* and *procrastination* around a self-created difficulty and attempts to master it. Obsessions and compulsions.	• Rationalization • Undoing
	4. *Constructing obstacles* by focusing on a symptom and blaming failure on it. Usually the least severe form of safeguarding because there is some success	• Rationalization • Inhibition

1. Depreciation is a strategy that the neurotic employs to devalue other people so that in comparison to self they are not seen as superior or as threats. A similar maneuver involves overvaluing self in relationship to others. Instead of expressing hostility directly toward competitors, the neurotic can accomplish the same end by inflating their own importance relative to others. Other people are perceived as inferior, just as when they are depreciated directly, but the neurotic can console the self by implying they are not disparaging other people, only comparing them to their own magnificent self (1913, p. 268).

In a similar way, the neurotic can depreciate others subtly by comparing real people to impossible ideal standards. Adler also described a more subtle, form of depreciation.

He observed that neurotic people can be overly solicitous for the welfare of others. They behave as if they are altruistically concerned that the people in their lives are exposed to dangers, confusions, and demands that only they can help them master. The neurotic seems to believe that without his or her help, other people are incapable of caring for themselves:

> They always give advice, want to do everything themselves, find new dangers and never rest until the other person, confused and discouraged, confides himself to their care. Neurotic parents thus create much damage.... The neurotic aspires to make the laws for the others. (1913, p. 269).

This kind of loving concern hurts. With friends like the neurotic people Adler is describing, we do not need enemies.

2. Accusation involves a more direct expression of anger. The neurotic feels unconsciously deprived and frustrated by others, and embarks on subtle blaming of others. The person blames parents, siblings, or fate for their own difficulties. Adler referred to this strategy as the "Cinderella" fantasy because, like Cinderella, the person looks for someone, a "Prince Charming," to take responsibility and to be the source of well-being and happiness. In Freud's terms, *accusation* may be considered a form of displacement and is often found combined with the defense of rationalization in some people to avoid responsibility for their actions.

3. Self-accusation is putting the blame for one's misfortunes on self, but doing it in such a way that it attracts attention, sympathy, concern, or help from others. Unconsciously, the neurotic person who accuses self also provokes guilt as a kind of atonement for being inferior. Self-accusation, making oneself a pitiable target of criticism can also be a way of inducing guilt in others—trying to make them feel guilty for one's misery. The comparable Freudian mechanisms are turning-against-the-self, reversal, and asceticism.

Distancing Strategies

The neurotic person can also safeguard self-esteem by developing **distancing strategies**, which involve restricting his or her participation in life. The person protects his or her self-image by avoiding challenges that are threatening or potentially anxiety-provoking (cf. Maslow's *Jonah complex*, Chapter 13). Adler described four overlapping distancing strategies:

1. Moving backward is a strong indicator of the basic conflict of the neurotic person because he or she is caught between wanting success and wanting to avoid failure. As a result, the person becomes motivationally frozen. The person "moving backward" can either do nothing or develop symptoms that symbolically signify doing nothing, such as mutism (can't talk), hysterical paralyses (can't move), abulia (can't decide), agoraphobia (can't go out into the world), anorexia (can't eat), or amnesia (can't remember). According to Adler, the person can also display severe anxiety attacks or even criminal behavior. Comparable, but not identical Freudian defenses are fixation and regression.

2. Standing still is not much different from "moving backward"; the person shows the same motivationally frozen attitude, but the symptoms are less dramatic. The person again uses the neurotic symptom as a way of not allowing self to be evaluated or judged. Examples are complaints of weak memory, insomnia that produces fatigue and prevents work, or an inability to concentrate while studying for an exam. In effect, the neurotic opts out of making a credible effort to succeed. The trigger for such behaviors is some life demand, such as an examination, a job task, or a relationship demand. When the external demand or test is removed, the safeguarding strategy disappears. Analogous Freudian defenses are inhibition and regression.

3. Hesitation is the "back and forth" strategy of safeguarding by procrastinating so that whatever effort the person makes, it is "too late." The person may unconsciously create his or her own difficulties, and then, just as unconsciously, create a way of mastering it that becomes a neurotic symptom. Washing compulsions, touching compulsions, leaving things unfinished, destroying nearly completed work because it has to be done over to be right are all ways of wasting time and never committing oneself to be evaluated. Analogous Freudian mechanisms are undoing and rationalization.

4. Construction of obstacles is similar to hesitation and to the strategy of excuses because the person looks for problems, such as illnesses, that will prevent him or her from expending effort. The person rationalizes by saying, "If only I wasn't handicapped by such and such, I could have achieved so much more." The obstacle in such cases is a challenge that could have been overcome even with only partial effort so that the person can say, "Oh, what I could have done had I not been ill."

The Completed Transition

In the final stage of his theorizing, Adler developed a more positive view of the striving for perfection. He eventually viewed such perfection as a "victorious adaptation to the external world." He conceived of perfection-striving as a basic evolutionary process of adaptation to life's circumstances, one that was selected by Darwinian principles. Adler had maintained continuity with his earliest notions of organ inferiority and the striving to compensate and win a sense of superiority. By the assumption of an inherent biological trend toward better adaptation (i.e., toward perfection), Adler also maintained the goal-seeking or **teleological** aspect of his personality theory.

The development of the various stages of Adler's view of perfection-striving are summarized in Table 4.3. It may be of some help to compare the contents of Table 4.3 with the items outlined previously in Table 4.1.

SOCIAL INTEREST AND THE TASKS OF LIFE

Even though the striving for perfection is common to normal and neurotic personalities alike, the neurotic's motives are isolated from any interest in the rest of humanity.

Table 4.3   Transitions in Adler's Conception of Human Motivation

Motive or personality goal	Antecedent or cause
1. Organ inferiority	Physiological-environmental interaction
2. Aggression drive	Frustrated biological needs and perceived helplessness
3. Masculine protest	Cultural attitudes toward "maleness," and feelings of passivity or inferiority
4. Superiority striving	Evolutionary trend toward successful adaptation; personal feelings of inferiority
5. Perfection striving	Subjective interpretation of life's meaning, life's values, the fictional final goal

Adler's concept of social interest is very similar to Erik Erikson's concept of *generativity* (Chapter 8). Both of them are very concerned with the overall impact of the person's life on the world. Erikson would place generativity, the concern for the well-being of coming generations, as a quality that develops during adulthood, after a person has established an identity and entered into a committed relationship. For Adler, social interest was the essential ingredient of a healthy approach to life. He did not limit its importance to a specific period of development. Erikson was, of course, aware of Adler's concept of *social interest* when he formulated his own theory.

Indeed, they are isolated from any interest, even in those closest to them. Adler indicated the essentially normal sympathy of feeling for one's fellow humans by a German term he coined, ***Gemeinschaftsgefuhl***. Adler favored the term **social interest** as the best approximation in English (Ansbacher & Ansbacher, 1956, p. 134).

Adler thought that the normal person's trait of social interest is missing in the neurotic person:

> It is always the want of social feeling, whatever be the name one gives it—living in fellowship, co-operation, humanity, or even the ideal-ego—which causes an insufficient preparation for all the problems of life. (Adler, 1964, p. 110)

Adler asserted that only a person with strong social interest could successfully solve the basic problems of life. Adler conceived each of these life tasks as a universal problem of living. He grouped life tasks under three categories:

- *Occupational Tasks:* In the selection and pursuit of a vocation as a productive mode of existence, a person "arrives at a feeling of his worth to society, the only possible means of mitigating the universally human feeling of inferiority. The person who performs useful work lives in the midst of the developing human society and helps to advance it."
- *Societal Tasks:* In this instance the goal is to make a positive difference in the society in which one finds oneself. One works with others to build a better community, society, or world.
- *Love Tasks:* The relationship between the sexes is the last significant "task" to be mastered. "On his approach to the other sex and on the fulfillment of his sexual role depends his part in the continuance of mankind" (Adler, 1933, p. 132).

Adler emphasized the relatedness of the three tasks:

> The three problems are never found apart, for they all throw cross lights on one another. A solution of one helps toward the solution of the others, and indeed we can say that they are all aspects of the same situation and the same problem—the necessity for a human being to preserve life and to further life in the environment in which he finds himself. (Adler, 1933, pp. 132–133)

The individual who embodies a healthy social interest is expressing an empathic attitude toward life: "To see with the eyes of another, to hear with the ears of another, to feel with the heart of another" (Adler, 1956, p. 135).

INDIVIDUALITY, SOCIAL INTEREST, AND STYLE OF LIFE

Adler chose the phrase **individual psychology** to identify his system. This term indicates the subjective and individual nature of a person's goal striving, the creativity of human psychological adaptation, and the wholeness of personality. And then, individuals subordinate all drives, needs, and strivings to their **style of life**, the very pattern of their existence as social beings as they create it:

> The goal of superiority, with each individual, is personal and unique. It depends upon the meaning he gives to life; and this meaning is not a matter of words. It is built up in his style of life and runs through it like a strange melody of his own creation. ... Understanding a style of life is similar to understanding the work of a poet. A poet must use words; but his meaning is more than the mere words he uses. The greatest part of his meaning must be guessed at; we must read between the lines. ... The psychologist must learn to read between the lines; he must learn the art of appreciating life-meanings. (Adler, 1931, pp. 57–58)

To the degree that individuals have developed a high degree of social interest, their strivings for superiority will be shaped into a style of life that is warmly receptive of others and focused on friendship and interpersonal ties. They will be characteristically expectant that other people are similarly warmly receptive of them and are therefore sources of satisfaction and pleasure.

The specific style of life that a person develops is the general approach to the world and to others he or she adopts. It is exemplified best in how a person chooses to cope with threatening situations. Adler illustrated his meaning with the following analogy:

> Perhaps I can illustrate this by an anecdote of three children who were taken to the zoo for the first time. As they stood before the lion's cage, one of them shrank behind his mother's skirts and said, "I want to go home." The second child stood where he was, very pale and trembling, and said, "I'm not a bit frightened." The third glared at the lion fiercely and asked his mother, "Shall I spit at it?" The three children really felt inferior, but each expressed his feelings in his own way, consonant with his style of life. (1931, p. 50)

One's style of life is the product of a creative personality trend in the direction of wholeness and integration.

> Every individual represents both a unity of personality and the individual fashioning of that unity. The individual is thus both the picture and the artist. He is the artist of his own personality, but as an artist he is neither an infallible worker nor a person with a complete understanding of mind and body; he is rather a weak, extremely fallible, and imperfect human being. (Adler, 1956, p. 177; see also 1930, p. 24)

In Adler's view, therefore, the individual is a creative and active constructor of his or her personality. As Adler noted however, like any creative process, this one is always a "work in progress."

Adler's Typology of Personality

Adler developed a theory of personality types based on the degree of social interest (and corresponding empathic capacity) and activity level. For Adler, the most important factor was not whether a person had a deep sense of inferiority. After all, according to him, some degree of an underlying sense of inferiority was universal. It existed in everyone. What was most important in Adler's individual psychology was to what extent a person developed a constructive or a destructive style of life in response to this sense of inferiority.

BOX 4.3   *Only Connect . . .*

In Chapter 17 we shall find that one tenet of evolutionary psychology is that much altruistic behavior has been selected as part of the evolutionary process. Freud based his ideas on classical Darwinian evolutionary theory, which focused on the survival value of reproductive and aggressive behavior and did not include biologically-determined altruism. The more recent inclusive fitness or "selfish gene" hypotheses indicate selective advantage to some altruistic behaviors. Adler, much more than Freud, emphasized the importance of altruistic behavior with his development of the concept of *social interest*.

In addition to the all-important, constructive-destructive dimension, Adler further defined and categorized an individual as a **ruling-dominant type**, **getting-leaning type**, **avoidant type**, or **socially useful type**. Clearly the socially-useful type would be the most constructive. Descriptions of the four specific types of this typology are:

1. *The Ruling-Dominant Type:* These personalities are assertive, aggressive, and active. They manipulate and master the life situation and the people in it. Their activity levels are high but are combined with a minimal degree of social interest and little capacity for empathy. The danger is that their activities will be directed into antisocial behaviors.

2. *The Getting-Leaning Type:* These types of individuals expect others to satisfy their needs and to provide for their interests; they may be said to "lean on" others. The getting-leaning types are combinations of a low level of social interest, little capacity for empathy, and low activity levels.

3. *The Avoidant Type:* These individuals are inclined to achieve success by circumventing a problem, by withdrawing from it. In effect, they achieve mastery by avoiding defeat. Their level of social interest and capacity for empathy is as low as that of the getting-leaning types, but their activity levels are even lower.

4. *The Socially Useful Type:* This personality type is the healthiest of them all in Adler's view. The socially useful person attacks problems head on with a realistic appraisal of their difficulty. This type is socially oriented and prepared to cooperate with others to master the tasks of life. Thus, the socially useful person has a combination of high activity level, a high degree of social interest, and high empathic capacity (based on Adler, 1935, pp. 167–168).

EARLY RECOLLECTIONS AS INDICATORS OF STYLE OF LIFE

Adler thought that one of the most significant ways of understanding patients was to explore their earliest recollections. We have already seen an application of this technique to aspects of Adler's own life. The incidents, feelings, and people that an individual recalls from early in life are significant as a result of the selectivity of such memories. Current meanings and understandings are expressed in the memories that are available for recall. Thus, if one lives one's life "as if" others are always trying to humiliate one, the memories one is likely to recall are those of humiliation or those that can be interpreted as humiliating experiences (Adler, 1956, p. 351). A person's memories "represent his 'Story of My Life'; a story he repeats to himself to warn him or comfort him, to keep him concentrated on his goal, and to prepare him by means of past experiences, so that he will meet the future with an already tested style of action" (Adler, 1931, p. 73).

Adler considered the most significant early recollection as the one that a person chooses to verbalize first. This incident will reveal the basic life attitude, "his first satisfactory crystallization of his attitude." Adler in no way accepted the individual's recollections as statements of fact. He seems, rather, to have treated them more as a form of a projective test whereby the individual's *perceived meanings*, not the objective truth of the memory, are the key indicator.

ORDINAL POSITION WITHIN THE FAMILY AS INDICATOR OF STYLE OF LIFE

Adler used the **birth order** of children within a family as a diagnostic indicator. Adler pointed to the myriad differences that exist between the first born and the last born, to the differences between an only child and a child with many siblings, and so on. *First born, second born, youngest child*, and *only child* are considered distinctly different and significant roles by Adler.

Adler's observations seem to describe some aspects of the behavior of many people, but they are by no means universally relevant. Merely examining birth order does not elucidate the pattern of relationships within a family nor does it take account of the personalities of the parents, the nature of their parenting, or many other factors. Adlerian birth-order analysis is transparently a very generalized and often inaccurate approach to understanding a given individual. We present Adler's typology with the understanding that it has many limitations. One of the problems is that Adler assumes a standard married, two-parent household with traditional roles. Many changes have occurred in typical family structure since Adler's time. Increased numbers of divorces, blended families, stay-at-home-fathers, working mothers, and single-parent families have limited the applicability of Adler's theory. We might consider preserving Adler's general idea that a child's role in the family affects his or her development of life style, but such a role is based on much more than simply birth order. Family history and the complexity of relationships within the family must be taken into account.

First Born (Oldest)

Because it is first born, the oldest child lives a favored existence for a time as an only child. It is given central place until another child is born to remove its favored status. Adler comments,

> Now he must share the attention of his mother and father with a rival. The change always makes a great impression and we can often find in problem children, neurotics, criminals, drunkards, and perverts that their difficulties began in such circumstances. They were oldest children who felt deeply the arrival of another child; and their sense of deprivation had molded their whole style of life. (1931, p. 144)

Though skillful at gaining attention, the oldest child eventually learns that mother is too busy, too harassed, or too unconcerned to tolerate its demands. It turns to father. By directing attention-getting behaviors to father, the deprived oldest child seeks to "reproach his mother" (1931, p. 146). The outcome of this family struggle is that the oldest child "trains himself for isolation." It masters the technique of surviving alone and independently of the need for anyone's affection or attention. Because the happiest time of life was before the birth of the new child, oldest children often show an unusual interest in the past. "They are admirers of the past and pessimistic over the future" (1931, p. 147).

A healthy outcome is also possible. An oldest child may imitate father and mother in their attentions to the other children. As such imitation progresses, the oldest becomes a helper to the younger children or a mother or father figure to playmates.

Second Born

From birth, a second-born child is raised in a world in which mother divides her attention and ministrations between her two children. This second child's existence is the more favored of the two since it has, so to speak, a pacemaker in the form of an older brother or sister. It is thus stimulated, or perhaps provoked, to match the older child's exploits:

> He behaves as if he were in a race, as if someone were a step or two in front and he had to hurry to get ahead of him. He is under full steam all the time. (Adler, 1931, p. 148)

When, however, the oldest child, the pacemaker, beats the younger sibling, the younger child is likely to feel incompetent. The most difficult combination occurs when the oldest is a boy and the second child is a girl. If the girl beats the older boy at his own game, he fares worse than if the younger child had been another boy. On the other hand, if the older child sets a pace to which the girl cannot match her stride, her personal and culturally reinforced feelings of inferiority will be intensified. Generally, however, the second child is the conqueror, using direct and devious means to surpass the pacemaker (Adler, 1929b, p. 106).

The Youngest Child

Although in a large family each succeeding child dethrones the previously born one, the last or youngest can never be removed from its pampered position. This child has many pacemakers, but because it retains the position of the thoroughly *pampered child*, the baby of the family group, it often outstrips its brothers and sisters in achievements.

Adler thought, however, that the second largest proportion of problem children come from the group of youngest:

> The reason for this generally lies in the way in which all the family spoils them. A spoiled child can never be independent. He loses courage to succeed by his own effort. Youngest children are always ambitious; but the most ambitious children of all are the lazy children. Laziness is a sign of ambition joined with discouragement; ambition so high that the individual sees no hope of realizing it. (1931, p. 151)

Because of the multiplicity of its pacemaker models, the youngest child is driven to desire success in everything. Because universal accomplishment is unlikely, he or she may be discouraged and give up.

The Only Child

The only child's rival is the father. Pampered by the mother because she is afraid of losing her child, the only child becomes "tied to the mother's apron strings." In later life, when no longer the center of attention, this enforced timidity and passivity will operate to the child's detriment.

> Only children are often very sweet and affectionate, and later in life they may develop charming manners in order to appeal to others, as they train themselves in this way, both in early life and later. ... We do not regard the only child's situation as dangerous, but we find

that, in the absence of the best educational methods, very bad results occur which would have been avoided if there had been brothers and sisters. (Adler, 1929b, pp. 111–112)

EVALUATING ALFRED ADLER

Adler's Legacy

Adler anticipated many later developments in psychoanalytic theory, humanistic theory, cognitive psychology, and even social learning theory. A large portion of what Adler wrote and thought that was criticized by the orthodox Freudians has become mainstream ego psychology or accepted into humanistic or cognitive-behavioral psychology. Adler focused on some of the blind spots in the psychoanalytic conception of human beings well before the development of ego psychology. Adler's chief contribution was to provide the framework for a unified, holistic account of personality. His view of people as creative was along the lines that Carl Rogers, Abraham Maslow, and other humanistic theorists (Chapter 13) would later pursue (Mosak & Maniacci, 1999).

Adlerians train therapists in institutes and in professional graduate programs around the world. Recent trends in psychotherapy including the method of coaching and focusing on formulating and reaching goals follow in Adler's footsteps. Adler's optimistic approach to the possibility of change in people who have had difficult early circumstances facilitates the development of therapeutic programs for the disadvantaged.

Adler reached out to the general public through his many appearances. He often presented counseling or therapeutic sessions with individuals in front of an audience for educational purposes. His democratization of the previously elite institution of Freudian psychoanalysis anticipated psychology's goal of "giving away" psychology.

Refutability of Adler's Concepts

It is of some historical interest that Karl Popper's criterion of refutability was created in part as his response to the ideas of Adler and Freud. Popper conceived of the idea of refutability when he realized that the theories of Freud, Adler, and Karl Marx could explain any kind of human behavior. Popper's account of how he first came to the concept of refutability was related directly to his interest in Adler's work. Popper (1965, p. 35) said that he was, in fact, "much impressed" by his experience of working with Alfred Adler in 1919 when he discussed a case with Adler and found that Adler could account for a child's behavior easily with his theory of inferiority feelings. Popper asked Adler how he could be so sure of his interpretation, and Adler replied, "Because of my thousand fold experience." Popper responded wryly, "And with this new case, I suppose, your experience has become thousand-and-one-fold" (1965, p. 35). Popper was not simply being sarcastic. The interchange with Adler set Popper thinking:

> ... every conceivable case could be interpreted in the light of Adler's theory, or equally of Freud's. I may illustrate this by two very different examples of human behavior: that of a man who pushes a child into the water with the intention of drowning it; and that of a man who sacrifices his life in an attempt to save the child. Each of these two cases can be explained with equal ease in Freudian and in Adlerian terms. According to Freud the first man suffered from repression (say, of some component of his Oedipus complex), while the second man had achieved sublimation. According to Adler the first man suffered from feelings of inferiority (producing perhaps the need to prove to himself that he dared to commit some crime), and so did the second man (whose need was to prove to himself that he dared to rescue the child). *I could not think of any human behavior which could not be*

Figure 4.1 Alfred Adler speaking to a receptive audience in Sweden. Consistent with his concepts of *Gemeinschaftsgefuhl* (literally "fellow-feeling") or social interest, Adler believed it was important to reach out to the public in many countries with his ideas. He no doubt would use television or the Internet to reach people if he were alive in today's world. The approach of current television psychologists is, at least, partly in the spirit of Adlerian openness and enthusiastic coaching.

interpreted in terms of either theory. It was precisely this fact—that they always fitted, that they were always confirmed—which in the eyes of their admirers constituted the strongest argument in favor of these theories. (Popper, 1965, p. 35, italics added)

What Popper realized is that precisely the apparent comprehensiveness of the theories—that they apply to and are confirmed by so much—is their greatest weakness. To be compatible with any outcome is to predict no one outcome (see also Stepansky, 1983, pp. 37ff. for a similar view of Adler's difficulties with refutability).

There are sections of Adler's thinking that have been (and others that could be) subject to empirical testing. Adlerian-derived variables such as the degree to which a person is goal-directed, has the trait of social interest, suffers from inferiority feelings, is a ruling-dominant type, a getting-leaning type, an avoidant type or a socially useful type, or uses any one of a number of safeguarding mechanisms can be measured with the development of a variety of appropriate tests and observations.

Informed or inspired by Adler's thinking, some research has already been done on the personality correlates or effects of birth position. The results of such research do indicate in a general way that there is some relevance for personality of a person's birth-order in a family, but the effect clearly depends on many factors including the subjective perceptions of the family members, cultural and economic factors, and the specific dynamics and history of an individual family.

Adler's Conception of Human Agency

Almost from the beginning, Adler argued that a person was not trapped by personal history, biology, or social circumstances. Each person has the ability to alter or adapt creatively to these conditions. When we read Adler's essays, our impression is that he was actually angered by people who passively accept their limitations or who create their own obstacles in order to safeguard their self-esteem.

It might be argued that Adler allowed for a balance between environmental determinism and choice as, for example, in his concept of organ inferiority. But by the final phases of his theory construction, he emphasized a person's power to choose, capacity to interpret, and willingness to try to change the conditions of his or her life in the direction of social interest. Adler saw genetic, physical, or environmental limitations as challenges to overcome. "If life gives you lemons, make lemonade," was his approach to life.

The Idiographic versus Nomothetic Nature of Individual Psychology

As the very term *individual psychology* suggests, the major focus of Adler's theory is idiographic. Adler stressed the individual's unique and creative interpretation of reality as the most important element of his understanding of psychology. And, like the other thinkers who share psychoanalytic propositions, Adler's own efforts were largely clinical and educational and involved working with individual cases. There are also some very important nomothetic concepts, which partly balance this idiographic emphasis. For example, his thoughts about birth order represent a nomothetic typology. Also, concepts such as the inferiority complex and superiority strivings are viewed as generally applicable, although the specific content of a person's inferiority complex or superiority strivings can be individualized.

SUMMARY

As a child, Alfred Adler had been singularly sensitized to cues indicating his own frailty and powerlessness. Poor health prevented him from competing successfully with his older brother and peers in the athletic pursuits of boyhood. Repeated brushes with death impressed Adler with the fragility of human life and with the necessity for struggling against imposed helplessness. His resentment toward his mother and brother led to his conviction that hostility had to be controlled and replaced by a healthy concern for others. In his later theory of personality, Adler referred to this essential quality of the healthy personality as *Gemeinschaftsgefühl* (social interest).

Having joined Freud's intellectual circle in Vienna in 1902, Adler never completely committed to psychoanalysis and slowly drew further apart from orthodox Freudian theory. By 1911 the split between Freud and Adler reached a climax, and Adler set off to develop his own school of individual psychology. His differences from Freud were many, but key theoretical discrepancies can be discerned in the following six areas:

1. The ego was not the handmaiden of the id, but an independent, creative entity capable of proactive coping.

2. The Oedipus complex was not primarily a sexual phenomenon but an indication of the boy's attempts to gain competence, superiority, and power as possessed by the father.

3. Narcissism was not a retraction of energy into the ego as a protective self-interest, but an unhealthy, antisocial, and egocentric withdrawal of interest in others. Mental health is typified by *social interest* or constructive concern and activity to promote the well-being of others.

4. Personality could not be studied piecemeal or in fragments of discrete id, ego, or superego functioning; the human person is a whole entity, striving toward self-determined goals.

5. Dreams are attempts to create a mood that will induce awake dreamers to take action they were previously reluctant to pursue; dreams are not

satisfactions, as Freud held, but attempts to solve problems from waking life.

6. Freud's mature view of the inherent evil of human nature offended Adler's optimistic philosophical convictions of innate human goodness.

For Adler, the central core of personality is a state of perceived inferiority for which the individual feels compelled to compensate by striving for superiority. The notion of inferiority compensation underwent several changes in Adler's thinking. In order of their development, they are:

1. **Organ inferiority**
2. **Aggression drive**
3. **Masculine protest**
4. **Superiority striving**
5. **Perfection striving**

Adopting Vaihinger's concept of fictional finalism, Adler postulated that all persons construct or adopt goals and engage in goal-directed behaviors. The meaning of individuals' lives can be understood only by comprehending the goals toward which they strive.

Adler developed a typology of personality organized on the principles of activity level and degree of social interest. Four personality types were described: ruling-dominant, getting-leaning, avoiding, and socially useful. Adler believed that only the socially useful personality type, embodying a high degree of social interest and a high degree of activity, was healthy enough to master successfully the three types of life tasks: occupational tasks, societal tasks, and love tasks.

Adler's diagnostic indicators employed in psychotherapy included the analysis of early recollections and the interpretation of the child's ordinal position within the family. Early recollections are important indicators because they reveal the central concerns and unconscious goals (fictions) of the personality through its conscious choice of key memories. Application of Adler's birth order theory should take into account the actual role of children within specific families.

Evaluation of Adler's theory indicates that many, but not all, of its concepts are non-refutable. In fact, Karl Popper created the criterion of refutability largely out of consideration for the capacity of Freud's and Adler's theories to be compatible with nearly any human behavior. Adler is a strong proponent of an active agency conception of human motivation and behavior, as evidenced in his adoption of Vaihinger's "as if" process of creativity. Many aspects of individual psychology are highly individualized or idiographic. Other aspects, such as Adler's typification of the differential psychologies of people with different birth orders, are nomothetic. In addition to the continuing existence of Adlerian institutes, Adler's legacy is in line with the contemporary emphasis on cognitive interventions, therapeutic optimism, educating the public about psychotherapy, and directive and coaching approaches in counseling and psychotherapy.

FOR FURTHER READING

Two readily accessible paperbacks by Adler that express his ideas in a very clear way are *What Life Could Mean to You and Understanding Human Nature*. Both were published by Hazelden Information and Education Services (Center City, MN, 1998).

Adler for Beginners by Anne Hooper and Jeremy Holford (New York: Writers and Readers, 1998) is an excellent, deceptively simple, comic-book style summary of Adler's life and work.

Harold Mosak, an eminent Adlerian therapist, and Michael Maniacci have recently written a book that highlights the connections between Adler's thought to current trends in psychological theory and practice—*A Primer of Adlerian Psychology: The Analytic-Behavioral-Cognitive Psychology of Alfred Adler* (New York: Brunner/Mazel, 1999).

Adler's definitive work is *The Practice and Theory of Individual Psychology* (London: Routledge, 1999). It was originally published in 1924.

Additional Adlerian bibliographic and Internet sources are indicated on the *Beneath the Mask* web page for Chapter 4. This can be found on the John Wiley's higher education web page: www.wiley.com/college/sollod

GLOSSARY

Accusation: Blaming others for one's own short-comings and failures.

Aggression drive: (Adler) One of the two major drives, along with the sex drive.

Aggressive strategies: Strategies involving feeling or expressing hostility toward others or self in order to safeguard self-esteem. This hostility can consist of *depreciation, accusation*, and *self-accusation.*

Avoidant type: Individuals who consistently avoid or ignore problems or challenges.

Birth order: Different birth orders create different situations to which children must adjust, and that adjustment may influence personality development and adherence to specific lifestyles.

Compensation/overcompensation: A process by which a perceived weakness or frailty is both denied and converted into a strength.

Confluence of drives: Drives enter into a "confluence", an amalgam of interaction whereby each separate component drive is subordinated to the whole.

Depreciation: A devaluing of the accomplishments of others in order to safeguard one's own self-esteem.

Distancing strategies: The neurotic strategy of safeguarding self-esteem by restricting one's participation in life. The person protects his self-image by not exposing himself to challenge, or by not entering a situation where there is some risk of failure. Four distancing strategies are termed *moving backward, standing still, hesitation*, and *construction of obstacles.*

Ego: (in Adler's theory) The center of a person's sense of wholeness; the source of autonomy and creative processes.

Excuses/rationalizing strategies: Excuses and rationalizations that serve the purpose of escaping life's demands or of avoiding the burden of feeling responsible for performing at one's best.

Feelings of inferiority: A sense or feeling that one has of being inferior, which Adler asserted was universal.

Fictional finalism: The process of inventing or formulating a goal and working toward its fulfillment.

Gemeinschaftsgefuhl (literally "fellow-feeling"): The feeling of connectedness with and sympathy for one's fellow humans, translated by Adler as *social interest.*

Getting-leaning type: Individuals who expect others to satisfy their needs. They attain personal goals by relying on others for help.

Individual psychology: A term used to identify Adler's theory to distinguish it from other approaches. It stresses that each person, as an integrated whole, engages in goal-directed behavior.

Inferiority complex: An individual's sense of helplessness, of powerlessness, beginning in infancy and childhood.

Integrative amalgam: A term used to indicate the confluence of drives.

Masculine protest: Attempt by both males and females to compensate for feelings of inferiority. Over-compensatory striving to demolish dependency, to assert autonomy, and to achieve superiority.

Need for affection: An integrative amalgam composed of a confluence of parts of the drives to look, to touch, and to listen.

Oedipus complex: (in Adler's theory) An only partly sexual rivalry felt by a son toward his father. Much of this rivalry has to do with overcoming a sense of inferiority and attaining a sense of power and superiority.

Organ inferiority: A damaged, diseased, or defective organ, usually accompanied by inferiority feelings.

Perfection striving: The desire to develop, to strive, and to achieve perfection.

Philosophy of "as if": According to the philosopher Hans Vaihinger, the idea that terms, concepts, hypotheses, goals, theories, laws, generalizations, etc., are fictional inventions.

Ruling-dominant type: A personality type composed of individuals who are assertive, aggressive, and active. They strive for personal superiority by trying to exploit or control others.

Safeguarding strategies: Adlerian defensive strategies to protect self-esteem from interpersonal threats. They come in three classes: *excuses* or *rationalization strategies, aggressive strategies*, and *distancing strategies.*

Self-accusation: Putting the blame for one's misfortunes on self, but doing it in such a way that it attracts attention, sympathy, concern, or help from others.

Social interest: Adler's preferred translation of *Gemeinschaftsgefuhl*; desire to contribute to the welfare of others and to society. It has a different meaning than sociability.

Socially useful type: Individuals who actively confront and solve problems in a pragmatic and thoughtful manner. Such people are socially oriented and prepared to cooperate with others.

Striving for superiority: Striving for autonomy and masculinity to compensate for a sense of inferiority. The fundamental urge to achieve a sense of competence and self-fulfillment.

Style of life: The consistent approach people have in coping with a variety of situations. This term, in Adler's theory, does not refer to consumer behavior.

Teleological: Goal-directed, purposeful; examining behavior in terms of its goals.

Chapter 5

Carl Gustav Jung

Analytical Psychology

It seemed to me that I was high up in space. Far below, I saw the globe of the earth, bathed in a gloriously blue light.

Carl G. Jung, *Memories, Dreams, Reflections*

[Whether He is] Called or not, God is present.

Translation of the Latin carving over the doorway of Jung's home at Kussnacht.

We need more understanding of human nature because the only real danger that exists is man himself.

Jung, *interviewed in 1959.*

Carl Gustav Jung   Born: 1875   Kessnil, Switzerland
                              Died: 1961   Kussnacht, Switzerland

---

About Jung's Analytical Psychology

Carl Gustav Jung was for a short time Freud's hand-chosen successor. But personal and intellectual differences eventually led to a break between Freud and Jung, with Jung subsequently developing his own theories and therapeutic approach. Much of Jung's picture of the human personality was derived from his affiliation with Freud, so the familiar concepts of unconscious motivation, neurotic defenses, and human conflict will also be found here. Jung's importance lies very much in the many ideas that differed markedly from Freud's. He labeled his approach **analytical psychology,** to distinguish it from Freud's psychoanalytic approach. Some basic concepts of analytical psychology are these:

- Jung agreed with Freud that energy dynamics were important to the psyche, but he thought the fundamental energy, or libido, was not specifically sexual in nature but, rather, a more general type of energy.

147

- The personal unconscious described by Freud overlays what Jung termed the "collective unconscious," which consists of universal images and inherited behavioral proclivities (instincts).
- All aspects of a person's psychological makeup, including all conscious and unconscious aspects, are part of a whole, the psyche.
- One's social role is an important but largely surface aspect of the psyche.
- The psyche is guided toward becoming a harmonious and integrative whole. Many crises and conflicts can be considered part of the teleological or purposive process of growth and development instead of merely as forms of pathology.
- Spiritual growth is central to personality development.
- Jung developed a typology of personality or temperaments to help understand and categorize differences in how people experience and approach life.

Much of Jung's thinking emerged from his personal experiences. Even though many clinicians would consider these experiences, which included visual and auditory hallucinations, to be pathological, Jung used them creatively and productively in developing his theories. Jung maintained an often tenuous hold on reality while exploring worlds of meaning emerging from what he termed the collective unconscious.

EXPERIMENTAL STUDY OF WORD ASSOCIATIONS

Jung and Freud exchanged a number of letters and published articles during their association. After a visit by Jung to Freud's home early in 1907, Freud began to consider Jung his successor. That visit involved an intense exchange of ideas between Jung and Freud. On April 7, Freud wrote to Jung, "that you have inspired me with confidence for the future, that I now realize that I am as replaceable as everyone else and that I could hope for no one better than yourself, as I have come to know you, to continue and complete my work" (Freud & Jung, 1974, p. 27). Part of Freud's enthusiasm for his younger colleague rested in part on Jung's published acknowledgment that Freud's ideas had been useful in his own clinical work. Jung had independently engaged in empirical studies that led to conclusions consistent with Freudian hypotheses and findings. Instead of using hypnosis and the concentration technique, Jung used the **word association test** in experimental situations to access unconscious meanings. (See Table 5.1.) Only later would Freud develop the clinically based method of free association to help unravel the hidden contents of the unconscious.

Jung's method involved word association experiments to demonstrate and explore unconscious mental processes. Researchers prior to Jung had used word association tests to explore associative thinking. Jung discovered that the word association method could also aid in uncovering the specific contents of an individual's psychological difficulties. This was done by recording and exploring content areas in an individual subject that produced hesitation, perseveration, or total inhibition of response. This application of the word association test was a precursor of using standardized stimuli in psychological testing to discover the makeup of specific individuals.

Jung became quite adept in the use of the word association test for discovering unconscious complexes. He quickly saw that his word association studies could offer empirical support for some of Freud's psychoanalytic concepts. Subject's inhibitions and long **reaction times** to Jung's list of stimulus words, along with their heightened physiological responsivity, could serve as quantitative evidence of latent ideas that could not be directly expressed but nonetheless produced demonstrable effects.

Table 5.1   Jung's List of Stimulus Words

1. head	26. blue	51. frog	76. to wash
2. green	27. lamp	52. to part	77. cow
3. water	28. to sin	53. hunger	78. friend
4. to sing	29. bread	54. white	79. happiness
5. death	30. rich	55. child	80. lie
6. long	31. tree	56. to pay attention	81. department
7. ship	32. to prick	57. pencil	82. narrow
8. to pay	33. pity	58. sad	83. brother
9. window	34. yellow	59. plum	84. to fear
10. friendly	35. mountain	60. to marry	85. stork
11. table	36. to die	61. house	86. false
12. to ask	37. salt	62. darling	87. anxiety
13. cold	38. new	63. glass	88. to kiss
14. stem	39. custom	64. to quarrel	89. bride
15. to dance	40. to pray	65. fur	90. pure
16. village	41. money	66. big	91. door
17. lake	42. stupid	67. carrot	92. to choose
18. sick	43. exercise book	68. to paint	93. hay
19. pride	44. to despise	69. part	94. contented
20. to cook	45. finger	70. old	95. ridicule
21. ink	46. dear	71. flower	96. to sleep
22. angry	47. bird	72. to beat	97. month
23. needle	48. to fall	73. box	98. nice
24. to swim	49. book	74. wild	99. woman
25. journey	50. unjust	75. family	100. to abuse

From Jung, 1909a, p. 440.

EMOTIONAL COMPLEX INDICATORS

Unlike prior researchers, Jung arranged the list of words used for association into a sequence that elicited maximum emotional reactions. In later experiments, Jung and his colleagues used additional procedures beside the simple stopwatch timing of the subject's reactions. Sometimes the subject's respiration rate was measured along with a recording of **galvanic skin response (GSR).** The GSR measures the skin's decrease in resistance to electrical current during sensory and emotional changes, a variable akin to one of the measures used in the modern "lie detector" or polygraph.

Usually, the stimulus word that triggered the subject's hesitation or inability to respond was connected symbolically with a deeply personal and threatening set of ideas or experiences. Jung's word association test was tapping the same phenomenon as Freud's method of free association—experiences that were threatening were found to resist conscious awareness. Such latent difficulties were often collections of various thoughts held together by common themes. Jung coined the term **complex** to describe such a grouping of hidden thoughts and defined the concept as a personally disturbing constellation of ideas connected together by an identifiable theme (Jung, 1913, p. 599). The individual caught up in a conflict over relations with his or her father would be said to have a "father complex"; the individual experiencing anxiety and frustration in sexual matters would be characterized as having a "sex complex."

Complexes are revealed in word association experiments through a number of diagnostic signs:

- Longer than average reaction time
- Repetition of the stimulus word by the subject
- Mishearing of the stimulus word as some other word
- Expressive bodily movements like laughing or twitching
- Reaction composed of more than one word
- Very superficial reaction to stimulus word, as in rhyming to the sound: e.g., to sin—subject responds with "to win"
- Meaningless reaction: made-up words
- Failure to respond at all
- Perseveration of response: continuing to respond to previous word even after new stimulus word is presented
- Major alteration of responses when list is administered for second time
- Slips of the tongue or stammering

In addition to these 11 unique patterns of response, Jung also discovered characteristic and stable differences between men and women and between more educated and less educated subject's responses. In Jung's laboratory, women characteristically took longer to respond to the stimulus words than their male counterparts at both educational levels. Jung also found that more educated people responded faster than less educated ones.

DISCOVERING A CASE OF CRIMINALLY NEGLIGENT HOMICIDE THROUGH THE WORD ASSOCIATION TEST

Jung developed a variation of the word association test even for criminal cases. He thought that it was sometimes possible to discover the guilt or innocence of an accused person by careful interrogation based on word lists that included critical words relating to key aspects of the crime (Jung, 1905, pp. 318 ff.). Jung and his associates also employed the word association tests for comparisons of unconscious complexes among members of a family and found striking similarities among different individuals. In this discovery of family complexes one can see the foreshadowing of the idea of family dynamics, and even the seed of family approaches to psychotherapy, which would come into its own only many decades later.

One of Jung's clinic patients, a 30-year-old woman, had a depression of psychotic proportions. She was also labeled as schizophrenic. Most of the hospital staff agreed that her prognosis was poor. Jung thought otherwise. To obtain more insight into her inner experience and complexes, he administered a form of the word association test.

Some of her responses are graphically indicated in Figure 5.1. Each of the words graphed has a reaction time that exceeds the average reaction time for an educated woman. The height of the bars indicates the relative differences in length of reaction time above the mean for educated women. Most outstanding of the woman's responses was her inability to offer any reply to the word "obstinate."

Jung proceeded by confronting the patient with the results of her word association test. He asked her to comment on the various stimulus words that had produced the longest reaction times. To "angel," the woman replied, "Of course, that is my child whom I have lost." She then displayed great emotional upheaval. To "obstinate," she

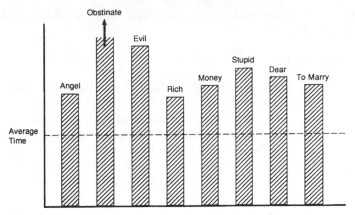

Figure 5.1 Relative reaction time for critical stimulus words.

responded, "It means nothing to me." To "evil," she again refused to comment. But to the word "blue" (not illustrated in the graph) she replied, "Those are the eyes of the child I have lost." Jung asked her why the child's eyes had so impressed her: "They were so wonderfully blue when the child was born." Jung noticed that this last reply was accompanied by much emotion. He again asked her why she was upset: "Well, she did not have the eyes of my husband."

A tragic story unfolded: The child's eyes had so upset her mother because they resembled the eyes of a former lover. In her hometown, the woman had fallen in love with a wealthy young aristocrat. Coming from a "common" background, the girl and her parents had concluded that an engagement and then marriage with the aristocrat was not feasible. At the insistence of her family, she married another young man. She was happy until the fifth year of the marriage. At that time, a friend from her hometown visited her and brought upsetting information: her present marriage had hurt and displeased the wealthy aristocrat she had once loved. For the first time she realized that he had also loved her. She realized that she could have fulfilled her dreams by marrying him. Her mind quickly repressed these hard-to-accept thoughts and associated feelings.

Two weeks later, she was bathing her two children, a small boy and the older, blue-eyed girl. She noticed the girl sucking on a bath sponge. The woman knew she should stop the child because the town's water supply was thought to be contaminated with typhus, and she had not boiled the bath water. She hesitated to take the sponge away from the girl's mouth. Shortly thereafter, the girl got typhoid fever and died.

The mother's act of letting the girl suck on the infected sponge, in Jung's view, was unconsciously motivated. The unconscious purpose was symbolically to deny her marriage through murder of the first child. Jung confronted her with the fact of what he considered to be her actual homicidal motivation. At first, she had no conscious inkling of what Jung considered to be the significance of what she had done. After working with Jung on the tragic story that had unfolded by exploring the meaning of her associations to critical stimulus words, she began to experience guilt and remorse. Within three weeks she was sufficiently recovered from her depression to be released from the hospital. Jung concluded,

> I traced her for fifteen years, and there was no relapse. That depression fitted her case
> psychologically; she was a murderess. . . . I practically saved her from the punishment of

insanity by putting an enormous burden on her conscience. For if one can accept one's sin, one can live with it. (Jung, 1968, p. 61)

JUNG'S CONCEPT OF LIBIDO

Initially, Jung and Freud agreed on what was to be found in the unconscious part of the mind: namely, repressed, unacceptable sexual and aggressive strivings and threatening experiences. As Jung continued his explorations of the unconscious, he found it increasingly difficult to accept Freud's insistence that sexual motives were the only basis of neurosis (Jung, 1961, Chapter 5). Early in their relationship, Jung questioned the central Freudian concept of libido as a general pleasure drive rooted exclusively in sexuality. Early in their relationship Jung wrote to Freud and inquired,

Is it not conceivable, in view of the limited conception of sexuality that prevails nowadays, that the sexual terminology should be reserved only for the most extreme forms of your "libido," and that a less offensive collective term should be established for all the libidinal manifestations? (Freud & Jung, 1974, p. 25)

For Jung, then, the fundamental psychic energy was still to be termed **libido,** but his conception of this primal force differed from the classical psychoanalytic view. For Jung, libido was a neutral and nonsexualized or general psychic energy (1912, p. 137). Libido is a form of energy, and, as in Freud's theory, may be channeled, suppressed, repressed, blocked, or expressed. In all cases, however, it is to be understood as a dynamic life force not purely as a sexualized energy. Jung's divergence from Freud's emphasis on the sexual nature of libido was one of the major issues leading to Jung's eventual decision to leave the Freudian fold.

THE PRINCIPLES OF EQUIVALENCE AND ENTROPY

Jung agreed with Freud that psychic energy obeys the **principle of equivalence.** It never ceases to exist, despite transformations in form. Repressed ideas embodying psychic energy simply find substitute expression in equivalent symbolic forms (Jung, 1948, p. 19; 1912, pp. 143–144). Unlike Freud, Jung did not regard these transformations as necessarily neurotic. Rather, Jung defined such modifications as potentially healthy channelings or "canalizations" of libido, that is, as transfers of psychic energy to mythic symbols.

Jung's principle of equivalence was based on the first law of thermodynamics—that energy is neither created nor destroyed but only transformed. According to this law, repressed libido is not destroyed but turns up elsewhere in the psyche. A good example is a student who represses sexual fantasies and redoubles efforts at community service. This represents not the destruction of energy but a shift of an equivalent amount of energy elsewhere in the psyche.

Jung also formulated a psychological principle based on the second law of thermodynamics, the law of **entropy,** which states that, in a physical system, energy will flow from the more energized matter to the less, eventually achieving a state of balance. The **principle of entropy** implies that psychic energy also flows from the most intensely energized ideas, archetypes, and complexes to those that are less energized. Ultimately, the mental system strives to an equalization of differences (1948, p. 26). Thus, for example, an individual who overemphasizes one way of approaching life will find, over the years, that other areas receive more energy. For example, a "macho" male may gradually get in touch with his more sensitive and artistic side; a compliant young woman may get in touch with her more assertive sense of self.

LEARNING FROM ANCIENT MYTHOLOGY

The Sun's Phallus

Jung had the following enigmatic encounter with a schizophrenic 30-year-old clerk in 1906. Staring out the window of the hospital corridor, the young patient beckoned Jung to his side. If you half shut your eyes, he told Jung, and stared at the sun, you could see the sun's phallus, or penis. If you then moved your head side to side, the sun's phallus would also move. The young man concluded his strange remarks to Jung with the matter-of-fact assertion that *the movement of the sun's phallus was the origin of the wind* (Jung, 1931, pp. 151–152; 1912, pp. 100, 157; and 1936, pp. 50–51).

Jung originally dismissed the episode as one more strange hallucination or fantasy characteristic of schizophrenia. Four years later, however, in 1910, while researching in the field of mythology, Jung came across a book that reproduced the rituals of the ancient Mithraic Greek religious cult. Professor Albrecht Dieterich, the author of the book, quoted one of the cult's visions:

> And likewise the so-called tube, the origin of the ministering wind. For you will see hanging down from the disc of the sun something that looks like a tube. And towards the regions westward it is as though there were an infinite east wind. But if the other wind should prevail towards the regions of the east, you will in like manner see the vision veering in that direction. (Quoted in Jung, 1931, pp. 150–151)

Jung was startled by the striking similarity between this ancient pre-Christian myth and the young schizophrenic clerk's hallucinatory vision. Jung reasoned that the clerk could not have read Dieterich's book since he had been institutionalized before its publication. Nor could Jung explain the similarity as a product of the young man's educational and cultural experience. He had, after all, only the equivalent of a secondary school education and had not engaged in foreign travel. Further mythological study convinced Jung that the notion of a sun phallus, or its equivalent, a divine phallus, was a common theme in many cultures of the past. Jung wondered how to account for the presence of this myth in the unconscious and conscious mind of a contemporary schizophrenic. The details of this particular case provided some clues for Jung in his later development of the concept of archetypes (Jung, 1959).

The Snake Dream

Another of Jung's patients, a young military officer, succumbed to a hysterical neurosis characterized by three symptoms. First, he suffered severe attacks of pain in the chest. Second, he experienced several episodes of choking "as if there were a lump in his throat." Finally, he was unable to walk normally because of stabbing pains in his left heel (Jung, 1931, p. 146).

In psychotherapy with Jung, the source of the first two symptoms was uncovered and followed the usual patterns of hysterical neurosis. The young man had been hurt and humiliated by a love affair that terminated when the girl became engaged to another man. He had denied his hurt and shattered self-esteem, but unconsciously he felt that "his heart was broken," and the idea that she had terminated the affair was "hard to swallow." Thus, as Freud had suggested, a painful experience had been converted into a painful and symbolic cluster of bodily symptoms. Though the pain in the throat and the choking attacks, along with the chest pains, were eliminated when these feelings were made conscious, the young soldier's third symptom, a stabbing pain in his left heel, remained intractable.

Jung turned to analyzing the man's dreams. The officer reported a dream in which he was bitten in the heel by a snake and instantly paralyzed. Analysis of the dream revealed the expected associations of the girl as a "snake" who had betrayed him; of a mother who had overprotected and thus "crippled" him; of a certain tendency to "girlishness" in himself for which he overcompensated by joining the military. But Jung thought that he detected something more fundamental, more primitive and universal in the man's dream. It was as though the Genesis saying: "And I will put enmity between thee and the woman, and between thy seed and her seed; it shall bruise thy head, and thou shalt bruise his heel . . ." had been transformed by the man's unconscious mind into a personal mythic symbol of his recent romantic upset.

Jung speculated that the soldier, who was not religious, must have had some scanty knowledge of the Bible dormant in his unconscious mind (1931, p. 147). The Bible story had provided just the right medium for conversion of a personal conflict into an opportunity to express a deeper sentiment in allegorical fashion (Jung, 1968, p. 116). The soldier's unconscious chose a universal myth to express his pain.

Consequently, Jung was convinced that a part of the unconscious mind, as exemplified by the sun's phallus fantasy, *transcends* the personal experiences of the individual. This unconscious subsystem, which he termed the collective unconscious embodies some of the past experiences of humanity in general. Moreover, that same transpersonal unconscious domain may *also* employ personal experience as a vehicle for mythological, allegorical expression of age-old themes, as exemplified by the soldier's snake dream. Jung wrote that, " . . . for the dream of the snake reveals a fragment of psychic activity that has nothing whatever to do with the dreamer as a modern individual . . ." (Jung, 1931, p. 148). Such a dream could not be a product solely of the soldier's personal experiences. Fantasies like the sun's phallus and the snake dream could have originated only in the individual's resonance with the cumulative experiences of humanity.

VISIONARY AND CREATIVE OR JUST CRAZY?

Jung's writings contain arrays of mythological themes found in the dreams, paintings, and fantasies of normal as well as abnormal personalities. But there was an even more fundamental source of Jung's conviction that a suprapersonal unconscious exists. In his autobiography, *Memories, Dreams, Reflections*, written just before his death in 1961, Jung provided his readers with a series of rare and penetrating glimpses into his inner life. The entire book is laden with gods, spirits, and fantasy figures that populated Jung's inner mental life. Jung reported that between 1913 and 1917 he was seized by a series of vivid dreams, visions, fantasies, and mystical experiences. Many of these would have met the formal characteristic of hallucinations, that is, "the apparent perception of sights, sounds, etc., that are not actually present."

Jung was also convinced that " . . . there are things in the psyche which I do not produce, but which produce themselves and have their own life" (1961, p. 183). One particular figure, whom Jung named Philemon, was striking in appearance:

> Suddenly there appeared from the right a winged being [Philemon] sailing across the sky. I saw that it was an old man with the horns of a bull. He held a bunch of four keys, one of which he clutched as if he were to open a lock. He had the wings of a kingfisher with its characteristic colors. (1961, pp. 182–183)

Jung did not interpret the dream but tried to impress it upon his memory or, one might say, "to honor its reality" by painting it. During the time he was painting that memory, he discovered in his garden a dead kingfisher bird. "I was thunderstruck, for kingfishers are quite rare in the vicinity of Zurich and I have never since found a dead one" (1961, p. 183).

Jung considered such an unusual coincidence to be meaningful and he eventually proposed the principle of **synchronicity** to refer to such an unusual thematic coincidence of apparently unrelated aspects of life. These are events occurring around the *same time* that are related through meaning but with no apparent physical cause-and-effect sequence. For example, one might dream of the death of a relative with whom little contact has been had in recent years. A day after the dream, word arrives announcing that relative's death. The two events, dream and the relative's death, are not related causally. The dream did not cause the relative's death any more than the future demise could have caused an anticipatory dream. Jung's explanation of synchronicity was that unconscious themes can penetrate many different aspects of an individual's experience: dreams, personal events, hunches, even snippets of conversation one might "accidentally" overhear. (1952).

What are the implications of Jung's ideas about synchronicity for our lives? If you accept his theory, synchronicities point to deeper meanings to which we should pay attention. An incidence of synchronicity is like a universal exclamation point that makes us attend to the meanings that are entering our experience. On the other hand, one might consider such events to be mere randomly determined coincidences, without any particular meaning. Jung's assumptions concerning his concept of synchronicity seem impossible to prove or disprove empirically. Whether one is attracted to the idea of synchronicity or not seems more a question of personal experiences than of scientific evidence.

For Jung, the significance of the Philemon figure also lay in the insight that such an apparition represented a reality beyond his personal experiences and even beyond the personal unconscious mind. During the fantasies he experienced hearing Philemon say things that Jung realized he himself had not consciously thought.

> ... I understood that there is something in me which can say things that I do not [consciously] know and do not intend, things which may even be directed against me. (1961, p. 183).

The Philemon fantasy occurred between the middle of December and early January 1913, shortly after Jung's bitter and unsettling break with Freud. Jung saw himself poised on the edge of a precipice. Visions and fantasies or, more clinically, visual and auditory hallucinations, had been bombarding his consciousness. Jung knew that he might be on the verge of being overwhelmed by the unconscious contents of his mind and he was determined to hang on to his sanity.

> It was most essential for me to have a normal life in the real world as a counterpoise to my strange inner world. ... My family and my profession remained the base to which I could always return, assuring me that I was actually an existing, ordinary person. The unconscious contents could have driven me out of my wits. (Jung, 1961, p. 189)

Opinion is divided over whether Jung's descent into his dreams and fantasies was voluntary, or whether it was an involuntary form of psychopathology. Interestingly, there is a long history of people who dealt creatively with the very ingredients that would make most people mad. There are examples of *creative illness* in the lives of Emily Dickinson, Vincent Van Gogh, Friedrich Nietzsche, and William Blake for example. Such individuals are antedated by the role of shamans in traditional tribal society. Shamans would enter into the worlds of dreams, fantasies, and visions and emerge not only intact but also with information important to society. In the West, the long tradition of saints, prophets, and healers goes back to Biblical times. The history of religion would not be the same without the influence of visionaries and their visions or other sources of inner knowledge.

The prophetic, shamanic role is one that Jung sometimes assumed for the modern world. Based on the dreams of his patients, he prophesized World War I. He foresaw the demise of Soviet Communism before many others and commented extensively on what he considered basic aberrations in the modern way of life. Shortly before his death in 1961, he expressed concerns about the possibility of a nuclear holocaust (Jung, 1959). The Cuban missile crisis occurred shortly thereafter.

Jung's Boyhood Experiences

From the evidence of his memoirs and from information provided by his biographers, two related and, at times, intertwined themes arose in Jung's experience before the age of 12. The first theme was Jung's belief that certain thoughts, dreams, visions, and fantasies he periodically experienced were truly important, externally derived revelations, secret wisdom that only a few, rare people were privileged to acquire. A second was his experience and growing conviction that he was actually two persons. It is worth noting that, in contrast to these themes, Jung characterized himself as leading a vigorous, "rugged" life in the country and being able to physically intimidate other kids who tried to bully him (Jung, 1959). He was a dreamer but was not ungrounded.

Sensing the Mystery of Being

As a boy, Jung often played by himself around a large chunk of stone jutting from a garden wall. Frequently, when alone, Jung would sit on this stone and pass the time in meditation and reverie. His experiences reflected more than just a theoretical question, but came from a state of awareness in which he was not identified with his embodied self:

> "I am sitting on top of this stone and it is underneath." But the stone also could say "I" and think: "I am lying here on this slope and he is sitting on top of me." The question then arose: "Am I the one who is sitting on the stone, or am I the stone on which he is sitting?" This question always perplexed me, and I would stand up, wondering who was what now. The answer remained totally unclear, and my uncertainty was accompanied by a feeling of curious and fascinating darkness. (Jung, 1961, p. 20)

Jung thought his apparent ability to shift his sense of his center of awareness to this chunk of stone was his first discovery of the "mysterious" in life. Opinion is divided on whether such experiences represented a pathological departure from ordinary reality or a higher level of awareness. Jung's own view was that a spiritual yearning for the unchanging and even for immortality lay behind this experience.

> . . . it was strangely reassuring and calming to sit on my stone. Somehow, it would free me of all my doubts. Whenever I thought that I was the stone, the conflict ceased. "The stone has no uncertainties, no urge to communicate, and is eternally the same for thousands of years," I would think, "while I am only a passing phenomenon which bursts into all kinds of emotions, like a flame that flares up quickly and then goes out." I was but the sum of my emotions, and the Other in me was the timeless, imperishable stone. (Jung, 1961, p. 42)

Jung's sense of a deep connection with what was mysterious and hidden to others made him less open to the formal religious doctrines he heard. When the very religious adults around him (his father was a minister and his mother a minister's daughter) tried to "pump" religious teachings into him, Jung would think: "Yes, but there is something else, something very secret that people don't know about" (1961, p. 22).

Jung as a Boy and as a Wise Old Man

As a school boy, Jung began to experience himself and be convinced that he was *both* the child he objectively seemed to be *and also* an authoritative wise old man who had lived in the eighteenth century. The precise imagery of Jung's other personality seems to have been connected with a piece of terra-cotta sculpture that depicted a well-known medical doctor of the day and his patient. So powerful was his sense of a past life that, as an eleven-year old doing his schoolwork, he would occasionally write "1786" instead of the correct date, 1886.

Jung's conviction that he himself consisted of two different individuals may have emerged originally during a scolding he received from a friend's father for some misbehavior related to the man's boat.

> ...I was seized with rage that this fat, ignorant boor [i.e., the friend's father] should dare to insult ME. This ME was not only grown up, but important, an authority, a person with office and dignity, an old man, an object of respect and awe. Yet the contrast with reality was so grotesque that in the midst of my fury I suddenly stopped myself, for the question rose to my lips: "Who in the world are you, anyway?"... Then, to my intense confusion, it occurred to me that I was actually two different persons. One of them was the schoolboy who could not grasp algebra and was far from sure of himself; the other was important, a high authority, a man not to be trifled with. ... This "other" was an old man who lived in the 18th century, wore buckled shoes and a white wig, and went driving in a fly with high, concave rear wheels. ... (Jung, 1961, p. 34)

One function of Jung's sense of himself as two persons thus appears to have been as a means of coping with feelings of vulnerability.

Jung's Experience of Opposites in His Parents

Jung reports that his father, a pastor of the Swiss Reformed Church, developed a morose personality due to a deep crisis of faith (1961, p. 73). Toward the end of his life, the Reverend Dr. Paul Jung became extremely concerned and even preoccupied with real or imagined health problems. Jung's father also had a more positive side. Jung described him as tolerant, approachable, and kind. His religious views as a pastor were traditional and not at all extreme (Jung, 1959).

Jung's mother, Emilie, was, on the surface, an opposite personality to his father. Some of Jung's childhood sorrow stemmed from his experience of frequent parental disputes. Jung was convinced that his mother also possessed or was possessed by two personalities: one, the observable character of the pleasant, plump housewife. The other personality was that of a witch, prophetess, and seeress who communicated with spirits. Jung described his mother in this way:

> By day she was a loving mother, but at night she seemed uncanny. Then she was like one of those seers who is at the same time a strange animal, like a priestess in a bear's cave. Archaic and ruthless; ruthless as truth and nature. (1961, p. 50)

The "uncanny" personality in his mother seems to have emerged only at special moments. "She would then speak as if talking to herself, but what she said was aimed at me and usually struck to the core of my being, so that I was stunned into silence" (1961, p. 49). Early on, Jung decided to keep his own inner life hidden from his mother

---

| BOX 5.1 | *Only Connect...* |

Jung's view of some dreams and visions as gifts to be experienced, re-experienced, artistically represented and cherished is far from Freud's idea of dreams as disguised transformations of taboo thoughts and feelings. Jung's approach emphasizes *dream appreciation* as distinguished from Freudian *dream interpretation*. Jung's view is very similar to that of traditional cultures, which viewed dreams as gifts from the spirits or gods. In such cultures, a dream or vision might be a sought-after and treasured experience with possible significance for the entire society. Alfred Adler (Chapter 4) had a more practical view of dreams as assisting the ego to take action.

---

because he was unsure just how much control the uncanny personality exerted over the housewife personality (cf. Atwood & Stolorow, 1977, p. 199).

Jung's experience of the opposites within his parents' personalities and the opposite qualities of each parent might be viewed as reflecting a fundamental way that his experience was structured. It is not clear that the qualities of his parents *caused* him to have such a view. Jung's way of endowing people with two or opposite personalities also appears to be involved in his pattern of coping. Whatever the cause or function, dualities such as the ones Jung experienced would become an important feature of the concept of archetypes that Jung was to formulate as a personality theorist.

Two Memorable Experiences as an Adult

Among his other accounts of dreams and visions, Jung reports a vivid dream vision or what some might term an "out-of-body-experience." In the dream, he experienced himself as many miles above the earth:

> Far below my feet lay Ceylon, and in the distance ahead of me the subcontinent of India. My field of vision did not include the whole earth, but its global shape was plainly distinguishable and its outline shone with a silvery gleam through that wonderful blue light. ...Later I discovered how high in space one would have to be to have so extensive a view—approximately a thousand miles! The sight of the earth from this height was the *most glorious thing I had ever seen*. (Jung, 1961, pp. 289–290, italics added)

It is worth noting that Jung had this experience *prior* to the famous photographs taken from space showing earth as a "blue marble."

In his memoirs, Jung reports that, when he was 69 years of age, he had a dream of seeing a yogi meditating. His dream led him to wonder whether he was dreaming the yogi or rather whether the yogi was dreaming Jung:

> When I looked at him more closely, I realized that he had my face. I stared in profound fright, and awakened with the thought: 'Aha, so he is the one who is meditating me. He has a dream, and I am it.' I knew that when he awakened, *I would no longer be*. ...In the opinion of the "other side," our unconscious existence is the real one and our conscious world a kind of illusion, an apparent reality. (Jung, 1972, p. 323, italics added)

Thus, throughout his life, Jung experienced both the irrational as well as the rational as partners in the events of the psyche. He ultimately learned to value the mysterious as much or more than the merely logical.

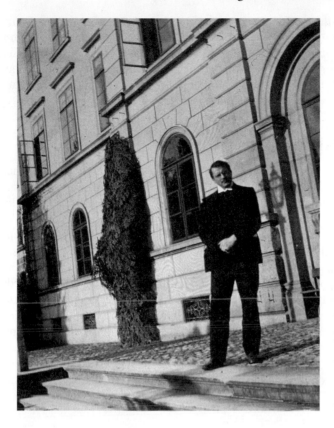

Figure 5.2 Jung in 1910. This photo was taken when Jung was in his mid-30s, around the time he conducted his word association experiments and about three years before his unsettling break-up with Freud.

JUNG AND FREUD: FROM ADMIRATION TO BITTERNESS

It is necessary, at least very briefly, to discuss the development of difficulties in the relationship between Jung and Freud. Jung drew much from Freud's concepts. In fact, after Freud's death, he wrote, "Without Freud's psychoanalysis, I wouldn't have had had a clue" (as quoted in McLynn, 1997). After a period of cooperation with Freud, however, Jung began to question Freud's ideas and further develop his own.

After an initial period of mutual admiration, there was growing and intense ambivalence between the two men. Meeting in 1909, Freud, for example, thought Jung harbored a death wish against him and fainted in Jung's presence (McLynn, 1997, p. 135). By 1913, the break with Freud and the Freudians had become permanent. As we have seen, this period also signaled Jung's development of the most distinctive aspects of his own theorizing and his own personal voyage into the depths of what he termed the "collective unconscious."

Finally, in the 1930s, after many years of bitterness between the two camps, Jung wrote anti-Freudian and apparently anti-Semitic statements. Though not an outright Nazi, many people saw Jung as, at the very least, morally neutral or opportunistically accommodating when it came to fascism. Jung understood that his approach to psychiatry, unlike Freud's and unlike Freud himself, was compatible with the anti-Semitic Nazi ideology. Jung's theory of archetypes allowed him to see many aspects of a vicious totalitarian system as simply the expression of long hidden archetypal themes, such as that of the mythical Teutonic personage Wotan (McLynn, 1997), Jung said Hitler was "just a hero myth" (Jung, in Evans, 1976, p. 86).

Jung and Freud thus ultimately came to see their theories as opposed and themselves as rivals. There was, to the end, no reconciliation between the two, even though Jung tried to donate funds to help Freud leave Vienna to flee from Nazi persecution. In spite of his decades-long competition with Freud, Jung thus attempted to aid him. In what must have been an upsetting interaction, Freud refused the money that Jung's cousin brought to his door (McLynn, 1997).

JUNG'S PHILOSOPHICAL BACKGROUND

Jung had a deep philosophical background. The philosopher who early influenced him was Arthur Schopenhauer, who highlighted the tragedies and ironies of human experience (*Memories, Dreams, Reflections*, p. 69). Many of the ideas of the philosopher Immanuel Kant had an impact on Jung's approach to personality theory. Freud on the other hand, had a strong background in biology, laboratory research and Darwinian evolutionary theory. This background contributed to his primarily scientific worldview. Some consequences of this difference were that Jung felt superior to Freud in his knowledge of philosophy and that Jung was not inclined toward a reductionistic or materialistic approach to understanding human experience. Their differences regarding such concepts as the libido, the collective unconscious, synchronicity and the purpose of life can be seen as rooted in their fundamentally different approaches to understanding reality. The fact that Jung and Freud had a falling out is not so surprising given these differences. What is more surprising is the fact that, early on, some of their ideas converged and they were a cooperative team, if only for a few years.

STRUCTURE OF THE PSYCHE: EGO, PERSONAL, AND COLLECTIVE UNCONSCIOUS

Partly based on his clinical observations with schizophrenic patients such as the young visionary clerk, along with his own self-analysis, Jung developed some additional differences with Freud in his understanding of personality. In Jung's view, a major problem that Freud had not solved was how to explain those fantasies and dreams that embodied symbols and themes unlikely to be part of an individual's strictly personal experiences. As has been noted, Jung began by formulating the existence of a *collective unconscious* in addition to Freud's ego and *personal unconscious* as part of the psyche. He also significantly modified Freud's ideas of the personal unconscious and its functions.

In Jung's theory, the **psyche** ["soul" in Greek] is the *sum total of all the conscious and unconscious contents of the mind*—including the conscious ego, thoughts and feelings, memories, surface and deeper emotions, the personal unconscious, the collective unconscious, and a multitude of archetypes including the most spiritual. The psyche is far more extensive than the individual's own individual experience and personality. Within the psyche, there is space for all the psychodynamics, transformations, and growth about which Jung theorizes.

The Conscious Ego

For Jung, the **conscious ego** corresponds roughly to what Freud meant by the same term. Functioning as the conscious part of personality, the ego includes all external sense impressions, thoughts, and awareness of feelings and bodily sensations. Consciousness consists of all those internal and external events that are within our awareness at a given moment.

The Personal Unconscious

Jung's second division of the mind, the **personal unconscious,** is largely similar and partly different from what Freud termed the *unconscious*. Jung conceived of the personal unconscious as the necessary surface aspect of the unconscious.

Jung agreed with Freud that the personal unconscious contains ideas and impulses that have been actively withdrawn from consciousness by repression. Such content is kept unconscious because it involves repressing motives, the awareness of which would be threatening to the ego (1931, p. 151). This part of Jung's personal unconscious corresponds in a general way to Freud's *dynamic unconscious*.

Jung also included mental content which, through disuse or inattention, does not at the moment occupy awareness, but which can become conscious at will. (Freud would have called such momentarily latent content *preconscious*.) Even out of awareness, however, all the activities that normally take place consciously also are recorded unconsciously (Jung, 1931, p. 144). Therefore, the personal unconscious also consists of all those contents that became unconscious simply because they lost their intensity and became seemingly forgotten memories.

Jung viewed the personal unconscious as having different functions from Freud's dynamic unconscious mind. For Jung, the personal unconscious has *both* retrospective and prospective aspects. It is oriented both by the individual's past and also by anticipations of the future. Jung noted that his patients often had dreams that could aptly be described as "forward looking" in the sense that, though the individual was not yet aware of his or her decision or feelings, a dream revealed that the unconscious had already solved some problem or made some decision (1916, p. 255).

The **prospection function** may aid the individual's adaptation to life. For example, an individual may be confronted with a seemingly insoluble problem. In the morning, a solution may pop suddenly into mind as if the problem had been continuously worked on while the individual was sleeping. Jung also thought that people could have accurate *precognitive* hunches about future events, sometimes based only on intuitive, inner knowing (Jung, 1961).

In addition, Jung's personal unconscious has a **compensatory function.** When an individual's conscious attitude leans too one-sidedly in a single direction, the unconscious may *compensate* for the imbalance by producing dreams or fantasies that emphasize the opposite tendency (Jung, 1916, pp. 252–253). For example, a person with a sedate existence may have dreams involving exciting adventures. Compensation may also be seen in dreams that make available to consciousness all that was subliminal or not attended to during the day.

The Collective Unconscious

At a deeper level than the personal unconscious lies the *impersonal* or *transpersonal* unconscious. This transpersonal domain is "detached from anything personal and is common to all men, since its contents can be found everywhere" (Jung, 1917, p. 66). Jung termed this layer of the unconscious the **collective unconscious.**

Stored within the recesses of the collective unconscious are the primordial images and ideas that have been common to human beings. These images represent

---

BOX 5.2 *Only Connect . . .*

Jung's concept of archetypes anticipated the concept in the neurosciences of mental modules and in evolutionary psychology (Chapter 17) that organisms, including humans, have inherited proclivities to behave in certain ways. These concepts are very similar to Jung's theories of archetypes and the collective unconscious. Very few personality theorists 30 years ago imagined that some of the more "far out" and least validated of Jung's notions would be reinforced by future scientific developments.

---

possibilities of action; *predispositions* to respond to external events in specific ways, and potentialities of shaping experience in certain directions. They are, in short, flexible templates, or models, for current experience to follow. Jung termed these important contents of the collective unconscious **archetypes** (Jung, 1936, pp. 66 ff.).

ARCHETYPES AND THEIR ORIGINS

Jung concluded that the contents of the collective conscious are inherited from the sum total of all human experience. He surmised that certain human experiences have been common throughout the ages. As an example, the rising and setting of the sun surely did not escape the notice of even the most primitive humans.

> One of the commonest and at the same time most impressive experiences is the apparent movement of the sun every day. We certainly cannot discover anything of the kind in the unconscious, so far as the known physical process is concerned. What we do find, on the other hand, is the myth of the sun-hero in all its countless variations. It is this myth, and not the actual physical process, that forms the sun archetype. The same can be said of the phases of the moon. The archetype is a kind of readiness to produce over and over again the same or similar mythical ideas. Hence it seems as though what is impressed upon the unconscious were exclusively the subjective fantasy-ideas aroused by the physical process. We may therefore assume that the archetypes are recurrent impressions made by subjective reactions. (Jung, 1917, p. 69)

Archetypes, in this view, are the cumulative effect of perpetually repeated experiences on the human nervous system's development. It is not the memory of the actual physical experience itself that Jung thought was inherited. Rather, he thought that the repetitive subjective reaction to the event is somehow impressed on unconscious mental processes. It is this internal state, this predisposition to react in a similar way to repetitions of the physical event, that is transmitted to future generations. Thus, Jung thought that the archetypes in the collective unconscious originated as residues of ancestral emotional life (Jung, 1917, p. 77).

Jung's concept of the development of the collective unconscious and its contents are closely related to the discredited Lamarckian theory of evolution, which asserted that acquired characteristics can be inherited. In Lamarck's view, parental experiences or at least the learning that accrued from them could be transmitted to offspring. As no mechanism for such an effect has been discovered, modern biologists do not accept the view that characteristics or experiences acquired in an organism's life are biologically or genetically passed on to offspring.

In recent decades, the pendulum has begun to swing in a direction more sympathetic to Jung's idea of archetypes, even though his Lamarckian notions of other origin are still discredited. Contemporary sociobiologists and evolutionary psychologists agree that people and other organisms have sometimes complex instincts; neuropsychologists and some cognitive psychologists refer to the inheritance of modules, which are part of the hardwiring of the brain. They view the underlying mechanism for the origin of such instincts and modules as the differential selection of variations in genetic makeup and neural wiring. This Darwinian explanation is consistent with contemporary biology (see Chapter 16).

Jung eventually devoted a significant part of his life to discovering and elucidating scores of specific archetypal images as they appeared in mythological stories, dreams, fantasies, and in paintings. The following are among the most frequently appearing and psychologically significant in analytical psychology.

The Mother Archetype

The Mother archetype may be elicited from an individual's collective unconscious in response to a real mother, mother-in-law, grandmother, or stepmother. Even figurative mothers may provoke the emergence of the Mother archetype as symbolized by a wife, Divine Mother (Virgin Mary), an institution, or any event, place, or person associated with fertility and fruitfulness. Most students react to their college or university (Alma Mater) in terms of this mother archetype. We refer to our "mother country" and "mother language." The Mother archetype can be positive or negative, light or dark, good or evil. For example, the goddess of fate (Moira) can be kind and generous, or remorseless and heartless. Evil-Mother archetype symbols abound: for example, the witch, the dragon or any devouring and entwining animal (Jung, 1938, p. 82). Thus the Mother archetype includes both the loving and the terrible mother.

The Trickster or Magician Archetype

Jung explored the figure of the Trickster or Magician through a variety of myths, most notably in Native American mythology. A characteristic of this mythical figure is his fondness for sly jokes, malicious pranks, and his dual nature: half animal, half human. This figure appears in various guises throughout mythology, folk tales, and literature.

The Hero Archetype

According to Jung, a clear expression of the symbol-making capacity of the collective unconscious is the figure of the Hero and its opposite, the demon (e.g., Anti-Christ, Satan). Hero myths are common to many cultures and tend to share the same characteristics. The Hero defeats evil, slays the dragon or monster, usually near water, suffers punishment for another, or rescues the vanquished and downtrodden (Jung, 1917, p. 99). To provide only one of scores of examples in popular culture, Luke Skywalker played the hero role in *Star Wars*. Totalitarian dictators are often experienced by their followers in terms of the hero archetype.

The Shadow Archetype

Within our personal unconscious there are repressed, unacceptable motives, tendencies, and desires. There is thus within us an inferior, undesirable aspect to our personality. Jung calls this side of our inner life the **shadow archetype,** the "dark half" of personality. It is the side of ourselves that we would prefer not to recognize. The Shadow is common to all people. It is both a personal and a collective unconscious phenomenon (Jung, 1968, pp. 21–22).

Mythologically, Shadow symbols include demons, devils, and evil ones. This archetype may be evoked in our relations with another when we feel terribly uncomfortable with a person but are unable to specify exactly what provokes the distress. We might sense, for example, an immediate dislike for some people we hardly even know. In such cases we may be projecting our shadow side onto them because we recognize in these persons something that we do not like in ourselves (Jung, 1917, p. 95). In the case of war, one side may project their shadows upon the enemy, who might be seen as cunning, treacherous, and sinister. People usually see their own side as clever, courageous, and righteous. In popular culture, the *Star Wars* character Darth Vader is a good example of the Shadow archetype; he contains unacceptable qualities of evil and cunning. Although Darth Vader starts out as Anakin Skywalker, Luke's father and former Jedi warrior and hero, he is tempted by power and gives in to his dark side.

It takes psychological insight and sometimes personal courage to deal with the Shadow archetype. If we fail to recognize the "inferior" dark side of ourselves, there is the possibility of separation of the Shadow from the conscious experience of the ego. In this case, our personality would be incomplete, truncated. Harmonious and balanced psychological development involves becoming aware of and accepting the existence of our shadow qualities. We may come to recognize that we are not entirely free of what we consider the bad or evil traits we see in others.

The Animus and Anima Archetypes

During the period when Jung was experimenting with the descent into his unconscious, he asked himself the question "What am I really doing?" Abruptly, a "voice" within said: "It is art." Jung was astonished and somewhat annoyed—astonished because the voice was a woman's, and annoyed because he did not agree with her assessment.

> Then I thought, "Perhaps my unconscious is forming a personality that is not me, but which is insisting on coming through to expression." I knew for a certainty that the voice had come from a woman. I recognized it as the voice of a patient, a talented psychopath who had a strong transference to me [i.e., an inappropriate but strong attachment to her therapist]. She had become a living figure within my mind. (Jung, 1961, p. 185)

Jung struck up a conversation with this new feminine personality, which rapidly turned into an argument over whether Jung's exploration of his unconscious was science, art, or something else. The conflict was resolved when Jung insisted to his inner feminine personality that what he was doing was neither science nor art; it was nature. He now encouraged her to speak through himself and felt both awed and perturbed:

> I was greatly intrigued by the fact that a woman should interfere with me from within. My conclusion was that she must be the "soul," in the primitive sense, and I began to speculate on the reasons why the name "anima" was given to the soul. Later I came to see that this inner feminine figure plays a typical, or archetypal, role in the unconscious of a man, and I called her the "anima." The corresponding figure in the unconscious of woman I called the "animus." (Jung, 1961, p. 186)

It was only a short step from this experience for Jung to propose the existence of universal, gender-based opposites: Accordingly, no man could be entirely masculine or exclusively male. Feminine elements, attitudes, and intuitions are part of every man's character. This is not often apparent because, traditionally, men strive to repress their weak, soft, feminine traits.

The projected image of femininity from a man's collective *unconscious* is his **anima**—as is a woman's *conscious* experience of what are considered feminine qualities. The anima determines a man's relationship to women throughout his life and shapes his understanding of those relationships. In a sense, a man's first repressed and then projected anima compensates for the otherwise one-sided masculine nature of his personality. Likewise, the woman has her inherited masculine image, her **animus,** which is also the conscious sense of masculine qualities in a male. Jung suggested that the opinions of the animus in both men and women have the character of solid unassailable convictions. The moods of the anima are often expressed in sudden changes in temperament, or character.

A danger of the anima and the animus archetypes lies in the possibility that the entire psyche may come under the exclusive sway of either one of these images (Jung, 1917, p. 209). Without recognition of their inherent opposites, all humans regardless of gender are incomplete.

One can question the degree to which Jung's formulation of the animus and anima archetypes reflected the role of men and women in Western society in the nineteenth and early part of the twentieth century. In a society with a greater opportunity for women to be more autonomous and independent, Jung's model seems to express mostly traditional gender roles. It is possible to disengage the meanings of anima and animus from the specifics of gender and refer to them as more general psychological characteristics, which may be conscious to one extent or another in both men and women.

The Persona Archetype

Persona is Latin for the mask that actors in Roman and Greek drama wore to depict their roles (see Chapter 1). Thus the **persona** in Jung's theory is the front we present to others because social living makes demands for certain kinds of behavior. Society establishes certain expectations and certain roles around which we must shape our public selves, and behind which we hide our "private" selves (Jung, 1917, p. 192).

There are *individual differences* in the role or roles the individual will role-play, but the existence of the persona archetype itself is universal and impersonal. The persona is an ideal image, a desirable actor's part, a compromise between the individual and humanity as a whole, past and present, as to what a person should appear to be (Jung, 1917, p. 158). The specifics are filled out by the individual himself or herself.

To understand the importance of the persona in the psyche, all one has to do is think of all the energy and thought each of us puts into honing the image that we present to the world and how much we depend on others presenting us with their personas. When we meet someone for the first time, we are very uncomfortable unless we have clues as to their identity, who and what they are. A person who has not formed a clear persona image can be seen as drifting, distant or even threatening. Someone too attached to some aspects of the persona may view everything he or she experiences too narrowly in terms of a specific social role. As is the case with other archetypes, there is potential danger when the persona "takes over" the psyche.

Other Archetypes

Jung discovered a whole array of archetypes in his work with clients, his personal introspective work, and his study of mythic and religious symbols and themes. Just for starters, there are the Eternal Child (a youthful and creative Peter Pan-like archetype), the Wise Old Man, the Trickster, Wotan, and the Hero archetypes. A sensual Bacchus-like figure is another archetype, as are a Venus- or Aphrodite-like archetype. One clue to archetypal identities is the panoply of ancient or tribal gods and goddesses, each representing a different aspect of the psyche.

ARCHETYPES, POPULAR CULTURE, AND SOCIETY

Another way of uncovering archetypes is to examine the themes behind the most popular and energized figures of contemporary popular culture, our current "tribal gods and goddesses." People like Elvis Presley, Marilyn Monroe, John F. Kennedy, and Princess Diana have elicited projections of archetypal themes by the public. Jungian archetypal themes are evident in characters such as Harry Potter, Luke Skywalker, Darth Vader, The Phantom of the Opera, Peter Pan, and an almost endless array of others.

Jung thought that groups of people, even whole civilizations, might project the meanings of a given archetype at a specific point in history. The course of that civilization may then move in the direction of the archetypal theme that emerges. For example, a satanic or demonic archetype may have made its appearance during the years of the rise to power of the Nazis. The reverse may, of course, also occur. A return to religious commitment or faith may be preceded by an emergence of the God archetype. This might have been the case, for example, during the Second Great Awakening in American history, a religious revival in the early 1800s that transformed American society and led to the woman's suffrage and abolitionist movements.

JUNGIAN ATTITUDE TYPES: FREUD THE EXTROVERT AND ADLER THE INTROVERT

Jung began to see the differences between the views of Freud, Adler, and himself as an interesting and important problem to be solved. He eventually began to see that not only were Freud and Adler different in intellectual skills and theoretical viewpoint, but also, more important, each had a distinctly different type of personality. What emerged from this effort to understand the differences between theories was first an understanding of the personality theorists themselves and finally, Jung indicated, to his theory of psychological types (Jung, 1921).

For Freud, according to Jung, the key element is the individual's conscious and unconscious relationship to people and things in the external world (1917, p. 41). For Adler, as interpreted by Jung, the focus is more subjective with the accent on the individual's striving for inner security and compensation for perceived personal inferiority.

Adler, it seemed to Jung, was an *introvert* whereas Freud appeared to be more of an *extrovert*. Jung described **introversion,** which he considered the first attitude and **extroversion,** which he termed "the second attitude."

> The first attitude [introversion] is normally characterized by a hesitant, reflective, retiring nature that keeps itself to itself, shrinks from objects, is always slightly on the defensive and prefers to hide behind mistrustful scrutiny. The second [extroversion] is normally characterized by an outgoing, candid, and accommodating nature that adapts easily to a given situation, quickly forms attachments, and, setting aside any possible misgivings, will often venture forth with careless confidence into unknown situations. (Jung, 1917, p. 44)

Thus Freud and Adler were bound by their own personality type to see only one viable interpretation of the psychology of others.

Jung also proposed that the differences between introverts and extroverts in relation to subjective and objective experience were not absolute. Jung did not think that a persona could be 100 percent one type or the other. He saw the degree of introversion and extroversion to be changeable. At times, some introverts will become more interested in the objective, external world, when that world affects their inner lives.

Conversely, extroverts can become more interested in the subjective world when the objective world has caused them disappointment.

In addition to the attitude types of introversion/extroversion, Jung proposed the existence of four functional personality types: (1) sensation; (2) thinking; (3) feeling; (4) intuition.

THE FUNCTIONS OF THE PSYCHE

Jung gave the name *ectopsychic* to those functions of consciousness directed outwardly to the world and *endopsychic* to the functions of the unconscious in its relations with the ego (1968, p. 11). We omit a discussion of endopsychic functions here because they were not emphasized in Jung's theory.

Ectopsychic Functions

The **ectopsychic functions** were those that Jung emphasized in constructing his introversion/extroversion typology. They are four in number. The *first ectopsychic function is sensation*, "which is the sum total of external facts given to me through the functions of my senses" (Jung, 1968, p. 11). Thus sensation is concerned with orientation to reality: "Sensation tells me that something is; it does not tell me *what* it is" (Jung, 1968, p. 11; 1921, p. 461, definition 47).

The *second ectopsychic function is thinking* and is complementary to sensation, for thinking "in its simplest form tells you what a thing is. It gives a name to the thing" (Jung, 1968, p. 11; 1921, p. 481, definition 53). For Jung, the term thinking was to be restricted to "the linking up of ideas by means of a concept, in other words, to an act of judgment, no matter whether this act is intentional or not" (1921, p. 481).

The *third ectopsychic function is feeling*. For Jung, the concept of feeling had a somewhat restricted meaning. "Feeling informs you through its feeling-tones of the values of things. Feeling tells you, for instance, whether a thing is acceptable or agreeable or not. It tells you what a thing is worth to you" (1968, p. 12). Feeling may give rise in isolated circumstances to mood, an emotional state of acceptance or rejection. Thus feeling is a subjective process that is independent of external stimuli (Jung, 1921, p. 434, definition 21).

The *fourth and last ectopsychic function is intuition or inner knowing*. Intuition is composed of hunches about the origins and the prospects of a thing (Jung, 1968, p. 13). Jung pointed to the conditions, familiar to almost everyone, under which we use intuition: "Whenever you have to deal with strange conditions where you have no established values or established concepts, you will depend upon that faculty of intuition" (1968, p. 14). Intuition is therefore the psychological function that mediates perceptions in an unconscious way so that our experience of intuitive problem solutions is that they spring on us suddenly, without conscious intent (Jung, 1921, p. 453, definition 35).

Rational Versus Irrational Functions

The four ectopsychic functions can be further classified as either **rational** or **irrational functions** depending on how much reasoning or judging is involved. Hence, **sensation** and **intuition** are classified as irrational because conscious reasoning is, by Jung's definitions, virtually absent in these functions. By contrast, **thinking** and

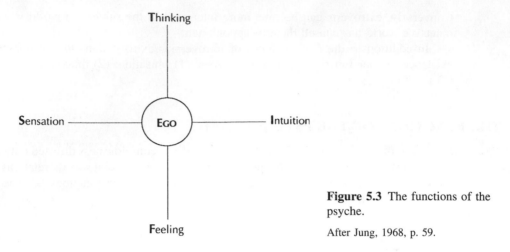

Figure 5.3 The functions of the psyche.

After Jung, 1968, p. 59.

feeling are classified as rational functions because both involve the judgmental process and the "supremacy of reason" (Jung, 1921, pp. 359ff.; 1968, p. 12). Feeling is therefore considered a rational function in this typology, at variance with the commonly held conception that feelings are often irrational. Each of these four functional types may dominate the basic introvert or extrovert attitude orientation. The four ectopsychic functions and their relationships in the psyche are summarized in Figure 5.3. The combined attitude and function typology devised by Jung is shown in Figure 5.4.

THE EXTROVERT TYPES

The extrovert is focused on external objects instead of subjective experience. Extroverts are strongly influenced by their social surroundings, and their beliefs are therefore shaped by the opinions and values of those close to them. The extreme extrovert can be overly focused on objects and might completely lose the sense of an autonomous self in them (Jung, 1921, p. 336). Thus, in Jung's view, the most typical neurosis of the extrovert is hysteria, as hysterical reactions are essentially attention-getting, dependent

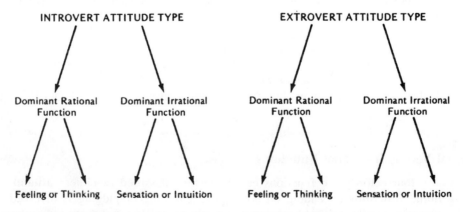

Figure 5.4 The Jungian combined attitude and function typology.

attitudes toward people and things in the environment. Influenced by Jung's theory of extroversion and introversion, the psychologist Hans Eysenck (see Chapter 16) has marshaled a good bit of confirmatory empirical evidence.

Extrovert Thinking Type (Rational)

Thinking extroverts are also "captured" by external ideas and objects; they are unable to escape their influence in solving problems. They may give the impression of a certain shortsightedness or lack of freedom in the drawing of logical conclusions because they refuse to go beyond the objective facts at hand.

Thinking extroverts subjugate everything to the intellect, refusing to see any other principle for themselves or others to follow than the power of their own decision making. Their moral code is correspondingly rigid and intolerant of exception. Their struggle is for objective and valid universal truths (Jung, 1921, p. 347). "Oughts" and "musts" dominate the thinking extroverts' approach to values, and their thinking tends to be dogmatic.

Since thinking is their superior function, the feeling side of their lives is suppressed. Key concise trait descriptions are that they are *objective*, *rigid*, and *cold*.

Extrovert Feeling Type (Rational)

According to Jung, dominance by the feeling function is most characteristic of women (Jung, 1921, p. 356). Like thinking extroverts, *feeling extroverts* seek harmony with the external world. Their thinking function is hidden behind a facade of loud gushing talk and intense displays of extravagant emotionality. They have a tendency to make friends easily and to be influenced by the feeling-tone of social situations. They are often described as *intense, effervescent*, and *sociable*.

Extrovert Sensation Type (Irrational)

Sensation extroverts search for new sensory experiences (1921, p. 363). They may refine their sensory powers to a high pitch so that they are not merely gross sensual types, but rather connoisseurs of fine wines and discriminating judges of art. Sensation extroverts are usually good company, for they suppress any tendency to introspection and self-concern, favoring instead minute attention to objective, external detail. They tend to be well adjusted to reality and concerned for the welfare of others. Key trait descriptions are *realistic*, *sensual*, and *jolly*.

Extrovert Intuitive Type (Irrational)

Intuitive extroverts have difficulty maintaining interest in any one thing for very long. Usually, this type of person flits from one new idea to another and stays with each only until the novelty wears off. This individual tends to make decisions without much conscious, reflective thought. Yet such persons' decisions are likely to be good ones because intuitive extroverts can use their intuition to access the wisdom of their own unconscious. Their consideration for the welfare of others is weakly developed. However, intuitive extroverts are valuable to society because they have the capacity to inspire confidence and enthusiasm for new causes and undertakings. Key trait terms describing the intuitive extrovert are *visionary, changeable*, and *creative*.

Jung's typological theory has led to the development of popular approaches to testing and consulting. Web sites based on the dimensions Jung outlined have proliferated, and one can find a number of well-researched tests of Jungian types. Foremost among these are the Myers-Briggs test and the Keirsey temperament survey. One can also find descriptions of the major Jungian types using a four letter code, **I**(ntroversion) or **E**(xtroversion), (i)**N**(tuition) or Sensation, **T**(hinking) or **F**(eeling and **J**udging) or **P**(erceiving). Jung described himself as an Introverted, iNtuitive, Thinking, and Perceiving type of personality. Descriptions of this type of

personality can be found by entering the letters INTP and the word "type" in an Internet search engine. It is possible to explore your understanding of your own personality and those of people you know with these descriptions.

When applying this approach to personality, it is important to realize that these typologies represent oversimplified versions of Jung's thinking. Jung insisted that there were no pure types, for example, no pure introverts or pure extroverts. According to Jung, a person's type is not fixed but often changes in the course of life history, through maturation and different experiences. (Jung, 1959)

THE INTROVERT TYPES

The introvert attitude, you may recall, implies that, even though such individuals are aware of external conditions, they are focused on their subjective reactions. The introvert focuses inward to understand the significance of external events. Jung saw himself as an introvert and indicated that it was difficult to be an introvert in modern society, which he viewed as largely extroverted (Jung, 1959).

Introvert Thinking Type (Rational)

Concerned with abstractions and with the creation of theories, the *thinking introvert* has a tendency to ignore the practicalities of everyday living. "His judgment appears cold, inflexible, arbitrary, and ruthless, because it relates far less to the [external] object than to the subject [himself]" (Jung, 1921, p. 384).

The thinking introvert develops an intense desire for privacy. Some key terms to describe the introverted thinking type are therefore *intellectual, impractical*, and *private*.

Introvert Feeling Type (Rational)

The extreme *feeling introvert* seems to have no concern for the feelings or opinions of others. There is an air of superiority and critical neutrality in the feeling introvert's relationships. Emotional expression is kept to a minimum, for the feeling introvert's emotions are intense and troublesome. Key trait descriptions are *silent* and *indifferent*.

Introvert Sensation Type (Irrational)

The *sensation introvert* type is focused on the changing flux of external events. Their subjective reactions are of paramount importance, for the only thing that matters to the sensation type of introvert is their personal reaction to objective sensory events. Such individuals' thinking and feeling functions are not developed. They evaluate their sense impressions in terms of clear-cut categories of good and evil—only in terms of what seems good and evil for them. They sometimes are distant from the outer world and misinterpret reality. They remain calmly undisturbed under most circumstances. They are often described as *passive, calm*, and *artistic*.

Introvert Intuitive Type (Irrational)

The *introvert intuitive* type of person tends to be aloof and unconcerned about concrete reality or external events. They present the stereotypical picture of the "peculiar artist" or the slightly "mad genius" whose productive efforts result in beautiful but strange creations. Inaccurate perception is the main problem for intuitive introverts. They often interpret their perceptions in ways that will satisfy the inner self. Thus they may become estranged from those around them and be viewed as a "wise person gone wrong" or as a "crank and oddball." Key descriptive traits are *mystic, dreamer*, and *unique*. Incidentally, Jung saw himself as an introvert intuitive type (Jung, 1959).

THE PROCESS OF INDIVIDUATION

Jung also spent a good deal of the latter part of his life exploring the processes by which a person becomes a complete individual. He also investigated the process of individual psychological **differentiation,** by which each person develops their own pattern of traits as well as an idiosyncratic relationship with their personal unconscious and the collective unconscious. He called the process of harmonizing the unconscious with the conscious ego and accessing the meaning of the variety of the components of the psyche, **individuation** (1939, p. 287). Some key concepts related to the process of individuation are the transcendent function, active imagination, and enantiodromia—the *play of opposites*.

The Transcendent Function

Jung thought that each psyche has an innate tendency, the **transcendent function,** to pursue inner harmony. The transcendent function is the motive force for the individual to come to terms with all aspects of the self. It guides the need to accept the content of the unconscious as "mine" (Jung, 1916, p. 73). Individuation and the transcendent function work together. Individuation refers to the attainment of full development of all sides of oneself into a unique whole. The transcendent function is the guiding force behind this process.

Active Imagination

Jung's method of helping his patients to attain individuation involved the process of **active imagination.** Jung instructed his patients in the art of consciously focusing on dream images or on fantasy figures. Active imagination might best be considered a form of visualization or meditation for the purpose of attaining self-knowledge. Through the process of active imagination, Jung's patients could examine many formerly hidden aspects of their psyches.

Enantiodromia: The Play of Opposites

Within every personality, Jung discerned many usually conflicting, discordant, and antagonistic opposites. Thus, for the anima, there is the animus; for the good mother archetype, there is the evil opposite; for introversion, there is extroversion; for thinking, sensation; for sensation, feeling; and the Shadow is opposite to the persona archetype. Sometimes, Jung approached opposites as complementary aspects of reality. For example, causal explanations of dreams could be balanced by synchronistic or precognitive explanations. In other words, dreams can be analyzed not only in terms of the past, but also in terms of the future.

Jung derived the term **enantiodromia** from Heraclitus, a fifth-century B.C. Greek philosopher, to label the *play of opposites* in human experience. Enantiodomia literally means "running counter to" (1921, p. 425, definition 18). Initially, Jung restricted the term to mean only the emergence of an unconscious function or idea that was opposite to a conscious dominant function. Eventually, however, Jung began to see the development of personality as a goal-directed or **teleological** enterprise, marked by a striving toward the equal development of all parts of the psyche. Thus, opposites must surface and coalesce in the psyche. Each of us should not only develop the function of rationality, but also should accept our irrationality. We should not only be aware of qualities we have that we think are ideal but also recognize the shadow characteristic in ourselves. Successful individuation means the acceptance of inherent opposites. Individuation is such an involved process that it necessarily can come to fruition only in one's mature years.

DEVELOPMENT OF THE SELF: A TELEOLOGICAL VIEW OF LIFE

Throughout life, the psyche's development is focused on the attainment of the reconciliation of opposites. For Jung, individual psychological development does not proceed haphazardly. It is purposive or teleological. Within the fully differentiated, individuated psyche, a final psychological organization develops that embodies all the discordant elements, slighting none, emphasizing all equally. Jung defined the **self** as the archetype representing a psyche which has become such a balanced and harmonious whole. Because the self is a totality, it must embody both light and dark, good and evil. Fully individuated persons can freely accept both aspects of their psyches and can willingly strive to unite the two into wholeness. For Jung, the goal of psychotherapy, indeed, the goal of the well-lived life, is the attainment of wholeness, balance, and harmony.

Jung asserted that the representation of Christ in the Bible is a quintessential symbol of the self.:

> As an historical personage Christ is unitemporal [once in time] and unique; as God,
> universal and eternal. Likewise the self: as the essence of individuality it is unitemporal and
> unique; as an archetypal symbol it is a God-image and therefore universal and eternal (Jung,
> 1950b, p. 63).

Even this divinely archetypal figure of the self is a composite of opposites: Christ and Anti-Christ, God and Satan, the Prince of Light and the Prince of Darkness (1950b, p. 44). Thus the self, that totality of opposites, that unique combination of perfection and baseness, was prefigured in humanity's mythology and religion by symbols of the God-man.

Jung regarded the need for religion, for God, as an inherent motive directed toward self-fulfillment. He thought that people expressed an inherent need for wholeness by their belief in an omnipresent, omniscient, and omnipotent reality. Without God or a symbolic equivalent of God to which to aspire (such as an ideal or even a political figure who is seen as godlike), people are forever condemned to the incompleteness of their own existence. This aspect of Jung's theory reveals one of the most important functions of Jungian psychology in the modern world—to preserve a sense of the spiritual outside of the traditional formulations and institutions of religion. One might term his approach "spiritual" but not "religious."

One major impact of Jung's emphasis on spirituality on contemporary society was his influence on the founding of Alcoholics Anonymous (AA). With its many offshoots, this organization has profoundly affected the lives of millions of alcoholics and other addicted individuals throughout the world. In the early 1930s, Jung had a conversation with a former patient—"Rowland H"—who was also an alcoholic. Jung stated that conventional medical treatment would not help him but that he could overcome his alcoholism if he had a spiritual conversion. This patient did follow through with the suggestion and his example, through a variety of contacts, led to the founding of Alcoholics Anonymous. (Jung, 1961/1987, pp. 19–21)

In a letter to AA's founder in 1961, Jung alluded to his assessment of Roland H's alcoholism:

> His craving for alcohol was the equivalent, on a low level, of the spiritual thirst of our being for wholeness, expressed in medieval language as the union with God. . . . You see, "alcohol" in Latin is *spiritus* and you use the same word [spiritual or spirits] for the highest religious experience as well as for the most depraving poison. The helpful formula therefore is: *spiritus contra spiritum* [the spirit against spirits]. (1961/1987, p.21)

Expressions of the Self's Harmonies: Mandalas Paintings

Jung found in his explorations of mythology and alchemy that the self archetype, or harmonious personality, was often symbolized by a **mandala.** *Mandala* is a Sanskrit word meaning "circle." Jung observed a variety of figures resembling mandala in various mythologies, religious rituals, and in the dreams and fantasies of his patients. Sometimes the mandala is divided into four segments, around which is drawn the characteristic circular enclosure. Jung himself was energized at times to paint mandalas to express understanding of his psyche.

Jung's own mandala paintings show his efforts at psychological healing and growth. His paintings demonstrate his strivings to mold unity and order within himself, Two of Jung's own mandala paintings are reproduced in Figures 5.5 and Figure 5.6. In

Figure 5.5 Four archetypes of the self, painted by Jung.

Source: Jung, 1950a.

Figure 5.6 Window on eternity, painted by Jung.

Source: Jung, 1950a.

Figure 5.5 the representation of interlocking circles, with human figures in the four most peripheral circles, was intended by Jung to illustrate four complementary aspects of the self. To the right and left of center are two female figures, with the left woman representing the "dark" side of the anima and the right one symbolizing the nurturing aspect. The top and bottom peripheral circles contain the Wise Old Man archetype and the Trickster archetype, respectively. The sixteen "globes" surrounding the center star are symbolic "eyes," and stand for "observing and discriminating consciousness" (Jung, 1950a, p. 374).

The "Window on Eternity" as shown in Figure 5.6 is at once the final and the most harmonious of Jung's mandalas. It is a refined and symmetrical expression of spiritual unfolding. In the delicately balanced harmonies of this mandala, Jung discerned a mythic expression of the self as the reconciler of opposites. The precise juxtaposition of colors and shadings and the fourfold spatial division of the circle symbolize the psyche's ultimate goal of harmony.

EVALUATING CARL JUNG

Jung's work has had a continuing influence on psychotherapeutic practice and in the humanities and creative arts, possibly even more than in the field of psychology. There are numerous Jungian institutes throughout the world. Many scholarly investigations are animated by Jungian theory. Expressive artists and writers find inspiration in Jungian archetypal explorations. Jung's work, with its emphasis on instincts, anticipated the work of evolutionary psychologists. He was also far ahead of his time in emphasizing cross-cultural approaches to personality.

Jung's reputation has been tainted among those who are convinced that he either unwittingly or deliberately contributed to Nazi anti-Semitism. How relevant this factor is for evaluating his work and his theories is a very difficult question. One conclusion is that his theories, in their acceptance of all facets of human behavior—both good and evil—provide neither a complete nor a satisfactory moral, ethical compass.

Refutability

Jung's contributions include both empirical and non-empirically based ideas. Jung's early work with the word association test was certainly empirical, and though the standards of evidence have grown more stringent than they were in Jung's day, his basic research technique would qualify as a refutable way to test his hypothesis of psychological complexes.

Jung's conception of personality types, especially the fundamental dimension of introversion-extroversion, is eminently testable. Eysenck's work (e.g., 1967; Eysenck & Eysenck, 1985), which we review in Chapter 16, has certainly established the basic dimension and its correlates in the laboratory. However, beyond only the most elementary trait descriptions, Eysenck's concepts of introversion and extroversion differ from those of Jung. Nevertheless, taking Jung's ideas about this dimension, there is at least one paper-and-pencil personality test devoted to measuring the Jungian personality types and their attitudinal correlates (Myers, 1972). Moreover, the descriptions that Jung gave of the types, subtypes, and attitudinal variations lend themselves to a variety of empirical tests using already available psychological instruments.

What of Jung's most original and central ideas? The *collective unconscious* and *synchronicity*, to name two, are not stated in empirically testable forms. By definition, synchronicity is an acausal concept, and we have to admit that it would be extremely challenging (if not impossible) to come up with an empirical test of this concept.

Interestingly, one of Jung's most elusive concepts, *archetypes*, has recently re-emerged in a different guise in the form of cognitive modules, or inherited predispositions to process information and experience in pre-programmed ways. Consideration of this type of hardwiring is becoming a more important part of contemporary neuroscience and evolutionary psychology (see Chapter 16).

Jung's Conception of Human Agency

Jung's work anticipated much of the later ideas of humanistic and existential theorists such as Abraham Maslow, Carl Rogers and Rollo May (Chapters 12 and 13), in their emphasis on the person's active creation of meaning. The ideas of Jung's later years focus on the self, on actualizing the self, and on a holistic conception of personality that is quite consistent with humanistic psychology in flavor and conception. Jung believed, apparently, in determinism, the determinism of our primordial ancestry and our personal history. However, he emphasized that the person's responsibility lies in an active synthesis of the discrete parts of his or her life into a harmonious whole. This synthesis is an activity, not merely of the persona, but of the whole psyche, guided in the process of individuation by the archetype of the self.

Jung's emphasis on the spiritual side of life, his concern with teleology or goal-oriented behavior, and his willingness to see the determinants of behavior in a person's remote past, personal past, and future strivings certainly argue for a complex, largely active conception of human agency.

Jung's Combined Idiographic and Nomothetic Emphases

Jung envisioned his theory as providing a nomothetic basis for understanding behavior by transcending the individual, by going beyond the immediate past, and by allowing for the influence of the future. In a way, his concepts of the collective unconscious and synchronicity are the clearest examples of a nomothetic or universal focus in personality theory. Concepts such as enantiodromia, the various archetypes, the collective unconscious, the principles of entropy, equivalence, and opposites are also nomothetic or generally applicable. As we have indicated here, they are very difficult if not impossible to test.

On the other side of the coin, Jung clearly proposed idiographic concepts that have fared better in empirical research. His word association procedure is an idiographic one by definition. His psychoanalytic-like analysis of dreams and symptoms is, like its psychoanalytic cousin, highly individualized. And Jung's conception of the self as the psychological structure that harmonizes the conflicting pulls of an individual life proceeding toward self-actualization is largely idiographic.

SUMMARY

Beginning his career in the tradition of classical clinical psychiatry, Carl Gustav Jung soon developed a tool of investigation that brought his thinking close to that of Sigmund Freud. The word association test, in Jung's innovative hands, revealed that normal and neurotic subjects harbored latent and inexpressible ideas and feelings. These *complexes*, as Jung called them, could be objectively demonstrated in the pauses, hesitations, and inhibitions of the subjects as each reacted to a list of stimulus words.

Eventually, however, Jung pursued a path different from Freud's when he found himself unable to accept the exclusively sexual nature of Freud's *libido*. With his own patients, Jung discovered residues of human history and prehistory in their fantasies. His own childhood experiences with visions and alternative personalities had prepared him to accept the possibility that some psychic content might arise from sources external to the individual. His self-analysis (from 1913 to 1917) of the dreams, visions, and nightmares that flooded his consciousness convinced him more strongly that a higher power was responsible for at least some of the content of mental life. He therefore postulated a personal unconscious similar to Freud's concept, and a collective unconscious that transcends the personal experiences of the individual.

Within the collective unconscious, there are stored inherited predispositions to respond with great emotion to specific events. These predispositions, which Jung called *archetypes*, include the animus and anima, the hero, God, the shadow, and the persona. Jung considered the archetypes solid evidence of the innate symbol-making tendency humans had inherited from their ancestors.

In trying to resolve the differences between himself and Freud, and between Freud and Adler, Jung postulated two personality types: the introvert and the extrovert. Introverts are characterized by their withdrawal from social stimulation, their intensely subjective interest in things intellectual, and their reliance on the power of their own feelings. The extrovert, much the opposite, is dominated by objective, external reality and is socially oriented. In addition to these attitude types, Jung proposed four functions: thinking and feeling (rational), and intuition and sensation (irrational). Introverts and extroverts each can be dominated by one or more of these functions, leading to an eightfold combined typology.

In his later years, Jung came to emphasize the spiritual side of humanity's existence. Jung postulated that to achieve full *individuation*, as he called it, a person must form a psychological organization that can reconcile all of the opposing and contradictory trends within the psyche. To this reconciler of opposites, Jung gave the name *self*. He created usually symmetrical figures called mandalas to represent and facilitate the harmonious development of the self.

An evaluation of Jung's theory indicates that some parts are, in principle, testable, especially his early work on word association and his conception of personality types. Jungian theory is essentially an active agent theory. We should note, however, that the active agent in Jung's theory is not the egoistic personality or persona, but the entire psyche, itself, including both unconscious and conscious elements. Jung's theory is a complex blend of nomothetic universals (e.g., collective unconscious, archetypes) and idiographic particulars (e.g., introversion, the self).

FOR FURTHER READING

Jung's popular *Memories, Dreams, Reflections* (New York: Vintage, 1989) is a wonderfully readable, unpretentious, revealing and intriguing autobiography. The most readable of Jung's writings that summarize his concepts is *Analytical Psychology:* *Its Theory and Practice* (New York: Pantheon, 1968).

Further additional readings on Jung and Jungian psychology are described in the *Beneath the Mask* web site at www.wiley.com/college/sollod

GLOSSARY

Active imagination: The conscious process of focusing on dream images or on fantasy figures to facilitate psychological insight and personal transformation.

Analytical psychology: The term Jung gave to identify his personality theory and therapeutic approach. This term was in contradistinction to the Freudian *psychoanalytic approach* and to Adlerian *individual psychology*.

Anima: An archetype; consisting of the female component of the psyche. Includes the positive characteristics of warmth and intuitive understanding and the negative components of moodiness and irrationality.

Animus: An archetype consisting of the male component of the psyche. On the positive side it includes the ability to reason and use logic to solve problems, and on the negative side it leads to argumentativeness and social insensitivity.

Archetypes: Jung's term for universal themes or symbols that are a residue of ancestral emotional life. They lead to predispositions to behave and to experience reality in certain ways.

Collective unconscious: For Jung, that part of the psyche that is presumed to contain representations of the collective experiences of humanity. It is the depository of instincts and archetypes that go beyond one's own personal experience.

Compensatory function: The activities of the personal unconscious to compensate for the imbalance that occurs when an individual's conscious attitude leans too one-sidedly in a single direction. The unconscious may compensate for this imbalance by producing dreams or fantasies that emphasize the opposite tendency.

Complex: In Jungian theory, a set or collection of interrelated ideas or fantasies that are highly valued by the individual and which reside in the personal unconscious. Such thoughts are usually united by a common underlying theme.

Conscious ego: The conscious part of the psyche. It consists of all those internal and external events that are within our awareness at any given moment, including all sense impressions and self-awareness.

Differentiation: The psychological process by which individuals develop their unique patterns of traits and idiosyncrasies.

Ectopsychic functions: The four functions of consciousness that are directed outwardly to the world. Those functions are sensation, thinking, feeling, and intuition.

Enantiodromia: The play of opposites within every personality. Jung discerned a multiplicity of conflicting themes, discordant opposites, and antagonistic forces that individuals faced in their pursuit of individuation or wholeness.

Entropy: A law of physics that states that energy will flow from the most to the least energized areas. In Jungian theory, the principle of entropy implies that the least energized archetypes or human potentials will acquire energy in the course of life.

Extroversion: The tendency to be externally oriented, confident, outgoing, and accommodating.

Galvanic skin response (GSR): The skin's decrease in resistance to electrical current during sensory and emotional changes.

Individuation: This is the full development of all aspects of the psyche into a unique and harmonious whole. In this process, the individual comes to experience and express the various components of his or her psyche.

Introversion: The tendency to be internally oriented, reserved, reflective, and socially inhibited or circumspect.

Libido: In Jungian theory, the libido is a general life energy, of which sexual urges are only one aspect. This life force or energy manifests itself in our diverse feelings, thoughts, and behaviors. Libidinal energy can be shaped, channeled, suppressed, repressed, blocked, or expressed.

Mandala: In Jung's theory, a circular figure that represents the synthesis or union of opposites within the psyche that takes place when individuals reach self-realization. It is the symbol of wholeness, completeness, and perfection. It can be imagined as a symbolic representation of the self.

Personal unconscious: The region of the mind or psyche that contains the individual's experiences that have been blocked or repressed from conscious awareness. It is comparable but not identical to Freud's *dynamic unconscious.*

Persona: The archetype that consists of the "mask" we wear in order to function adequately in interpersonal relationships. This mask or public face takes as many forms as the roles we engage in on a regular basis.

Principle of entropy: Second law of thermodynamics, which states that there is a tendency to equalize energy within a system. Thus elements of unequal strength seek psychological equilibrium within the psyche.

Principle of equivalence: First law of thermodynamics, which states that the amount of energy in a system is neither created nor destroyed but only transformed. Thus an increase in psychic functioning in one area of interest or preoccupation will lead to a compensatory decrease in functioning in another part of the psyche.

Prospection function: In Jungian theory, the prospection function is the "looking ahead" and sometimes even precognitive function of the unconscious mind.

Psyche: In Jung's theory, the sum total of all aspects of the personality, including all conscious and unconscious components. To Jung, the psyche transcends time and space.

Rational/irrational functions: The four ectopsychic functions can be further classified as rational or irrational, depending on the degree of judgment or reasoning involved.

Reaction times: The time an individual takes to respond to a stimulus word in the word association test.

Self: In Jung's theory, a psyche that has achieved balance and has developed into a harmonious whole. In addition, *self* is a term used for the part of the psyche that provides guidance toward wholeness.

Sensation intuition: Modes of apprehending the world without evaluation or interpretation. Those two manners of responding are classified as irrational because conscious reasoning is virtually absent. They do not involve logical thought processes.

Shadow archetype: The archetype that represents the dark, evil, and repulsive side of human nature. The shadow archetype is universal, but its specific contents vary individually. It is often projected onto other people.

Synchronicity: The meaningful coincidence of two or more outer or inner events (e.g., dreams or visions). They may occur around the same time but have no apparent cause-and-effect connection.

Teleological: Goal-directed. In Jung's theory, the development of the psyche is directed toward the goals of balance and harmony.

Thinking feeling: Modes of making judgments or evaluations of events. These types of responding are classified as rational because they involve the supremacy of reason, and the assessment of the worth of an experience.

Transcendent function: The driving force behind individuation, the innate tendency to pursue inner harmony.

Word association test: A test developed by Jung in which individuals are presented with stimulus words and asked to give responses to them. This method helps to uncover latent emotional difficulties by exposing content areas that produce hesitation, perseveration, or total inhibition of response.

Chapter **6**

Anna Freud

Widening the Scope of Psychoanalysis:
Ego Psychology

> ... *[the] earliest environmental influences on the child create states that are comparable to deficiency illnesses on the physical side.*
>
> Anna Freud

> *I was always looking outside myself for strength and confidence, but it comes from within. It is there all the time.*
>
> Anna Freud

Anna Freud   Born: 1895 Vienna, Austria
             Died: 1982 London, England

About Ego Psychology

Psychoanalytic ego psychology extended Freudian theory to include the ego's capacity to cope proactively with the physical and interpersonal environment.

In this view, people are motivated not only from reduction of the tension from id impulses but also from the sense of active mastery in surmounting life's obstacles. Significant maladjustment is not exclusively the result of intrapsychic conflict or imbalance but is also present in persons who have not met the developmental challenges of dealing with the world outside of the self.

Anna Freud began her explorations in her psychotherapeutic work with children. She gradually altered the theory of the ego from that of the helpless rider of the id horse described by Sigmund Freud into a more intelligent rider concerned with the best routes to travel. She changed the psychoanalytic focus on the past experiences of adults to an emphasis on the current environments of children and their capacity to respond to the difficulties they faced.

LEGITIMIZING EGO PSYCHOLOGY

Whereas Sigmund Freud reconstructed his patients' childhoods from their adult recollections, Anna Freud observed her child patients in the act of constructing their adult reminiscences. Sigmund Freud liberated his patients from ignorance of their own pasts. Anna Freud labored to nurture her patients' mastery of their present challenges. In many ways, Anna followed directly in her father's footsteps yet, in so doing, she also developed new directions of theory and practice.

For Anna Freud, widening the scope of psychoanalysis meant applying the fundamental discoveries of her father to new realms of behavior, to children, to adolescents, to pediatrics, to family law, and to modified techniques in education and child care (A. Freud, 1972, 1978a). A widened psychoanalytic theory of the ego does not include leaving behind her father's conception of the power of id instincts, his portrait of the ego as a survival-contingent outgrowth of the id, and his conviction that, after all, the ego rider leads the id horse where the id horse wants to go. But the story of Anna Freud's work is not the history of a student completely devoted to her father and teacher, who were one and the same. It is a narrative of brilliant innovation, revision, and creation accomplished almost reluctantly (Young-Bruehl, 1988, p. 208ff. and Chapter 11). As part of her acceptance speech for an honorary doctorate from Jefferson Medical School in 1964, Anna Freud viewed her psychoanalytic career and pictured an essential difference between herself and many other contemporary psychoanalytic theorists:

> In contrast to many colleagues, I was never concerned one-sidedly with id, ego, or superego, but always with the interactions between them. The dynamics of mental life which fascinated me, to my mind, found their clearest expression in the defense organization of the ego, with the attempts of the rational personality to deal with the irrational. (1967, pp. 514–515)

Anna Freud's position in the history of psychoanalysis has two aspects. In her primary role as Sigmund Freud's chosen and personally groomed intellectual heir, she was the keeper of the keys, custodian of the faith, and conservator of tradition. Balanced against these protective and understandable daughterly motives was her competing role as an independent theorist, who explored new territories. Her family heritage led to a protective attitude toward classical psychoanalysis. It also supported an adventuresome curiosity, a self-confidence and an aura of credibility that helped her make and promulgate new discoveries. She was, after all, not only a Freudian; she was a Freud.

PERSONAL SOURCES: FROM BEING UNWANTED
TO BECOMING INDISPENSABLE

By the time Sigmund and Martha Freud realized that Martha was again pregnant, they had already agreed that their fifth child, Sophie, was to be their last. Indeed, the initial phase of Martha's pregnancy was misinterpreted and welcomed as an early onset of menopause (Roazen, 1969, p. 40; 1971, pp. 52 ff. and pp. 436 ff.; Young-Bruehl, 1988, p. 35 ff.). When it became clear that the pause in Martha's menstruation was not the end of fertility but the beginning of new life, Freud found himself hoping for another son. He wrote to his friend, Wilhelm Fliess, in October 1895, "You will not have any objection to my calling my next son Wilhelm! If he turns out to be a daughter, she will be called Anna" (S. Freud, 1954, p. 130). He was she, as Freud and Martha learned on the afternoon of December 3, 1895. With evident disappointment and potential rejection, Freud announced Anna's birth to Fliess:

> If it had been a son I should have sent you the news by telegram. But as it is a little girl of the name of Anna, you get the news later. (S. Freud, 1954, p. 136; see alternate form of this quotation in Freud, 1985, p. 153)

Despite this birth announcement to Fliess, Freud eventually became fond of all of his children. Anna, his youngest and last child, would grow up to become the intellectual heir Freud was unable to find in Jung, Adler, Rank, or in any of his other male psychoanalytic colleagues.

On the basis of his thorough researches which drew on a variety of sources, the biographer Paul Roazen (1968, 1969, 1971) pieced together the probable personal history of Anna Freud's eventual entrance into her father's discipline. Roazen's findings have not gone unchallenged. (Anna Freud herself found Roazen's work objectionable, as reported by Young-Bruehl, 1988, p. 432ff.). We follow Roazen's account supplemented with some of Sigmund Freud's letters here.

Young Adulthood: Training Analysis with Freud

Sometime before 1918, when Anna was in her early twenties, she entered into analysis with her father. This unique relationship apparently continued for several years (Dyer, 1983, p. 26, feels that the duration was somewhat shorter; Roazen, 1971, p. 439; Young-Bruehl, 1988, gives the most complete and compelling account. See especially Young-Bruehl, 1988, p. 171). Sigmund Freud thus functioned in the acutely contradictory roles of Anna's father and psychoanalyst. Roazen described the consequences for Anna Freud's development in this way:

> Freud's motives may have been the very best, but medically and humanly the situation was bizarre. As her analyst, he would inevitably mobilize her feelings of overvaluation, while at the same time invading the privacy of her soul; he added new transference emotions to their relationship, without the possibility of ever really dissolving them. A genius who was also naturally an immense figure in his daughter's fantasy life, as her analyst he tied her permanently to him. (1971, p. 440; italics added)

Today, such a dual relationship would be universally considered an unprofessional ethical violation and would lead to severe sanctions, including the loss of one's license to practice medicine. One can easily doubt whether such psychoanalysis could have been effective. Could a parent be objective? What motives would lead a parent to psychoanalyze his own child? Are there no other and more satisfactory ways of passing on an intellectual tradition? What kind of example is provided with such rule-violation? How could a daughter feel free to give voice to a range of feelings toward her father

---

BOX 6.1   *Only Connect . . .*

Freud broke the rules he himself created for the proper conduct of a psychoanalyst by taking his own daughter into such a relationship. Some theorists have suggested that he must have placed special importance on having a trustworthy and competent intellectual heir. By so teaching his daughter the techniques of his profession, Freud bequeathed to her his place as leader of the psychoanalytic movement. Talk about countertransference!

when her father was the therapist? One can construct a very long list of questions to which one cannot imagine ethically or intellectually satisfactory answers.

One source for understanding the meaning of her analysis with her father is Anna Freud herself. In a letter advising a friend, Eva Rosenfeld, to enter treatment with her father, whom Eva already had known in a social context, Anna made these poignant remarks:

> You know, there is no contradiction in your undergoing analysis in a place that you would prefer to come to for love's sake alone. I did the same thing, and perhaps because of it, the two things became inextricably bound together for me. In the end you will realize: it is the only way to go into analysis. Right now you are troubled by the feeling that where you love you would like to be especially good. You will see that being good and being in analysis finally amount to the same thing. (A. Freud, 1929/1992, letter 8, p.112)

Anna Freud began attending her father's lectures, and she was permitted to join the important Wednesday seminars of the Vienna Psychoanalytic Society (Roazen, 1971, p. 438). She was even given her first exposure to classical psychiatry by being allowed to attend rounds in the psychiatric teaching hospital of Vienna, under Professor Wagner-Jauregg, a friend of Sigmund Freud's from his own medical school years (A. Freud, 1967, p. 512). Heinz Hartmann, known later as the father of ego psychology, served as a second assistant on these psychiatric rounds. In May 1920, two years after her training analysis by one account, Sigmund accepted Anna as a full-fledged and accepted member of the Vienna Psychoanalytic Society. He confirmed her new role by bestowing on her one of the special rings that signified membership in his exclusive inner circle (Dyer, 1983, p. 32).

Anna as an Early Analyst

By 1923, having already presented her first psychoanalytic paper to the society the previous year, Anna Freud was ready to enter psychoanalytic practice (A. Freud, 1922). Her first paper was an extension of one of her father's own essays on "beating fantasies" devised by children. The elder Freud (1919) had written a paper entitled "A Child Is Being Beaten" in which he described the fantasies of several of his female patients for what they reveal of the plasticity of sexual motives. Freud's analysis shows that the fantasy-like daydream of his patients, which pictured an older person beating or punishing a child, is a disguised substitute for a repressed sexual wish.

Anna Freud's (1922) own first published contribution to psychoanalysis is an extension of the beating fantasy analysis with a major difference from her father's work. The female patient she describes in the paper is most certainly herself (Young-Bruehl, 1988, pp. 103ff.). Anna Freud describes the progressive fantasy stories of a girl from preschool age through adolescence in which the central theme is "a child is being beaten." Her 1922 paper reveals some of the personal experiences on which Anna Freud based her therapeutic method for working with children. The girl described in her paper eventually developed a set of "nice fantasies" that she thought had little or no connection with the "beating fantasies" she found so distressing. In fact, the nice fantasies were more deliberate on the surface, more under voluntary control. But, as Anna Freud reveals in the paper, through analysis, the patient learns that the "nice stories" are thinly disguised continuations of the beating fantasies.

Anna Freud analyzes the progression from the beating fantasies to the "nice stories" as a study in repression and sublimation, two defense mechanisms she would later describe in much detail. She implies that the girl is developmentally more mature at

Figure 6.1 Anna Freud and her famous father in the Dolomite region of Italy, 1927. They appear happy together. Anna was devoted to her father.

the point when she can recognize the connection between the earlier unwanted beating fantasies and her even more defensive "nice stories." Anna Freud points out that the girl eventually turned her combination beating fantasies and "nice stories" into a creative and more rationally controlled enterprise by writing a compelling short story that she could share with others. In this early paper, the theme of creative mastery of conflict as a basic motive is already clearly in evidence—a theme that she later extended in the theoretical concept called "developmental lines."

Anna's Adulthood: Anna's Antigone Played to Freud's Aging Oedipus

Eventually, Anna Freud became indispensable to her father, especially during the last 16 years of his life, when he was battling cancer of the mouth. She was his emissary to psychoanalytic societies throughout the world, and she delivered his papers when his prosthesis, designed to replace excised oral tissue, impaired her father's ability to speak. She typed his correspondence daily and administered to his personal and medical needs. That task required daily inspection of Freud's surgically brutalized mouth for any signs of new growth. Anna Freud accompanied her father on his journeys to Paris for radium treatments, on visits to his surgeon in Berlin, and on much-needed holidays in the woods to pick mushrooms and wild strawberries (Jones, 1957; Schur, 1972; Young-Bruehl, 1988, p. 118). Anna Freud was devoted to her father's comfort and care.

Sigmund Freud himself understood how dependent he had become on Anna. He chose an appropriate metaphor to describe the relationship between them. In his correspondence of the mid-1930s, Freud would refer to Anna as his "faithful Antigone," alluding to the dutiful and courageous daughter of the blind and ill Oedipus in Sophocles' plays. For example, in a letter to Arnold Zweig in 1934, Freud wrote,

> But it cannot have remained concealed from you that fate has granted me as compensation for much that has been denied me the possession of a daughter who, in tragic circumstances, would not have fallen short of Antigone. (Freud/Zweig, 1970, p. 66)

Thus, in Freud's mind, with Anna as his Antigone, he was the ailing and aged Oedipus. Like the blind Oedipus led by his faithful Antigone, Sigmund Freud's contacts with the outside world were made through Anna's skilled touch. In a letter to Lou Andreas-Salome, he also managed to express fatherly pride in a peculiarly objective—almost depersonalized—way that echoes the equally curious tone of his announcement of her birth to Fliess 40 years before:

> I of course rely more and more on Anna's care, just as Mephistopheles once remarked:
>
> > In the end we depend
> > On the creatures we made.
>
> In any case, it was very wise to have made her. (Freud [1935], 1960, p. 425)

From being an unexpected and unwanted daughter, Anna Freud had finally matured into an independent and intelligent adult:

> She has grown into a capable, independent person who has been blessed with insight into matters that merely confuse others. To be sure, for her sake I would like—but she must learn to do without me, and the fear of losing vital parts of my still intact personality through old age is an accelerating factor in my wish. (Freud/Zweig, 1970, p. 140)

Freud partly expressed his wish not to die and, in so doing, indicated his concern that Anna required his continued presence. But the wish for immortality gave way to a more realistic appraisal. Freud finally realized that the ravages of his illness and age would ultimately render him unable to act as protecting father to Anna and as founding father of psychoanalysis. Anna's growing independence and mastery of psychoanalytic theory and practice assured him that she would continue to prosper and so, in consequence, would aid his intellectual progeny—the psychoanalytic endeavor.

The Central Themes: Devotion, Protection, and Reluctant Innovation

Three fundamental themes governing the course of Anna Freud's work emerge from her life history. First, Anna found her whole life centered in one person and became intellectually and emotionally focused on her relationship with her father. Freud's own need for emotional and intellectual intimacy intensified the momentum of their growing mutual dependence.

The second relevant theme of Anna Freud's life history is her understandably protective and conservative approach to psychoanalytic theory. Anna Freud regarded her father's basic discoveries as foundation stones that cannot be discarded or greatly modified without demolishing the entire edifice they support. She cogently argued that psychoanalysis historically achieved its uniqueness and value as the study of the whole personality in both its unconscious and conscious components (A. Freud, 1936, pp. 3–5; 1969). Restricting investigation to one aspect of personality functioning or ignoring instinctual factors in favor of environmental-cultural ones severely distorts and violates psychoanalytic procedure and theory.

The third and last theme that is discernible in Anna Freud's life history follows from her first two themes and her own creativity and innovativeness. Anna Freud was caught between genuine loyalty to and belief in her father and his work and the compelling evidence of her own discoveries in child analysis and ego function. Thus, she never presented her contributions as revisions or modifications of psychoanalytic theory. She envisioned her own work as more in the nature of subtle refinements, sophisticated clarifications, or shifts in emphasis. Yet, despite her tendency to minimize the newness of her ideas as a solution to the conflict between her loyalty and creativity, genuinely new discoveries and fresh ideas are found in Anna Freud's writings. Some of these ideas have profoundly influenced other psychoanalytic workers to alter the course of contemporary psychoanalysis, moving the evolution of theory in directions never contemplated by Sigmund Freud in his lifetime.

There is no better way to illustrate and to summarize this enduring conflict between Anna Freud's loyal protectionist attitude and her own hard-won discoveries than to quote an instance of her own vacillating prose:

> ...It is important to remember that some forty years ago, long before the time when cooperation with academic workers could have played a part, psychoanalytic child study itself had already *transgressed the strict confines* of the psychoanalytic technique and situation, and had created its own field of direct observation, in its own way. It is true that all the important data on which psychoanalysis has built its view of childhood...were derived from the analytic setting itself, reconstruction from the analyses of adults, and later from the analyses of children. But immediately after the discoveries were made, a host of observers set to work, outside of the analytic setting, unsystematically indeed, and following the opportunities offered by life situations as they arose, but providing in time a mass of useful data, which served to check and countercheck, add to or refute the analytic findings proper. (A. Freud, 1951a, pp. 139–140; italics added)

Anna Freud's muted claims for originality and independence of child analysis, her special branch of the discipline, are inseparably interwoven in this passage with her dutiful recognition of the primacy of classical psychoanalysis. Yet she ends the passage with the admonition to remember that the data of child analysis have the special status of serving as the "countercheck" by which classical theory is confirmed or refuted.

WIDENING THE SCOPE OF ANALYSIS: LITTLE PATIENTS' PROBLEMS

By extending psychoanalytic technique from the reconstruction of childhood events in adults to direct exploration of children's life histories as they live them, Anna Freud quickly made two discoveries. Little patients are often exuberant free spirits but lackadaisical in free-associating. As might be expected, the use of disciplined verbal-analytic technique with small children, with small vocabularies and limited verbal skills, is not a promising undertaking. Furthermore, unlike adults, child patients typically do not perceive themselves as needing aid, do not comprehend the role of a psychoanalyst, and present themselves for treatment only at the urging or command of parents. Because traditional psychoanalysis required that patients be intellectually and emotionally engaged in their own treatment, child patients constituted a formidable challenge (A. Freud, 1927, p. 6; 1945, p. 8).

How do we decide when a child requires psychoanalysis? One viewpoint, represented by other child analytic workers in the 1920s and 1930s, was that any emotional or intellectual disturbance in the child would benefit from psychoanalytic treatment. Anna Freud's own early view during this same period was that psychoanalysis was indicated only for children in whom a full-blown childhood neurosis was strangling further development (A. Freud, 1927).

After considerable experience, Anna Freud conceptualized the criteria for treatment of children. For adult patients, the severity of neurotic disturbance is indicated by the degree of damage to their capacities to lead a conflict-free love life and to work productively with satisfaction (A. Freud, 1945, p. 15). These criteria are inapplicable to children. Childhood involves cognitive, emotional, and behavioral development:

> In childhood there is only one factor of such central importance that its impairment through a neurosis calls for immediate action; namely, the child's ability to develop, not to remain fixated at some stage of development before the maturation process has been concluded. (A. Freud, 1945, p. 17)

The broadening in theory to encompass the facts of childhood change was required by the demands of child patients whose unconscious processes were not accessible by strictly verbal procedures. The refocusing of theory was necessitated by the shift from treatments for outright pathology to therapy for developmental, transitional impairments (A. Freud, 1968). Thus the criterion by which a child's need for analytic treatment was to be assessed was no longer the presence of explicit neurotic symptoms. Threatened fixation to some single phase of development became a sufficient indicator to warrant analytic intervention.

MAKING THE CHILD ANALYZABLE: THE PREPARATORY PHASE

Prior to Anna Freud's work with children, Melanie Klein (Chapter 7) of the Berlin School of Psychoanalysis had used a method for treating children almost exactly the same as adult psychoanalysis (Sayers, 1991, p. 153). Anna set about to develop a therapeutic method more suited to children. Many of the approaches and methods she developed were fundamentally different from the more orthodox or conventional Freudian approach developed by Klein. It could be argued that, even though Anna Freud's techniques with children differed from her father's techniques with adults, her work was nonetheless in keeping with Freudian theory. This was possible because children were not simply little adults. There were major differences between the psyches of children and the adults with whom Sigmund Freud was more familiar. Melanie Klein, following the letter of Freudian technique, may have not "gotten it" as well as Anna Freud.

Coming from her experiences as a teacher of children (A. Freud, 1952), Anna Freud understood the importance of engaging children's interest at the outset and the necessity of winning their respect for the superior skills of the adult participant. In the early years of formulating usable principles of child analysis, Anna Freud felt the necessity of a lengthy preparatory phase of give-and-take relationship building before analytic work was begun. This preparatory phase was made more elaborate later with her addition of a "metapsychological assessment" procedure based on direct observation of a child and reports by others who were able to observe the child's family interactions.

Engaging the Child's Self-Interest; Establishing the Analyst's Usefulness

Initially, Anna Freud undertook a preparatory period of "breaking the child in" for analysis by helping the child see the need for the treatment, view the analyst as helpmate and ally, and develop a genuine resolve to endure the difficulties of self-exploration. In practice, these goals are transformed into creative strategies. The analyst helps the child gradually develop insight into the child's difficulties and elicits greater and greater cooperation. In these efforts, the analyst expresses sincere interest and good wishes for the child's eventual self-management. To illustrate, consider Anna Freud's skillful approach to a ten-year-old boy presented for treatment by his parents for a variety of anxieties, nervous states, tendency toward lying and fabrication of stories, and for a series of thefts. With some children, the analyst may assume the role of helpful ally against a hostile adult world or of potential helpmate in dealing with inner misery. For this child, no such partnership could be proposed. His attitude from the outset was one of hostile rejection of his proposed analyst, and, on the surface at least, he was not interested in looking at or changing any aspect of himself.

At first, Anna Freud spent their time together merely mirroring his moods. When he appeared cheerful, she was cheerful; when he was serious or depressed, she acted seriously. At one point, he preferred to spend the entire session under a table in the room, an activity that Anna Freud treated with no special attention. She merely lifted the tablecloth to speak with him as though it were the most ordinary conversation. Simultaneously, however, she also subtly demonstrated the superiority of her adult skills and wisdom:

> If he came with a string in his pocket, and began to show me remarkable knots and tricks, I would let him see that I could make more complicated knots and do more remarkable tricks. If he made faces, I pulled better ones; and if he challenged me to trials of strength, I showed myself incomparably stronger. (A. Freud, 1927, p. 12)

Throughout their conversations, Anna Freud followed his every whim and choice of topic, with no subject too delicate or too adult for discussion. "My attitude was like that of a film or novel meant to attract the audience or reader by catering to their baser interests" (1927, p. 12). Thus, Anna Freud succeeded not only in making herself interesting to the boy but also in learning about his interests, attitudes, and typical behaviors and activities.

A second stage in this preparatory work began when Anna Freud demonstrated that she could be useful to the boy in many small ways, such as by typing letters for him, by eliciting and writing down his daydreams, and by making small toys during their therapy sessions. In the process of recording daydreams, the analyst could also learn something about the child's fantasy life. Anna Freud remarked concerning another of her patients, "...I zealously crocheted and knitted during her appointments, and gradually clothed all her dolls and teddy bears" (1927, p. 13). If we take this last statement as typical, it suggests that such a preparatory phase is relatively long-lived and requires much patience until the child patient finally becomes committed to the therapeutic process.

Establishing the Analyst's Power and the Child's Vulnerability

The third stage of the preparatory period had its origins in yet another skillful maneuver designed to augment the boy's growing value for his analyst. "I made him realize that being analyzed had great practical advantages; that, for example, punishable deeds have an altogether different and much more fortunate result when they are first told to the analyst, and only through him to those in charge of the child" (A. Freud, 1927, p. 13).

Eventually the boy relied on Anna Freud to protect him from punishment for his rash acts, to confess to his parents for him, and to restore stolen money before he was caught. The chief result of this stage of preparation was that Anna Freud had now become not only interesting, helpful, and wise, but powerful as well, a person "without whose help he could no longer get along" (1927, p. 13). At this point came the crucial moment when Anna Freud could finally request his complete cooperation in unveiling his treasured and guarded secrets. She could demand of him the equivalent of the adult analytic rule: Tell all. Keep no secrets.

The preparatory phase concludes when children have developed sufficient insight to recognize the necessity of external aid for their difficulties. Indeed, child patients must learn to understand that they have difficulties. The only clear signal of sincere willingness to attempt extended and painful self-exploration comes when the child has experienced his or her own vulnerability and needs to invest the analyst with complete and trusting dependence. In short, the analyst works very hard during the preparatory stage to establish a strong, positive transference relationship.

The analyst must become the child's ego ideal in order for treatment to proceed and eventually to succeed. The analyst then displaces the parents from this role and usurps much of their authority: "Before the child can give the highest place in his emotional life, that of ego ideal, to this new love object which ranks with the parents, he needs to feel that the analyst's authority is even greater than theirs" (A. Freud, 1927, p. 60). In some cases, where the parents themselves are either the source of the child's difficulties or are negatively disposed to the treatment, it becomes necessary for the child analyst to work actively against their influence.

THE CHILD ANALYSIS: PROPER TECHNIQUES

Once an affectionate and dependent attachment to the analyst is established, analytic treatment of the child, with its special focus on the unconscious, may begin. The success of the analysis depends heavily upon the firmness of this attachment, for "Children, in fact, believe only the people they love, and make efforts only for the love of such people" (A. Freud, 1927, p. 40). The question naturally arises of how to provide analytic interpretations in the absence of free-associative verbal products. What does the analyst interpret?

Interpretation of Fantasy and Dreams

One avenue of approach that immediately suggests itself is the play activities of the child. The Berlin school of child analysis headed by Melanie Klein employed the technique of play interpretations. Anna Freud rejected this road to the child's unconscious because it implies that a child's manipulations of toys and construction of play fantasies are equivalent to adult verbal productions in the analytic situation, a proposition for which there seemed little justification (1927, p. 38). Compared to verbal expressions, the analyst dealing with play may have difficulty understanding when a behavior is symbolic and when it is merely play.

At the beginning of her work with children, Anna Freud employed two tools adopted from adult psychoanalysis but in greatly modified form. The first of these approaches was the reliance on the child patients' verbal reports of their fantasies and dreams. As in adult analysis, these productions were treated as symbolic derivatives of unconscious processes, and they were therefore subject to interpretation. In this activity, Anna Freud clearly drew on her own experience analyzing her own "beating fantasies" and "nice stories." With some children, direct encouragement of fantasy stories was employed, as in the case of a little girl patient who was asked to close her eyes and "see pictures" that she would then describe to Anna Freud. In a similar way, the analyst and child patient discuss the child's dreams, and with practice, the child becomes accustomed to seeking hidden meanings in his or her own productions.

Maintaining and Interpreting the Child-Analyst Relationship

The second tool of child analysis in the initial period of Anna Freud's development of the technique was the interpretation of the relationship between herself and her patient. In adult analysis, the transference relationship and the development of a full-blown transference neurosis was necessary for therapy to succeed. With a child patient, as we have seen, the transference relationship embodies an essentially positive, affectionate quality that is not inherent to adult psychoanalysis. In fact, though negative feelings toward the analyst will eventually emerge, Anna Freud regarded these as temporary interferences that should be dealt with promptly to prevent rupture of the delicate bonds that hold the child to the therapist (1927, p. 41). The only really productive work with children, she concluded, takes place in an atmosphere of positive emotional attachment.

The child's transference relationship to the analyst is different from the adult's in other important ways. Unlike adult counterparts, child patients are still in the formative stages of their real relationships with their parents or guardians and other important people. They do not recall, reexamine, and relive these relationships in analysis as part of the past; they live them in the present. Outside the analytic room, their pleasures and pains still largely depend on those who affect them in daily life. Analysts who attempt to interpose themselves in this scheme of things have to share the children's affection for their parents as well as the hostilities, disappointments, and idealizations they have for their parents. By contrast, the analyst of adult patients becomes the full target of feelings reconstructed from the patient's past. The adult analyst becomes momentarily a blank screen onto which the patient can project unresolved and unrealistic feelings carried over from the patient's early parent–child interactions.

Figure 6.2 Anna Freud at her desk. The books and objects in this photograph indicate Anna's wide-ranging interests and scholarly activities. Like her father, she was a theorist and a prolific writer in addition to her psychotherapeutic role.

The situation is further complicated in cases where children have little or no real affection from their parents. Emotionally deprived children may obtain a caring and affectionate relationship from their analysts that they have not experienced at home. Such children do not project a fantasized reenactment of their emotional relationships onto the analyst (A. Freud, 1927, p. 45).

> For these reasons the child forms no transference neurosis. In spite of all his positive and negative impulses toward the analyst, he continues to display his abnormal reactions where they were displayed before—in the home. Because of this the child analyst must not only take into account what happens under his own eye, but also direct his attention to the area where the neurotic reactions are to be found—the child's family. (A. Freud, 1927, p. 46)

Child analysis involves understanding and interpreting interpersonal bonds both in and outside of the analytic situation. In addition to understanding these relationships from the child patient's view, the analyst might also be able to explore the viewpoint of the adults with whom the child has their most intimate contacts. Child analysts often violate a rule of adult analysis in their reliance on and active seeking of information about the patient from outside sources.

Delicate Balance Between Permissiveness and Authority

If, as Anna Freud was discovering, children's neurotic disturbances were so dependent on their present relationship to the people and things in their own worlds, then it must follow with inevitable logic that:

- Childhood neurosis is not limited to conflicts among the id, ego, and superego but includes the distorting and paralyzing influences of the environment;
- Children's egos and superegos are not only weak by virtue of unconscious conflict but also as a result of lack of maturation.

As a result of these factors, the results of child analysis would appear to be fragile. One might ask, "If the analyst succeeds in liberating the conflicted instinctual forces of the child's id, will the environment provide a healthy context for continued growth? If the superego and ego are not fully mature and are not sufficiently experienced in modulating these liberated unconscious forces, will the environment, especially the parents, provide understanding acceptance and support for this unruly transition to emotional health?" In the case of an adult, the analyst need not be overly concerned with the fate of impulses freed from repression, because the normal adult's ego is able to take charge of them, manage them, and accept them for what they are. In the child's case, however, liberated impulses may easily find themselves translated into action.

To illustrate: A young girl that Anna Freud was treating had gotten to a stage of her analysis in which she was producing a wealth of anal fantasies, marked by use of particularly vulgar imagery and language. The child saw her analytic sessions as a period of freedom, a "rest hour" during which all of this repressed and suppressed anxiety-producing fantasy material could be openly expressed in the seclusion of the analytic room. However, she eventually began to carry her fantasies, her "dirty" jokes, and her anal language into situations beyond the analytic "rest hour." Alarmed, the parents consulted Anna Freud, who took the matter lightly, suggesting that they neither reject nor condone such misbehavior but merely let it pass unnoticed. The advice backfired! Without external condemnation, the little girl reveled in her anal verbalizations, especially at the dinner table, where they produced the most dramatic effect:

I had to acknowledge that I had made a mistake, in crediting the child's superego with an independent inhibitory strength that it did not possess. As soon as the important people in the external world had relaxed their demands, the child's superego, previously strict and strong enough to bring forth a whole series of obsessional symptoms, suddenly had turned compliant. . . . I had changed an inhibited, obsessional child into one whose "perverse" tendencies were liberated. (A. Freud, 1927, p. 63)

It is clear that the child analyst cannot depend on the strength of the patient's ego to stay out of trouble. Experienced child analysts learn to steer skillfully between

Figure 6.3 Anna Freud at age 85 with her dog, Jo-Fi. This photograph indicates the affectionate and caring side of Anna Freud's personality.

two dangerous extremes. On one side, they have to tease unconscious material into consciousness. On the other side, the child analyst must somehow prevent the freed impulses from creating total anarchy in the child's life, a real threat in the light of the child's underdeveloped superego. They must educate children to employ healthy strategies for dealing with their heretofore frightening impulses. "The analyst accordingly combines in his own person two difficult and diametrically opposed functions: he has to analyze and educate, that is to say, in the same breath he must allow and forbid, loosen and bind" (A. Freud, 1927, p. 65).

THE THEORETICAL YIELD: NEW MEANINGS FOR FAMILIAR ANALYTIC CONCEPTS

It became increasingly clear to Anna Freud that child analysis involved more than merely applying orthodox psychoanalytic theory to children. Her earliest work with the technique laid the groundwork for important new areas that promised not only to establish child analysis as an independent, special branch of psychoanalysis but also to open the door to fundamental modifications of classical theory.

The Therapeutic Alliance: Awe and Trust

The first theoretical yield derived from the fact that child analysis could not be undertaken with the usual methods of free association, dream interpretation, and transference analysis. Children's strivings to grow, to mature, to change, to master inner and outer reality could lead to the modification of classical techniques or to the development of new ones. Anna Freud learned the importance of a long preparatory phase designed to establish the analyst as an important, dependable, even indispensable person. With a mixture of awe and trust, the child would come to accept the analyst as a very special kind of teacher, namely, as a specialist in self-knowledge and as an ally. Although the adult analytic patient may fantasize this kind of relationship with the therapist, it is only the child patient who lives it.

Beyond Structural Conflict: Developmental Vulnerability

Second, the fact of a child's plasticity, the continual growth toward maturity, forces the child analyst to focus not on overt neurotic symptoms but on the distant goal of future healthy functioning. Anna Freud and her colleagues soon recognized that crystallized neurotic syndromes were only a small fraction of the problems of childhood. Developmental disturbances, threats to continued maturing, both physical and psychological, were most often areas of concern. Moreover, even when overt indicators of serious pathology were present, these often had a very different significance in the context of a child's life than they did in an adult, whose psychological makeup was largely formed.

What Anna Freud and her coworkers eventually developed was a formalized system of diagnosis for children. It emphasized the developmental sequence of personality formation and malformation. The diagnostic system highlighted serious threats to the completion of personality growth while minimizing those that were less serious (A. Freud, 1970b, pp. 163ff.). In effect, doing analytic therapy with children had enabled Anna Freud to go beyond the classic conception of neurosis and maladjustment as primarily a result of intrapsychic conflict. Children often have disturbances that stem from difficulties in the process of psychological maturation.

Metapsychological Assessment

Third, Anna Freud had learned an important lesson from the length of the preparatory period required to make a child analyzable. Not only do child patients need a relatively long time to convince them of the value of analysis, but therapists also need a substantial period of assessment to understand each child's conflicts, deficits, and strengths. What was needed was a way to make such assessments at the outset. In general, psychoanalysts did not favor observational and formal interviewing techniques modeled on the academic tradition of psychological testing. However, the new field of child analysis seemed to require some compromise with formal academic psychology. Eventually, just such an assessment procedure was developed and formalized into what is termed a **metapsychological profile** (A. Freud, 1965a, 1965b; W.E. Freud, 1972; Laufer, 1965).

The metapsychological profile is a psychoanalyst's way of organizing all of the information obtained about a patient during a diagnostic assessment. *Metapsychological* is applied as a descriptive term to this procedure because the diagnostician attempts to integrate the findings into a coherent picture of the person's dynamic, genetic, economic, structural, and adaptive functioning (see Chapter 3 for a discussion of metapsychological viewpoints).

Recall that the:

- *dynamic* meaning of a psychological event refers to the conflictful nature of the competing drive energies as the ego attempts to provide satisfaction for the id;
- *genetic* viewpoint refers to the multiple developmental experiences in the course of a person's life history that converge to produce a particular symptom, meaning, or defense;
- *economic* is meant to indicate the degree of drive intensity and changes in quantity of instinctual energy over time;
- *structural* (or, earlier, topographical) viewpoint seeks to understand the interactions among the various structures or agencies of the mind as the ego, id, and superego perform their tasks; and
- the *adaptive metapsychological* viewpoint focuses attention on the ego's capacity to enable the person to resolve inner conflict and "fit in" with external reality's demands in a healthy way.

Metapsychological profiles have been developed for infants (W.E. Freud, 1972), for adolescents (Laufer, 1965), and for adults (A. Freud, 1965a; A. Freud, H. Nagera, & W.E. Freud, 1965). The baby, adolescent, and adult profiles require somewhat different kinds of data from those required by the child profile. For example, the baby profile requires assessments of bodily functions such as sleeping, eating, and elimination. Adult profiles focus on the possible interferences of the patients' conflicts and regressions with their sexual functioning and with their ability to work productively.

The version we present here was designed for children (A. Freud, 1965b). Table 6.1 outlines the major categories of the child's metapsychological profile. The categories in Table 6.1 range from biographical information, such as family background and current environmental situation, to descriptions of drive functioning, to diagnosis based on an integration of all preceding metapsychological viewpoints.

The significance of the metapsychological profile is threefold:

- It is standardized. It provides a uniform set of explicit instructions to gather specific behavioral and psychological data.

Table 6.1   Outline of Metapsychological Profile of the Child

I. REASON FOR REFERRAL—arrests in development, behavior problems, symptoms.

II. DESCRIPTION OF CHILD—personal appearance, moods, manner.

III. FAMILY BACKGROUND AND PERSONAL HISTORY—life history, family constellation.

IV. POSSIBLY SIGNIFICANT ENVIRONMENTAL INFLUENCES

V. ASSESSMENTS OF DEVELOPMENT

    A. Drive Development

       Libido and aggression distribution toward self and others.

    B. Ego and Superego Development

       Ego functions, age appropriate behavior, defensive balance, emotional balance.

VI. GENETIC ASSESSMENTS (Regression and Fixation)

Behavior, fantasy, and symptoms from which can be inferred the level of psychosexual development that has been reached or whatever regression or fixation to earlier stages is indicated.

VII. DYNAMIC AND STRUCTURAL ASSESSMENTS

Classify internal and external conflicts as to source in ego-id, ego-superego, or ego-reality clashes.

VIII. ASSESSMENT OF GENERAL CHARACTERISTICS

    A. Frustration Tolerance

       Ability to ensure tension, drive blocking, and capacity to employ adaptative defenses.

    B. Sublimation Potential

       Ability to neutralize sexual and aggressive urges and channel them into healthy activities.

    C. Attitude to Anxiety

       Use of defenses against fears of external and internal stimuli; degree of capacity to master inner and outer fears and stress situations.

    D. Progressive versus Regressive Forces

       Estimate ability to continue to develop, to profit from learning and treatment, to move forward to next developmental level.

IX. DIAGNOSIS

Integrate findings on degree of ego health, conflicts, frustrations, developmental level, superego severity, presence of organic disease, role of environment.

Based on A. Freud, 1965b, pp. 138–147.

- It requires the diagnostician to integrate those observations and supplementary life history data into a picture of the overall functioning and developmental status of the child's personality. Patterns of consistency and inconsistency emerge, as do areas of adequate and deficient development.

- It requires sophisticated use of psychoanalytic developmental theory, drive theory, and ego theory to derive metapsychological meaning from it. Psychoanalytic theory is used as a conceptual guide to diagnosis and as a predictive guide to specific therapy.

The metapsychological profile thus integrates theoretical propositions and observable clinical phenomena into a coherent psychological "map."

The Inescapable Limits of Child Analysis: Unchangeable Lives

The fourth theoretical yield from Anna Freud's work with children was her discovery that one could pursue therapeutic exploration too far. Other analysts who entered the field of child therapy often pursued personality disturbances in children to their very roots in the first year of life. In trying to go beyond manifest disturbances to the earliest antecedents of personality, the child analyst runs the risk of prolonging the

Anna Freud was the first of a number of women who exemplified a characteristically feminine, and in her case, maternal approach to understanding personality and conducting psychotherapy. Unlike her father, she emphasized creating a caring and nurturing environment for children. She focused on the impact of parental neglect and social upheaval on children and even initiated homes that provided a protective and caring environment for children who had lost or were separated from their parents. Anna Freud was a caring woman who spoke and acted on behalf of the well-being of children.

analysis indefinitely. Furthermore, such analyses, extending to the very beginning of the child's short life, may very well run headlong into *unchangeable* constitutional or environmental givens of personality:

> In my opinion, these earliest environmental influences on the child create states that are comparable to deficiency illnesses on the physical side. While the effects of such early deprivation can be mitigated by later favorable influences, they cannot be undone or reversed or solved in a new more age-adequate way, as conflicts can: this means that they are not in the true sense of the word a legitimate object of analytic effort. (A. Freud, 1970a, pp. 18–19)

Anna Freud thus acknowledged that child analysis does not prevent all psychological misery. Certain environmental and constitutional givens cannot be undone. Specific elements of the human condition may mar a child's life, yet remain beyond the reach of even the most well-intentioned efforts. Failure to recognize these real limits leads to the unrealistic aspiration of extending a child's analysis through the full period of development and well into adulthood.

Significance of Contemporary Social Reality: Bulldogs Bank Children

A fifth theoretical yield from Anna Freud's work was her discovery that the analytic practitioner must recognize that, unlike adults, children are more dependent on and more easily influenced by their current external realities. The child analyst must be prepared to accept the proposition that child patients' current dependencies on parents, their conflicts with siblings and peers, and their relationships to teachers and other authority figures are all reflected in their disturbances. Unlike adult analytic patients whose neurotic disturbances are almost entirely internalized and have their causes largely in past relationships or prior unresolved conflicts, children can be disturbed to a great degree by their present relationships in present reality:

> In treatment, especially the very young reveal the extent to which they are dominated by the object world, i.e., how much of their behavior and pathology is determined by environmental influences such as the parents' protective or rejecting, loving or indifferent, critical or admiring attitudes, as well as by the sexual harmony or disharmony in their married life.... *The child analyst who interprets exclusively in terms of the inner world is in danger of missing out on his patients' reporting activity concerning his—at the time equally important—environmental circumstances.* (A. Freud, 1965b, pp. 50–51; italics added)

The child analyst must recognize that the little patient's disturbances do not necessarily exclusively reflect what has gone wrong, been distorted, or been blocked in the realm of the child's internal world. A child's disturbances may very well reflect his or her links to reality (A. Freud, 1958, p. 127).

The importance of children's external environments and their abilities to cope with grave threats was impressed on Anna Freud in her work with children separated from their parents during World War II in the London bombing raids. Children, with the consent of their parents, were evacuated from areas of extreme danger and relocated in safer foster homes outside the bombing zone. Suddenly, thousands of children who had never before been separated from home and family were under the guardianship of strangers (A. Freud, 1953, p. 511). Other less fortunate children experienced the death of a family member or members through the devastation wreaked on London by German air attacks. Such children had witnessed death and destruction firsthand and, therefore, had been even more traumatically separated from their parents or other loved ones.

In 1940 Anna Freud collected financial contributions from several sources to open and staff a children's center in Hampstead, London. Eventually a babies' rest center and a country house in Essex were also opened and were filled with evacuated children. Collectively known as the Hampstead Nurseries, Anna Freud's residential homes were designed not as institutional settings but as substitute homes that would provide security, mothering, and love for the children (A. Freud & D. Burlingham, 1944).

The effects of separation took their greatest toll on the youngest children and infants. Children between 5 and 12 months responded with all manner of bodily disorders, ranging from eating difficulties, sleep disturbances, and feeding problems to respiratory troubles and loss of recently acquired abilities such as talking and walking. Other children evidenced uncontrollable grief reactions and resisted all contact. When reunited with their mothers or provided with a substitute mother, most of these grief-stricken infants returned to normal emotional responsivity and behavior. In Anna Freud's view, the disaster of war and evacuation had demonstrated the validity of psychoanalytic hypotheses concerning the central importance of the mother-child relationship (1958, p. 515).

Some years later, in August 1945, six young children finally reached England. They were German-Jewish orphans whose parents had been killed in gas chambers shortly after their births and then were evacuated from place to place and from family to family. For three years they had actually been held in a German concentration camp. One can only imagine their sufferings under such conditions. A former contributor to Anna Freud's Hampstead Nurseries donated a year's tenancy of a country house in Sussex named Bulldogs Bank. Together with Sophie Dann, one of the nurses in charge of Bulldogs Bank, Anna Freud published an account of their group life (A. Freud, 1951b).

> The Bulldogs Bank children functioned as a unit; no child wished to be separated from the others, nor would the group allow any of its members to be parted. Their insistence on being constantly together caused some difficulty in the staff's plans to treat them as individuals. For example, John, the oldest (3 years, 10 months), needed only to push away his plate at dinner for the other five children to cease eating. Unlike normal children, this group of orphans showed no envy, jealousy, or rivalry among themselves. They would spontaneously take turns at games, equally share every treasure, and were acutely sensitive to each other's needs and feelings. (A. Freud, 1951b, p. 174)

The **Bulldogs Bank children** rarely attacked or hurt one another during their first few months at the country house. Disputes were typically word battles, which ended in a massed attack against any outsider, such as an interfering adult. Their way of expressing aggression was less sophisticated than would be expected for children of their age. Biting and spitting were the usual modes of expressing anger, although sometimes they urinated on the floor or into their clothes to express their feelings. All of these behaviors are regressive, that is, characteristic of much younger children. But after a few weeks, they were able to add hitting and smacking adults to their growing repertoire.

Positive relations with adults were first made on a group basis. They began to expect that adults should act the way they did. For example, the children eventually began to insist that the adults take their turns or share. Then they expressed concern about the adults' feelings. Finally, individual personal attachments to the adults began to appear and had the quality of child-parent relationships.

The children had been exposed to terror and deprivation during their stay in concentration camps. Though they usually expressed no clear memories of their past, they evidenced signs of their experiences. For example, all six children were terrified of dogs, probably because of the concentration camp guard dogs. "Once, when he met a strange large dog on a walk, John bit his lip in his terror and thought that the dog had bitten him when it bled" (A. Freud, 1951b, p. 216). In a similar way, the children were afraid of large trucks, presumably because they resembled concentration camp vans. That the children did not show an even greater range of fears and anxieties is probably attributable to their close cohesion and mutual support, through which each member drew strength from the others. Anna Freud and Sophie Dann summarized their observations in this way:

> They were deprived of mother love, oral satisfactions, stability in their relationships and their surroundings. They were passed from one hand to another during their first year, lived in an age group instead of a family during their second and third year, and were uprooted again three times during their fourth year. . . . The children were hypersensitive, restless, aggressive, difficult to handle. They showed a heightened autoeroticism and some of them the beginning of neurotic symptoms. But they were neither deficient, delinquent, nor psychotic. They had found an alternative placement for their libido [i.e., each other] and, on the strength of this, had mastered some of their anxieties and developed social attitudes. (1951b, pp. 228–229).

Thus, even in children who were severely deprived and traumatized, Anna Freud recognized the efforts they made for psychological survival in a devastating environment.

Mastery of Life Tasks: Developmental Lines

The sixth and last theoretical yield from Anna Freud's child analytic work was her observation of how the ego masters problems posed by life. **Developmental lines** is Anna Freud's term for a developmental sequence of id-ego interactions. As they proceed along these developmental lines, children outgrow, in gradual steps, their dependence on external controls and gain in **ego mastery** of internal and external reality (A. Freud, 1965b, p. 63). The focus is not only on the ego's growing mastery, for the id drives are the primary impetus for the ego's alertness to inner and outer demands.

Developmental lines may be thought of as reliable sequences in the child's maturation from dependency to relatively complete independence, from irrationality to rationality, and from passivity to activity. These lines of development reveal the ego's attempts to confront life situations successfully, without painful retreat and without overly defensive inhibition. Such life situations include separation from mother, birth of a brother or sister, illness, school, peer relations, play, emergence of sexual interest at puberty, and, of course, love (A. Freud, 1962, p. 34).

The six developmental lines (Table 6.2) are:

1. From Dependency to Emotional Self-Reliance
2. From Suckling to Rational Eating
3. From Wetting and Soiling to Bladder and Bowel Control

Table 6.2 Six Developmental Lines

I. Dependency to emotional self-reliance	*II. Suckling to rational eating*
1. Biological dependence on mother; no recognition of separation between self and other. 2. Need-fulfilling relationship, with mother seen as partially externalized satisfier. 3. Object-constancy phase, in which image of mother is retained even when she is not present. 4. Pre-oedipal, clinging stage, marked by fantasies of dominating the love object. 5. Phallic-oedipal phase, marked by possessiveness of parent of opposite sex and rivalry with same-sexed parent. 6. Latency phase with lessening of drive urgency, denigration of parental models, transfer of libido to peers, groups, authority figures. 7. Preadolescent phase of return to early attitudes of need-fulfilling relationship with love object. 8. Adolescent phase, marked by struggle to win independence and break ties with childhood love objects (parents), and need for establishing genital primacy.	1. Being nursed by schedule or on demand. 2. Weaning from breast or bottle initiated either by infant or by wishes of mother; new food. 3. Transition from being fed to self-feeding; "food" and "mother" still identified with each other. 4. Self-feeding, disagreements with mother about quantity; meals as battlegrounds for other difficulties of mother-child relations. 5. Infantile sexual theories shape attitude toward food: fantasies of impregnation through mouth, pregnancy fear (fear of getting fat). 6. Fading of sexualization of feeding, with pleasure in eating regained or increased; more self-determination of eating habits.
III. Wetting and soiling to bowel and bladder control	*IV. Irresponsibility to responsibility in body management*
1. Complete freedom to wet and soil is controlled by mother, not self 2. Anal phase of child's direct opposition to control of elimination by others; feces treated as precious "gifts" to mother; battle of wills for toilet training. 3. Identification with parental rules, self-control of bladder and bowel; cleanliness concerns based on learned disgust and shame. Orderliness and tidiness interests based on anal regularity. 4. Cleanliness concerns pursued for their own sake, regardless of parental pressures; autonomous ego and superego control of anal drives.	1. Aggression turned from self to external world. Self-injury from biting, scratching, picking limited by focus on external objects; child recognizes causes of self-induced pain. 2. Ego advances of understanding cause-effect principles, delay of dangerous wishes, recognition of external dangers such as fire, heights, water. 3. Voluntary endorsement of rules of hygiene and medical necessity; avoidance of unwholesome foods, bodily cleanliness, compliance with doctor's orders only when fear or guilt enforces it. Belief that mother can restore endangered health.

(continued)

Table 6.2 *(continued)*

V. Body to toy and play to work	VI. Egocentricity to companionship
1. Infant play is body sensuality in fingers, skin, and mouth of own or mother's body with no clear distinction between the two.	1. Selfish, narcissistic outlook, in which other children do not matter or are seen as disturbers and rivals for parental love.
2. Sensual properties of own and mother's body transferred to some soft object; e.g., teddy bear, blanket.	2. Other children related to as lifeless objects or toys, to be manhandled and roughly treated with no response expected from them.
3. Clinging to one specific "soft" object grows into general liking for such cuddly things; but all are inanimate objects and do not retaliate for toddler's ambivalent handling.	3. Other children seen as helpmates in tasks; duration of partnership determined by task requirements.
4. Cuddly objects used now only at bedtime; other toys for day play.	4. Other children seen as equals and partners in their own right; they can be admired, feared, or competed with, loved, hated, or identified with. True companionship desired.
5. Pleasure in finishing play activities, and pleasure in achievement.	
6. Play grades into work via hobbies, daydreams, games, proficiency sports. Child can inhibit own impulses.	

Based on A. Freud, 1965b, pp. 64–85.

4. From Irresponsibility to Responsibility in Body Management
5. From the Body to the Toy, and From Play to Work
6. From Egocentricity to Companionship

Anna Freud's introduction of the concept of developmental lines is an original contribution to psychoanalysis. The concept of lines of development as formulated by Anna Freud focuses attention on the ego's capacity to adapt to life's demands; those demands can be situational, interpersonal, or personal. Thus, Anna Freud has brought classic psychoanalytic theory closer to looking at the world of relationships and away from an exclusive focus on intrapsychic dynamics.

THE EGO DEFENDS ITSELF: PROFILES OF MASTERY AND VULNERABILITY

In the early phase of her development of a modification of the analytic method for application to children, Anna Freud searched for a way to shorten the diagnostic stage of the preparatory period. The first step in that direction came with her investigation of ego defenses as indicators of instinctual change. Although the instinctual dynamics themselves are not directly observable, the ego's reaction to them is apparent from an examination of the individual's defenses.

In 1936 Anna Freud published her classic monograph, *The Ego and the Mechanisms of Defense*. This book was largely responsible for legitimizing the interest of psychoanalysts in ego functioning. She stated the justification for interest in ego defenses:

> If we know how a particular patient seeks to defend himself against the emergence of his instinctual impulses, i.e., what is the nature of his habitual ego resistances, we can form an idea of his probable attitude toward his own unwelcome affects. (A. Freud, 1936, p. 32)

BOX 6.3 *Only Connect...*

When you examine Table 6.2, you will notice that some of the items reflect actual behaviors that can be observed, such as "Being nursed by schedule or on demand." Other items reflect imagining what a child must be thinking and feeling, such as "Pre-oedipal, clinging stage, marked by fantasies of dominating the love object." This hybrid combination of operationally defined, observable items and other items that can only be inferred indicates both Anna Freud's immersion in psychoanalytic theory as well as her attention to the actual behaviors of infants and children as they respond to their surroundings.

Anna Freud began to systematize and expand the whole range of Sigmund Freud's many writings and pronouncements on the topic of ego defenses. These ranged from his earliest conception of repression as the fundamental ego maneuver in the face of instinctual threat to his later elaboration of secondary defense strategies. For the first time, the patients' maneuvers for adjusting to their social and biological needs, and their typical techniques of expressing emotional reactions came under direct scrutiny. All of these ego functions, many of them involving observable behaviors, had been largely ignored or neglected by analysts in favor of what they presumed to be more valuable knowledge to be gained by study of unconscious drives. Defenses had been viewed merely as obstacles to a clear view of the unconscious.

Defenses as Diagnostic Indicators

Consider the paradox that confronts the psychoanalyst treating patients who navigate the obstacles of their lives with the aid of massive psychological defenses. Such patients have come to therapy because they feel that their lives are constricted, joyless, and devoid of spontaneity. Yet, so long as a patient's defenses hold, the analyst confronts an apparently intact personality, which does not need psychoanalysis. It is ironic that only when the defenses fail and unconscious material reemerges into awareness that the analyst may discern trouble in the depths:

> So long as the defenses set up by a person's ego are intact, the analytic observer is faced by a blank; as soon as they break down, for example, when repression fails and unconscious material returns...a mass of information about inner processes becomes available.
> (A. Freud, 1969, p. 125)

Defenses are successful protectors of the personality precisely because the ego remains unaware that it is defending itself.

In Anna Freud's terms, the ego's defenses are silent and invisible (1936, p. 8). Repression, for example, is only apparent by the absence of drive components that we expect to be present in a normal person. The child who is all sweetness and goodness, with no evidence of hostility, jealousy, or anger is most likely one whose ego has been enfeebled by massive repression against anger and aggression. Thus, the ego defenses are observable only by inference when the individual's behavior evidences signs of missing customary id derivatives. Looked at from the developmental point of view, people's defenses reveal their personal history of ego development, that is, life stories of mastering or succumbing to their passions, needs, wishes, and urges (1936, p. 21; Sandler & A. Freud, 1985).

Motives for Defense

Following her father's lead (S. Freud, 1926), Anna Freud distinguished three sources of danger to which the ego responds defensively. First, in the case of the adult neurotic, there is the danger of superego dissatisfaction with the way the ego seeks to provide gratifications to id sexual and aggressive strivings. The irony of this form of anxiety is that the ego itself does not regard the sexual or aggressive impulses against which it so actively defends itself as dangerous or condemnable. "The instinct is regarded as dangerous because the superego prohibits its gratification, and if [the instinct] achieves its aim, it will certainly stir up trouble between the ego and superego" (A. Freud, 1936, p. 55). Because the superego is capable of setting up a rigid and unattainable ideal standard, the neurotic's ego works to renounce all sexual and aggressive impulses to a degree that is incompatible with good mental health. The neurotic ego thus serves the superego to an exaggerated extent, even at the cost of internal conflict.

Second, in the case of the child neurotic, who has not yet formed a severe superego, the ego may come to fear the danger of the outside world. Fearing the instincts because the parents have prohibited their expression, the child's ego is reacting to fear of their displeasure. This more "objective" anxiety is nevertheless sufficient to trigger the ego's defensive maneuvers against sexual and aggressive impulses (A. Freud, 1936, p. 57).

Third, there is the ego's fear of the danger of the strength of unconscious impulses. Sigmund Freud thought that this fear resulted from the ego's differentiation from the id in infancy and its gradual separation from the id's primary process by the development of its own reality-oriented secondary process of logical thought. Thus, when an instinct becomes too strong, the ego experiences the impulses as a threat to its independence, as a signal of the danger of being flooded by id primary process chaos (S. Freud, 1923a, p. 57). Rather than submit helplessly to invasion, the ego brings defenses into play. In a few sentences, Freud concisely summarized the three kinds of anxiety that trigger ego defenses and the difficult situation in which the id finds itself:

> Thus the ego, driven by the id, confined by the superego, repulsed by reality, struggles to master its economic task of bringing about harmony among the forces and influences working in and upon it; and we can understand how it is that so often we cannot suppress a cry: "Life is not easy!" If the ego is obliged to admit its weakness, it breaks out in anxiety—realistic anxiety regarding the external world, moral anxiety regarding the superego, and neurotic anxiety regarding the strength of the passions in the id. (S. Freud, 1933, p. 78)

In Anna Freud's hands, analysis of ego defensive functioning became a very sensitive diagnostic tool. For the child analyst, severely limited in the use of free association, defense analysis became the indispensable means to an understanding of the child's personal history of instinctual development (A. Freud, 1936, pp. 37–39; Sandler & A. Freud, 1985). By permitting the deduction of the specific id passion, the period of life when it emerged, and the specific kind of blockage erected by the ego against it, defense analysis opened the way to the hidden depths of the child's life history.

Anna Freud listed ten ego defenses hinted at or described by her father, and five elaborations of her own. Table 6.3 provides a definition and an illustration of each of these **classic defenses.** It should be pointed out that other psychoanalysts have many others, so that the total number of possible ego defenses is considerably larger than those represented in the table.

Table 6.3   Anna Freud's Ten Ego Defenses

Defense mechanism	Definition and characteristics	Illustration
1. REPRESSION [Motivated Forgetting]	Abrupt and involuntary removal from awareness of any threatening impulse, idea, or memory. Most dangerous and one of the most archaic defenses, repression or denial is the prerequisite for any of the other defense mechanisms listed below.	Adolescent girl feeling guilty over her sexual impulses, frequently "blocks" on her boyfriend's name when introducing him to family and friends.
1A. DENIAL [Motivated Negation]	Blocking of external events from entry into awareness, when perception of such stimuli is symbolically or associatively related to threatening impulses. Denial abolishes dangers "out there" by negating them.	A recent widow continues to set a place at the table for her deceased husband. She also fantasizes frequently about conversations she is having with him.
2. ASCETICISM [Renunciation of Needs]	Characteristic of puberty, asceticism is more of a character style than a defense. Preadolescents feel overwhelmed by their emerging sexual impulses and protect themselves by repudiating all desires, all pleasures. In extremes, adolescents may "mortify" themselves by limiting sleep and food intake, and retaining urine and feces as long as possible.	The adolescent who embarks on what seems to be a "fad" diet, or "fad" interest in rigorous physical exertion may be attempting to control his or her impulses.
3. PROJECTION [Displacement Outward]	Attribution to another person or object one's own unacceptable impulses, wishes, or thoughts. Then, these impulses become "ego-alien" as though not a part of self.	A husband who has barely resisted the temptation to be unfaithful to his wife, begins to be chronically suspicious about her fidelity to him.
3A. ALTRUISTIC SURRENDER [Sacrifice Self]	A form of projection in which the person fulfills his or her own needs vicariously by identifying with the satisfactions of another; in extreme form, person may even give up own ambitions to allow another to be fulfilled.	An employee who was too timid to ask for a raise for herself became a militant advocate for the rights of another worker, expressing extreme assertiveness.
3B. DISPLACEMENT [Redirection of Impulse]	Redirection of impulses, usually aggressive ones, onto a substitute target when the appropriate target is too threatening.	A young woman, who in childhood was very envious of her brother's relationship with their mother, could only express her feelings of rage toward other females, typically other female relatives.
4. TURNING-AGAINST-SELF [Self-as-Object or Target]	Redirection of impulses inwardly against oneself instead of outwardly toward the appropriate target. Usually results in masochistic feelings of inadequacy, guilt, depression.	Same woman as above (3B) also turned her hatred toward mother inward, becoming self-accusatory, passive, surrendering, and inferior feeling.
5. REACTION-FORMATION [Believing the Opposite]	Transformation of unacceptable impulses into their opposites and more acceptable forms; usually has the quality of "The Lady doth protest too much." Hate into love; love into hate.	A child who had been aggressive toward her mother became overly concerned for her safety, for her mother's welfare, and became excessively worried that some harm would befall her mother.

(continued)

Table 6.3   (*continued*)

5A. REVERSAL [Active into Passive]	Similar to reaction-formation, reversal transforms an impulse from an active to a passive mode. Also similar to Turning-Against-Self.	Sadistic impulses may become masochistic, with the self as passive target of aggression and sexual impulses.
6. SUBLIMATION [Acceptable Substitutes]	Transformation of an impulse into a socially productive and acceptable form.	A war veteran who had enjoyed his soldiering became a policeman who preferred assignments in the most dangerous neighborhoods.
7. INTROJECTION [Taking Within]	Incorporating into one's own behavior and beliefs the characteristics of some external object or admired person.	The adolescent who adopts the traits, mannerisms, and speech of an admired teacher. The widow who adopts items of apparel from her deceased husband, along with his tastes in food and entertainments.
7A. IDENTIFICATION-WITH-THE-AGGRESSOR [Adopting Feared Traits]	Adopting the traits or mannerisms of a feared person or object.	A little girl who was afraid to walk down the dark hallway of her house for fear of meeting a ghost solved the problem by "booing" her way down the hall: "You just have to pretend that you're the ghost who might meet you."
8. ISOLATION [Stripping of Emotion, Meaning]	Characteristic of obsessive-compulsive neurosis, unacceptable impulses are retained in consciousness but divested of emotion and separated from connecting ideas to achieve an emotional-intellectual quarantine.	Seventeen-year-old boy with acute masturbation guilt, divided all his thoughts into acceptable and unacceptable ones. Both categories of ideas could not be thought simultaneously without unacceptable ideas contaminating acceptable ones. (Fenichel, 1945)
9. UNDOING [Magical Cancellations]	Characteristic of obsessive-compulsive personality, who performs magical gestures or rituals, to cancel unacceptable thoughts or acts, once the thought or act has been completed.	Same boy as above (8), had to perform rituals whenever unacceptable and acceptable thoughts occurred together. For example, he had to recite the alphabet backwards whenever he had a sexual thought, or turn around and spit whenever he met another boy he knew also masturbated.
10. REGRESSION [Developmental Retreat]	Probably not really a defense, so much as a primitivization of behavior in face of stress: return to earlier modes of response when confronted with anxiety.	At his first separation from mother upon hospitalization for a tonsillectomy, Timmy began thumb-sucking and soiling his pants, deeds he "outgrew" two years earlier.

Based on A. Freud, 1936; Undoing and Isolation examples from Fenichel, 1945; Sandler & A. Freud, 1985.

A FINAL WORD ON ANNA FREUD

Anna Freud's work represents one possible solution, or more precisely, a group of solutions, to the unfinished problems bequeathed by Sigmund Freud. The character of Anna Freud's solutions was threefold.

First and foremost, she attempted to enlarge the boundaries of classical psychoanalysis with direct considerations of ego functioning in social reality without abandoning the bedrock of psychoanalytic instinct theory. For Anna Freud, the ego is still in partnership with the id, still bound primarily to fulfill its tasks at the id's behest. But the ego is also capable of some independent functioning in the areas of life mastery.

Second, Anna Freud systematized what had been insights scattered throughout her father's work. Thus her attention to ego defenses, her adaptation of the psychoanalytic method for therapy with children, and her metapsychological classification scheme. All are based on classic theoretical formulations. At the same time each of these achievements transcends classical theory in significant but sometimes subtle ways. The key modification was her emphasis on viewing personality development as more affected by the environment, as more easily shaped by interpersonal relations, and as more fluid than classical theory would have it.

Third, Anna Freud's work is far removed from the implicit neurological assumptions of Sigmund Freud's creation. For Anna Freud, children, and presumably also adults, are active, assertive, and masterful. They need not be perpetual victims of their internal conflicts or of their overwhelming environments.

THE LEGACY OF ANNA FREUD

Anna Freud has bequeathed an enormous multifaceted legacy. While she preserved the important findings of her father, she also developed his ideas to studying the ego's pattern of activity with external reality. Her psychotherapeutic work with children was pioneering. She can be credited for beginning the work of psychoanalytically informed child psychotherapy. This approach involved considerable creative and thoughtful modification of adult psychoanalytic technique.

Her idea of measuring stages of child development in many areas, which she termed "developmental lines" was an innovative study of child development and a forerunner of an abundance of developmental theories and measures that are still applied today. Instead of merely theorizing about child behavior and psychodynamics, she engaged in actual observations of children's behavior in a wide range of environments. Her "metapsychological analysis," which integrated many areas including an individual's history, environment, psychodynamics and behavior, was a precursor of the assessment and diagnostic procedures of contemporary school and clinical psychologists. Equally important, her thoughtful compassion and attention to the needs of children as well as her convincing rationales for the importance of children's well-being has affected the approach of generations of mental health professionals working with children.

Later in her life, Anna Freud extended her work to informing the legal system, particularly the area of family law, to take into account what had been the largely ignored emotional and developmental needs of children (A. Freud & Burlingham, 1973; Sayers, 1991, pp. 190–195). She emphasized not the parents' wishes but the maintenance of the child's beneficial attachments. Her foray into jurisprudence endeavored to have a positive impact on quality of the environments with which children would have to cope. Her ideas in this regard do not seem so striking today, but they represented a real advance over the practices of the time.

EVALUATING THE PSYCHOANALYTIC EGO PSYCHOLOGISTS

Anna Freud and other theorists whom we classify as ego psychologists explicitly attempted to preserve classical psychoanalysis. They certainly developed new ideas but they invariably did not claim originality. By contrast, the neo-Freudian thinkers we examine later had no great concern for the preservation of classical analysis. Thinkers such as Horney and Sullivan aimed to change classical analysis. Instead, Anna Freud indicated that her ideas were derived from Freud's theories.

Refutability of Psychoanalytic Ego Psychology

Anna Freud did little to provide a basis for the empirical researcher. There is much in what we have seen that cries out for testing, but there are so few ways to translate ego psychology into testable hypotheses. An exception appears to be Anna Freud's concept of developmental lines, which is based in part on observations of children. Possibly, her descriptive categorization of ego defenses could lead to empirical research.

Psychoanalytic Ego Psychologists' Conception of Human Agency

The greatest difference between classical psychoanalysis and the ego psychologist considered in this chapter concerns the issue of active versus passive human agency. The person is seen as largely reactive in classical psychoanalytic theory. The ego psychologists see humans as partly passive agents, but also as partly active agents who are capable of influencing the nature of the reality with which they interact. They have a more balanced view.

Anna Freud's conception of developmental lines emphasizes themes of mastery that partially free the ego from its passive stance in relation to the id and to reality. In this view children are seen as actively striving to master developmental tasks in different areas of functioning. Their development can be thwarted as a result of environmental deprivation or regress in response to loss and trauma.

Idiographic and/or Nomothetic Emphases—Anna Freud's Personality Theories

Anna Freud's theory is focused on understanding the dynamics of individuals and is largely clinically focused and largely idiographic. She does indicate some general stages that apply to all individuals, but her focus, even here is on the specific case.

SUMMARY

Like Freud's classical approach, ego psychology represents a collective attempt to understand both normal and abnormal human functioning. Like Sigmund Freud's ego psychologists, Anna Freud aimed to clarify the connection and the conflict between reason and passion. But unlike Freud, she gradually shifted psychoanalysis away from its focus on drives and instinctual satisfaction and more toward a concern with reason and masterful coping.

Anna Freud, Freud's self-chosen psychoanalytic conservator, legitimized ego psychology by her clinical and theoretical contributions. She preserved her father's legacy while, at the same time, making significant and original contributions to the direction of psychoanalysis. Through her work with child patients, with war orphans, and with children separated from their parents, Anna Freud was able to transcend classical drive theory without demolishing it. Her focus on the ego and its ability to cope with external challenges was an addition to Sigmund Freud's intrapsychic focus. She developed a diagnostic classification system predicated on the plasticity of the child's healthy strivings toward increased maturity. She further elaborated and expanded Freud's understanding of ego defenses. Her most original contribution to psychoanalytic theory has been her elucidation of developmental lines, sequences of psychological and physical growth organized along the paths of dependency to independence, from irrational to rational, and from passive to active relations with reality. Developmental lines suggest an important interactionist vantage point from which to account for psychological functioning, a viewpoint neglected in classical Freudian theory.

Anna Freud's work relied, more than that of classical psychoanalysts, on direct observations of behavior. She modified Freudian psychoanalytic technique in order to be therapeutically effective with children. Her approach seems superficially contradictory to psychoanalysis, but it is based on her understanding that children are significantly affected by *present environmental factors* rather than being largely affected by *intrapsychic residues of past experience*, as in classical psychoanalysis. She worked to provide environments in which deprived and traumatized children could experience safety and care. In such circumstances, she noted that children had the resilience to overcome their developmental fixations.

Anna Freud's development of a comprehensive model of assessment, the metapsychological profile, was a precursor of contemporary psychodiagnostic approaches. Her assessment process consisted of integrating findings from many sources—including an inventory of important events in the life of the patient, observations in a variety environments, a range of psychological tests, and psychodynamic formulations. Her legacy includes a concern for the well-being of children. Her advocacy of the psychological welfare of children has affected our understanding of the importance of parenting and influenced the mental health professions, as well as the legal system and other governmental agencies in their approach toward children.

Anna Freud did little to provide a basis for the empirical researcher as many of her ideas are hard to operationalize. Two possible exceptions are her concept of developmental lines and her categorization of ego defenses. Anna Freud, like other ego psychologists had a more balanced view of active versus passive human agency than was the case in classical psychoanalysis. She saw children as very much affected by the environment but also able to be resilient and to face up to environmental challenges. Her view was that there was interaction between the environment and individual activity. Her approach has a largely idiographic and clinical focus.

FOR FURTHER READING

Anna Freud's most important books and papers, of which there are many, have been collected into a seven-volume collection, *The Writings of Anna Freud* (New York: International Universitites Press, 1965–1974). Also, a biography by Young-Bruehl, *Anna Freud: A Biography* (New York: Summit Books, 1988), is available. There is a need for a more thorough and balanced biography of Anna Freud.

Additional suggestions for further readings on Anna Freud and ego psychology can be found on the web site associated with Chapter 6 at www.wiley.com/college/sollod

GLOSSARY

Bulldogs Bank children: The collective name given to six children who were survivors of a Nazi concentration camp. Anna Freud cared for them in a house in England called Bulldogs Bank. She learned much about the resiliency of the personality from them.

Classic defenses: Repression, denial, asceticism, projection, altruistic surrender, displacement, turning-against-self, reaction formation, reversal, sublimation, introjection, identification-with-the-aggressor, isolation, undoing, and regression.

Developmental lines: Reliable sequences of development during which children outgrow dependence on external controls and gain in ego mastery of internal and external reality. Anna Freud listed six separate developmental lines:

1. From Dependency to Emotional Self-Reliance
2. From Suckling to Rational Eating
3. From Wetting and Soiling to Bladder and Bowel Control
4. From Irresponsibility to Responsibility in Body Management
5. From the Body to the Toy, and From Play to Work
6. From Egocentricity to Companionship

Ego mastery: The ego's ability effectively to deal with both internal drives and external reality. Ego mastery involves the individual's growing awareness of inner and outer demands.

Metapsychological profile: Developed first by Anna Freud, it is the psychoanalyst's way of organizing all of the information obtained about a patient during a diagnostic assessment. It integrates the findings into a coherent picture of the person's dynamic, genetic, economic, structural, and adaptive functioning.

Psychoanalytic ego psychology: An approach that focuses on the unique properties of the ego in guiding a person's capacity to master the demands of life, not just react to them. An extension of Freudian theory, it addressed inconsistencies between the classical Freudian drive theory and observations that people often are able to transcend their drives and impulses.

Chapter 7

Melanie Klein & Donald W. Winnicott

The Psychoanalytic Heritage: Object Relations Theories

...the infant's longing for an inexhaustible and ever-present breast stems by no means only from a craving for food...

Melanie Klein

I once risked the remark, 'There is no such thing as a baby'....A baby cannot exist alone, but is essentially part of a relationship.

D. W. Winnicott

Melanie Klein   Born: 1882 Vienna, Austria
                         Died: 1960 London, England

About Object Relations Theories

Object relations theorists such as Melanie Klein and Donald W. Winnicott started with modest revisions but eventually transformed Freudian theory and psychoanalytic practice more completely than did the ego psychologists. This chapter focuses on the contributions of two of the most well known of these theorists.

Melanie Klein pictured the subjective world of the infant as a chaotic mixture of internalized images of people and parts of people. The child's imagination, spurred by anxiety and anger, transforms these images into sometimes terrifying phantasies of good and bad objects.

Donald W. Winnicott, a pediatrician and child psychoanalyst, learned from Melanie Klein about the infant's internal world of object relations. Winnicott was less focused on psychopathology and included his understanding of children's capacity for healthy spontaneity.

WHAT ARE PSYCHOANALYTIC OBJECT RELATIONS THEORIES?

The term *object relations* is derived from Freud's (e.g., 1917b; 1921; 1923a) drive theory, as discussed in Chapter 3. Freud referred to the specific actual satisfiers of drives as the "objects" of the drive. For example, different foods are considered *objects* of the hunger drive. Later, in *The Ego and the Id,* Freud theorized that the ego could incorporate lost or renounced love objects as internal images. By creating such images, the ego diminishes the id's frustration at the loss. Freud concluded that many qualities of the ego are formed by incorporating lost love objects. In this process, the ego introjects or assumes some features of love objects that are no longer actually available. (Freud, 1923a, pp. 29 and 30; see also Freud, 1917b)

The interpersonal emphasis of the term *object relations* only gradually evolved. Whereas Freud's main efforts had been spent explaining how the ego achieved the aims of the id drives, theorists such as Melanie Klein and Donald W. Winnicott focused on the infant's interpersonal strivings for safety, love, empathy, admiration, and trust. Freud's drive model was thus supplanted by a theory of intimate relationships. The term **object relations** thus came to be understood as the person's actual relationships with "objects" (mostly people) beyond the subjective world of the self. To qualify as a psychoanalytic object relations theory, a theory also must include private and unconscious meanings associated with a person's pattern of object relations.

PSYCHOANALYSIS AS PEDAGOGY: EDUCATING ERICH

Without an M.D. or a Ph.D., Melanie Klein was nonetheless encouraged by her psychoanalyst, Sandor Ferenczi (1873–1933), to observe children's educational development and relate her observations to psychoanalytic theory. Her own son Erich was her first subject. Lacking training in either psychological assessment or empirical research methods, Klein's earliest contributions were enthusiastic and largely uncritical confirmations of Freudian psychoanalytic theory and child psychoanalysis.

Freud had argued for the special theoretical importance to psychoanalysis of such childhood neuroses and had proposed that every adult neurosis has origins in childhood neurosis (Freud, 1918, p. 9). Klein agreed with this view and saw psychoanalysis or an "upbringing with psychoanalytic features" in childhood as necessary preventative therapy (Klein, 1931/1975a).

Dating from her earliest observations and psychotherapy with children, Klein emphasized children's imaginative reconstruction of reality. As an early and articulate feminist, she also countered Freud's emphasis on penis envy and male psychodynamics with a greater appreciation of the importance of womb envy, the female breast, and the maternal role.

KLEIN'S DISCOVERY OF "PHANTASY"

Melanie Klein discovered that from the very earliest moments of life, children construct what she termed *phantasies*—Klein used the word **phantasy** to mean the infant's unconscious world of the "unreal real" (Klein, 1937/1975a, p. 221). Phantasy with the

---

BOX 7.1   *Only Connect . . .*

Klein's theory anticipates some ideas later proposed by cognitive psychologists (Chapters 12 and 13). Her theory indicates that it is not the actual reality of stimuli to which babies respond but rather the meanings that they *perceive*. A

Kleinian emphasis not stressed in later cognitive approaches is the importance of phantasy or imagining as a source of baby's experience of the world.

"ph" spelling, as distinguished from fantasy, describes for Klein unconscious thoughts and wishes that are not necessarily reality (cf. Mitchell 1986, p. 22). Presumably, she reserved the alternate spelling of the word *fantasy* for conscious, imaginative constructions.

In Klein's concept, phantasy creates the world of imagination. Through phantasizing, the baby tests out and primitively construes its experiences of inside and outside. External reality can gradually affect and modify the unrealistic sense of reality that phantasy creates (Mitchell, 1986, p. 23).

Klein's Adultlike Interpretation of Phantasy

Klein's early approach to interpretations of children was direct and sometimes blunt (Klein, 1961). With clinical experience over a long period, Klein eventually learned to offer more skillfully phrased and timed interpretations. Klein believed that direct interpretation and sympathetic acknowledgment of the child's phantasies strengthened the child's ability to deal with conflicting feelings such as love and hate for the same person (cf. Segal, 1992, p. 59).

One prominent feature of Klein's interpretative style is that she treated the child's verbal expressions during play as equivalent to adult free associations. She encouraged verbalization by providing an assortment of toys, including human and animal figures, building blocks, and toy vehicles of all kinds. She even used ordinary objects in the therapy room. Klein did not limit her interpretations only to what the child said. She thought that the child's actual behavior with the toys represented, sometimes even symbolized, unconscious ideas, wishes, and phantasies. Klein believed that the themes expressed in play are similar to those in dreams and thus are especially suitable for interpretation (Klein, 1926/1975a, p. 134).

Correcting Freud's Male Emphasis

Klein made every effort to correct Freudian theory regarding his view of the significance of female behavior and anatomy. For example, she believed that Freud was mistaken in his theoretical neglect of the mother's role. Freud's version of psychosexual development focused on the male. For example, he emphasized the significance of the penis for both genders with his concepts of castration anxiety and penis envy. By contrast, Klein assigned major significance to the loving or rejecting breast, which became the enduring core of Klein's mother-centered psychoanalytic theory (cf. Hughes, 1989; pp. 174–175). Melanie Klein intended to balance Freud's theories with a focus on the importance of the female (cf. Sayers, 1991, pp. 3–20 and pp. 261–268).

Klein's emphasis on the importance of the breast was not completely at variance with Freudian theory. Freud had also acknowledged the importance of the breast in his writings. Consider his well-known passage:

A child's first erotic object is the mother's breast that nourishes it; love has its origin in attachment to the satisfied need for nourishment. There is no doubt that, to begin with, the child does not distinguish between the breast and its own body; when the breast has to be separated from the body and shifted to the "outside" because the child so often finds it absent, it carries with it as an "object" a part of the original narcissistic libidinal cathexis. This first object is later completed into the person of the child's mother, who not only nourishes it but also looks after it and thus arouses in it a number of other physical sensations, pleasurable and unpleasurable. By her care of the child's body she becomes its first seducer. In these two relations lies the root of a mother's importance, unique, without parallel, established unalterably for a whole lifetime as the first and strongest love-object and as the prototype of all later love-relations for both sexes. (Freud, 1940, p. 188)

DEVELOPMENT OF THE OBJECT WORLD

Attachment: Love and Hate at the Breast

The most important object in an infant's world, initially the only object, is the breast. Concerned exclusively with the gratification of needs, an infant is limited to two major categories of experience: pleasure (gratification) and pain (frustration). If the baby is being gratified by the breast, the baby loves it and has phantasies of a pleasant kind regarding the breast. When babies feel frustrated at the breast, their phantasies are of attacking this breast. In these aggressive phantasies, the baby wishes to bite and to tear up the mother and her breasts, and to destroy her in other ways as well (Klein, 1937/1975a, p. 308).

The infant's relationship to the breast, and therefore to the world, is nearly completely an oral, passive-incorporative orientation. There is very little reality-based active initiative or differentiation between self and not-self. Consequently, the child's phantasy world focuses on the breast as its "object of constant desire." The breast is possessed by incorporation:

> In phantasy, the child sucks the breast into himself, chews it up and swallows it; thus he feels that he has actually got it there, that he possesses the mother's breast within himself, in both its good and bad aspects. (Klein, 1936/1975a, p. 291)

In this phantasy of incorporation, the baby experiences that the breast-in-the-mouth is part of self; breast and baby are perceived as one and the same.

Development from Part Objects to the Whole Person

The object world of the very young infant consists of part-objects, some of which are gratifying, some frustrating, some welcoming and some hostile, some inside and some outside. Infants gradually perceive the world to consist of **good objects** (satisfying and pleasurable) and **bad objects** (frustrating and painful). Good (gratifying) objects are idealized. Phantasy elevates them to absolute goodness. Bad objects are phantasized into representations of distilled hate. Because the mother's breast is sometimes a satisfier, and sometimes a frustrator of the infant's oral needs, the way breast-feeding and weaning are handled by the mother strongly influences how the child learns to manage emotions of love and hate.

An infant's undeveloped cognitive abilities permit it to attach to a part of a person or even to parts of his or her own body. The infant treats the part as the whole. The experience of the mother in early infancy thus need not be the whole, real person. Initially, the experience of mother is little more than of a nipple protruding from a breast (Klein, 1936/1975a, p. 290). According to Klein's theory, the infant experiences that **part-object** either as the source of all goodness or as the agent of all that is frustrating:

> The baby's mother is both desired and hated with all the intensity that is characteristic of the early urges of the baby. In the very beginning he loves his mother at the time when she is satisfying his needs for nourishment. She alleviates his feelings of hunger, and gives him sensual pleasure, which he experiences when he is sucking at her breast. This gratification is the initial part of the child's sexuality. The meaning of the situation suddenly is altered when the baby's desires are not gratified. Hatred and aggressive feelings are aroused and he becomes dominated by the impulses to strike out at the object of all his desires and who, in his mind, is linked with everything he experiences—good and bad alike (Klein, 1937/1975a, p. 306).

Parallel with maturation in the infant's emotional life is the child's growing sophistication in perceiving its love-objects. Some time after four or five months of life, mother is transformed from a collection of part-objects to a **whole object.** Good and bad breasts become experienced as good and bad mothers. Now the clash of love and hate—the fear of being attacked by a gratifying but frightening object—is transferred to the mother as a whole person.

The infant now undergoes an intensification of its conflicts about good and bad objects. It is difficult to cope with a good-mother-who-is-also-sometimes-a-bad-mother. One strategy might be to protect the good object by attacking the bad. Annihilate bad mommy before she attacks you. However, such infantile logic clashes with the perception that *good* and *bad* are no longer experienced as separate part-objects. Mommy is a whole person. In Klein's view, the infant must calculate that it might destroy the loving good object even while intending only to destroy the persecutory bad object. The dim awareness that the love-object is in danger leads to the infant's guilty realization that he or she is dangerous to the mother (Klein, 1936/1975a, p. 295). Guilt feelings are thus added to the pain of the conflict between love and hate.

INFANTILE SADISM AND THE OEDIPUS COMPLEX

In Klein's theory, the infant interprets hostile objects as persecuting and attacking (1936/1975a, p. 293). To defend itself, the infant incorporates as much of the safe and gratifying good breast as possible, eventually extending its "greedy" impulses to the mother's entire body. Erotic and aggressive impulses are fused into **infantile sadism,** an actively aggressive stance toward love-objects.

Klein's thoughts and observations led her to conclude that the Oedipus complex is triggered in the infant during weaning, a period of maximum frustration typified by sadistic impulses. In her earliest papers, Klein (1921/1975a; 1928/1975a) had first reported observations that indicated the presence of a sadistic superego in infants as early as age two. In contrast to Freud's view of genital dominance in the Oedipal phase, Klein believed that the dynamics of the classic Oedipus complex emerge only when they build on these earlier, more amorphous and more unruly pre-genital sadistic impulses (Klein, 1929/1975a, p. 212; 1933/1975a, p. 251). Eventually, Klein (1933/1975a) conceptualized the origins of the superego and a rudimentary Oedipus complex as occurring even earlier—in the first six months of life.

In summary, the views of Freud and Klein regarding the nature and origin of the Oedipus complex are markedly different. Freud saw the Oedipus complex as developing during the phallic stage and arising from a male child's sense of rivalry with his father. Klein thought the Oedipus complex was a response to frustration during the oral stage.

The Epistemophilic (Love of Knowledge) Instinct

The infant's ego is undeveloped and poorly equipped to understand the nature of the oral and anal impulses that are mounting in intensity. Feeling overwhelmed in the face of these unruly urges, the infant's ego is nevertheless intensely curious about them. Because of the importance she attributed to the child's sexual curiosity, Klein called it the *epistemophilic* (love of knowledge) *instinct.*

But about precisely what is the child so curious? Klein's clinical interpretations led her to believe that infants, as well as younger children, caught up in a confusing swirl of oral, anal, and emerging genital impulses, are curious about those same processes in the love-object. Therefore, the child's urge to know is directed at first to the mother's body, which the child believes is the site of all sexual processes. In Klein's theory, the young child phantasizes that inside the mother's body are feces, sexual organs, and even father's penis. Still incorporative in its relation to the world and dominated by aggression, the child is not only curious about mother's body and its contents, but desires strongly to take possession of it. Klein called this phase of development the **femininity phase** because infants of both genders actively identify with the mother they seek to possess (Klein 1928/1975a, p. 189). Both infant boys and infant girls desire to possess the mother's "special sexual organs." Put another way, children of both genders experience "breast envy" and "womb envy."

The infant's intense sexual curiosity meets initially only with frustration because its primitive ego lacks the language ability to ask questions about sexual urges and body parts. Even when the child becomes able to formulate some basic questions, frustration is rekindled because the child realizes that most of the more complex and interesting questions remain unaddressed (Klein, 1928/1975a, p. 188). Early and late frustrations turn to anger and indignation. Stifling of the child's sexual curiosity can generalize over time to include an inhibition of all forms of curiosity. Haunting general feelings of being inept and incapable may result. Anger over "not knowing" may impede the child's development of generalized intellectual competency and skills needed to meet the demands that life makes.

The Oedipus Complex in Boys

Klein thought that *womb envy* was more important than penis envy as a universal Oedipal motive. The breasts and vagina were also sexual organs of interest to the boy. Full of aggressive and sadistic urges as well, the male infant not only wants to learn about these organs and to possess them, but also to injure or destroy them. Yet, the infant also is fearful of retaliation for its hatred. In addition, Klein suggests that the mother, too, can be part of the male child's castration fears:

> The boy fears punishment for his destruction of his mother's body, but, besides this, his fear is of a more general nature....He fears that his body will be mutilated and dismembered,

and that he will be castrated. Here we have a direct contribution to the castration complex. In this early period of development the mother who takes away the child's feces signifies also a mother who dismembers and castrates him. Not only by means of the anal frustrations which she inflicts does she pave the way for the castration complex: in terms of psychic reality she is also already the castrator. (Klein 1928/1975a, p. 190)

To illustrate these fears for oneself, one can imagine an infant lying frightened and helpless as his mother, perhaps forcefully, cleans his behind of fecal material. Such a scene is very different from the picture of an infant sucking contentedly at the breast.

Klein further hypothesized that infants of both genders phantasize that the mother incorporates orally one or more of father's many penises. As a result, infants envy the mother, but also fear what might be inside her. For the boy, the mother-who-incorporates-father's-penis is a "woman with a penis," that is, an amalgam of father and mother. It does not go unnoticed by the boy that mother has "taken" a penis from a man. In short, mother can be a dangerous, castrating person (Klein, 1928/1975a, pp. 131, 245).

Overlapping toilet training, during which the mother must at least partially frustrate the child's anal impulses as she sometimes has frustrated its earlier oral urges, the femininity phase rekindles feelings of intense anger toward the frustrator. Klein (1928/1975a, p. 189 ff.) believed that this new **anal frustration** is in fact a "second trauma" that prompts the child eventually to devalue the frustrating love-object. Children of both genders may thus be prompted to withdraw from the mother and move toward the father.

Under the influence of his emerging genital impulses, the boy desires his mother as a love-object. He already experiences her as a frustrator of his oral and anal needs, and his accumulated feelings of hatred are now amplified to encompass genital urges. To make matters more difficult, an early and incomplete version of castration anxiety in the form of jealousy and fear of the father makes itself known, although full castration fear at the hands of the father will not materialize until later, around the ages of four and five years. Now, however, as early as age one or two years, the male child is caught on the horns of a three-pronged dilemma: desire to possess the mother, hatred of her as a frustrator-castrator, and an amorphous fear that father will take revenge.

The boy's sexual curiosity grows. His insecurity over not being able to have a baby because he has no womb is concealed behind a facade of ever-escalating curiosity about wombs. He can become an expert on where babies come from even if he cannot have one. Hence, the boy directs his sexual urges and fears into curiosity and information gathering. In this way, intellectual challenges, at which eventually he can feel superior, displace the anatomical deficiencies that made him feel inferior (Klein, 1928/1975a, p. 191). The use of his mind helps him deal with his "womb envy."

The Oedipus Complex in Girls

After weaning, the girl turns away from her frustrating mother and is further encouraged to devalue her mother by the anal deprivations she feels mother imposes. Klein proposed that the girl infant unconsciously senses her vagina and other sexual equipment as soon as the stirrings of the Oedipal impulses begin (Klein, 1928/1975a, p. 192). Unlike her male counterpart, Klein believed that the female infant gains little gratification from masturbation for these newly emerging genital impulses. Envy and hatred of the mother arise because the girl believes that mother not only possesses the father but also the father's penis. As time progresses, the more classical form of Oedipal dynamics (actually Electra dynamics) appear as the girl grows more attached to father, experiences his attentions erotically, and becomes increasingly resentful of mother.

The little girl's epistemophilic impulse is first roused by the Oedipus complex; the result is that she discovers her lack of a penis. She feels this lack to be a fresh cause of hatred for the mother, but at the same time her sense of guilt makes her regard it as a punishment. This embitters her frustration in this direction, and, in its turn, exercises a profound influence on the whole castration complex (Klein, 1928/1975a, p. 193).

> Analogous to the boy's castration anxiety in the full Oedipus complex described by Freud, the girl, too, has a primal fear. She desires to empty her mother's body of all its goodness, including the father's penis she imagines within it, feces, and other children. Nevertheless, the girl phantasizes that the mother may turn the tables on her to retaliate by emptying the child's body of these good things. In short, the mother can attack the self and destroy, devour, or annihilate it. Klein regarded this terrible fear of being destroyed by mother to be the fundamental and universal danger situation among woman. At later stages of development, this fear of an attacking mother is transformed into a fear of losing the real mother (Klein, 1929/1975, p. 217).

Mother-as-love-object is thus closely associated with guilt and anxiety. Consequently, Klein thought that the infant girl finds that she can identify with the father more easily than with the mother. The plot thickens as the female infant's guilt leads her to try to form a new love relationship with mother. This effort bears the hallmarks of overcompensation and reaction formation. She overdoes it to the point of being saccharine and ungenuine. This new attempt at a loving relationship is doomed as the girl experiences a fresh round of hatred and rivalry with her mother for father's attentions. The girl finally gives up her attempts to identify with father. Instead, she comes to view father as a love-object from whom she can obtain love and to whom she may give love without necessarily being like him. More or less by default, mother becomes the girl's object of identification (Klein, 1928/1975a, pp. 193–194).

HOW IT ALL TURNS OUT: KLEIN'S FIRST THEORY OF THE SUPEREGO

Ultimately, the girl models herself on her *phantasy* of the mother in both its cruel and nurturing aspects. "From the early identification with the mother in which the anal-sadistic level so largely preponderates, the little girl derives jealousy and hatred and forms a cruel super-ego after the maternal imago" (Klein, 1928/1975a, p. 195). Fortunately, as the little girl matures and as her genital impulses assume dominance over the oral and anal sadism of early infancy, she identifies more and more with mother's nurturing, kind, and generous qualities. She even phantasizes an idealized image of the "bountiful mother" who may be more a product of wish than reality.

The boy's development is along similar lines with a slightly different outcome for his superego. Initially, the boy also acquires a severe superego modeled on the cruel-sadistic image he has constructed of mother-breast in phantasy. Moreover, like his female counterpart, maturity finds the boy incorporating in a more modest way the kinder, nurturing aspects of the maternal image. But boys ultimately have to identify more strongly with *father*. The idealized father image now becomes dominant in the boy's superego.

Klein (1927/1975a; see especially 1928/1975a, pp. 197 ff.) argued early in her career that her account of the Oedipus complex, including the infant's hatred and its origins in an early, cruel superego, did not contradict Freud's model. She believed that her ideas extended Freud's without substantially challenging his basic views. As

Klein's ideas continued to evolve, she began gradually to consider hatred as a less important factor in development than did Freud. Other psychoanalysts could see that she was taking Freud's ideas and transforming them into her own (e.g., A. Freud 1927, pp. 37–40; and A. Freud, 1952/1992, p. 63; Freud & Jones, 1993, pp. 621 ff., see especially Freud's letters to Jones, #508, p. 624; and letter #509, pp. 627 ff).

Disagreements between Melanie Klein and Anna Freud

For Klein, a child's play is an equivalent to free association in the adult and is thus suited for direct interpretation. As we saw in Chapter 6, Anna Freud did not regard child analysis as a simple equivalent of adult psychoanalysis. She insisted on a specialized technique, a phase of preparation for analysis, and only then did she interpret the child's verbal associations elicited by play. Anna Freud avoided interpreting the play activity itself. In all respects, Anna Freud emphasized the unique developmental requirements that make working analytically with children different from working with adults. Given this fundamental divergence in orientation to the task, Melanie Klein's therapeutic technique was at variance with Anna Freud's in four major ways:

First, Klein's interpretations were often based on symbolic meanings derived from her theory. She treated the child's games and play with toys as direct representatives of the phantasy objects her theory postulates in the child's unconscious. In working with children, Klein used the child's play with toys and objects in the room for interpretation of symbolic meanings. Anna Freud thought that symbolic interpretations imposed meanings on the child's actions rather than elucidating their inherent meaning. Such a technique, she thought, amounted to "wild analysis," in which the child's thoughts and actions would be steered into compliance with Kleinian theory. Anna Freud's own technique for child analysis (see Chapter 6) emphasized the child's actual verbal productions during play or story telling. Interpretations were limited to the immediately available evidence emerging from the child's associations after a period of preparation in which the child is made comfortable with and instructed in the procedure. Very young children were not considered suitable candidates for psychoanalysis precisely because they were not yet sufficiently verbal.

Second, for Anna Freud, the transference relationship with a child is different from adult transference because the child's past relationships are necessarily also its current relationships (A. Freud, 1927, pp. 39 ff. and p. 45). From Melanie Klein's point of view, transference is transference. Object relationships begin almost from birth in Klein's view of infancy. Thus early object relations, real and phantastic, are sufficiently plentiful to form the basis of a child's transferential relationship to the therapist. Just as in adult psychoanalysis, the analyst must interpret the transference (A. Freud, 1952/1992, p. 63).

Third, Klein suggested that Anna Freud saw children as very different from adults, whereas she herself saw very little reason to treat a child patient differently from an adult patient. Using her own play technique with toys and drawings, Melanie Klein thought that she had been able to access the most primitive layers of the child's unconscious, an achievement that lay outside the range of Anna Freud's more verbal technique. It seemed to Klein that Anna Freud's method minimized the psychoanalyst's role as the interpreter of the child's unconscious conflicts. Instead, the analyst operating with Anna Freud's technique becomes an educational role model who encourages a positive, even submissive, transference relationship with the child. Because of the analyst's failure to establish a "true analytic situation," the child becomes unable and unwilling to make its deepest feelings known (Klein, 1927/1975a, pp. 153–154, 167).

Fourth, from Anna Freud's viewpoint, the Kleinian approach led to excessive pathologizing and at times, unwarranted attributions of aggressive motives to the child.

The dispute between Anna Freud and Melanie Klein resulted in divisions in the profession of child analysis. In London, psychoanalysts and their students identified themselves as Anna-Freudians, Kleinians, or Middle-groupers.

ANXIETY: FIRST MODIFICATIONS
OF KLEIN'S DEVELOPMENTAL THEORY

With growing experience and an increased number of observations from child analyses, Melanie Klein modified her basic formulations about the development of the superego and Oedipus complex. The changes took three forms. She added detail about the content of the child's phantasies, changed the developmental timing of them, and slightly reduced the role of aggression in all of them. The first change resulted in a significant population explosion of the infant's internalized objects whereas the second change pushed back the origins of personality structure to the earliest days of life. Klein postulated the existence at birth of a rudimentary ego, superego as well as innate Oedipal-like motives. Klein supplemented her emphasis on the importance of aggression as the primary motive of infancy with some small degree of consideration of envy, guilt, anxiety, and love.

Fear of One's Own Destructive Impulses: Projection

In amplifying her reasons for the severity of the infant's superego, Klein elaborated her theory of internalized objects. Her observations led her to believe that a regular part of a child's life centers on fears of phantastic frightening figures who threaten to dismember, devour, or "tear the child to pieces." Klein believed that the terrifying characters of fairy tales are transformed by phantasy into personalized constructions of real objects in the child's life:

> I have no doubt from my own analytic observations that the real objects behind those imaginary, terrifying figures are the child's own parents, and that those dreadful shapes in some way or other reflect the features of its father and mother, however distorted and phantastic the resemblance may be. (Klein, 1933/1975, p. 249)

If a child unconsciously equates the parents with wild beasts and fairy tale monsters, then the child clearly is not identifying with actual parents as they exist in reality. Instead, the child is identifying with transformed images of the parents unconsciously created by the child. The cruelty and sadism of the child's superego thus derives secondarily from identifying with the cruelty of these transformed and imaginary objects. The primary transformation of the objects into malevolent persecutors, recall, was a product of the child's innate sadism. But how does a child's fear mount to a level that can transform loved ones into menacing object images?

Klein's answer is that the child's immature ego is frightened of its own innate sadism. The danger of being destroyed by one's own death instinct is so terrifying that the immature ego mobilizes against the death instinct what libido or life instinct it has available (Klein, 1932/1975b, pp. 126 ff.) Then, using the relatively primitive defense of projection, the ego directs the uncontainable aggression outward onto external objects. In this way, the infant's fear of its own internal impulses becomes, in part, a fear of external objects (Klein, 1932/1975b, p. 128). Now the infant believes that the objects want to destroy self rather than vice versa. Projections grow into persecutors. The infant's internalized and externalized objects have become ravaging terrorists within. In reality, the fear that the infant experiences is the dread of its own destructive urges toward love-objects. Consequently, "... his fear of his objects will always be proportionate to the degree of his own sadistic impulses" (Klein, 1933/1975a, pp. 251).

The weapons of the child's sadism are ordinary infantile equipment and activities mutated by phantasy into agents of destruction. Thus wetting by urination becomes equivalent to drowning, cutting, stabbing, and burning; feces are equated with missiles and direct-contact combative weapons. With development, the more knowledgeable child can perceive feces as poisons and toxins of all sorts. The penis itself can be a target of injury or a weapon with which to inflict it. And there are the always available standbys of biting, chewing, and spitting, which can become interchangeable equivalents of devouring, dismembering, and annihilation (Klein, 1930/1975a, pp. 219–220, 226).

With the focus thus firmly on sadism and fear as the motivating force, Klein moved the timing of the origins of the superego to the child's first oral introjections of objects, that is, to the first few months of life.

Oral, Urethral, and Anal Sadism: Cannibalizing Mother

In her reformulation, Klein continued to rely heavily on innate aggression as a primal motive. However, she tempered this reliance with a consideration of the child's fears of its own aggression and its displacement of that aggression onto phantastic internalized and external objects. She eventually tempered sadism further with considerations of love and guilt. For now, however, the content of the child's sadistic phantasies was given greater elaboration and increased developmental precision.

Taking Freud at his word once again, Klein distinguished between an early oral-sucking aggressive phase and a later oral-sadistic phase. In the first part of the first year of life during the oral-sucking phase, the child phantasizes taking the breast within itself; in the somewhat later oral-sadistic phase, the child imagines chewing it up, devouring the breast cannibalistically. In this later phase, presumably late in the first year, oral and aggressive needs are simultaneously gratified by the same phantasy. In the second and third years of life, the child enters the anal-sadistic phase in which the necessary focus on elimination becomes tied to aggressive urges once more. Klein believed that elimination of feces took on the meaning for the child of eliminating the love-object—a "forcible ejection" of it—linked to destructive desires (1933/1975a, p. 253). Between the oral-sadistic phase and the anal-sadistic phase, Klein discerned a transitional urethral-sadistic phase and its associated phantasies.

In its oral-sadistic phantasies the child attacks its mother's breast, and the means it employs are its teeth and jaws. In its urethral and anal phantasies it seeks to destroy the inside of the mother's body, and uses its urine and feces for the purpose. In this second group of phantasies the excrements are regarded as burning and corroding substances, wild animals, weapons of all kinds, etc.; and the child enters a phase in which it directs every instrument of its sadism to the one purpose of destroying its mother's body and what is contained in it. As regards choice of object, the child's oral-sadistic impulses are still the underlying factor, so that it thinks of sucking out and eating up the inside of its mother's body as though it were a breast (Klein, 1933/1975a, pp. 253–254).

When the child phantasizes attacking the insides of the mother, he or she thereby attacks a great many internalized objects. By extension of its infantile phantasy logic, Klein argued, the infant is attacking an entire world peopled by objects hostile to the self, including the father, mother, brothers, and sisters. "The world, transformed into the mother's body, is in hostile array against the child and persecutes him" (Klein, 1929/1975a, p. 214). Destroy or be destroyed becomes the infant's strategy, but it is a strategy fraught with guilt and anxiety.

HATE VERSUS GUILT: REPAIRING THE RAVAGES OF SADISM

As the child matures toward the genital phase of development in the fourth and fifth years of life, innate sadism diminishes because life-affirming and creative motives take precedence. With these normal developments comes the emergence of the child's capacity for pity, sympathy, and empathy (Klein, 1929/1975a, p. 214). In short, authentic object love becomes possible.

From Part-Object Introjections to Whole Object Identification

Initially, as we have seen, the infantile ego is capable only of identifying with part-objects, and often these partial persons are equated in phantasy with body processes and products such as feces, breasts, and penises. With development, the infantile ego becomes capable of perceiving and identifying *with* whole objects that more closely approximate reality. More important, given the choice, the ego more readily identifies with and incorporates good rather than bad objects because good objects can provide pleasure for the id and because bad objects installed into the self are likely to create pain. From the ego's point of view, preservation of the good internalized object is synonymous with survival of the ego (Klein, 1935/1975a, p. 264). Said differently, the ego is now capable of understanding that loss of or damage to the good object threatens its own existence.

> With this change in the relation to the object, new anxiety-contents make their appearance and a change takes place in the mechanisms of defense. The development of the libido also is decisively influenced. Paranoid anxiety lest the objects sadistically destroyed should themselves be a source of poison and danger inside the subject's body causes him, in spite of the vehemence of his oral-sadistic onslaughts, at the same time to be profoundly mistrustful of the objects while yet incorporating them. (Klein, 1935/1975a, p. 264)

The infant repeats again and again the act of incorporating the good object. Each repetition is also a compulsive test of an object's goodness as the infant tries to disprove its fears about the object. In this way, the infant fortifies itself against persecutory objects and can phantasize about protecting the good objects by safeguarding them within the self.

Protecting the Good Object: Paranoid versus Depressive Anxiety

To the child's dismay, repetition does not lead to success or finality. The child soon discovers that he or she cannot protect internalized good objects from the sadism of internalized bad ones. Anxiety develops about the dangers that lie in wait for internalized good objects, including a phantasy that the inside of the body can be a poisonous place in which good objects perish (Klein, 1935/1975a, p. 265). Every real and imagined act of destruction that objects have enacted against one another, including parental sexual relations, which the child views as an act of violence, are seen as sources of continuing danger to the good object.

One irony, lost on the child, is that its new capacity to identify with whole objects occurs simultaneously with the development of its awareness that it cannot protect them from persecuting bad objects or from the id.

> It requires a fuller identification with the loved object, and a fuller recognition of its value, for the ego to become aware of the state of disintegration to which it has reduced and is continuing to reduce its loved object. The ego then finds itself confronted with the psychic reality that its loved objects are in a state of dissolution—in bits—and the despair, remorse and anxiety deriving from this recognition are at the bottom of numerous anxiety-situations. To quote only a few of them: there is anxiety how to put the bits together in the right way and at the right time; how to pick out the good bits and do away with the bad ones; how to bring the object to life when it has been put together; and there is the anxiety of being interfered with in this task by bad objects and by one's own hatred, etc. (Klein, 1935/1975a, p. 269)

Another irony is the close link between love and destruction. For at this stage of his development, loving an object and devouring it are very closely connected. A little child who believes, when its mother disappears, that he has eaten her up and destroyed her (whether from motives of love or of hate) is tormented by anxiety both for her and for the good mother which he has absorbed.

> It now becomes plain why, at this phase of development, the ego feels itself constantly menaced in its possession of internalized good objects. It is full of anxiety lest such objects should die. Both in children and in adults suffering from depression, I have discovered the dread of harboring dying or dead objects (especially the parents) inside one and an identification of the ego with objects in this condition. (Klein, 1935/1975a, p. 266)

Thus, for Klein, even the apparent love and empathic concern that develops with the maturation of the infant's ego has a selfish basis. The child fears that its good objects may die and is terrified that such dead objects will reside within the self. Every event that signals loss of the real, good mother in the world of reality also indicates the potential loss of the internalized good mother in the world of phantasy. The feelings of sadness or remorse that result from imagining loss of the loved object is what Klein initially called depressive anxiety. At its core, depressive anxiety is a kind of sadness about the fate of the good object.

However, paranoid anxiety over what the objects might do to the self also develops. Never secure in their possession of the good object, children cannot be certain about the goodness and stability of the good object. Instead, paranoid fears and doubts can prevail. Even if good objects of the real world are not actually lost, it is nevertheless possible, the anxious and suspicious child believes, that bad objects of the phantasy world can still mount an assault on them. In Klein's account, the alternatives the child faces in viewing the world are a lose-lose proposition.

PARANOIC AND DEPRESSIVE POSITIONS: KLEIN'S FIRST THEORY

A child's self-involved fears take one of two forms. When the central anxiety assumes the form of persecution of the ego itself—a fear that one's own ego is at risk of attack—then the anxiety is described by Klein as the **paranoic position.** If, however, the central fear is that the good object is at risk because internalized bad objects might destroy it, the prevailing feeling is melancholy and therefore is considered the **depressive position** (Klein, 1935/1975a, p. 269).

Persecution and Pining

The feelings of sorrow in the depressive position reflect a desire to regain or repair the lost or damaged love-objects. Klein called this whole constellation of melancholy emotions "pining." The depressive position constitutes anxiety that internalized bad objects will persecute and destroy internalized good objects, defends against these fears, and subjectively experiences longing or pining (Klein, 1945/1975a, p. 349). It is characteristic of the depressive position to be anxious and remorseful about the plight of the damaged loved object, whereas the person in the paranoiac position is vigilant and fearfully alert to the possibility that a disintegrated object may reunify to emerge again as a persecutor (Klein, 1935/1975a, p. 272).

Positions of Development from Paranoid to Depressive

Fear of one's own annihilation, the paranoiac form of anxiety, is the developmentally earlier and more primitive form because its danger situation—annihilation—is innate. Fear of losing the good object by destruction or mutilation, the depressive form of early anxiety, is developmentally later and more complex because its danger situation requires a comprehension of whole objects, empathy for them, and a sense of guilt for one's own role in the process of loss. The depressive and paranoiac forms of early anxiety to perceived danger situations are actually a normal developmental personality progression, but one that is never completely surpassed with age or totally resolved in the sense that ordinary developmental stages are customarily outgrown. For that reason, Klein referred to these personality processes as the depressive position and the paranoid position, rather than "stages" of melancholy and persecutory anxiety (Klein, 1935/1975a, p. 275n; see especially the last paragraph of the end notes in 1952/1975c, p. 93).

MANIC AND DEPRESSIVE POSITIONS IN ADULT PSYCHOPATHOLOGY

Klein theorized that the adult psychopathologies of manic excitation and depression could be understood as derivatives of the paranoiac and depressive positions of childhood. In classical theory, Freud had argued that manic behavior was the ego's way of defending itself against feelings of depression at the loss of a love-object. Klein held the view that the ego is seeking refuge from depressive feelings and trying to escape its tortured relationships with internalized love-objects. To do so, the ego attempts to take control of its love-objects by dominating them. The ego supplements the familiar paranoid and depressive positions by adopting a manic position that serves the additional defensive aim of denial.

Omnipotence and Denial

The sense of omnipotence observable during some adult manic episodes is the central feature, Klein suggested, of this psychotic level of psychopathology. For Klein, the normal developmental version of the "manic position" also hinges on the child's belief in its own omnipotence. The person destined to be manic in adulthood attempted early in infancy to deny the presence of the internalized persecuting objects it had incorporated into the self. Even more painfully, the infantile ego of the person heading toward mania denied its dependence on good objects as well. This defense of denial also has to accomplish an additional aim. The manic person uses denial to obliterate all recognition of danger to good objects from the persecution of internalized bad objects. Freud had pictured personality dynamics as conflict between the id, ego, and superego. Klein widened the war to include conflicts between real and internalized phantasy objects:

What in my view is quite specific for mania is *the utilization of the sense of omnipotence for the purpose of controlling and mastering objects.* This is necessary for two reasons: (a) in order to deny the dread of them which is being experienced, and (b) so that the mechanism (acquired in the previous—the depressive-position) of making reparation to the object may be carried through. By mastering his objects the manic person imagines he will prevent them not only from injuring himself but also from being a danger to one another. His mastery is to enable him particularly to prevent dangerous coitus between the parents he had internalized and their death within him. (Klein, 1935/1975a, pp. 277–278; italics in original)

Infantile denial no longer works for the manic adult, even though the infantile sense of magical omnipotence lingers. Adult psychopathology results when the manic patient believes that he or she has destroyed the internalized love-objects and also magically believes he or she can reconstitute them at will.

Omnipotence and Devaluation: The Power of Life and Death

Omnipotence is coupled with the defense of devaluation whereby the adult belittles the worth and importance of its internalized objects. Contempt replaces love. "This *disparagement of the object's importance and the contempt for it* is, I think, a specific characteristic of mania and enables the ego to effect that partial detachment which we observe side by side with its hunger for objects" (Klein, 1935/1975a, p. 279; italics in original). By detaching itself from its loved objects, the ego advances its development beyond the more dependent depressive position, but it does so at the price of increased anxiety and the need for perpetual vigilance. The new burden that has been presented to the ego is that it must gain mastery over its objects. Merely hungering for them and worrying about their safety are no longer sufficient. Sometimes, however, mastery over the persecuting and malevolent internalized objects includes killing them—with the intention, perhaps, of resurrecting them later.

At a deeper level, the dynamics of the manic position reveal the fundamental ambivalence of children toward their internalized objects. Klein argued, as we have seen, that the infant eventually has to form a more realistic perception of the parents as real objects in the real world. To do so, it must maintain the separation between incorporated good and bad phantasy objects. However, learning and development are making clear to the infantile ego that good and bad are often aspects of the same object, not separate objects as it once thought.

Splitting in Normal Development

As the child relates with increasing appropriateness to the real mother, there is the danger that the phantasy good and bad mother-breast will also unite into one contradictory and unmanageable object. To prevent this intolerable and confusing internal state, the ego splits the images, as Klein describes the process, into permanently separate and opposite object images. Notice that the splitting mechanism is aimed at the internal world of phantasy objects rather than the external world of actual people. Now the child can treat the internalized objects as simple instances of good or bad, loved or hated, while it puts increased trust in the more complicated real people who exhibit both qualities simultaneously (Klein, 1935/1975a, p. 287).

The child now vacillates between depressive worry and manic omnipotence. Troubling thoughts that the good objects will be destroyed are warded off by manic efforts to exert mastery over them. Splitting the phantasy objects into separate good and bad images helps confine this vacillation to the internal world of phantasy objects, and paves the way for the child to relate appropriately to its real objects. In Klein's view, when splitting is used as a strategy to protect the internalized good objects from the internalized bad ones, it is a normal component of personality development. Healthy adaptation to reality requires that the child perceive its real objects accurately and trust them more than its primitive phantasy objects as it matures to adolescence (Klein, 1945/1975a, pp. 348 ff.). This concept is consistent with Freudian theory, even if Klein's techniques do not seem to be.

Splitting as a "Flight to the Good"

Klein described a secondary defense as a "flight to the good" by which the child can vacillate between its external love-objects and its internalized love-objects. If the flight is directed inwardly to the good but internalized phantasy objects, then the result is separation from reality and potential psychosis. On the other hand, if the person's flight is directed outwardly to the good but external real objects, there is the potential either for normal development or for slavish and neurotic dependence on others. In either case, the flight mechanism is the child's way of resolving its depressive and paranoiac anxieties. Thus development of the defense of splitting, for Klein, is a normal developmental process.

At this stage of her thinking, Klein used the term **splitting** in a narrow way to refer to the separation of good and bad objects in the child's phantasy. Subsequently, as we shall see, Klein (1946/1975c) elaborated her account of splitting to include *structural splits* in the child's id, ego, and self. In fact, she later makes clear that the infant cannot split its image of the love-object without splitting its own ego into good and bad components as well. A particular split-off part of the id, Klein will later propose, becomes the prison of psychoticlike and terrifying object images that seek to devour the child.

Triumph and Guilt in the Manic Position

If psychological development is normal, a balance is achieved between love and hate as the child's objects are unified into whole and more realistic images. With time, the child develops the desire to outgrow its dependencies, to rival the achievements of its admired love-objects, and to master fears of its own destructiveness. Eventually, mastery strivings become dominant. The child wants to reverse the parent-child relationship so that it can attain power over the parents, exceed their achievements, and even subjugate them in phantasies of power and humiliation. Envisioning a time when the parents will have changed into helpless beings, like little children, as they become weak, old, and frail adults, the child relishes its future triumph. But the ego also experiences these phantasies of triumph with feelings of guilt (Klein, 1945/1975a, 351–352).

Triumph and guilt can impede the child's progression out of the depressive position because they compete with and block the ego's reparative work of restoring the damaged loved objects. Without the reparative work of normal mourning for lost or abandoned love-objects, normal emotional development and healthy independence are put at risk. This destructive aspect of the manic position mobilizes the child's sadism and focuses it not only on healthy urges to be masterful, but also on desires to humiliate and destroy the parental figures. Nevertheless, there is good news as well as bad. Triumph over one's objects can also promote emotional, intellectual, and physical growth. "The child's growing skills, gifts and arts increase his belief in his constructive tendencies, in his capacity to master and control his hostile impulses as well as his 'bad' internal objects" (Klein, 1940/1975a, p. 353). Triumph thus can lead to genuine mastery and ultimately to the capacity for authentic love.

Of the three positions—paranoiac, depressive, and manic (psychotic)—Klein regarded the depressive position as the central feature of infantile development. The ways in which the child learns to resolve its depressive anxieties and establish real relationships with real objects is crucial to normal personality functioning (Klein, 1935/1975a, p. 289).

LOVE, GUILT, AND REPARATION

By the late 1930s, Klein was expanding her analysis of love and guilt. Klein began to emphasize that infants have spontaneous feelings of love and empathy for others, a different stance from her previous pronouncements. In addition to all of the negative emotions that infants experience, she pointed out, they can routinely feel love and gratitude toward the mother for the care she provides. Klein now introduced the importance of the concept of love. Following Freud's lead, Klein viewed the emotion of love as a derivative of the life instincts, ever present and opposing the destructive urges of the death instinct:

> Side by side with the destructive impulses in the unconscious mind both of the child and of the adult, there exists a profound urge to make sacrifices, in order to help and put right loved people who in phantasy have been harmed or destroyed. In the depths of the mind, the urge to make people happy is linked up with a strong feeling of responsibility and concern for them, which manifests itself in genuine sympathy with other people and the ability to understand them, as they are and as they feel. (Klein, 1937/1975a, p. 211)

Restoring the Good Object: Restitution as Self-Serving Love

Guilt drives love in the Kleinian world. Because the child's ego is identified with the good object and can empathize with its plight, the ego is motivated to make restitution to the good object for all of its previous acts of sadism against it. As the superego develops, furthermore, the child's phantasies of attacking its objects are met with guilt. Feelings of regret surface in the child's awareness for the imagined damage it has inflicted. Desires to "make good"—engaging in the processes of **reparation/restitution**—emerge in the infant mental economy, fueled equally by love and guilt (Klein, 1933/1975a, p. 254).

The infant's empathy for and identification with the love-object also permits it to profit from its concern for the love-object's welfare. Whatever sacrifices the child makes for the sake of the loved one, it is simultaneously making for itself because it identifies with the love-object. As adults, we complete the circle by assuming the role of caring parents where once we were cared-for children. In so doing, we reenact the love we received from our own mothers and now give to our children. In Klein's view, we also expiate our infantile guilt for the damage we imagine we, so long ago, inflicted on our mothers (Klein, 1937/1975a, p. 314). When successful, the infant's reparative efforts open the child to the possibility of loving new objects without fear or guilt. "Thus making reparation—which is such an essential part of the ability to love—widens in scope, and the child's capacity to accept love and, by various means, to take into himself goodness from the outer world steadily increases" (Klein, 1937/1975a, p. 342).

The mother who turns the tables and excessively identifies with her child presents an alternative scenario. Caught up in a resurgence of her own infantile unconscious guilt for the harm she once wished on her love-objects, the mother is attempting to revive a loving relationship to her own mother through her child. She becomes overly self-sacrificing because she sees far too much of herself in the child and far too much of her mother in the role she plays toward her child. Instead of repairing the damage to her own phantasy objects, however, the overly indulgent mother deprives her child of those experiences that will permit it to mature and become psychologically differentiated. "It is well known that a child who has been brought up by a mother who showers love on him and expects nothing in return often becomes a selfish person" (Klein, 1937/1975a, p. 318).

PROJECTION + IDENTIFICATION = SPLITTING REVISITED

Klein revised her earlier views by concluding that splitting was a universal process of defense against normally occurring, psychoticlike anxiety states. Klein wanted to make the implicit link between splitting and the paranoiac and depressive forms of anxiety more explicit.

Revision of the Paranoiac Position to the Paranoid-Schizoid Position

In an earlier version of Klein's theory, the infant splits the love-object into a good and bad object to isolate its own sadism to one aspect of a part-object rather than risk destroying the whole. The infant also splits its relationships with the object into love and hate—love for the good and hate for the bad object. Klein now elaborated this twofold concept of splitting and extended its reach from the early splitting of object relationships to the splitting of personality structures, the self, and feelings.

To reflect the changes, she renamed the "paranoiac position," now to be called the **paranoid-schizoid position.** Schizoid personality phenomena—dysfunctions of empathy, love, and hate in relating to objects and to the self—became for Klein a convenient synonym for all manner of personality pathologies; thus she included the term schizoid in the newly named paranoid-schizoid position.

How Shall I Split? Let Me Count the Ways

From the very beginning of life, Klein now asserted, the ego's experience of its own fear of annihilation is the foundation of anxiety. Anxiety is always experienced in connection with objects. In the paranoid-schizoid position, the infant projects all of its fears onto part-objects, transforming them into hated persecutors. Other significant sources of anxiety included in Klein's new view are the trauma of birth and the frustration of bodily needs. Even these anxieties are experienced from the earliest moments as linked to objects or projected onto them (Klein, 1946/1975c, pp. 4–5; Klein, 1958/1975c, pp. 23 ff.).

Splitting the Object: *Defending Against Annihilation*

In the early days and weeks of life, the normal state of the early ego is a lack of cohesiveness. Its natural tendency toward integration alternates with a tendency toward disintegration when confronted with the enormity of its own destructiveness (Klein, 1946/1975c, p. 4). This vacillating pair of opposite tendencies underlies the mechanism of splitting.

Some of the infant's annihilation fear is not projected outwardly onto objects. A residual component of the death instinct lurks within and magnifies the primitive

| BOX 7.3 | *The Defense of Splitting in Clinical Work* |

Development of the defense of splitting is, in Klein's theory, a normal aspect of a child's development. But splitting is not a mature defense for adults. Patients who rely on this defense in inpatient settings are often a challenge to the staff, particularly if staff members are not knowledgeable about the defense of splitting. Such patients may go to one staff member and complain about another, who they view as rejecting or deficient; then they may turn around and go to the other staff member and complain about the first. They are thus hard to pin down and their behavior can magnify disagreements and conflicts among staff members.

ego's feelings of helplessness. As such helplessness mounts, the ego's natural tendency toward disintegration is accelerated. Thus threatened, the ego attempts to defend itself in one of three ways: by externalizing (projecting) the threat, by denying it altogether, or by **splitting the object** perceived to be the source of the threat into good and bad images. Klein regarded this most elementary form of splitting as a defense directed to the control of annihilation anxiety under the impact of the death instinct. Splitting dichotomizes the internalized phantasized and the perceived external object into good and bad. Splitting also bifurcates the child's relationships to these images into love-and-hate/desire-and-fear. The destructive impulse and its associated anxiety is thus defensively dispersed, deflected, and isolated from the good objects and from self-identified-with-good-objects.

Splitting the Ego: *The Idealized Breast and the Superego*

In her revised formulation, Klein suggested that the ego could not split the object without also **splitting the ego** itself (1946/1975c, pp. 5–6; see also 1958/1975c). When the infant takes into himself the "good" and satisfying breast, this phantasy object is experienced as whole or integrated. In contrast, the split-off "bad" and frustrating breast is experienced as fragmented, "broken into bits." Good feelings that derive from having a satisfying object inside one can be disrupted by the anxiety of having a fragmented and poisonous bad object also inside. To enhance the effectiveness of splitting as a defense against the bad objects, the infantile ego idealizes the goodness of the good object images. "Idealization is bound up with the splitting of the object, for the good aspects of the breast are exaggerated as a safeguard against the fear of the persecuting breast" (Klein, 1946/1975c, p. 7).

A secondary motive also governs idealization of the good object. Because the infant is also driven by its instinctual needs for food and love, it strives for unlimited gratification from an inexhaustible and always bountiful object, the idealized breast. Klein proposed that the process of idealization of split-off parts of the ego underlies the formation of the earliest superego. By the end of the first six months of life, splitting the breast into good and bad images, idealizing the good aspect, and identifying with it constitute the formation of the earliest and most primitive superego (Klein, 1958/1975c, p. 239). Said another way, one aspect of splitting the ego is the creation of the superego.

> In my view, the splitting of the ego, by which the super-ego is formed, comes about as a consequence of conflict in the ego, engendered by the polarity of the two instincts [i.e., life and death]. This conflict is increased by their projection as well as by the resulting introjections of good and bad objects. The ego, supported by the internalized good object

and strengthened by the identification with it, projects a portion of the death instinct into that part of itself which it has split-off—a part which thus comes to be in opposition to the rest of the ego and forms the basis of the superego. (Klein, 1958/1975c, p. 240)

For Klein, the superego is a product of very early splitting of the ego and phantasized incorporation of the good (satisfying) and bad (frustrating) mother, rather than, as Freud's version would have it, the repository of the image of the father who punishes by castration.

The bad object is kept as distant as possible from the bountiful object. Toward this end, the infant's ego may use denial to obliterate awareness of the very existence of the bad object, along with any frustrating situations linked in phantasy to the bad object. But this very selective obliteration of reality works only because the infant temporarily experiences itself as all-powerful—capable of materializing gratification by the mere experience of desire.

In the process of annihilating recognition of the bad object, an entire set of object relations is obliterated and along with them a part of the ego that supported those relations (Klein, 1946/1975c, pp. 7). In short, phantasy objects, reality objects, the relationship to both, and the part of the ego active in the process are all split off and denied.

Splitting the Id: *Dividing Conscious from Unconscious*

Another structural split is needed to cope with the incorporated and terrifying bad object images that the infant has split off from the sadistic strivings of its ego—**splitting the id.** In this way, the unmanageable terrifying persecutory objects—derived, you will recall, from the phantasy transformations of the mother and father—are "relegated to the deeper layers of the unconscious", to the split-off section of the id (Klein, 1958/1975c, p. 241). Two benefits result. First, the split-off aspect of the ego destined to become a superego is better tolerated once these horrific images are dissociated into the deeper unconscious. Second, "extremely bad" images are not assimilated or accepted into either the superego or the ego. They remain dissociated as split-off id contents, or what Freud considered primal repressions.

Klein pointed out that ego splitting is different from id splitting. The ego has to fuse together contradictory images and drives to create its split-off part of the superego. When the id splits, in contrast, images have to be "defused" so that the bad images are divorced from the good and then split off or dissociated. In short, the first kind of splitting associated with the ego ultimately results in a synthesis whereas the second kind associated with the id results in dissociation or in primal repression (Klein, 1958/1975c, pp. 243 ff.).

For Klein, even the adult defense mechanism of repression is a kind of splitting whereby the fully integrated adult ego "divides itself off" from unconscious threat. Consequently, one might suppose that yet another sense in which Klein used the concept of splitting is the division of conscious from unconscious mental content as contrasted with defensive structural splitting.

Splitting the Self: *Projective Identification*

As development proceeds, Klein theorized that the early oral incorporative and aggressive impulses are joined by anal and urethral aggressive impulses. The good object—idealized breast—and the mother's body as an extension of the breast become the targets of the infant's attacks. This is termed **splitting the self.**

The phantasized onslaughts on the mother follow two main lines: one is the predominantly oral impulse to suck dry, bite up, scoop out and rob the mother's body of its good contents. . . . The other line of attack derives from the anal and urethral impulses and implies expelling dangerous substances (excrements) out of self and *into* the mother. Together with these harmful excrements, expelled in hatred, split-off parts of the ego are also projected on to the mother or, as I would rather call it, into the mother. These excrements and bad parts of the self are meant not only to injure but also to control and to take possession of the object. In so far as the mother comes to contain the bad parts of the self, she is not felt to be a separate individual but is felt to be *the* bad self. (Klein, 1946/1975c, p. 8; italics in original)

There is even a bonus to be had in all this projection and splitting: To the degree that the infant can idealize the good parts of self it has projected, it can reincorporate not only the original good aspects but the intensified and idealized ones it has created. It is truly a give and take world for the infant. Normal development, Klein suggested, is an exquisitely delicate balance of optimal degrees of introjection and projection (Klein, 1946/1975c, p. 11).

Because the infant can project self-content into the object and then take it back by identification, Klein termed the process **projective identification.** In a way, the infant gets what it gives: predominantly hostile projections result in primarily hostile identifications. But another aspect of projective identification is that the intention of the infant is forcibly to enter the object to take control of it. This strategy can backfire during the identification part of the cycle. When identification is at its height, the infant ego may feel that others are controlling it, or can take retribution for the violent intrusion, or that its own body and mind can be controlled by others (Klein, 1946/1975c, p. 11).

Schizoid Object Relations: Guilt, Narcissism, and Projective Identification

Because the infant projects the split-off hated part of the self into the object, it eventually realizes that it has placed the object in jeopardy. The infant feels guilty, at least to the small degree that it can experience responsibility, for others who are representatives of the sadistic parts of the self. On the other hand, the projection and splitting enable the infant to permit the "bad" object to carry some of the guilt.

There is also a narcissistic element in projective identification. The infant, after all, is also projecting good aspects of the self, often idealized, into the object. Objects are loved and admired because they are so like the self. Correspondingly, the despised parts of the self can be "split off" and projected into others. Perceived as resembling the unacceptable self, objects embodying the unacceptable projections are transformed into targets of hatred. In either case, the schizoid position from which some infants never emerge assures that their later object relations will be marked by themes of control. For narcissistic self-protection, the infant must dominate the people who carry its projected, split-off self-fragments.

If the infant fails to resolve the paranoid-schizoid position on its way to the depressive position, there is also the possibility that later character development will be marked by a degree of artificiality and lack of spontaneity in relating to others. This characteristic "coldness" of the schizoid style reflects a severe disturbance of a self that has failed to reintegrate the split-off and projected aspects by identification with the available good objects. The various ways in which Klein applied the term splitting to the developmental process are summarized in Table 7.1.

Table 7.1   The Meanings of Splitting in Klein's Theory

Splitting type	Definition and functions
Object	Good-satisfying breast split from the bad-persecuting breast. *Infant's earliest defense against "bad" objects.*
Object relations	The infant can "hate" the bad and "love" the good object (breast). *Defense against guilt for sadistic urges to destroy the good object.*
Ego	Because the infant "incorporates" objects into itself, there is necessarily a split in the ego that parallels splits in the object and relations to the object. *Structure building: Split-off parts are destined to become the superego but only if they can be reintegrated.*
Id	Terrifying and persecuting phantasy objects that the infant has projected onto the parents are "split off" from the rest of the unconscious and pushed to the "deepest" area of the id. *Defensive dissociation: These split-off images are never reintegrated and are like "primal repressions."*
Self	Split-off and hated "bad" parts of the ego and self are split off and projected into the mother to injure her and take possession/control of her. Some good parts of self are also split off and projected into mother: excrements intended as "gifts of self." *Structure building through projective identification and defensive protection against bad objects.*

REPARATION: THE LINK BETWEEN POSITIONS

The depressive position is the central feature of normal development, for the way in which the infant resolves its depressive longings sets the pattern for its later intimate interpersonal relationships. When the infant can introject a "complete" object near the end of the first six months of life, the split between good and bad (and those corresponding splits in the self and ego) are narrowed. The infant begins to construct a more realistic picture of people. Because loved and hated aspects of the breast and mother are now not so widely separated, the infant experiences a sense of loss or mourning when the whole object is not available. An increased sense of guilt for sadistic urges toward the object is the price to be paid for this achievement, a developmental advance that marks the infant's entry into the depressive position (Klein, 1946/1975c, p. 14).

The Drive to Reparation Promotes Ego Integration

The depressive position, Klein now proposed in more detail, has a beneficial early effect of integrating the fragmented ego that has been weakened by its earlier paranoid-schizoid phase of excessive projection and splitting. Depression, an infantile reaction to the phantasized damage inflicted on the love object, engenders strivings to repair or restore the object. This "drive to reparation" exhibited by the infantile ego during the second six months of life will remain in effect for the next several years of childhood. As the child's growing ability to process reality more realistically enhances its adaptation to the world, the depressive position is "worked through" as part of normal emotional development. However, if the earlier paranoid-schizoid position has not been successfully navigated, a successful resolution of the depressive position is also jeopardized. Under these circumstances, the impact of the depression and anxiety of the depressive position may thus mark not a developmental progression but the onset of a vicious circle:

> For if the persecutory fear, and correspondingly schizoid mechanisms, are too strong, the ego is not capable of working through the depressive position. This forces the ego to regress to the paranoid-schizoid position and reinforces the earlier persecutory fears and schizoid phenomena. Thus the basis is established for various forms of schizophrenia in later life; for when such a regression occurs, not only are the fixation-points in the schizoid position reinforced, but there is a danger of greater states of disintegration setting in. Another outcome may be the strengthening of depressive features. (Klein, 1946/1975c, p. 15)

Klein was adamant that during normal development no precise line could be drawn between the feelings of persecution experienced in the paranoid-schizoid position and guilty anxiety in the depressive position. One slowly grades into the other, and elements of both positions persist in later life.

ENVY AND GRATITUDE: THE FOREVER GENEROUS, TOLERANT, AND BOUNTIFUL BREAST

From the infant's point of view, the good breast is an inexhaustible and ever-present source of all that is satisfying. The good breast is the most powerful ally the infant can recruit to protect itself from its own destructive urges. So powerful, so generous, so satisfying is the good breast that the infant envies it and suspects that the good breast selfishly keeps for itself some of its unlimited milk, love, and power (Klein, 1957/1975c, p. 183).

Envy, Jealousy, and Greed Distinguished

Klein distinguished among the meanings of three related terms: envy, jealousy, and greed. **Envy** is an angry feeling that another person possesses and enjoys something desirable. The envious person wants to take away the object of desire, and failing that, to spoil the object of envy so that no one can enjoy it. **Jealousy,** by contrast, is found in the love relationship between two people. When one of the people feels that love is in danger of being taken away by a rival, he or she becomes *jealous* of the rival. The loved object itself is not the target of the emotion and is in no danger of being harmed. **Greed,** a related term, indicates an impetuous and insatiable craving that exceeds what the loved object can give and what the greedy person actually needs (Klein, 1957/1975c, p. 181). In short, the envious person cannot tolerate someone else's possession of the good, the jealous person is fearful of losing the good, and the greedy person is never satisfied by any amount of goodness.

Primary Envy of the Breast

Klein now extended her earlier descriptions of the effects of frustration to include the infant's feelings of envy for a mean and grudging breast that is seen as depriving the infant by keeping for itself what the infant wants: milk, care, love. But the good breast can also be envied. "The very ease with which the milk comes—though the infant feels gratified by it—also gives rise to envy because this gift seems something so unattainable" (Klein, 1957/1975c, p. 183).

Envy Expressed as Grievances in Analysis

Klein pointed out that a parallel to this infantile envy exists within the transference relationship to the psychoanalyst in therapy. For example, when the analyst provides an interpretation that brings relief and changes the patient's mood from despair to hope, some patients respond with angry and destructive criticism of the analyst. The interpretation, initially experienced as enriching and nourishing, is quickly experienced as "not good enough." Focusing on often trivial details, the envious patient is full of criticisms of the psychoanalyst:

> The envious patient grudges the analyst the success of his work; and if he feels that the analyst and the help he is giving have become spoilt and devalued by his envious criticism, he cannot introject him sufficiently as a good object nor accept his interpretations with real conviction and assimilate them. (Klein, 1957/1975c, p. 184)

Feeling guilty for devaluing the help given him in analysis, the envious patient also feels unworthy to benefit from the analysis.

A different but related devaluing maneuver is typical of the paranoid person. Particularly prone to concealing the split-off hostile and envious parts of self from the analyst, the paranoid patient exacts a kind of sneaky revenge against the helpful therapist who expects the patient to be grateful. The paranoid patient cannot permit the self to experience any gratitude to the therapist or incur any psychological debts to the therapist. Instead such patients have abundant needs to devalue the therapist by defeating the analyst's efforts and spoiling whatever good might come of the process. A kind of perverse sadistic, but self-defeating, pleasure is experienced by disparaging the analyst's efforts. This strategy of spoiling the therapeutic relationship is fed by split-off feelings of envy the patient experiences relative to the therapist. Pathological envy thus prevents any possibility that the analyst's interpretations can be meaningfully assimilated.

A defense against recognizing unbearable envy is employed by patients who become confused and express their open doubts about the meaning of interpretations. Their confusion is a way of substituting expressions of doubt for open criticism of the analyst. Klein hypothesized that such confusion stems from the earliest possible object-relationship disturbances. Such patients, as infants, were unable to keep apart the images of the good and bad breast because the strength of their paranoid-schizoid and depressive fears were overwhelming. Such infants do not separate feelings of love and hate and are thus confused about what might be a good (safe) breast and what might be a bad (persecuting) breast. Infants who cannot adequately maintain the split between good and bad never know whether they will suck or be sucked dry, bite or be bitten.

For both kinds of patients, the infantile origins of their contemporary envy include feelings that the breast was not available when wanted or that it provided milk too quickly or too slowly. Such infants may have turned away from the breast to suck their own fingers for a time. When they finally accepted the breast, they may not have drunk enough to satisfy hunger. Some infants overcome their grievances and eventually enjoy feeding, but others seem unable ever to be satisfied even by a satisfactory breast, just as some patients seem unable to accept what good the psychoanalyst can provide (Klein, 1957/1975c, p. 185). At the core, however, what the infant most wants from the bountiful breast, and entertains grievances for not having gotten, is a sense of safety and, in addition, security from its own destructive and frightening urges.

Excessive Envy: Spoiling the Breast

Envy aims to spoil the primary envied object. Sadistic attacks on the breast are intensified by envy, sometimes to the point that the object utterly loses its value. The breast has become "bad" by being bitten. Greed, envy, and persecutory anxiety, all linked together, intensify one another and increase the level of the infant's destructive impulses toward the mother. The good object is never completely or reliably introjected. Doubts about the reliability, goodness, and generosity of the good object have repercussions for later object relationships. Adults who have been unable to completely introject the good object exhibit poor judgment about others, sliding into and out of inappropriately intimate relationships repetitively.

Gratitude and Love: Breast Bliss and Self-Trust

The infant who can overcome its own destructive impulses, incorporate a stable and nurturing object image of the good breast and good mother, can love. There is, Klein acknowledged, some pleasure to be had at the breast for most infants. Full gratification at the breast means that the infant feels it has received from its loved object a unique gift (Klein, 1957/1975c, p. 188). Gratitude is also the basis of trust. When the infant feels grateful for the sustenance and security provided by the breast, it begins an object relationship based on positive feelings for and trust in the object. Such feelings become the foundation for later feelings of connectedness with other people, pleasure in their happiness, and trust in their capacities to reciprocate. Reliable mothering increases the likelihood that such trust will develop.

Freud (1905) described the infant's "bliss" in sucking at the breast as the prototype of all later sexual satisfactions. Klein expanded this Freudian concept to suggest that bliss at the breast is even more widely influential in permitting later intimate relationships, feelings of love for others, and feelings of being fully understood by others. Perhaps even more important, she theorized that investing the good object with one's feelings of trust permits the infant to begin developing a sense of trust in self (Klein, 1957/1975c, p. 188).

DEFENDING AGAINST ENVY: THE MOST DEADLY OF SINS

Klein proposed the importance of envy and gratitude toward the end of her career. One indicator of the importance she placed on these new concepts was her insight into the reasons why envy could be viewed as the worst sin.

> I would even suggest that it [envy] is unconsciously felt to be the greatest sin of all, because it spoils and harms the good object which is the source of life. . . . The feeling of having injured and destroyed the primal object impairs the individual's trust in the sincerity of his later relations and makes him doubt his capacity for love and goodness. (Klein, 1957/1975c, p. 189)

When the infant's ego feels overwhelmed by envy, it may resort to an array of primitive defenses against envy. Some of these defenses may develop into adult personality features that have the potential to disrupt interpersonal relationships. Klein enumerated eight defenses against envy:

- *Idealization.* Klein originally described the infant's efforts to idealize the good breast as a protection against the persecution of the bad breast. Now she expanded her concept to include **idealization** as a means of protecting self from envy of the good object. She indicated that for children in whom the normal splitting process of the object into good and bad has failed, "Strongly exalting the object and its gifts is an attempt to diminish envy" (Klein, 1957/1975c, p. 216).

- *Confusion.* Recall the confusion and doubting of the resistant patient in therapy. For the infant who cannot achieve the normal splitting of the object, confusion between good-and-bad/love-and-hate is the result. "By becoming confused as to whether a substitute for the original figure is good or bad, persecution as well as the guilt about spoiling and attacking the primary object by envy is to some extent counteracted" (Klein, 1957/1975c, p. 216). In extreme form, such confusion may lay the groundwork for psychotic-level states of delusion and obsessive indecision later in adulthood.

- *Flight from mother to other.* Both infants and adults may learn to avoid admired people because they are reminders of the primary envied object, mother. In this way, they protect the breast (and mother) from the destructiveness of their envy. Somewhat later in life, such behavior may lead to promiscuous relationships as the person flees from one love-object to the next (Klein, 1957/1975c, p. 217).

- *Devaluing of the object.* Spoiling and **devaluation** are inherent in envy. A devastated or spoiled love-object need not be envied. Even idealized objects are subject to such devaluation. Indeed they may be especially vulnerable to such devaluation. A sense of ingratitude and the expression of complaints about the object's failings accompany devaluation.

- *Devaluing of the self.* Some adults are unable to use or exploit their own talents and abilities. By denying their own competencies, they avoid envy of and rivalry with admired figures who may provide occasions for unflattering competitive comparisons. As we have seen, even in analysis, the patient may admire and therefore envy the psychoanalyst. Only by further devaluing the self can some patients maintain any relationship with the analyst.

- *Greed for the good.* By greedily and rapaciously incorporating the good and admired object, the infant can believe that it possesses the object and controls it totally. Therefore, all the object's good attributes have become its own.

- *Arousing envy in others.* A frequent adult maneuver to conquer envy is to arouse it in others. In one stroke, the situations of envious subject and envied object are reversed. Klein suggested that this method is particularly ineffective because it backfires, creating worries of being persecuted. Another reason why this defense is so fragile, Klein suggested, is its link to the depressive position. "The desire to make other people, particularly loved ones, envious and to triumph over them gives rise to guilt and to the fear of harming them. The anxiety stirred up impairs the enjoyment of one's own possessions and again increases envy" (Klein, 1957/1975c, pp. 218–219).

- *Stifling love and intensifying hatred.* One way to prevent envy is to deny love for the admired object and express hatred for it instead. Freud had referred to such transformations of impulses into their opposites as the defense of reaction formation. In this way, the most painful combination of love, hatred, guilt, and envy is avoided. On the surface, the hatred may not be evident, but a degree of studied indifference or coldness toward others is observable. An allied maneuver is simply to withdraw from all intimacy.

For the infant who cannot work through the paranoid-schizoid persecutory position adequately, these defenses may signal later severe disturbances of personality.

However, for the infant who achieves the depressive position and is able to work through its feelings of depression and guilt, the outcome is more favorable. Such an infant can learn not only to contain its own destructive impulses, but also to care for, rather than envy, the admired object.

SOME PERSONAL SOURCES OF KLEIN'S VISION OF THE INFANT'S WORLD

Klein envisioned the infant's subjective world as a frightening place of psychoticlike phantasy, need, and wish. Driven by fear, sadism, hate and more hate, triumph, and envy, the Kleinian infant seemingly experiences little happiness. Even triumphs lead, not to ultimate satisfaction, but to guilt. For the Kleinian infant, life is hard: frighteningly difficult to endure or master, nearly impossible to comprehend, and stingy in its rewards. Small wonder that Klein thought infants were angry.

Klein's views of the infant's subjective world are speculative and inferential. But what was her sense of the experience of infancy that guided her inferences? When Melanie was four years old, her nearest sibling in age, Sidonie (age 8), died from a particularly virulent form of glandular tuberculosis. The two had enjoyed an especially close relationship. Sidonie treated her younger sister with memorable kindness, in sharp contrast with their older siblings, who had less tolerance for their youngest sister and often made Melanie the target of their teasing.

Sidonie's death was the first of many that Melanie Klein would experience through her long life, and each of the losses she endured fed her earliest fears of illness and death (Grosskurth, 1986, p. 15). Substantial periods of unresolved mourning, feelings of anxious vulnerability over her own health, and episodes of overt depression recurred throughout her adult life. These symptoms probably had their origins in these early experiences of illness and death (cf. Sayers, 1991, p. 206). As we shall see, young Melanie's feelings of physical vulnerability and susceptibility to illness were often preyed upon, if not actually manipulatively concocted, by her mother.

An Intrusive Mother and Detached Father

Libussa Deutsch Reizes (1852–1914), Melanie's mother, was a smart, strong-willed, energetic but very intrusive person. Twenty-four years younger than her husband, Libussa was in her mid-twenties when the couple settled in an Austrian town to raise their first three children. By 1882, the year Melanie was born, the family had relocated to the capital city of Vienna. Moriz Reizes (1828–1900), Melanie's father, was a general medical practitioner. Melanie and her mother noted that his family was of lower status than the maternal side of the family. Melanie regarded her mother's clan as "full of knowledge and education," whereas the paternal relatives were largely the objects of scorn (Grosskurth, 1986, p. 7).

Melanie wanted to feel close to her father and to note things about him she could admire, such as his knowledge of at least ten languages. But she had few memories of happy moments with him and no recollections of her father ever playing with her. She attributed this neglect largely to his age (an "old fifty") during her childhood. A favorite childhood anecdote about her father told of his brave conduct during a cholera epidemic in a Polish village. Nevertheless, as a Polish-Jewish doctor in an anti-Semitic Vienna, Moriz's medical practice failed. The family regarded Moriz as ineffectual, invisible, and irrelevant.

Libussa Reizes was clearly the dominant member of the family. Melanie grew up observing firsthand a matriarchy that no doubt shaped much of Melanie's attitude toward her mother, motherhood in general, and herself in particular (Grosskurth, 1986, pp. 7, 18). To bolster the family's finances, Libussa opened a retail shop where she sold both plants and reptiles with substantial success. In Melanie's view, her mother's efforts were crucial to the family's survival (Sayers, 1991, p. 206).

As he aged, Melanie perceived her father growing increasingly ineffectual and detached. In her recollection, her father had grown not only old but also became senile. Moriz Reizes died of pneumonia on April 6, 1900, and his passing created even greater financial stresses for the family. Libussa seems to have spent the rest of her life worrying about money and about Melanie's alleged poor health.

Melanie was 17 years old when her 21-year-old second cousin, Arthur Klein, proposed marriage (Grosskurth, 1986, p. 19). Melanie had plans to go to medical school like her father, but she abandoned these when she met Arthur. Arthur and Melanie decided to postpone their marriage for a few years, until economic circumstances stabilized and Arthur could earn a comfortable living. He was then a student preparing for his degree in chemical engineering, and his prospects seemed very good. Over a period of years, however, Melanie found herself trapped in a very long engagement to a man she found she actually did not love.

The next decade and a half was a period during which Melanie finally got married and became a mother. As a mother herself, Klein was often depressed and distracted, with the apparent result that her children created angry phantasies about her. She was still stifled by her domineering mother and sustained many devastating losses of those she loved. In her early thirties, during a continuing period of unhappiness, Melanie read Freud's (1900 and 1901) brief essay "On Dreams" and became convinced that she had found the answer to her own personal distress. In addition to the emotional relief that Freudian therapy seemed to promise, psychoanalysis as an intellectual pursuit might provide a substitute way to achieve her long blocked professional interests in a medical career (Grosskurth, 1986, p. 68).

Melanie sought psychoanalytic treatment for her ongoing depression, recently intensified by the death of Libussa, with the eminent Hungarian psychoanalyst Sandor Ferenczi (1873–1933). Ferenczi was not just another Budapest analyst. For a long period, Ferenczi was a confidant and close associate of Sigmund Freud. Ferenczi underwent personal analysis with Freud in 1914 and 1916. Sometime around 1914, it was Sandor Ferenczi who first suggested to his patient Melanie Klein that child analysis would profit from her unique skills. Figure 7.1 shows Melanie around the period of her analysis with Ferenezi.

The Implications of Klein's Personal Sources

Melanie's experiences with the dominating and intrusive Libussa Reizes surely fueled her anger. The utter detachment of the nearly invisible Moriz Reizes could only facilitate Libussa's fabrication of the Reizes matriarchy. Melanie's yearning for a competent father was thwarted. Her mother and brother convinced Melanie that she had been an "unexpected" child and the "heaviest burden" to her mother. Klein's belief that she had been the unplanned and begrudgingly loved child among her more favored siblings instilled deep curiosity about her life in addition to anger. This search for self-knowledge and, ultimately, healing became her life-long quest.

The concept of mother-as-evil-devouring-witch was not entirely unprecedented in her experience and not all that difficult to accept. She understood that the maternal

Figure 7.1 A sad-looking Melanie Klein. This photograph was taken around the time Melanie Klein suffered a series of losses and sought psychotherapy for depression with the psychoanalyst, Sandor Ferenczi.

(Grosskurth, 1986, opp. p. 148).

phantasy image created by children was determined in large part by the character of the relationship between mother and child at that time. And so it must be, she reasoned, for all children. There can be little doubt that Melanie applied this reasoning to her own conflicted feelings toward Libussa, and thereby insulated her mother from a great deal of anger. Used in this way, the concepts of phantasy and split objects are both theoretical constructs and personally protective rationalizations.

Also, as an adult, Melanie's experiences with her own children led to the discovery that mothers can be seen as evil, devouring witches, or as trustworthy, comforting companions. As she had experienced her own mother, Melanie Klein must have been experienced as intrusive and manipulative by those of her children she employed as psychoanalytic patients. It is small wonder that Klein proposed the fear of being attacked, devoured, or annihilated by mother as the fundamental and universal danger situation among women.

For Klein specifically, the path to psychoanalysis was paved with chronic depression and intolerable feelings of unworthiness. She was especially alert to those feelings in others. If anger is the first reaction to feeling unwanted or inferior, the second is curiosity.

Creative thinkers transcend the immediate grievance to question the meaning of what they experience. Such people want to know if others share similar personal pain, and if so, how is it similar? Klein found herself focusing on this version of the puzzle: How can relationships be so contradictory? It was clear to her that even the earliest relationships generate pleasure along with pain. They generate chaos and thereby instigate a need for order. Relationships trigger rage, but rage provokes guilt and anxiety. Love and admiration put the infant on the fast track to envy. These contradictory experiences were the ones Melanie Klein knew best and most intimately and chose to universalize.

A FINAL WORD ON MELANIE KLEIN

Melanie Klein learned from her own relationships that the people to whom one is most attached are also the people who can provoke the most profound anger and the deepest envy. Hatred of one's nearest intimates inevitably leads to guilt. More painful still, when these people are gone, through death or alienation, only the residue of unresolved guilt grounded in the finality of loss remains constant. The raw power of feeling, not reason, is at the heart of the Kleinian worldview. Melanie Klein's emphasis on the irrational is evident in her insistence on chaotic infantile phantasy, aggression, love, and guilt-driven reparation.

D. W. Winnicott   Born: 1896 Plymouth, England
Died: 1971 London, England

A COMMONSENSICAL AND CREATIVE CHILD ANALYST

Pediatrician turned child analyst, Donald Woods Winnicott brought common sense and a wry spontaneity to the treatment of children. D. W. Winnicott was restrained in his rhetoric, pragmatically playful in his clinical style, and fiercely protective of his intellectual independence. Above all other qualities, Winnicott was gifted in the art of communicating with children. He could be playful with youngsters, and he had the knack of helping them feel safe and secure in his presence.

Three anecdotes provide a glimpse into Winnicott's therapeutic approach. The first, which we label "the squiggle" indicates his down-to-earth, use-what-you-got technique with children. The second. "the spatula," displays Winnicott's charm, a graceful mix of whimsy and wit. The "niffle" section provides a close-up view of Winnicott's personal style.

The Squiggle

When beginning to work with a child, Winnicott often drew a random-appearing line or an elaborate but ambiguous doodle on paper. He then invited a child to "make something" from this squiggle and then encouraged the child to talk about the drawing and what it might mean. Then it was Winnicott's turn. He encouraged the child to create a squiggle, which Winnicott, with his talent for drawing, could turn into a meaningful picture. Winnicott's creations were often better than anything the child could accomplish with squiggles, and he was not reticent about pointing out this fact. Figure 7.2 illustrates Winnicott's use of squiggles with a 12-year-old patient named Patrick.

Winnicott sometimes enjoyed completing the child's squiggle with a wry or comic picture accompanied with humorous comments or even patently absurd, Dr. Seuss-like word play. Squiggle by squiggle, Winnicott permitted the child to tell the story of his or her world without hurry, often disjointedly, always interactively. After several "consultations" with Dr. Winnicott, previously inhibited children learned to express themselves through play.

Figure 7.2 Squiggle drawings of a 12-year-old boy. Patrick made the elephant in the left frame (1) from a squiggle drawn by Winnicott. The middle frame (3) shows Winnicott's transformation of Patrick's squiggle into what Patrick called "mother holding a baby." Sometime later, Patrick made the unusual picture on the right (11) from Winnicott's squiggle. He described it as person "who slipped into some dog food," and was probably mocking someone, perhaps Winnicott. The bottom corner inset of each frame shows the probable outlines of the starting squiggles, which are more apparent in the originals as variations of line density.

(Winnicott, 1965b, pp. 344, 346).

The Spatula

Winnicott invented a different technique to enable infants to communicate. The waiting room outside his office in the Paddington Green Hospital was often full to bursting with mothers and their infants. One by one, they entered Winnicott's consulting room to make a rather lengthy walk from the door to the desk and chair where the mother was invited to sit with her infant on her lap. The long walk provided Winnicott with an opportunity to observe the mother's handling of her child and the demeanor of both as they entered for the consultation.

He then invited the mother and her infant to sit together next to a table on which he had placed a shiny, steel tongue depressor, a "spatula." Winnicott instructed the mother and any observers present in precisely how to behave, especially about the necessity to restrict their natural eagerness to prompt the infant.

> . . . I ask the mother to sit opposite me with the angle of the table coming between me and her. She sits down with the baby on her knee. As a routine, I place a right-angled shining tongue-depressor at the edge of the table and invite the mother to place the child in such a way that, if the child should wish to handle the spatula, it is possible. Ordinarily, a mother will understand what I am about, and it is easy for me gradually to describe to her that there is to be a period of time in which she and I will contribute as little as possible to the situation, so that what happens can fairly be put down to the child's account. You can imagine that mothers show by their ability or relative inability to follow this suggestion something of what they are like at home; if they are anxious about infection, or have strong moral feelings against putting things to the mouth, if they are hasty or move impulsively, these characteristics show up. (1941/1992, pp. 52–53)

Eventually, Winnicott's "set situation," as he called it, grew into a process suitable for personality assessment of mother and child. Despite Winnicott's instructions to remain silent and motionless, some mothers did not go along with the stated guidelines. Winnicott observed, for example, mothers who "have a rooted objection to the child's mouthing and handling of objects," and communicated their disgust to their infants in subtle and not so subtle ways. Impulsive-anxious mothers could not restrain their eagerness to reassure and comfort their babies. Such over-eager reassurance often had the paradoxical effect of interfering with the child's spontaneous efforts to cope with the situation. Competitive mothers saw the set situation as a test of intelligence. These mothers intrusively coached and prodded their infants toward what they thought was "success" in grasping the spatula (1941/1992, p. 59).

Based on his observations of infants ranging from 4 to 13 months, Winnicott described three stages. The beginning one, called the period of hesitation, consists of initial stillness and expectancy with little overt action. In the second stage, the infant grasps the spatula and exhibits confidence and satisfaction in taking possession of and exerting control over it. Finally, the infant becomes playful, deliberately dropping the makeshift toy to hear it clang on the floor. Some infants in this third stage even engage the collaboration of an adult to "lose" and "find" the dropped spatula repeatedly. Table 7.2 provides a more detailed summary of a typical child's progress through the three stages.

Table 7.2   Behavior of Normal 4- to 13-Month-Old Infants in Winnicott's "Set (Spatula) Situation"

Stage	Infant behavior	Evidence of anxiety
1. Period of hesitation (*Expectation and stillness*)	• Holds body still. Expectant but not rigid. • Touches spatula, hesitantly, warily. • Wide-eyed with expectation, watches adults. • Sometimes withdraws interest and hides face. • Momentary hesitation to summon courage and accept reality of own desire to touch the spatula.	Inhibited. Buries face in mother's lap. Ignores spatula completely or immediately seizes and throws spatula.
2. Confident and collaborative play (*Possession and control*)	• Reaches for spatula decisively. • Excitement and interest mirrored in changes in baby's mouth: inside becomes flabby, saliva flows copiously, tongue looks thick and soft. • Explores spatula with mouth. • Free/flexible body movements linked to the spatula. • Exhibits confidence that he/she possesses the spatula and is in (magical?) control of it. • Plays with spatula, bangs it on table or on nearby metal bowl to make as much noise as possible. • Wants to play at being fed with adult as collaborator, but is upset if adult "spoils" game by really taking spatula into mouth. • Not obviously disappointed that spatula is inedible.	Persistent, prolonged hesitation. Brute force needed to bring spatula close to infant or put it in baby's mouth with resulting distress, crying, colic, or screaming.
3. Riddance and restoration (*Loss and return*)	• Drops spatula as if by mistake. • Pleased when it is retrieved. • Deliberately drops it after restoration. • Enjoys aggressively getting rid of spatula, especially if it makes sound when dropped.	Persistent (compulsive) repetition of riddance and restoration, with no evidence of boredom or waning interest.

Based on the description in Winnicott, 1941/1992.

Winnicott thought that the first stage in Table 7.2, or period of hesitation, was especially significant in revealing infants' typical emotional reactions to unfamiliar situations. For most normal infants, the period of hesitation can be more precisely described as only a moment of expectation. Normally infants, Winnicott observed in thousands of instances, rapidly overcome their initial hesitancy because desire and curiosity grow more intense than anxiety. As self-confidence grows, action replaces indecision. Delight displaces delay. Anxiety evaporates. The prize is seized. Drooling and cooing accompany the spatula as it enters the baby's mouth. Winnicott also observed that anxious infants had difficulty mastering their hesitation and often prolonged their delay indefinitely. In contrast, some anxiously impulsive infants circumvented the period of hesitation altogether and immediately seized the spatula to throw it to the floor.

When Winnicott wrote his first paper describing his deceptively simple observational technique, he was still in the early phases of learning about child psychoanalysis. Melanie Klein's ideas loomed large in Winnicott's training, and he attempted to interpret the symbolic meaning of the spatula for the child. He hypothesized that the spatula signified to the infant a breast, a penis, and even a person or "bits" of a person (1941/1992, p. 61). Fortunately, Winnicott's empirical predilections and good sense eventually prevailed over his early enthusiasm for Kleinian speculations. He could see that the "set situation" was a window on the infant's interpersonal transactions and emotional maturity (1941/1992, pp. 64–65).

The Niffle

Five-year-old Tom was injured while on vacation with his family and evacuated to a distant city to be hospitalized. His mother accompanied him, but eventually left Tom alone in the hospital. Tom found it hard to sleep without what he called his "niffle." His niffle was a square of woven material derived from a wool shawl. In fact, there had been three niffles, but only one of them was Tom's special niffle. He could distinguish his special niffle from the other two even in the dark (Winnicott, 1996a/1996, p. 105). Returning home, Tom's mother tried to ship the special niffle to her son's hospital, but the niffle failed to arrive and was never seen again.

Eventually Tom recovered and rejoined his family, but he seemed not to be the same child. He became oppositional toward his mother, and resisted being dressed and cleaned by her. Tom acted in an annoying way and spoke with a peculiar high-pitched voice. Tom's mother was especially irritated by this voice. When questioned by Winnicott, Tom summed it all up: "But I wish I had this little niffle. It makes me feel . . ."—at which point Tom was at a loss for words. Winnicott understood the strength of Tom's emotional reaction to his loss.

We have all seen children attached to their teddy bears, comforted by soft blankets they drag around with them, and their delight in other cuddly things. Winnicott understood that the teddy bears, blankets, and niffles of this world had the function of bridging the gap between children's dependence on their mothers and their capacity for independence. Winnicott termed such objects **transitional objects.** Tom experienced the disappearance of his niffle as a profound loss of love, security, and trust.

UNCONVENTIONAL PSYCHOANALYSIS: THE PEDIATRIC CONSULTATION MODEL

Winnicott's primary professional training was in pediatrics. Throughout his career, even after years of preparation as a child analyst, Winnicott thought of himself as both a pediatrician and a psychoanalyst. Each professional identity, he believed, informed and enhanced the other (e.g., Winnicott, 1965a, pp. 140–141; Kahr, 1996; Phillips, 1988). "I am a pediatrician who has swung to psychiatry," Winnicott wrote, "and a psychiatrist who has clung to pediatrics" (1948c/1992, p. 157). He sought nothing less than his own synthesis of two antagonistic traditions. Successful management of this novel, not to say subversive, blending of clinical roles elevated Winnicott to a unique position in medical and psychiatric circles.

Unlike Winnicott, the typical child analyst did not take detailed histories of the patient and patient's family, did not physically examine the patient, nor directly observe the child-rearing environment provided by the parents. The child analyst's role did not include brief consultation to provide child-rearing advice to the parents or make focused, often educational, interventions (Winnicott, 1963/1965a; 1958/1965c).

Elements of a Winnicottian Consultation

Much of Winnicott's experience was gained in relatively brief consultations with parents and children, especially during the time of World War II, and frequently in a hospital clinic setting. In these consultations, Winnicott provided a number of services, including diagnosis, advice on child care, and recommendations for placement or specialized treatment. Khan (1975/1992, p. xvii) places the number of children and family members seen by Winnicott in consultation over a period of four decades at an amazing sixty thousand.

Winnicott viewed few of the children for whom he consulted as appropriate candidates for standard psychoanalysis. He thought that ". . . analysis is [only] for those who want it, need it, and can take it" (1962a/1965a, p. 169). Winnicott preferred a consultative style characterized by precision focus, rapid tempo, and brief duration. He might engage in a single "diagnostic-history-taking-recommendation-session" or a series of comparatively leisurely meetings with a child, typically over the span of several weeks or months, but sometimes extending for years (Winnicott, 1957/1965c).

Take a History, Make a Diagnosis

Winnicott believed it was necessary to obtain a complete and chronologically ordered narrative of the child's life. Such history taking included the usual elements of presenting problem, chronology of developmental landmarks, parental descriptions of the child's problem, the child's description of the problem, and sometimes even direct observation of mother and child (or father and child) playing together. But the purpose of taking the history was not the mere gathering of data:

> It was as a practicing pediatrician that I found the therapeutic value of history taking, and discovered the fact that this provides the best opportunity for therapeutics, provided that the history-taking is not done for the purpose of gathering facts. Psycho-analysis for me is a vast extension of history-taking, with therapeutics as a by-product. (Winnicott, 1963/1965a, pp. 198–199)

Diagnosing the patient's difficulty correctly was a central feature of Winnicott's work. His diagnosis began by taking the patient's history, but continued throughout their work together. Changes in the patient's behavior, alterations to the patient's circumstances, and changes in the quality of the therapeutic relationship signaled Winnicott to alter his diagnosis and sometimes his therapeutic strategy.

Take Charge, Take Notes, Take Your Time

From the vantage point of medical practice, Winnicott was a firm believer in taking charge of the consultation. As both a pediatrician and as a psychodynamic psychotherapist, Winnicott assumed that it was his responsibility to provide a structured setting in which both the child and parents felt safe enough to communicate the meaning they placed on the child's distressing symptoms. The responsibility of the clinician is to be reliable, truthful, calm, and authoritatively knowledgeable (Winnicott, 1961/1990, p. 235).

Use What Is Available: As Little as Needed, as Simply as Possible

Winnicott was creative in enlisting the aid of the child's parents, teachers, or caseworker to carry out treatment plans in the child's daily environment. Winnicott was sensitive to the need for economy and efficiency in the treatment of childhood disorders, a sensitivity that he carried over into his psychoanalytic practice as well (Winnicott, 1955/1989). Even when working analytically, Winnicott strove to make his interpretations as brief as possible. He usually limited himself to one interpretation per session (1962a/1965a). He did not hesitate to mix standard analytic method with other procedures that met the needs of specific patients. He sometimes intervened directly into the patient's daily life. He aimed to provide more stability and security for those who were fragile and in need of such support (e.g., Little, 1990).

Don't Be Eager to Be Clever. Don't Talk Too Much. Listen.

Winnicott learned a lesson then very unusual in medical education from a teacher of pediatrics—Dr. Thomas Horder—at St. Bartholomew's Hospital. The lesson was to listen to his patients. Horder told Winnicott: "Don't you go in with your wonderful knowledge and apply it all. Just listen. They'll tell you quite a lot of things. You'll learn if you listen" (C. Winnicott, 1983/1991, pp. 188–189). Winnicott took the advice both for his pediatric consultations and, later, for his approach to psychoanalysis. When he was tired, he sometimes found himself talking too much in analytic sessions. At such times, he described himself as having drifted into a "teaching session" rather than "doing psychoanalysis." He even quipped that whenever he found himself using the word moreover, he knew he had drifted again (Winnicott, 1962a/1965a, p. 167). As Winnicott put it toward the end of his life,

> If only we can wait, the patient arrives at understanding creatively and with immense joy, and I now enjoy this joy more than I used to enjoy the sense of having been clever. I think I interpret mainly to let the patient know the limits of my understanding. (1968b/1989, p. 219)

Normal Life Is Normally Difficult. Symptoms Are Easier.

Winnicott recognized that even a child's aberrant behavior often had multiple functions. Symptoms can communicate various meanings that are not always abnormal. Bed-wetting, for example, is

> ...a common enough symptom which almost everyone has to deal with who has to deal with children. If by bed-wetting a child is making effective protest against strict management, sticking up for the rights of the individual, so to speak, then the symptom is not an illness; rather it is a sign that the child still hopes to keep the individuality which has been in some way threatened.

> Or take refusal of food—another common symptom. It is absolutely normal for a child to refuse food. I assume that the food you offer is good. The point really is that a child cannot

always *feel* the food to be good. A child cannot *always* feel that good food is deserved. (Winnicott, 1964a, p. 127; italics in original; see also 1964c)

Sometimes, Winnicott stated, the best course of action for the child therapist is to do nothing. Waiting for the child's growth and maturity to attenuate the problem is often effective. Active intervention in what appears to be seriously pathological behavior is sometimes not necessary if the parents can provide an adequate and loving environment for the child to master his or her distress.

> A normal child can employ any and all of the devices nature has provided in defence against anxiety and intolerable conflict. The devices employed (in health) are related to the kind of help that is available. Abnormality shows in a *limitation* and *rigidity* of the child's capacity to employ symptoms, and a relative lack of relationship between the symptoms and what can be expected in the way of help. (1964a, p. 126–127; italics in original)

Winnicott repeatedly emphasized that symptoms are often indicators of the healthy child's ability to battle against disease and other adversities. Only when such symptoms are linked to failure of the child's natural defenses can we assume the presence of abnormality.

Why Normal Life Is Difficult: From Illusion to Disillusion

Under the best of circumstances, the developing infant is challenged by a succession of disappointments. Winnicott first pointed to the child's experience of the clash between its inner world of fantasy and the outer world of reality. With varying degrees of disappointment, babies learn that what they want is not always provided. Wishes are frustrated by the facts of reality (1964a, p. 128).

Second, babies learn that destructive urges and thoughts that are frightening sometimes accompany the feeling of excitement (1964a, p. 128). As the infant slowly recognizes and increasingly loves the person who supplies food, care, and affection, its spontaneous urges to devour and use up the good it receives from that person become increasingly troubling. "And, along with this, there comes a feeling that there will be nothing left if everything has been destroyed; and what happens then, should hunger return?" (Winnicott, 1964a, pp. 128–129). Consequently, the baby's eagerness for food disappears. Inhibition can replace the infant's healthy greediness for food. Wise mothers intuitively know that simply "playing for time" is all that is needed to allow the baby to overcome its inhibitions.

Third, the infant quickly discovers a new source of life's difficulties. "Only too soon, added to other troubles are those that belong to the child's recognition that there is also father to be reckoned with" (Winnicott, 1964a, p. 129). Perhaps, the discovery of siblings adds additional fuel to the fire. Jealousy rears its ugly head. The illusion of exclusive possession of mother dissolves into the disillusionment of a shared, sometimes unavailable, love-object.

Fourth, the child's inner world of imaginary friends and foes, fantastic fairies and animals, and magical battles won and lost is an illusion that the child can omnipotently control. With time however, the stresses and strains of controlling this inner world are revealed in all manner of bodily aches, pains, and upsets (Winnicott, 1964a, p. 130). Such aches, pains, and upsets are normal reflections of internal ups, downs, triumphs, and failures. The wise mother and father support the child's struggle to reconcile inner and outer worlds. They might, for example, acknowledge that they, too, could see an imaginary friend.

Imaginative play need not be shameful. Setting a place at the table for the friend, or at bedtime even tucking child and companion in for the night strikes some as pandering to the child's eccentricity, but the alternative is to invalidate the child's healthy childishness. Hence, parents who scoff at their child's imaginary world and its creatures are expecting maturity to occur prematurely.

In Winnicott's description of it, life is hard. Early experiences are fraught with difficult things to learn, and often evoke disappointment because disillusionment is unavoidable. Such experiences, however, are normal, and momentary signs of psychological distress are not indications of abnormality. The degree to which a child remains sufficiently able to be playful through all of the adversities and disappointments of early life is a measure of that child's normality.

Commitment to Pediatrics

Winnicott's early papers consisted of pediatric medical advice, admonitions to parents to trust their own abilities and those of their children, and psychological insights about development drawn from Freud (e.g., Winnicott, 1931a/1992, 1931b/1992, 1936/1992, 1944/1992). Winnicott had a wry, homey, avuncular style honed to perfection in a series of radio broadcasts during World War II. That same style, an entertaining and disarming mix of authority, wit, and soothing nurturance, continued to serve him well in print when his broadcasts were turned into papers and books (Winnicott, 1993, especially Chapter 1). He was widely in demand as a speaker throughout his career, and he never failed to provide a humorous and psychologically informed slant on practical pediatric problems and issues.

Winnicott's knowledge and experience as a pediatrician broadened his vision as a child psychiatrist and supported his understanding of child psychology. Pediatric practice taught him the importance of patience in treating children. Most important, Winnicott was realistic and had reasonable expectations for the children he treated:

> The best that can happen is that the person who is being analyzed gradually comes to feel less and less at the mercy of unknown forces both within and without, and more and more able to deal in his or her own peculiar way with the difficulties inherent in human nature, in personal growth, and in the gradual achievement of a mature and constructive relationship to society. (Winnicott, 1945b/1996, p. 12)

Winnicott gradually theorized more and more based on his own clinical experience and insights. He got away from being influenced very much by the theories of others and finally developed an object relations theory that, more often than not, stands traditional ideas on their heads.

EARLY THEORY: THE KLEINIAN INFLUENCE

At the outset of his psychoanalytic career, Winnicott had also assimilated the classic formulations of Freud both from his reading and from his personal analysis with James Strachey (1887–1967), an eminent British psychoanalyst and Freud's chief translator. During the analysis, Strachey recommended to Winnicott that he seek out Melanie Klein to learn more about the application of psychoanalysis to children (Winnicott, 1962b/1965a). Winnicott took Strachey's advice and made contact sometime in 1932, about two years before the end of his analysis (Kahr, 1996, p. 58).

Winnicott's View of Melanie Klein

Winnicott found that Klein's work provided important insights about emotional functioning at the very earliest periods of infancy. As we have seen, Klein was extending psychoanalysis to earlier and earlier periods of infancy on an almost daily basis. For a time, Winnicott found this Kleinian direction a congenial and enlightening path to follow. His own observations as a pediatrician had already paved the way for his ready acceptance of the idea that children could be emotionally ill with roots extending well before the Oedipal period of ages five and six.

Winnicott saw Klein as an admirable teacher who could be flexible and attentive to the details of the cases he brought for supervision. He retained Melanie Klein as a clinical supervisor for the better part of six years, from 1935 to 1941 (Kahr, 1996, p. 59). More than 20 years later, Winnicott summarized the significance of his experiences with Melanie Klein:

> Klein was able to make it clear to me from the material my patients presented, how the capacity for concern and to feel guilty is an achievement, and it is this rather than depression that characterizes arrival at the depressive position in the case of the growing baby and child. Arrival at this stage is associated with ideas of restitution and reparation, and indeed the human individual cannot accept the destructive and aggressive ideas in his or her own nature without the experience of reparation, and for this reason the continued presence of the love object is necessary at this stage since only in this way is there opportunity for reparation. This is Klein's most important contribution, in my opinion, and I think it ranks with Freud's concept of the Oedipus complex. (1962b/1965a, p. 176)

In a narrative 20 years later, Winnicott alluded to his growing independence from Klein's thinking and from her approach:

> Since those days a great deal has happened, and I do not claim to be able to hand out the Klein view in a way that she herself would approve of. I believe my views began to separate out from hers, and in any case I found she had not included me in as a Kleinian. This did not matter to me because I have never been able to follow anyone else, not even Freud. (1962b/1965a, p. 176)

On December 4, 1935, Winnicott presented his membership paper entitled "The Manic Defence" to the British Psychoanalytic Society. This, his first psychoanalytic paper, was largely an elaboration of one of Melanie Klein's central concepts. Giving such a presentation carried the weight of a commencement ceremony in psychoanalytic circles. It marked the culmination of Winnicott's long preparation to become a qualified psychoanalyst and indicated his acceptance as a full member of the society.

Candidates for membership were required to present original theoretical or clinical ideas, but the wise aspirant understood that the content of the presentation had to fall within specified parameters. Applicants first had to demonstrate that their ideas were derived from or consistent with Sigmund Freud's concepts. A candidate also had to acknowledge intellectual debts to the influential senior psychoanalysts in the candidate's area of specialization. There was a demand for originality within the context of a developing tradition of psychoanalytic thought. One's ideas should be original but not too original or too threatening.

The Manic Defense: Inner and Outer Reality

In his original paper on this topic, Winnicott (1935/1992) artfully redefines Klein's manic position to moderate her emphasis on the absolute power of the internal world. He argues that the developmentally normal manic defense against depressive feelings compels the defender to minimize, not maximize, as Klein would have it, the influence of internal object representations.

> Omnipotent fantasies are not so much the inner reality itself as a defense against acceptance of it. One finds in this defense a flight to omnipotent fantasy, and flight from some fantasies to other fantasies, and in this sequence a flight to external reality. This is why I think one cannot compare and contrast fantasy and reality. (Winnicott, 1935/1992, p. 130)

Winnicott was subtly paving the way for a fundamental alteration to Klein's ideas. Recall his argument that life is normally difficult. Winnicott asserted the importance of the difficult realities of life in development. As a direct consequence, he normalized the pathological-sounding—manic and depressive—developmental positions. Winnicott reasoned that manic defenses, for example, are part of ordinary living. They are inherent in the struggles all people make against the daily abrasions and sorrows of life.

> For instance, one is at a music-hall and on the stage come the dancers, trained to liveliness. One can say that here is the primal scene, here is exhibitionism, here is anal control, here is masochistic submission to discipline, here is a defiance of the super-ego. Soon or later one adds: here is LIFE. Might it not be that the main point of the performance is a denial of deadness, a defense against depressive "death inside" ideas, the sexualization being secondary.
> What about such things as the wireless [i.e., radio] that is left on interminably? What about living in a town like London with its noise that never ceases, and lights that are never extinguished? Each illustrates the reassurance through reality against death inside, and a use of manic defense that can be normal. (Winnicott, 1935/1992, p. 131)

For Winnicott, inner reality is an equal partner with outer reality, the world of ordinary life. "Life is hard," but that does not mean for Winnicott that strenuous coping with life's difficulties, including the struggle to feel alive in the face of death, is inevitably pathological. Winnicott depathologizes Klein's concept of manic defense by reframing it to encompass coping with life's unavoidable miseries. He elevates the external world to equal status with the inner world as a determinant of emotional development.

Depathologizing the Depressive Position: The Ruth and the Ruthless

In a later paper, Winnicott applied the same strategy to a fuller discussion of the Kleinian depressive position (Winnicott, 1954–1955/1992). He proposed that the Kleinian term depressive position was a poorly conceived name and suggested that the term, **stage of concern,** would be more accurate. Winnicott thus took a Kleinian concept that implied abnormality and changed it to indicate a more normal process. Winnicott agreed with Klein that the infant begins its relationship to the external object more or less "pre-ruth," that is, ruthless (pitiless) in attempting to satisfy its needs. With the whimsy of Lewis Carroll, Winnicott points out that the infant gradually passes from the pre-ruth stage to the stage of ruth (capable of pity).

PRIMITIVE PERSONALITY DEVELOPMENT: WINNICOTT STYLE

Despite his disagreement with some of Klein's concepts, Winnicott incorporated many of her ideas about the psychology of the earliest days of life. Winnicott's own observations as a pediatrician suggested that a series of important cognitive and emotional achievements occurred during the first five or six months of life. His observations of babies exploring the spatula had convinced him that infants of five months understood that the object for which they reach is localized in space and separate from themselves. Furthermore, the baby who thrusts the spatula into its mouth is necessarily aware that there is an "inside me." Deliberately dropping the spatula demonstrates that "he knows he can get rid of something when he has got from it what he wants from it" (1945a, p. 148). Parallel to these achievements, the infant of five or six months

> ... assumes that his mother also has an inside, one that may be rich or poor, good or bad, ordered or muddled. He is therefore starting to be concerned with the mother and her sanity and her moods. In the case of many infants there is a relationship as between whole persons at six months. Now, when a human being feels he is a person related to people, he has already traveled a long way in primitive development. (Winnicott, 1945a, p. 148)

Winnicott concluded that Klein's depressive position involves cognitive and emotional developments that have nothing to do with defensive maneuvers against depression. Winnicott began describing what happens before the stage of concern at five or six months. He eventually determined that the five- or six-month-old child has developed in three areas: personality integration, personalization, and realization.

Personality: From Muddled to Cuddled

Winnicott hypothesized that at the very beginning of life, personality is in a primal state of "unintegration." With absolute literalness, Winnicott meant that in the earliest days of life there is no *person* to embody an integrated personality. There are only biological needs and potentials. "What is there is an armful of anatomy and physiology, and added to this a potential for development into a human personality" (Winnicott, 1968a/1987, p. 89). Unintegrated infants do not comprehend themselves or others as whole people. **Unintegration** has a different significance than the term, *disintegration.* **Disintegration** lies on an altogether different conceptual dimension—the dimension of psychopathology—rather than occupying the opposite end of the same dimension as unintegration. *Unintegration* is a nonpathological term.

Personality integration begins quickly and spontaneously after birth, and requires two sets of experiences to go forward smoothly. The first is the baby's own internal world of need and drive, which by their infinite repetition become the stabilizing routines of life around which a personality can form. Needs and drives provide reassuring experiences that signal one is alive. As long as mother and other caretakers satisfy the infant's needs reliably, survival is not threatened, and the natural process of integration proceeds unhindered. The inexorable repetition of appetite arousal and satisfaction gradually grows familiar and welcomed.

The second organizing area of experience is the care the infant receives. The baby is handled, bathed, fed, rocked, named, called by name, and cuddled. Each of these repetitive events helps bring order to internal confusion. From these scattered fragments of need, maternal response, cuddling, and predictable care, a gradual synthesis of identity emerges. "Me" and "not-me" begin to have meaning for the infant. Mother can provide physical and a kind of emotional cuddling, or what Winnicott termed **holding.** As Winnicott used the term, holding elevates cuddling to a primary means of communication between infant and mother. Holding the infant securely in both the physical and psychological senses of the term enables the securely held infant to organize its urges, wishes, and fears into predictable experiences.

Personality integration continues to evolve with time, but the feeling of being not quite whole does not frighten the securely held infant:

> There are long stretches of time in a normal infant's life in which a baby does not mind whether he is many bits or one whole being, or whether he lives in his mother's face or in his own body, provided that from time to time he comes together and feels something. (Winnicott, 1945a, p. 150)

Personalization: From Cleaning to Weaning

Satisfactory **personalization** leads to the feeling that the infant is in his or her own body. *Personalization,* as Winnicott employed the term, is the achievement of a personality completing the process of integration by taking possession of the body in which it finds itself and becoming increasingly comfortable with ownership. As with integration, biological needs and maternal care guide the process of personalization so that the evolving personality has a "place" to reside. Mother's attention to physical care and cleanliness quietly helps the infant reach the understanding that he or she has a body, resides in it, and is sometimes in control of it. In short, the infant achieves a sense of personalization.

Put another way, the infant particularizes its inventory of recognizable physical equipment by personalizing each component. The particular "person" is either self or not-self. For example: This waving digit is my finger because I can make it go in my mouth for a good suck, but this digit tickling my tummy is not mine because I can't stop it. This wiggling pink thing that lies just out of reach is my toe, but this bigger one that I can reach—and bite—is not mine because I don't feel bitten and because Daddy is doing the yelling.

Schizophrenic and near-psychotic people, who may abruptly feel uncomfortable with their own bodies or develop the delusion that they are not in their bodies, sometimes experience **depersonalization.** A less pathological variation of depersonalization is the belief that something is alarmingly and abruptly different, "not right," or "not real" about my body. An even less serious variation of depersonalization, in fact a common occurrence of childhood, is the creation of imaginary companions. Some children even use an imaginary companion as a magical defense to bypass the anxieties of childhood associated with eating, digestion, retention, and expulsion (Winnicott, 1945a, p. 151). One of the authors of this text, in fact, had a friendly and playful imaginary companion named Mortimer, who accompanied him at mealtime quite often.

Realization: From Dreaming to Scheming

The third major early personality development is learning to take account of external reality. Rather than employ the standard psychoanalytic term, "reality testing," Winnicott chose to call this achievement **realization.** Winnicott explained how he thought such realization could be achieved in the nursing situation. Mother and baby each bring to the nursing situation their own capabilities and needs. The mother brings knowledge, tolerance, and adult judgment. The baby brings absolute dependence, need, and a readiness for hallucinatory gratification. Sights, sounds, smells, and touches experienced with each real feeding teach the baby what it can and cannot conjure up when the real object is not present but real need is exerting itself (1945a, p. 153). Eventually, over substantial periods of time, the mother helps her infant accept and tolerate the limitations of reality, and to enjoy the real satisfactions that such acceptance makes possible.

In the earliest phase of life, objects seem to act according to magical laws. The object exists when desired, approaches when approached, and vanishes when not wanted. Vanishing is a terrifying experience for the infant because it represents annihilation. From this dreamlike world of magic the infant progresses to the real world of planned actions.

The change from dreaming to scheming is paralleled by the nature of the changes in the infant's relationship to the object. Initially, following Klein, Winnicott proposed a "ruthless" stage prior to the stage of concern in which the infant expects mother to tolerate its aggressiveness in play. Without this experience of a tolerant caretaker, the infant can show its ruthlessness only in dissociated states. In later life, ruthlessness can be shown only in states of disintegration marked by abrupt regression to the primitive and magical world of infancy. In short, ruthless relations to objects may reappear in psychotic-level psychopathologies.

ENVIRONMENTAL EMPHASIS: "THERE'S NO SUCH THING AS A BABY"

Winnicott put the focus of child emotional development on what he termed the nursing couple: *a child in relationship with a mother.*

> *"There is no such thing as a baby."* I was alarmed to hear myself utter these words and tried to justify myself by pointing out that if you show me a baby you certainly show me also someone caring for the baby, or at least a pram with someone's eyes and ears glued to it. One sees a "nursing couple."

> In a quieter way today I would say that before object relationships the state of affairs is this: that the unit is not the individual, the unit is an environment-individual-set-up. By good-enough child care, technique, holding, and general management, the shell becomes gradually taken over and the kernel (which has looked all the time like a human baby to us) can begin to be an individual. (Winnicott, 1952, p. 99)

Winnicott's insistence that babies can be understood psychologically only in relation to their environments, specifically the "ordinary devoted mother," was an important corrective to Melanie Klein's often one-sided emphasis on the infant's instincts.

Holding: Primary Maternal Preoccupation of the Ordinary Devoted Mother

Winnicott hypothesized the existence of a special psychological state called "primary maternal preoccupation." Among its characteristics are:

> It gradually develops and becomes a state of heightened sensitivity during and especially towards the end of pregnancy.

> It lasts for a few weeks after the birth of the child.

It is not easily remembered by mothers once they have recovered from it. I would go further and say that the memory mothers have of this state tends to become repressed. (Winnicott, 1956/1992, p. 302)

Winnicott thought that the **primary maternal preoccupation** provides a specific adaptive context for her newborn to flourish and mature. The mother is sensitized to the newborn's state and she can empathically put herself in the infant's place. She comes to know her infant's needs and capabilities as she knows her own. In short, the primary maternal preoccupation results in a close identification of mother with her infant (Winnicott, 1960/1965a, p. 147).

For their part, infants bring their biological constitution, innate developmental tendencies (conflict-free ego functioning), motility, and drives. Mother's heightened empathy permits the kind of silent communications that enable the infant's "innate equipment" to unfold, helps the infant experience free movement for the first time, and encourages the child to take ownership of its body and sensations (personalization). In short, the mother provides a "good-enough" adaptation to the infant's absolute dependency.

... from these silent communications we can go over to the ways in which the mother makes real just what the baby is ready to look for, so that she gives the baby the idea of what it is that the baby is just ready for. The baby says (wordlessly of course): "I just feel like ..." and just then the mother comes along and turns the baby over, or she comes with the feeding apparatus and the baby becomes able to finish the sentence: "... a turn-over, a breast, nipple, milk, etc., etc." (Winnicott, 1968a/1987, pp. 100)

Winnicott grouped maternal caretaking practices under the general, and metaphorical, label of holding. In its literal sense, the mother holds her infant securely in her arms while feeding, cleaning, and playing with it. This tight and intimate physical closeness provides the initial and most basic level of holding. At a metaphorical level, holding involves a number of interconnected, more emotional communications from mother to child. Holding communicates to the infant that it is alive—"I am seen and I exist"—as the child feels mirrored in the mother's facial expressions and reactions (Winnicott, 1962c/1965a, p. 61). Inherent in these mirroring experiences are the infant's gradual realization that there is another, someone who is not me, who reacts to me. Personality integration, as we have seen, gets its impetus from these "holding" communications.

Holding and the Unthinkable Anxieties

Holding provides a safety net for the infant to survive the earliest and most terrifying first fears. Influenced again by Klein, Winnicott described a series of infantile **unthinkable anxieties,** or primordial fears, that date to the earliest days of life. Unlike Klein, Winnicott saw these "anxieties" as normal developmental phases, not as derivatives of the death instinct. More important, unthinkable anxieties are precursors of psychopathology only with the failure of mother's holding functions. Typically, however, the combination of maternal holding and an unthinkable anxiety leads to normal personality integration, personalization, and realization. The unthinkable anxieties are:

- Going to pieces
- Falling forever
- Having no relationship to the body
- Having no orientation
- Complete isolation because there is no means for communication

Winnicott added the last item in the list some years after his initial formulation (1962c/1965a, p. 58; and 1968a/1987, p. 99). Maternal holding is the totality of the mother's loving physical and emotional care that, to extend Winnicott's metaphor, prevents the infant from toppling over the abyss of unthinkable anxiety.

Winnicott pointed out the parallel to the psychoanalyst's "holding" interpretations in therapy. The analyst's words sometimes are less significant than the nonverbal and spontaneous message that the analyst and the patient are both alive and continue to be real. For example, Winnicott related the incident of the patient who dug her nails into the back of his hand during an intense moment in therapy.

> My interpretation was: "Ow!" This scarcely involved my intellectual equipment at all, and it was quite useful because it came *immediately* (not after a pause for reflection) and because it meant to the patient that my hand was alive, that it was part of me, and that I was there to be used. Or, shall I say, I can be used if I survive. (Winnicott, 1968a/1987, p. 95)

A **good-enough mother,** in Winnicott's vocabulary, provides encouragement and support for the infant's "going on being" (Winnicott, 1956/1992, p. 303). The mother protects the infant from "impingements." Impingements are any experiences that jeopardize "going on being." They can stem either from the external environment or originate in occasional maternal failures to provide "good-enough" care. Unreliable need satisfaction, prolonged separation, intolerance of infantile neediness and aggression, or an inability to make the infant feel safe are all forms of impingement because they threaten spontaneous and normal developmental progress (Winnicott, 1968a/1987, p. 95). Winnicott's focus in this part of his theory is on maternal actions that enhance healthy personality formation. The infant must feel safe enough to be spontaneous, secure enough to be able to take risks vis-à-vis the difficulties of reality, even to be able to "afford to die" (Winnicott, 1956/1992, p. 304). The good-enough mother makes "normally difficult life" tolerable, manageable, and capable of being mastered:

> . . . without the initial good-enough environmental provision, this self that can afford to die never develops. The feeling of real is absent and if there is not too much chaos the ultimate feeling of futility. The inherent difficulties of life cannot be reached, let alone the satisfactions. If there is not chaos, there appears a false self that hides the true self, that complies with demands, that reacts to stimuli, that rids itself of instinctual experiences by having them, but that is only playing for time. (Winnicott, 1956/1992, pp. 304–305)

Winnicott's concept of the **False Self** seems to have originated from two sources. First, Winnicott had a keen interest in working therapeutically with severely regressed adult patients who were psychotic or near psychotic. Winnicott saw the dependency needs of the infant reemerge in an exaggerated form in a type of personality splitting in his adult schizophrenic and borderline patients. In particular, one patient described to Winnicott how she had felt all her life that she had not been real, and felt as though she had been looking for her true self (1960c/1965a, p. 142). From the patient's point of view, the first two years of her analysis had been conducted between what she called her "caretaker self" and Winnicott. This caretaker self had sought out treatment, protected the patient during the early phases, gradually handed over its role to Winnicott, and hovered nearby to resume caretaking whenever Winnicott failed to "hold" the patient safely.

The second basis of Winnicott's concept of the False Self was his experience with apparently cheerful children who visited his hospital clinic. Nevertheless, these children were, at the same time, presented for psychological treatment by their parents, often with maternally described problems of depression, listlessness, anger, and apathy. The marked discrepancy between direct observation and maternal report caught Winnicott's attention:

> It took me years to realize that these children were entertaining me as they felt they must also entertain their mothers, to deal with the mother's depressed mood. They dealt with or prevented my depression or what might be boredom in the clinic; while waiting for me they drew lovely colored pictures or even wrote poems to add to my collection. I have no doubt that I was taken in by many such cases before I eventually realized that the children were ill and were showing me a false self organization and that at home the mother had to deal with the other side of this, namely the child's inability to keep up counteracting the mother's mood all of the twenty-four hours. Indeed the mother had to endure the hatred belonging to the child's sense of having been exploited and of having lost identity. (Winnicott, 1969/1989, pp. 247–248)

Winnicott discovered that some of these entertaining children had developed their False Selves not only to cheer up their depressed mothers, but also to fend off her hatred of them (1969/1989, p. 249; 1948 d/1992, pp. 91–92). We return to the concept of the mother's unconscious hatred of her child shortly. It is of some benefit at present, however, simply to note that Winnicott links the three concepts of maternal depression, hatred, and the False Self.

Origins of the False Self: The "Not-Good-Enough" Mother

Winnicott eventually hypothesized that the primary purpose of the False Self is defense of the True Self. It is like a mask or a shell that others perceive as real, and can totally conceal the True Self.

The origins of the False Self are in failures of the mother-infant relationship during the phase prior to the integration of the infant's personality (1960/1965a, p. 145). The "not-good-enough" mother fails to hold her infant securely and reliably. She may permit external reality to "impinge" on the infant's world before the infant is ready. Or she herself may intrusively impinge on that world in a way that the infant cannot tolerate. Such "errors" of maternal care fail the infant in two ways. First, the "not-good-enough mother" does not validate or help make real her infant's spontaneous gestures. She does not mirror in her responses her empathic understanding of the infant's needs or wonderment at her infant's successes. In Winnicott's terms,

> The mother who is not-good-enough is not able to implement the infant's omnipotence, and so she repeatedly fails to meet the infant gesture; instead she substitutes her own gesture which is to be given sense by the compliance of the infant. This compliance on the part of the infant is the earliest stage of the False Self, and belongs to the mother's inability to sense her infant's needs. (1960/1965a, p. 145)

The second failure of the not-good-enough mother is that she does not help her infant link its spontaneous gestures with observable effects in reality, including her own reactions. Thus the infant is unable to reach the stage of giving up a sense of omnipotence in an imagined or hallucinatory world in favor of dealing with the real world. In extreme cases, where the maternal failures occur from the very beginning of existence, the infant's survival may be in question. More often, however, the not-good-enough mother is not "bad enough" to disrupt infant survival totally. Instead, the infant complies with the maternal environment by creating the mask of the False Self:

> Through this False Self the infant builds up a false set of relationships, and by means of introjections even attains a show of being real, so that the child may grow to be just like mother, nurse, aunt, brother, or whoever at the time dominates the scene. The False Self has

---

BOX 7.5   *Only Connect . . .*

Winnicott's concept of "not-good-enough mother" can be related to Erikson's (Chapter 8) concept of *ritualism* of the role of mother, whereas the "ordinary devoted mother" can be seen as exemplifying the *ritualization* of the maternal role. Winnicott's thinking also paralleled and anticipated the development of existential and humanistic approaches to personality. In existential and humanistic terms (see Chapters 9 and 10), we might consider the False Self to represent an inauthentic mode of being, which has arisen as a result of a lack of genuine connectedness with an empathic and caring mother.

> one positive and very important function: to hide the True Self, which it does by compliance with environmental demands. (Winnicott, (1960/1965a, pp. 146–147)

Ultimately, the chief defensive efforts of the False Self are directed to protecting the True Self from exploitation, manipulation, and unjust demands. The most "unthinkable" anxiety of all is thus fended off: annihilation of the True Self.

Levels of Organization of the False Self

Winnicott distinguished five different "levels" of False Self personality organization. They are organized along a spectrum of severity extending from gross maladaptation to ordinary healthy adaptation. Table 7.3 summarizes the levels of False Self organization.

Extremely Maladaptive: Mask

In this instance the False Self is organized as real and observers see and relate only to this real False Self as it takes over relationships in work, love, play, and friendships. The True Self is completely masked. With time, however, the False Self shows signs of failure because life continues to present situations in which a whole person is required.

Table 7.3   Winnicott's Levels of False Self Organization

False self	*True self*	*Consequence*
Extremely Maladaptive: *Mask*	Completely hidden beneath an utterly compliant False Self.	False Self fails when life demands a whole spontaneous person.
Moderately Maladaptive: *Caretaker*	Permitted secret life, regarded as potential self.	Preservation of individual in abnormal environments. Minimal spontaneity, aliveness.
Minimally Adaptive: *Defender*	Waits for safe/desirable conditions to reveal True Self.	Possible suicide if hope for safe conditions is lost; little aliveness.
Moderately Adaptive: *Imitator*	Identifies with caring or productive objects as models.	Successful life, but without realness, aliveness.
Adaptive: *Facilitator*	Normal socialization for politeness and self-restraint	Humility, modesty, social success.

Moderately Maladaptive: Caretaker

The False Self defends the True Self and even serves as its protector or caretaker. The True Self is dimly acknowledged as a potential self and is permitted, in Winnicott's terms, to have a "secret life." Winnicott's constant search of the healthy silver lining exhibited itself most clearly when he wrote of the moderately pathological False Self that it is:

> "...the clearest example of clinical illness as an organization with a positive aim, the preservation of the individual in spite of abnormal environmental conditions" (1960/965a, p. 143).

Minimally Adaptive: Defender

The False Self can serve as a defender against exploitation of the True Self, biding its time until proper conditions for the emergence of the True Self can be found. If safe conditions are not encountered, the False Self may defend the True Self literally to death: suicide. When there is no hope left that the True Self can emerge safely, then the False Self can mobilize the psychological equivalent of a scorched earth policy. The False Self attempts or carries out suicide with the paradoxical intention of preventing the annihilation of the True Self by accomplishing the absolute destruction of the entire self.

Moderately Adaptive: Imitator

A False Self is organized within the personality, but is modeled on caring, productive, and protective people. Although the person feels as though he or she is sometimes not really real, or continually searching for him- or herself, the False Self comprised of benign identifications can negotiate a very successful life.

Adaptive: Facilitator

The False Self is organized normally as ordinary elements of socialization, including polite behavior, personal restraint, false-but-charming modesty, and deliberate control over personal wishes and urges. Without this benign False Self, a kind of socially sophisticated alter ego, the unvarnished True Self would not achieve a place in society as successful or as satisfying.

The True Self: Aliveness

The **True Self,** in Winnicott's view, is real, spontaneous, and creative. It originates in the "aliveness" of the body tissues and functions, especially the beating of the heart and the regularity of breathing (Winnicott, 1960/1965a, p. 148). At the beginning, the True Self is linked to the primary process thinking of the unconscious and is therefore not responsive to external reality (see the discussion of primary process thinking in Chapter 3). At core, True Self is a synonym for the "experience of aliveness."

Initially little more than sensory motor aliveness, the True Self grows more complex and develops its own links to reality. At first, reality is understood as a projection of the inner world. Somewhat later, reality is actually "real" in the sense of having an objective, outside-the-self, existence. Finally, the strengthened True Self becomes able to tolerate two kinds of momentary breaks in personal continuity. First, physical trauma such as brief separations from mother or physical illness do not have the devastating effect after the emergence of the True Self that they would have had prior to it. Second, normal False Self experiences, such as being taught to say "thank you" when the child hardly feels thankful, are taken in stride as part of ordinary socialization without the integrity of the True Self. In this sense, everyone develops a normal social mask or False Self which functions to provide superficial compliance in social contexts where conformity is routinely required (Winnicott, 1964d/1986, p. 67). Functioning in this way, the False Self is a social compromise.

An intermediate level of functioning of the False Self that lies between healthy compromise and pathological defense is to be found between dreaming and reality. People who develop a compliant self, a self capable of manipulating symbols and language can use their skills to play roles deliberately, entertainingly, and convincingly in the world of drama. The False Self becomes a sublimation of the True Self rather than a defender. However, when the split between the True and False Selves is large, the person is impoverished in the use of symbols, language, and cultural skills.

The greatest danger of the successful False Self is that it will be too successful. By hiding the True Self, the False Self may bury its potentialities so deep that they are no longer accessible, no longer constitute the core of the person's "going on being." A "too successful" False Self ironically may result in the very obliteration of the True Self that it was originally created to prevent.

Transitional Objects and Transitional Phenomena

A **transitional object,** in Winnicott's sense, is anything—even a part of the child's own body, such as a fist or thumb—to which the child relates (Winnicott, 1959/1989, p. 53). It is, in Winnicott's phrase, the child's "first not-me possession." Early on, the infant's own tightly balled fist in the mouth is explored with tongue and lips in pretty much the same way as the breast or bottle are explored and comprehended. Later in development, external objects—rattles, stuffed toys, and the like—will become transitional objects with which the infant, guided by the sensitive assistance of the attuned mother, establishes a relationship.

At first, when the infant's needs are aroused, it provides its own objects on demand (the fist or thumb in the mouth). Sometimes the infant's crying and other signs of distress or excitement prompt the mother to provide the nipple or bottle. From the child's point of view, the very desire to have something actually causes the satisfaction of that desire. To the infant it appears that the subjective wish is sufficient to create the gratification.

> The infant thus has a sense of magical omnipotence. On some occasions, the infant will "conjure" up an image of what it wants, and because the sensitive mother is attuned and can read her child's signals of curiosity or distress, she provides in a seemingly magical way the exact object desired: a teddy bear, rattle, blanket, or the like. Winnicott calls this seemingly magical satisfaction of a wish the "moment of illusion."

> The mother, at the beginning, by an almost 100-per-cent adaptation affords the infant the opportunity for the illusion that her breast is part of the infant. It is, as it were, under the baby's magical control. The same can be said in terms of infant care in general, in the quiet times between excitements. Omnipotence is nearly a fact of experience. The mother's eventual task is gradually to disillusion the infant, but she has no hope of success unless at first she has been able to give sufficient opportunity for the illusion.

> In another language, the breast is created by the infant over and over again out of the infant's capacity to love or (one can say) out of need. A subjective phenomenon develops in the baby, which we call the mother's breast. The mother places the actual breast just where the infant is ready to create, and at the right moment. (Winnicott, 1971, pp. 12–13)

Besides the breast, other "objects," such as a teddy bear or a favorite blanket, are dimly recognized by the infant as not belonging to the infant's body ("not me"). However, they are not necessarily fully comprehended as belonging to the outside world or to another person either (Winnicott, 1971, p. 2). Such objects are transitional in the senses of:

- *Place:* bridging inner and outer
- *Agency:* bridging hallucinatory omnipotence and dependency on a real external agent
- *Separateness:* bridging not-me and me

What is important for Winnicott is not the object itself, but the process of transition between subjective hallucination and objective reality testing. These objects are not completely magical nor are they completely real. They are transitional.

> I have introduced the terms "transitional object" and "transitional phenomena" for designation of the intermediate area of experience, between the thumb and the teddy bear, between the oral eroticism [sic] and true object relationship, between primary creative activity and projection of what has already been introjected, between primary unawareness of indebtedness and the acknowledgement of indebtedness (Say: ta! [i.e., "thanks"]). (Winnicott, 1951/1992, p. 230)

Thus, for Winnicott, transitional objects and phenomena are fundamentally intermediate between reality and illusion, landmarks on the road to full acceptance of the real. However, there are "rules of ownership" over the transitional object that the infant carefully exercises:

- The infant assumes rights over the object, and we agree to this assumption. Nevertheless, some abrogation of omnipotence is a feature from the start.
- The object is affectionately cuddled as well as excitedly loved and mutilated.
- It must never change, unless changed by the infant.
- It must survive instinctual loving, and also hating, and, if it be a feature, pure aggression.
- Yet it must seem to the infant to give warmth, or to move, or to have texture, or to do something that seems to show it has vitality or reality of its own.
- It comes from without from our point of view, but not so from the point of view of the baby. Neither does it come from within; it is not an hallucination.
- Its fate is to be gradually allowed to be decathected, so that in the course of years it becomes not so much forgotten as relegated to limbo. By this I mean that in health the transitional object does not "go inside" nor does the feeling about it necessarily undergo repression. It is not forgotten and it is not mourned. It loses meaning. . . . (Winnicott, 1951/1992, p. 233)

Winnicott assumed, that at least for some infants in some circumstances, the transitional object served as a symbol for a part-object. That is, a piece of cherished blanket might symbolize the nurturing breast for some infants; for others it may symbolize feces (1951/1992, p. 236). Yet the fundamental purpose remains the same: Transitional objects are the infant's first tools in negotiating the gap between the illusion of magical creation of desired objects and the disillusion that such objects have their own existence.

The infant eventually learns to distinguish between "me" and "not-me," between "inner" and "outer," and between illusion and reality. Reality in the form of external frustration and obstacles makes itself known. And the mother herself will become a real object with whom the infant establishes a mutual relationship. Out of this relationship will come important psychological understandings about trust in self, trust in others, and how to relate to people.

EXPLORING DEEPER QUESTIONS

Near the end of his life, Winnicott turned his attention toward paradoxical aspects of living and dying. The concepts of survival, creation, and annihilation had renewed fascination for the aging pediatrician. Always the master of puns and paradoxes, Winnicott now grew increasingly philosophical. His thinking became more abstract and drawn toward the philosophical implications of psychoanalytic concepts. In this frame of mind, Winnicott introduced a distinction between using and relating to an object. The distinction embodied his last concerns in a formulation that elevated psychological paradox into metaphysical existentialism. The theme of survival was placed squarely at the center of the circle of creation, destruction, and recreation—the universal cycle of birth, death, and renewal.

The Cycle of Aliveness: Using an Object

Winnicott's formulation of transitional objects and phenomena already had laid the foundations for the recognition of the significance of paradox in object relations:

> I should like to put in a reminder here that the essential feature in the concept of transitional objects and phenomena . . . is the *paradox, and the acceptance of the paradox:* the baby creates the object, but the object was there waiting to be created and to become a cathected object. I tried to draw attention to this aspect of transitional phenomena by claiming that in the rules of the game we all know that we will never challenge the baby to elicit an answer to the question: did you create that or did you find it? (Winnicott, 1968b/1989, p. 221)

What Winnicott had accomplished in formulating the concept of transitional phenomena was to diffuse the usual psychoanalytic focus. Instead of the traditional understanding of the external world as interesting only to the degree that it is a projection of the internal world, Winnicott studied the external world on its own terms. Transitional phenomena are the bridge between inner and outer worlds. To exist at all, they require an interaction between subjective and objective reality. Transitional objects are paradoxically both projections and discoveries. Part illusion, part perception, transitional phenomena belong to the middle ground between unreal and real. They are projections sent into the objective world by an infant who creates them in the subjective world; but projections are, by definition, projected onto something. That suitable something is always also an accessible something. It is a something that happens to be available at exactly the moment the baby is ready to create. In this metaphysical sense, then, the baby repeatedly creates and recreates its image and experience of the breast as love-object (Winnicott, 1951/1992, p. 238).

Winnicott now argued that a baby progresses from relating to using the love-object. The transition between relating and using presupposes destroying the object in fantasy. The specific sequence follows this logic: In the first phase, **relating to the object** requires that the infant advance from magical understanding of the object's existence as a projection under omnipotent control to realistic comprehension of the object as a real, independent, objectively existing entity. Mother becomes a person. At that point, following Melanie Klein's hypotheses, the baby's innate destructiveness meets an obstacle it had never before encountered. Real objects survive fantasies of destruction.

Indeed, the most significant developmental advance in distinguishing between fantasy and reality comes from this very stubborn refusal of real objects to be obliterated by wishing. "Aha!" says the infant, "total destruction is not total destruction" for objects that really exist and continue to exist. The attempt at destruction—and most important, the failure of the attempt—is the trigger for the infant to place the object outside subjective reality and squarely into the world (Winnicott, 1968b/1989, p. 223). Winnicott summarized the paradoxical logic of his hypothesis in this way:

> This is a position that can be arrived at by the individual in early stages of emotional growth only through the actual survival of cathected objects that are at the same time in process of becoming destroyed because real, becoming real because destroyed.... (1968b/1989, p. 223)

and

> *There is no anger* in the destruction of the object to which I am referring, though there could be said to be joy at the object's survival. From this moment, or arising out of this phase, the object is *in fantasy always* being destroyed. This quality of "always being destroyed" makes the reality of the surviving object felt as such, strengthens the feeling tone, and contributes to object-constancy. The object can now be used. (1968b/1989, p. 226; italics in original)

A main effect of Winnicott's hypothesis was to shift the emphasis in psychoanalysis away from the theory that the infant's understanding of external reality is based primarily on its own projections. In accord with his long-standing emphasis on the facilitating environment, Winnicott's **using the object** concept split the focus equally between internal and external reality.

But what, precisely, does it mean to say that the infant progresses from relating to using the object? Winnicott argued that the infant's realization that the object survives its attacks—without retaliating—enables the baby not only to believe in its external existence, but also to trust the object. An object that survives the most intense destruction the infant can muster and that does not strike back is a "good-enough" mother whose reliability and trustworthiness are usable—helpful—in learning how to cope with life.

PERSONAL SOURCES FROM WINNICOTT'S CHILDHOOD

The majority of Winnicott's biographers agree that he had a strong identification with his mother and an empathic bond with all mothers (especially C. Winnicott, 1978, 1989; see also Goldman, 1993; pp. 47ff.; Jacobs, 1995; Kahr, 1996; Phillips, 1988). Winnicott's own childhood has been described by his second wife Clare as "too good to be true" in the particular sense that Donald was loved, knew he was loved, and thought of himself as lovable (1989, p. 9). He grew up fundamentally happy and secure. To judge from the substance of the theory he left behind, his vision of humanity was certainly individualized by his experiences—even, necessarily, idiosyncratic ones—but it does not appear to have been driven by psychopathology.

Mothered by Many

Donald Winnicott was born in 1896 in Plymouth, England. He was the youngest of three children and the only son born to John Frederick Winnicott and Elizabeth Martha Woods. The Winnicott family belonged to the Wesleyan Methodist Church (Phillips, 1988, p. 23). Clare Winnicott (1983/1991, p. 184) pointed out that the Methodist tradition is one of strong independence, self-reliance, and nonconformity, characteristics that certainly describe Winnicott himself.

Winnicott recalled as an adult that: ". . . in a sense I was an only child with multiple mothers and with a father extremely preoccupied in my younger years with town as well as business matters" (quoted in C. Winnicott, 1989, p. 8). Clare Winnicott recalled that Donald had thought he did not have enough contact with his own father: "So he says, 'I was left too much to all my mothers. Thank goodness I was sent away at thirteen!' " (1983/1991, p. 185). In fact, the members of the Winnicott household in which Donald grew up were almost exclusively female. Two older sisters, his mother, a nanny, sometimes a governess for his sisters Violet and Kathleen, his Aunt Delia and another aunt, a cook, and several parlor maids populated the Winnicott household, and all "doted" on Donald (Kahr, 1996, p. 5). All the Winnicott females loved children and all of them, well into their elderly years, maintained the knack of playing and talking with youngsters (C. Winnicott, 1983/1991).

This unusual childhood situation of being a little boy enveloped by mothers and virtually deprived of a father seems to have left an indelible impression on Winnicott's psychological development, resulting in a powerful female identification. First of all, because young Donald received so much affection from so many women with whom he interacted in a reliable manner, he felt protected, safe, and secure, and this emotional stability provided him with a solid foundation for a sturdy, productive, and creative adult life. Secondly, the preponderance of women in Winnicott's childhood stimulated his fascination with the inner world of the female (Kahr, 1996, p. 6).

Donald's Mother: Elizabeth Woods

Donald's actual mother is a biographically indistinct figure about whom few details are known. There is some evidence that Elizabeth Woods struggled with episodes of depression throughout her life and that Donald's distant father expected his son to care for and cheer up his mother (Kahr, 1996, p. 10). Clare Winnicott quoted her husband's observation that ". . . it is probably true that in the early years [my father] left me too much to all my mothers. Things never quite righted themselves" (C. Winnicott, 1989, p. 8; see also C. Winnicott, 1978, p. 24). At the age of 67, Winnicott wrote a poem about his mother entitled "The Tree," which he sent to his brother-in-law with a note acknowledging the hurt he felt in composing it:

> Mother below is weeping
> weeping
> weeping
> Thus I knew her
> Once, stretched out in her lap
> As now on dead tree
> I learned to make her smile
> to stem her tears
> to undo her guilt
> to cure her inward death
> To enliven her was my living.
>
> (quoted in Phillips, 1988, p. 29)

The tree referred to in the title was the special place to which the young Donald retreated to do his homework. Phillips (1988) points out that there is religious symbolism in Winnicott's choice of metaphor:

In the poem Winnicott clearly identifies himself with Christ, and the Tree of the title is the Cross. . . . The chilling image of himself 'stretched out on her lap/As now on dead tree,' by omitting the definite article suggests that once it is dead it is no tree in particular, as anonymous as dead wood. (Phillips, 1988, pp. 29–30)

His poetry alludes to the role that the young Winnicott played in combating his mother's "deadness." The poem also poignantly expresses themes that occupied Winnicott professionally for his entire career:

- feeling fully alive versus feeling dead numbness,
- maternal depression experienced by the child as aggression,
- the needs of the child for maternal holding,
- the protective role of a superficially compliantly cheerful False Self, and
- the False Self as caretaker.

Winnicott understood that at the beginning and at the end of his life that he had made "...a living out of keeping his mother alive" (Phillips, 1988, p. 30).

Donald's Father: Sir John Frederick Winnicott

John Frederick Winnicott was a successful merchant, specializing in women's corsets. He was a religious man with a strong faith who attended church regularly. John Winnicott was twice elected mayor of the town of Plymouth and was knighted in 1924 (Phillips, 1988, p. 23). "Sir Frederick," as he became known, was active in town politics and the business community, and even became Manager of the Plymouth Hospital and Chairman of the Plymouth Chamber of Commerce. Despite these accomplishments, John Frederick felt insecure throughout his adult life about his lack of formal education (Phillips, 1988, p. 23). His aspirations to become a member of Parliament foundered on lifelong learning difficulties, which John Frederick believed had robbed him of the confidence to enter the world of politics outside his local community (Kahr, 1996, p. 4).

For all of his success in local business and politics, John Frederick was a distant parental figure and not a good or close father to Donald. His relationship with Donald was formal rather than intimate, and sometimes surprisingly authoritarian. Indeed, John Frederick could be so insensitive to his son's needs that Donald risked the humiliation of his father's rejection for even minor infractions of proper decorum. On one occasion, 12-year-old Donald used the word drat as an expletive during the noonday meal:

> ...my father looked pained as only he could look, blamed my mother for not seeing to it that I had decent friends, and from that moment he prepared himself to send me away to boarding school, which he did when I was thirteen. (quoted in C. Winnicott, 1989, p. 8)

There is some indication that the nature of John Frederick's rejection and teasing was linked to issues of Donald's masculinity or sexuality. When Donald was only three, he ascended the grassy slope in the garden armed with his child-sized croquet mallet prepared to exact revenge and make a piece of personal family history. In the tall grass, he bashed flat the nose of a wax doll called "Rosie" that belonged to his sisters. Rosie was a particular source of irritation to young Donald because his father often teased him with the doll by parodying a popular song of the day in a voice intended to taunt:

> Rosie said to Donald
> I love you
> Donald said to Rosie
> I don't believe you do.

(quoted in C. Winnicott, 1989, p. 7)

Winnicott (1989, p. 7) says that he "knew the doll had to be altered for the worse, and much of my life has been founded on the undoubted fact that I actually did this deed, not merely wish it and planned it." Ironically, his father relieved some of his son's guilt by heating the wax of the doll's head with a series of matches and remolding it into a more or less recognizable face.

> This early demonstration of the restitutive and reparative act certainly made an impression on me, and perhaps made me able to accept the fact that I myself, dear innocent child, had actually become violent directly with a doll, but indirectly with my good-tempered father who was just then entering my conscious life. (Winnicott, quoted in C. Winnicott, 1989, p. 8)

Winnicott clearly and defensively presents the memory of his father as an admirable, even-tempered, helpful man for whom he felt only admiration and love. Yet it was the father who provoked humiliation by repeated teasing of his son.

Implications of Winnicott's Childhood

Winnicott's affinity for and empathy with mothers, his tight focus on mothering, rather than parenting, and his own impressive talents "mothering" and "holding" his patients were consistent with his personal experiences with "multiple mothers" and his family tradition of nurturing children.

At least three inferences can be drawn from the sample of episodes we have reviewed from the early life of D. W. Winnicott. First, compared to most of the theorists we examine in this book, Winnicott had a happy, secure, healthy childhood in a warm and loving family. For this reason, Winnicott's vision of personality development emphasizes spontaneous collaboration between children and their parents rather than the conflicts that are enacted between them.

Second, Winnicott's freedom from childhood insecurity was not immunity from other forms of maternal rejection. Although the definitive biography has yet to be written, the existing body of life history data make it clear that Winnicott's sensitivity to failures in maternal "holding" stemmed from his own experiences trying to vitalize an emotionally numbed and depressed mother.

Third, Winnicott's theory mentions the contributions of fathers to the development of their children—but just barely. Fathers are not in the Winnicottian spotlight just as Sir Frederick was not in his son's daily life.

A FINAL WORD ON D. W. WINNICOTT

D. W. Winnicott followed a line of independent thinking as he blended approaches from pediatric medical practice and psychoanalysis. More than the other object relations theorists, he was a careful observer of the actual behavior of infants and children. Like Anna Freud (Chapter 6), he adjusted his behavior so as to strengthen the relationships between his young clients and himself. He also emphasized the healthy aspects of behaviors that Melanie Klein and other theorists might have dismissed as simply pathological.

EVALUATING OBJECT RELATIONS THEORY

Like the parent theory from which these object relations models emerged, each of them shares the strengths and weaknesses of psychodynamic formulations.

Refutability of Object Relations Theory

The major focus of object relations theorists is the presumed unconscious dynamics (sometimes even of a barely verbal infant) rather than the observable interpersonal transactions of relationships. As a result of this focus, most of their hypotheses are untestable. What presumably transpires in the mind of the baby as it interacts with its mother is largely inferential.

Some inferences are more reasonable than others, but reasonableness is not equivalent to refutability. Klein's formulations appear on close examination to be wanting both in the consistency of their logic and in the vast distance between her inferences and the observations on which they are presumably based. Winnicott's proposals, influenced by Klein, lie closer to pragmatic common sense. Unfortunately, however, with the exception of the concept of the transitional object, Winnicott's hypotheses are also inferences about unconscious dynamics that are far from the possibility of empirical test.

Reactive vs. Active Human Agency in Object Relations Theories

Klein's formulation preserves substantial elements of the classical drive theory and its reliance on a reactive model of the nervous system. Kleinian babies are tense infants who reactively discharge their drives onto available objects. Winnicott, on the other hand, views people from the earliest days of their lives as collaborative constructors of social reality. Winnicott's concepts of the infant's progress from omnipotent magical thinking to object relating and on toward using the object by constructing it, destroying it, and happily rediscovering it surviving in reality are active agent concepts.

The Idiographic Emphasis of Object Relations Theory

Shared with orthodox psychoanalysis is the goal of understanding the individual. Personality development, and the ways in which it can go wrong, are strictly "one person at a time" phenomena for object relations theorists. A goal, largely unattained, is also to discover generalizable regularities of behavior.

SUMMARY

Object relations theory advanced Freud's orthodox model in two ways. First, a more ambitiously developmental perspective based on direct clinical work with children was introduced into psychoanalysis. Second, Freud's passing references to the ego's propensity to retain the character of its lost objects were expanded substantially. Intimate relations, rather than drive gratification, became both the medium and the message of psychoanalysis. Unlike the neo-Freudians, whom we consider in later chapters, the object relations theorists wanted to preserve as much of orthodox psychoanalysis as they could.

Melanie Klein

Beginning with the observations of her own children, Melanie Klein's earliest formulations were more or less overly enthusiastic educational applications of classical theory. She initially presented her formulations as "psychoanalytic educational upbringing" designed to be a kind of prophylaxis of the child's mind. In a number of other ways, Klein took Freud at his word, and then extended the words beyond anything Freud intended. She soon pushed psychoanalytic understanding backwards in time to the earliest days of life, where eventually she found a fully functioning ego, superego, and a remarkably active aggressive drive. She credited even the youngest children with an active unconsciously imaginative capacity, called "phantasy." Phantasy images are real to the infant, as real as the people from whom they are derived and on whom they will eventually be projected. Klein's work is sometimes seen as a feminist corrective to Freud's male-dominated theory. In contrast to Freud's emphasis on the importance of the penis for both genders, Klein placed the female breast, the child's first love and most enduring love-object, at the center of her psychological world.

Klein's conception of the infant pictures an inherently aggressive, sadistic, and opportunistic creature who becomes frightened by its own aggression. To protect itself from the retaliation it imagines its love-objects might enact, the infant splits objects into good and bad. The worried infant anticipates persecution from its bad objects and idealizes its good ones for protection.

With time, Klein moderated the role of aggression in her theory, supplementing it with formulations of anxiety, guilt, envy, and reparation. The infant was now understood as envying the good object (breast) because of its bountiful goodness. Phantasies of destroying the good object not only evoke anxiety but also provoke guilt feelings. The need to repair the love-object emerges and the infant omnipotently believes that it can accomplish this magical feat.

These various landmarks in the infant's progress toward conceptualizing the mother as a real person were called "positions" by Klein to emphasize that they are ongoing, lifelong processes. The first developmental position was called the *paranoid position* because the central anxiety is the infant's fear of its own annihilation. By a convoluted twist of logic, Klein argued that the infant fears that the destroyed object may reconstitute itself inside the infant and reinitiate its persecution. At a later moment in development, anxiety or concern for the welfare of the object becomes dominant. When the infant comprehends that the mother-as-a-person is in jeopardy from its own rage, the *depressive position* is entered. Now the baby's central concern is to protect the good object from its own attacks and those mounted against the mother by internalized bad objects. To supplement the reparative defensive strategy, the ego may temporarily adopt what Klein called the *manic position*. This developmental phase is marked by the need to take omnipotent control over the object, dominating it by exerting the power of life and death over it, and protecting it from its own sadistic impulses.

Although Klein originally proposed splitting as an elementary and primitive infantile defense against the recognition that good and bad object are one, she elaborated the concept into a series of complex developmental maneuvers. *Splitting* eventually referred to object division (good and bad), ego defensive splitting or repressive dissociation, object relations splitting (love and hate), and even splitting of enduring personality structures such as the id and superego.

A supplementary and related defense is *projective identification,* whereby the infant identifies with the split-off good object and distances itself from the split-off bad object. But the target of the projection, mother, may find that the infant behaves in ways that subtly coerce her behavior into conformity with the infant's projection. Projective identification can thus be a kind of self-fulfilling prophecy by which the projector manipulates the projectee to comply with the wish embodied in the projection.

Klein's model of infant development relies on major inferences about the infant's mind. It strikes many observers that Klein's specific deductions tell us less about the infant's mind than they do about what was on Klein's mind. To the extent that this is true, they are Klein's own projections.

D. W. Winnicott

Trained as a pediatrician, Donald Woods Winnicott brought to psychoanalysis a pragmatic sensibility rooted in common sense. He had a gift for communicating with children and often could employ the simplest of games as diagnostic assessments. The squiggle game and his observations of babies mouthing a shiny tongue depressor (the "spatula") were part of Winnicott's consultative approach to child psychiatry.

He transferred that same flexible, spontaneous attitude to his psychoanalytic clinical work and to his theoretical formulations. Influenced by Melanie Klein, Winnicott was nevertheless adamant in trying to maintain his intellectual and creative independence. He understood infants as collaborators rather than as sadistic aggressors. While he found value in Klein's developmental "positions," he made every effort to depathologize them by focusing on the achievements of the infant in coping with its interpersonal world. Life is normally difficult, Winnicott argued, and most babies momentarily display some forms of behavior that appears pathological. But on closer examination, coupled with a willingness to tolerate momentarily eccentric or disruptive behavior, adults soon discover that most children can cope with life's real difficulties if their mothers can provide sufficiently secure and comforting *holding.*

The basic developmental tasks for the infant whose mother provides the physical and metaphorical holding that facilitates development are threefold: integration, personalization, and realization. *Integration* refers to the organization of personality facilitated by the mother's attention to satisfying her infant's needs reliably. *Unintegration,* the Winnicottian opposite of integration, is a primordially natural phase of development that the infant does not find distressing. *Personalization* is Winnicott's term for the infant's achievement of linking inner and outer reality by recognizing the boundaries of its own physical body. By this he meant that the baby "personalizes"—takes possession of—its body with help from mother's ministrations so that "this is my finger" begins to have real meaning. Finally, *realization* was Winnicott's term for the baby's acceptance of external reality as real, as objective and as enduring contrasted with the inner world of fantasy. Here the mother helps her child achieve "disillusionment": the understanding that illusion, however satisfying, is simply not shared reality.

Winnicott suggested that the *"good-enough mother"* provides enough security to permit her child to master its own aggression, come to grips with life's real difficulties, and develop a spontaneous, authentic self that he termed the *True Self.* By contrast, "not good-enough" mothering, exhibited, for example, by the depressed, psychiatrically ill, or neglectful mother, promotes the development of a protective masklike self, called the *False Self.* Children can develop differing levels of False Self protection that vary in degree of maladaptiveness. At the extremely maladaptive end of the continuum is the False Self, which functions to conceal completely the spontaneous True Self in an effort to protect it from manipulation in social contact. At the opposite end of the spectrum, most children develop a kind of socially cooperative False Self that serves to facilitate social success rather than to wall off the True Self. Between these extremes, children find healthy and not-so-healthy ways of protecting their inner lives from "impingement" and potential betrayal. But it was Winnicott's belief that the more protectively powerful the False Self grew, the less "alive," spontaneous, and playful could the True Self feel.

As part of her skilled and empathic "holding," the good-enough mother provides just those things that the baby needs at just those moments when the baby is ready for them. In Winnicott's famous phrase, "There's no such thing as a baby," babies are best understood as an integral part of the "nursing couple." Winnicott envisioned the mother-child relationship as a collaboration of two very unequal partners. The mother's task is to "shrink down" to baby size to understand her infant's needs because the baby cannot expand to adult size to tell her what they might be. The good-enough mother provides sufficient holding for the baby to master its most primitive fears, the unthinkable anxieties:

- Going to pieces,
- Falling forever,
- Having no relationship to the body,
- Having no orientation, and
- Complete isolation because there is no means for communication.

Along the way, the infant learns the difference between those parts of self and mother that belong to "me" and those that are "not-me." Once this division between inner and outer reality is achieved, the infant can tolerate increased separation from its love-objects. To bridge the separation, a *transitional object,* the infant's first "not-me" possession will be "created" in collaboration with the mother. A bit of soft blanket, a stuffed toy, even a handkerchief or piece of clothing ("the niffle"), can serve the role of transitional object. It is baby's choice in cooperation with a mother who facilitates and supports the choice.

Toward the end of his life, when personal survival was at issue, Winnicott created one final developmental distinction between relating to and using an object. On the basis of a dream evoked by reading Jung's autobiography, Winnicott came to the insight that the infant has to fantasize destroying its love object to discover that the object in reality nevertheless survives. This infantile discovery permits the infant not only to relate to the object in a dependent way, but also to trust sufficiently in the reliability and durability of the object to use the object to facilitate its own growth toward independence. As Winnicott pointed out, the progression from relating to using involves creation by destruction.

In all, ego psychology has greatly expanded the confines of classical theory. No longer is a human being an "assembly of minds" or a battlefield on whose terrain the battalions of the mind erect obstacles, conduct assaults, and sustain defeats. No longer is psychoanalytic psychology restricted to study of unhealthy personalities. The whole span of life, from birth through adulthood, and the whole range of possible adaptations, from inhibited and fearful withdrawals to psychotic and fragmented separations from reality to masterful and efficacious coping, are accepted as suitable areas for a general psychoanalytic psychology to explore.

Taken as a loosely related group of ideas, object relations theories share the strengths and weaknesses of their parent model, classical psychoanalysis. They rely on untestable, irrefutable inferences about the infantile mind. The theorists in this chapter both re-conceptualize humans as active agents—with Winnicott viewing people as more active than Klein. They are ideographically focused on the individual case.

FOR FURTHER READING

A thorough, readable overview of object relations theories is Frank Summers' *Object Relations: Theories and Psychopathology* (New York: Academic Press, 1994). Phyllis Grosskurth has contributed an excellent, encompassing biography of Melanie Klein in *Melanie Klein: Her World and Her Work* (Cambridge, MA: Harvard University Press, 1989).

Further suggested readings about object relations theory as well as about the approaches of Melaine Klein and Donald W. Winnicott are presented in the web site associated with Chapter 7: www.wiley.com/college/sollod

GLOSSARY

Melanie Klein

Anal frustration: During toilet training, the mother partially frustrates the child's anal impulses. This experience prompts the child to devalue the frustrating love-object.

Bad objects: Objects that are frustrating, unfulfilling, or painful and often experienced as persecuting and attacking.

Depressive position: The child's prevailing melancholy or depressive feeling that is derived from the fear of losing the good object by destruction or mutilation.

Devaluation: Belittling the worth and importance of internalized objects. Contempt replaces love. Such devaluation enables the ego to effect partial detachment from the love object.

Envy: An angry feeling that another person possesses and enjoys something desirable. The infant develops feelings of envy when the mother's breast is begrudging, depriving him or her of ample milk, care, and love.

Femininity phase: A phase in which infants of both genders actively identify with and envy the mother they seek to possess.

Good objects: Objects that are gratifying, satisfying, or pleasurable. Such objects are idealized in phantasy.

Greed: An impetuous and insatiable craving that exceeds what the loved object can give and what the greedy person actually needs. The greedy person is never satisfied by any amount of goodness.

Idealization: The infantile ego's attitude of "strongly exalting the object" and what it provides. The good breast is idealized as a protection against the persecution of the bad breast. Klein also added that idealization serves to diminish envy of the good object.

Infantile sadism: An actively aggressive stance toward love-objects. In their imagination, children attack the object, rob it of everything it contains, and devour it.

Jealousy: An attitude that occurs when a person feels that love is in danger of being taken away by a rival.

Object relations: In Freud's theories objects were considered aims of id drives; later theorists defined object relations as the person's actual relationships with and subjective views of "objects" (mostly people) beyond the subjective world of the self.

Paranoic position: The fear of one's own annihilation, fear that one's own ego is at risk of attack.

Paranoid-schizoid position: Dysfunctions of empathy, love, and hate in relating to objects and to the self may be found in schizoid personality phenomena. The infant "splits" its relationships with the object into love and hate—love for the good and hate for the bad object.

Part-object: A part of a person, often the mother's breast, that itself becomes an object with which the infant or child relates.

Phantasy: For Klein, the infant's unconscious world of the "unreal real." The child's phantasy world, which may not correspond to external reality, is nonetheless the child's reality.

Reparation/restitution: A desire to protect the object or person that was once mutilated or annihilated in sadistic phantasies. It is guilt-driven reparation. Destructive impulses in the unconscious mind mingle side by side with spontaneous feelings of love and empathy for others in the conscious mind.

Splitting: Originally used by Klein to indicate the separation of good and bad objects in the child's phantasy. Subsequently, Klein elaborated to include structural splits in the child's id, ego, and self.

Splitting the ego: The split that occurs when good feelings arise from internalized satisfying objects, but anxiety arises from internalized fragmented and poisonous bad objects.

Splitting the id: Refers to unmanageable, terrifying, persecutory objects, derived from the phantasy transformations of the mother and father, are "relegated to the deeper layers of the unconscious." The horrific images are dissociated into the deeper unconscious.

Splitting the object: The splitting of the object perceived to be the source of the threat into good and bad images.

Splitting the self/projective identification: Identification with external objects. The infant projects self-content into the object and takes it back by identification.

Whole object: An object seen as having both good and bad qualities and having its own continuing existence.

D. W. Winnicott

Depersonalization: The feeling of being mildly or extremely uncomfortable with one's body. A person might develop the delusion that he or she is not "in" his or her body. In a milder variation, there can be the belief that something is alarmingly different, "not right," or "not real" about one's own body.

Disintegration: A frightening unintegrated state caused by developmental failure. This state is often associated with psychotic-level psychopathology.

False Self: A sense of self in which the feeling of being real is absent. The False Self masks and hides the True Self. The True Self does not feel secure enough to surface and display its facets spontaneously. The False Self may serve as caretaker, defender, imitator, or facilitator of the True Self.

Good-enough mother: A mother who "holds" her infant securely in her arms while feeding, cleaning, and playing with it. She provides warmth, reliability, and sameness. She provides encouragement and support for the infant's "going on being."

Holding: A physical and psychological process that enables the infant securely to organize his or her muddled urges, wishes, and fears into predictable experiences. The mother's holding is a primary means of communication between a mother and her infant and promotes comfort and stability. It fosters the beginnings of personality integration.

Personalization: The process of becoming increasingly comfortable with ownership of the body and its sensations. Satisfactory personalization leads to the feeling that the infant is "in" his or her own body.

Primary maternal preoccupation: The mother's sensitization to the infant's needs toward the end of pregnancy and shortly after birth. It results in a close identification of the mother with her infant.

Realization: Learning to take account of external reality. Sights, sounds, smells, and touches experienced with each real feeding teaches the baby what it can and cannot conjure up when the real object is not present. The baby learns to accept and tolerate the limitations of reality.

Relating to the object: Realistic comprehension of the object as a real, independent, objectively existing entity. Mother becomes a person. In Kleinian terms, real objects survive fantasies of destruction.

Stage of concern: Winnicott proposed that the Kleinian term "depressive position" be renamed the "stage of concern" to indicate the greater awareness of the good object. The infant begins to feel concern and empathy for its love-objects.

Transitional objects: Objects that bridge the gap between the child's dependence on its mother and its need to progress to independence. Teddy bears, blankets, and other cuddly things are often transitional objects.

True Self: The core self, or, the True Self is a synonym for the "experience of aliveness." The True Self is real, spontaneous, and creative.

Unintegration: At the beginning of life, the stage before a "person" begins to exist. All that exists is a bundle of biological needs and potentials. Winnicott said, "There is no such thing as a baby."

Unthinkable anxieties: Those anxieties having to do with going to pieces, falling forever, having no relationship to the body, having no orientation, or complete isolation due to inadequate communication. The mother's loving physical and emotional care prevents the infant from unbearable anxiety.

Using the object: The infant's realization that the object survives its attacks—without retaliating—enables the baby not only to believe in its external existence, but also to trust the object.

Chapter 8

Erik Homburger Erikson

Psychoanalytic Ego Psychology: The Centrality of Identity

A sense of self-control without loss of self-esteem is the ontogenetic source of free will.

Erik H. Erikson, *Identity, Youth and Crisis*

...healthy children will not fear life if their elders have integrity enough not to fear death.

Erik H. Erikson, *Childhood and Society*

Erik Homburger Erikson   Born: 1902   Frankfurt-am-Main, Germany

Died: 1994   Harwich, Massachusetts

About Erikson's Ego Psychology

Erik Homburger Erikson's work consists of two major and closely related contributions: a psychoanalytic ego psychology and a psychosocial life span theory of development. The focus for Erikson, as for the other ego psychologists, is on the person's interactions and relationships with others. Instincts and needs are seen as important, but the chief concern for Erikson is how the person interprets and acts upon them. He also accords to the environment an important role in facilitating or obstructing healthy psychological development.

Central to Erikson's formulation are his concepts of:

- Ego identity formation by which Erikson means the development of a clear sense of who and what one is within the cultural and environmental framework in which one finds oneself.
- Epigenetic stages of psychosocial development. These were originally derived from Freud's psychosexual stages but go beyond them by considering ego development within the context of a person's psychosocial environment.

- The developmental progression of the human life cycle from infancy to old age.
- Ego strengths, which mark each of eight stages of human development; they are virtues such as hope, will, purpose, and wisdom.

Erikson's work led to a psychotherapeutic focus on an important aspect of personality not strongly emphasized by prior theorists: What is the person's conception of him- or herself? It also led to reconsidering much psychopathology in terms of the process of identity formation.

Each stage of Eriksonian personality development includes different insights and emphases. Erikson's contributions thus constitute one of the most comprehensive personality theories.

IDENTITY'S ARCHITECT

Erikson has been called "Identity's Architect" (Friedman, 2000). This terminology reflects Lawrence J. Friedman's comprehensive biography of Erikson's life and his published works. As will be discussed further in this chapter, Erikson, in contrast to Freud, shifted emphasis away from instinctual drives as determinants of behavior and personality formation, to understanding how identity is shaped across the entire life cycle from birth to death. He proposed that the developmental and aging process presents a series of normatively occurring challenges associated with different ages and phases of life. He broadly used the term *crisis* to characterize the unique nature of each of the eight stages that he thought defined the human life cycle.

> And it may be a good thing that the word crisis no longer connotes impending catastrophe, which at one time seemed to be an obstacle to the understanding of the term. It is now being accepted as designating a recurring turning point, a crucial moment, when development must move one way or another, marshaling resources of growth, recovery and further differentiation. (1968, p. 16)

The concept of further differentiation is crucial to understanding Erikson's ideas about personality formation. Further differentiation has specific meaning within Erikson's framework of how ego processes and identity changes as persons face the tasks and choices that confront them from birth to death.

> Furthermore, the process described is always changing and developing: at its best it is a process of increasing differentiation, and it becomes ever more inclusive as the individual grows aware of a widening circle of others significant to him, from the maternal person to 'mankind.' The process begins somewhere in the first true 'meeting' of mother and baby as two persons who can touch and recognize each other, and it does not 'end' until a man's power of mutual affirmation wanes. (1968, p. 23)

The idea of a "widening circle" of significant others is a metaphor. It is similar to the visual image produced when a stone is thrown into a pool of still water and the ripple effect causes concentric circles from the point of the stone's entry, to the outer limits of the ripples themselves. So, beginning at birth, the process of identity and personality formation begins and continues in a relatively fluid way until the last stage of the life cycle where each individual faces the reality of their own death and the end of living.

In a more specific sense, Erikson's use of the "widening circle" metaphor refers to familial, social, cultural and natural forces that influence a person's development at any given point in the life cycle. For example, some may have broken families, alcoholic parents, or early parental loss due to illness; some may have close-knit families and communities and others may live in rural, isolated geographical areas where social contact is limited; others may have strong ethnic backgrounds with expected ways of valuing and believing; some may have to serve during wartime in times of national emergencies (e.g., World War II) or in political wars such as Vietnam, the Persian Gulf or Iraq. These types of events help shape how the person forms a sense of personal identity which may have many different configurations (e.g., identity integration versus identity confusion, positive versus negative self-identity, etc.). Thus, the historical and social context of events are among the central determinants of identity formation.

Consistent with his psychoanalytic training, Erikson's works reflect the use of psychodynamic language. Important here is that the central concept of individual identity is part of ego functioning, the cognitive aspects of memory, intelligence, information processing, executive functioning, and capacity for self-reflection and understanding. Thus, in describing the task of the ego, Erikson notes:

> We may reformulate the ego's task (and maybe, the ego) by recognizing it as one of three indispensable and ceaseless processes by which man's existence becomes and remains continuous in time and organized in form. The first of these—first because it was studied originally through Freud's transfer of biological and physiological modes of thought to psychology—is the *biological process,* by which an organism comes to be a hierarchic organization or organ systems living out its life cycle. The second is the *social process,* by which organisms come to be organized in groups which are geographically, historically or culturally defined, what may be called the *ego process* in the organizational principle by which the individual maintains himself as a coherent personality with sameness and continuity both in his self experience and in his actuality for others. (1968, p. 73)

As an ego task, the psychological principle of self dynamics is to maintain a coherent personality and to sustain a sense of self sameness and continuity across time and life events at different stages of the life cycle. In this regard, how does Erikson define identity? He describes two types of identity which are integrally related to each other.

> But here it is necessary to differentiate between personal identity and **ego identity.** The conscious feeling of having a personal identity is based on two simultaneous observations: the perception of self-sameness and continuity of one's existence in time and space and the perception of the fact that others recognize one's sameness and continuity. What I have called ego identity, however, concerns more than the mere *fact* of existence; it is as well, the *quality* of this existence. Ego identity, then, in its subjective aspect, is the awareness of the fact that there is self-sameness and continuity to the ego's synthesized methods, *the style of one's individuality,* and that this style coincides with sameness and continuity of one's meaning for significant others in the immediate community. (1968, p. 50)

This quote illustrates the complexity of Erikson's psychodynamic thinking. In a more simple way, personal identity is how other people see us as unique persons with certain characteristics of personality, coping and adaptation that define our uniqueness. Ego identity, in contrast, is our internal, subjective awareness of how we attempt to master experiences and challenges in life (i.e., ego's synthesizing methods) and that this "style of one's individuality" is recognized by peers, significant others and the community in which social relations occur. However, it should be noted that identity can and does change in varying degrees across the course of the life cycle. As will be discussed, Erikson considered adolescence as the period when the structure of identity began to mold, as a consequence of childhood development, into a more coherent form. Knowing "who I am, what my role in society is, and who I am to become" is the central task of this phase of personality formation and it extends from the teenage years into early adulthood. Moreover, Erikson avoided defining ego identity in a single definition:

> I can attempt to make the matter of identity more explicit only by approaching it from a variety of angles. At one time, then, it will appear to refer to a conscious sense of individual identity; at another, to an unconscious striving for a continuity of personal character; at a third, as a criterion for the silent doings of ego synthesis; and finally, as a maintenance of an inner solidarity with a group's ideals and identity. (1959, p. 102)

We will review further considerations of ego identity and the self later in the chapter.

LIFE HISTORY SOURCES OF THE IDENTITY HYPOTHESIS

In 1970, Erikson published an autobiographical essay in which he traced some aspects of his own identity formation. Erikson employed the facts of his own life history to illustrate the concept of **identity crisis** and the ultimate resolution of his crisis in forming an acceptable personal identity. Erikson provided glimpses into the motives that underlaid his own intense interest in the concepts of identity and identity crisis.

Erikson's biological father abandoned his mother, Karla (maiden name *Abrahamsen*), before Erik's birth. She then divorced before Erik was born. She subsequently married Theodor Homburger, a physician, before Erik's birth. Throughout childhood, Erikson's mother and stepfather Theodor "kept secret from me the fact that my mother had been married previously . . ." (Berman, 1975, p. 27). Both Karla and Theodor were Jewish, whereas Erik's biological father apparently was a tall, light-skinned gentile.

Sometime after the age of three, Erikson developed the beginnings of his later identity crisis. Further intensification of his identity crisis was produced when, as a schoolboy, he was referred to as a "goy" (gentile) in his stepfather's temple, whereas his schoolmates identified him as a Jew (Berman, 1975, p. 27). Erikson thus developed a sense of "being different" from other children, and he entertained fantasies of being the son of "much better parents" who had abandoned him. Because his mother and stepfather, Dr. Homburger, were Jewish, Erikson's Scandinavian heritage of blue eyes, blond hair, and "flagrant tallness" enforced and intensified his feeling of somehow not belonging to his family. Thus, a conflicting family heritage, discordant social expectations and prejudices, and his own sense of not belonging to the family in which he grew up combined to create for Erikson an acute sense of identity confusion.

Erikson's kindly stepfather, Dr. Homburger, allowed young Erik to take the last name "Homburger." His eventual choice of a last name, "Erikson," reflected his wish to create his own identity. In effect, the name "Erik Erikson" signified, "Erik, son of Erik." It was a way of saying, "I have created my own identity." Erik kept "Homburger" as a middle name.

At puberty, Erikson rebelled against his stepfather's expectation that he would follow in his footsteps and also become a doctor. After graduation from a *gymnasium,* the equivalent of high school in the United States, Erikson entered art school. Later, as a young man with the tentative identity of an artist, Erikson moved frequently throughout Europe. He was, like many a hippie later in the 1960s, independent of social pressures for success and conformity: "I was a 'Bohemian' then" (1975, p. 28). At around this time, young Erikson was in the throes of what he would later term an "identity crisis."

> . . . the choice of the occupational identity of "artist" meant, for many, a way of life rather than a specific occupation . . . and, as today, it could mean primarily an anti-establishment way of life. Yet, the European establishment had created a well-institutionalized social niche for such idiosyncratic needs. A certain adolescent and neurotic shiftlessness could be contained in the custom of *Wanderschaft* [journey or excursion]. . . . To be an artist, then, meant to have at least a passing identity, and I had enough talent to consider it for a while

an occupational one. The trouble was, I often had a kind of work disturbance and needed time. *Wanderschaft* under those conditions meant neurotic drivenness as well as a deliberate search, even as today dropping out can be a time either of tuning in or of aimless negativism.... No doubt, my best friends will insist that I needed to name this crisis and to see it in everybody else in order to really come to terms with it in myself. (1975, pp. 25–26)

With the help of a youthful friend, Peter Blos, who later became a psychoanalytic expert on adolescence (e.g., Blos, 1962, 1970), Erikson finally overcame his crisis. He learned to work regular hours. Joining the faculty of a school in Vienna, Erikson met the circle around Anna Freud and her father, Sigmund Freud. Erikson must have been a brilliant and impressive young man because, to his own surprise, he was quickly accepted by Freud's psychoanalytic circle. At first, he tenaciously held on to his identity as "artist" rather than changing it completely to "psychoanalyst." The fact that psychoanalysis then "collected at least a few men and women who did not quite belong elsewhere" admirably suited Erikson's unconsciously formed identity of "outsider."

It must be obvious now what Freud came to mean to me, although, of course, I would not have had words for it at the time. Here was a mythical figure and, above all, a great doctor who had rebelled against the medical profession. Here also was a circle which admitted me to the kind of training that came as close to the role of a children's doctor as one could possibly come without going to medical school. What, in me, responded to this situation was, I think, some strong identification with my stepfather, the pediatrician, mixed with a search for my own mythical father. (Erikson, 1975, p. 29)

Erikson's professional association with the early Freudians was the outcome of a set of unique personal and historical circumstances. Psychoanalysis was at that period in its history outside of the medical establishment. Erikson found in this group of brilliant outcasts a congenial solution to the conflict between his "Bohemian" identity and his growing need for commitment to a productive cause. If medicine treated psychoanalysis as an unwanted stepson, leading psychoanalysts, including Freud, accepted Erikson wholeheartedly.

Erikson sought neither a Ph.D. nor an M.D. He was accepted into Freud's circle not by virtue of his educational background but because of the recognition of his brilliance and insightfulness. Erikson did receive formal training under Anna Freud in psychoanalysis with children (she was also his training analyst).

Erikson's eventual identification with the field of psychoanalysis fit his psychological makeup. As a psychoanalyst, Erikson would be able to remain aloof from medicine in accord with his own need to be a creative outsider, yet he still was able to engage in clinical work like his stepfather. Erikson's successful resolution of his identity crisis was the psychological basis for nearly 50 years of productive clinical and theoretical work.

CLINICAL SOURCES OF THE IDENTITY HYPOTHESIS: WAR VETERANS

Erikson left Europe in 1933 to come to the United States. He taught at Harvard for three years. Later, during World War II, he worked for a time at Mt. Zion Veterans' Rehabilitation Clinic in San Francisco. In treating soldiers sent there, largely from the Pacific front, Erikson first coined his now famous phrase "identity crisis." This term described the chaotic, profoundly confused mental state of soldiers hospitalized for "battle neurosis," or what we would today term posttraumatic stress disorder. Erikson described these soldiers as having lost their sense of identity and also suffering from anxiety and vulnerability to different types of stimuli (1968, p. 66).

> Most of our patients, so we concluded at that time, had neither been 'shell shocked' nor become malingerers, but had through the exigencies of war lost a sense of personal sameness and historical continuity. They were impaired in that central control over themselves for which, in the psychoanalytic scheme, only the 'inner agency' of the ego could be held responsible. Therefore, I spoke of a loss of ego identity. Since then, we have recognized the same central disturbance in severely conflicted young people whose sense of confusion is due, rather, to a war within themselves . . . (1968, p. 17)

> Anxiety and anger were provoked by anything too sudden or too intense, a sudden sensory impression from outside, an impulse, or a memory. A constantly "startled" sensory system was attacked by external stimuli as well as by somatic sensations: heat flashes, palpitation, cutting headaches. Insomnia hindered the nightly restoration of sensory screening by sleep and that of emotional rebinding by dreaming. . . . Above all, the men felt that they "did not know any more who they were": there was a distinct loss of ego identity. The sense of sameness and continuity and the belief in one's social role were gone. (1968, pp. 66–67)

Erikson reported a case of a marine who had suffered loss of ego identity sometime after discharge from the service. The soldier told Erikson of a particular incident during an assault on a beachhead under enemy fire. Lying in the darkness, the soldier had experienced intense anger, rage, disgust, and fear at the military's failure to provide supportive air cover and naval reinforcements. He was stunned to realize that he and his group of marines had to take the enemy's fire "lying down." As a medical officer, Erikson's patient had been unarmed on that beachhead. His memories of the rest of the night on the beach were vague and incomplete. The soldier stated that medical corpsmen were ordered to unload ammunition instead of attending to medical duties. One night, he recalled, he was forced to take a submachine gun—an unusual weapon for a medic. The remainder of what transpired was a blank. He woke up the next morning in an improvised field hospital. He was suffering from severe fever. That night, the enemy attacked from the air. He found that he was unable to move or to help others. He did not go blank at this time and was aware of his fear. After evacuation from the beach, he succumbed to raging headaches, chronic anxiety, and "jumpiness" in response to any sudden sound or sensory impression.

Later, in therapy with Erikson, the young ex-marine was able to trace his difficulties back to the time he had been forced to brandish a submachine gun. At this time, he had also observed his superior officer violently angry, swearing, and perhaps a little afraid. He told Erikson that the officer's behavior had disillusioned him. He thought such an outpouring of rage and anger by an officer was shocking conduct. Erikson wondered why this soldier was so outraged by anger in others. Was it necessary for him to see himself and others as such paragons of strength that they were immune to anger or fear?

The soldier's free associations led back to a critical childhood incident in which his mother, in a drunken rage, had pointed a shotgun at him. He took the gun from her, broke it in half, and threw it out the window. He subsequently sought the protection of a fatherly person, his school principal. Remorseful and frightened by the violent episode, he promised never again to drink, swear, indulge sexually, or touch a gun (Erikson, 1950, p. 41). Later, as a soldier faced with the stress of battle, his sense of personal identity as a good, moral, and benevolent person crumbled. Standing with a submachine gun in his hands and watching his superior officer explode with violent oaths were behaviors inconsistent with the identity he had formed as a civilian.

In Erikson's view, three factors conspired to provoke the young man's battle neurosis. First, his sense of having a shared identity with other soldiers was threatened by their panic and anger on the beachhead. Second, the constant assault on the soldier's bodily integrity by the real dangers of the battle, combined with his fever, led to a breakdown of his ego's capacity to ward off and control external stimuli. Third, there was loss of his inner sense of personal continuity or ego identity. His officer's anger and fear along with his own possession of a gun served further to undercut his sense of identity, his sense of who he was and what his values were.

His lifelong adherence to idealized moral values had served as a defensive bulwark against disturbing life circumstances. Now, in battle, these defenses were crumbling as he began to feel fear, rage, and panic (Erikson, 1950, p. 43). Erikson summarized his findings in this way:

> What impressed me most was the loss in these men of a sense of identity. They knew who they were; they had a personal identity. But it was as if, subjectively, their lives no longer hung together—and never would again. There was a central disturbance of what I then started to call ego identity. At this point it is enough to say that this sense of identity provides the ability to experience one's self as something that has continuity and sameness, and to act accordingly. In many cases there was at the decisive time in the history of the breakdown a seemingly innocent item such as the gun in our medical soldier's unwilling hands: a symbol of evil, which endangered the principles by which the individual had attempted to safeguard personal integrity and social status in his life at home. (1950, p. 42)

Thus Erikson's developing concept of ego identity helped him understand the psychological impact of soldiers' involvement in combat.

ANTHROPOLOGICAL SOURCES OF THE IDENTITY HYPOTHESIS: THE OGLALA SIOUX

After the war, Erikson accepted an appointment with the Yale Institute of Human Relations within the medical school. Under the leadership of John Dollard, Erikson was able to secure financial support for a field trip to South Dakota to study child-rearing practices among the Oglala Sioux Tribe at the Pine Ridge Indian Reservation.

Teachers in the government-sponsored education program complained of a variety of character defects in the Native American children they taught:

> Truancy was the most outstanding complaint: when in doubt Indian children simply ran home. The second complaint was stealing, or at any rate gross disregard of property rights, as we understand them. This was followed by apathy, which included everything from lack of ambition and interest to a kind of bland passive resistance in the face of a question or of a request. Finally, there was too much sexual activity, a term used for a variety of suggestive situations ranging from excursions into the dark after dances to the mere huddling together of homesick girls in boarding-school beds....The discussion was pervaded by the mystified complaint that no matter what you do to these children, they do not talk back. They are stoical and non-committal. (Erikson, 1950, p. 125)

Erikson detected in his discussion with these teachers a deep and unconscious "fury" that clouded their professional judgments. So disappointed, so discouraged, and so disillusioned were many of the teachers at their lack of success with these children that they had come to regard their failures as the fault of some inherent "Indian" personality flaw. Erikson surmised that the difficulty lay elsewhere.

Erikson undertook a historical investigation of Sioux tribal identity. The members of the Oglala Sioux lived on land allotted to them by the federal government. They had been militarily defeated and subdued. When the Sioux had ranged over their land, the buffalo was central to their nomadic hunting existence. The early white settlers disturbed the hunting grounds with their homesteads and domesticated cattle, and they "playfully, stupidly, slaughtered buffalo by the hundred thousands" (Erikson, 1950, p. 116). When gold fever struck Americans, they invaded the Sioux's holy mountains, game preserves, and winter refuge. An appeal by Sioux leaders to U.S. Army generals was of little help in setting matters right.

The outcome of the resulting chronic warfare between settlers and Sioux was epitomized in the tragedy of two massacres. General Custer's decisive defeat by Sioux warriors was avenged years later at Wounded Knee by the Seventh Army cavalry's massacre of a small band of Sioux they outnumbered four to one. Erikson summarized this climax to the gradual erosion of tribal identity.

> The young and seething American democracy lost the peace with the Indian when it failed to arrive at a clear design of either conquering or colonizing, converting or liberating, and instead left the making of history to an arbitrary succession of representatives who had one or another of these objectives in mind—thus demonstrating an inconsistency which the Indians interpreted as insecurity and bad conscience. (1950, p. 117)

Sioux culture came under massive assault. Government policies of establishing reservations, controlling the education of Sioux children, and imposing the values of larger society undermined Sioux identity. In fact, even Native American religious practices were illegal during the time Erikson was working with them. Dependency, fearfulness, chronic suspicion, and despair were some results of U.S. government policies to indigenous people.

In Erikson's view, the crux of the problem was primarily the shock of contact between the two cultures. White, middle-class values modeled by the educators and government advisers were singularly inappropriate to the needs and traditions of Native Americans. Teachers undermined traditional child-rearing practices, and families were forced to reconsider the meaning and the value of their existence. Erikson recounted many examples of the psychologically confusing and harmful effects of the government educational system. One poignant illustration serves here:

> During school time the child is taught cleanliness, personal hygiene, and the standardized vanity of cosmetics. While having by no means fully assimilated other aspects of white female freedom of motion and of ambition which are presented to her with historically disastrous abruptness, the adolescent [Indian] girl returns home prettily dressed and clean. But the day soon comes when she is called a "dirty girl" by mothers and grandmothers. For a clean girl in the Indian sense is one who has learned to practice certain avoidances during menstruation; for example, she is not supposed to handle certain foods, which are said to spoil under her touch. Most girls are unable to accept again the status of a leper while menstruating. (1950, p. 131)

Thus, as in his clinical work with American soldiers, Erikson found that the concept of identity was essential for understanding the plight of the Oglala Sioux children.

THE EGO IDENTITY HYPOTHESIS
AND PSYCHOANALYTIC THEORY

As we shall note in the coming sections, the development of a sense of identity is an important ego activity. Erikson observed in the cases of the traumatized World War II soldiers that their disorders could not be traced to their earliest psychosexual stages. A Freudian model of the psychiatric disorders of war veterans would have traced them to such vulnerabilities. Erikson believed that the soldiers' war experiences were sufficient to explain their pathology. He developed what would be termed the

ego identity hypothesis. The experiences were such as to undermine the ego's efforts to maintain a consistent, meaningful sense of ego identity. In other words, the soldiers' pathology occurred because of disruptive events during adult life—not as a result of events during infancy or early childhood. Likewise, with the Oglala Sioux, Erikson did not trace the psychopathology he found to poor parenting of Sioux infants, but rather to events that took place mostly during latency or early adolescence. It was difficult for Sioux youngsters to form coherent ego identities out of discordant experiences.

The psychotherapeutic implications of Erikson's insights are profound. A therapist who applies Erikson's theory is encouraged to consider the environmental challenges at each stage of life and how the person has dealt with and is dealing with them. Also worth considering is the nature and adequacy of the specific identity that an individual has formed.

Much of this therapeutic work can refer to contemporary behavior and current environmental challenges as well as characteristic coping patterns. Similarities to the approaches of Anna Freud, Karen Horney and Alfred Adler are apparent in Erikson's work.

PSYCHOSOCIAL DEVELOPMENT: AN EPIGENETIC SEQUENCE

Although Erikson was trained as a psychoanalyst, indeed his training analyst was Anna Freud, he emphasized different personality dimensions from those of classical psychoanalytic doctrine. Erikson worked to broaden Freud's emphasis on *psychosexual* development and instinctual dynamics with a consideration of *psychosocial* development.

In his theory of the eight stages of the life cycle, Erikson uses an analogy of embryonic development to explain the epigenetic development of personality and the vicissitudes of identity formation.

> When we try to understand growth, it is well to remember the *epigenetic principle* which is derived from the growth of organisms *in utero*. Somewhat generalized, this principle states that anything that grows has a ground plan, and that out of the ground plan the parts arise, each part having its time of special ascendancy, until all parts have arisen to form a functioning whole. This, obviously, is true for fetal development where each part of the organism has its critical time of ascendance or danger of defect.... But here too, it is important to realize that in the healthy child, given a reasonable amount of proper guidance, can be trusted to obey inner laws of development, laws which create a succession of potentialities for significant interaction with those persons who tend and respond to him and those institutions which are ready for him. While such interaction varies from culture to culture, it must remain within the proper rate and the proper sequence which governs all epigenesis. (1968, pp. 92–93)

Erikson received wide recognition for his specification of the stages through which the ego develops. In response to the crises initiated by the biological and social givens of life, the child's ego matures in an **epigenetic** sequence of combined psychosexual and **psychosocial stages.** The term *epigenesis* is used wherever there is a stepwise sequence of development that is genetically determined but requires specific environmental conditions for successful completion. For example, gardeners know that a plant requires certain conditions to sprout from seeds and to develop roots, stems, and finally produce seeds of its own. The structures that develop are predetermined by the plant's genetic makeup, but their successful unfolding is made possible by the presence of environmental factors, such as sunlight and rain.

For Erikson, it is the social environment that influences how the biologically determined psychosexual characteristics of the infant develop. To Freud's oral, anal, phallic, and genital stages, Erikson couples interpersonal crises that guide the flowering of these biologically determined developments. For Erikson, the person's interpersonal milieu is the psychosocial half of the developmental equation, an aspect that pre-ego psychologists neglected. Freud interpreted human behavior largely as the result of a clash between the ego and the biological drives of the id on one side and the requirements of the superego on the other. Ego psychologists, such as Erikson, focus on the interaction between the ego-id-superego, taken as a whole, and the external, social world.

VIEWING ERIKSON'S EPIGENETIC THEORY OF IDENTITY FORMATION

Figure 8.1 presents a schematic model of Erikson's theory of the epigenetic development and the self-structure (Wilson, 2006). The model illustrates both *ontogenetic* and the unfolding process of epigenetic development. First, ontogenetic development refers to the natural history of an organism from birth to death. Epigenetic development, as noted, refers to the progressive development across the eight stages of the life cycle as identity and personality emerges, forms a self-structure, and a differentiated sense of personal identity. In terms of epigenetic stages the following can be discerned:

- Each stage influences the unfolding sequence,
- Each stage accumulates identity components,
- Ontogenetic development is natural history of life course trajectory,
- Life course trajectories may be altered by trauma,
- Identity differentiation is an ongoing process determined by successive stages of adulthood.

Figure 8.1 also indicates that ego identity occurs throughout each stage of development, starting with the first psychosocial growth crisis, "trust versus mistrust" and continues sequentially to the second, "**autonomy versus shame/doubt,**" until the last stage, "integrity versus despair." In this sense, each of the eight stages has the potential to reconfigure a person's sense of self and ego-identity. Moreover, given that Erikson defined each normatively occurring stage as a "crisis," identity and personality can be altered, transformed or reconfigured as a result of the tasks and life-events by which the person is challenged. In this way, Erikson believed that change was possible in each stage of development, including unresolved conflicts, fixations, repressions and "old issues" in life that could potentially find new solutions and be incorporated within a new and modified identity structure and sense of self.

As Figure 8.1 illustrates, Erikson believed that the fifth stage, beginning in adolescence, was pivotal for identity formation. As such, this stage (approximately ages 13–23) is the transitional one between childhood and young adulthood. For this reason, he named this stage "identity versus identity confusion and role confusion," as the task of ego development is to make choices that have significant long term consequences for the forthcoming stages of life. To use an analogy, if we think of human development as a malleable block of clay being shaped by an artist, then the first four stages of life begin to give form and structure (give shape) to the clay. By the fifth stage the structure is "roughed out" but not completely finished in details. However, at stage five the artist or persons shaping the clay have less importance or impact and the burden to complete the structure shifts to the object created. That object is now animated from within to find a way to give architectural details that will give identity to what has

Figure 8.1 Erikson's Theory of Epigenetic Development of Identity and Self-Structure.

Source: John P. Wilson, © 2006.

been created from the beginning to this stage of development. To be clear, however, the process of identity formation is an ongoing one in Erikson's theory—not a static entity that ends with stage five and whatever outcomes occur, positive or negative. Each person, at the end of stage five segues into the sixth stage and beyond, as identity formation continues to differentiate in accordance with the epigenetic principle, until the end of stage eight, integrity vs. despair, and the end of life.

It is possible at this point to discern within Erikson's work several trends that are characteristic of psychoanalytic ego psychology:

- Erikson has conceptualized the ego as the source of the person's awareness of self. The ego also develops a sense of continuity. The ego has a realization of itself as an "I."
- One of the ego's major tasks is to develop and maintain a sense of personal identity.
- Erikson emphasizes the individual's conscious adjustments to interpersonal influences.
- Erikson builds upon the instinctual theoretical framework developed by Freud, by adding his own epigenetic psychosocial conception of personality development.
- Motives may originate in unconscious or repressed id impulses, yet these motives may become free of the id drives from which they originated. This idea, as we shall see in Chapter 11, is very similar to Gordon Allport's concept of "functional autonomy." It recognizes that, even though adult behaviors might have originated from early drives and immature motives, they could have subsequently become motivated by mature goals.

THE LIFE CYCLE: EIGHT STAGES OF HUMAN DEVELOPMENT

The center of Erikson's developmental model of personality is a sequence of **eight stages of ego development.** The first five stages in Erikson's scheme build on and broaden Freud's psychosexual stages (Erikson, 1950, 1959, 1968). In Erikson's model, relatively successful resolution of a specific crisis is the necessary preliminary to advancement to the next. These eight crisis periods can be grouped into four broad life periods: The four divisions of Table 8.1 represent a condensation of Erikson's scheme in which he distinguishes between early and later childhood, and between young adulthood and adulthood proper (cf. Erikson, 1959, p. 120).

Table 8.1 Life Cycle Ego Crises

Infancy	*Childhood*	*Adolescence*	*Adulthood*
1. Trust versus mistrust (oral)	3. Initiative versus guilt (phallic)	5. Identity versus role confusion (early genital)	6. Intimacy versus isolation (genital)
2. Autonomy versus shame, doubt (anal)	4. Industry versus inferiority (latency)		7. Generativity versus stagnation
			8. Ego integrity versus despair

Note: Corresponding Freudian psychosexual stages appear in parentheses.

Each of the eight psychosocial crises includes both positive and negative elements. It is sometimes mistakenly assumed that negative and positive outcomes are mutually exclusive. Erikson has pointed out, however, that it is important to experience and incorporate *both* negative and positive aspects of each crisis. A degree of mistrust, of shame, of guilt, and other negative aspects of development are normal consequences of dealing with the challenges of life. Without any degree of suspicious caution or mistrust, for example, a child would be very vulnerable to harm. Each crisis is favorably resolved when there are more positive than negative elements incorporated into the person's identity (Erikson, 1968, p. 105).

Ritualization versus Ritualism: The Way We Do Things

Erikson hypothesized a pair of **ritualizations** and **ritualisms** for each of the eight psychosocial crises. A ritualization, the positive member of each pair, is a custom that is part and parcel of the pattern of life within a culture. Stemming initially from the ego's capacity for playfulness, ritualizations confirm one's sense of identity, one's sense of belonging to a particular culture. A good way to understand what Erikson meant by ritualization is to consider its origins in evolutionary biology. Erikson borrowed the term *ritualization* from Julian Huxley's description of the "ceremonial" acts of certain animals, such as the greeting ceremonies of some bird species (Erikson, 1982, p. 43). Erikson emphasizes in his uses of the term ritualization the "informal and yet prescribed interplay between persons. While such interplay may not mean much more . . . than 'this is the way we do things,' it has, we claim, adaptive value for all participants and for their group living" (1982, p. 43). An example might be the friendly interaction that occurs as part of a family meeting. This idea anticipated some concepts of the field of evolutionary psychology, which will be covered in Chapter 17.

On the negative side, each ritualization is balanced by ritualism, which is a form of behavior involving estrangement from self and from one's community. Ritualisms indicate the ambivalent character of all human relationships. The loving mother, for example, also has a potentially dark side that threatens abandonment and separation. A ritualism is a ritualization that has become stereotyped and mechanical, an empty ceremony devoid of meaning and lacking the power to bond individuals. It is a pattern of coldly going through the motions without the appropriate emotions.

The balance between love and the fear of separation can have either a positive or negative balance. The ideal balance for each ritualization, in each developmental stage occurs when the negative or ritualistic aspect is present but outweighed by positive aspects. This is parallel to the ideal balance between trust and mistrust.

The Psychosocial Ego Functions of Ritualization

Ritualizations serve at least seven important psychosocial functions:

1. *Social function:* Ritualization elevates need satisfaction to a communal context by joining personal desire and right to the group's shared sense of the importance and justice of its desires and rights.
2. *Destiny function:* In teaching a sanctioned way of doing simple and daily things, ritualization transforms the infantile sense of omnipotence into a joint sense of destiny.
3. *Worthiness function:* Ritualization deflects feelings of unworthiness onto outsiders, both in and out of one's culture.

4. *Interpreting function:* Ritualization puts emerging cognitive patterns in the service of a general vision shared by the community; it also cultivates the cognitive capacity to discern the "right" class of things and people from the "wrong" one.

5. *Sanctification function:* Each successive stage of ritualization helps develop essential aspects of all ritual sense.

6. *Moral function:* Ritualization develops the experience of social differentiation between good behavior and wrongful acts.

7. *Identity function:* Ritualization provides the psychosocial foundation for the gradual development of an independent identity.

ACQUIRING A SENSE OF TRUST VERSUS MISTRUST: HOPE

The earliest sense of identity arises from an infant's contact with its mother or caregivers in the feeding situation (Erikson, 1968, p. 105). Throughout the first year of life, an infant's most crucial contacts with reality are those mediated by the person attending to the infant's needs. When these attentions have been given willingly, lovingly, and reliably, and in quick response to the infant's cries, it is more likely that the infant will develop a sense of the environment as trustworthy and predictable (Erikson, 1950, pp. 247 ff.; 1959, p. 56). The opposite is also true: Erratic and unreliable parenting is more likely to result in an attitude of mistrust.

The trusting infant's experiences have been marked by consistency, continuity, and sameness in the mother's or caregiver's responses:

> Such consistency, continuity, and sameness of experience provide a rudimentary sense of ego identity which depends, I think, on the recognition that there is an inner population of remembered and anticipated sensations and images which are firmly correlated with the outer population of familiar and predictable things and people. (Erikson, 1950, p. 247)

When the baby's first teeth begin to emerge, a parent's patience is often tested. Seeking to bite and to grasp desirable objects and persons, infants explore the boundaries of their capacities to trust and be trusted. Consequently, Erikson stressed that the sense of basic trust is not restricted to a perception of the outer world as trustworthy, "but also that one may trust oneself and the capacity of one's own organs to cope with urges; and that one is able to consider oneself trustworthy enough so that the providers will not need to be on guard lest they be nipped" (Erikson, 1950, p. 248).

The infant's sense of trust is often robust enough to withstand parental restrictions or prohibitions, especially if they are consistent and reasonable. As long as parental commands and prohibitions communicate to the infant that the parents know what they are doing, minor frustrations and repeated "no, no's" are not harmful. Only discipline that is administered without confidence and without consistency can result in damaged trust (Erikson, 1950, p. 249). On the opposite side of the coin, an infant who has failed to experience predictable parenting behavior may develop a basically mistrusting attitude. Successful development during the first year of life involves acquiring a preponderance of basic trust. The trusting infant looks forward eagerly to new challenges.

Erikson proposed a developmental schedule of psychological virtues (1964, pp. 111 ff.). Successful resolution of the crisis at each stage leads to the attainment of a specific virtue. For example, the infant who acquires a sense of basic trust has also acquired the virtue of hope. The acquisition of various virtues indicates the ego's growing capacity for strength, restraint, and courage (Erikson, 1964, p. 113). In Erikson's own words, "I will call 'virtue,' then, certain human qualities of strength, and I will relate them to that process by which **ego strength** may be developed from stage to stage and imparted from generation to generation" (1964, p. 113).

For the infant who finds itself and its environment trustworthy,

> *Hope is the enduring belief in the attainability of fervent wishes, in spite of the dark urges and rages which mark the beginning of existence.* (Erikson, 1964, p. 118; italics in original)

Because, at the first stage of development the trusting infant's desires and wishes have met with reliable and generally positive responses from a trustworthy interpersonal environment, the future development of the person is marked by hope—for all types of positive experiences, achievements, and successes.

The ritualization characteristic of the trust-mistrust stage centers on the significance of the interaction of mother or caregiver and child. Every day the infant is exposed to the repeated ritual of its mother's approach, her smiles, her voice, her nursing behavior, her cuddling. The infant experiences the **ritualization of the numinous** (or awesome) quality of the mother's presence as evidenced by her facial expression, voice quality, and the feel of her touch. The whole series of infant care events is highly stylized and superimposed on the periodicity of the infant's physical needs. By her care and reliable concern, the mother confirms the infant's "I-ness" while she also helps the infant to overcome fears of aloneness (Erikson, 1977, pp. 86ff).

According to Erikson's theory, the ritualism possible at this stage is **idolism**, a distortion of the numinous reverence into adulation or worshipful adoration. An illusory image of perfection binds the idolizing infant to the mother. Instead of the mutuality of affirmation and recognition, idolism results in dependence and in an inflexible attribution to the mother of impossibly unreal human perfection.

ACQUIRING A SENSE OF AUTONOMY VERSUS SHAME AND DOUBT: WILL

Near the age of 18 months, the infant gains more precise control over its muscles. An increased capacity for self-control accompanies this development. The child begins to experiment with two modes of muscular action: holding on and letting go (Erikson, 1950, pp. 251 ff.). Such an infant may repeatedly drop an object to the floor and then repeatedly grab and drop it again when it is retrieved.

This period of muscular exertion and experimentation occurs during the Freudian anal stage. Besides holding on to and letting go of objects, the child also begins to learn how to retain feces and urine until an appropriate, parentally approved, time and place is reached to let them go. Depending on the way the parents handle this pivotal experience, the child learns either that holding on and letting go are powerful weapons to be employed against overly demanding parents, or that elimination is "a relaxed 'to let pass' and 'to let be' " (Erikson, 1950, p. 251). Parental guidance at this stage should ideally be firm and at the same time protective of that sense of trust achieved during the previous oral stage:

> Firmness must protect [the child] against the potential anarchy of his as yet untrained sense of discrimination, his inability to hold on and to let go with discretion. As his environment encourages him to "stand on his own feet," it must protect him against meaningless and arbitrary experiences of shame and of early doubt. (Erikson, 1950, p. 252)

The crisis of this stage of ego development revolves around the child's need to achieve a sense of independence or willful autonomy in controlling its bodily functions and physical activity. Early experiences of self-control will set the pattern for the capacity to make free choices. A child that has been repeatedly and excessively *shamed* is most likely to become an over-controlled adult.

"Shame supposes that one is completely exposed and conscious of being looked at: in one word, self-conscious. One is visible and not yet ready to be visible . . . " (Erikson, 1950, p. 252). Thus the child who has learned control over self by having been made to feel small or shameful for unavoidable lapses wins only a "hollow victory." Shamed beyond the limits of its trust, such a child learns to distrust those who are doing the shaming. Instead of learning to regard the products of its body as dirty or evil, the child may come to regard its tutors as evil. Harsh parental demands for self-control have a further negative consequence: *Doubt.*

Erikson vividly explicates this sense of doubt concretely as a form of "watching one's butt":

> Where shame is dependent on the consciousness of being upright and exposed, doubt . . . has much to do with a consciousness of having a front and a back—especially a "behind." For this reverse area of the body, with its aggressive and libidinal focus in the sphincters and in the buttocks, cannot be seen by the child, and yet it can be dominated by the will of others. The "behind" is the small being's dark continent, an area of the body which can be magically dominated and effectively invaded by those who would attack one's power of autonomy. (Erikson, 1950, p. 253)

The child who attains a favorable ratio of autonomy to shame and doubt is likely to develop a capacity for willful self-control. Reasonable tolerance and realistic firmness shown to the child by the parents result in reasonable self-tolerance and realistic self-firmness (Erikson, 1959, p. 70). The quality of ego strength that emerges during the establishment of a sense of autonomy corresponds to the virtue of *will:*

> *Will . . . is the unbroken determination to exercise free choice as well as self-restraint, in spite of the unavoidable experience of shame and doubt in infancy.* (Erikson, 1964, p. 119; italics in original)

In this stage of autonomy versus shame, the ritualization that develops centers on the ego's capacity to discriminate good from bad. Erikson terms this capacity **judicious ritualization;** here the child learns what is culturally sanctioned and what is out of bounds (Erikson, 1977, p. 92). During this stage, autonomous behavior may test the limits of peer and adult tolerance. Before this stage, the child's deeds and misdeeds were the responsibility of the parents; now he is trained to "watch itself."

Sometimes, parents predict the child will turn out badly unless the limits of good behavior are followed. Such negative prophecies may be the self-fulfilling roots of an adolescent's negative identity. The child may very well develop in accordance with parental fears, not their hopes.

> Behind the dreaded traits, of course, are often images of what the parents themselves had been tempted to become and therefore doubly fear the child might turn out to be—*potential*

traits, then, which the child yet must learn to imagine in order to be able to avoid them. (Erikson, 1977, p. 95)

The ritualism that parallels judicious ritualization is **legalism:** "the victory of the letter over the spirit of the word and the law" (Erikson, 1977, p. 97). Legalism is marked by self-centered displays of righteousness and a moralistic insistence on right over justice. A legalistic individual may learn to use the letter of the law to justify bad behavior. Such an individual might be motivated not by a sense of rightness but by shrewdly manipulative selfishness.

ACQUIRING A SENSE OF INITIATIVE VERSUS GUILT: PURPOSE

Resolving the crisis of autonomy, the child of age four or five enters the next phase of ego development with a firm sense that he or she is a person, an "I" (Erikson, 1959, p. 74). The child now also discovers what kind of person he or she is. The crucial question for the child is to decide which of the parents will be the object of identification. Freud characterized this stage of development as phallic, and the chief crisis as the solution of the Oedipus or Electra complex.

Three important developments during this stage bring the child closer to the point of crisis:

1. The range of movement is widened by the capacity to walk rather than crawl;
2. The use of language is more precise "to the point where he understands and can ask about many things just enough to misunderstand them thoroughly;"
3. Language and locomotion combine to permit the child to expand the imagination, even to the point of being frightened by his or her own thoughts (Erikson, 1959, p. 75).

The key characteristic of this stage is the child's growing capacity to initiate actions, thoughts, and fantasies. The child develops the capacity to plan and to reflect on the consequences of self-initiated activities. He or she can experience jealous rage against siblings or others who are perceived as threats. For the male child in a traditional two-parent family, the sense of exclusive domination of mother's attention is imperiled when he realizes that father is a stronger, more powerful competitor. To resolve these Oedipal strivings, the boy internalizes the imagined prohibitions of his father. The prohibitions become the basis of the superego or conscience (see the discussion of the superego in Chapter 3). With the formation of the superego, the child usually consolidates its identification with the same-sexed parent and acquires the gender-specific behaviors of that model.

During this stage, too, the child learns to cooperate with other children. The child may plan projects and participate actively in games and social interaction. The child also imitates desirable adult role models. Hopefully, a favorable balance between initiative and guilt is established. As the child discovers what it can do, it also continues to realize what is permitted, what it may do (Erikson, 1959, p. 75). Nowhere is this balance between ability and expectancy more apparent than in imaginative play:

> Play is to the child what thinking, planning, and blueprinting are to the adult, a trial universe in which conditions are simplified and methods exploratory, so that past failures can be thought through, expectations tested. (Erikson, 1964, p. 120)

The main addition to the ego's strength that results from a successful resolution of the crisis during this stage is the virtue of *purpose:*

Purpose ... is the courage to envisage and pursue valued goals uninhibited by the defeat of infantile fantasies, by guilt and by the foiling fear of punishment. (Erikson, 1964, p. 122; italics in original)

Purpose requires the internalization of the sense of right and wrong, that is, with the inner adoption of external moral and ethical guidelines. The child's ego may now make judgments and plans that in the past had to be made for it.

The initiative versus guilt stage of development incorporates a **ritualization of a sense of authenticity.** Entering the play stage of childhood, girls and boys learn to create dramatic elaborations of their inner and outer conflicts. This dramatic element allows a child to relive, correct, recreate, and rework past experiences, and to anticipate future ones. The child can experiment dramatically with a variety of roles. A genuine sense of inner guilt—the capacity for self-condemnation—develops as the child toys with fantastic events and roles it could not possibly enact in "real life."

An awareness of congenial roles, comfortable situations, and satisfactory coping strategies emerge during play. Finally, a sense of authenticity emerges. Such authenticity involves a feeling of what "I *want* to be" and what "I realistically *can* be."

Impersonation is the ritualism of the dramatic element. It is a form of disconnected role-playing that is untempered by realistic shame and guilt. "To be denied a true chance of authenticity ... can force children (and youths) to compulsively assume the role of shameless evildoers—as preferable to being either nameless or overly typed" (Erikson, 1977, p. 103). Such an impersonating child lacks and does not develop a genuine commitment to any one role.

ACQUIRING A SENSE OF INDUSTRY VERSUS INFERIORITY: COMPETENCE

In the first stage of basic trust, personality focuses around the conviction, "I am what I am given." During the crisis of the second stage involving autonomy, personality is centered on the belief that, "I am what I will." At the third stage, when the sense of initiative reaches critical proportions, the nucleus of personality is, "I am what I can imagine I will be."

With the emergence of the fourth psychosocial crisis of industry versus inferiority, the central theme for personality development becomes "I am what I learn" (Erikson, 1959, p. 82). This fourth stage takes place along with the child's first school experiences.

In school, the child is expected to focus on often impersonal and abstract subjects and, at least in class, taming imagination in the service of productive learning (Erikson, 1950, p. 258). Corresponding to the Freudian latency period, the child in this stage discovers that how one is valued in school is becoming increasingly important.

Children ideally realize that completing a task requiring steady attention and diligence is intrinsically rewarding (Erikson, 1950, p. 259). They learn to use tools of the culture and to become familiar with current technology. The key danger here is that some children may despair of success. They may develop a sense of inadequacy and inferiority and may even lose some of the accomplishments of their previous ego crises. Such children may not be able to identify with productive adult models.

A successful resolution of the crisis between industry and inferiority leads to the development of a new strength, the virtue of *competence:*

Competence ... is the free exercise of dexterity and intelligence in the completion of tasks, unimpaired by infantile inferiority. (Erikson, 1964, p. 124; italics in original)

Children learn "by virtue of" their trust, autonomy, initiative, and industry that confident, independent, and active productivity is satisfying.

The industry versus inferiority stage is marked by the **ritualization of formality.** Becoming accustomed to school tasks and the necessity for successful "making" and "producing," the youngster learns the value of methodical performance (Erikson, 1977, p. 103).

> [In school] . . . with varying abruptness, play is transformed into work, game into
> competition and cooperation, and the freedom of imagination into the duty to perform with
> full attention to the techniques which make imagination communicable, accountable, and
> applicable to defined tasks. (Erikson, 1977, p. 104)

School introduces children to the socially appropriate forms of producing, competing, and cooperating. When children master the formal aspects of work, they learn to feel worthwhile, deserving of praise, success, gain, and acceptance. They learn that hard work, initiative, and perseverance are necessary for meaningful accomplishments.

The ritualism side of formality is **formalism,** the forgetting of the purpose of methodical performance in favor of mere proficiency. As Karl Marx suggested, a "craft-idiot" is one who denies the human significance of his or her skills and becomes enslaved to the trappings of efficient method (Erikson, 1977, p. 106). Formalism is adherence to technique and blindness to purpose and meaning.

ACQUIRING A SENSE OF IDENTITY VERSUS
ROLE CONFUSION: FIDELITY

By the time childhood is over, the child's ego has ideally assimilated a grown-up sense of industry. In reaching this point in development, the adolescent has constructed a sense of his or her own sameness. This sense of continuity is the foundation of ego identity.

At this time, the earlier developmental crises are echoed and the person's sense of sameness is questioned all over again.

> In their search for a new sense of continuity and sameness, adolescents have to refight many
> of the battles of earlier years, even though to do so they must artificially appoint perfectly
> well meaning people to play the roles of adversaries; and they are ever ready to install
> lasting idols and ideals as guardians of a final identity. . . . The sense of ego identity, then, is
> the accrued confidence that the inner sameness and continuity prepared in the past are
> matched by the sameness and continuity of one's meaning for others, as evidenced in the
> tangible promise of a "career." (Erikson, 1950, pp. 261–262)

In Erikson's view, the adolescent period is a socially sanctioned interval of role experimentation. A full and healthy ego identity can emerge only when previous identifications are integrated. The varying senses of identity formed in infancy, childhood, and in the school years can merge to become a comfortable and workable whole. Identity is not formed in a vacuum, however. The identity ideally should be formed in such a way as to fit within the framework of society. A youngster may want to be a rock star, but in order to become one, his musical style must attract an audience. Erikson has contributed thoughtful idiographic studies of Mahatma Gandhi (Erikson, 1969) and Martin Luther (Erikson, 1962). In these studies, he explored their creative formation of historically important identities.

In proper perspective, the **psychosocial moratorium** of adolescence (and occasionally, young adulthood) permits a young person to explore a range of opportunities without the necessity of immediate commitment. For the adolescent who has failed to integrate all previous crisis solutions, the moratorium on final role choice permitted by society to its young is extended to a paralyzing and interminable era of confusion. Like Erikson with his own youthful identity crisis as an outsider, confused adolescents cannot become what their lives have prepared them to be:

> The prime danger of this age, therefore, is identity confusion, which can express itself in excessively prolonged moratoria; in repeated impulsive attempts to end the moratorium with sudden choices, that is, to play with historical possibilities, and then to deny that some irreversible commitment has already taken place.... The dominant issue of this, as of any other stage, therefore, is that of the active, the selective, ego being in charge and being enabled to be in charge by a social structure which grants a given age group the place it needs—and in which it is needed. (Erikson, 1963, p. 13)

Thus the sense of identity means "being at one with oneself," and harboring an affinity for one's community, both for its history and for its future (Erikson, 1974, p. 27). But with this positive sense of identity there is necessarily a negative aspect to one's sense of self. Each adolescent consequently harbors a negative identity. Healthy resolution of the identity crisis enables adolescents to discard their negative identity. However, for the adolescent who does not develop a positive ego identity,

> The loss of a sense of identity often is expressed in a scornful and snobbish hostility toward the roles offered as proper and desirable in one's family or immediate community. Any part or aspect of the required role, or all parts, be it masculinity or femininity, nationality or class membership, can become the main focus of the young person's acid disdain. (Erikson, 1959, p. 129)

Negative identity choices are most easily discerned among troubled or "disturbed" adolescents. Such young people willfully choose to become everything that parents and teachers had expressly indicated as undesirable. A **negative identity** is thus "an identity perversely based on all those identifications and roles which, at critical stages of development, had been presented to the individual as most undesirable or dangerous, and yet also as most real" (Erikson, 1959, p. 131). For example:

> A mother who is filled with unconscious ambivalence toward a brother who disintegrated into alcoholism may again and again respond selectively only to those traits in her son which seem to point to a repetition of her brother's fate, in which case this "negative" identity may take on more reality for the son than all his natural attempts at being good: he may work hard on becoming a drunkard and, lacking the necessary ingredients, may end up in a state of stubborn paralysis of choice. (Erikson, 1959, p. 131)

According to Erikson, vindictive choices of negative roles around which to integrate one's sense of self represent a desperate attempt to regain some control over one's fate. Many adolescents faced with chronic **identity diffusion,** an unclear and often fluctuating sense of who one is and what one's purpose is, I would "rather be nobody or somebody bad, or indeed, dead—and this totally, and by free choice—than be not-quite somebody" (Erikson, 1959, p. 132).

Despite the dangers of adolescent identity diffusion, the majority of ego-integrated youth evidence attainment of another form of ego strength, the virtue of *fidelity:*

> *Fidelity is the ability to sustain loyalties freely pledged in spite of the inevitable contradictions of value systems.* (Erikson, 1964, p. 125; italics in original)

Healthy youths, from their springboards of firm self-identities and strong egos, develop a high sense of duty to the tasks of rendering reality faithfully to themselves and to their culture. For youths who have attained the strength of fidelity, life becomes the living out of their established core identities. They actually are the roles they play.

Like other theorists, Erikson employed the theatrical imagery of the actor and his mask of roles. For healthy "faithful" adolescents, the actor's mask is adjusted precisely to the actor's face. The danger in the roles to which adolescents turn in their experimentation with the multiple identities their life offers is that the role may become more real than the actor's core:

> But what if role-playing becomes an aim in itself, is rewarded with success and status, and seduces the person to repress what core-identity is potential in him? Even an actor is convincing in many roles only if and when there is in him an actor's core identity—and craftsmanship. (Erikson, 1974, p. 107)

During the adolescent identity-formation period, the individual undergoes **the ritualization of commitment to an ideology**. Adolescence is the time to integrate the conflicting self-images that have developed since infancy in some formal "confir- mation" procedure. A formal rite of passage is needed to mark clearly the adolescent's transition from childhood to adulthood. Adolescents must be made to experience what Erikson calls "solidarity of conviction," that is, a sense that they belong to the gener- ation of youth as distinguished from their elders (Erikson, 1977, p. 107). Adolescents often develop their own rituals of belonging, marked outwardly by the distinction of their clothes, preferences for music and literature, and sometimes hostility to adults. By their adoption of the work ethic of their culture, adolescents implicitly adopt its ideological style. They are ready to exclude and repudiate all alien ideologies (Erikson, 1977, p. 107).

The ritualism of this phase is **totalism,** "a fanatic and exclusive preoccupation with what seems unquestionably ideal within a tight system of ideas" (1977, p. 110). Ritual- ism is a partial regression to the idolism of infancy. Adolescents now find themselves a cause, an idea, a group to which they can totally commit themselves unthinkingly and in which they run the risk of losing themselves.

ACQUIRING A SENSE OF INTIMACY VERSUS ISOLATION: LOVE

With entrance into young adulthood, the person becomes willing to risk his or her newly established identity by fusing it with the identities of others. "He is ready for intimacy, that is, the capacity to commit himself to concrete affiliations and partnerships and to develop ethical strength to abide by such commitments, even though they may call for significant sacrifices and compromises (Erikson, 1950, p. 263).

A firm sense of personal integrity based on the fusion of past bodily and social identifications allows the young adult to face the fear of ego loss in situations and relationships that call for self-sacrifice. Thus the young adult can experience intimate social interactions ranging from intense friendships or physical combat to hesitant sexual experimentation.

The danger of this period is that young adults may not be ready for the demands of intimacy. They may be unwilling to lend themselves to intimate sharing with another, and thus retreat into personal isolation.

In the shift among combative, cooperative, and intimate interpersonal relationships, new adults must learn not only to adopt personal formulas for intimate cooperation, but also their own unique modes of productivity.

In Erikson's view, healthy genital sexuality that marks this stage is characterized by:

1. mutuality of orgasm
2. with a loved partner

BOX 8.2 *Only Connect...*

Freud was once asked what he thought the healthy person should be able to do well. His curt answer was "Lieben und arbeiten" (to love and to work) (Erikson, 1950, p. 265). Compare this answer with Erikson's fourth and sixth developmental stages. Freud's formula, "to love and to work," is more complicated than is at first apparent. Freud and Erikson meant to indicate that the healthy adult personality is able to absorb himself or herself in intimate sexual fulfillment while simultaneously maintaining the independence of spirit necessary for productive and fulfilling work.

---

3. of the other sex
4. with whom one is able and willing to share a mutual trust
5. and with whom one is able and willing to regulate the cycles of
   a. work
   b. procreation
   c. recreation
6. so as to secure to the offspring, too, all the stages of a satisfactory development. (Erikson, 1950, p. 266)

Some aspects of this part of Erikson's theory now seem very dated and even biased. His specifications regarding healthy genital sexuality can be seen as unfairly excluding same-sex couples and couples who do not engage in child-rearing. Erikson's assertion that mutuality of orgasm is a necessary indication of genuine intimacy is an assertion without empirical evidence.

The key virtue attending the successful resolution of the conflict between intimacy and isolation in this stage is *love:*

> Love ... is mutuality of devotion forever subduing the antagonisms inherent in divided function. (Erikson, 1964, p. 129; italics in original)

Love is thus the ego strength to share one's identity with another for "mutual verification."

Growing from the core of intimacy achieved in this stage is the **affiliative ritualization** (Erikson, 1977, p. 110). Affiliation indicates that the identity achieved thus far is compatible with the identities of people in one's life. The young adult finds a partner with whom to share enthusiastic opinions and scathing judgments, and with whom to establish an enduring affiliation promising a productive and procreative life (1977, p. 110).

The ritualism counterbalancing the affiliative element is **elitism,** a sense of narcissism shared with others that leads to membership in formal or informal groups that exclude others. According to Erikson, such elitism is an isolating trend rooted in infantile idolism.

ACQUIRING A SENSE OF GENERATIVITY VERSUS STAGNATION: CARE

"Mature man needs to be needed, and maturity needs guidance as well as encouragement from what has been produced and must be taken care of" (Erikson, 1950, p. 267). Mature adults thus need to feel some concern for the next generation, especially as exemplified by their own offspring. Because children are the products of the intimate

> BOX 8.3 *Only Connect...*
>
> The possible evolutionary basis for a generative stage of development has been highlighted by evolutionary psychology (Chapter 17). In addition to working for the survival of one's own progeny, the *inclusive fitness* theory indicates the selective advantage accruing to genes of people who enhance the overall fitness of those around them. The *kin selection* concept indicates the evolutionary value of aiding those who are related, especially young offspring. Thus, altruism directed toward the next generation (generativity) would be selected in the evolutionary process.

fusion of bodily and personal identities of the parents, each has a "libidinal investment" in their offspring.

Being a parent does not, in itself, ensure the attainment of a sense of **generativity.** What is needed is the ability to extend oneself, literally to give oneself to the future. Erikson chose the term *generativity* to indicate the capacity to transcend immediate self-related interests in favor of generations to come (Erikson, 1968, p. 138).

The main danger of this stage lies in the inability of some otherwise mature adults to find value in guiding and aiding the next generation. A pervasive sense of **stagnation** or boredom then characterizes their approach to a variety of life tasks. Life is viewed as unsatisfying and without much meaningful activity. A feeling exists that accomplishments and even interpersonal intimacies lack relevance to one's sense of identity.

The ego's strength in meeting the necessities of life is increased in the generative adult by the development of the virtue of *care:*

> Care is the widening concern for what has been generated by love, necessity, or accident; it overcomes the ambivalence adhering to irreversible obligation. (Erikson, 1964, p. 131; italics in original)

By postulating the stage of generativity and the attainment of the virtue of care, Erikson has extended the Freudian psychosexual stages beyond genital sexuality. Care assures for the mature ego the right to be needed and the privilege to need the young. Thus care includes not only work for those persons whom one has created, but for all of humanity's created works as well.

The hallmark of the adult generative period is what Erikson calls the **generational ritualization** (1977, p. 111). This ritualization is a composite of a variety of adult ritualizations, including the parental, the teaching, and the curative. Generational means that the adult must be prepared to exercise authority with a conviction that "I know what I am doing" and receive reassurance from the various cultural images of authority, such as God, kings, and one's own parents, that "I am doing it right."

The corresponding ritualism of the adult period is **authoritism,** a self-convinced but spurious seizing of authority. Instead of functioning as a just transmitter of ideal values and as a sanctioned judge of evil, the adult who yields to authoritism becomes an oppressive model of insensitivity.

ACQUIRING EGO INTEGRITY VERSUS DESPAIR: WISDOM

The climax of the life cycle is reached when the foundations of infantile trust have made possible their adult counterpart: **ego integrity.** Adults who have been cared for, who have cared for others, can now care for themselves. The fruit of the previous seven stages ripens in adults whose egos can accept their life cycles "as something that had to be and that, by necessity, permitted of no substitutions: it thus means a new, a different love of one's parents" (Erikson, 1950, p. 268).

Adults in whom ego integrity has fully blossomed realize that their individual lives are but one life cycle in the flow of history. They are convinced that what had to be, was—and was satisfying. The danger is that the ego may have failed to integrate the crisis resolutions of the previous seven stages. The fear of death that emerges means that the individual is unable to accept his or her life cycle as the ultimate and one and only meaning that living embodies. **Despair** of what has been implies that what has been, has been in vain. Despair is the protest of a person who is not yet satisfied with a life that has never been satisfying. Despair indicates unwillingness, paradoxical as it may be, to end a life that has failed to achieve fulfillment and that now culminates as the sum of a thousand little miseries.

The most important gift parents can provide their children is the strength, shown in their own example, to face ultimate concerns like death without the disintegrating effects of fear: "Healthy children will not fear life if their elders have integrity enough not to fear death" (Erikson, 1950, p. 269). Thus the virtue that serves as the hallmark of the climactic stage of the life cycle is *wisdom:*

> Wisdom . . . *is detached concern with life itself, in the face of death itself.* (Erikson, 1964, p. 133; italics in original).

Adults who embody the kind of integrity that Erikson describes are wise in the sense that they view their limited lives as a totality that transcends petty disgust at the feeling of "being finished." They are able to transcend the despair "of facing the period of relative helplessness which marks the end as it marked the beginning" (Erikson, 1964, p. 134).

This last stage of the life cycle brings us to the **integral ritualization,** literally an ability to integrate the previous phases into a confirmation of the life thus led. To have achieved the ego strength of wisdom means that the important achievements of

Table 8.2   Crises, Ego Strengths, and Ritualizations of the Life Cycle

Cycle	*Ego crisis*	*Ego strength*	*Ritualization range*
Infancy	1. Trust versus mistrust	Hope	Mother-child mutual recognition: Numinous to idolism
Early childhood	2. Autonomy versus shame and doubt	Will	Good-bad discrimination: Judicious to legalism
Childhood (play age)	3. Initiative versus guilt	Purpose	Dramatic elaboration: Authenticity to impersonation
Childhood (school-age)	4. Industry versus inferiority	Competence	Methodical performance: Formality to formalism
Adolescence	5. Identity versus role confusion	Fidelity	Solidarity of conviction: Ideology to totalism
Young adulthood	6. Intimacy versus isolation	Love	Complementarity of identities: affiliative to elitism
Mature adulthood	7. Generativity versus stagnation	Care	Transmission of values: Generational to authoritism
Old age	8. Ego integrity versus despair	Wisdom	Affirmation of life: Integral to sapientism

(Based on Erikson, 1950, 1977, 1978.)

the previous seven stages are synthesized and consolidated into the awareness that new ideas, new meanings, new persons have been personally created. In a real way, these creations are immortality—for the individual and for the human group. The ego that has achieved the ritualization of the integral affirms life, and the person of old age realizes a new affinity for what was childish. This paradox is expressed beautifully in the lines of William Blake that Erikson used as his book epigraph and title: "The Child's Toys and the Old Man's Reasons Are the Fruits of the Two Seasons" (Erikson, 1977).

The ritualism of this stage is a distortion of wisdom that Erikson names **sapientism,** "the unwise pretense of being wise" (Erikson, 1977, p. 112).

Table 8.2 summarizes the eight stages of the life cycle and their various crises, strengths, and ritualizations.

APPLYING ERIKSON'S STAGE THEORY

When we apply Erikson's stages to our lives or to the lives of other people, some interesting conclusions emerge. First, it is not necessary to resolve each stage completely one hundred percent positively. For example, a good amount of healthy mistrust is a beneficial trait as is the capacity to identify those situations in which either trust or mistrust is warranted. A certain degree of basic trust does need to be established in order to provide a foundation for further development. Otherwise, trust-mistrust issues might continue to dominate a person's experience.

The stages seem more flexible than Erikson actually proposed. The timing of stages is not necessarily strictly sequential or invariant. Individual and cultural differences play a role in determining the course of development. Some people may put off the stage of developing an occupational identity until later in life or even go through a whole new identity crisis while switching to a new field in midlife. In many instances, adult women who have finished child-rearing go through the same soul-searching that Erikson indicated is typical for younger people. Adolescents and young adults may demonstrate generativity in the form of community service projects or other ways of improving the world. Even the virtue of wisdom may be found in those younger people who are "wise beyond their years."

When applied in a flexible manner, Erikson's developmental model provides general categories and guidelines by which we can more fully understand the patterns of psychological growth. Knowledge of them is a rich resource for anyone trying to understand psychological development over a lifetime.

SOME CONCLUDING REMARKS ON ERIKSON

Erikson's psychosocial scheme of the life cycle has provided the conceptual tools for the analysis of the lives of significant historical figures. Erikson has thus examined the process of identity development in the lives of Martin Luther (1962) and of Mahatma Gandhi (1969). In both cases, Erikson sought to identify the historical, social, and psychological forces that uniquely combined with accidental circumstance to produce a human personality that changed the course of history.

Psychohistory, as this form of psychological and historical investigation has come to be called, has gained a wide foothold in a broad array of academic disciplines. It is not within the scope of this chapter to review this literature. But it is important to recognize the far-reaching acceptance Erikson's ideas have had. The concepts of identity, identity crisis, life cycle, ego strength, and psychosocial development, all pioneered by

Erikson, have found their way into quarters where orthodox psychoanalytic doctrine would be most unwelcome. Perhaps one reason for the great respectability of Erikson's concepts in the eyes of critics lies in the stimulating impact of Erikson's ideas in many fields.

EVALUATING ERIK ERIKSON

Erikson's theory is a most widely read, taught, and written-about theory. We would be hard put to find a general psychology text or an adolescent or child psychology text in the United States that does not give substantial space to his ideas. Erikson's ego psychology has been welcomed in places where Freud's theory would be most unwelcome. People from different disciplines, with vastly different expectations about psychological theories of human nature, find in Erikson what they are looking for, even if each of them seeks something different. Developmental psychologists find a stage-phase theory of psychological growth; psychoanalysts find a Freudian account of identity formation; humanists find a holistic conception of the life span; theologians find cogent observations on aging and death; and social learning theorists find a cognitive translation of Freudian developmental tasks. The list could be expanded. But the point is that Erikson was a man of great erudition, with the humanist's eye for the uniqueness of personality, the psychoanalyst's ear for the unconscious personal meaning, and the artist's flair for bold but elegant statement.

Refutability of Erikson's Concepts

Erikson's concepts are easily translated into cognitive and emotional constructs, independent of the psychoanalytic assumptions from which he started. The most research productive of Erikson's concepts has been his notion of identity and identity formation. Some years ago, James Marcia (1966) devised a set of criteria and a way to measure various degrees of crystallized identity formation in young people. Since then, there have been a variety of empirical, sometimes predictive, studies based on the Marcia-Erikson measures of identity status (e.g., Marcia, 1993; Marcia & Friedman, 1970; Rowe & Marcia, 1980).

In summary, Erikson's theories thus score relatively high in refutability. However, much of the theory is so philosophical and general that large portions appear not to be testable.

Erikson's Concept of Human Agency

Erikson has a balanced conception of human agency. On the one hand, as a Freudian theorist, Erikson regards unconscious processes and social reality as determining variables that shape the person. But, as we have seen, Erikson also portrays development as a matter of some personal choices, which implies an active agent view. How shall we characterize Eriksonian theory, then? It is a matter of judgment, based largely on whether one emphasizes the Freudian component to the theory or the cognitive component. Because Erikson has stressed repeatedly his allegiance to the basic psychoanalytic formulations, especially for the first four developmental stages, we can speculate that Erikson's view of people is more of a passive agent view—people are shaped by reality—than an active agent view. But it is a close call.

The Idiographic-Nomothetic Balance in Erikson's Theory

Erikson's theory deals with universals. His conception of the stages/phases asserts a universal human developmental scheme. As we have seen, Erikson even reiterated Freud's "anatomy is destiny" dictum and thereby earned a great deal of criticism. His conception of identity formation clearly has nomothetic components, some of which have received testing, as we discussed.

By the same token, Erikson has argued convincingly that each of us solves the crisis of a given developmental stage uniquely, in terms of our given social, historical, and familial context. His early clinical work with soldiers, Native American children, and his own psychoanalytic patients, along with his interest in psychohistory (Martin Luther and Gandhi, for example) are testimony to the idiographic, single-case concerns of his work.

In Erikson, as in few other theories, we find the idiographic perspective well balanced with the potential for nomothetic or generally applicable "laws" that can be tested.

SUMMARY

Erik Homburger Erikson's work falls within the realm of psychoanalytic ego psychology by virtue of the theory's stress on the ego's integrating and stabilizing influences in the person's life history, but he might just as well be considered an object relations theorist. Identifying himself closely with orthodox psychoanalysis, Erikson nevertheless has transcended classical Freudian instinct theory. He portrays the ego from a psychosocial perspective as the hub of individual identity. As the ego matures through life crises, it gains strength to master in increasingly sophisticated ways the puzzles posed by inner and outer reality. Perhaps Erikson's continued self-identification with psychoanalytic theory and his desire to preserve its essential elements were fostered by his own gratefulness for his early acceptance into the Freudian mainstream. His adolescent role confusion, the culmination of his development as an outsider, was greatly reduced by his commitment to the role of psychoanalyst. Feeling neither completely Jewish nor completely Scandinavian, the young Erikson had long wondered who his real father was, why he did not fit in either with his Jewish family or his non-Jewish schoolmates, and what he would ever become.

Erikson conceptualizes the healthy personality as one who, in Freud's words, is able to work and to love. That is, the healthy functioning personality has the capacity to share intimacy with another and to work fruitfully, with personal satisfaction. A healthy social milieu, initially provided by the parents, aids the individual to accept the inexorability of his or her own development. Erikson calls such acceptance of one's life a "sense of ego integrity."

Erikson has proposed that such integrity or ego strength is achieved in an unalterable sequence of psychosocial stages. Beginning in infancy, the child's ego must first learn to trust itself and others to become autonomous and self-sufficient. With trust and autonomy come the virtues of hope and will, forms of ego strength that foster sufficient security for the child to risk the potential disappointment that hope entails, and sufficient independence of spirit for children to dare to initiate willingly their personal adaptation to their inescapable realities. Once these fundamental ego strengths are acquired, the child is able to acquire, in sequence, a sense of initiative (purpose), a sense of industry (competence), a sense of identity (fidelity), a sense of intimacy (love), a sense of generativity (care), and, finally, a sense of integrity (wisdom).

During the various phases in the acquisition of these ego strengths or virtues, the maturing person will also be exposed to age-appropriate ritualizations and ritualisms through which comes a special kind of learning, the mastery of "the only proper way to experience and to do things" in that person's culture. In the trust-mistrust stage, there is the ritualization of mother-child recognition; in the autonomy-doubt stage, the child learns good-bad discriminations, followed by acquisition of the ability to elaborate dramatically conflicts and concerns in the initiative-guilt phase of middle childhood. By the school-age years, the ritualization of methodical performance is acquired, allowing the child to progress into adolescence with a more or less perfectly formed "worker" image that will be further shaped by the ritualization of shared convictions with other adolescent children. Young adulthood brings exposure to the complementary identity of one's intimate partner, with whom, by mature adulthood, the person seeks to perform the ritualization of transmitting values to the next generation. Old age, finally, sees a return,

in Erikson's view, to the playfulness of childhood in the wise old person's affirmation of the life he or she has led.

An evaluation of Erikson reveals a theory that has the potential for refutable constructs and an established capacity for generating productive research. Erikson also achieves a balanced view of human agency in which social, biological, and cultural variables are seen as determinants, but the individual is capable of choice within these limits. Erikson's theory embodies a well-balanced concern for nomothetic or universal psychological "laws" with some traditional psychoanalytic concern for the uniqueness of the individual, especially in the areas of clinical application and psychohistory.

FOR FURTHER READING

Erikson's most comprehensive treatment of both his early and later theorizing is contained in *Childhood and Society* (New York: Norton, 1993). In *Insight and Responsibility* (New York: Norton, 1994) Erikson considers the various "virtues" that may arise through healthy resolution of the eight psychosocial developmental crises.

Robert Coles has provided a detailed account of the personal and historical influences that shaped Erikson's ideas in *Erik Erikson: The Growth of His Work* (Boston: Little, Brown, 1970). More recently, he has put together *The Erik Erikson Reader* (New York: Norton, 2000), which contains a wide spectrum of Eriksonian writings. Richard I. Evans, in Vol. 8 of his famous "Dialogs" series, interviews Erikson and provides commentary on his work. Evans' interview comprises *Dialog with Erik Erikson* (New York: Harper & Row, 1996).

A good summary of his stages (including an introduction to a ninth stage) can be found in *The Life Cycle Completed* (New York: Norton, 1997). This book is worth consulting for the new emphases that have emerged as Erikson himself writes from the perspective of old age; the extended edition was coauthored posthumously by his widow, Joan Erikson, and contains a brief introduction to a possible

ninth stage. A more artful and literary approach to Erikson's conception of the eight stages may be witnessed in the collection of papers, including his own analysis of an Ingmar Bergman movie, edited by Erikson under the title *Adulthood* (New York: Norton, 1978).

Young Man Luther (New York: Norton, 1993) and *Gandhi's Truth: On the Origins of Militant Nonviolence* (New York: Norton, 1993) are two of Erikson's books that transcended the world of psychology and dealt with historical events and cultural change from the perspective of individual development and life history.

Two volumes give some indication of the scope of Erikson's research and thinking on the concept of identity and some of its philosophical underpinnings. The collection of papers edited by Jane Kroger in *Discussions on Ego Identity* (Hillsdale, NJ: Lawrence Erlbaum, 1993) presents a wide range of interpretations of identity. The compendium edited by J. E. Marcia and his colleagues, *Ego Identity: A Handbook for Psychosocial Research* (New York: Springer-Verlag, 1993) provides a thorough survey of recent research, Marcia's most recent thinking, and several samples of ongoing projects.

GLOSSARY

In the glossary for this chapter, the definitions for the various ritualizations are paired with terms defining the corresponding ritualisms. For example, the definition for the ritualization of the numinous is paired with the definition of idolism, its corresponding ritualism.

Autonomy versus shame and doubt: Second psychosocial stage. With increased voluntary muscular control comes the capacity for increased self-control. The child begins to experiment with holding on or letting go. If the parents mishandle toilet training, a sense of shame and doubt will result instead of a sense of willful autonomy. If the developmental task is resolved positively, the virtue of will emerges.

Ego identity: A person's clear sense of "who I am, what my role in society is and who I am to become." The sense of ego identity includes the sense of continuity of self, including one's values, purposes, and role in society. A clear sense of identity—either positive or negative—enables a person to sort out the relevant from the irrelevant and to have a clear guide to behavior.

Ego identity hypothesis: Erikson's theory that much adult pathology, originally that of wartime veterans, occurred because life experiences undermined the ego's efforts to maintain a consistent, meaningful sense of identity. In other words, their pathology occurred because of disruptive events during adult life—not as a result of events during infancy or early childhood.

Ego integrity versus despair: Eighth psychosocial stage. Those who have adapted successfully to the triumphs and disappointments of life can look back on a constructive journey with a sense of completion and fulfillment. The person who has led an overly disappointing life is not contented, and thus will experience despair. If the outcome of this stage is positive, the resulting ego strength is wisdom.

Ego strength: A virtue that could develop from each of Erikson's eight developmental stages. Those virtues—states of goodness or growth orientedness—are: hope, will, purpose, competence, fidelity, love, care, and wisdom.

Eight stages of ego development: These refer to a series of sequential psychosocial stages that begin in infancy and extend through life to old age. Each psychosocial stage involves a developmental crisis that can be resolved positively (strengthening the ego) or resolved negatively (weakening the ego).

Epigenetic: A term drawn from the field of biology. It is used wherever there is a stepwise sequence of development that is genetically determined but requires specific environmental conditions for successful completion. Erikson applied the concept of epigenetic stages to human psychological development.

Generativity versus stagnation: Seventh psychosocial stage. This stage of adulthood involves finding meaningful activities by extending one's sense of self into future generations. It involves passing on one's skills, knowledge, experience, and even possessions to the next generation. The main danger of this stage lies in the inability of some adults to find value in guiding and aiding the next generation. A sense of stagnation or boredom then sets in. If the outcome is positive, the virtue is care.

Identity crisis: An inner conflict, usually during adolescence, during which a person's identity in one or more areas of life is unclear.

Identity diffusion: An unclear and often fluctuating sense of who one is and what one's values and goals are.

Identity versus role confusion: Fifth psychosocial stage. Individuals strive to find out who they are and who they are not. They must sort out their sexual, ideological, and occupational orientation. Identity confusion may include problems of a conflicting self-image, an inability to establish intimacy with others, an inability to adhere to tasks, and a rejection of family or community values. If the outcome is positive, the virtue that ensues is fidelity.

Industry versus inferiority: Fourth psychosocial stage. The child learns to complete tasks with diligence and perseverance, and to acquire new intellectual and technological skills as well as social skills for cooperative endeavors in the future. If the outcome is positive, the ego strength is competence. If the child is ridiculed in his or her efforts, or does not receive praise and appreciation, the child will acquire a sense of inadequacy and inferiority.

Initiative versus guilt: Third psychosocial stage. If the parents encourage the child's self-initiated fantasies, ideas, and behaviors, it develops a lively curiosity and a strong sense of initiative. If they stifle or ridicule the child's behavioral or ideational initiative, it will develop guilt feelings whenever it strives for independence and goal-orientedness. If the outcome is positive, the ego strength is purpose.

Intimacy versus isolation: Sixth psychosocial stage. In this stage, a person becomes willing to risk his or her newly established identity by fusing it with the identities of others. It is the capacity to commit oneself to concrete affiliations and partnerships. If one avoids close contacts and withdraws into oneself, a feeling of isolation ensues. If the outcome is positive, the virtue that emerges is love.

Negative identity: Refers to a commitment to aspirations, values, and roles that are deemed unacceptable by society. The individual makes undesirable or dangerous choices. A person may be inclined to choose a negative identity to relieve a state of chronic identity diffusion.

Psychosocial moratorium: A period during which a person, usually an adolescent or young adult, explores a range of opportunities without the need for immediate commitment.

Psychosocial stages: Four childhood and four adulthood stages of development that Erikson added to Freud's oral, anal, phallic, latent, and genital psychosexual stages. The combined psychosexual and psychosocial stages are epigenetic stages of development.

Ritualisms: Mechanical and stereotyped activities—just "going through the motions" without including feelings or a sense of deeper meanings. Ritualisms lead to an individual's estrangement from the self and from the community.

Ritualizations: The "informal and yet prescribed interplay between persons, with adaptive value for all participants and for their group living." These patterns of behavior confirm the meanings held by individuals and by the larger society.

The affiliative ritualization versus elitism: The ritualization in which a young adult finds others with whom to share enthusiastic opinions and scathing judgments, and with whom to establish an enduring affiliation—promising a productive and procreative life. The comparable ritualism is elitism, which is a sense of shared narcissism with a few select people. It leads to exclusion and isolation.

The generational ritualization versus authoritism: This ritualization is a composite of a variety of adult ritualizations, including the parental, the teaching, and the healing. Generational indicates that the adult must be prepared to exercise meaningful authority with conviction. The corresponding ritualism, authoritism, indicates that the adult becomes insensitively authoritarian.

The integral ritualization versus sapientism: The integral ritualization involves the ability to unify all the previous phases into a confirmation of the life thus led. It synthesizes all the important achievements of the previous stages. The corresponding ritualism is a distortion of wisdom called sapientism, "the unwise pretense of being wise."

The judicious ritualization versus legalism: The judicious ritualization is one in which the child learns the significance of rules, laws, and societal norms. The comparable ritualism is legalism, which is marked by self-centered displays of righteousness and moralistic insistence on right over justice.

The ritualization of a sense of authenticity versus impersonation: The child tries on a variety of roles, and both positive and negative roles are used to reconfirm appropriate behaviors and frown upon inappropriate behaviors. Eventually the child discovers the role that is just right for him or her. This is called the ritualization of a sense of authenticity. The comparable ritualism is impersonation, which occurs when the child uses ungenuine role-playing, that is, becomes the role he or she is playing without shame or guilt.

The ritualization of commitment to an ideology versus totalism: The ritualization of commitment to an ideology involves the search for a religious, political, or other set of beliefs that give meaning to his or her life. The adolescent is faced with integrating all the conflicting self-images that have developed since infancy. The corresponding ritualism is totalism, "a fanatic and exclusive preoccupation with what seems unquestionably ideal within a tight system of ideas." Adolescents now find themselves a cause, an idea, a group to which they can totally commit themselves unthinkingly and in which they run the risk of losing their sense of self.

The ritualization of formality versus formalism: The ritualization of formality occurs when the youngster learns the appropriate ways of doing tasks, and learns the value of methodical performance, which includes real skills and knowledge. The comparable ritualism is formalism, which occurs when the person ignores or forgets the human significance of his or her skills, and becomes overly concerned purely with technological proficiency.

The ritualization of the numinous versus idolism: In the mutual recognition and affirmation of the mother and child interaction, the infant experiences the ritualization of the numinous (awesome) quality of her presence. If the infant's normal respect for the mother becomes distorted, the ritualism of idolism unfolds. Such idolism involves a kind of hero worship or putting the mother "on a pedestal."

Trust versus mistrust: First psychosocial stage. When the mother's attentions have been given willingly, lovingly, and reliably, the infant is more likely to develop an attitude of basic trust. The infant who failed to experience reliability, continuity, and sameness is much more likely to develop a sense of basic mistrust. The ego strength that emerges is the capacity to hope.

Chapter 9

Harry Stack Sullivan

Interpersonal Theory

Properly speaking, a man has as many social selves as there are individuals who recognize him and carry an image of him in their mind. To wound any of these images is to wound him.

William James

We are all much more simply human than otherwise.

Harry Stack Sullivan

Love begins when a person finds another person's needs to be as important as his own.

Harry Stack Sullivan

| Harry Stack Sullivan | Born: 1892 Norwich, New York |
| | Died: 1949 Paris, France (at a mental health conference) |

About Sullivan's Interpersonal Theory

Harry Stack Sullivan was among the most open and integrative of the neo-Freudians. In addition to being strongly influenced by Sigmund Freud, Sullivan read widely and drew from theorists, researchers, and clinicians including Carl Jung, Jean Piaget, Alfred Adler, William Alanson White, George Herbert Mead, and Kurt Lewin.

Sullivan's theory and therapeutic approach emphasized the following concepts and themes:

- Sullivan asserted the fundamental humanity and similarity of all people, including those suffering from forms of schizophrenia.
- Psychological development proceeds through three modes of experiencing the world: the prototaxic mode, the parataxic mode, and the syntaxic mode. Such development leads to a reduction of cognitive and emotional egocentrism and to an increasing use of cause-and-effect logic.

- In Sullivan's theory, an individual's personality arises out of interpersonal experiences. The most significant of these is the mothering-infant relationship.
- The ways in which the mothering one responds to an infant's behaviors result in the development of three personifications of the self: the "Good-Me," the "Bad-Me," and the "Not-Me."
- In Sullivan's theory anxiety is viewed as socially and interpersonally based.
- The self-system or self-dynamism, is a cluster of security operations that the infant develops in order to minimize anxiety and to gain the greatest satisfaction from interaction with others.
- Sullivan's view of homosexuality was more accepting than was typical of the mental health establishment of his day. He considered close bonding with other boys to be a common phase of male development.
- Therapeutic interaction with patients—including psychiatric inpatients—should include caring, respect, validation of their positive qualities.

THREE MODES OF EXPERIENCE: PROTOTAXIC, PARATAXIC, SYNTAXIC

Sullivan's developmental theory focused first on the ways infants and young children and adults experienced the world—what he termed their "modes of experience." Developing infants and children do not completely abandon one mode of experience when they move on to another, more mature mode of experience. In Sullivan's theory, earlier modes of experience thus may continue to coexist with more mature ones.

The Prototaxic Mode: Serial Sensation

Sullivan used the terms **prototaxic mode** to indicate an infant's earliest mode of experience (1953b, p. 29). For the first few months of life, the infant's world is composed of a stream of sensory experience without order or consistency. Each sensory experience in the prototaxic mode of experience is isolated from and uncoordinated with other sensory experiences. The world thus is perceived, or "prehended" as Sullivan would say, as a flux of unconnected and discrete moments of sensation (1953b, p. 108). In other words, the world is felt to be a "buzzing, blooming confusion."

An infant in the prototaxic mode of experience is unable to generalize from one event to another. Experiences may occur with some regularity, but the infant is not able to comprehend that one event usually accompanies, precedes, or follows another. When the infant is hungry, "mother-with-bottle," what Sullivan called the "mouth mother," appears as if by magic. The infant does not understand that its own crying may have led the mother to decide that feeding time is at hand. A neglected, unfed infant would experience discomfort in the form of pangs of hunger, but it would not have the capacity to connect such sensations with the mother's failure to provide food.

The Parataxic Mode: Sequential Sensation

The **parataxic mode** of experience begins to emerge when the infant starts perceiving events as having a temporal connection. Repeated cycles of mounting hunger tension and its reduction when food is available lead eventually to the infant's anticipation that its hunger will be satisfied by the mothering person (Sullivan, 1953b, p. 38). The infant is now able to respond differentially to different stimuli based on experience (Sullivan,

1953b, pp. 82–83). For example, the infant is able to see that the *same* person might minister to *different* needs: The mother who provides a nipple when the baby cries with hunger is the same mother who brings a blanket if it cries when feeling cold.

Though **egocentrism** or cognitive-emotional self-centeredness is diminished during this stage, the infant still tends to judge events only by their effects on itself, what they do for and to itself. Sullivan also proposed that parataxic thinking is accompanied by the ability to differentiate the body from the rest of the world (1953b, p. 163). This differentiation gradually leads to the development of the personification of self called the "Not-Me."

A residue of parataxic thinking may occur in older people along with more mature modes of experience. For example, many superstitions are based on parataxic reasoning. If a gambler on a losing streak at the roulette table suddenly strikes it lucky, he or she might assume that the person who just sat down nearby was the cause of the good fortune.

The Syntaxic Mode: Causal Sensation

The **syntaxic mode** of experience corresponds to logical, analytical thought. Syntaxic experience of reality requires the ability to understand physical and spatial causality and the ability to predict causes from knowledge of their effects. It involves a logical synthesis of past, present, and future experience. Syntaxic experiencing is characteristic of much (but not all) adult functioning.

Sullivan pointed out the importance of the early use of signs, symbols and a few words—the beginnings of language—at the very emergence of the syntaxic mode of experience. This begins after an infant's first year of life:

> ...the first instances of experience in the syntaxic mode appear between, let us say, the 12th and the 18th month of extrauterine life, when verbal signs—words, symbols—are organized which are actually communicative. (Sullivan, 1953b, p. 184)

and

> ...I should stress that syntaxic symbols are best illustrated by words that have been consensually validated. A consensus has been reached when the infant or child has learned the precisely right word for a situation, a word which means not only what it is thought to mean by the mothering one, but also means that to the infant. (Sullivan, 1953b, pp. 183–184)

Sullivan also emphasized the predictive function of syntaxic thought (1953b, p. 233). Older children and adults use language to label and store information from experiences for use in understanding future novel events.

BOX 9.1 *Only Connect...*

In the developmental part of Sullivan's theory, there are clear parallels to Vygotsky's and Piaget's earlier theories of cognitive development. In all these models of development, there is a progression toward the infant's and child's greater understanding of cause and effect and a reduction in cognitive egocentrism.

George Kelly's personal construct approach (Chapter 14) and Bandura's social cognitive theory (Chapter 15) and other theories with a cognitive emphasis also focused on the active processes of coding and storing information in order to predict a person's behavior from the regularities of past experience.

THE DEVELOPMENT OF PERSONALITY:
AN INTERPERSONAL EMPHASIS

Sullivan's early theorizing about the origins of personality and personality dynamics drew on concepts such as *anxiety* and *defense mechanisms* that were an integral part of Freudian theorizing. Sullivan, however, modified the meaning of these terms and traced their origins not to intrapsychic processes (such as those between the ego and the id) but rather to interpersonal dynamics beginning as early as infancy.

Sullivan's theory replaced Freud's emphasis on the importance of physiological drives as a motivating force. Instead, Sullivan focused on the individual's experiences resulting from their *interpersonal interactions*. He defined two polar opposite experiential states: absolute euphoria and absolute tension. **Absolute euphoria** is roughly similar to total peace, complete freedom from anxiety or a sense of neediness, a state of utter well-being experienced, for example, by the infant in the state of deep sleep after feeding (Sullivan, 1953b, p. 35). Sullivan defined **absolute tension** as the "maximum possible deviation from absolute euphoria" as, for example, being in a state of acute anxiety or panic. In Sullivan's theory, the developing individual is motivated by the desirability to move in the direction of experiences of absolute euphoria and the wish to avoid experiences of absolute tension.

Avoiding or getting away from experiences of anxiety is a major factor in the development of what Sullivan termed the **self-system** or **self-dynamism.** The self-system or self-dynamism, is a cluster of security operations, roughly analogous to defenses in psychoanalysis, that the infant develops in order to minimize anxiety as well as to gain the greatest satisfaction from interaction with others.

The Interpersonal Origins of Anxiety

Early in his theorizing, Sullivan focused on a central question, "How does the experience of **anxiety** originate?" Sullivan began by stressing that some anxiety originates with the mother and can be communicated from mother to child.

> It is demonstrable that the human young in the first months of life...exhibits disturbed performance when the mothering one has an "emotional disturbance."...Whatever the infant was doing at the time will be interrupted or handicapped—that is, it will either stop, or it will not progress as efficiently as before anxiety appeared....I have reason to suppose, then, that a fearlike state can be induced in an infant under two circumstances: one is by the rather violent disturbance of his zones of contact with circumambient reality; and the other is by certain types of emotional disturbance within the mothering one. (Sullivan, 1953b, pp. 8–9)

Sullivan next asserted that anxiety did not proceed only in a one-way direction from mother to child. He emphasized the reciprocal relationship between mother's and child's tensions: Not only does the mother's anxiety communicate itself to the infant, but tension arising in the infant can induce tension in the mother, (1953b, pp. 39–41). *Thus, from the earliest moments of life, anxiety and tension involve interpersonal relationships.*

An infant who is still in the prototaxic mode of experience does not yet differentiate itself from its environment, but experiences itself and its world as one global, fused mass. Its experience of anxiety is diffuse and fragmented, isolated from other experiences. To the infant in the parataxic mode of experience, the anxiety of the mother or mothering person seems the same as its own anxiety. Infant and mother are linked by a kind of **empathic resonance**, the capacity of an infant or a child to feel the mother's feelings, and vice versa.

Since it cannot differentiate the experience of anxiety from other unpleasurable tensions, the infant possesses as yet no specific means of reducing the anxiety on its own. Just as the infant relies on the mother to satisfy bodily needs, the infant relies on the mothering one to reduce his or her anxiety.

Experiencing the Nursing Situation

Like Freud, Sullivan recognized the importance of development during the period that Freud termed the "oral stage." Instead of Freud's focus on psychosexual development, Sullivan's emphasis was on the infant's *experience* of nursing, out of which emerged his or her model of the mothering person. Nursing begins while the infant experiences reality in the prototaxic mode of experience. At this stage, its perceptions consist only of momentary and fleeting states of sensory awareness. One of the most important sensory experiences for the nursing infant is that of "nipple-in-the-lips." The infant comprehends or, in Sullivan's term, "prehends" the nipple-in-the-lips event as a series of discrete bodily sensations including tactile, thermal, and olfactory stimuli.

Over time, the infant's prototaxic, and later parataxic, experience of discrete sensations gradually leads to a personification of the mother or of the mothering person. This person becomes identified with the primary transactions with the infant in the feeding situation and the infant's experience of it.

Depending on the degree of satisfaction supplied by the mothering person's feeding behavior, the infant develops one of several different **personifications** of the nipple-in-the-lips mothering one:

1. *Good-and-satisfactory nipple* personification is the nipple in the lips that supplies milk when the infant is hungry [Good Mother].
2. *The good-but-unsatisfactory-nipple* personification is the nipple that supplies milk when the infant is not hungry [Good Mother].
3. *Wrong-nipple-in-the-lips* is an unsatisfactory nipple because it does not supply milk when the infant is hungry; infant rejects this nipple and searches for a better nipple [Bad Mother].
4. *Evil-nipple* is the nipple of an anxious mother who communicates a profound degree of anxiety and tension; this tension is a signal for avoidance; "not that nipple in my lips" [Bad-Anxious Mother]. (Based on Sullivan, 1953b, p. 80.)

Thus, the nursing situation is an important prototype for the development of the infant's relationships with future **significant others**, a term Sullivan used to indicate those people who have important interpersonal relationships with an individual.

> ...the infant is bound to have two personifications of any mothering person (Good and Bad Mother), barring the most incredible good fortune, and ...the infant in the earliest stages of life need have only two personifications for any number of people who have something to do with looking after him. (Sullivan, 1953b, p. 122)

DIFFERENTIATION OF SELF FROM THE UNIVERSE

Toilet training is a clearly interpersonal situation that involves the learning of new personifications about oneself and about one's own body. The way in which the mothering one responds to the infant's body—with disgust, with delight, or with simple acceptance—will be the key determinant in the infant's personification of itself. Coupled with these interpersonal effects are the infant's first clues that its activities

Thinking About ... Sullivan's portrayal of infant-nipple relationships

Tracing back feelings in adult situations to infantile experience might be seen as an example of a reductionistic or even a rather far-fetched approach to personality. One way of thinking about Sullivan's emphasis on the infant-nipple relationship is that it is a metaphor or, as mentioned in the text, even a prototype for the experience of nurturance or lack of nurturance in human relationships. A patient's transference to a psychoanalyst can be viewed by a Sullivanian as a derivative of the pattern of nursing that the patient experienced in infancy.

For example, feelings associated when others are giving unnecessary or unwanted support or advice could be traced to or seen as similar to the (real or imagined) "good-but-unsatisfactory-nipple" experience. Likewise, feelings that occur if the individual needs guidance but receives indifferent treatment can be compared or traced to the "wrong-nipple-in-the-lips" situation.

One can also see in Sullivan's theory something akin to a behavioral or social-cognitive approach in which early conditioning or experience of the environment has a continuing impact on later behavior. Sullivan's idea of experiencing a "Good Mother" or a "Bad Mother" is consistent with Jung's idea that archetypes come in pairs, and that the Mother Archetype has two sides, the loving mother and the witchy or bad mother (cf. Chapter 5).

gradually lead to the discovery of the difference between its own body and the external world. For example, the infant lies in the crib and studies the movement of its own hands. The infant may grasp an object, bring it unsteadily to its mouth, and then insert it into its lips. The infant soon discovers that it is not a nipple; but it also discovers that *its own hand* has brought about the event. When, moreover, it brings an *empty* hand to its mouth, and sucks the thumb, the infant learns an even more important lesson:

> ... That the thumb is uniquely different from any nipple by reason of being *in itself* a source of zonal sentience. *The thumb feels sucked*. (Sullivan, 1953b, p. 136)

Sucking the thumb is also different from the nursing situation in an important way: Unlike an attempt to bring mother-with-satisfactory-nipple on demand, the infant's attempts to bring the thumb to his or her mouth are always successful and unvaryingly satisfying.

> The thumb-in-the-lips is dependable, and is independent of evoking the good mother; the infant can bring it into being, as it were, without cooperation—in isolation from any of his personifications, whether of the good mother or the bad mother. (Sullivan, 1953b, p. 139)

By its experiences with self-evoked satisfactions, the infant learns to foresee and to control some of its own behaviors. More important, the infant learns that it exists—that it has a certain independence. However, when the infant seeks further exploration of its own body in the genital or anal zones, the mother may respond with anxiety or anger. Her behavior evokes the infant's personification of the bad mother. The infant quickly discovers that he or she is not independent of the mothering one's "forbidding gestures," which direct the infant not to experience certain parts of itself.

PERSONAL SOURCES OF SULLIVAN'S EMPHASIS ON HUMAN RELATIONSHIPS

Harry Stack Sullivan's early life may very well have sensitized him to the theme of boyhood loneliness. Harry Stack Sullivan was different from other boys in his village in rural New York State. He was an Irish Catholic in an all-Protestant community; he was an only child, emotionally isolated from unaffectionate parents; and most important, he was considered homosexual in a place and at a time when there was not the slightest shred of acceptance for gays and lesbians.

The other children at school and in his rural village never accepted young Harry. Sullivan's social isolation seems to have been a mixture of shyness that triggered withdrawal and compensatory disdain for his schoolmates (Swick-Perry, 1982; cf. Thompson, 1962). He was thus shy, socially awkward, and eccentric. Perry reports a poignant image of the lonely boy standing in a pressed serge suit in the church courtyard after attending Sunday Mass:

> He seemed miserable. . . . This standing alone on the edge of a group is a picture of Sullivan that persists. While close friends remember him as merry and witty in a social setting, people who saw him in situations of less intimacy think of him as testy and caustic—and often obviously miserable. Junior colleagues, who saw him usually in seminars, are apt to discount the idea that he could be kind and merry. (Swick-Perry, 1982, p. 89)

Growing up on an isolated farm was a lonely experience for Sullivan. One consolation was that, as a young boy, he became attached to horses. In fact, throughout his life, he used the symbol of two horses' heads within a circle—one facing up and the other facing down—as his personal emblem. Sullivan used this design for the front cover of the books he would publish in the field of mental health (Chapman, 1976, p. 21).

Sullivan's Relationship with his Parents

Harry's mother was the most important figure in his early life. He had been her third child; the two previous children died in infancy. Ella Sullivan was a semi-invalid who

Figure 9.1 Harry Stack Sullivan with his parents, Ella and Timothy, about 1925. All three seem reserved and self-contained. The image of Timothy's dour expression and folded arms and legs is consistent with Harry's description of his father as "remarkably taciturn."

Source: Perry, H. S. (1982). *Psychiatrist of America: The Life of Harry Stack Sullivan*. (Cambridge, MA: Belknap Press of Harvard University.)

appears to have been profoundly depressed and sufficiently disturbed to require periods of hospitalization for psychiatric treatment (Swick-Perry, 1982). She mysteriously disappeared when Harry was about two-and-a-half years old. At that time, Harry's grandmother took over his care. Eventually, however, mother and son were reunited.

Harry's relationship with his father was distant, and Sullivan described him as "remarkably taciturn." Harry was nearly 30 years old before he was able to establish a somewhat closer relationship with his father. At this late date, Sullivan had come to understand that his mother had gotten in the way of his getting to know his father.

Young Harry's Bullying Buddy

At the age of eight-and-a-half, Harry found friendship with an older boy of 13. Chapman (1976) suggests that the relationship was probably homosexual. However, another biographer, Swick-Perry (1982, p. 89), has argued on the basis of more thorough research that the relationship was not homosexual. At the time, however, the people of Sullivan's hometown viewed Sullivan and his buddy as homosexuals. The boys become even closer in the face of such rejection and ostracism.

For Harry, the relationship with Clarence was one of trust and tenderness. Clarence, on the other hand, seems to have been a manipulative bully. Years later, Harry recalled that early relationship with more pleasure than pain, whereas Clarence appears to have come to hate his one-time chum. Both Clarence and Harry became psychiatrists. Perhaps it was their own awareness of the psychological pain of rejection that influenced their choice of career.

In his first book, withheld from publication for a variety of reasons until 23 years after his death, Sullivan wrote of the sexual adjustment of the isolated preadolescent:

> Three special cases of isolation call for comment. The first and most unfortunate is that of boys who, because of serious deviation of personality growth, are excluded from gangs and chumships. Those whose progress was fair into the juvenile era are one class. One of these boys is usually clearly conscious of his "difference" from the other boys, of being an "outsider," of his being distrusted, if not despised, by the "regular fellows." Often he has earned a nickname cruelly indicative of the most conspicuous social manifestation of his limitation.... His self-respect is gravely impaired. His authority-attitudes are upset. His schoolwork suffers. If he can he becomes loosely associated with some other "failures," often under quasi-leadership of an older, badly beaten boy. It may be that the boy is so unhappy that he submits to manipulation for criminal purposes. It may be that, while he is incapable of submitting himself thus far, he is glad to participate in activities clearly damaging to those who "belong." (Sullivan, 1972, pp. 177–178)

The autobiographical nature of this theoretical discussion is further strengthened by a later passage in which he describes the case of boys isolated merely by virtue of their geographical location. The typical rural community enforces this kind of loneliness, Sullivan states, and the boy usually suffers a prolongation of adolescence:

> Fantasy processes and the personification of subhuman objects are called on. Loyalty is developed to abstract ideals, more or less concretely embodied in fanciful figures, rather than to concrete groups. The capacity for sympathy becomes peculiarly differentiated because of the elaboration of its underlying tendencies in loneliness, among fanciful objects. (Sullivan, 1972, p. 180)

This passage may help us understand Sullivan's adoption of the horse emblem as his personal symbol. His own loneliness as a child may have resulted in loyalty to "personified subhuman objects" that also represented abstract ideals which were symbolized in his personal symbol.

Earlier in the same book, Sullivan was even more overtly autobiographical in speaking of a rural community where he had observed firsthand the matter of gang sexuality:

> ...a large number of the early adolescents participated in overt homosexual activities during the gang age. Most of them progressed thereafter without let or hindrance to the customary heteroerotic interest in later adolescence. Some of the few boys in this community who were excluded from the gangs as a result of their powerful inhibitions, who missed participation in community homosexual play, did not progress to satisfactory heterosexual development. (Sullivan, 1972, p. 171)

It is not unreasonable to assume that Sullivan was alluding here as well to his own exclusion from gang friendships. In this passage, he attributes the development of a homosexual identity in adulthood to a lack of opportunity to engage in "community homosexual play" as an early adolescent.

Unpromising Beginnings in College and Medical School

Having won a state scholarship to Cornell University in the fall of 1908, Sullivan entered college at the age of 16. After only two terms at Cornell, he was suspended for failure in all his subjects. He also seems to have been involved in some illegal activities that included tampering with mail sent to other students (Swick-Perry, 1982). Another version depicts young Harry as selling something illegal through the mail. The exact facts are not known, but a biographer, Swick-Perry, suggests that he may have been involved in the schemes of older students who attempted to obtain chemicals illegally by ordering them on stolen drugstore stationery. (1982, p. 146)

In any event, Harry left Cornell and dropped out of sight for two years. Swick-Perry (1982) states that Sullivan suffered a schizophrenic psychotic episode during this time and was probably hospitalized at Bellevue in New York City. In his writings, Sullivan (see especially 1972) makes oblique reference to the fact that he had personal experience with "schizophrenic states." It is quite possible that the events of his own life history at this time led to the professional interest he would have as a young physician in understanding and treating schizophrenic patients.

In 1911, Sullivan gained entrance to an unaccredited medical school in Chicago. Only 19 years old when he began medical school, he was barely able to afford tuition. His medical school education included little psychiatric study. Incidentally, psychiatry was a subject in which Harry received some of his lowest grades. Although graduating within four years, Sullivan did not actually receive his diploma until he could pay his final tuition. In order to save some money, Sullivan worked as a physician for insurance and steel companies in Illinois and Indiana. After two years, he was able to redeem his diploma.

Sullivan's Creative Contributions and Rise to Prominence

Eventually, Harry Stack Sullivan became affiliated with a branch of the federal government that worked with war veterans. In 1921, he accepted a position as liaison officer at St. Elizabeth's Hospital in Washington, D.C. At St. Elizabeth's, Sullivan received wide exposure to psychiatric cases and seems to have acquired his knowledge of psychiatric procedure by on-the-job training and attending lectures. He was mentored by Dr. William A. White, a prominent American psychiatrist, who helped him obtain a position at Baltimore's well-regarded Sheppard and Enoch Pratt Hospital.

There, Sullivan demonstrated his creativity in clinical work by devising a number of novel procedures for working with schizophrenic patients. Sullivan's creativity and the value of his work was quickly recognized, and he rapidly acquired a major reputation for excellence in the field of psychiatry.

Humanizing Our Approach to Schizophrenia: The One-Genus Postulate

Sullivan's approach to clinical work emphasized the common humanity of those with severe psychopathology.

> In approaching the subject of mental disorder, I must emphasize that, in my view, persons showing mental disorder do not manifest anything specifically different in kind from what is manifested by practically all human beings. (Sullivan, 1956, p. 3)

Sullivan's emphasis on the continuity of mental processes from normality through psychosis led him to a memorable philosophical statement of human similarities:

> *Everyone and anyone is much more simply human than otherwise, more like everyone else than different* (1962, Frontispiece) [italics added].

This concise statement was originally called *the species identity theorem* by Sullivan in his early unpublished notebooks, and later eventually termed the **one-genus postulate:**

> . . . the differences between any two instances of human personality—from the lowest-grade imbecile to the highest-grade genius—are much less striking than the differences between the least-gifted human being and a member of the nearest other biological genus. Man—however undistinguished biologically—as long as he is entitled to the term, human personality, will be very much more like every other instance of human personality than he is like anything else in the world. (1953b, pp. 32–33)

Because "everyone and anyone is much more simply human than otherwise," Sullivan thought it necessary to rescue psychiatry from the "ivory tower myth" of objective, uninvolved commitment to "scientific" truth finding (1964, p. 15). For Sullivan, the psychiatrist is certainly a scientific observer of behavior, but he is also **a participant observer** who is no less human, no less involved, no less of a participant, and no less changed than the patients he treats. As Sullivan pithily summarized his concept, "The crying need is for observers who are growing *observant of their observing*" (1964, p. 27, italics added). The one-genus postulate also led to more interactive and humane treatment of schizophrenics and other mental patients, who were often treated in isolated long-term wards.

BOX 9.3 *Only Connect . . .*

Sullivan's *one-genus postulate* is consistent with the findings of modern genomics, the study of the genome. Of the 3 billion-or-so-long molecular chemical code for the human genome, only an average of 0.01 percent distinguishes one person from another. We are almost completely alike in terms of our genetic makeup. We are, in fact, 99.99 percent similar. The 0.01 percent that is different may account, however, for major physical and behavioral differences such as sickle cell anemia and schizophrenia.

Sullivan's Unique Ward: For Males Only

Sullivan designed a ward at Sheppard-Pratt to provide a corrective preadolescent-male society for schizophrenic patients. Sullivan had already concluded that a period of homosexual interaction in puberty could be part of healthy male development. He also assumed that many male schizophrenic patients had prior homosexual conflicts (Swick-Perry, 1962, p. xii). These ideas were part of Sullivan's rationale for having an all male staff, which he thought could encourage openness about such issues (Swick-Perry, 1962, p. xxi; see also Sullivan, 1962, pp. 104 and 251). In addition, Sullivan encouraged the staff members to share their own experiences of any preadolescent homosexual activity and to indicate that such activities are not depraved but simply represent a specific stage of developmental.

Sullivan selected only male aides and instructed them in the art of relating to patients. He was ahead of his time in relying on what today we would refer to as "paraprofessionals" as an integral part of the treatment team. Sullivan reasoned that **schizophrenia** had its origins in initially unhealthy interpersonal relations (Chapman, 1976, p. 45). His goal was to establish healthy human relations between the staff and patients as a therapeutic procedure.

Approximately 80 percent of the patients on Sullivan's ward substantially improved. We cannot ascertain, however, whether the effectiveness of his treatment actually specifically validated his theories of schizophrenia. For one reason, his patients were selectively chosen, a factor that might have increased his success rate. Patients may have improved because there was a high level of interaction with staff. They received a lot of attention and were treated sensitively and with an expectation that they would improve. This was far from the indifferent treatment and low expectations that usually greeted schizophrenic patients in ward settings.

As a creative therapist, one who thought "outside of the box," Sullivan demonstrated a "fine disregard" for the rules and procedures of classical psychiatry (White, 1977, p. 317 Clarence Schulz (1978) points out that Sullivan's style was not focused on "helping" the patient or on trying to make him feel more comfortable. Rather, the patient was treated as a collaborator who knew his problems better than the psychiatrist. Sullivan would often confront a patient directly with the illogicalities of his statements or with his deliberate untruths. He would attempt to show the patient the nature of his evasions, and Sullivan could sometimes be deliberately sarcastic to make a point.

Unlike the typical Freudian analyst, Sullivan frequently had a stenographer present to record his interviews with patients. At one point, he wired a concealed microphone in his office to another room so that his secretary could record the sessions (Swick-Perry, 1962, p. xxi). Excerpts of verbatim transcripts of Sullivan's sessions with three patients at Sheppard-Pratt during the period 1923 to 1930 have been published (Schulz, 1978).

BOX 9.4 *Only Connect . . .*

In considering Sullivan's collaborative approach to psychotherapy, one might keep in mind that other therapists have also relied, to one extent or another, on the patient's own efforts to seek health. As we have seen in Chapters 2 and 3, Freud first started with hypnotic techniques but then used the pressure or concentration technique and finally developed free association. In this process, he increasingly depended on patients' own thinking and insight.

Theorists as varied as Anna Freud, George Kelly, Carl Jung, Carl Rogers, Gordon Allport, and Erik Erikson also emphasized a person's own inclinations toward mastery and growth.

Sullivan's Later Years: Personal and Professional Developments

In 1927, Sullivan took care of a 15-year-old boy who lived with him until Sullivan's death on a trip to Paris in 1949. Swick-Perry (1982, p. 209) reports that the boy had been brought to Sullivan for treatment after he had been found in a kind of catatonic pose on the street. For more than 20 years, this young man, James Inscoe Sullivan, served as confidant, household staff, cook, and office staff combined. Sullivan regarded Jimmie as his "beloved foster son" (Swick-Perry, 1982, p. 211).

Sullivan moved to New York City in 1930 and opened a successful private psychiatry practice. During this period, he received what was probably his first psychoanalysis with Clara Thompson, a student of Sandor Ferenczi, a well-known Freudian analyst. Sullivan joined the psychoanalytic movement but did not accept classical Freudian theory and practice. His preferred approach emphasized interpersonal factors (as opposed to Freud's intrapsychic emphasis). He also advocated the interdisciplinary integration of ideas from the social sciences. He helped to found the interpersonally-oriented William A. White Foundation in New York, which has been an influential supporter of alternatives to classical Freudian psychoanalysis in New York until the present time.

Back in Washington in 1939, Sullivan's interests expanded to having an impact on promoting peace and mental health internationally. He was involved in founding the World Federation for Mental Health, which was a means for him to implement his pro-social goals. On January 14, 1949, while attending a meeting of the World Federation of Mental Health in Paris, Sullivan suffered from a cardiovascular event (stroke or heart attack) and died.

In the course of his life, Harry Stack Sullivan had emerged from the loneliness and isolation of his childhood. After an unpromising start, he fashioned a career that helped many other vulnerable people and contributed to a more sympathetic understanding and compassionate treatment of mental illness.

PERSONIFICATIONS OF SELF: GOOD-ME, BAD-ME, NOT-ME

For Sullivan, it was clear that the most important kinds of learning occur in the discovery that some behaviors eliminate or reduce the intensity of interpersonal anxiety (1953b, p. 152). The **gradient of anxiety** ranges from relatively mild tension-evoking behaviors to behaviors that elicit such intense feelings of emotion that they are best described as "uncanny," "*awe*-full," or "*dread*-full."

Good-Me Personification

All those infant behaviors to which the mothering one has responded with tenderness, praise, emotional warmth, or physical reward become amalgamated into a self-perception of **Good-Me.** The Good-Me personification is thus a product of satisfying or pleasing interpersonal relations with this significant other, the mothering one (1953b, p. 162). The Good-Me personification is largely conscious and usually indicated in verbal behavior by everything to which a person can freely apply the pronoun "I," as in "I am ... " or "I would like to be ... " or "I have. ... "

Bad-Me Personification

Increasing degrees of anxiety and tension on the part of the mothering one are often responses to certain behaviors of her infant: touching objectionable parts of its body, unruly crying, refusing to eat certain foods, struggling over bodily care such as bathing. All those behaviors that cause increasing tension in the mother also evoke anxiety in the infant. Over time, these undesirable, anxiety-provoking behaviors become amalgamated into the personification of the **Bad-Me.** The Bad-Me personification is also conscious to a large degree, but it may merge into behaviors that are unconscious because they evoke stronger degrees of anxiety.

Not-Me Personification

The **Not-Me** personification is a more elusive concept. The "Not-Me" consists of a dissociated cluster of feelings and images that does not belong to one's everyday self. It is the part of personality that is rarely experienced consciously by the normal person, except perhaps during dreaming. For the schizophrenic, on the other hand, experience of the Not-Me personification is continual. Thus the Not-Me lies outside the realm of description by language. It is a product of intense, "uncanny" emotion in the parataxic mode:

> This [Not-Me] is a very gradually evolving personification of an always relatively primitive character—that is, organized in unusually simple signs in the parataxic mode of experience, and made up of poorly grasped aspects of living which will presently be regarded as "dreadful," and which still later will be differentiated into incidents which are attended by awe, horror, loathing, and dread. (Sullivan, 1953b, p. 163)

The feelings of dread and terror, disgust and loathing that attend the Not-Me personification are difficult to place in words. These feelings were originally attached to certain behaviors and perceptions that resulted from forbidding gestures and expressions of anxiety from the mothering one. To a greater or lesser extent, all personalities have a Not-Me personification, a part of one's own self that seems alien and hideous.

In the development of the normal personality, according to Freud's theory, the erotic and autoerotic impulses of childhood are repressed at the time of the resolution of the Oedipus complex. In addition, the child's normally uninhibited desire to play with and to smear his own feces is abandoned after learning shame and disgust lessons from parents or parenting figure. In one of Sullivan's patients, most of his erotic impulses lingered on in consciousness, but only in a dissociated form. This psychotic patient evidenced, among other dissociated systems, strong homosexual and incestuous impulses so loathsome and frightening to him that they had been split off from the rest of consciousness. Particularly problematic was his habitual masturbation accompanied by fantasies that could be described in the normal personality only as Not-Me:

> He masturbated frequently, to the accompaniment of homosexual anal phantasies. *On an occasion when about 17*, he, having inserted a candle into the rectum "to increase satisfaction," as the orgasm approached, withdrew the candle and thrust it into his mouth. The orgasm, he remembers vividly, was very powerful. This recollection was strongly resisted. He had never repeated the procedure. (Sullivan, 1962, p. 36; italics in original)

The disgust and revulsion we experience upon reading of this schizophrenic person's behavior is some evidence of the uncanny Not-Me nature of the oral-anal impulses.

In Sullivan's theory, the close association between the mouth and the anus for the infant is not connected with disgust or revulsion until shame, learned through anxiety, is established. From that point, the early willingness to manipulate feces, to smear them, or to raise them to the mouth evokes intense horror. Any connection between

BOX 9.5   *Only Connect...*

Sullivan's "Bad-Me" and "Not-Me" personifications of self correspond in content and function to Carl Jung's (Chapter 5) Shadow archetype. Like these personifications of self, the Shadow archetype is that part of the psyche that normally is not incorporated into the person's sense of self and consists of qualities that the individual considers negative or alien.

The purported origins of the Bad-Me and Not-Me personifications of self differ from Jung's idea of the origins of the Shadow archetype. Sullivan saw these personifications of self as a result of experiences in early infancy. Jung thought, however, that the Shadow, like other archetypes, arose out of the experiences of humanity during its long history.

Sullivan's "Good-Me" is similar in meaning and function to Jung's Persona archetype.

oral and anal impulses and genital sexual activity is likewise deeply submerged. In effect, these impulses have become Not-Me:

> The not-me is literally the organization of experience with significant people that has been subjected to such intense anxiety, and anxiety so suddenly precipitated, that it was impossible for the then relatively rudimentary person to make any sense of, to develop any true grasp on, the particular circumstances which dictated the experience of this intense anxiety. (Sullivan, 1953b, p. 314)

As in some other parts of Sullivan's theory, much of what he says here seems to be related to specific cultural and societal norms. In today's culture, some parents take a more relaxed, less anxious, and certainly less punitive response to an infant's touching his or her genitals or anus or playing with feces than did parents during Sullivan's childhood. No doubt, this change has been caused by a greater acceptance of bodily functions and sexuality. Such increased acceptance in turn has come about, at least in part, by the efforts of theorists such as Freud and Sullivan. Sullivan's theory would predict an impact of such changes in parenting on the personality of today's adults.

THE SELF-SYSTEM: SECURITY OPERATIONS

From its experiences with reward and anxiety, with forbidding and tender gestures, the infant learns important lessons: Its own anxiety can be reduced by certain specific behaviors that are approved by the mothering one; and its own anxiety is sometimes increased to an unbearable degree by behaving in ways that she disapproves. In effect, it learns that it is desirable to be the Good-Me; undesirable to be the Bad-Me; and unthinkable to be the Not-Me.

To maintain the division between "good" and "bad" forms of living, the infant learns to interact only in certain ways with the significant others of its world. The habitual pattern of behaviors that the infant develops to gain the greatest satisfaction and to keep anxiety at a minimum in dealing with significant others is the **self-system,** or **self-dynamism.** The self-system is thus a cluster of **security operations.**

In Sullivan's attempt to establish a scientific conception of interpersonal relations, he chose the term **dynamism** to indicate habitual patterns of behavior like the self-system because he thought it was a term indicating objective, neutral observation. For Sullivan, the study of the personality is based on understanding the organism's energy transactions with the world of things and people. Sullivan defined dynamism in psychological and biological terms:

...the ultimate entity, the smallest useful abstraction, which can be employed in the study of the functional activity of the living organism is the dynamism itself, *the relatively enduring pattern of energy transformations which recurrently characterize the organism in its duration as a living organism.* (1953b, p. 103)

The concept of dynamism may be thought of in psychological terms as a *habitual reaction pattern.* Sullivan again emphasized his fundamental belief that we are all "much more simply human than otherwise" by suggesting that minor variations in habitual reaction patterns were relatively unimportant. It was his opinion that such variations were merely "the envelope of insignificant particular differences." Thus his earliest definition of personality was constructed along these same lines:

Personality is the relatively enduring configuration of life-processes characterizing all of the person's total activity pertaining to such other persons, real or fantastic, as become from time to time relevant factors in his total situations. (1972, p. 47)

In Sullivan's final, definitive lectures on his conceptualizations, he changed the definition of personality somewhat to emphasize the concept of person-to-person contact as the fundamental unit of study:

Personality is the relatively enduring pattern of recurrent interpersonal situations that characterize a human life. (1953b, pp. 110–111)

Sullivan has viewed **personality** as composed of a series of interpersonal dynamisms, *habitual patterns of relating to others.* Originally founded on the need to reduce anxiety and obtain satisfaction for needs, the self-system is the dynamism of "educative experience called into being by the necessity to avoid or to minimize incidents of anxiety" (1953b, p. 165). The self-system's sole function is to aid the infant in reducing anxiety, first with the mothering one and later, as an adult, with all significant others.

Unfortunately, the self-system also embodies some troublesome characteristics. Since it is the product of parental censure and praise, it embodies the prevailing cultural standards by which the parents themselves have been molded. The self-system, therefore, functions to screen the child's repertoire of possible behaviors and to focus them into a smaller number of socially acceptable ones. Thus, the self-system narrows attention to those aspects of living that generate praise and blame, and it attempts to perpetuate only those experiences that are least likely to generate anxiety. In this sense, the self-system is a stumbling block to growth:

[The self-system] permits a minute focus on those performances of the child which are the cause of approbation and disapprobation, but, very much like a microscope, it interferes with noticing the rest of the world. When you are staring through your microscope, you don't see much except what comes through that channel. So with the self-dynamism, it has a tendency to focus attention on performances with the significant other person which get approbation or disfavor. (Sullivan, 1953a, p. 21)

The self-system prevents awareness of all experiences, all impulses, that are not relevant to parental approval and disapproval. Experiences that generated parental approval become part of the Good-Me; experiences that generated disapproval become part of the Bad-Me. Experiences that generated large doses of disapproval or intense disfavor are dissociated from the personality and relegated to the Not-Me. The self-system is a selective filter, restricting attention, and consequently personality growth, to the reflected appraisals of others (Sullivan, 1953a, p. 29). Sullivan called this process of filtering *selective inattention.*

SELECTIVE INATTENTION

Selective inattention may occur in emergency situations, for example, when it is necessary to focus awareness only on the problem at hand. In this case, selective inattention is a very adaptive and useful response. But when selective inattention to important aspects of living is habitual in the service of allaying anxiety, it is a mechanism of defensive perception, a security operation. Sullivan added this concept to the long list of defenses developed by Freud, Anna Freud, and others.

To illustrate, Sullivan reported an experience with a patient who provided an elegant and extreme example of selective inattention. Sullivan had been seeing this patient every week for a number of years and soon became accustomed to the man's ritualistic way of beginning the therapeutic hour. Each week the patient would recount an experience he had while on the train en route to Sullivan's office. Each week it was the same experience. And each week the man reported the experience with the same fresh amazement, as if none of the other reported experiences had happened. Sullivan commented,

> I had heard it perhaps two hundred times when one day, for some reason or other, all the factors added up in my mind and I interrupted before he finished. After he had recounted his fantasy of kissing some man and then biting a piece out of his ear I said, "And you were amazed!" He said, "Yes, what do you mean?... I *was* amazed. But why did you say so? What do you know about it?" [Sullivan responded:] "Why, only that you have told me the same story two or three hundred times...." (1956, pp. 44–45)

To a large extent, selective inattention resembles Freud's mechanisms of denial and repression. But Sullivan saw selective inattention as an integral part of the self-system's functioning. On this basis, Sullivan proposed a **Theorem of Escape:**

> The self-system unlike any of the other dynamisms... is extraordinarily resistant to change by experience. This can be expressed in the theorem that *the self-system from its nature... tends to escape influence by experience which is incongruous with its current organization and functional activity*. (1953b, p. 190)

As maturity is attained, whole segments of activity related to anxiety are kept away from the self-system. As with the train-riding man, parts of the self are isolated from the rest of the personality. Though we behave in particular ways, we may be reluctant to recognize all our actions as our own or to incorporate new experiences into the self.

ME-YOU PERSONIFICATIONS

Even in maturity, the individual's self-system and its processes of selective inattention shape conceptions of the self and of significant others. For example, consider the possibilities inherent in the multiple relationships of Mr. A to Mrs. A in the course of their married life. Both partners' self-systems are differently attuned to reality. To maintain self-images founded on others' reflected appraisals, they may respond to **personifications** of the other, not to the reality of the other's presence. As the conditions of the interpersonal situation change, Mr. A's image of his wife will shift. He may personify her one moment as the illusory image "loving and tender wife-mother" and in the next situation she will become for him the illusory image "feminine viper and tauntress." Likewise, Mrs. A responds not to the objective Mr. A but to a series of multiple "you's" she has created in relationship to her personification of herself, her "me" image.

The six epochs and the predominant mode in each epoch are:

1. infancy   (prototaxic mode)
2. childhood   (parataxic mode)
3. juvenile   (mostly syntaxic mode, partly parataxic)
4. preadolescence   (syntaxic mode)
5. early adolescence   (syntaxic mode)
6. late adolescence   (syntaxic mode)

Infancy

Extending roughly from birth to the development of language, the period of infancy is primarily prototaxic in nature. The infant experiences reality as a discrete flux of momentary states. The infant does not differentiate self from the world; his or her experience of reality is global, diffuse. Most significant of the developments of infancy are the personifications of self and significant other. Good-Me, Bad-Me, and Not-Me have already been surveyed as well as the personifications of the Good and Bad Mother (nipple). Out of its experiences with the significant others of its world, the infant develops a particular orientation to the world. These dynamisms can include apathy and somnolent detachment when the infant's experiences with the mothering one have been anxiety-provoking and frustrating.

The term **apathy** refers to the capacity of the infant to deal with emergency situations of unsatisfied needs by developing a withdrawing "I don't care" orientation to its own experiences of hunger, thirst, and pain (Sullivan, 1953b, p. 55).

Somnolent detachment literally means the separation from reality that occurs by being sleepy. In effect, the infant's withdrawal response of apathy may be extended to cope with anxiety situations that are persistent and prolonged. From the infant's point of view, somnolent detachment involves not only a "don't care" attitude about objects of need satisfaction but also a forthright indifference to the significant persons who are responsible for neglect of desires. Apathy is called out by aggravated and unsatisfied needs; somnolent detachment is evoked by prolonged anxiety in interpersonal contacts (Sullivan, 1953b, p. 57).

Childhood

The childhood epoch extends roughly from the acquisition of language to the appearance of a need for playmates or what Sullivan termed "compeers" (1953b, p. 33; 1953a, p. 37). Though language is present, it is sometimes used in some very magical, parataxic ways:

> ...in so far as a verbal statement by a child is taken by the acculturating adults to have a superior quality of reality to other of his behavioral acts, the child is being trained to be incapable of dealing with life.... In a good many homes, the following kind of statement is a conspicuous ingredient in the alleged education of the young: "Willie, I told you not to do that. Now say you are sorry."... If Willie dutifully says he is sorry, that is supposed to markedly mitigate the situation, although it is something that Willie is almost absolutely incapable of understanding. (Sullivan, 1953b, pp. 200–201)

Another important development of the childhood epoch is the possibility for the child to undergo what Sullivan called a **malevolent transformation** (1953b, p. 213):

> A child may discover that manifesting the need for tenderness toward the potent figures around him leads frequently to his being disadvantaged, being made anxious, being made

fun of. . . . Under those circumstances, the developmental course changes to the point that the perceived need for tenderness brings a foresight of anxiety and pain. The child learns, you see, that it is highly disadvantageous to show any need for tender cooperation from the authoritative figures around him, in which case he shows something else; and that something else is the basic malevolent attitude, the attitude that one really lives among enemies. . . . (Sullivan, 1953b, p. 114)

Later, in adolescence, some children have learned that their world is hostile and unfriendly. They may, therefore, deliberately behave in ways that make it difficult for anyone to show them affection and kindness. They have learned not to express any need for tenderness, and they often treat others in a hostile manner.

On the positive side, the epoch of childhood is marked by a number of "as if" performances or role-playing the significant behaviors modeled by parents. "As if" performances may eventually be practiced as defensive maneuvers by a child who has been exposed to manipulative and anxiety-provoking parenting.

Instead of a healthy identification with parents, children may play roles to conceal their real feelings in the dramatization of behaviors demonstrated by mother and father (1953b, p. 209). In a dramatization, the "as if" performance shifts to children acting as if they actually were the parents. For the most part, however, dramatizations are an essential and normal part of the childhood epoch, and they facilitate adoption by the child of each one's appropriate male or female role.

The second kind of "as if" performance is the technique of seeming preoccupied with something in order to be left alone. Children learn to behave "as if" some activity were highly important to them, riveting their attention and demanding all their energy. In actuality, the seeming preoccupation is really a technique of avoiding disturbing and painful interactions with anxiety-provoking significant others, or it is a means of escaping their demands (1953b, p. 210).

The changing role of playmates clearly marks the transition from childhood to the juvenile epoch. In childhood, the need for a playmate was essentially **egocentric**, even selfish. Children play side by side, but they do not necessarily interact. A child's awareness of a playmate or playmates is usually less important than the child's own ideas and pursuits. The child may even invent an imaginary playmate to satisfy his or her own wishes. A need for genuinely cooperative play and for mutuality of experience emerges during the juvenile period (Sullivan, 1953b, p. 226).

The juvenile epoch extends from the grammar school years through that phase when the child experiences a need for an intimate relationship with a same-sexed "chum." Most of the juvenile's experiences are in the syntaxic mode; language has become the chief tool for coping with the demands of authority.

Education and the authority figures of the school play a significant role in the juvenile's life. The chief contributions to personality development occur through two avenues of social activity.

1. **Social subordination** occurs when the child learns to respect and to obey a succession of parental authority substitutes: a teacher, a crossing guard, the gym coach, and so on.
2. **Social accommodation** involves learning to accept and tolerate familial and social diversity through exposure to a variety of new and significant others.

Preadolescence

The key characteristic of preadolescence is the strong emergence of a trend already present in the juvenile epoch: the need for a close friend or what Sullivan termed a "chum" of the same sex. The preadolescent epoch begins with the establishment of a friendship with a same-sexed peer to the emergence of an interest and a need for a partner of the opposite sex.

The significance of the need for a chum is in the character of the relationship. For the first time, the chum is a person who has equal importance to self. His or her interests, needs, and fantasies are on the same level of importance as those of the preadolescent. The preadolescent has developed a real sensitivity to the needs of the other person.

> And this is not in the sense of "what should I do to get what I want," but instead "what should I do to contribute to the happiness or to support the prestige and feeling of worth-whileness of my chum." (Sullivan, 1953b, p. 245)

The relationship that develops between chums is termed collaboration because each of the chums validates the personal worth of the other. They collaborate mutually to validate desires, conceptions of the world, and interpretations of the self:

> Because one draws so close to another, because one is newly capable of seeing oneself through the other's eyes, the preadolescent phase of personality development is especially significant in correcting autistic, fantastic ideas about oneself or others. (Sullivan, 1953b, p. 248)

Early Adolescence

Early adolescence is characterized by feelings of "lust" (1953b, p. 263). Most adolescents have experienced orgasm, and the feelings of sexual arousal are a new and continual component of the self-image. A variety of collisions between the feelings of lust and the needs for security and intimacy often occur. It is typical of adolescence in modern secular society that burgeoning sexual needs cause a reevaluation of the self-image in the light of growing doubts about sexual competence and proficiency.

> Ridicule from parents and other elders is among the worst tools that are used on early adolescents. Sometimes a modification of ridicule is used by parents ... and this modification takes the form of interfering with, objecting to, criticizing and otherwise getting in the way of any detectable movement of their child toward a member of the other sex. (Sullivan, 1953b, p. 268)

There are also collisions between the need for intimacy and lustful feelings. Adolescents often feel awkward and clumsy in their first advances to a member of the other sex, particularly so when that person has already been idealized and idolized. Groups of male adolescents may distinguish between "good" girls and the more permissive ones. When there is a double standard, sexual intercourse or genital stimulation is thought to apply only to the latter group, with the "good" girls reserved as more or less potential marriage partners.

Biographical material on Sullivan's childhood indicates that his description of the whole adolescent epoch was consistent with his own painful struggle in the area of male sexuality. One might question to what extent his developmental theory of early adolescence largely reflects culturally determined behaviors rather than being universal.

Late Adolescence: The Mask

Late adolescence extends from the focused expression of genital sexual activity through the establishment of a full repertoire of adult interpersonal relations (1953b, p. 297). The predominant mode of experience is syntaxic. The most important behavioral characteristics of late adolescence are the establishment of vocational identity or the decision to pursue an educational course leading to some professional role.

For the first time, adolescents may experience real "restrictions in living." Inhibitions or hindrances based on past developmental failures or other handicaps stemming from their past emotional interactions may curtail their range of adult choices for a job, for education, or for a mate. Respect for self must be based on learned respect for others. Without this mutuality of concern and performance, the adolescent is likely to develop a variety of techniques for isolating and preventing further development to full maturity.

To cope with the puzzling inner and outer changes that they experience, adolescents on the threshold of adulthood may experiment with aspects of all the "selves" they have been up to now. Sullivan described this compartmentalization of character with the metaphor of the mask in the first book he wrote:

> The adolescent may begin the "life behind a mask" that tends to characterize numbers of our urban denizens. The mask, however, requires so much energy for its successful maintenance that personality growth is apt to end with its successful construction. As the necessities for masking certain motivations vary from one to another interpersonal situation, it may be easier to avoid further integration of the self, and to develop, from this point onward, specialized accommodations and interests for various groups. (Sullivan, 1972, p. 201)

In effect, such an adolescent has failed to integrate the many self-conceptions and reflected appraisals that constitute the personality into a functioning unity. Instead, an artificial facade that may fit into some peer groups is developed.

EVALUATING HARRY STACK SULLIVAN

Harry Stack Sullivan is frequently considered a neo-Freudian, but he does not fit that label easily. Unlike the other neo-Freudians, Sullivan did not actually rebel against Freud's ideas, rather, he merely ignored those he found uncongenial. Sullivan was an eclectic borrower from many other theorists. He had a broad range of interests in the social sciences, linguistics, and anthropology. Findings or concepts from each of these fields are, in some way, integrated into his theory. But Sullivan was first and foremost a psychiatrist whose primary duty was the treatment of patients, and much of his focus was clinical rather than theoretical. His interpersonal theory arose out of this clinical, social, and scientific mixture.

Refutability of Sullivan's Concepts

Because the main thread that runs through Sullivan's ideas is a psychodynamic one, he shares with other psychoanalytically oriented theorists a general lack of refutability that such theories embody. Many of his main concepts, however, are in principle testable, but not in the form he stated them. For example, his conception of the self-system as a group of self-protective processes with selective inattention as the "motor" of self-protection could be re-conceptualized in testable cognitive and perceptual terms. But his more abstracted and psychodynamic constructs, such as the "Not-Me" and the "Bad-Me," are couched in non-observable referents and are beyond empirical testing. Sullivan's theory, however useful clinically, has not generated empirical research.

Sullivan's emphasis on the psychological causation of schizophrenia has been largely refuted. Recent research and clinical advances have pointed to a superabundance of dopamine as being a major causal factor in schizophrenia. Medications that reduce dopamine levels reduce schizophrenic symptoms. To what extent environmental or psychological factors, such as ones to which Sullivan alludes, may result in too much dopamine has not been determined. As far as improving the life of schizophrenic patients, demonstration of the value of Sullivan's work in therapeutic wards is handicapped by the lack of comparison or control groups. Given that many of Sullivan's patients improved, we therefore do not know whether such improvement is a result of the specifics of his treatment approach or simply of a kind, caring, and respectful environment. He should, in any case, be given a good deal of credit for not "giving up" on or warehousing his schizophrenic patients.

Sullivan's Conception of Human Agency

Sullivan has an essentially interactive viewpoint with respect to personality functioning. He emphasized that personality develops in social interaction, so that without the multiple perspectives of others' views of self, the self would be empty. But Sullivan also acknowledged that each person constructs his or her own interpretations of others, the "personifications" supported by selective inattention, and he believed that each person acts on that set of beliefs. The balance, therefore, appears to be toward an active and even interactive agency viewpoint. Interpersonal relationships shape us, and we have the power to shape our relationships.

The Nomothetic Aims of Sullivan's Theory

More than other psychodynamic theorists, Sullivan emphasized the importance of human relationships and the influence of cultural variables. His theoretical focus was nomothetic. But, as a clinician, his focus on individual psychopathology and its treatment raised idiographic issues.

On balance, Sullivan's theory would be classed as nomothetic, but, unfortunately, a nomothetic theory that has yet to generate empirical validation for its generalizations. His scheme of development through the various epochs from infancy to adolescence would certainly lend itself to nomothetic research, but no one has taken up the challenge of conducting such research.

SUMMARY

Sullivan viewed personality as the set of characteristic and habitual interpersonal relations that mark a human life. The most significant of these is the mothering-infant relationship. Because the mother or mother figure can communicate anxiety to the infant, and because the infant's needs arouse in her a corresponding need to show her infant tenderness, Sullivan characterized the relationship as an "empathic linkage." The ways in which the mothering one responds to the infant's behaviors shapes the three personifications of the self: Good-Me, Bad-Me, and the uncanny Not-Me.

Sullivan also emphasized the unity of human endeavor in his *one-genus postulate:* "We are all much more simply human than otherwise." Thus, even psychotherapists are to be conceptualized as *participant observers*, for they, too, bring to the therapeutic relationship strictly human experiences and qualities.

As infants progress through the various stages of growth and psychological development, they experience reality in vastly more abstract ways than were possible in their first months of existence. Sullivan conceptualized three levels or modes of experiencing in the earliest years:

1. The infant's first perceptions of self and the universe are fused, vague, and in continuous flux. Called the *prototaxic mode*, this early form of experience is primarily sensory and predominantly egocentric.

2. In the *parataxic mode*, temporal contiguity is interpreted as causality.

3. Finally, the child begins to enter the *syntaxic mode* in which reality is interpreted on its own terms, and the most important tool that the child brings to bear is language.

Sullivan's conception of me-you patterns of personification was yet another indication of his growing sense of the importance of social interaction for psychiatry. Sullivan's emphasis on the importance of interpersonal experiences along with his understanding of early stages of thought and experience led to his insightful, humane, and empathic approach to schizophrenic patients.

Sullivan divided personality development into six epochs: infancy, childhood, juvenile, preadolescence, early adolescence, and late adolescence. The significant advances represented by the successive stages center on the increasing emphasis on more sophisticated modes of experiencing reality and on the growing need for intimate relationships with significant others.

Our evaluation of Sullivan's theory suggests that it is a largely untestable one, with a few exceptions, such as his concept of selective inattention, his developmental scheme, and his notion of "personifications." These concepts would require creative research to derive an empirically testable version from Sullivan's imprecise theoretical prose. Sullivan aimed to be nomothetic in his theory-building, but large segments of the theory are fundamentally idiographic.

The most important aspect of Sullivan's view of personality was that he pointed out that, from early infancy, this is a world of interpersonal relations. Our feelings and emotions—both painful and joyful—are tied up with our interactive relations to significant others. In his view, our basic ways of dealing with life emerge from our earliest and deepest experiences with others.

FOR FURTHER READING

Sullivan's major work, *The Interpersonal Theory of Psychiatry* (New York: Norton, 1968), is a combined series of lectures.

Two major biographies are available. They are Helen Swick-Perry's *Psychiatrist of America: The Life of Harry Stack Sullivan* (Cambridge, MA: Belknap Press of Harvard University, 1962) and A.H. Chapman's *Harry Stack Sullivan: The Man and His Work* (New York: Putnam, 1976).

Additional bibliographic and Internet sources are indicated on the *Beneath the Mask* web page for Chapter 9. This can be found on the John Wileys higher education web page: www.wiley.com/college/sollod

GLOSSARY

Absolute euphoria: A state of complete well-being, roughly similar to total peace, complete freedom from desire and need. Like absolute tension, a hypothetical extreme that rarely occurs.

Absolute tension: The "maximum possible deviation from absolute euphoria" as, for example, experiencing terror or panic.

Anxiety: Sullivan asserted that the experience of anxiety has its origins in an infant's interpersonal experiences. A mother who is tense and fearful passes on those feelings to her vulnerable infant.

Apathy: A withdrawn "I don't care" orientation to an infant's experiences of unsatisfied needs such as hunger, thirst, and pain.

Bad-Me: A personification that is made up of those experiences that have been punished or disapproved of by the mother. It stems from unpleasant or embarrassing interpersonal relationships, and it contains those behaviors of which we are ashamed. This self-image is associated with feelings of anxiety.

Dynamism: Energy transformations that become habitual behavioral patterns of relating to others that characterize the individual throughout life.

Egocentric: In childhood, the absorption in one's own play, ideas, and pursuits. Awareness of a playmate is usually less important.

Egocentrism: Being absorbed in one's own ideas or needs; lacking awareness or attentiveness to the reactions or experiences of others. In Sullivan's theory, such developmentally based egocentrism is characteristic of childhood.

Empathic resonance: The capacity of an infant or child to feel the mother's feelings, and vice versa.

Good-Me: A personification that consists of those aspects of ourselves we feel good about, and for which we have been praised in the past. This self-image is associated with feelings of security resulting from a nurturing, satisfying, and pleasing relationship with a mothering figure.

Gradient of anxiety: A means of an infant's gauging the desirability of its various behaviors. The gradient of anxiety ranges from relatively mild tension-evoking behaviors to behaviors that elicit intense negative emotions.

Malevolent transformation: The development of a malevolent attitude toward others. This change in attitude can occur when children have been denied tenderness and affectionate care. They come to repress any need for tenderness and treat others with hostility and unfriendliness.

Not-Me: A personification that is made up of those inchoate and threatening aspects of ourselves, from which we dissociate and keep in the unconscious. This personification of self embodies all the unacceptable behaviors that are accompanied by "uncanny" feelings of anxiety.

One-genus postulate: The concept that "Everyone and anyone is much more simply human than otherwise, more like everyone else than different." Sullivan focused on the continuity of mental processes from normality through psychosis.

Parataxic mode: The perception of events in a temporal sequence, one after the other. The infant comes to expect an event by what immediately precedes or follows it.

Participant observer: Sullivan's concept that the clinical investigator is not only a scientific observer but also an involved participant who is insightful regarding his or her own reactions.

Personality: A series of interpersonal dynamisms, habitual patterns of relating to others, originally designed to reduce anxiety and obtain satisfaction.

Personifications: Mental images we have of ourselves and other people. Also, conceptions of the self that are formed in the relationship with the mothering figure.

Prototaxic mode: The simplest and crudest mode of experiencing reality at the beginning of life in which the infant's experience is limited to a constant stream of sensory events over which it cannot impose order or consistency.

Schizophrenia: A variety of disorders characterized by bizarre, seemingly unconnected cognitive and verbal processes and often of psychotic proportions. Sullivan focused on psychological causation, whereas contemporary psychiatry emphasizes the biochemistry involved in this syndrome.

Security operations: The process of denying or distorting interpersonal experiences that contradict or upset an individual's self-image.

Selective inattention: A method of ignoring or rejecting stimuli, which serves to alleviate the influence of anxiety-provoking stimuli. This defense mechanism may lead to distortion of reality.

Self-system/self-dynamism: A cluster of security operations. It begins when the infant begins to develop a habitual pattern of behaviors in dealing with others, to minimize anxiety and to gain the greatest satisfaction.

Significant others: Those people who have important interpersonal relationships with an individual.

Social accommodation: In Sullivan's view, the second of the two main factors leading to development during the juvenile years. It involves learning to accept and tolerate familial and social diversity through exposure to a variety of new and significant others.

Social subordination: In Sullivan's theory, one of the two main factors leading to development during the juvenile years. It consists of the respecting and obeying a succession of authority figures.

Somnolent detachment: Literally, the separation from reality that occurs by being sleepy. From the infant's point of view, somnolent detachment involves not only a "don't care" attitude but also a forthright indifference to those who are seen as responsible for neglecting the infant's desires.

Syntaxic mode: Adult, logical, and analytical thought processes. The experience of reality in the syntaxic mode includes the ability to predict cause and effect.

Theorem of Escape: Sullivan's theorem that the self-system tends to escape the influence of experiences that are incongruous with its current organization and functional activity.

Chapter 10

Karen Horney

Psychoanalytic Social Psychology

For the very reason that love in our civilization is so rarely a genuine affection, maltreatment and betrayal abound.

Karen Horney, *Our Inner Conflicts*

Karen Horney   Born: 1885   Blankenese, Germany
                             Died: 1952   New York, New York

About Horney's Social Psychoanalytic Approach

Karen Horney began as a psychoanalytic theorist. However, she soon found classical Freudian ideas too restrictive in their emphasis on sexual and aggressive motives. She widened and modified classical psychoanalysis with her concepts of:

- Childhood as a period of anxious helplessness and hidden anger toward all-powerful but indifferent adults.
- Neurotic strategies to cope with the anxiety and anger that alienate the person from the true self; the neurotic person is not comfortable in his or her own skin but must avoid, attack, or completely comply with others.
- Male envy of the ability of women to give birth (womb envy) and to breast-feed.
- A desexualized Oedipus complex, in which the key issues are power and love rather than sexuality and guilt.
- The importance of culture, not biology, in determining personality makeup and areas of conflict.

Horney transcended Freudian classical theory in her search to understand people based on factors other than the gratification of sexual and aggressive drives.

ANXIOUS IN A HOSTILE WORLD

Alfred Adler (Chapter 4) had earlier emphasized that children correctly perceive themselves to be weak and insignificant in the face of powerful "giants" such as parents, other adults, as well as stronger or smarter peers. Some of Adler's ideas served as the jumping-off point for Horney's conceptions. Horney's concept of basic anxiety is similar to Adler's notion of the inferiority feelings of childhood. Like Adler, Horney also asserted that one of children's most important experiences is an awareness of their vulnerability and dependence.

There are significant differences, however, between Horney's and Adler's approaches. Adler considered inferiority feelings to be an inevitable and *universal* aspect of human nature. In Horney's theory—what she termed the **basic anxiety**—was seen as a result of hostility and mistreatment, especially by parents. "It [the basic anxiety] may be roughly described as a feeling of being small, insignificant, helpless, deserted, endangered, in a world that is out to abuse, cheat, attack, humiliate, betray, envy" (Horney, 1937, p. 92). Horney thought such a hostile environment was prevalent but certainly *neither inevitable nor universal*. In fact, theorists such as Anna Freud and Karen Horney have helped many people develop a deeper appreciation of the importance of becoming loving and nurturing parents.

Another difference between the two approaches is that Adler stressed that hostility was not the only outcome of inferiority feelings. He thought that more constructive choices were possible. Adler's *The Practice and Theory of Individual Psychology* (Totowa, NJ: Littlefield, Adams, 1999) provides some comparisons of Adler's theory with Horney's ideas.

The "Basic Evil" Also Leads to Basic Hostility

To Horney, a coldly indifferent, often hostile, rejecting and domineering attitude of a child's parents, is what she termed the **basic evil.**

> The basic evil is invariably a lack of genuine warmth and affection. A child can stand a great deal of what is often regarded as traumatic—such as sudden weaning, occasional beating, sex experiences—as long as inwardly he feels wanted and loved.... *The main reason why a child does not recieve enough warmth and affection lies in the parent's incapacity to give it on account of their own neuroses.* ... We find various actions or attitudes on the part of the parents which cannot but arouse hostility, such as preference for other children, unjust reproaches, unpredictable changes between overindulgence and scornful rejection, unfulfilled promises, and not least important, *an attitude toward the child's needs which goes through all gradations from temporary inconsideration to a consistent interfering with the most legitimate wishes of the child*, such as disturbing friendships, ridiculing independent thinking, spoiling its interest in its own pursuits ... *altogether an attitude of the parents which if not in intention nevertheless in effect means breaking the child's will.* (1937, pp. 80–81; italics added)

Horney wrote at length on the types of mistreatment of children by their parents. Some parents, she asserted, dominate their children in part by teaching them to be generally fearful. They impress their children with the "great dangers of life": germs, cars, strangers, other children, and on and on. In consequence, such children become apprehensive lest they be unable to survive in such a dangerous world without their parents' help. Furthermore, they learn to fear the parents themselves because they have the awesome power to evoke images of dangers.

A child who is subjected to parental indifference, interference, and inconsistency usually develops not only the *basic anxiety* but an attitude of deep resentment, or what Horney termed **basic hostility.**

In 1937, Horney provided a definitive statement defining the basic anxiety and indicating its relation to basic hostility.

> The condition that is fostered or brought about by the factors I have mentioned...is an insidiously increasing, all-pervading *feeling of being lonely and helpless in a hostile world*....This attitude as such does not constitute a neurosis but it is the nutritive soil out of which a definite neurosis may develop at any time. Because of the fundamental role this attitude plays in neuroses I have given it a special designation: the *basic anxiety*; it is inseparably interwoven with a *basic hostility*. (Horney, 1937, p. 89; italics added)

Both the *basic anxiety* and a *basic hostility* are thus consequences of the *basic evil* of parental mistreatment.

Anxious Attachment: Repressing Basic Hostility for Survival and Security

Unloving and uncaring parents leave children feeling dependent, frightened, helpless or guilty. Such feelings get in the way of their being capable of fully experiencing their basic hostility or of expressing their anger at being so poorly treated (Horney, 1937, p. 85). The result of having hostility and anger seething within is that the child feels *unworthy of affection* and a resulting sense of *anxious attachment* to the rejecting parents.

The relationship of some children toward an uncaring adult is like a statement to the effect that, *"I have to repress my hostility because I need you"* (Horney, 1937, p. 86). Repressing expressions of hostility to adults, a child may then displace those hostile feelings against a safe target, his or her own self. For other children, repression of hostility is a product of fear of their intimidating parents. Their behavior signifies that, *"I have to repress my hostility because I am afraid of you"* (Horney, 1937, p. 86). Finally, children whose parents express superficial or phony affection may nonetheless cling desperately. Their relationship signifies, *"I have to repress my hostility for fear of losing love"* (Horney, 1937, p. 86). In all these situations, a child seeks to sustain satisfying contact with parental figures.

Other children respond to the "basic evil" by developing a compliant attitude as a self-protective defense. If children come to feel that they can survive only by complying with others and by placating them—*"If you love me, you will not hurt me"*—they may solve their survival problems by offering the world a passive, nonassertive, appeasing personality (Horney, 1937, p. 97).

Other children may develop the attitude that life is a struggle, which must be fought by maintaining an aggressive stance toward others: *"If I have power, I shall not be hurt"* (Horney, 1937, p. 97). These children's characteristic interaction with others involves keeping others at arm's length or by exerting dominance over them.

BOX 10.1 *Only Connect...*

We see in Horney's theory an awareness of the same dynamic that Anna Freud (Chapter 6) and later social psychologists have pointed out in the concept of *identification with the aggressor*. One example of this pattern is the "Patty Hearst syndrome," in which a person identifies and actively cooperates with a person holding him or her hostage. Other examples are what happens in an abusive parent/child or marital relationship, both of which Karen Horney herself experienced first as a child and then as a wife.

Last, children may solve the conflict between unexpressed basic hostility and basic anxiety by withdrawal from others: *"If I withdraw, nothing can hurt me"* (Horney, 1937, p. 99). Such children avoid any significant emotional interactions.

NEUROTIC[1] NEEDS AND TRENDS

The child has been made aware that his or her feelings of hostility and anger cannot be openly displayed. He or she represses them to avoid further parental indifference, inconsistency, or withdrawal of love. The child comes to anticipate the world and its people as a source of pain and anxiety. Out of these anticipations the child develops rigid, compulsive, and indiscriminate strivings, which Horney termed **neurotic needs,** to predict, control, and survive a hostile world.

Neurotic needs differ from those experienced by psychologically more normal people. Such needs:

- evidence disproportionate intensity,
- are indiscriminately applied to others,
- evidence an extreme disregard for reality, and
- show a tendency to provoke intense anxiety when unsatisfied.

Karen Horney further elaborated that the neurotic personality is governed by one or more of ten **neurotic trends.** These are the associated strategies to satisfy the neurotic needs. Each neurotic trend is directed toward interpersonal control and coping. These ten neurotic needs (Horney, 1942, pp. 54–60) and their associated strategies or "trends" are as follows:

1. *The neurotic need for affection and approval:* an indiscriminate desire to please others and to be liked and approved of by others. The person's "center of gravity" is in others, not in self.

2. *The neurotic need for a "partner" who will take over one's life:* a partner who will fulfill all expectations the neurotic has in life; who will take responsibility for good and evil, success and failure. The neurotic so inclined has a tendency to overvalue "love" because love can solve everything.

3. *The neurotic need to restrict one's life within narrow borders:* a necessity to be undemanding and contented with little; a need to remain inconspicuous, belittling one's potential.

4. *The neurotic need for power, for control over others, and for a facade of omnipotence:* domination over others craved for its own sake; essential disrespect for others; indiscriminate adoration of strength and contempt for weakness; belief in the power of reason and intelligence; extreme value placed on foresight and prediction; tendency to relinquish wishes and to withdraw because of dread of failure.

---

[1]The term *neurotic* is not a current diagnostic label. Many people formerly labeled as neurotic would be considered to be suffering from some form of anxiety disorder, a more behaviorally defined term. Horney often used the term *neurotic* to indicate patterns of extreme and inflexible approaches to life. The current diagnostic term most similar to Horney's meaning is *personality disorder*. Such a label indicates a deeply ingrained, inflexible, and maladaptive pattern of behavior. The person usually has little or no insight into such a behavior pattern (APA, 2000, 685–729). Three personality types very similar to Horney's descriptions are *dependent personality disorder*, *obsessive-compulsive personality disorder*, and *avoidant personality disorder*.

5. *The neurotic need to exploit others and get the better of them:* others evaluated primarily according to whether they can be exploited or made use of; dread of being exploited or made to look "stupid."

6. *The neurotic need for social recognition or prestige:* self-evaluation dependent entirely on public acceptance; all things and people evaluated only in terms of prestige value.

7. *The neurotic need for personal admiration:* inflated image of self; need to be admired not for what one possesses or presents in the public eye but for the imagined self.

8. *The neurotic ambition for personal achievement:* self-evaluation dependent on being the very best lover, athlete, writer, worker—particularly in one's own mind—recognition by others being vital too, however, and its absence resented.

9. *The neurotic need for self-sufficiency and independence:* necessity never to need anybody, or to yield to any influence, or to be tied down to anything; necessity to avoid any closeness that involves the danger of enslavement.

10. *The neurotic need for perfection and unassailability:* ruminations or recriminations regarding possible flaws; relentless driving for perfection; feelings of superiority over others because of being perfect.

Some overlaps and similarities can be found among the ten needs and the associated strategies to satisfy these needs, the neurotic trends. Horney devoted a great deal of her later theoretical efforts to grouping these ten discrete trends into clusters and categories descriptive of particular personalities.

Horney distinguished her theory of neurotic trends from those of the other theorists with whose ideas she was most familiar:

> Freud believed that the [neurotic] disturbances generate from a conflict between environmental factors and repressed instinctual impulses. Adler, more rationalistic and superficial than Freud, believes that they are created by the ways and means that people use to assert their superiority over others. Jung, more mystical than Freud, believes in collective unconscious fantasies, which, though replete with creative possibilities, may work havoc because the unconscious strivings fed by them are the exact opposite of those in the conscious mind. *My own answer is that in the center of psychic disturbances are unconscious strivings developed in order to cope with life despite fears, helplessness, and isolation.* I have called them "neurotic trends." (1942, p. 40; italics added)

Horney eventually grouped neurotic trends into *three* categories: *compliance, aggression,* and *withdrawal.* Some neurotic personalities are individuals who have the tendency of compliance and try to please and pacify others. At the opposite extreme, there are some who are typically hostile or display aggression toward others. Yet a third form of interpersonal strategy is exemplified by neurotic individuals who remain coldly aloof and detached. These people experience the world and other people as essentially troublesome and unjustly demanding. Their solution is withdrawal from significant interaction with others.

PERSONAL SOURCES OF THE BASIC ANXIETY AND BASIC HOSTILITY HYPOTHESES

Karen Horney's lucid portrait of a child's resentment to parental indifference and of helplessness in the face of a hostile world reflects her own experiences. We turn now to a consideration of Karen Horney's life story to trace the roots of her special sensitivity to children's feelings of rejection and their strategies for coping with them.

Karen Horney was born in 1885 to a German ship's captain, Berndt Wackels Danielson, and his second, much younger wife, Clotilde. Captain Danielson already had four children by his previous marriage. The captain's children did not accept his new wife, and they resented the two children born into the second marriage, Berndt and his younger sister, Karen. Moreover, the marriage between the dominant, authoritarian and sexist sea captain and his young bride was a difficult one. When Karen was almost twenty years old, Clotilde Danielson finally separated from Captain Danielson (Quinn, 1987, p. 20; Rubins, 1978, p. 8).

Young Karen's Unhappy Family Life

When Karen's brother Berndt was born, he fulfilled the family tradition by carrying on the family name. He was a boy, he was wanted, and he became his parents' darling (Rubins, 1978, p. 10). Karen's birth, four years later, came at a time when the relationship between her parents had grown abrasive. "Karen questioned whether she had really been wanted" (Rubins, 1978, p. 11).

Captain Danielson sought to impose a particularly strict and narrow interpretation of Biblical teachings on his wife and children. On occasion, after a long period of silent Bible reading, he would erupt into one of his frequent explosions of anger and throw his Bible at his wife. The children later referred to their father as *der Bibelschmeisser* (the Bible-thrower), when he was not present (Rubins, 1978, p. 11). Captain Danielson believed that men were created intellectually and morally superior to women and should have more privileges and status. "What was permitted the male could not be tolerated in the female. His son Berndt would be allowed freedom, privilege, education; these were not necessary for his wife or youngest daughter" (Rubins, 1978, p. 11).

Danielson's wife, nicknamed "Sonni," was beautiful and sophisticated. Karen's relationship with her mother was close, loving, and devoted. Sonni often came to the girl's rescue in disputes with the father. Rubins (1978, p. 13) speculates she identified with her daughter's talents and wishes, thus vicariously fulfilling her own blocked ambitions. As the children grew older, they—along with their mother—formed a "protective alliance" against their father (Rubins, 1978, p. 13).

In her childhood, Karen generally felt deprived of affection. Her coping style up to the age of eight was to behave "like a little lamb" (Rubins, 1978, p. 13). Once, she even placed some of her toys on the street for some poorer child to find. She told no one about her altruistic deed because self-sacrifice was her way of being the good child she hoped her parents would love. (See Horney's semi-autobiographical case history and comments in Horney, 1950, p. 20, and 1942, pp. 190 ff.)

During her school years, Karen was an unhappy child. She found her home life intolerable. She was also self-conscious and displeased with her appearance even though she was considered strikingly good-looking. She seized upon schoolwork and achievement as a way of compensating for her unhappiness at home and with her appearance. "As she said years later to her daughter, 'If I couldn't be beautiful, I decided I would be smart'" (Rubins, 1978, p. 14A).

At puberty, Karen displayed open and excessive affection toward her brother Berndt. Such displays contrasted with her more genuine feelings of resentment toward him. Berndt found his sister's loving protestations embarrassing and rebuffed her. His rejection proved overwhelming for Karen: "It was a blow to her pride; . . . she felt ashamed and humiliated" (Rubins, 1978, p. 14).

After Karen showed signs of depression, the family doctor told her parents that the strain of schoolwork caused her depression. Her parents then transferred her to a lower grade. As a response, Karen vowed to be first in her class always!

By the age of 12, she had decided on a career in medicine. This career was almost unheard of for women at the time. Karen's sexist father predictably opposed her pursuit of a medical career, but Karen's mother was encouraging. With the support of her brother and mother, Karen finally convinced her father to provide the tuition to enter a preparatory program. Karen promised in writing to ask nothing more of her father if he would help her attain the goal of a medical education (Rubins, 1978, p. 21).

On the whole, Karen felt rejected by her father and less loved than her brother Berndt. Nonetheless she did have some positive feelings toward her father and had some good times with him. She admired and respected him and was caught up in the romantic vision of his far-ranging sea travels. For his part, in addition to providing some financial support for her academic progress, Captain Danielson took his daughter to accompany him on at least three lengthy voyages aboard his ship. He also occasionally brought her gifts from his travels (Rubins, 1978, p. 12).

An Antireligious Rebellion

Given her family background, it is not surprising that Karen had conflicting feelings toward religion while growing up. She questioned some fundamental religious beliefs. At one point, Berndt lovingly guided her to one way of understanding what to her was the contradiction contained in the belief that Jesus was both man and God. Karen confided to her diary: " 'Something like a stone fell from my heart. . . . He [Jesus] became dearer to me' " (Rubins, 1978, p. 18).

Her struggles with religious belief were a continuing theme. At the time of her confirmation, religious authority merged in her thinking with her father's domineering and abusive authoritarianism, yet she still expressed a yearning for spiritual faith. Karen wrote in her diary:

> It must be grand to have a father one can love and esteem. The Fourth Commandment stands before me like a specter, with its "Thou shalt." I cannot respect a person who makes us all unhappy with his hypocrisy, egocentricity, crudeness and illbreeding. . . . [These are] indescribable days for Mother and us under the fearful domination of the master of the house and our pastor. Pen and paper would rebel against writing down anything so coarse and mean. Confirmation was no blessing for me. On the contrary, it was a great piece of hypocrisy, for I professed belief in the teachings of Christ, the doctrine of love, while carrying hatred in my heart (and for my nearest at that). I feel too weak to follow Christ. Yet I long for the faith, firm as a rock, that makes oneself and others happy. (Quoted by Rubins, 1978, p. 19; see also Horney, 1980, p. 37)

As Rubins notes, Karen could not openly express her lack of respect for her father and what she saw as his hypocrisy (1978, p. 19). As she confided years later to her friend Franz Alexander she did not feel capable of "'standing up to the frightening gaze of my father's blue eyes'" (Rubins, 1978, p. 19).

Horney's Relationship with Her Husband and Children

In 1906, Karen Danielson entered a medical school in Freiburg. It was one of the few medical schools in Germany that admitted women, and Karen was the only woman in her class. Even in this all-male environment, Karen relished a new-found sense of freedom and independence. During this exciting time, she became friends with Oskar Horney, an economics student on vacation from his own studies at the University of Brunswick. Karen was attracted to Oskar, a stern man who radiated confidence and physical strength. She engaged in an intimate correspondence with him, one in which she expressed her changing attitudes toward her mother. Sonni had become, in her daughter's less idealized view, basically a good person but one who was also coldhearted and lacking in self-control (Rubins, 1978, p. 31).

In 1909, Karen and Oskar were married. He had graduated law school and was employed by an investment firm. By 1910, Karen was pregnant with her first child, Brigitte. Shortly before Brigitte's birth, Sonni suffered a stroke; she died one week later in February 1911. Karen graduated from medical school in 1913. Thus, in a relatively short space of time, Karen had experienced profound changes—her marriage, a death, and the giving of new life. She also had successfully pursued her career goals. It is not surprising, with all of these stressors and given her susceptibility, that she became depressed.

At this time, she was also undergoing her own personal psychoanalysis with Karl Abraham in preparation for a career in psychiatry. The net effect of all these experiences, along with the reexamination of childhood conflicts necessitated by the analysis, has been well summarized by Rubins (1978, p. 38):

> Karen's ambivalent feelings toward her father, her dependency upon her mother and her struggle to free herself from this dependency, her longstanding resentment at playing a secondary role to her brother, the conflict within herself between the roles of assertive professional woman and the compliant childbearing homemaker—all these had to be confronted.

> The outcome of her psychoanalysis was not satisfying and, given the quality of her marital relationship, did not alter the pattern of relating to her husband. Karen remained depressed. She even asked in a letter to her analyst, "Does not the real work begin after the analysis? The analysis shows one her enemies but one must battle them afterwards, day by day" (Quinn, 1987, pp. 157 ff. and pp. 193 ff; Rubins, 1978, p. 39).

Karen and Oskar Horney eventually had three daughters. Karen had found in Oskar a man who repeated the domineering severity of Karen's father. Karen was acquiescent even when he became physically abusive. One Christmas dinner, Marianne, the middle daughter, leaned back too far in her chair at the table. Grabbing hold of the tablecloth, she pulled with her to the floor an entire new dinner service and the elaborate meal as well. Oskar spanked Marianne viciously with a dog whip. Brigitte, the eldest, cried in sympathy, but Karen showed no outward reaction to her daughter's plight (Rubins, 1978, p. 51). All three of the girls recalled that Karen generally exhibited a detached indifference toward them.

> She would not interfere with their growing up, with their comings and goings. But the children felt that this noninterference might have bordered at times on neglect: Their clothes were often too long or too short; their stockings did not fit. A governess was no longer needed now that they were all in school, and the maids did not look after them personally. (Rubins, 1978, p. 83)

And this cold and indifferent behavior was that of a mother who herself had been so desperate for parental warmth and affection as a child.

Karen's marriage gradually began to disintegrate over personality differences and the burden of professional obligations. In 1923, Oskar's investments collapsed and his salary (in inflated currency) from his bankrupt firm was worth little. He borrowed heavily, contracted encephalomeningitis during a business trip to Paris, and eventually returned home as a broken, defeated, spiritless man. He became morose, withdrawn, and argumentative. As their finances deteriorated, so did their marriage. In 1926, Karen and her daughters separated from Oskar by moving into a small apartment with their few possessions. Some ten years later, Karen filed for divorce, which finally became official in 1939.

Berndt's Death

Throughout her life, beginning with her brother's rejection of her effusive protestations of love for him in adolescence, Karen Horney suffered periodic bouts of dejection bordering on depression. In 1923, at the height of her husband's financial difficulties, her brother Berndt died of pulmonary infection. He was 40 years old, and she was devastated at the senselessness of his death. Profound depression was the consequence. Writing to Georg Groddeck some months after Berndt's death, Karen expressed a curiously ambivalent kind of acceptance.

> ... in the beginning I considered [the death of my brother] as something totally senseless—he belonged to those people who seem to burst with the joy of living. In the face of this, after many weeks I arrived at the conclusion: something in him had wanted to die. That insight I tend to accept in general and I have only one suspicion about it, and that is that it is too much of what we want to believe. (Quoted in Rubins, 1978, p. 72)

The loss of her idealized yet resented brother was overwhelming for Karen. Shortly after Berndt's death, while on vacation at the beach with her family and friends, Karen went alone for a swim. When she failed to return after more than an hour, Oskar found her clutching a piling in deep water, ruminating on whether to end her life or swim back to the beach (Rubins, 1978, p. 87). Oskar and his friends had to plead to convince Karen that her life was worth living.

The death of her brother evoked profound depression in Karen. A possible explanation was that Berndt's death fulfilled her darkest childhood wishes for his death and simultaneously triggered the most intense adult guilt: self-punishment in suicidal longings.

Summarizing Karen Horney's Personal Problems

Overall, the central issues in Karen Horney's life centered around her profound sense of inadequacy and guilt-provoking resentment toward her parents and her brother for making her feel that way. In summary, three related themes emerge in her life history.

First, her sense of her own unwantedness and unattractiveness initially had produced a compliant, meek, over-eager-to-please child. From this stance of selflessness emerged a rebellious, skeptical, and defiant young woman, who sought by her intellectual achievements to compensate for her presumed weaknesses and to exact revenge with the evidence of her hard-won competence.

Second, Karen found herself almost unwittingly married to a man who bore more than a superficial resemblance to the authoritarian father she so resented. Avoiding confrontation, she proved unable to stand up to her husband's abusive behavior toward one of her daughters.

Third, achieving in a frowned-upon profession for women in the early 1900s, Karen adopted psychoanalytic theory, drew what intellectual and emotional sustenance she could from it, and then abandoned some of its central tenets in favor of her own insights. She rebelled against paternalistic psychoanalysis in much the same way as she had rebelled against religion and her father's conception of it, and through that revolt, against the father himself. As Rubins (1978, p. 113) tactfully phrased it: "It was the same old conflict within her that she had experienced so often before, how to be aggressive yet friendly and loving at the same time."

We turn now to the case history of "Clare," which, there is some reason to believe, contains some thinly disguised autobiographical elements of Karen Horney's own life. According to Rubins (1978, p. 17), we can catch a glimpse of Karen Horney's view of her own struggle in this case.

AN ILLUSTRATIVE CASE: CLARE, AN UNWANTED CHILD

Despite several of her mother's abortion attempts, "Clare" was born into an unhappy marriage. Her parents' first child, a boy, had been born at a time when the marriage was a happy one, and in some ways he remained the main object of parental approval and affection. Not that Clare was in any material way mistreated or abused. She always received the same quantity and quality of gifts, trips, lessons, and educational opportunities as her brother.

But in less tangible matters she received less than the brother, less tenderness, less interest in school marks and in the thousand little daily experiences of a child, less concern when she was ill, less solicitude to have her around, less willingness to treat her as a confidante, less admiration for looks and accomplishments. (Horney, 1942, p. 49)

Always away from home, Clare's father, a doctor, became the object of the mother's ridicule and loathing. Clare's mother was so bitter that she often expressed open death wishes against her husband. Clare felt that the safest course was meekly to acquiesce to her mother's expressions of rage (Horney, 1942, p. 49). The most immediate result of the family atmosphere on Clare's development was her lost opportunity to develop a sense of confidence and self-trust. As Clare matured, her feelings of unworthiness and her sense of total unlikableness grew:

> This shift from essentially true and warranted accusations of others to essentially untrue and unwarranted self-accusations had far-reaching consequences.... And the shift meant more than an acceptance of the majority estimate of herself. It meant also that she repressed all grievances against the mother. If everything was her own fault, the grounds for bearing a grudge against mother were pulled away from under her. (Horney, 1942, p. 50)

Clare thus relinquished any possibility of genuine rebellion against the injustice of her own treatment at the hands of her family. Instead, she became a "joiner," a compliant member in the circle of admirers surrounding her powerful mother. "By admiring what in reality she resented, she became alienated from her own feelings. She no longer knew what she herself liked or wished or feared or resented" (Horney, 1942, p. 51). In short, she began to act on the premise "that it is safer to admire others than to be critical."

Clare was overly modest and had a tendency to "put herself in second place," and to judge herself more critically than others did. On the surface, she lived life largely to appease and placate others. But beneath the surface, she developed a need to surpass others, to beat them at their own game. That need remained out of consciousness. It would have been dangerous to express and thus had to remain submerged.

BOX 10.2 *Only Connect...*

The distinction between the mother's treatment of Clare and of her brother is illustrative of Erik Erikson's (Chapter 8) concepts of *ritual* and *ritualization*. *Ritualization* involves meaningful participation and real bonding, but Erikson used the term *ritual*, to describe stereotyped, mechanical, empty and fundamentally meaningless interactions. Rituals involve no more than "going through the motions."

At the age of 30, Clare felt the need for psychoanalytic treatment. As an editor for a magazine, she had not fulfilled her ambition to write fiction. Her life and interests had become so constricted in the service of her compliant approach to others that she was able to perform only the routine editing work that her employer requested but was unable to engage in her own creative writing.

Fortunately, an incident occurred that helped Clare in her psychoanalysis to develop insight into the degree of her compliant and self-effacing behavior. She had developed a plan for improving the magazine, a plan she knew to be sound but that would occasion much protest and argument from other members of the staff. During the staff meeting at which she was to present her plan, Clare experienced several moments of panic. She even had to leave the room at one point because of a sudden, apparently psychogenic, attack of diarrhea. However, when the discussion began to favor her proposal, she was able to control herself and the panic diminished. After her plan proved successful in operation, she received much recognition and acclaim. Instead of viewing her success as an important milestone, however, she viewed it only as a lucky escape from great danger.

Eventually, with continued analytic treatment, Clare was able to recognize that a striving for security motivated her self-effacing behavior. She came to enjoy her successes and to take pride in her considerable abilities. A final indication of her slowly burgeoning self-confidence and realistic pride was embodied in a dream she had during the final phase of her psychoanalysis:

> ... she drove with her friend in a strange country and it occurred to her that she, too, might apply for a driver's license. Actually she had a license and could drive as well as the friend. The dream symbolized a dawning insight that she had rights of her own and need not feel like a helpless stranger. (Horney, 1942, p. 84)

DESPISED REAL SELF, IDEAL SELF, AND THE ACTUAL SELF

When children are confronted by the intense conflict between their feelings of help-lessness and repressed hostility toward their parents, they develop a defensive way of perceiving themselves. When parents are inconsistent and indifferent in their reactions toward their children, children are made to feel that their self is despicable, unlovable, and unworthy. This results in what Horney considered the **despised real self.** Children's repressed hostility turns against the self to further buttress the notion that they are unlovable and unworthy. This despised real self is not real at all. Since the picture they hold of their self is based on false evaluations by others, it is "real" only to the extent that they believe it (Horney, 1945, p. 98). When their image of this *real self* is this negative, it would more appropriately be designated as the *despised real self*.

Children necessarily begin to defensively restructure the image of the despised real self into an image of the **idealized self** or **ideal self** they should be. They do this in order to survive in a hostile world and gain needed love and approval.

> In contrast to authentic ideals, the idealized image has a static quality. It is not a goal toward whose attainment he strives but a fixed idea, which he worships. . . . The idealized image is a decided hindrance to growth because it either denies shortcomings or merely condemns them. *Genuine ideals make for humility, the idealized image for arrogance.* (Horney, 1945, p. 99; italics added)

The idealized self substitutes for genuine self-confidence and pride. It is based on a wishful-thinking style. This unrealistic ideal fills the mind of the adult neurotic with a population of "shoulds":

Forget about the disgraceful creature you actually *are* [i.e., the despised real self]; this is how you *should* be.... He should be the utmost of honesty, generosity, considerateness, justice, dignity, courage, and unselfishness. He should be the perfect lover, husband, and teacher. He should be able to endure anything, should like everybody, should love his parents, his wife, his country; or, he should not be attached to anything or anybody, nothing should matter to him, he should never feel hurt, and he should always be serene and unruffled. He should always enjoy life; or, he should be above pleasure and enjoyment. He should be spontaneous; he should always control his feelings. He should know, understand, and foresee everything. He should be able to solve every problem of his own, or of others, in no time. He should be able to overcome every difficulty of his as soon as he sees it. He should never be tired or fall ill. He should always be able to find a job. He should be able to do things in one hour which can only be done in two to three hours. (Horney, 1950, p. 65; italics in original)

This seemingly endless list of things neurotics feel they ought to be or do was termed by Horney the **"tyranny of the should"** (1950, pp. 65 ff.). The idealized self-image eventually becomes converted into an ideal self, no longer to be recognized as a fiction. It is now seen as a state of being that is nearly impossible to attain (Horney, 1950, p. 158). Nevertheless, the neurotic is compelled to strive toward this unreachable ideal in what Horney called the "search for glory" (1950, p. 23). Indeed, the ideal self slowly becomes more real to the neurotic than the despised "real" self ever was. The idealized self becomes the **comprehensive neurotic solution,** for it actualizes the fantasized image by which all problems can be solved and all difficulties surmounted. With the creation of the ideal self, the neurotic "solves" the conflict between feelings of basic anxiety and hostility; he or she learns to deal with the world and its people through the shoulds of the ideal self.

In writing about the *tyranny of the should*, it seems as though Horney was alluding to her father's rigid standards of conduct and impossible demands for moral perfection. Horney, no doubt, was expressing to some degree her own experience of these demands, as well as her striving to surpass her more favored brother.

In her later work, Horney created a further distinction among the images neurotics have of themselves. Originally Horney used the term *real self* to indicate the damaged self-image produced in children by indifferent parents. Horney later changed the usage somewhat by employing **real self** to designate the true core of a person's being, his or her very center of existence. The real self harbors all the potential for growth and health: "clarity and depth of his own feelings, thoughts, wishes, interests; the ability to tap his own resources, the strength of his will power, the special capacities or gifts he may have; the faculty to express himself, and to relate to others with his spontaneous feelings" (Horney, 1950, p. 17). It is this core that is damaged by parental indifference. The goal of the real self is the striving for self-realization, that is, the accomplishment

---

BOX 10.3   *Only Connect...*

Carl Rogers' later development of his personality theory (Chapter 13) included many ideas very similar to those engendered by Horney. For example, his concepts of conditions of worth, perceived self, and ideal self are very consistent with Horney's formulations, even though his outlook on life was much more optimistic. Horney like Rogers, also stresses the idea that people have a natural tendency for personal growth and psychological health. In a very real sense, Horney's work, though having its origins in Freudian thinking, is a precursor of humanistic psychology and well ahead of its time.

Table 10.1   Our Different Conceptions of Self

1. **Despised real self:** False conceptions of one's competence, worth, and lovability based on belief in others' evaluations, especially those of the parents. Negative evaluations may reinforce one's sense of helplessness.
2. **Real self:** The true core of one's being, containing potential for growth, happiness, will power, special capacities and gifts, and the urge for "self-realization," that is, the need to be spontaneously what one truly is.
3. **Actual self:** the objectively existing person, with physical and psychological characteristics seen independent of subjective distortions.
4. **Ideal self:** The perfect or near perfect sense of self that a person wishes to be *or imagines that he or she actually is* as a compensation for feelings of vulnerability in a hostile world.

of the person's own values and aims in life. In this sense, Horney began to use the term *real self* to indicate a "possible self," that is, a self that the individual can realistically learn to express. To a large extent, this real self is a product of the person's own perceptions, his or her own interpretations of what he or she is. Horney distinguished this subjectively real self from the person's objective reality as observed by others. Horney used the term **actual self** to describe the totality of everything that the person "really" is.

In summary, the real self is the core of the person's existence as he or she perceives it and perhaps despises it; the ideal self is a glorified image of what he or she should be, an image that is impossible to attain; the actual self is the sum of objectively observable characteristics of the person at one moment in time.

It should be pointed out that for Horney the goal of psychotherapy was to provide the individual with the means to free the real self, to accept its character, and to allow it full and spontaneous expression without the curtailment of learned defensiveness (Horney, 1946, pp. 202 ff.). Table 10.1 summarizes the differences among the real, actual, and ideal selves.

THE CORE NEUROTIC CONFLICT: ALIENATION FROM REAL SELF

The pervasive anxiety and helplessness experienced in childhood, coupled with basic hostility that cannot be expressed, causes an alienation of the individual from his or her real self. This **core neurotic conflict** is furthered by the adoption of an idealized self at the expense of one's spontaneity, self-trust, and independence. Since other people are dangerous actors in what is seen as a dangerous world, neurotics adopt defensive strategies for dealing with them: "He feels what he *should* feel, wishes what he *should* wish, likes what he *should* like" (Horney, 1950, p. 159; italics added).

> In other words, the tyranny of the should drives him frantically to be something different from what he is or could be. And in his imagination he is different—so different, indeed, that the real self fades and pales still more. Neurotic claims, in terms of self, mean the abandoning of the reservoir of spontaneous energies. Instead of making his own efforts, for instance, with regard to human relations, the neurotic insists that others should adjust to him. (Horney, 1950, p. 159; italics in original)

Three consequences of the individual's alienation from his or her real self can be discerned in the neurotic's feelings of being removed from himself or herself (Horney, 1950, pp. 159–161). These are the ways in which a neurotic person's relation to his or her own real self can be distorted:

1. *Abandonment of responsibility for one's own behavior:* The neurotic comes to feel that "I am driven instead of being the driver" (1950, p. 159).

2. *Active moves away from the real self:* The person's creative forces lie fallow as he or she succumbs to the idealized self and the search for glory embodied in "shoulds"; the ideal image must be the ever unreachable goal since only by investing all energy in such strivings can the despised real self be left behind.

3. *Active moves against the real self:* The individual experiences bouts of self-hate, with the idea of "being oneself" becoming terrifying and appalling. The neurotic has an unconscious interest in not being him—or herself, in not having a clear self-perception.

INTERPERSONAL COPING STRATEGIES: MOVES TOWARD, AGAINST, AND AWAY FROM OTHERS

Unlike Freud, who saw conflict between repressed instincts and the forces of the ethical side of personality as the core of neurosis, Horney viewed her concepts of interpersonal and intrapersonal conflict as central:

> They [i.e., the conflicts] operated between contradictory sets of neurotic trends, and though they originally concerned contradictory attitudes toward others, in time they encompassed contradictory attitudes toward the self, contradictory qualities and contradictory sets of values.... (1945, p. 15)

Horney thought that neurotic symptoms and interpersonal strategies are attempts to resolve basic conflicts. Compulsive and indiscriminate strivings, contradictory and conflicted needs for perfection, power, affection, and independence are all anxiety-allaying techniques with the purpose of maintaining the alienation between the despised real self and the ideal self, and between the real self and significant others. The ten neurotic trends or needs began to be more comprehensible to Horney as *clusters of strivings* directed toward dealing with people and their demands. Horney organized the ten needs into three patterns of traits, illustrated by the three hypothetical personalities with which we began this chapter. Let us now examine those three character types from the perspective of Horney's concept of self-alienation.

Moving Toward People: The Self-Effacing Solution

Horney had early termed one solution to neurotic conflict as **moving toward people** (Horney, 1945, pp. 48 ff.). This solution—as in the case of "Clare"—involves an individual manifesting the neurotic traits that are part of a compliant interpersonal stance. These traits include intense needs for affection and approval, a need for a partner in the form of friend, husband, wife, or lover, and a necessity to be undemanding, restricting one's life within narrow borders:

> In sum, this type needs to be liked, wanted, desired, loved; to feel accepted, welcomed, approved of, appreciated; to be needed, to be of importance to others, especially to one particular person; to be helped, protected, taken care of, guided. (Horney, 1945, p. 51)

The goal of the **compliant type** is a surface need to be in harmony with others, to avoid friction. But contradictory trends may also be served by this strategy. Compliance on the surface may mask a strong inner need to compete, to excel, to dominate (Horney, 1945, p. 56). Below the surface, within the real self, unrecognized rage, anger, and residual hostile sentiment boils. Occasionally, repressed anger will explode into fits of irritability or into temper tantrums. Or this individual may make demands on others to help "poor me." Of course, the compliant person never recognizes that such demands are manipulative of others, or that they are attempts to satisfy his or her aggressive strivings: "He cannot help feeling at times that he is so unfairly treated that he simply can't stand it any longer" (Horney, 1945, p. 58).

In her later statement of neurotic conflict (1950, pp. 214 ff.), Horney referred to the "moving toward others" strategy as the **self-effacing solution** to neurotic conflict. In effect, the self-effacing person has identified the ideal self with the restricted and subdued despised self:

> He is *his subdued self;* he is the stowaway without any rights. In accordance with this attitude he also tends to suppress in himself anything that connotes ambition, vindictiveness, triumph, seeking his own advantage. In short he has solved his inner conflict by suppressing all expansive attitudes and drives and making self-abnegating trends predominant. (Horney, 1950, p. 216)

The self-effacing type has idealized the qualities of suffering, helplessness, and martyrdom. Only by viewing oneself as "saintly" can one supply oneself with a good reason to endure the basic hostility one has never allowed oneself to express. If one is a saint, then it is reasonable that one must suffer. And suffering becomes even more enjoyable if one can spread the misery to others. Horney felt that the self-effacing "solution" was the most damaging because this strategy involves the most intense unhappiness.

Moving Against People: The Expansive Solution

The aggressive, expansive solution to neurotic conflict is based on a different view of life: on a belief that the world is a hostile place and that life "is a struggle of all against all . . ." (Horney, 1945, p. 63). Individuals with this view characteristically behave toward others in aggressive ways; they are best described as **moving against people.** They may have a facade of suave politeness and good fellowship that is designed to facilitate satisfaction of their needs for control and power. Aggressive individuals need to excel by exploiting others, to attain recognition by exerting dominance and power over those they perceive to be underlings. Success and prestige are the yardsticks to their sense of self-worth.

> Any situation or relationship is looked at from the standpoint of "What can I get out of it?"—whether it has to do with money, prestige, contacts, or ideas. *The person himself is consciously or semiconsciously convinced that everyone acts this way*, and so what counts is to do it more efficiently than the rest. (Horney, 1945, p. 65; italics added)

Where the compliant types who move toward others have a need for a mate or partner stemming from their feelings of helplessness, aggressive types desire a partner who can enhance their prestige, power, or wealth.

Horney later described this type who "moves against" people as the **expansive solution** to neurotic conflict: the appeal of mastery (1950, pp. 187 ff.). In almost every respect, the expansive solution is the direct opposite to the self-effacing solution. The expansive type glorifies and cultivates in himself or herself everything that leads to mastery of others (1950, p. 214).

> The appeal of life lies in its mastery. . . . He should be able to master the adversities of fate, the difficulties of a situation, the intricacies of intellectual problems, the resistances of other people, conflicts in himself. The reverse side of the necessity for mastery is his dread of anything connoting helplessness; this is the most poignant dread he has. (Horney, 1950, p. 192)

Unlike the compliant, self-effacing type who identifies with the despised real self, the aggressive person has come to believe that he or she is the ideal self, that he or she is the glorified image toward which he or she strives. All the behaviors of the

aggressive type can be understood as attempts to actualize the ideal self (Horney, 1950, p. 192).

Moving Away from People: The Solution of Resignation

Those individuals who develop a protective "I don't care about anything" attitude practice the third "solution" to neurotic conflict, the **solution of resignation**. They become detached from human affairs and resigned to an emotionally flat life. For if they do not allow themselves to care about anything or anyone, they think that they will never be hurt. Horney characterized this individual's dominant strategy as **moving away from people** (1945, pp. 73 ff.). Resigned individuals evidence intense needs of self-sufficiency, perfection, and unassailability. They tend to restrict their lives within narrow confines much as the compliant types do, but for resigned individuals the motive is the need never to be dependent on anyone.

Neurotic detachment is considerably different from the normal feelings each of us experiences on those occasions when we would like to be alone with our own thoughts. The neurotic has persistent feelings of indifference and withdrawal based on an "intolerable strain in associating with people" (Horney, 1950, p. 73).

> What is crucial is their inner need to put emotional distance between themselves and others. More accurately, it is their conscious and unconscious determination not to get emotionally involved with others in any way, whether in love, fight, co-operation, or competition. They draw around themselves a kind of magic circle, which no one may penetrate. (Horney, 1945, p. 75)

By their resigned attitudes and detachment, neurotic individuals who move away from others have removed themselves from the "inner battlefield" of their own conflicts. Their "don't care" demeanor provides them with a sense of superior distance, haughty removal from their own and others' "petty" problems. They become onlookers at themselves and their lives to the degree that even in therapy they remain detached and view the process of their own inner explorations as "fascinating entertainment" (Horney, 1950, p. 261).

A consequence of this "moving away from others" is the total lack of any striving for achievement or success. They are considered the **detached type**. Unconsciously, they deny any desire to achieve success or to exert effort on their own behalf. They are hypersensitive to coercion or advice and they reject both in their attempts to remain independent.

Horney identified three modes of stilted and joyless living that characterize various subtypes of the resigned neurotic:

1. *Persistent resignation:* These individuals are characterized by a continual emotional inertia. They fulfill as few of the tasks of life as are necessary to guarantee their freedom. They may pass for essentially normal, though without any observable joy in living. Their persistent resignation may be only a mask covering a feeling of rebelliousness.

2. *Rebelliousness:* The appeal of freedom and independence from others is so strong for these individuals that they actively resist the "trivia" of life. They may turn their rebellion against the self and struggle against their own inner tyrannies and shoulds. In this sense, their rebellion may actually become liberating and therapeutic.

3. *Shallow living:* This type of individual "moves to the periphery of life;" he or she is without hope or any positive commitment. In worse condition than the persistently resigned type, the one engaged in "shallow living" finds life worthless.

Eventually he or she will settle for superficial enjoyments, "high living," without meaning or direction, or will pursue opportunistic success in business. But beneath the mask of sociability, this individual is merely a "well-adapted automaton" (Horney, 1950, pp. 286–287). He or she goes through the motions of life, but is without genuine concern or involvement.

The common denominator that binds the three types of resigned neurotic is vacillation between identification with the despised real self and identification with the glorified ideal self. Detached neurotics strive halfheartedly toward actualization of the ideal self, but fundamentally they have surrendered any hope of making the glorified image come true. In effect, they are unsatisfied with the despised self, but simultaneously afraid to strive toward the goals of the ideal self. They desire to be free from all demands, rather than to be free for the pursuit of desirable activities.

Horney's description of the three patterns of neurotic conflict-solution points to an important premise of her theory. Each of the patterns is designed to minimize anxiety in dealing with people. Thus, Horney's conceptualizations emphasize her position that the neuroses are evidence of damaged interpersonal processes. Horney summarized the three attitude types in these terms:

> As we have seen, each of the basic attitudes toward others has its positive value. In moving toward people the person tries to create for himself a friendly relation to his world. In moving against people he equips himself for survival in a competitive society. In moving away from people he hopes to attain a certain integrity and serenity. As a matter of fact, all three attitudes are not only desirable but also necessary to our development as human beings. *It is only when they appear and operate in a neurotic framework that they become compulsive, rigid, indiscriminate, and mutually exclusive.* (1945, p. 89; italics added)

The three attitude types are presented together with their dominant neurotic needs in Table 10.2.

Table 10.2 "Solutions" to Neurotic Conflict

Self-effacing solution:	*Expansive solution:*	*Resignation solution:*
Love "moving toward" (compliance)	Mastery "moving against" (aggression)	Freedom "moving away" (detachment)
Need for 1. Affection and approval 2. Partner to take control 3. Restriction of life to narrow borders	*Need for* 4. Power, omnipotence, and perfection 5. Exploitation of others 6. Social recognition and prestige 7. Personal admiration 8. Personal achievement	*Need for* 3. Restrictions of life to narrow borders[a] 9. Self-sufficiency 10. Perfection and unassailability
"*If you love me, you will not hurt me.*" Identification with the despised real self	"*If I have power, no one can hurt me.*" Identification with the ideal self	"*If I withdraw, nothing can hurt me.*" Vacillation between despised real self and ideal self

[a]Need 3 is repeated from the Self-effacing solution.
Based on Horney, 1945, Chapters 3,4,5; 1942, Chapter 2; and 1950, Chapter 3.

AUXILIARY CONFLICT SOLUTIONS

In addition to the basic attitudes for dealing with others, Horney suggested that several secondary or **auxiliary conflict solutions** might be employed by neurotic personalities in their striving for security. These techniques can be conceptualized as secondary defenses. The **secondary defenses** are techniques to buttress neurotic solutions to the core neurotic conflict. Unlike Freudian defenses, they are not designed to deal with id impulses but rather to protect the person from seeing what we would consider his or her character flaws.

Externalization

Though the neurotic personality seeks to bridge the distance between the idealized self and the real self, efforts to do so paradoxically broaden the gap. In the most extreme instance, the gap between the idealized self and the real self becomes so great that the person can no longer tolerate the discrepancy. He or she must turn to external factors for the solution: "The only thing left then is to run away from himself entirely and see everything as if it lay outside" (Horney, 1945, p. 116).

Externalization is the auxiliary neurotic defense technique by which individuals shift their "center of gravity" from the self to others. Although somewhat similar to the defensive technique described by Freud as projection, externalization is much more comprehensive, for it involves the shift outward to others not only of unacceptable feelings, but of all feelings, all emotion. Other people become the center of all of the neurotic's emotional life; these external individuals become the nucleus of all important strivings that would normally be directed to and experienced by the self, from the self to others. Other people become the center of all of the neurotic's emotional life. One focuses not on how what one thinks or feels but on the thoughts and feelings of others.

Thus, one may be angry with oneself but instead attribute the anger to another: He is angry with me. A profound consequence for dealings with others emerges from this tendency to externalize:

> When a person feels that his life for good or ill is determined by others, it is only logical that he should be preoccupied with changing them, reforming *them*, punishing *them*, protecting himself from *their* interference, or impressing *them*.... Another inevitable product of externalization is a gnawing sense of emptiness and shallowness.... Instead of feeling the emotional emptiness as such, the person experiences it as emptiness in his stomach and tries to do away with it by compulsive eating. Or he may fear that his lack of bodily weight could cause him to be tossed about like a feather—any storm, he feels, might carry him away. He may even say that he would be nothing but an empty shell if everything were analyzed. (Horney, 1945, p. 117; italics added)

Such an individual can forgo any feelings of humiliation, self-hate, or self-contempt, merely assigning these damaging functions to others. He or she still feels unworthy but now has provided a rational reason for the self-hatred: Others have no use for him or her since he or she is nothing.

Creation of Blind Spots

The magnitude of the difference between neurotics' ongoing behaviors and the idealized picture of themselves can sometimes be so great that outsiders marvel that they never detect the discrepancy. The fact that neurotics never consciously admit the difference is evidence for the existence of a **blind spot**, that is, the creation of a defensive "refusal to see" their own defenses.

A patient, for example, who had all the characteristics of the compliant type and *thought of himself as Christlike*, told me quite casually that at staff meetings he would often shoot one colleague after another with a little flick of his thumb. True enough, the destructive craving that prompted these figurative killings was at that time unconscious; but the point here is that the shooting, *which he dubbed "play,"* did not in the least disturb his Christlike image. (Horney, 1945, p. 132; italics added)

Compartmentalization

Similar to blind spots, **compartmentalization** involves pigeonholing one's life into rigid and exclusive categories: Thus, there is a compartment for friends, for enemies, for family, for outsiders, a compartment for professional activities separate from personal life, and so on (Horney, 1945, p. 133). The important point is that anything that occurs in one compartment cannot contradict, influence, or support what transpires in another. "Compartmentalizing is, thus, as much a result of being divided by one's conflicts as a defense against recognizing them" (Horney, 1945, p. 134). A widely cited example is that of the man who ruthlessly runs his business affairs during the week, taking no real interest in the hurt or humiliation he causes his competitors, and on Sunday serves as the deacon of his church. Religion and business are in separate compartments, and so too, unfortunately, is his humanity. Horney herself may be viewed as someone who compartmentalized. Her professional life involved helping people overcome the very conflicts that she continued to express in her personal life.

Rationalization

Horney treated the defense of **rationalization** pretty much as had other theorists, including Freud. "Rationalization may be defined as self-deception by reasoning" (Horney, 1945, p. 135). Thus, when the person rationalizes, he or she invents a good reason for some action where the actual reason would be unacceptable to his or her self-esteem. For example, the compliant type offers as the reason for "giving in" to others the desire to make them happy when, in fact, he or she seeks to bring them under his or her control. Where an altruistic reason is consciously offered, a desire for dominance lurks.

Excessive Self-Control

In her clinical practice, Horney found that the tendency for **excessive self-control** was so pervasive that she originally classed it among the ten neurotic trends or needs: the need to restrict one's life self-protectively within narrow borders. Individuals who are exerting excessive self-control are attempting to avoid emotions: They "will not allow themselves to be carried away, whether by enthusiasm, sexual excitement, self-pity, or rage.... In short, they seek to check all spontaneity" (Horney, 1945, p. 136).

Arbitrary Rightness

Some neurotics make important decisions arbitrarily—even those that have an impact on others—and then defend them with anything but thorough explanations. When questioned why a decision has been made, a typical answer would be, "Because I said so!" Horney felt that the most fertile type of personality for such **arbitrary rightness** was one with aggressive tendencies coupled with feelings of detachment from others

(1945, p. 138). For example, a neurotic may end a family dispute by preemptively declaring that he will do what he has already decided to do since he is right. He then storms off, effectively ending the argument by absenting himself to pursue a course of action chosen more in spite than by reason.

Elusiveness

Sometimes the only way neurotics can avoid the inherent contradictions of their lives is through **elusiveness**—to avoid making any decisions whatsoever. Completely opposite to the arbitrarily right neurotic, the elusive neurotic seeks never to be pinned down to anything, never to state any issue or opinion clearly. "They have a bewildering capacity to becloud issues. It is often impossible for them to give a concrete report of any incident; should they try to do so the listener is uncertain in the end just what really did happen" (Horney, 1945, p. 138).

Cynicism

To defend against the recognition of inner conflict, the neurotic may adopt **cynicism,** a cynical stance toward life and its traditional moral and ethical values. By treating such issues derisively, the neurotic can forestall any conflict over deciding what his or her own position is. In effect, he or she adopts the attitude "Do what you please, so long as you don't get caught" (Horney, 1945, p. 140).

In summary, the character attitudes of compliance, aggression, and withdrawal, coupled with secondary defenses or auxiliary conflict solutions, constitute what Horney termed a **protective structure.** This protective structure is designed to provide a sense of security, however falsely based, and the means to fend off threats to a person's idealized self-image. Neurotics pay a heavy price for having a strong and rigid protective structure: They do not realize their true potentialities and do not express their authentically felt needs. They fall short of what they could become.

HORNEY'S FEMINIST, CULTURALLY BASED MODIFICATIONS OF FREUDIAN THEORY

Horney radically differed from Freud in her views regarding motivation. For example, she reinterpreted the Oedipus complex as culturally rather than biologically determined. She saw it as resulting from jealousy and aggression within some families (1939, p. 84). For Horney, the roots of the Oedipal situation consisted largely of *interpersonal attitudes:*

> If a child, in addition to being dependent on his parents, is grossly or subtly intimidated by them and hence feels that any expression of hostile impulses against them endangers his security, then the existence of such hostile impulses is bound to create anxiety.... The resulting picture may look exactly like what Freud describes as the Oedipus complex; passionate clinging to one parent and jealousy toward the other or toward anyone interfering with the claim of exclusive possession.... *But the dynamic structure of these attachments is entirely different from what Freud conceives as the Oedipus complex. They are an early manifestation of neurotic conflicts rather than a primarily sexual phenomenon.* (1939, pp. 83–84; italics added)

Thus Horney desexualized the Oedipal conflict and transferred the dynamics of its emotional constellation into the realm of disturbed interpersonal relations.

Some years before Horney rejected the orthodox Freudian interpretation of the Oedipus complex, she applied it rather tellingly in the classic manner to the topic of marriage. Her comments contain echoes of her own marriage to Oskar Horney:

> In his paper on a case of female homosexuality, Freud says that there is nothing about which our consciousness can be so incomplete or false as about the degrees of affection or dislike we feel for another human being. This is quite especially true of marriage, it being often the case that the degree of love felt is overestimated.... Once again, the relation to the Oedipus complex provides a very much deeper explanation. For we see that the commandment and the vow to love and cleave to husband or wife with which one enters into matrimony are regarded by the unconscious as a renewal of the fourth commandment ["Honor thy father and thy mother"] in relation to the parents, and in this respect also—the suppression of hate and the exaggeration of love—the earlier experiences are compulsorily repeated with exactness in every detail. (Horney, 1967, p. 88)

The reference to the fourth commandment is reminiscent of Horney's diary entry on the same theme with reference to her difficulties with her father and with religious doubt. In the just-quoted passage, Horney, in a paper entitled "The Problem of the Monogamous Ideal," is apparently trying to justify to herself ill-fated marriages on the basis of resurrected Oedipal themes. Not surprisingly, she reworked this basic tenet of Freudian theory during her period of rebellion from psychoanalysis into a more interpersonal concept with which she had personal experience.

Along these same lines, Horney found Freud's concept of penis envy as an explanation of women's feelings of inferiority grossly inadequate. She concluded that Freud's ideas were based on his preconceived notions that he attempted to support with biased interpretations of flimsy evidence obtained from the case histories of neurotic women (1939, pp. 104 ff.). Horney also pointed out that, while psychoanalyzing male patients, she uncovered "womb envy" and formed

> ... a most surprising impression of the intensity of this envy of pregnancy, childbirth, and motherhood, as well as of the breasts and of the act of suckling. (1967, pp. 60–61).

Horney recast Freud's concepts of the determinants of patterns of personality. For Horney, personality development cannot be understood in terms of instinctual drives or biological factors. Personality is seen as developing within the context of an individual's familial interactions, wider interpersonal relationships, and even more general cultural environment. Penis envy and womb envy are not viewed as biological givens but as related to the culturally determined meanings of the male and female roles.

Refutability of Horney's Concepts

Horney's lucid and nearly behavioral descriptions of neurotic misery and the conflicts underlying neurotic striving beg for translation into empirically testable concepts. At the least, the psychometrically minded psychologist could develop personality assessment tests based on her descriptions. Beyond those descriptions, her synthesis of neurotic "styles" (moving toward, against and away from) have an untapped empirical potential.

Horney's Conception of Human Agency

In part, Horney portrays human agency as active, subjective, and only partly determined by drives, needs, or environmental pressures. She allowed that many adults have the potential to make free decisions, freely interpret their world, and freely make the kind of mistakes for which they suffer the burden of anxiety and alienation. For many others, however, early environmental influences are so strong that they have little ability to be aware of or to change their patterns of relating. These people, who Horney termed "neurotic," were the major focus of her theoretical and clinical work.

The Idiographic Emphasis of Horney's Approach

Horney clearly focused on clinical issues and psychopathology. Normal development is an afterthought in her work, and while she describes personality functioning with empathy and brilliance, her most dazzling concepts are those related to neurosis. With such a clinical perspective, it is not surprising that her theory is almost wholly focused on individual functioning and idiographic, almost phenomenological, concepts. Despite her concern with cultural differences and effects, the body of her work is idiographically focused.

She also was interested in patterns of coping and behavior. In looking at the similarities underlying behavior and the general types of choices that people make, there was also a nomothetic aspect to her work.

A FINAL WORD ON KAREN HORNEY

In recent years, Karen Horney's ideas have become largely overlooked by students and researchers of personality theory. Her contributions have been less valued, less frequently studied, and more rarely applied by researchers than those of other neo-Freudian theorists. The reason for this narrowing of interest in Horney's writings is difficult to understand. Certainly other theorists whose contributions were of lesser magnitude have retained their popularity. It would be difficult to find another personality theorist with whom to compare her lucid and brilliant descriptions of neurotic misery and excessive and compulsive striving for imaginary and defensive self-excellence. In addition, she was a theorist who expressed feminist concerns about the male-orientation of Freudian theory. That her lucidity and attention-compelling style derive their potency from her self-explorations should, in coming years, re-arouse at least scholarly historical interest in Karen Horney's body of writings. But, as may be said of any personality theory, until the creative researcher devises an empirical way of testing or applying Horney's ideas, it is unlikely that her work will become influential outside the clinical realm of intuitive and artistic understanding of troubled people.

SUMMARY

Karen Horney developed a psychoanalytically oriented interpersonal theory of personality and psychopathology. Fundamental to her conception of personality development and its distortion by neurotic strivings are two basic emotions: anxiety and hostility. When the parental attitude toward the child is cold, inconsistent, or abusive, the foundation is laid for the child to develop a sense of basic hostility toward the parents, and perhaps toward people at large. Because children cannot openly express their anger for fear of abandonment by these powerful "giants," they repress these dangerous feelings. Unable to recognize the hostility that boils below the surface, the child develops a facade of pleasing lovableness, a strategy Karen Horney herself had used as a child to cope with her anger and resentment toward her parents for favoring her brother. But such a strategy is usually doomed to failure, for the child's fear of abandonment and the resulting chaos of utter helplessness provoke a basic and enduring anxiety that shapes all dealings with significant people in the child's world.

Compulsive, indiscriminate, and unrealistic "neurotic needs" make their appearance in the child's character as desperate means to cope with what the child perceives as a hostile or indifferent world. Horney eventually grouped these ten needs into three compulsive patterns: moving compliantly toward, detachedly away from, aggressively against, or detachedly away from others. Horney also suggested that several secondary or auxiliary conflict solutions might be employed by neurotic personalities in their striving for security. These techniques can be conceptualized as secondary defenses. These defenses include what Horney termed arbitrary rightness, compartmentalization, the creation of blind spots, cynicism, elusiveness, and excessive self-control.

For Horney, the central neurotic conflict is alienation from self, a personal estrangement that has its roots in the stranglehold of the neurotic needs and coping strategies. The real self, in Horney's conception, is the source of all spontaneous personal growth toward happiness, health, and genuine love for others.

Horney conceptualizes neurotic individuals as developing idealized self-images, typically composed of a long list of things they *should* be. She wrote brilliantly of the "tyranny of the shoulds" by which the neurotic's life becomes distorted and constricted in an unending struggle to attain what is humanly impossible. Horney speaks of the person's alienation from real self in futile attempts to identify with an idealized and tyrannical self-image.

Horney's theories are largely nonrefutable, although some of Horney's concepts regarding personality style are more than ripe for translation into empirical referents. Horney's theory balances active and passive human agency, and demonstrates a largely idiographic focus on specific case histories.

FOR FURTHER READING

A good place to start is Karen Horney's own written work. In her first book, *The Neurotic Personality of Our Time* (New York: Norton, 1994), she lucidly describes neurotic patterns. Her *New Ways in Psychoanalysis* (New York: Norton, 2000) indicates her profound differences with Freudian psychoanalysis. Most comprehensive is Horney's *Neurosis and Human Growth* (New York: Norton, 1991).

An excellent and concise biography is Susan Quinn's *A Mind of Her Own: The Life of Karen Horney* (New York: Summit Books/Simon and Schuster, 1987).

Additional bibliographic and Internet sources are indicated on the *Beneath the Mask* web page for Chapter 10. This can be found on the John Wiley higher education web page: www.wiley.com/college/sollod

GLOSSARY

Actual self: The person physically and mentally as he or she actually exists, independent of anyone's perceptions.

Aggressive type: A personality disposition to use aggressive acts to actualize the ideal self image.

Arbitrary rightness: The secondary neurotic defense technique through which the individual chooses one solution or one position rigidly to ward off indecision or doubt.

Basic anxiety: A child's all-pervasive sense of being lonely and helpless in a hostile world.

Basic evil: The often hostile, rejecting and domineering attitude of a child's parents.

Basic hostility: Children's often hidden anger toward all-powerful but indifferent and manipulative adults. Many children must repress their anger and feelings of hostility to survive, resulting in internalized hostility.

Blind spot: The secondary neurotic defense technique through which the person refuses to see his or her own defenses. It deals with a marked discrepancy between one's actual behaviors and one's idealized self-picture.

Compartmentalization: The secondary neurotic defense technique by which the individual pigeonholes his or her life into rigid and exclusive categories. Anything that occurs in one compartment cannot contradict, influence, or support whatever transpires in another.

Compliant type: A neurotic's trend to be in harmony with others and to avoid friction. Compliance may mask a strong inner need to compete, excel, or dominate.

Comprehensive neurotic solution: The resolution of the conflict between feelings of basic anxiety and hostility by dealing with the world and its people through the shoulds of the ideal self.

Core neurotic conflict: The alienation of the individual from his or her real self. It leads the person to adopt an idealized self at the expense of one's spontaneity, self-trust, and independence.

Cynicism: The secondary neurotic defense technique through which the individual adopts a cynical stance toward life and society's traditional moral and ethical values. By believing in nothing in particular, the person avoids hurt or disappointment by others.

Despised real self: The child's view of him or herself as despicable, unlovable, and unworthy. This is a false conception of self that is derived from false negative evaluations by others of one's ability, worth, and lovability.

Detached type: The personality disposition to move away from others in defensive ways to protect self image and esteem.

Elusiveness: The secondary neurotic defense technique that involves avoiding making any decisions whatsoever. Completely opposite to the arbitrarily right neurotic, the elusive neurotic seeks never to be pinned down to anything, never to state any issue or opinion clearly.

Excessive self-control: The secondary neurotic defense technique by which the individual seeks to check all spontaneity. Emotional impulses are kept under control.

Expansive solution: The disposition to act towards others in aggressive ways to obtain personal goals.

Externalization: The secondary neurotic defense technique by which the individual shifts his "center of gravity" from the self to others. Other people become the center of all of the neurotic's emotional life; one focuses not on what one thinks or feels but on the thoughts and feelings of others.

Idealized or ideal self: The false sense of self constructed by the individual hurt by negative evaluations and parental indifference. This person strives for perfection in a wishful way to compensate for feelings of inadequacy and unlovability.

Moving against people: An expansive solution to the core neurotic conflict. The person handles the neurotic conflict by adopting an aggressive approach, which includes the tendency toward mastery and control, to dominate and exploit others. Such a person is viewed as an aggressive type.

Moving away from people: The adoption of a protective solution of resignation to the core neurotic conflict. Such an approach includes the tendency to become detached from human affairs and resigned to an emotionally flat life. Such a person is perceived as a detached type.

Moving toward people: A self-effacing solution to the core neurotic conflict. The person identifies with the despised real self. Horney described such an individual as a compliant type.

Neurotic needs: Rigid, compulsive, and indiscriminate strivings to predict, control, and survive a hostile world.

Neurotic trends: Strategies designed to overcome the fears, helplessness, and sense of isolation experienced by the neurotic person.

Protective structure: The protective structure in a person consists of character attitudes of compliance, aggression, or withdrawal as well as secondary defenses or auxiliary conflict solutions. In neurotics, the protective structure, developed to protect against threats to their idealized self-images, hinders personal growth.

Rationalization: The secondary neurotic defense technique through which the individual uses self-deception by reasoning. It offers plausible but inaccurate explanations to excuse one's failures or unacceptable tendencies, thus warding off anxiety.

Real self: In Horney's later theorizing, the essential core of a person's being and very center of existence. The real self contains all the potential for growth and health, including "the ability to tap his own resources, the strength of his will power, the special capacities or gifts he may have; the faculty to express himself, and to relate to others with his spontaneous feelings."

Secondary defenses/auxiliary conflict solutions: Techniques to buttress neurotic solutions to the core neurotic conflict. Unlike Freudian defenses, these are not designed to deal with id impulses, but rather to protect the person from seeing major aspects of his or her character and personality.

Self-effacing solution: The personality disposition to move towards others in style of personal suffering and martyrdom.

Solution of resignation: The personality disposition to act in a detached and withdrawn pattern of behavior.

Tyranny of the should: Domination by an often unrealistic view of what one should.

Chapter 11

Gordon W. Allport

Humanistic Trait and Self Theory

Whoso would be a man must be a nonconformist.

Ralph Waldo Emerson, *Essays*

Personality is like nothing else in the world, there is nothing with which it can be compared, nothing which can be placed on a level with it.

Nicholas A. Berdyaev, *Slavery and Freedom*

| Gordon W. Allport | Born: 1897 Montezuma, Indiana |
| | Died: 1967 Cambridge, Massachusetts |

About Allport's Humanistic Trait and Self Theory

Gordon Allport was a founder of the field of personality psychology in the United States. His emphases on the uniqueness of each person and the importance of individuality have enduring value. Among his core ideas are:

- Personality can be understood as a system made up of traits. As a dynamic system, the whole (personality) is more than the additive sum of is parts (traits), and each part is affected by its participation in the system.
- A personality trait is an actual neuropsychic structure that disposes a person toward specific kinds of action in certain circumstances.
- A person's experience of self and sense of purpose are unifying aspects of personality. Allport replaced Freud's use of the term ego with the broader concept of "proprium."

- The concept of functional autonomy indicates that motives may develop as a person matures. Although originally set in motion by infantile or childish motives, behaviors may function autonomously in new ways for new reasons in new situations.

- A psychologist understands another person most adequately by examining that person's life history—gathering information about the person from various sources and encouraging the person to contribute a thoughtful self-evaluation. This is far from the psychoanalytic approach of distrusting an individual's consciously held explanations of his or her own behavior. It also differs from the behavioral approach of emphasizing the history of environmental conditioning.

Allport worked within the tradition of the Harvard psychological clinic and in the spirit of personologists such as Henry Murray and Robert White. His contributions influenced the thinking of several generations of personality theorists and clinicians toward considering whole human lives in addition to specific motives, wishes, and actions. He stood for consideration of the organized complexity of the individual against the prevailing intellectual climate, which favored reductionistic psychoanalytic or behavioral approaches.

WAS YOUNG ALLPORT MISUNDERSTOOD BY FREUD HIMSELF?

After graduating college, where he took as many psychology courses as were available, Gordon Allport taught for a year at a college in Turkey. On his way back from Turkey, he had an opportunity to be in Vienna. Allport recounts that, at the age of 21, he sent Sigmund Freud a note announcing that while he, Allport, was visiting Vienna, Freud would no doubt be glad to make his acquaintance. In response to what Allport afterward labeled his "callow forwardness," Freud invited the assertive young American to his office with a reply in his own handwriting. Over four decades later, Allport recalled his visit with Freud to a class on Personality and Religious Development at the Boston University School of Theology:

> I went there, to the famous red burlap room with pictures of dreams on the wall. He opened the door and invited me into the inner sanctum, and sat there silent. You may not believe this possible, but I was not prepared for silence. It occurred to me it was up to me to say something, so I fished around in my mind and I told him about an episode on the tram car coming out. I had seen a little boy about four years old and the little boy, obviously, was developing a real dirt phobia. His mother was with him. She was a starched Hausfrau, terribly clean and purposive looking. And the little boy was saying: "I don't want to sit *there*! Don't let *him* sit near me, he's *dirty*." He kept this up all the time, and I thought it might interest Freud how early a phobia of dirt can get set. (Allport, 1962, p. 2; emphasis in original)

Freud responded by interpreting Allport's remarks.

> When I finished my story Freud fixed his kindly therapeutic eyes upon me and said, "And was that little boy you?" Flabbergasted and feeling a bit guilty, I contrived to change the subject. While Freud's misunderstanding of my motivation was amusing, it also started a deep train of thought. I realized that he was accustomed to neurotic defenses and that my manifest motivation (a sort of rude curiosity and youthful ambition) escaped him. For therapeutic progress he would have to cut through my defenses, but it so happened that therapeutic progress was not here an issue. (Allport, 1968, pp. 383–384)

Allport later told the Boston University class,

> ...*this time* he made a mistake, a bad mistake, thinking that I was a pathological case. (I may have been, but not in that particular respect.) I don't think he had ever seen a *well* person, if you know what I mean. He was so busy, he had all these neurotics coming around. So, he was not prepared for a normal personality—for a brassy young American tourist. He was prepared for the pathological, unconscious, resistant, defensive type of person. I don't think I perceived the importance of this experience until a few years later. (Allport, 1962; emphasis in original)

Allport further commented that the experience with Freud, "...taught me that depth psychology, for all its merits, may plunge too deep, and that psychologists would do well to give full recognition to manifest motives before probing the unconscious" (1968, p. 384). One might see in Allport's report of his early encounter with Freud evidence that he must have had an aversion to psychoanalytic interpretations even before he became a psychologist.

In his accounts of this episode with Freud, Allport did not indicate awareness that he might have been projecting his feelings about his meeting with Freud on the "little boy" (Allport) and the "dirty" man (who would have been Freud) that he had seen earlier that day. If so, then Freud's upsetting interpretation, "And was that little boy you?" would have been correct. Years later, Allport would tell his students, "As far as the unconscious was concerned, Freud went down deeper, stayed longer, and came up dirtier than anybody else." He *did* see Freud, at least to a certain extent, as a "dirty man."

"HOW SHALL A PSYCHOLOGICAL LIFE HISTORY BE WRITTEN?"

Allport stated the guiding questions that shaped his work in personality: "How shall a psychological life history be written? What processes and what structures must a full-bodied account of personality include? How can one detect unifying threads in a life, if they exist?" (1968, p. 377). Although these were questions that governed his lifelong theorizing and research, Allport modestly admitted toward the end of his life: "I still do not know how a psychological life history should be written" (1968, p. 377). The individual person was a subject of enduring mystery and fascination for Allport.

As a mature scholar, Allport championed research and assessment strategies that emphasized exploration of readily accessible information, thoughts, and feeling:

> When we set out to study a person's motives...I see no reason why we should not start our investigation by asking him to tell us the answers as he sees them. (1960, p. 101)

Allport believed that direct questioning frequently results in more information than either projective testing or psychoanalytic interviewing. Commenting on the prevailing motivational theories in the 1950s, Allport pointed out that psychologists thought that conscious verbal reports were untrustworthy. Indeed, psychologists were often interested in the roots of patients' motives rather than trying to understand present strivings. Allport did not deny the existence or significance of unconscious motives or the importance of infantile experiences. Rather, he wanted to supplement such a focus with an emphasis on a person's current conscious self-evaluation.

Allport taught that reliance on theories of personality should be tempered with a willingness to apply them flexibly and nondogmatically. He emphasized that whole persons are more complex than our often over-simplifying explanations. Allport urged psychologists to abide by two principles (1968, p. 23):

1. *"Do not forget what you have decided to neglect."* If a theory accounts for some findings, do not lose sight of what remains unexplained.
2. *"Theorize in such a way that what is true in any region of mental life can be verified to be so."* This is Allport's statement of the important principle of refutability.

TOWARD A PERSONALISTIC PSYCHOLOGY

Allport was challenged by the difficulty of combining science's traditional interest in universal laws with psychology's presumed focus on the unique individual. In *Personality: A Psychological Interpretation* (1937), his first book on the field of personality, Allport wrote:

> The outstanding characteristic of man is his individuality. He is a unique creation of the forces of nature. Separated spatially from all other men he behaves throughout his own particular span of life in his own distinctive fashion. It is not upon the cell nor upon the single organ, nor upon the group, nor upon the species that nature has centered her most lavish concern, but rather upon the integral organization of life processes into the amazingly stable and self-contained system of the individual creature. (1937, p. 3)

Allport indicated that, in its attempts to seek regularities in nature, science has focused on whole classes of phenomena. From this perspective, the individual is regarded only as an instance or an example of a universal principle. For scientific psychologists, processes like intelligence, perception, and learning are regulated by general laws. It is their job to discover how these laws apply despite individual differences among subjects.

In contrast to the classic scientific strategy, Allport preferred the rationale and methods of **personalistic psychology:**

> The chief tenet of [personalistic psychology] is that every mental function is embedded in personal life. In no concrete sense is there such a thing as intelligence, space perception, color discrimination or choice reaction; there are only *people* who are capable of performing such activities and of having such experiences.... Nor can motives ever be studied apart from their personal setting; they represent always the striving of a total organism toward its objective. (Allport, 1937, p. 18; italics in original)

Idiographic and Nomothetic Approaches

The distinction between the investigation of general or universal laws, and the application of such laws to the individual case occupied Allport's attention throughout his career. He adopted from the philosopher Wilhelm Windelband (in Allport, 1937, p. 22) the term **idiographic** for the study of individuals and **nomothetic** to describe a concern for general principles. Probably to correct a perceived imbalance in research methodology, Allport asserted that his chief interest was the development of methods and concepts that take account of the complexity of individual cases. But, as a personalistic psychologist, or personologist (Murray, 1938), Allport also took the point of view that idiographic (particular) and nomothetic (general) methods and concepts should ultimately be combined:

> [The psychological study of individuality] will not be content with the discovery of laws pertaining to mind-in-general, but will seek also to understand the lawful tendencies of minds-in-particular. The personologist seeks to understand individual consistency; that is, uniformities and regularities in individual behavior. The concern is always for the whole of personality as it exists in real people (Allport, 1960, pp. 146–147).

Suggestions for an Adequate Theory of Personality

Allport's emphasis on the importance of the individual case and the necessity to understand the whole person led him to formulate criteria by which to judge the adequacy of any personality theory (1960, pp. 20 ff.):

1. Does the theory construe the human personality as actually existing within the functioning organism? To Allport, personality is more than a hypothetical construct. It actually *is*. Personality, for Allport, is not explainable exclusively in situational terms or in terms of others' opinions of the person. An adequate personality theory recognizes that personality is *biophysical*, having both psychological and physiological components (Allport, 1960, p. 21). It "... has internal structures and substructures which 'cause,' or partially cause, behavior" (1960, p. 25). This view is contrary to the behavioral approach, which focuses on observable stimuli and responses to the exclusion of inferred internal processes or structures.

2. An adequate personality theory will regard motivation "as normally a fact of present structure and function, not merely as an outgrowth of earlier forces" (Allport, 1960, p. 20). Allport disagreed with psychoanalytic theories that regarded motivation largely as a product of the person's past. Such formulations reduce the multiplicity of human motives to a few basic drives, needs, wishes, or vectors. Allport's view was that such reductionism does not aid in understanding any actual personality (1960, p. 27).

3. The satisfactory personality theory will employ units of analysis "capable of living synthesis" (Allport, 1960, p. 20). Allport criticized the method of reducing personality to a set of measurable variables without the eventual goal of resynthesizing the measurements into a whole picture: "To say that John Brown scores in the eightieth percentile of the 'masculinity-femininity' variable, in the thirtieth percentile on 'need for achievement' and at average on 'introversion-extroversion' is only moderately enlightening. Even with a more numerous set of dimensions, with an avalanche of psychometric scores, patterned personality seems to elude the psychodiagnostician" (1960, p. 30).

4. The acceptable personality theory will "allow adequately for, but not rely exclusively upon, the phenomenon of self-consciousness" (Allport, 1960, p. 20). "[S]elfhood is the central presupposition we must hold in examining the psychological states of human beings" (Allport, 1960, pp. 34–35).

Allport advocated an *open system* model of personality (1960, Chapter 3). Such a theory stresses past, present, and future-oriented motives and goals. The individual is viewed as proactive as well as reactive. The open-system approach acknowledges that people sometimes strive for more than the status quo. Allport's view was that people strive toward self-enhancement and growth rather than act largely from a sense of deficiency.

PERSONAL SOURCES OF ALLPORT'S EMPHASIS ON UNIQUENESS AND INDEPENDENCE

Allport did not go along with Freudian or behavioral reductionism regarding adult motives. Someone's motives could no doubt have had childish origins, yet that person could function adaptively or creatively in the present. In his mature theorizing, Allport called this conception of motivation "functional autonomy." Allport may have drawn the concept of functional autonomy at least in part from his own life, where it is clearly relevant.

On Swallowing a Dictionary: Competing for Recognition

Gordon Allport was born November 11, 1897, in Montezuma, Indiana, to a Scottish American medical doctor, John Edwards Allport, and his wife, Nellie Edith Wise. Gordon was the youngest of four brothers. Family life was marked by "plain Protestant piety and hard work" (Allport, 1967, p. 4). Allport's father stressed a humanitarian outlook on life, expressed in his fundamental rule: "If every person worked as hard as he could and took only the minimum financial return required by his family's needs, then there would be just enough wealth to go around" (1967, p. 5).

Allport's brothers were much older than he was. Gordon was introverted and had few boyhood friends, "for I never fitted the general boy assembly. I was quick with words, poor at games." At the age of 10, a schoolmate expressed the prevailing opinion of young Gordon: "Aw, that guy swallowed a dictionary" (1967, p. 4). Allport then knew he was an "isolate," though "I contrived to be the 'star' for a small cluster of friends."

For Allport, the road to acceptance as a valued individual was intellectual achievement. But even this avenue was fraught with competition. His high-achieving, older brother, Floyd, graduated from Harvard about the time Gordon finished high school. Floyd suggested that Gordon attend Harvard, and though he made the decision to apply belatedly, Gordon was accepted "after squeezing through the entrance tests." After his first final examinations produced an array of D's and C's, young Gordon redoubled his efforts to earn all A's at the year-end exams.

After college graduation, when Allport returned from his travels, including his visit with Freud, his work for the doctorate in psychology at Harvard seemed less challenging: "Back at Harvard I found that the requirements for the Ph.D. degree were not stiff (not nearly stiff enough), and so with only two years' additional course work, a few examinations, and the thesis, I qualified for this degree in 1922 at the age of 24" (1967, p. 8). He had, at last, mastered Harvard's academically challenging environment and was now on a par with his brother Floyd.

When Floyd published a classic textbook on social psychology, Gordon's view was critical: "His *Social Psychology* (1924) was too behavioristic and too psychoanalytic for my taste" (1967, p. 12). Gordon and Floyd Allport rarely collaborated professionally, and they published only two papers together. Gordon Allport commented "Apart from these two papers we never collaborated, even though we have occasionally helped each other with criticism" (1967, p. 12).

Atwood and Tomkins (1976) have pointed to the pattern in Allport's life of first following in his brother's footsteps and then striving for autonomy:

> If we assume that this pattern of similar behavior [by Gordon imitating Floyd] was the outcome of an identification based on envy, it would mean that Allport's education and career choice were, in large measure, "functionally dependent," i.e., motivated by the infantile aim of participating in his brother's greatness and thereby overcoming his own feelings of inferiority. Some insight into why it should have become necessary for him to abandon this aim and make his work functionally autonomous is suggested by another emphasis in his theoretical writings—the uniqueness of the individual. To the extent that his life was directed and determined by the emulation of his brother, his own identity as a separate person (his uniqueness) was likely to have been compromised. In the service of asserting his identity, then, he opposed the identification with his brother by declaring that his interests had become independent of their origins. (Atwood & Tomkins, 1976, p. 175)

Atwood and Tomkins therefore suggested that Allport's emphasis on his own personal uniqueness was an ego defense. They thus presented a Freudian analysis of Allport, who was himself critical of Freud's ideas.

Allport's View of His Own Personal Uniqueness

Throughout his autobiography, Allport mentions his poor ability in the hard sciences. He considered Floyd talented in these subjects and others: "Floyd was a stricter logician and more systematic in his use of method than I. It should also be said that he had artistic, musical, and manual giftedness that I lacked" (1967, p. 12). What special talent, then, did Gordon himself possess? He hints that he and his brother differed drastically but then ambivalently withdraws the distinction: "Over the years we pursued our own ways, but because of our common and unusual surname and divergence of points of view we managed to confuse students and the public. Were there one or two Allports?" (1967, pp. 12–13).

Most emphatically, there were two. But one of them was a social psychologist and the other was a personality psychologist who struggled to wrest his chosen, self-created field from that of social psychology:

> In my thinking there is a sharp distinction between personality and social psychology. One must think of personality as a biophysical or biopsychical structure. It may be modified by the field, but it *is* something. Social psychology is everything else. (Allport, paraphrased by Brewster-Smith, 1971, p. 353; italics in original)

Allport dismissed the genetic fallacy of disproving a proposition by demonstrating its personal origins in the believer's life experiences. It is difficult to read his statement without seeing some degree of personal justification in it:

> The plain truth is that origins can tell nothing about the validity of a belief. Neither can origins characterize the mature belief as it now exists, nor explain its part in the present economy of life. One of the best musicians I know took up his profession originally, in part at least, because he was taunted in childhood for what seemed to be his tone-deafness. In psychological parlance, he "overcompensated" for the defect. But that incident has absolutely nothing to do with the present structure or dynamics of his life-absorbing interest.... Were we to gauge our evaluations by origins we would disparage the eloquence of Demosthenes because his oratory served as a compensation for his tendency to stammer.... And the fact that many psychologists take up their science because of personal maladjustments would make psychology worthless. (Allport, 1950, pp. 109–110)

Allport himself created a valuable and unique theory of personality out of his unique constellation of personal experiences and motives. His theory's validity is not lessened by an examination of its personal origins. Allport followed his brother to Harvard as an undergraduate and then followed him again through Harvard graduate study, even imitating his brother's field of specialization. But Gordon Allport's study of psychology was deliberately a world apart from Floyd's brand of psychology. In organizing the field of personality study, Gordon sought to rescue his special domain from the hands of his brother, the social psychologist. In one stroke, he built a theory to reflect the uniqueness and independence of the person and, at the same time, established his own uniqueness and independence among the Allports.

PERSONALITY: ALLPORT'S DEFINITION

Allport's emphasis on an open-system personality theory was an outgrowth of his earliest conceptualization of **personality:**

> Personality is the dynamic organization within the individual of those psychophysical
> systems that determine his unique adjustments to his environment. (1937, p. 48)

In devising his definition, Allport devoted a good deal of effort to synthesizing the
varied usages of the term *personality* into a coherent and workable concept. Allport's
definition of personality has four major criteria:

1. The first emphasis involves the usage of the term **dynamic organization.** Allport meant to stress that personality is always an organized whole, a whole
   that is constantly changing (dynamic). Personality is thus self-regulating and
   continually evolving (1937, p. 48).

2. The phrase *within the individual* was intended to indicate that personality is
   something "real"—something that resides within the skin. Personality is not an
   abstraction, nor is it a scientifically convenient fiction or hypothetical construct.
   It really exists.

3. The term **psychophysical systems** was meant to convey a recognition of the
   fact that personality has roots in the physical, chemical processes of the body's
   glands and nervous system. The term *psychophysical* reminds us that personality
   is neither exclusively mental nor exclusively neural.

4. The phrase *unique adjustments to his environment* emphasizes both Allport's
   conviction that psychology must attend to the individual personality as the individual adapts to changing psychological or physical environments.

In his 1961 revision of his major work, Allport modified his personality definition
by substituting a new phrase for the previous "unique adjustments to his environment." The modified definition now ended with the phrase, "characteristic behavior
and thought" (1961, p. 28). The alteration broadened the concept of personality as
involving more than adjustment to personal and physical environments. Thus Allport
recast his definition in 1961: "We not only adjust to our environment but we reflect
on it. Also, we strive to master it, and sometimes succeed. Behavior and thought,
therefore, make both for survival and for growth."

The Concept of Traits: Personal Consistency

The basic component in Allport's concept of personality was the **personality trait.**

> A trait is ...*a neuropsychic structure having the capacity to render many stimuli
> functionally equivalent, and to initiate and guide equivalent (meaningfully consistent) forms
> of adaptive and expressive behavior*. (1961, p. 347; italics in original)

In this definition Allport asserted that traits are indeed real, that they are rooted in
nervous system functioning, and that they guide behavior. A trait lends consistency to
personality by allowing the person to respond similarly to a wide array of situations,
that is, renders diverse stimuli "functionally equivalent." For Allport, traits are rather
complex enduring dispositions to respond to one's environment in particular ways.
A trait is always established within the personality through a combination of innate
physical attributes and acquired environmental habits (1937, p. 292).

Allport illustrated his conception of trait development and function with the following example:

> A young child, finding that his mother is nearly always present to satisfy his wants,
> develops for her an early affective attachment (conditioning). But later other social contacts
> likewise prove to be conducive to this child's happy and successful adjustment: playmates,
> for example, or family gatherings, or crowds at the circus.... The child gradually comes to

BOX 11.1   *Only Connect ...*

Contemporary cognitive psychology's concept of *schema* is very similar, if not identical, to Allport's concept of trait. A cognitive schema is capable of evaluating stimuli in a way that leads to certain actions. It identifies patterns in stimuli and it may lead to meaningfully consistent patterns of behavior. We might well consider Allport an incipient cognitive psychologist, ahead of his time.

seek people, rather than to avoid them. A trait (not an instinct) of gregariousness develops. The child grows eager for social intercourse; he enjoys being with people. When isolated from them for some time, he misses them and becomes restless. The older he grows the more ways he finds of expressing this gregarious interest. He seeks to ally himself with groups of people at the lodge, at the theater, at church; he makes friends and keeps in touch with them, often entertains them, and corresponds with them.... Sociability has become a deep and characteristic quality of this individual's personality. Its expression is variable; a wide range of equivalent stimuli arouse it. (1937, pp. 292–293)

Thus the child's trait of gregariousness or sociability renders many stimuli equivalent and guides many behaviors into equivalent forms of expression. The way in which Allport conceptualized a trait's mediation between diverse stimuli and the individual's characteristic and uniform responses to them is illustrated in Figure 11.1.

As Figure 11.1 indicates, the child's trait of gregariousness allows diverse situations like theater-going, church-going, letter-writing, and family gatherings to be occasions in which an individual may express his or her pervasive outgoing social involvement. The behaviors that constitute personal style are varied because they are particular responses to the specific characteristics of each social situation. But all behaviors share the common denominator of gregariousness or sociability. Thus, the trait of

Figure 11.1 Trait as mediator between stimuli and responses.

gregariousness indicates a person's "characteristic behavior and thought" in the face of diverse circumstances. In commonsense terms, we often say that John or Jane did something "typical" of them. To be able to make such a judgment, it was first necessary to have observed John or Jane behaving in a consistent fashion in different situations. Traits are inferred as the basis of this personal consistency over situations.

Cardinal, Central, and Secondary Traits

Allport indicated that, within the context of an entire network of traits that compose a personality, some traits play major roles and some play minor roles. In rare cases, a particular trait is so outstanding, so pervasive that nearly all of an individual's activities can be traced to it. A trait of this significance is readily apparent. Such pervasive, dominantly influential traits are termed **cardinal traits** (Allport, 1937, pp. 337 ff.).

A cardinal trait, such as *Christlike or Machiavellian*, is so unifying that all other traits are subordinate to it. A cardinal trait is not found in a large percentage of people. Cardinal traits are not necessarily good, nor is it necessarily good to have a cardinal trait. Some saintly people like Mother Teresa and some tyrants such as Hitler are examples of people with cardinal traits. What they have in common is only a highly focused personality.

Central traits have an important role in the personality. They represent patterns of behavior that typify major areas of a person's functioning. "Central traits are those usually mentioned in careful letters of recommendation, in rating scales where the rater stars the outstanding characteristics of the individual, or in brief verbal descriptions of a person" (Allport, 1937, p. 338). Some typical characteristics that would likely be central traits are conscientiousness, level-headedness, laziness, industriousness, sense of responsibility, or irresponsibility.

Secondary traits are less generalized, less consistent, and less influential in the overall guidance of behavior than central traits. Such secondary traits are evoked by a narrower range of equivalent stimuli and direct a more restricted range of equivalent responses than central traits (1937, p. 338). Some typical secondary traits might refer to tastes in food, music, or clothing. Being well-groomed is usually considered a secondary trait. But determining whether a trait is central or secondary depends not so much on the trait itself, but on its importance within the personality.

Depending on the specific person or life situation, a given trait may be cardinal, central, or secondary. For example, a comedian's sense of humor might be central to their identity or even to their career whereas, for another person, a sense of humor may be less important. A given trait, such as love of music, might be a central trait in a musician and a secondary trait for someone else. An accountant's precision with numbers might be a central trait, whereas, for an artist, the same trait of precision might be of secondary importance. The fact that you shine your shoes regularly might represent a secondary trait; yet for a person who is obsessively concerned about neatness and cleanliness, such behavior might represent a central trait.

Individual and Common Traits; Personal Dispositions

Allport distinguished between individual and common traits. **Individual traits** are those unique to an individual whereas **common traits** are those shared by many people. Allport accurately noted that two people could not have precisely the same trait (1937, p. 297). Thus, even though two individuals may be said to possess the trait of politeness, the personal style with which this common trait will be expressed is at least a little different in each person. In this sense, every trait is an individual trait. Yet, for all practical purposes, individuals do share some patterns of behavior. It is possible, for example, to speak of generally polite people. In this more practical sense Allport concluded that the term *common trait* may be applied. In 1961 Allport introduced some terminological changes into his theory of traits. To emphasize his fundamental distinction between individual and common (aspects of) traits, Allport chose to re-label the individual trait as a *personal disposition* (1961, p. 358). Allport employed the following definition of **personal disposition:**

> *A personal disposition is a generalized neuropsychic structure (peculiar to the individual), with the capacity to render many stimuli functionally equivalent, and to initiate and guide consistent (equivalent) forms of adaptive and stylistic behavior.* (1961, p. 373)

Allport emphasized that,

> Every man is in certain respects: a. like all other men (universal norms), b. like some other men (group norms), c. like no other men (idiosyncratic norms). (1961, p. 13)

He continued by indicating that this individuality is not only a matter of individual traits, but represents the unique organization and dynamics of each and every person:

> Although we accept the formula of three sets of norms, we should guard against one pitfall. This approach might mistakenly imply that the individual as such is only a handful of residual, and perhaps negligible, idiosyncrasies.... The facts are otherwise. [A given person] Sam, to be sure has many attributes characteristic of the human species, and many that resemble his cultural fellows: *but he weaves them all into a unique idiomatic system.*... The organization of the individual life is first, last, and all the time a primary fact of human nature. (1961, pp. 14–15; italics in original)

This is a clear statement of Allport's idiographic focus. Each person is viewed as unique, one of a kind. The study of an individual, in his view, is the proper and most appropriate area of investigation for psychology. We will see how this view is applied in his single case strategy for studying individuals.

PERSONAL DOCUMENTS: AN IDIOGRAPHIC APPROACH TO LIFE HISTORY

Personal documents may take many forms: autobiographies, diaries, letters, interviews, even literary productions (Allport, 1942, 1961). "The personal document may be defined as *any self-revealing record that intentionally or unintentionally yields information regarding the structure, dynamics, and functioning of the author's mental life*" (Allport, 1942, p. xii; italics in original).

Individuals create self-revealing personal documents out of a variety of motives. For example, adolescents often keep detailed diaries or personal journals recounting their innermost thoughts, feelings, and aspirations. Such a document is often so revealing that the most grievous sin a parent can commit is to violate its secrecy.

The motives that impel individuals to create self-revealing productions are varied. Allport described 13 motives that might underlie such productions (1942, pp. 69–75):

1. *Special pleading:* To argue in a convincing way some self-serving or self-justifying premise.
2. *Exhibitionism:* A single-minded desire to display one's virtues and vices.
3. *Desire for order:* Compulsive need to record the circumstances of one's day.
4. *Literary appeal:* Desire for aesthetic and artistic satisfaction.

5. *Securing personal perspective:* A personal "taking stock" of one's life, achievements, failures, and so on.

6. *Catharsis:* A need to secure relief from tension and anxiety by writing when relief through direct action is unattainable.

7. *Monetary gain:* Personal revelations for prize competition, for payment in an experimental investigation, and so forth. Payment does not rule out, however, the validity of the self-revelations.

8. *Assignment:* School task imposed for some educational or therapeutic reason.

9. *Assisting in therapy:* Production of personal document for therapist to assist in one's own cure.

10. *Redemption and social reincorporation:* "Confessions" of an ex-criminal, spy, alcoholic, and so on. Generally such confessions are motivated by a genuine desire for forgiveness and acceptance.

11. *Public service:* Desire to achieve public or social reform.

12. *Desire for immortality:* "Battle against oblivion," or a desire not to be forgotten after death.

13. *Scientific interest:* Though not necessarily created for this reason, personal documents sometimes arc donated to psychologists with the intention of furthering science.

This diverse array of motives suggests the methodological problems that historians, sociologists, anthropologists, or psychologists face when they decide to study evidence of this sort. All of these personal documents suffer from varying degrees of lack of candor, defective recollection on the part of the writer, and from conscious or unconscious self-concealment. Nonetheless, it was Allport's conviction that personal documents were a valuable source of answers to the question: "How shall a psychological life history be written?"

To assess the value of a personal document, the psychologist must ask how useful it is in meeting three goals of science: understanding, prediction, and control beyond the level of unaided common sense (1942, p. 148). It was Allport's judgment, after a thorough survey of the literature relating to research on personal documents, that their use was well justified.

> Personal documents are good if they serve the comparison of lives, one with another, leading to statistical generalizations and to an understanding of uniformities of behavior. But they are good also if standing one by one they provide concrete evidence of the nature of single lives from which all psychological science is derived; if they yield evidence of pluralistic causation; if they give clinicians and practitioners a sounder basis for work; and if they enhance the understanding, prediction, and control of individual lives (which is all that science ultimately demands). (Allport, 1942, p. 59)

Allport's evaluation suggests that personal documents may be treated in research with a variety of conceptualizations and methods. Analyses ranging from impressionistic characterizations, psychoanalytic hypothesizing, and direct content analysis to sophisticated statistical and factorial assessments arc, in principle, possible. But two significant points about Allport's advocacy of personal document research bear mention: First, by definition, the study of personal documents is the idiographic strategy of assessing the unity, uniqueness, and consistency of the individual. Second, this single-case approach treats personality investigation as an attempt to comprehend the person from a subjective perspective—that is, trying to understand the viewpoint and experience of each individual.

AN ILLUSTRATIVE CASE:
ANALYSIS OF JENNY GOVE MASTERSON'S LETTERS

Within four years of the publication of his monograph on the use of personal documents in psychology, Allport published a series of letters that revealed the story of a
mother–son relationship from the mother's point of view (Allport, 1946). The letters
were presented to Allport by a young couple, identified as Glenn and Isabel, because
they felt the letters might be valuable for the field of psychology. A pseudonymous
"Jenny Gove Masterson" wrote the letters. The correspondence between Glenn and
Isabel and Jenny began in March 1926, when Jenny was 58 years old, and ran its
course of 301 letters. The correspondence ended with Jenny's death at the age of 69.

In 1965, Allport made the "Jenny Masterson" letters more widely available by
publishing some of them in book form along with several types of psychological
analysis of Jenny's personality. Allport posed the following challenges to psychologists:

> To me the principal fascination of the Letters lies in their challenge to the reader (whether
> psychologist or layman) to "explain" Jenny—if he can. Why does an intelligent lady behave
> so persistently in a self-defeating manner? When and how might she have averted the
> tragedy of her life? Could proper guidance or therapy at an appropriate time have helped
> alter the rigid course of her conduct? Was the root of her trouble some wholly unconscious
> mechanism? (Allport, 1965, p. viii)

Some brief details about "Jenny's" life are in order here. "Jenny Gove Masterson"
was born in Ireland of Protestant parentage in 1868. Migrating to Canada when Jenny
was five years old, the Gove family took up residence in Montreal. Her mother worked
hard to preserve the family's sense of Irish culture and tradition. Jenny grew up in a
family with five younger sisters and one younger brother. Her father died when Jenny
was 18. Jenny became a telegrapher to support her family. Unfortunately, Jenny and
her siblings did not get along well. By the time Jenny was 27 years old, bitter quarrels
and disputes resulted in disintegration of the family. Jenny married an American railway inspector, Henry Masterson, a marriage that angered her family because he was
divorced.

Jenny and Henry Masterson moved to Chicago, where Jenny found herself in an
enforced idle existence. "She complained that she was being 'kept' by a man. She
quarreled more than once with her husband over this issue, but he, like most men of
his day, was firmly set against a wife seeking employment" (Allport, 1965, p. 3). The
issue was not resolved at the time of Henry Masterson's death in 1897, when Jenny
was 29 years old. A month after her husband's death, Jenny gave birth to her only
child, a son named Ross.

After many years of a close relationship with his mother, Ross left home for
college "back East" at Princeton. Jenny continued to work to support Ross's tuition
and miscellaneous expenses. In Ross's sophomore year, the United States entered
World War I, and Ross enlisted in the ambulance corps. Before his departure for
France, Jenny visited Ross and met his college friends, including Glenn and Isabel,
her later correspondents. When Ross returned from France in 1919, he found himself
disoriented. Ross returned to college, obtained his college degree, and subsequently
failed in some business endeavors.

Ross and Jenny had many quarrels. One encounter occurred after Jenny learned of
his marriage, which he had kept secret from her, "... she drove him out of her room
with violent denunciations and a threat to have him arrested if he ever tried to see her
again" (Allport, 1965, p. 6).

Jenny later renewed her contacts with Ross's college friends, Glenn and his wife Isabel, and requested permission to "keep in touch" with them. Her motives for this renewed acquaintance with Glenn and Isabel seem to have been a mixture of nostalgia for the days when "Ross was all hers" and a need to maintain a source of information about Ross's whereabouts.

Jenny's Personality: Samples of Her Letters

Writing to Glenn and Isabel on the occasion of Ross's visit to her room with his second wife, Jenny described the scene as follows:

> Ross brought this same woman and her brat to my house one Sunday evening and I was angry and told him that if he ever brought any more prostitutes to my house I would have them both arrested. Anyone, short of a fool, would know what she was at one glance. (Allport, 1965, p. 9)

In her letter of January 5, 1927, Jenny recalled her childhood:

> My father dropped dead one day, and had no provision made for his family—7 of them, all under 18. Not one in the house capable of earning a penny. It was my salary that kept the house going. . . . No one ever denied it, or pretended to think otherwise, and when I dared to marry the man I had been in love with for years, but dreaded to take my money out of their house . . . why, they said I was like the cow that gave the milk and then kicked the pail. (Allport, 1965, p. 27)

In June 1928, Jenny gave vent to one of her characteristic outbursts of pessimism and martyrdom:

> Anyway I am firmly convinced that I am "through" and ought to step out. I have done all, of any use, that it is possible for me to do in this world. Whether it was for good or bad it is over and done and nothing can change it now, "The moving finger writes, and having writ moves on" and my days for possible usefulness are past. I should step out, but am a coward. To suppose that Ross needs me would be indeed a joke. (Allport, 1965, p. 50)

In 1929 Ross underwent surgery for a tumor on his inner ear and for an "abscess on the outer covering of the brain." During his convalescence, he stayed with "one of his women." About two months after the operation, Jenny received word that Ross had died in a sudden relapse. She was to outlive her son by eight years. Glenn was summoned to attend the funeral and cremation of Ross's body. After the ceremony, Glenn accompanied Jenny back to her room. Ending an hour of respectful silence, Jenny spoke, "The body is consumed, now we'll have a good steak dinner" (recollection of Isabel, in Allport, 1965, p. 153). Jenny wrote to Glenn and Isabel, following Ross's death:

> After a while I shall count up all my riches—after the horror of this loss becomes blunted a bit—you know "the years roll by and on their wings bear healing"—wounds do not remain open for always—and then I shall count up my riches—such wonderful friends—*such* friends—the glory of the sun and the stars—the sigh of the sea—the laughter of little children. (Allport, 1965, p. 73; italics in original)

An Analysis of Jenny's Personal Dispositions

Allport's perennial question: "How shall a psychological life history be written?" can, as always, be answered on two levels. A psychologist may decide to analyze the letters with regard to nomothetic (general-universal) results. Jenny's letters could be analyzed today to see to what extent she fits within some *DSM-IV* diagnostic category, such as Paranoid Personality Disorder. This diagnosis would indicate overall patterns of behavior but would not be adequate for understanding Jenny as an individual. The psychologist who wished to form an impressionistic portrait of Jenny as a unique person might take a different approach. Such a psychologist might ask a series of judges to read the Masterson letters and to put Jenny's outstanding traits in their own words. Then a "trait portrait" could be formed. It would be based on areas of agreement among the judges.

Allport reported the results of the latter type of investigation undertaken by himself with 36 judges. These 36 people used a total of 198 trait names to characterize Jenny. Loosely clustered, the 198 items fell into nine categories (Based on Allport, 1965, pp. 193–194):

1. *Quarrelsome-Suspicious* (e.g., distrustful, paranoid, opinionated)
2. *Self-centered* (e.g., selfish, jealous, possessive, martyr complex)
3. *Independent-Autonomous* (e.g., hardworking, stubborn, calculating)
4. *Dramatic-Intense* (e.g., emotional, rigid, serious, violent)
5. *Aesthetic-Artistic* (e.g., intuitive, fastidious, expressive)
6. *Aggressive* (e.g., ascendant, domineering, self-assertive)
7. *Cynical-Morbid* (e.g., pessimistic, sarcastic, despondent)
8. *Sentimental* (e.g., loyal, affectionate, maternal)
9. *Unclassified* (e.g., intelligent, witty, whimsical)

Clearly, some of the categories are contradictory, and some overlap. Yet nearly all the judges agreed that the prominent traits in Jenny's personality were: *suspiciousness, self-centeredness, autonomy, a dramatic nature, aggressiveness, morbidity, and sentimentality.*

Allport reported a more elaborate study of Jenny's letters by one of his students. Jeffrey Paige (in Allport, 1965, pp. 199 ff.) used a computer lexicon of social science terms to analyze Jenny's letters. Containing nearly 3,000 items, the coding system used by Paige reduced Jenny's letters to a small number of labels that summarized large classes of phrase usage in Jenny's writing. For example, Jenny employed many phrases to express her aggression, hostility, open rage, and opposition to Ross and his women. All of these phrases were coded into a single category signifying aggression. Once programmed in this way, the computer was asked to sort out several kinds of data from Jenny's letters.

Paige found, using the first 56 letters up to the death of Ross, eight factors that embodied Jenny's most prominent traits (1965, pp. 200–201). Listed in order of decreasing frequency of expression, these traits were

1. aggression
2. possessiveness
3. need for affiliation
4. need for autonomy
5. need for familial acceptance
6. sexuality
7. sentience (love of art, literature, natural beauty)
8. martyrdom

Clearly, there is much overlap between the judges' impressionistic analyses of Jenny's letters and the computer-derived traits.

Computer-derived data reveal further information. Jenny expresses more affection for Glenn than for Isabel; she makes more requests of Glenn for advice than of Isabel. But the computer had some trouble with items tagged "Good" and "Bad." For example, the statement: "I have a truly noble son, an honor to his college, his friends, his family"—a sarcastic comment—is labeled "Good" by the computer. Apparently sarcasm was not labeled by the computer's programming.

One can see why Allport concluded that little is gained by sophisticated statistical and factorial analyses of individual persons. The impressionistic judgments of Jenny's personality provide as much information on most issues as the computer-derived traits. Yet analysis with the aid of a computer program does lead to more detailed results. The two approaches could readily become complementary.

CRITICISMS AND ALLPORT'S RESPONSES

Allport's insistence that an adequate personality psychology must be based on attempts to understand the individual case evoked a great deal of criticism. The main issues in the controversy centered on Allport's distinctions between the idiographic and nomothetic scientific strategies. Part of the controversy, too, concerned Allport's conceptualization of traits as the fundamental units of study.

Falk (1956), whose ideas were repeated by later critics, suggested that there is no real dispute between nomothetic and idiographic goals in science. Study of unique events is not essential to the formulation of scientific theory. Furthermore, Falk argued, the idiographic approach is a necessary preliminary method to the development of generalizations, for the observation of single events always precedes the construction of laws. But, Falk suggested, general laws are adequate, when properly applied, to the task of understanding the unique personality.

Robert Holt (1962) extended the objections to Allport's emphasis on the idiographic in his idiographic-nomothetic distinction. He labeled Allport's point of view a "romantic personology." Holt concluded that there was no logical basis for establishing a special branch of natural science for the study of the unique personality because such a study is, by definition, not scientific. Holt suggested that Allport had confused art and science in his attempts to achieve comprehensive understanding of single persons. The feeling of fully understanding a person is more suitable to an artist. Scientists, by contrast, are satisfied when they can reliably predict and control the events they study.

Holt also pointed out that it is theoretically impossible to conceptualize something that is unique. If a given personality were unique, heretofore never experienced, a totally unique trait name would have to be coined or some unique combination of existing trait names would have to be employed. A combination of trait names, though, would hardly satisfy Allport because it would fail to capture the personal element in personality.

The concept of traits as the fundamental units of personality has also been subject to its share of criticism. B. F. Skinner, in the tradition of radical behaviorism, objected to postulating inner mechanisms to explain observable behaviors. From a behavioral viewpoint, traits, needs, or instincts are not necessary to explain observed responses.

> When we say that a man eats *because* he is hungry, smokes a great deal *because* he has the tobacco habit, fights *because* of the instinct of pugnacity, behaves brilliantly *because* of his intelligence, or plays the piano well *because* of his musical ability, we seem to be referring to causes. But on analysis these phrases proved to be merely redundant descriptions. A single set of facts is described by the two statements: "He eats" and "He is hungry." A

> single set of facts is described by the two statements: "He smokes a great deal" and "he has the smoking habit." (Skinner, 1953, p. 31; italics in original)

Thus, from the behaviorist point of view, postulating traits of personality is merely a redundant statement of the behavior that has already been observed.

Allport was aware of these criticisms of his trait theory and responded to what he considered to be the valid points of his critics. He wrote in his autobiography, "I know in my bones that my opponents are partly right" (1968, p. 405). He eventually came to the conclusion that ". . . my earlier views seemed to neglect the variability induced by ecological, social, and situational factors. This oversight needs to be repaired through an adequate theory that will relate the inside and outside systems more accurately" (1966, in 1968, p. 63). He subsequently revised his trait theory to make it more adequate.

"TRAITS REVISITED": HEURISTIC REALISM

In a 1966 restatement of trait theory, Allport conceded that trait theory would have to be made more sophisticated, more predictive, and more empirically testable if it was to survive as a useful construct in contemporary psychology. To further this aim, he proposed a new approach to theory building, which he termed **heuristic realism.** Heuristic realism has two guiding assumptions. First, the personologist *chooses* to believe that "the person who confronts us possesses inside his skin generalized action tendencies (or traits) and that it is our job scientifically to discover what they are" (1968, p. 49). Second, heuristic realism asserts that owing to the complexity of the objects or events observed, and because present methods are not completely adequate, the goal of scientifically conceptualizing personality's realness cannot be fully successful. Yet the heuristic realist proceeds "as if" success were possible, for only by making the attempt will progress toward knowledge of the person be attained. By introducing the concept of heuristic realism, Allport held to the position that it was worthwhile to try to understand the individual personality, even though a complete, perfectly accurate understanding might be out of reach.

Recently, many of Allport's most criticized views have been vindicated. Thomas Pettigrew, a leading social psychologist and former student and colleague of Allport, has recently written,

> . . . many of Gordon's initial proposals for addressing basic problems now exist in our literature with new labels and enlarged meanings. . . . Consider the much derided concept of functional autonomy. The notion that motives can become independent of their origins was widely considered heretical in 1937. Slowly, psychology came to accept the phenomenon if not the formulation. (1999, p. 415)

Pettigrew also mentions the fact that Allport's trait theory was in fact more interactionist and dynamic than portrayed by his contemporary critics.

THE MATURE, HEALTHY PERSONALITY

In his 1937 statement of his position, Allport criticized psychology's lack of interest in the **mature or healthy personality** and elaborated on the concept of maturity. One characteristic of maturity is the capacity to defer momentary needs, pains, or desires in favor of reaching long-term goals. Setbacks or defeats do not easily deter mature persons. The pursuit of personally meaningful goals represents **self-extension** (1937, p. 213). A mature person is capable of going beyond self to invest energies in pursuits beyond immediate self-interest. Allport related his concept of maturity to limitations in the thinking of behaviorists. He wrote, "...true maturity leads us to do things for reasons that are not mechanically enslaved to the principle of reward and punishment" (1961, p. 96).

The psychologically mature person also has the capacity for **self-objectification** (1937, p. 214). Allport defined self-objectification as "that peculiar detachment of the mature person when he surveys his own pretensions in relation to his abilities, his present objectives in relation to possible objectives for himself, his own equipment in comparison with the equipment of others, and his opinion of himself in relation to the opinion others hold of him" (1937, p. 214). The capacity for self-objectification is tied to insight and to a sense of humor. A third attribute of being mature is the development of *unifying philosophies of life*. Mature people live their lives according to guiding principles.

Allport proposed a developmental model to account for maturity. It appears to be generally relevant, although it is not the only model on the scene (see Erikson, Chapter 8).

Emergence of the Self in Infancy

The first sense of self to evolve, according to Allport, is the **bodily self.** To illustrate, consider the infant of five or six months who manages to get its foot into its mouth for a two- or three-toothed bite: "If he hurts his foot he cries but has no idea at all that *he* has hurt *him*" (1961, p. 112). But with the passing of time, many such bodily sensations are experienced as recurrent and reliable aspects of *me*. Combined with these sensations are the frustrations of desires and wants that originate in external agents, like mother. "A child who cannot eat when he wants to, who bumps his head, soon learns the limitations of his too, too solid flesh" (1961, p. 112).

The emerging certainty that "I am the *same person*" as time passes is what Allport termed **self-identity.** He thought that self-identity depends on the child's developing capacity for language. For with the possibility of employing words to think and to communicate, the regularity, the solidity, and the sameness of existence become apparent. "He hears constantly 'Where is Johnny's nose?' 'Where are Johnny's eyes?' 'Good Johnny,' 'John naughty'" (1961, p. 115). With the repetition of his name in various contexts, the child develops the capacity to refer to himself with a name. He also becomes aware of the continuity of his self-identity.

Parents often have difficulty with the two- to two-and-a-half-year-old because the child resents anyone taking over his or her prerogatives:

> A two-year-old went to the bathroom with his father to have his face washed. Saying, "Let me," he struggled to turn on the faucet. He persisted without success. For a time the father waited patiently, but finally "helped" the child. Bursting into screams of protest the child ran from the bathroom and refused to be washed. His father had spoiled everything. (Allport, 1961, p. 118).

A sense of **self-esteem** begins to acquire importance near the end of the second year of life and becomes critical for healthy development in the third year. At the same time the child undergoes what parents call negativism, saying "No!" to nearly every important demand that the parents make. In effect, the child regards every adult proposal or demand as a threat to its integrity. "To him it seems safer to resist any adult proposal in advance, as a protection to dawning self-esteem" (Allport, 1961, p. 119). So, by the end of the third year of life, three aspects of self have emerged: the bodily self, self-identity, and self-esteem (with accompanying pride and stubbornness).

Emergence of Self in Later Childhood

From four to six years of age, the child consolidates and refines the three aspects of self that have already emerged. At this time, the child's cognitive and emotional egocentricity is readily apparent. As Piaget described, the child believes that the sun follows it, "that God, or Santa Claus is a Being whose primary duty is to serve his interests" (Allport, 1961, p. 122). Slowly, however, the child experiences the fourth aspect of selfhood, **self-extension.** For example, the child begins to understand the meaning of possession: "This ball is mine, he is my Daddy" and so on. The "ball" and the "Daddy" are each seen as an extension of self. Important during this period, too, is the developing awareness of the child that its parents want it to be a certain kind of self. The child's **self-image** begins to become important and definite. The child of five or six years begins to realize the difference between being "good" and being "naughty."

From ages six to twelve, the child's sense of an extended self and its self-image are enhanced by experiences with peers in the school setting. The child learns what is expected of it in regions beyond the security of the family situation. The child learns to shift gears as it moves from family to outside situations so that, for example, rough-and-ready talk with peers is restrained to a more polite form of conversation at home. By the 12th year the child is capable of reflective thought and hypothetical or "as if" reasoning, and this achievement also marks the child's realization that self is a thinker and a judger—in short, a "rational coper" (1961, p. 124).

The **self-as-rational-coper** corresponds in Allport's view to Freud's "ego." This aspect of the self, like the Freudian ego, attempts to deal with external reality, mediate between the demands of one's impulses, and act according to the restraints of society (parents, teachers). In this sense, not all of the self-as-rational-coper's activities are conscious. Some of its attempts to mediate between need and reality may be unconscious and defensively oriented in its striving to maintain self-esteem. In this area, Allport has incorporated much of Freudian thinking.

Identity and Beyond

The period of adolescence is marked by what Erikson (Chapter 8) calls an "identity crisis." The central question for the adolescent is: "Just who am I?" or "Am I a child or an adult?" In attempts to form an identity, adolescents play various roles, trying on each for size and discarding those with which the emerging sense of self-identity clashes.

> The search for identity is revealed in the way an adolescent tries on different masks. He first develops one line of chatter, then another, one style of hairdress and then another (always within the range permitted by the peer group). He imitates one hero and then another. He is still searching for a garb that will fit. What he really wants is not yet fully present—his adult personality. (Allport, 1961, p. 125)

After adolescence, choosing to direct one's life into realistic and appropriate channels eventually becomes a central concern. "Paring down the self-image and aspirations to life-size is a task for his adult years" (1961, p. 126). This last aspect to emerge within the slowly evolving self is what Allport calls **propriate striving,** meaning literally, "self-governing motivations." In addition to its other aspects, the self (proprium) is the proprietor or governor that has ownership and responsibility for the outcome of one's life. The central theme of a life, the dominant goals of a life history, are the essence

Table 11.1 Aspects of the Proprium

Development Period	Proprium Characteristic	Personality Function
First year	Bodily self	Sensation-perception of physical pains, pleasures, and limitations.
Second year	Self-identity	Continuity of experience made possible through language.
Third year	Self-esteem	Pride in accomplishment; independence and negativism.
Four to six years	Self-extension	Abstract concept of possession: "mine."
Four to six years	Self-image	"Good" and "naughty" selves; sensitivity to praise and blame.
Six to twelve years	Self-as-rational-coper	Realistic solving of life's tasks; mediator between needs and reality.
Twelve years through adolescence	Propriate strivings	Ownership and acceptance of feelings, needs, thoughts; self-defined life goals.
Adulthood	Self-as-knower	The totality of all previous aspects of the proprium: awareness of self.

of propriate striving. Thus the content of a person's propriate strivings consists of who a person wants to be, and what he or she wants to become.

Propriate striving is a process that leads to the unification of personality and is characteristic of healthy functioning.

> Propriate striving distinguishes itself from other forms of motivation in that, however beset by conflicts, it makes for unification of personality.... The possession of long-range goals, regarded as central to one's personal existence, distinguishes the human being from the animal, the adult from the child, and in many cases the healthy personality from the sick. (Allport, 1955, pp. 50–51)

"Me, Myself, and I" and More: The Proprium

Because each of the emerging aspects of self is experienced as relevant, as personal, as "owned," Allport suggested substituting the term **proprium** for the term self or ego (1955, p. 40). The first seven aspects of the proprium consist of the bodily self, the self-identity, self-esteem, extended-self, self-image, self-as-rational-coper, and self-as-proprietor. Table 11.1 summarizes the ages at which different aspects of the proprium develop.

A key characteristic of the proprium is its warm or intimate quality, the feeling of being really a part of *me:*

> Personality includes these habits and skills, frames of reference, matters of fact and cultural values that seldom or never seem warm and important. But personality includes what is warm and important also—all the regions of our life that we regard as peculiarly ours, and which for the time being I suggest we call the *proprium*. The proprium includes all aspects of personality that make for inward unity. (Allport, 1955, p. 40)

A last aspect, **self-as-knower,** goes beyond the first seven aspects of the proprium and unifies them as objects of awareness:

> "Who is the I who knows the bodily me, who has an image of myself and sense of identity over time, who knows that I have propriate strivings?" I know all these things and, what is more, I know that I know them. But who is it who has this perspectival grasp? (Allport, 1961, p. 128)

Allport indicated that the self-as-knower is inherent to the structure of the person. It was not to be conceptualized as a "little man" or *homunculus* inside the person, but *rather as the totality of the person as process, as an entity that is becoming* (1961, p. 130; 1955, p. 53). Yet Allport readily admitted that the concept of self-as-knower still left a residue of mystery.

> It seems on the whole sounder to regard the propriate functions of wanting, striving, willing as interlocked with the total personality structure. They are felt as self-relevant, but are not caused by a separate agent within the personality. As for the knower, whether it is simply an inference we make at a high level of complexity... or whether it is necessary to postulate a pure knower, a continuing transcendental self... is a riddle we have not solved. (1961, p. 138)

FUNCTIONAL AUTONOMY: ALLPORT'S THEORY OF MOTIVATION

Allport objected to prevailing trends in motivational theory, particularly Freudian explanations, that rely almost exclusively on the person's past unconscious needs to account for his or her present status (1960, Chapters 6, 9). Allport preferred, in keeping with his emphasis on individuality, to view adult motives in terms of the person's contemporary situation and feelings. The most important concept he developed in this regard was that of **functional autonomy.** Allport proposed that new sets of motivations for behaviors may develop that are functionally autonomous or freed from their original motivations.

Allport pointed to a variety of everyday motives, freed of their initial sources, which continued to function as ends in themselves. "An ex-sailor has a craving for the sea, a musician longs to return to his instrument after an enforced absence, a city-dweller yearns for his native hills, and a miser continues to amass his useless hoard" (1937, p. 196). Although the sailor may have first gone to sea to earn a living, he is now financially secure. Yet, he continues to desire to go to sea.

Allport indicated that his development of the concept of functional autonomy was a direct response to his early encounter with Freud:

> ...you can see the impact of my encounter with Freud as the origin of my idea that adult motivation is not necessarily a channeling or conditioning, or overlay of cathected instincts or infantile motivations or fixations. The result was the concept of functional autonomy.... This was a direct answer to Freud, for Freud had thought that I was suffering from an infantile trauma. I wasn't.... He didn't perceive my contemporary motivation. His error impressed me very much, so that I kept working on the problem of motivation from a point of view of the developing adult. (Allport, 1962, p. 5)

In his presentation to a class at Boston University in 1962, he continued:

> I'm not denying or disparaging at all the Freudian contribution. But, Freud's theory to my mind just is not adequate, because some people *do* grow up *sometimes*, in *some* respects and be adult and normal in personality function. That is the focus of my concept of functional autonomy...as well as much subsequent writing. (Allport, 1962, p. 5).

Allport presented the **Zeigarnik effect** as an example of functional autonomy. Bluma Zeigarnik (1927) noted that subjects will often spontaneously resume tasks that they failed to complete during an experiment. Working with the task has become functionally autonomous of the original experimental requirements.

Functional Autonomy: Allport's Theory of Motivation **367**

BOX 11.2 *Only Connect...*

Allport was proposing a distinction similar to Maslow's later notion of the difference between deficiency and growth motivation (cf. Chapter 13). Propriate functionally autonomous motives may be viewed as goal-directed growth motives; perseverative functionally autonomous motives would be viewed as deficit motives in Maslow's hierarchy of needs.

Peter Bertocci (1950) criticized Allport's conception of functionally autonomous motives for its all-inclusiveness. Bertocci questioned the logic of Allport's concept because it seemed to imply that any motive could become autonomous if repeated often enough. Furthermore, Bertocci suggested that even if motives could become functionally autonomous with repetition, there was no limiting principle to prevent the creation of completely independent, competing motives.

In the light of these and other criticisms, Allport restated his concept to bring it into line with other developments of his theory. In 1961, he defined functional autonomy more broadly:

> *Functional autonomy... refers to any acquired system of motivation in which the tensions involved are not of the same kind as the antecedent tensions from which the acquired system developed.* (1961, p. 229; italics in original)

To modify his original conception further Allport proposed two types of functional autonomy: **perseverative functional autonomy** and **propriate functional autonomy.** In each of these forms of functional autonomy, the original motivational system is replaced by a new one. But there is a major difference between the two.

A motive becomes perseverative or self-repeating by developing roots in some biochemical or neurological process. Forms of perseverative functional autonomy include addictions to drugs, alcohol, or tobacco, the tension induced by the Zeigarnik effect, and a child's circular activities like dropping a spoon repeatedly as long as mother returns it. For example, a person may begin smoking to gain the acceptance of peers. A short time later, the underlying motivational system may involve nicotine dependence and physiologically-based withdrawal symptoms.

Propriate functional autonomy, by contrast, does not depend directly on any feedback mechanism or biochemical processes. Here, the self (proprium) determines which motives will become functionally autonomous. Consider, for example, a student who originally undertakes a field of study because it is required. He may continue to study it beyond the externally enforced requirements. He may discover the field is connected toward his ideals and plans for the future. A miser who begins to hoard and amasses a huge fortune—perhaps on the basis of a Freudian fixation at the anal level—may ultimately increase his wealth with philanthropy in mind.

Propriate functionally autonomous motives come about, according to Allport, for three main reasons:

1. *Principle of organizing the energy level:* People need new motives to consume their available energies. If existing motives have been satisfied, new ones will develop. For example, one might be a successful businessperson who enters the world of politics or a middle-aged employee who begins a new enterprise.

2. *Principle of mastery and competence:* People have the need to do more than passively react to their environment. They have the need to master it and thus experience a sense of competence in tackling the tasks of life.

3. *Principle of propriate patterning:* The self, or proprium, is the pattern or template on which functionally autonomous motives are shaped, directed, and unified.

EVALUATING GORDON ALLPORT

Gordon Allport was a founder of the academic field of personality psychology. It was his 1924 college course in personality, followed by his 1937 book, *Personality: A Psychological Interpretation* that put the subject of personality on the academic psychology map. He wrested the study of personality from the field of psychopathology and from the clinic and hospital. The present course you are taking and others like it are descendants of Allport's original Theories of Personality course taught at Harvard.

In his teaching, Allport emphasized the dynamic organization of the components of personality. He was convinced that personality was complex and could not be studied piecemeal. He first proposed the concept of refutability (testability) of theories, the active-passive dimension in evaluating human agency, and the idiographic-nomothetic distinction. As evidenced by this text, these concepts continue to be of value in the field of personality theory.

Allport pioneered the study of normal and psychologically healthy individuals and people's strengths as well as pathologies. He opposed the reductionistic psychoanalytic and behavioral approaches at a time when they predominated.

Allport's concept of trait was an incipient cognitive formulation and, as such, decades ahead of its time. Intensive studies of individuals, begun by Allport and other personologists, continue to have a very modest place in published research. The idiographic approach is more important in confidential applications such as executive selection, clinical assessment, and classified studies of powerful world leaders for governmental purposes.

In addition to his work in the area of personality, Allport also pioneered the study of the psychology of religion. His theory of intrinsic and extrinsic religiosity has generated continuing research and theoretical discussion. His own interest in religiosity as an area of study countered the fashions of his day and provided a foundation for the later work of many others. Allport also contributed to the understanding of prejudice and discrimination.

From the beginning, Gordon Allport was a ruggedly independent thinker who did not conform to the prevailing Freudian and behavioral emphases in psychology. He spent his professional life as a scholar with a serious commitment: to study the normal

---

BOX 11.3 *Only Connect . . .*

The third force, humanistic psychology (see Chapter 13), which would emphasize individuality and growth rather than pathology, has some roots in Allport's ideas. He wrote, " . . . how wrong we have been in viewing the process of growth as a reaction to past and present stimuli, neglecting the dynamics of futurity: of orientation, intention, and valuation" (Allport, 1955, p. 76).

The newly developing positive psychology movement also owes much to Gordon Allport's pioneering work. He had the insight that, " . . . we have paid more attention to the pathology of becoming than to its normal course, focusing upon disease rather than health, upon bad citizenship rather than good, and upon prejudice rather than tolerance and charity" (Allport, 1955, p. 33).

person in a way respectful of individuality. His work affirmed the human capacity for development and personal growth.

Refutability of Allport's Theory

Allport's ideas were largely refutable and intentionally so. After all, he was the person who first stressed the importance of the refutability of psychological theories. Accordingly, his work did lend itself to research, to experimental design, and to observational and correlational tests. Nonetheless, Allport's theories did not always withstand empirical tests. As we have noted, refutable theories may, at times, be refuted. For example, Allport's original concept of traits had to be modified on empirical grounds. Early research showed that situational factors (rather than traits) seemed largely responsible for people's often inconsistent behavior. Allport eventually developed a more sophisticated theory emphasizing interaction between traits and environment.

Emphasis on Active Human Agency

Allport's conception of personality included an elegant affirmation of active human agency. He rebelled against the determinism of Freudian psychology and was also opposed to behavioral reductionism. Allport's conception of personality as an open system stressed the human capacity for rational decision making and for creative problem solving. Like leading humanists such as Abraham Maslow and Carl Rogers, Allport emphasized the human capacity for seeking and overcoming challenges and for continued and active growth.

Allport's Focus on the Idiographic

Allport first brought the terms *idiographic* and *nomothetic* into psychology from philosophy. He also argued for combining idiographic with nomothetic factors in the field of personality psychology. Later, Allport's humanism and his interest in and respect for the individual pushed his efforts in the direction of the development of idiographic research methods—an area that had not been emphasized by other psychologists. His book, *Letters from Jenny* (1965), is a case in point. In it, Allport exemplified the use of personal documents as research data, a method that by definition is idiographic.

SUMMARY

Allport's early experience in an interview with Freud that he himself had engineered seemingly had lasting effects on his conceptualization of people and their motives. Refusing to accept the Freudian thesis that all motives can be reduced to a few basic unconscious drives, Allport proposed that motivational research should at least begin with an assessment of the individual's own estimates of his or her motives. *"How shall a psychological life history be written?"* became, for Allport, the abiding focus of his personality theory. Perhaps the single most important advice Allport had for psychologists was "Do not forget what you have decided to neglect." Allport's emphasis on individuality led him to adopt from the philosopher Windelband the distinction between idiographic and nomothetic strategies of acquiring knowledge. Allport argued that the two strategies should be blended to achieve what he called "full-bodied understanding of personality." Yet Allport's emphasis was largely on the idiographic. Allport conceptualized traits as the fundamental units of individual consistency.

Distinguishing between common traits and individual traits, Allport stressed that any individual possesses a unique organization of these personal dispositions to characteristic behavior and thought. A trait functions to mediate between larger classes of stimuli and equally large classes of response. The trait of sociability, for example, serves to render many diverse situations functionally equivalent by initiating a range of meaningfully consistent behaviors. Allport was careful to stress that traits are conceptualized as neuropsychic structures, that is, as real biophysical processes existing within persons.

The concept of traits was further organized into a hierarchy of cardinal, central, and a hierarchy of cardinal, central, and secondary traits. Cardinal traits are the master dispositions of personality, so pervasive and influential that they seem to color every activity of the person. Central traits are somewhat less pervasive and influential, but nevertheless exert strong directive influences on the person's characteristic ways of behaving. Secondary traits are the least influential forms of personal disposition.

Allport's abiding concern with the individual (idiographic) approach and with the concept of trait was criticized. Allport's restatement of his trait concepts stressed the need for heuristic realism in conducting research of an individual personality. The heuristic realist first recognizes that though he or she may be wrong, it is better to proceed as if traits were real entities residing in real, unique personalities. Second, though it is always a matter of approximation, and success is never certain, the heuristic realist realizes that it is better to make the attempt to understand individuals than to dismiss the idea as absurd.

Allport's personality theory also stresses the importance of individual personality unity and the fact that the person is always becoming, not just being. The sense of self that characterizes the mature, healthy individual is a gradual acquisition that proceeds through eight stages: (1) sense of bodily self, (2) sense of self-identity, (3) sense of self-esteem, (4) extension of self, (5) self-image, (6) self-as-rational-coper, (7) propriate striving, and (8) self-as-knower. The proprium, for Allport, is the final sense of self that develops in which the individual is capable of knowing and capable of knowing that he or she knows. In short, the self-as-knower poses the ultimate riddle of personality: How does the individual recognize that *he* or *she* is the person who is?

Closely connected with his concept of proprium was Allport's motivational theory of functional autonomy. Functional autonomy asserts that motives may continue to operate even when the original tensions on which they were based no longer operate. To modify the construct in the light of its subsequent criticism, Allport distinguished between two kinds of functional autonomy: perseverative and propriate. Perseverative functional autonomy involves biochemical or neurophysical processes that continue to operate through their own momentum or rhythm in the absence of the original deficit need that provoked them. Propriate functionally autonomous motives are those activities that serve some function of the self in its active striving for fulfillment.

Allport definitely took the position of human beings as active constructors of their lives. He supported the blending of idiographic and nomothetic strategies. In his own research, however, he encouraged idiographic methods more wholeheartedly, perhaps to correct for an existing imbalance in the field of personality studies.

FOR FURTHER READING

Allport's small volume, *Becoming: Basic Considerations for a Psychology of Personality* (New Haven: Yale University Press, 1955), expresses in clear form Allport's views on individuality and personal growth. It is a very popular and readable book and is in its umpteenth edition. It contains a historical survey of the use of the concept of self and Allport's recommendations for adopting the analogous concept of the proprium.

Allport's most comprehensive work in personality theory is to be found in two successive editions of the same work: *Personality: A Psychological Interpretation* (New York: Henry Holt, 1937), his first major contribution and still valuable as an introduction to his early ideas; and *Pattern and Growth in Personality* (New York: Holt, 1961), a revision of the former work that reflects Allport's changing views of such important concepts as functional autonomy and individual traits. A collection of Allport's midcareer papers may be found in *The Person in Psychology* (Boston: Beacon Press, 1968).

Allport's publication of Jenny Masterson's letters, *Letters From Jenny* (New York: Harcourt, Brace & World, 1965), provided psychologists with raw data on a unique personality that deserves the reader's careful attention. In a similar vein, Allport presents the benefits and limitations of personal documents in psychological research in *The Use of Personal Documents in Psychological Science* (New York: Social Science Research Council Bulletin, No. 49, 1942).

Allport's views on the crucial function of religion in the mature, healthy personality may be gleaned from his *The Individual and His Religion* (New York: Macmillan, 1971). Allport's book *The Nature of Prejudice* (Reading, MA: Addison Wesley, 1958) contributed much to the cause of social justice and civil rights and is still considered a classic in the field. A recent whole volume of The *Journal of Social Issues* (Fall 1999, Vol. 55, 3, Malden, MA: Blackwell Publishers) is devoted to reviewing and honoring Allport's contributions to psychology.

An interview of Allport is to be found in R. I. Evans's (Ed.) *Dialogue with Gordon Allport* (New York: Praeger, 1981) or in condensed form in Evans's *The Making of Psychology* (New York: Knopf, 1976).

Additional bibliographic and Internet sources are indicated in *Beneath the Mask* web page for Chapter 11. This can be Found on Wiley higher education web page: www.wiley.com/college/sollod

GLOSSARY

Bodily self: That sense of self based on one's physical senses and bodily reactions.

Cardinal traits: Traits that are pervasive, outstanding, and dominating. Only a few individuals have cardinal traits.

Central traits: Those five or ten traits that best describe an individual's personality. Such attributes are used to describe another person or to write a letter of recommendation.

Common traits: Generalized dispositions or shared traits, such as the capacity for gregariousness or aggressiveness.

Dynamic organization: The type of organization that characterizes personality, which Allport viewed as an organized whole that is constantly changing.

Functional autonomy: A process by which a behavior that was once set in motion by a basic motive comes to operate even when the original motive on which it was based is no longer present.

Heuristic realism: The useful working assumption that traits really exist even though the theorist realizes that this may not literally be true.

Idiographic: An approach in psychology that is concerned with identifying the unique combination of traits and other characteristics that best accounts for the personality of specific individuals. It consists of in-depth analyses of individuals, usually for clinical or evaluative purposes.

Individual traits: A term that can be applied to all traits. Each person has a personal style in expressing a common trait, such as gentleness. Moreover, a trait is always individual in that it must be viewed within the context of a person's unique organization of traits.

Mature or healthy personality: In Allport's view, a person who focuses on long-term goals over momentary needs or goals. Such a person has a

sense of self-extension, self-objectification, and a unifying philosophy of life.

Nomothetic: An approach to psychology that seeks to establish general laws of human functioning, that is, to understand the general variables and the behavior of people in general or groups of people. Most psychological research is nomothetic.

Perseverative functional autonomy: A behavior that becomes perseverative or self-repeating because it develops new motivational roots in some biological or neurological process. For example, a person who originally smokes to get the approval of peers may continue because of the development of an addiction to nicotine.

Personal disposition: Unique trait of an individual, a trait not shared with others.

Personalistic psychology: An approach to psychology that looks at every psychological process in terms of its occurrence within specific individuals. For example, instead of examining cognition or perception in general, the personalistic psychologist would focus on Jill's cognitions and cognitive process of Jack's perceptual field.

Personality: The dynamic organization within the individual of those psychophysical systems that determine his or her characteristic behavior and thought.

Personality trait: A continuing disposition to respond to one's environment in a meaningfully consistent way. Personality traits consist of neuropsychic structures that render stimuli functionally equivalent and lead to equivalent forms of adaptive and expressive behaviors.

Propriate functional autonomy: A behavior that continues because it develops new motivational roots that express the individual's propriate strivings or most cherished self-wishes or desired goals. A person who originally plays the violin because of parental pressure may continue as an adult because of a deep love of music.

Propriate striving: Striving for the attainment of personally meaningful goals.

Proprium: Allport's term for the self; it consists of the bodily self, self-identity, self-esteem, extended-self, self-image, self-as-rational-coper, self-as-proprietor, and self-as-knower.

Psychophysical systems: The physical and chemical structures and processes of the body's glands and nervous system, as well as associated psychological processes.

Secondary traits: Characteristics that are peripheral to the individual's personality, such as specific tastes in clothing, preferences for certain foods, or different musical affinities.

Self-as-knower: The last aspect of the proprium that surpasses, transcends, and unifies the other seven parts of the self through its awareness of the parts of the proprium. It is that sense of self that is aware of being and existing.

Self-as-rational-coper: That aspect of self that solves problems rationally and efficiently; knowledge that one is able to initiate strategies to attain present and future goals.

Self-esteem: Feelings about one's worthiness in the eyes of others and in one's own eyes. Based on a sense of competence or lack thereof.

Self-extension: Extension of one's sense of self. A person may extend his or her sense of self to his or her possessions, family, home, fellow humans, and country.

Self-identity: The aspect of the proprium that represents self-continuity. The regularity, the solidity, and the sameness of existence are apparent in self-identity.

Self-image: The reflected appraisals of other individuals that have become internalized; it also indicates one's own appraisal of one's virtues and weaknesses.

Self-objectification: The ability to perceive and measure realistically one's own abilities and shortcomings.

Zeigarnik effect: Named after Bluma Zeigarnik, the tendency of people to be motivated to complete an unfinished task. For Allport, the Zeigarnik effect was an example of a type of behavior that was functionally autonomous of its original motive.

Chapter 12

Rollo May

Existential Phenomenology

How are you able to live in a world where we are all alone, where we all die?

Rollo May (1989)

Freedom must be loving, and loving must be free.

Nicholas Berdyaev, *Slavery and Freedom*

| Rollo May | Born: 1909 Ada, Ohio |
| | Died: 1994 Tiburon, California |

About Rollo May's Existential Phenomenology

Some theories in personality psychology focus on narrow but manageable issues that can eventually be synthesized into a bigger picture. Rollo May has focused on broad, historically enduring, and deeply philosophical issues central to human experience. Some topics of ultimate meaning that May has addressed are indicated by some words in the titles of his books: Being, Death, Love, Evil, and Destiny.

Rollo May can be credited with bringing the ideas of largely European existential and phenomenological theorists to the attention of psychologists. Through the anthologies of writings that he edited and through his own contributions to existential phenomenological psychoanalysis, May shaped the thinking of psychologists, psychotherapeutic social workers, and other mental health professionals.

Central to May's conception of humanity are these ideas:

- Human beings are not like inanimate objects in that they experience themselves as conscious beings who experience a meaningful world.
- An individual's experience of the world—the physical world, the world of thoughts and ideas, and the interpersonal world—can be described directly,

without the use of abstract concepts that refer to impersonal processes or entities (such as repression, the id, the superego, or drive).

- Human beings can become aware of their own mortality. Such awareness that a person's life is finite emphasizes the importance of choice and commitment in the present.
- Anxiety is more than a form of psychopathology. One form of anxiety, existential anxiety, involves an individual's confrontation with the possibility of nonbeing, the possibility of being engulfed by a meaningless life.
- Human beings are always capable of change and development.
- People are, to a large extent, responsible for the meanings they experience and create. They have a great potential for good and evil, for creativity and destruction.

A LONELY YOUNG MAN, LOOKING FOR ANSWERS TO DEEP QUESTIONS

Rollo May described himself as having been an angry adolescent and rebellious in school. During his years at Michigan State College, May irked the school authorities with a student literature magazine he started and, at the suggestion of a friend, transferred to Oberlin College, a small liberal arts college in Ohio. His experience at Oberlin was positive and fed his interests in the humanities, especially Greek art and literature. He was hired by a *gymnasium* (a kind of high school and junior college) in Greece to teach English to boys between the ages of 12 and 18. He stayed in Greece for about three years teaching and studying art and painting.

> The boys were effusive, lovable, emotionally changeable. It was a case of an immediate love affair between the students and myself, but I was later to learn how unstable such adoration could be.... All this seemed to make my first year happy enough. But as the year went on I found that my habits and principles, coming from a typical small-town, midwestern childhood, such as hard work, fidelity, honesty and so on, stood by me less and less as the year progressed. (May, 1985, p. 6)

May grew lonely. There were only a few other Americans at the Greek school, and they soon ran out of things to talk about. Two new American teachers came on staff and "... the boys in the school found these new teachers to lavish their inconstant affection and charm upon" (May, 1985, p. 8). We can assume that feelings of rejection were now added to the loneliness May felt. May tried to work harder but found that the more effort he expended, the less effectively he taught. The loneliness was overwhelming:

> Finally in the spring of that second year I had what is called euphemistically a nervous breakdown. *Which meant simply that the rules, principles, values by which I used to work and live simply did not suffice anymore*. I got so completely fatigued that I had to go to bed for two weeks to get enough energy to continue my teaching. I had learned enough psychology at college to know that these symptoms meant that something was wrong with my whole way of life. I had to find some new goals and purposes for my living and to relinquish my moralistic, somewhat rigid way of existence. (May, 1985, p. 8; italics in original)

Had he been in America, May wrote that he would have sought psychotherapy at this time. Instead, a sympathetic couple teaching at the same school invited May to spend time at their home.

One late night in March, after a long talk with these new friends, May left the house and walked toward Mt. Hortiati—about ten miles away. May continued up the mountain alone in spite of a freezing rain. About six hours later he reached a plateau in the darkness and heard the barking of wolves. A pack of wolves circled around May a few times, but he reports that he was absorbed in his own inner turmoil and paid little attention to them. Fortunately for him, the wolves eventually left. May spent the rest of the night alone on the mountainside. At dawn, he made his way to the small village of Hortiati, woke up the café owner, and arranged to rent an upstairs room. After some sleep, May went down to the café, where some of the village men gathered around a stove to eat roasted fish, drink, and talk. May sat as near to them as he could "to keep warm" (1985, p. 10). He spent hours writing on the back of laundry slips he had carried from the school in his coat. Soon the village men became curious and asked about what May was writing. After his night in lonely contemplation, their reaction must have been quite jolting for the sensitive and impressionable May:

> I knew they would not understand if I talked about philosophy, and furthermore it wasn't quite true that I was writing that anyway. So I answered in my halting Greek, "I write, *what is life?*" They all leaned back with guffaws of laughter. One of them spoke out, "That's easy! If you have bread you eat, if you do not have bread you die." (May, 1985, p. 10)

May was far from familiar surroundings. He was distressed, lonely, feeling rejected and confused. In addition, the villagers' earthy philosophy, which was focused on meeting basic physical needs, must have been even more alienating. Young Rollo May was struggling for the survival of his own identity and searching for familiar landmarks by which to navigate this alien existence that threatened his understanding of the world and self. He climbed up the mountain again to contemplate the meaning of his existence. After two days, May started down Mt. Hortiati, this time to return to the home of his friends.

May spent some time around his friends' home walking in surrounding hillsides and meadows. On one day, he climbed a hill and found himself suddenly knee-deep in a field of poppies that were so beautiful, their "perfect movements seemed like children in a ballet" (1985, p. 11). He sketched those poppies that morning in 1932, and he made an important discovery that was to stay with him for many years:

> I realized that I had not listened to my inner voice, which had tried to talk to me about beauty. I had been too hard-working, too "principled" to spend time merely looking at flowers! It seems it had taken a collapse of my whole former way of life for this voice to make itself heard. (May, 1985, p. 13)

The drawing of the poppies, reproduced here in Figure 12.1 from May's book *My Quest for Beauty* (1985, p. 13), is a black-and-white pencil sketch of about a dozen flowers and foliage. Despite his description of his emotional state on that morning, the drawing is suggestive of a melancholy mood in the drooping stems of the flowers and the somewhat isolated quality of each of the individual flowers. Contrasted with other May drawings and paintings in the same book from other times in his life, the poppy drawing shows clear signs of the profundity of his distress and the depth of his depression at that time.

BOX 12.1   *Only Connect...*

Maslow's theory of the hierarchy of needs (Chapter 13) can be applied to Rollo May's experiences with the local people in Greece. They seemed to be interested only in meeting physical or physiological needs, whereas May was focused on trying to find beauty in his environment, thus trying to satisfy a higher level need or what Maslow would call a *B(eing)-need*.

Poppies, drawn at "White House,"
May 22, '32

Figure 12.1 Rollo May's drawing of a field of poppies in Greece, 1932, during his time of emotional crisis.

Source: May, 1985, used by permission.

Ironically, the chapter of the book following the one that describes this emotional crisis is "Beauty Has Kept Me Alive," which May hastily informs the reader is only a metaphorical statement, not a literal one. Yet the close association of the description of that depressed episode in his life and his later concern with nonbeing leads us to speculate about how closely May examined the issue of continued living during his crisis.

Beauty is harmony, as May explains later in the book, and harmony within himself, oneness with his own identity, with his fellows, and with nature (*Eigenwelt*, *Mitwelt*, and *Umwelt*) were to be theoretical concepts that would occupy most of May's later professional life. May's discovery of the beauty and peace that lay around him was his salvation.

Some years later, May recalled that, when he returned to America after his summer of crisis and searching in Greece, his interest in psychology centered on substantive issues and profound questions that he could not find addressed in most graduate psychology programs.

> American psychology, to which I came back, seemed naive and simplistic, omitting exactly what made life most rich and exciting. I longed for some community in which one could ask questions about the meaning of despair, suicide, and normal anxiety.... (May, 1973, p. 2)

May was looking for an approach outside of the traditions of American psychology. He was to find it in the writings of two related schools of thought, the existentialists and the phenomenologists.

The personal uncertainty he experienced had brought the young Rollo May to the edge of personal dissolution. There is every reason to believe that these experiences permanently sensitized May to the issues of existence, identity, and death, themes that were to occupy him for many years in his career as a psychologist and writer.

EXISTENTIAL PHENOMENOLOGICAL PSYCHOLOGY AND PSYCHOTHERAPY

The two philosophical traditions that inspired May, **phenomenology** and **existentialism**, were combined into a single approach to human nature, **existential phenomenological psychology**. The phenomenological tradition, pioneered by Edmund Husserl and Martin Heidegger, focused on the description of human experience as it appeared or unfolded without the application of explanatory or theoretical concepts. The idea of this approach was to "get back to the experience" itself. Concepts important in this approach, which we will define shortly, include terms such as *Dasein*, **Welt** (German for "world") *Mitwelt*, *Umwelt*, and *Eigenwelt*. The meanings of these terms, we will discover, are simpler and more basic than that of many psychological terms with which most people are more familiar. The existential philosophical tradition can be traced to thinkers such as the Russian novelist Fyodor Dostoyevsky, the Danish philosopher Søren Kierkegaard, and the French thinker Jean-Paul Sartre. The major emphasis in this tradition was that people had a responsibility for creating the meanings that they lived and for their commitments in various areas of life. In this view, people are in the ongoing process of **becoming**. In this process, people explore and develop their potentials and should bear responsibility for the choices they make. In a given situation, a person may choose to act creatively, courageously, generously, considerately, cowardly, or selfishly. Existential philosophers asserted that people should not deny their responsibility as conscious agents by referring to deterministic forces, whether they be internal drives or external intimidation.

The two threads came together in the work of psychiatrists such as the German émigré Ludwig Binswanger and the Swiss psychiatrist Medard Boss. Rollo May has been the most prominent exponent and popularizer of existential phenomenology in American psychology. For the existential phenomenologist, the central problem of human psychology is *being* and the person's awareness that someday he or she will *not be*. In metaphysics, a branch of philosophy, the study of being and reality is termed **ontology**. Many of Rollo May's (1958a, 1983) concepts and those of other existential phenomenological thinkers are ontological in character. That is to say, although the vocabulary sounds like familiar psychology—for example, *anxiety, guilt*, and *repression*—the terms are interpreted by the existential phenomenologist as reflecting the core processes of being and nonbeing.

May received his psychoanalytic training at the William Alanson White Institute and became a senior training analyst there. The White Institute was cofounded by Harry Stack Sullivan. How, then, did May reconcile the interpersonal psychoanalytic approaches of Sullivan and existential-phenomenological approaches? Rollo May achieved an integration by synthesizing those parts of psychoanalysis that are experientially based with an interest in the person's own view of reality. By avoiding the abstract psychoanalytic metapsychology of Freud's later years, May created a form of analytic existential phenomenology.

CONTRIBUTIONS OF EUROPEAN PHILOSOPHY

Rollo May began doing psychotherapeutic work and theorizing with the basic assumption that Freud's contributions to understanding human behavior, especially clinical phenomena, were largely correct (May, 1950/1970, 1960/1965). He gradually reached the conclusion, however, that Freud's concepts were philosophically unsophisticated and inadequate. May wanted to broaden the psychoanalytic horizon and emphasize a view of human nature that incorporated the ideas of a number of nineteenth and twentieth century existential and phenomenological European philosophers.

Modes of Being in European Existentialism

Ludwig Binswanger and other European existentialists and phenomenologists employed the German word *Dasein* to express an essential quality of human life. *Dasein* can be translated literally as "being" (*sein*) and "there" (*da*) (Binswanger, in May, 1958a, p. 315). The meaning of the term *world* (originally the German word *welt*) in this philosophical context is the structure of meaning and meaningful relationships in which a person exists (May, 1958b, pp. 56–59).

Dasein indicates that humans are beings who exist in relation to a specific time and place and in relation to specific meanings. Humans are actively involved in forming the meanings lived out in their existence (May, 1958a, p. 41). The existential phenomenologists refined their concept of *Dasein* or *being-in-the-world* by distinguishing three modes of world:

Umwelt, translated literally as "around-world," includes the biological drives, needs, and instincts of the individual. *Umwelt*, considered alone, corresponds to what we mean by the physical aspects of the world, including our body. May also defined **Mitwelt**:

> *Mitwelt* is literally the "with-world," the world of being-with-others, one's fellow humans. My *Mitwelt* includes the meaning I make out of my relationships with others, and they are also finding their own meanings in their relationships with me (May, 1958b, p. 63).

Eigenwelt, or "one's own world," is the mode of relationship to one's self. "It is a grasping of what something in the world—this bouquet of flowers . . . means to me" (May, 1958b, p. 63). Thus, the concept of *Eigenwelt* is not restricted to the inner, subjective world but includes one's subjective reactions to the world at large.

According to this viewpoint, the way to understand a person and their experience is to grasp these three worlds of experience *as they are experienced by the individual*, in a non-reductionistic fashion. One needs to understand how a person actually perceives and experiences the physical world, including his body, how the person experiences interpersonal relationships and the interpersonal world, and what constitutes the person's often private thoughts, feelings, and inner reactions. Existential phenomenologists are not interested in reducing or explaining such experiences by resorting to explanatory concepts such as *drives*, *cathexes*, or *libido*.

ONTOLOGICAL PRINCIPLES: "MRS. HUTCHENS"

May wanted to replace Freudian concepts with terms that more simply and directly referred to human experiences and that indicated the possibility of personal choice. For example, he reshaped Freud's concept of **the unconscious**.

> The "unconscious," then, is not to be thought of as a reservoir of impulses, thoughts, wishes which are culturally unacceptable; I define it rather as *those potentialities for knowing and experiencing which the individual cannot or will not actualize*; that it cannot be adequately comprehended in "*ego*" and "*not-ego*" terms, or even "self" and "not-self"; and that it inescapably raises the question of the human being's margin of freedom with respect to his

potentialities, a margin in which resides his responsibility for himself which even the therapist cannot take away. (May, 1960/1965, p. 178; see also May, 1983, pp. 17–18; italics in original)

It is clear that for May there is much value in psychoanalytic ideas, but that the concepts have to be transformed into first-person actions from their status as theoretical, third-person "things." The unconscious, in this example, is not a place, not a reservoir, not an internal structure. It is, rather, the process of the whole person in the acts of *wishing, fearing, knowing*, and *choosing not to know*. By these standards, a person does not "have defenses"; he or she defends against threats. Similarly, a "neurotic" person is not a person "with" a psychological disorder, nor can he or she be said to "have" symptoms. Rather, the person, along with all of his or her other human qualities, behaves anxiously or with a great deal of conflict because of the way he or she decides to interpret his or her life. A neurosis is not a condition that a person *has*. Rather, the term "neurosis" is a term that represents an ongoing pattern of choices that a person makes in order to preserve his or her own way of being or adjusting to perceived threat.

We can obtain an initial orientation to the six **ontological principles** that governed May's early views by following his account of the difficulties of "Mrs. Hutchens," one of the first patients May wrote about.

Principle One: Phenomenal Centeredness

May argues, as the European existential phenomenologists do, that genuine understanding of a person comes not from seeing people as composites of drives and deterministic forces nor by conceptualizing people as individual statistical units in the group we call humanity. If people are defined in this way for psychological understanding, "you have defined for study everything except the one to whom these experiences happen, everything except the existing person himself" (May, 1960/1965, p. 179).

May offers the extended example of one of his patients. "Mrs. Hutchens" is a woman in her thirties who presents herself as sophisticated, in control, and poised. But in her eyes, May detected "something of the terror of a frightened animal or lost child." She was referred for psychotherapy by her neurologist because of an hysterical tenseness of the larynx so severe that she could speak only in a hoarse whisper. May administered a Rorschach projective inkblot examination:

I have been given the hypothesis from her Rorschach that she has felt all her life, "If I say what I really feel, I'll be rejected; under these conditions it is better not to talk at all." (May, 1960/1965, p. 178)

As Freud discovered by the beginning of the twentieth century, hysterical symptoms rest on personal meanings, some of which are unconscious. A symptom is not random but is meaningfully related to the person's life experiences. Mrs. Hutchens's life history reveals an intimidating relationship with her authoritarian mother and grandmother, along with experiences that resulted in becoming guarded: choosing not to reveal any "secrets" at all. This background information is helpful in understanding some of the reasons why Mrs. Hutchens behaves as she does. But May argues that mere historical understanding is incomplete. Tracing the events in the development of Mrs. Hutchens's hysterical hoarseness does not provide an understanding of Mrs. Hutchens as she experiences her world. Her experience cannot be reduced to her history. Mrs. Hutchens must be grasped as an *existing person* with the "terror of a lost child" in her eyes along with her unique *continuing* reasons for *choosing to be* hoarse, controlled, guarded, and distressed. Ontological principle number one, **phenomenal centeredness**, describes the profoundly significant human core of subjectivity:

Phenomenal Centeredness:
Every person is centered in self and therefore lives, loves, hates, is creative or destructive, flexible or rigid, blind or perceptive by reason of that center.

Mrs. Hutchens can be understood only by grasping the world as *she sees it and lives it*. For Mrs. Hutchens, like every other existing person, organizes her understanding of reality and self through her experience of it. If we do not understand her experience, we do not understand her. Only by empathy and by avoiding theoretical abstractions can the observer get a glimpse of Mrs. Hutchens's world.

Principle Two: Courage for Self-Affirmation

May defines self-affirmation as the "courage to be," relying on the concepts of Paul Tillich, a theologian who influenced him greatly (May, 1973; Tillich, 1952). Without courage, according to Tillich, a person "loses being." It is courage that permits choice. Courage to be does not remove anxiety, according to Tillich. Nor can courage, by itself, lead to personality health. Rather, courage permits the healthy person to confront anxiety and avoid despair, as given in ontological principle number two, **self-affirmation and courage**:

Self-Affirmation and Courage:
Every existing person has the character of self-affirmation, which is the need to preserve his or her centeredness, and can mobilize courage to do so.

In Mrs. Hutchens's case, the possibility exists that she was confronted with three choices as she grew up. She could succumb to the authoritarian and frightening relationships and become what her elders wanted her to be. Or, second, she could rebel against their wishes and pressure, acting out her anger in some destructive way. Or, third, she could yield to despair, giving up hope and retreating from reality and life into nonbeing. What actually happened appears to be an outcome combining all three possibilities. Mrs. Hutchens has somehow found a way to avoid destructive rebellion, complete despair, and complete capitulation. What might conventionally be labeled as hysterical neurosis is, from this point of view, to be understood as an act of courage, an act of dignity, as well as a process of psychological dysfunction. Paul Tillich made these points well:

> Anxiety turns us toward courage, because the other alternative is despair. Courage resists despair by taking anxiety into itself. . . . He who does not succeed in taking his anxiety courageously upon himself can succeed in avoiding the extreme situation of despair by escaping into neurosis. He still affirms himself but on a limited scale. *Neurosis is the way of avoiding nonbeing by avoiding being.* In the neurotic state self-affirmation is not lacking; it can indeed be very strong and emphasized. But the self which is affirmed is a reduced one. (Tillich, 1952, p. 66; italics in original)

Mrs. Hutchens's previous therapist had, in fact, informed his patient that she was "too controlled" and "too proper." She became very upset and broke off treatment. The therapist, in a way, was correct, but he missed the essence of this controlled and proper person. Although these qualities can be seen as part of the "neurotic" process, the existential point is that they are Mrs. Hutchens. "Controlled" and "proper" and even the hysterical hoarseness are the adjustments to her life as she interprets it out of the center of her being. To interpret her personality qualities and behaviors as her "problem" is to attack precisely those ways of being in which she is centered and those ways of being that she has chosen to protect herself as a person.

There is to be found in Mrs. Hutchens's actions a further act of self-affirmation, **participation in other beings**. Mrs. Hutchens gathers the courage to seek out another therapist who could also demand that she change this center of being.

Principle Three: Participation in Other Beings

In seeking out her new therapist, Mrs. Hutchens confronts a new risk of losing her identity. "If the neurotic [person] is so afraid of his own conflicted center that he refuses to go out but holds back in rigidity and lives in narrowed reactions and shrunken world space, his growth and development are blocked" (May, 1960/1965, p. 181). Mrs. Hutchens sits with her new therapist:

> Now as Mrs. Hutchens talks hoarsely, she looks at me with an expression of mingled fear and hope. Obviously a relation exists between us not only here but already in anticipation in the waiting room and ever since she thought of coming. She is struggling with the possibility of participating with me. (May, 1960/1965, pp. 180–181 and 1983, p. 27)

Ontological principle number three, participation in others, formalizes this conclusion:

Participation in Other Beings:
All existing persons have the need and possibility of going out from their centeredness to participate in other beings.

May points out that it is also possible for the "neurotic" person to cope with the experience of threat to self by "overparticipating" in others. The neurotic might "lose self" by diffusing it in overidentification with others. In Mrs. Hutchens's case, she has enacted neither of these losses of self. She has acted from courage and pain to confront her conflicts. Understanding her in terms of a diagnostic classification would get in the way of a real understanding of her personal qualities and strengths (May, 1967/1979, p. 8).

Principle Four: Awareness

As May uses the term, **awareness** means alertness or vigilance. The person is wary of external threats and dangers. In the first few therapy sessions with May, for example, Mrs. Hutchens regards him as a threat. Lifelong vigilance underlies Mrs. Hutchens's guardedness. Ontological principle number four is:

Awareness:
The subjective side of centeredness is awareness.

In May's definition "awareness" is a form of self-protective, but not uniquely human vigilance (May, 1953, p. 75 ff.), which May believes has numerous counterparts in the vigilance systems of animals. It is probably best understood as an "early warning system" common to both animals and humans who feel themselves in danger. In humans, a more sophisticated level of awareness, the development of self-consciousness, has also been formed.

Principle Five: Self-Consciousness

Only a human can be self-conscious. Self-consciousness permits the person to transcend the immediate, concrete situation, to live in terms of the possible, and to use abstractions (May, 1960/1965, p. 182). But there are two sides to self-consciousness, for not only can a person be conscious of self as an active subject, a person can also be conscious of self as a passive object (May, 1967/1979, pp. 8 ff.).

As an example, May cites his own experience of writing a book under the pressure of a deadline. His first state of self-consciousness is bound by attention to externals. He looks at the clock, decides how much longer he will spend writing that morning, wonders how best to get the most done before his afternoon consultation hours begin, and he continues working. He realizes that something he has written might be criticized by a colleague and wonders whether to change the wording. He criticizes himself for worrying about what his colleague will think. He is aware that this thought is intruding on his writing. He refocuses on the writing, asking himself what is the best way to write this, what is the most efficient way to get it done, meet the schedule, make the ideas palatable to others?

As he continues to write, May becomes excited by a new idea. He enters a second state of self-consciousness. "Ah, here is something that has been playing around the fringes of my consciousness for years—what an alluring prospect to work it out now, form it, see where it leads!" (May, 1967/1979, p. 7). For a while, he is engaged in reorganizing the writing around the new idea. He wonders briefly whether his colleague will approve, then suddenly does not care because the idea is a good one. He looks at the clock and discovers that it is half an hour later than he had planned to stop.

In this brief episode, May has shown both kinds of self-consciousness. During the first part of the writing, musing about how to meet the deadline, setting time limits for himself, and wondering how best to phrase something so as not to offend a colleague, May has thought of himself as an object. But in the second phase of his writing, when the exciting idea has emerged, he becomes engaged in the idea and the process of working the idea through its many implications. His thinking reflects the change because he no longer experiences self as a "slave of time." In the second state, he is an active subject who is absorbed and engaged in what he does. Hence, we arrive at ontological principle number five, **self-consciousness**:

Self-Consciousness:
The uniquely human form of awareness is self-consciousness.

In a parallel way, May points out, a psychotherapist can be aware of his or her patient as an object or as a subject. If May were to be aware of Mrs. Hutchens as an object, he would focus on her life history, on the diagnostic category that best describes her difficulties, and on the information reported by her neurologist. Consequently, Mrs. Hutchens would be an object of his thought, but little empathic understanding of Mrs. Hutchens as an existing person would result. (May, 1967/1979, p. 8)

Principle Six: Anxiety and Nonbeing

From the existential point of view, human beings are unique in their capacity not only to be aware of self but also in their realization that the self will ultimately come to an end. Consciousness of death, of the possibility of the state of nonbeing is a powerful influence on the person's experience of self. Nothing so heightens the meaning of life as awareness of the possibility of dying.

> Death is . . . the one fact of my life which is not relative but absolute, and my awareness of this gives my existence and what I do each hour an absolute quality. (May, 1958b, pp. 48–49; see also May, 1961)

We come now to May's next ontological principle, **anxiety and nonbeing**:

Anxiety and Nonbeing:
Anxiety is the state of the person in the struggle against what would destroy his or her sense of meaningful being.

This understanding indicates that much of human anxiety arises from threats to one's sense of self and to the meanings to which one is committed. In the case of Mrs. Hutchens, May interprets her anxiety as arising from her confrontation with the imminent possibility of the death of a meaningful life. Her relationships to her mother and to her grandmother caused her to forfeit her independence and identity. May saw Mrs. Hutchens's anxiety as a sign that she realizes the threat of nonbeing in these relationships. Forfeiting one's identity is a descent into nonbeing—the death of the meanings important to the self (May, 1960/1965, pp. 183–184).

Transitional Summary

The six ontological principles we have discussed in the context of Mrs. Hutchens's therapy are a road map of the concerns that occupied Rollo May from the late 1950s until the end of his life almost 40 years later. The main themes of May's work are largely represented in these six major themes:

1. Every person is centered in self and lives life through the meaning he or she places on that center.
2. Every person is responsible for mobilizing the courage to protect the self, to affirm it and enhance its continued existence.
3. People need other people with whom they can empathize and from whom they can learn.
4. People are vigilant about potential dangers to their sense of selfhood.
5. People have self-consciousness; they experience themselves as both subject and object.
6. Anxiety originates, in part, out of a person's awareness that one's existence or sense of meaningful being can end.

THE PROBLEM OF NOTHINGNESS

"To grasp what it means to exist, one needs to grasp the fact that he might not exist . . ." wrote May, voicing one of the central concerns of the existential movement (1983, p. 105). As we have seen, such awareness is a dialectical process, for the awareness of death enhances one's sense of living. Life becomes real, vivid, and flavorful only when one confronts the possibility of nothingness. From this understanding of the significance of death comes May's definition of anxiety:

> Anxiety is *the experience of the threat of imminent nonbeing.*

and

> Anxiety is the subjective state of the individual's becoming aware that his existence can become destroyed, that he can lose himself and his world, that he can become nothing. (May, 1983, pp. 109–110; italics in original)

This ontological meaning of the term anxiety derives in part from the philosopher Kierkegaard, who, along with Freud and other European thinkers, used the German word **Angst** to describe this feeling of "losing being" (May, 1950/1970, p. 36), and in part the definition derives from theologian Paul Tillich's ideas (1952). Angst is not adequately translated into English by the word *anxiety*, for *angst* carries the connotations of "anguish" and "dread." As Tillich conceptualized the problem, "The basic anxiety, the anxiety of a finite being about the threat of nonbeing, cannot be eliminated. It belongs to existence itself" (1952, p. 39).

Ontological Anxiety in Contrast to Fear

May distinguishes between **ontological anxiety** and **fear**:

> The difference is that the anxiety strikes at the central core of his self-esteem and his sense of value as a self, which is the most important aspect of his experience of himself as a being. Fear, in contrast, is a threat to the periphery of his existence; it can be objectivated and the person can stand outside and look at it. (May, 1983, p. 110)

Anxiety has more profound effects than fear, according to May, for the experience of this emotion can overwhelm the person's "discovery of being," demolish the person's sense of time, dull the memory of the past, and even "erase the future" (May, 1983, p. 110). Anxiety can occur when a possibility for a new way of being opens for a person. That very possibility, even the possibility of positive change, is often anxiety-laden because it carries with it the seeds of destruction for the person's old way of being (May, 1950/1970, p. 36; 1983, p. 111). To give up the old is to give up security and induce angst. By the same token, to close oneself off from the possibility of change is to risk losing freedom.

Ontological Guilt

To pursue new possibilities of living is anxiety-provoking as we give up the familiar and with it our security. But to deny those possibilities, to deliberately fail to fulfill them to preserve security provokes what May termed **ontological guilt** (May, 1983, pp. 112 ff.). May points out that his conceptions of guilt and anxiety are both *ontological* conceptions. It other words, they are derived from basic qualities of "human being-ness." We can experience ontological anxiety precisely because we have choices, and our choices involve change and uncertainty. We can have ontological guilt because we might not have made the choices that were open to us, or that we might not have made the best choices. Ontological guilt is a non-neurotic form of guilt that accompanies awareness of our responsibility for our choices. Experiences of ontological anxiety and guilt stem from fundamental qualities of the human being and not from psychopathology, particular relationships, failures, or rule violations (May, 1983, p. 115).

May distinguishes among three ontological levels of guilt that correspond to the three modes of being discussed earlier in this chapter. Recall the *Umwelt* or the "world around" of natural drives and needs, the *Mitwelt* or the "with world" of being with others, and the *Eigenwelt* or one's "own world" of subjective meaning.

1. The first form of ontological guilt, then, corresponds to the *Umwelt* and is referred to as "separation guilt" in the sense of alienation or separation from the natural world. Our own technology continually distances us from nature, but the process is subtle and insidious so that we remain unaware of this kind of ontological guilt (May, 1958b, p. 54; 1983, p. 115).

2. The second form of ontological guilt corresponds to the *Mitwelt* (with world) and arises from "...the fact that since each of us is an individual, he necessarily perceives his fellow man through his own limited and biased eyes. This means that he always to some extent does violence to the true picture of his fellow man and always to some extent fails to understand fully and meet the other's needs" (May, 1958b, p. 54). May asserts that this kind of guilt is inescapable because we each have no choice but to see the world through our own eyes.

3. The third form of ontological guilt is equivalent to the *Eigenwelt* and returns us to our starting point of the person who forfeits potentialities in order to preserve security. That forfeiture produces ontological guilt at the most personal level.

Ontological guilt has four characteristics (May, 1958b, p. 55; 1983, pp. 115 ff.):

1. Everyone participates in ontological guilt because each of us distorts the reality of others and each of us fails to fulfill some of our possibilities.

2. Ontological guilt does not rely on cultural prohibitions. "Ontological guilt does not consist of I-am-guilty-because-I-violate-parental-prohibitions, but arises from the fact that I can see myself as the one who can choose or fail to choose" (May, 1958b, p. 55).

3. Ontological guilt is not neurotic or morbid. If a person can become aware of his or her ontological guilt, the person has an opportunity to accept it rather than repress it.

4. Ontological guilt does not necessarily lead to symptom formation. It might be the basis for constructive personality development. One possibility is that awareness of ontological guilt, an alertness to the vulnerability and universality of the human condition, leads to humility (May, 1958b, p. 55).

PERSONAL SOURCES OF MAY'S EXISTENTIALISM

If we take a step back from the ideas of Rollo May presented thus far, three broad themes emerge:

- First, May emphasizes the fragility of human life as well as its beauty. Like so many other personality theorists, much of May's professional concerns grew from his clinical work. There is, then, a thread of concern for the vulnerability of people to anxiety and despair and the struggle against helplessness. May's doctoral dissertation was the study of anxiety.

- The second theme that emerges from the theory thus far presented is May's profound concern with ultimate existence and death. His close association with theologian Paul Tillich is ample testimony to the importance of this theme in his work (May, 1973).

- The third theme we can trace is May's concern with loneliness and alienation in human existence. His ideas on the nature of ontological guilt that we have explored thus far can be understood as a concern with alienation from others and self, but a kind of alienation that is universal, inescapable, and experienced as profound loneliness.

BOX 12.2   *Only Connect . . .*

May's early personal history is similar to the difficult backgrounds of some of the personality theorists we have examined. His childhood, youth, and young adulthood were times of conflict, isolation, and emotional pain from which he sought relief in solitary communion with nature. Young May experienced anxiety and the pain of loneliness. Such themes are central to the philos-ophy of existential phenomenology, so it is not surprising that May was drawn to this school of thought and later devoted his professional career to this approach. May also shared with Karen Horney (see Chapter 10) an inability to lead a well-adjusted adult personal life in spite of his evident brilliance, prominence, personal psychotherapy, and intellectual insight.

These three themes are related. They evidence a great deal of coherence. Put succinctly, May's view of self, of others, and of the world emphasizes the needs for intimacy and acceptance, the human struggle against uncertainty and helplessness, and the confrontation with death and meaninglessness (nonbeing).

At the beginning of this chapter, we described the crisis that Rollo May experienced as a young man in Greece and indicated the important impact of these events and experiences. Now we are going to focus on some other aspects of May's biography. Additional personal roots of the themes in his work as a psychologist emerge as we review his life history.

May's Needs for Intimacy and Acceptance

Rollo May's childhood and family life were discordant and lonely. He was born April 21, 1909, in a small town in Ohio; the family moved to Michigan early in May's life. His father was a secretary for the YMCA and moved his family frequently. Rollo's immediate family consisted of five brothers and a sister who later became psychotic. The marital relationship was "discordant" with a rather unhappy family life as the result (Rabinowitz et al., 1989, p. 436). His experience of this family discord sparked May's interest in psychology and counseling and provoked escapes to the shores of the St. Clair River to watch the ships go by. May suggested that he learned more from the river than from his school years because the river was a "clean, deep, demonic, and beautiful friend" (quoted by Rabinowitz et al., 1989, p. 436). As a boy, Rollo found peace at the river, away from the sooty, noisy, industrial Detroit area in which he lived.

May's Confrontation with Helplessness and Death

After the emotional crisis we reviewed at the beginning of this chapter, May was on summer vacation from his job in Greece. He traveled to Vienna to study with Alfred Adler. His experience there was very positive. He even commented that Adler was "absolutely psychic in his therapy with children" (May in Rabinowitz et al., 1989, p. 67). May was also inspired by the work of Freud, Jung, and others, who were pioneers in developing psychoanalysis and related approaches.

He returned to America in 1933, with the intention of becoming a psychologist by taking a graduate degree at Columbia University. But the psychology program at Columbia was behavioral, not psychodynamic. Issues such as war, death, love, and hate were the questions that Rollo May wanted to investigate. So, after looking into the Columbia program, he decided not to apply (Rabinowitz et al., 1989, p. 436; May, 1973, p. 2).

May enrolled instead at Union Theological Seminary, where the questions in which he had become interested were being discussed by some of the many professors who had fled Nazi persecution in Europe. At this time, May began what was to be a long-lasting friendship with the theologian Paul Tillich, one of the European émigrés. At Union, May earned a bachelor's degree in divinity, but initially had no intention of a career in the ministry.

He was called home after graduation to "hold the family together" after his father left his mother (Rabinowitz et al., 1989, p. 437). Once home, he accepted a combined teaching and church position at Michigan State College in 1936. His interest in psychology and counseling combined, along with his brief studies with Alfred Adler (see Chapter 4), led to his lecturing on counseling procedures and to writing a book on counseling (May, 1939/1967a). May decided to return to graduate school again to study the process of counseling in more detail and enrolled in the clinically oriented psychology program at Teachers College of Columbia University.

Working hard in graduate school, researching his dissertation, and trying to earn a meager living by teaching part-time, May came down with tuberculosis. At that time, tuberculosis was a killer disease for which the only, usually ineffective treatment was complete rest. May spent most of the next two years in upstate New York in a tuberculosis sanatorium. During this extended period in the sanatorium, May had to confront the possibility of death from a disease about which medical science could do little. He gradually came to believe that his helpless and passive attitude was actually enhancing the disease process and decided to combat it. He reports that only when he took this more active stance did he recover:

> For a year and a half I did not know whether I would live or die. As best I could, I tried to do what my doctors instructed me to do. This meant, as I then interpreted it, accepting the program of rest and giving my healing over to others. I could only lie in bed, tracing with my eye patterns of light on the ceiling of my room, waiting for the monthly X-ray, which would tell whether the cavity in my lung had enlarged or decreased.
>
> But I found, to my moral and intellectual dismay, that the bacilli were taking advantage of my very innocence. This innocence had transformed my helplessness into passivity, which constituted an open invitation to the bacilli to do violence to my body. I saw, too, that the reason I had contracted tuberculosis in the first place was my hopelessness and sense of defeatism. . . . I could see in the apparently innocent patients around me in the sanatorium that passively accepting their powerlessness in the face of the disease meant dying. Not until I developed some "fight," some sense of personal responsibility for the fact that it was I who had the tuberculosis, an assertion of my own will to live, did I make lasting progress. (May, 1972, pp. 13–14; see also May, 1969, p. 239)

May described three types of patients he observed in the sanatorium. Some patients became passive and helpless. According to May, such patients "invite their own deaths" by essentially giving up the struggle for life (May, 1953, pp. 140 ff.). Other patients in the same sanatorium adhere to the prescribed regimen, but spend most of their time resenting their misfortune. Such people don't die, May observed, but they do not recover either. "Like rebels in any area of life, they remain on a plateau perpetually marking time" (1953, p. 141). Finally, there are those patients (one presumes this was the way May thought of himself) who confront the fact of their illness. They reflect on the meaning of their lives and try to understand what was wrong with their way of living before their illness. These patients use the illness as a means to new self-knowledge and self-discipline. "They are the ones who not only achieve physical health, but who also are ultimately enlarged, enriched, and strengthened by the experience of having had the disease" (May, 1953, p. 141).

He quotes the letter of a patient with tuberculosis. Given the allusion to overwork and three jobs, the letter could very well have been written by May himself:

> The disease occurred not simply because I overworked, or ran athwart some T.B. bugs, but because I was trying to be something I wasn't. I was living as the "great extrovert," running here and there, doing three jobs at once, and leaving undeveloped and unused the side of me which would contemplate, would read and think and "invite my soul" rather than rushing and working at full speed. The disease comes as a demand and an opportunity to rediscover the lost functions of myself. It is as though the disease were nature's way of saying, "You must become your whole self. To the extent that you do not, you will be ill; and you will become well only to the extent that you do become yourself." (May, 1953, p. 95)

May's confrontation with illness and the possibility of death led not to his demise but to a personal reorientation and to a productive and successful struggle to survive.

LOVE AND WILL

People have long sought either love or will power as the solution to many of the problems of existence. But, as May (1969) pointed out, these solutions no longer are effective in our society.

According to May, contemporary people usually believe that love and will are illusions. Contemporary life, according to May, has produced a schizoid withdrawal. He is not using the term *schizoid* in its diagnostic psychopathological meaning. Rather he is referring to a kind of empty numbness or apathy that people experience and can use as a way of avoiding or defending against the dilemmas of existence (May, 1969, pp. 27 ff.). If a person feels powerless or helpless to change his or her life, the concepts of will and love have little meaning. What is immediately lost is a concern for other people and a sense of concern for self.

Apathy and Violence

Violence can erupt out of such apathy. The person does not merely stagnate; he or she becomes increasingly apathetic and emotionally calloused.

> When I use the term "apathy,"...it is because its literal meaning is the closest to what I am describing: "want of feeling; lack of passion, emotion or excitement, indifference." Apathy and the schizoid world go hand in hand as cause and effect of each other. (May, 1969, p. 29)

May defines apathy as: "a condition in which men and women find themselves experiencing a distance between themselves and the objects which used to excite their affection and their will" (May, 1969, p. 29). A kind of numb indifference sets in as a protection against the depersonalizing, schizoid world. Such numbness breeds violence because

> When inward life dries up, when feeling decreases and apathy increases, when one cannot affect or even genuinely touch another person, violence flares up as a daimonic necessity for contact, a mad drive forcing touch in the most direct way possible. (May, 1969, pp. 30–31)

FOUR FORMS OF LOVING

From May's point of view (1969, p. 29), the opposite of apathy is love in its different forms. May distinguishes among four different **types of love**:

1. *Agapé* or *Caritas* or *Care*, the love devoted to the welfare of others; the prototype for which is the love of God for man. It is the foundation for all of the other forms of love.
2. *Sex* or lust, or what Freud called libido.
3. *Eros*, the biological drive to procreate.
4. *Philia*, or brotherly love and friendship.

Agapé or Care

For the person who evidences **Agapé** or who *cares*, things matter, people matter. There is a sense of relatedness between the person who cares and the object of care. The ancient Romans' Latin word is the root of our own: *Caritas*. Sometimes in theology the word *Agapé* is applied, as in the biblical account of God's *caring or love for humankind*. At the more human level, one cannot be indifferent if one cares. Care is essential from birth because the infant whose mother does not care will not survive. And caring can be directed toward self as well. If we do not care for ourselves, we neglect our health and well-being, producing injury and disease.

Care is associated with compassion and with empathy. It is likely that as infants we learn to care for others by the care we are shown. Care is also the foundation for wishing and willing, for we would not wish or will anything unless we care for it. But we must not assume that care is simply a feeling. It is, according to May (1969, p. 292), an ontological state, a state of being. It might lead to feeling and passion and even to motivated action, but the phenomenon of caring is part of being and the source of love and will. Caring is a form of intentionality in which the carer "throws his or her weight on the side" of another person. Caring is the prerequisite for love as it manifests itself in the remaining three forms: Sex, Eros, and Philia.

Sex: The Flight from Eros

May asserts that it is only in relatively recent times that **sex** has become as important as it is in our sexually obsessed culture. Up to Victorian times, the topic of sex was difficult to talk or write about. In Freud's day, sexuality was targeted for both personal and social repression. But, May argues, in the 1920s a revolution occurred. A belief developed in liberal circles that the opposite of sexual repression would have healthy effects. "In an amazingly short period following World War I, we shifted from acting as though sex did not exist at all to being obsessed with it" (May, 1969, p. 39). But, according to May, there are ironies in our newfound freedom with sex. Guilt and performance anxiety have been increased by the new emphasis on good technique and the implication that health requires a vigorous sex life. If you don't perform well, so this distortion goes, you are not healthy. There is also what May calls the new "puritanism" (spelled with a lowercase "p" to distinguish it from the historical Puritans):

> I define this puritanism as consisting of three elements. First, *a state of alienation from the body*. Second, *the separation of emotion from reason*. And third, *the use of the body as a machine*. (May, 1969, p. 45; italics in original)

This new "puritanism," according to May, involves depersonalized sexual activity that is devoid of caring, love, and passion. People use impersonal terms ("having sex" or "getting laid" rather than "making love" or, more simply, "love") to describe sexual intercourse. May's picture of sexual attitudes and behavior is one of depersonalized, mechanized, obsessive human interaction devoid of caring, relatedness, and joy.

What motives underlie such depersonalized, confused, and uncaring sexual preoc-cupations? May offers three major answers:

1. There is the motive of *trying to prove one's identity* based on a misguided egalitarianism of the sexes. "Egalitarianism is clung to at the price of denying not only biological differences—which are basic, to say the least—between men and women, but emotional differences from which come much of the delight of the sexual act" (May, 1969, p. 54).

2. Also involved is the need behind some sexual behavior to overcome isolation, loneliness, and feelings of emptiness: "...partners pant and quiver hoping to find an answering quiver in someone else's body just to prove that their own is not dead; they seek a responding, a longing in the other to prove their own feelings are alive" (May, 1969, p. 54).

3. Also, the need to prove oneself competent is often an underlying motive. A man, for example, may feel inferior or very insecure if his "technique" is unpracticed or not in line with the "latest" advice of media experts. Sex therapists have developed many remedies for sexual performance difficulties, some of which, in May's opinion, are more demeaning than the original sexual problem itself. Obsessive concern with performance ironically lessens sexual enjoyment.

What is missing in all of this, May asserts, is true passion—a desire to make love to one's partner because there is healthy lust, mature caring, and satisfying communication between the two people. In May's terms, sex has become superficial and disconnected from both the deep yearnings of *Eros* and the connectedness of *Caritas*.

Eros and Death

According to May, people have learned to anesthetize their deeper emotions in order to achieve better sexual performance. May sees sex as being used as a test of competence, and asserts that people often give up their identity in the search for intimacy. "We fly to *the sensation of sex in order to avoid the passion of* **eros**" (1969, p. 65; italics in original).

May explains that, in Greek mythology, Eros is the god of more than simply eroticism. Eros was one of the four original gods: Chaos, Mother Earth (Gaea), and Tartarus (the pit of Hell). According to the myths, Eros created life on earth. Eros is thus a progenitor, a creator, and the source of life. Eros involves yearning and a desire to transcend ourselves. Sex, for some people, is equivalent to orgasm, but Eros involves a sense of union with one's partner. Sex is surface satisfaction, whereas Eros involves delight in the beloved.

But there is a dark side to Eros as well. To love another, one must open the self to the possibilities of grief, sorrow, disappointment, and loss. To "fall" in love, one's reason is suspended in the service of Eros's passion. May pits the positive delight of love against the possibility of nonbeing or death:

> For death is always in the shadow of the delight of love.... When we love, we give up the center of ourselves. We are thrown from our previous state of existence into a void; and though we hope to attain a new world, a new existence, we can never be sure.... This experience of annihilation is an inward one and, as the myth [of Eros] rightly puts it, is essentially what *eros* does to us. To love completely carries with it the threat of annihilation of everything. This intensity of consciousness has something in common with the ecstasy of the mystic in his union with God: just as he can never be sure God is there, so love carries us to that intensity of consciousness in which we no longer have any guarantee of security. (May, 1969, p. 101; italics in original)

According to May, the relationship between love and death can be viewed in a number of different ways:

- Recognition of our own mortality heightens our appreciation of those things that give us pleasure.
- Both mythology and popular figures of speech ("I love you so much, I could die!") and psychotherapy patients' dreams and associations provide a metaphorical connection between love and death. The experience of orgasm, May suggests, is possible only when one can "let go" completely or surrenders one's being completely, as in death.
- There is a defensively disguised connection between love and death. It is possible, for example, to pursue obsessive concern with sex as a way of avoiding the fear of death. Or, along a different defensive pathway, the person may invest self so completely in sexual love that he or she can simply repress the fear of death. In contemporary society, whereas we rarely speak about death openly, it is usually easier and more acceptable to talk about sex.
- Sexual love is a way of "making ourselves infinite" in the face of our own mortality, the eventuality we fear most and speak of least (May, 1969, p. 106).

In short, May believes that many factors underlie a profound connection between love and death.

Philia: Brotherly Love and Friendship

Philia is friendship or *brotherly love*. It involves a kind of acceptance, in which the lover accepts, and enjoys, simply being with the beloved. In a way, Philia provides Eros with time to grow stronger and sink deeper roots (May, 1969, p. 317).

In turn, as Philia supports Eros, Agapé supports Philia. Agapé, recall, is a kind of esteem for the other in which there is no intention of getting something from the other. It is a genuinely disinterested love for another, modeled on the Biblical accounts of God's love for humans (May, 1969, p. 319). The New Testament renders the concept of Agapé as charity, which may be a poor translation but nevertheless conveys its selfless and altruistic quality. Philia needs Agapé in order to flourish, for the mutuality and acceptance embodied in Philia can flourish only when it is truly selfless. And, as we might expect, all three kinds of loving—Sex, Eros, and Philia—ideally rest on a foundation of Agapé—unselfish caring love.

GOOD AND EVIL

Through his many writings, May grapples with enduring and profound aspects of experience. Fear, anxiety, love, sex, death, being, and nothingness constitute just a partial list. May pictures humans neither as saints nor as sinners. He has consistently taken the position that humans are both good and evil. People are involved in a continuing struggle between good and evil, being and nonbeing, creation and destruction because of what May has emphasized is a *daimonic* element in human nature.

The Daimonic

The word *daimon* is to be distinguished from the more typical word *demon*. May is not using the term with any implication of some substantive thing or entity, such as a demon or devil, and he has clearly distinguished between the two (May, 1986b).

BOX 12.3 *Only Connect...*

Recall a similar concept to Philia in Harry Stack Sullivan's "chum" relationships of adolescence (see Chapter 9). The chum is the developing person's first opportunity to care for someone as much as he or she cares for self. Sullivan believed that prior to the "chum period" (approximately ages 8 to 12), the child is not capable of genuine love. Without the chum experience, Sullivan felt that heterosexual love relationships would be difficult to form (Sullivan, 1953b, pp. 223 ff.). In a way, Sullivan and May are both pointing to the necessity for learning mutuality and cooperative interaction with peers as a sound basis for loving, adult relationships. Out of the experience of "brotherly love" grows the possibilities of truly loving another.

The word can be spelled "demonic" (the popularized form), or "daemonic" (the medieval form often now used by the poets—Yeats, for example), or "daimonic" (the derivative from the ancient Greek word "daimon"). Since this last is the origin of the concept, and since the term is unambiguous in its including the positive as well as the negative, the divine as well as the diabolical, I use the Greek term. (May, 1969, p. 123n.)

The **daimonic** in May's usage is *"any natural function which has the power to take over the whole person"* (1969, p. 123). It can be a creative "taking over," as in lovemaking, or it can be destructive, as in sexual compulsion. What is daimonic in people can be the best that they are capable of, such as poetry, art, dance, literature, and ethical and religious convictions. The daimonic can be contagious, as when a charismatic figure exhorts others to his or her cause. The daimonic in us can even lead to ecstasy, as in the feeling of lovers for each other or the religious mystic's feeling of being swept away in the presence of the divine. But the daimonic can also be an expression of the worst in humans, the void of nothingness or nonbeing. The daimonic can assert itself in psychosis, or in a destructive cause.

According to May, when the daimonic is repressed in us, it tends to erupt in some other way. Violence is the daimonic unleashed without the balancing forces of reason and love. Freud's idea of the instinctual drives of the id is very similar to May's notion of the daimonic. May rightly credits Freud with detailing the power of the daimonic in his description of the dark urges and fantasies of which we are capable. When the daimonic takes over, the person's sense of self is no longer in control. Such a condition is revealed in psychotherapy when the patient says, "I felt like I had no control. I couldn't help myself" (May, 1969, p. 146 ff.).

WILL

Is it accurate to conclude that the daimonic is responsible for our actions, for our decisions? Are we the creatures of fate? Or do we intend our actions and therefore assume responsibility for our thoughts and actions? This is a question that May raises, the question of the existence of **will**.

Are We Responsible Agents?

May believes that Freud's greatest contribution was to peel away the illusion of what Victorians had termed "will power" to show that unconscious urges, drives, and wishes prompt much of our behavior. "Under his penetrating analysis, Victorian 'will' did, indeed, turn out to be a web of rationalizations and self-deceit" (May, 1969, p. 183).

Freud and other intellectuals fostered a tendency for people to view themselves as passive, pushed by forces for which they have little responsibility. This picture itself can undermine a sense of will and responsibility. It can become a self-fulfilling prophecy. People sometimes believe that even if they make decisions, exert effort, their actions will inevitably be futile in the face of deterministic forces that they cannot control.

Intentionality: The Subject-Object Bridge

May's proposed alternative to the deterministic conception of human action rests on European phenomenological philosophers' analysis of a way of knowing termed **intentionality.** Intentionality is a bridge between subject and object, between knower and known. It refers to the inextricable connection between our awareness and objects of awareness, the idea that there is no act of consciousness without an object of consciousness. One meaning of this concept is that our consciousness does not exist independent of the meanings and meaningful world we experience. Intentionality, therefore, is the person's ongoing and inevitable application of meaning to objects and people in his or her world, and to the experience of the world itself.

> [Intentionality] . . . is the structure of meaning which makes it possible for us, subjects that we are, to see and understand the outside world, objective as it is. In intentionality, the dichotomy between subject and object is practically overcome. (May, 1969, p. 225)

The concept of intentionality is a way of saying that we really cannot know a thing, unless we have, in some way, already participated in it. "I take this to mean that in the process of knowing, we are in-formed by the thing understood, and in the same act, our intellect simultaneously gives form to the thing we understand" (May, 1969, p. 225).

How does the concept of intentionality undermine the idea of determinism? The answer is that, from this point of view, the events in the world cannot be external causes of human behavior. Rather, even in the very experience of such events, acts of awareness and assignment of meaning are involved. The external events do not have inherent meaning. They are meaningful only as objects of intentional acts of consciousness.

May asserts that we inevitably impose our meanings on the people and things we observe. He (May, 1969, p. 224) gives the example of examining a house to rent. If the house hunter approaches the search for a suitable house in which to spend the summer months, issues such as how much sun the house gets, how soundly it is built, and whether there are guest rooms for friends will be paramount in shaping the meaning of *house* as "shelter." But if the house hunter examines houses from the viewpoint of a real estate speculator, then issues such as can a rundown house be fixed cheaply and resold for more than its purchase price, and can the house be made attractive to a particular group of buyers transform the meaning of house into "profit." Or, finally, if our house hunter is an artist looking for an aesthetically pleasing arrangement of house, hillside, and trees, the meaning of *house* becomes "beauty."

While considering the example given above, it is good to keep in mind that intentionality is an ontological concept, one rooted in our very being, regardless of whatever are the particular meanings that we might experience.

Will and Intentionality

Will and intentionality are linked. The connection between them is the fact that an intention and the resulting action are part of the same process. A willed action is implied by an intention, and an intention leads to the willed action. The only difference is when they occur. In the present, we are capable of intending a specific future action, as when we say, "I *will* go to England next week." The fact that the traveler projects an action for the future means that the meaning of this action already exists in his or her mind. When a person wills the action to be carried out—that action will embody the intention that preceded it.

May asserts that, in acts of intentionality and will, a person experiences his or her identity as an existing person. According to May, "I conceive—I can—I will—I am" (May, 1969, p. 243). The depression of some patients in therapy can be usefully understood as an incapacity to imagine their own futures: In effect, the patient says "I can't," and the therapist's job is to help the patient see the possibility for "I can." For it is in the "I will" and the "I can" that we are most authentically ourselves, most fully aware of our own existence, and most completely conscious of our identities.

Love and Will United

Loving and willing are not complete opposites, according to May. They are similar in that they both involve reaching out to someone or something and attempting to produce an effect. Love and will aim at influencing others. Both love and will are ways of molding, forming, relating to the world (May, 1969, p. 276). Love and will do not become united without our intention to unite them. An important task for adults is to unite love and will in their actions and in their speech to a variety of parental demands.

As any parent knows, children often exert their will in opposition to love. They say "no" loudly and clearly think of these developments as the emergence of individuality and independence. We usually think of these developments in a positive light. But, without the eventual development of the capacity to love and to care for others, children would grow into self-centered, narcissistic, and selfish individuals. Instead, most children learn also to deny self in a variety of tempting situations and to express caring, love, and consideration. Development involves learning to reach out to others, giving as well as getting.

As adults, we need to relearn, time and again, to combine love and will. May sees unifying love and will as an important developmental task. When it is accomplished, the result is mature integration and harmony.

FREEDOM

Freedom is defined as the capacity to make choices. If we do something without having made a choice, it is not a free action and does not have the same significance as a free choice would have. To take one example, May asks what value we would place on a person's love if we knew that the person was forced to love us (1981, p. 6). Unless love is given freely, it loses much of its value as love. In fact, one might question whether it would be love at all. People sometimes deny their freedom. One aspect of contemporary life is that people often say that they had no choice when anyone can see that they did choose a particular course of action.

Freedom of Doing

Freedom of doing is defined by May as "...the capacity to pause in the face of stimuli, from many directions at once, and, in this pause, to throw one's weight toward

There is a fundamental difference between May's idea of freedom of action and behavioral or psychodynamic views (see Chapters 2 and 3). The behaviorist would be inclined to look at a person's conditioning history in order to explain his or her choice of a product at a supermarket, whereas the analyst might refer to the satisfaction of a drive. Thus, a person with a proclivity to drink sodas might be seen as conditioned or as having oral cravings. The existentialists are open to the idea of individual freedom and choice, although they do not ignore the possibility that compulsions to behave in certain ways might occur in some cases.

this response rather than that one" (May, 1981, p. 54). It is the kind of freedom we experience in everyday activities when we make the myriad choices and decisions that constitute a day's activities. When we select one product rather than another from the supermarket's shelves, or when we watch one TV program rather than another, we are experiencing freedom of doing. One of the most interesting examples of freedom of doing is our ability to ask questions. The fact that questions occur to us implies that the question has more than one answer, or there would be no point in asking the question.

Freedom of Being

May distinguishes **freedom of being** as a second category of freedom that may also be called "essential freedom." Freedom of being is the origin of freedom of doing and goes to a deeper level of human existence. Instead of focusing on the act, or on the process of decision, freedom of being is concerned with the context of acts and the ability to choose one's attitude toward events whether one acts or not (May, 1981, p. 55).

May offers as an example the accounts of psychoanalyst Bruno Bettelheim, who was imprisoned in a Nazi concentration camp during World War II. Bettelheim had no freedom of action whatsoever, but he could choose his attitude toward his captors. Bettelheim could reflect, ponder, and ask spoken or unspoken questions about the situation and the people who controlled his daily life. Thus freedom of being is an inner, spiritual freedom that may or may not be reflected by external behavior.

DESTINY

Cooperating with Destiny

May resolves the conflict between determinism and freedom by conceptualizing these apparent opposites as dialectical, that is, as involved in reciprocal interaction. May is saying that the meaning of the terms *freedom* and *determinism* is each dependent on the other: One cannot be free from determinism unless determinism is possible, and one cannot be determined unless it is possible to remove a person's freedom (1981, p. 95).

> *Freedom and determinism give birth to each other. Every advance in freedom gives birth to a new determinism, and every advance in determinism gives birth to a new freedom.* Freedom is a circle within a larger circle of determinism, which is, in turn, surrounded by a larger circle of freedom. And so on ad infinitum. (May, 1981, p. 84; italics in original)

May thus acknowledges the possibility of determinism, but he prefers to use the term *destiny* to describe the limits of freedom for human beings. Billiard balls struck by other billiard balls are "determined" in the flight across the table. But humans are limited by their "destinies."

May defines **destiny** as the "pattern of limits and talents that constitutes the 'givens' in life" (1981, p. 89). May believes that it is through our very confrontation with these limits, with these "givens," from which our creativity and freedom emerge.

Destiny's Different Forms

Destiny (May's term for the limits of human freedom) has many levels, and each of the levels differs in the degree to which it yields to human intervention. May distinguishes four levels:

1. Cosmic destiny, sometimes termed "acts of God." Included here are birth, death, earthquakes, volcanoes, and other relatively unpredictable natural events that affect our lives but about which we can do nothing.

2. Genetic destiny, our inherited genome, which governs many of the physical traits with which we are born, including the color of our eyes or skin and our gender. Genetics may also play a role in the talents we have for art, music, mathematics, and so on. We can enhance or cooperate with our genetic givens to a degree, but there is little we can do to change what we inherit.

3. Cultural destiny, which includes the family, society, and culture into which we are born. We do not get to choose these "givens," although, through our attitudes and actions, we may greatly influence their effects.

4. Circumstantial destiny, which includes human events over which we individually have no control, such as the rise and fall of the stock market, or a terrorist act.

Figure 12.2 summarizes the spectrum of limitations that May envisioned as forms of destiny. As you move across the spectrum in Figure 12.2 from left to right, the degree of human control or choice increases.

May states that there are at least five ways that a person can relate to his or her destiny:

1. *Cooperate with destiny* and accept that one's life is shaped by it.
2. *Acknowledge destiny* in our limitations, such as height, weight, and death.
3. *Engage destiny* by actively seeking out the challenge of our limitations and trying to transcend them.
4. *Confront and challenge destiny* by attempting to see the most productive path that destiny provides and trying to overcome the destructive directions destiny tries to enforce.

Figure 12.2 Degrees of human intervention in destiny.

Drawn from a description in May, 1981, p. 91.

5. *Rebel against destiny* by refusing to accept it or cooperate with it. We can, for example, rage against death. It is not clear, however, what such "rebelling" can do to affect destiny.

Even if we cannot change certain limitations, we are free in how we relate to them.

EVALUATING ROLLO MAY

May's approach borrows heavily from psychoanalysis, ego psychology, philosophy, and theology. What he has created is an approach to human experience that includes an understanding derived from philosophical as well as psychological insights. The result is a set of ideas that encourages us to see ourselves as conscious beings capable of free choices. Many problems formerly considered psychopathological are viewed by May as inevitable consequences of having awareness and choice.

During the years since May's death, there has been a continuing interest in existential phenomenological psychology. At least one doctoral psychology program, at Duquesne University, is committed to this approach. It is also emphasized at the Saybrook Institute and by some scholars scattered throughout the United States and Europe. In addition, the past decade has shown an increase in the acceptance of the value of qualitative psychological research. Much of this research is in the phenomenological tradition of direct inquiry of subjects concerning their experiences. Such research might involve eliciting subjects' own accounts or narratives.

Refutability of May's Approach

Almost by definition, the existential phenomenologist would find the concept of scientific refutability inappropriate, if not irrelevant. However, because May has attempted to synthesize psychoanalytic ideas into his theory, there are some questions about refutability that pose themselves.

In May's earliest work on anxiety, the definitions he provides of normal and neurotic anxiety, and the hypotheses drawn loosely from psychoanalytic theory, surely lend themselves to empirical test. In fact, May's own doctoral dissertation, a part of which found its way into May's 1950 book on anxiety, was just such an attempt. But then there is the rest of May's work. What scientific psychological sense can we make of concepts such as *ontological principles, nonbeing,* and *will*? Because these terms and their associated ideas deal with unobservables, and with processes that do not have measurable empirical referents in action or thought, they remain outside the scope of refutability altogether. We are not even certain that the concept of refutability is the right question to ask about concepts such as these.

But even in this thicket of metaphysics there lurk some ideas that have a possibility of translation into refutable statements. *Destiny* may not of itself be a refutable concept, but what about the person's conception of destiny? Using May's hypothetical dimension of destiny, as illustrated in Figure 12.2, could we not devise a measure of people's reactions to the limitations that life hands them? Could we not develop a way of measuring the subjective reaction to destinies, such as the chance events of earthquakes, and the social constraints of other people's reactions to our handicaps and infirmities? In a way, the social learning theorists have begun to consider the power of destiny in shaping our perceptions of our lives. The social cognitive theorist, Albert Bandura (1986, 1989) avoids the term *destiny* in favor of either the term *chance* or *fortuitous events* (see Chapter 15).

On the whole, May's theory is comprised of a composite of largely nontestable ideas, with small pockets of potentially empirical constructs.

May's Conception of Human Agency

May's ideas on will, intentionality, destiny, and helplessness make it clear that he regards the person as capable of both active and passive agency. May's philosophical argument puts the body of his work on the side of an active agency conception of the person. May asserts that intentionality is an inherent aspect of the human being from which active willing emerges. May views much psychopathology (alienation, depression, despair, and violence) as the result of blocking the person's freedom. Mature personality integration is possible, therefore, in May's estimation, only when the person is free to exercise will in decision and in action.

May's Idiographic Focus

May's focus is a composite of particular and general, of specific and universal. At the most abstract, he deals with universals: existence, being, nonbeing, destiny, freedom, and so on. But he places the highest value on understanding the *individual's* unique embodiment of these universals. In fact, May's particular version of the existential phenomenological position emphasizes individual meanings, individual perceptions, and centeredness in the individual self.

May also borrows much from psychoanalysis, itself a highly idiographic account of people. Also, because such a large portion of May's work has centered on the clinical issues of treatment for psychological disorder, we would expect his focus to be idiographic rather than nomothetic. And because so much of the theory is couched in untestable terms, the usual relationship between degree of idiography and testability prevails: The more idiographic a theory is, the less likely will it generate empirical referents to permit its concepts to be tested.

SUMMARY

Rollo May attempts to blend the more clinical and experience-near ideas of psychoanalysis with the philosophical issues raised by the European phenomenologists and existentialists. His earliest efforts involved introducing existential phenomenological theory into American psychology. This approach focuses on ontological issues, that is, issues involving the conceptions of being. The person is conceptualized in such a way as to emphasize the ongoing, continuously becoming aspects of human personality. The existential phenomenological philosophers and psychologists distinguish among three modes of being:

- *Umwelt*, or the "around-world," meaning the natural world of biological urge and drive;
- *Mitwelt*, or the "with-world," meaning the social, interactive, interpersonal aspects of existence; and
- *Eigenwelt*, or the "one's own world," meaning the subjective, phenomenal world of the self.

May proposed six ontological principles, discussed in the context of the case of his patient, Mrs. Hutchens:

1. Every person is centered in self and lives life through the meanings he or she places on that center.
2. Every person is responsible for mobilizing the courage to protect the self, to affirm it, and enhance its continued existence.
3. People need other people with whom they can empathize and from whom they can learn.
4. People are vigilant about potential dangers to their sense of selfhood.
5. People have self-consciousness; they experience themselves as both subject and object.
6. Anxiety originates, in part, out of a person's awareness that one's existence or sense of meaningful being can end.

May defined anxiety as the active confrontation with nonbeing. Only the human person, he points out, is capable of envisioning a time when he or she will not be. The realization of one's own mortality is a powerful determinant of our behavior. When a person yields to anxiety and refuses to make choices or retreats from living, the result is feelings of helplessness, despair, and ontological guilt. Ontological guilt parallels the three kinds of being in the world, so that we can feel ontological guilt in a separation from the natural world (*Umwelt*), or experience guilt as alienation from self (*Eigenwelt*), or be aware of ontological guilt as alienation from others (*Mitwelt*).

We can trace the personal sources of May's interest in European existential and phenomenological philosophy in terms of his early discordant family life and subsequent sensitivity to loneliness, his personal confrontation with death when suffering from tuberculosis, and his personal desire to struggle against feelings of helplessness and despair at all costs.

May dealt with the theme of apathy in his discussion of love and will. He distinguishes among four kinds of loving:

1. *Agapé* or *Caritas* or *Care*, the love devoted to the welfare of others, the prototype for which is the love of God for man. It is the foundation for all of the other forms.
2. *Sex* or lust, or what Freud called libido.
3. *Eros*, the drive to procreate.
4. *Philia*, or brotherly love and friendship.

May argued that modern society has trivialized sexuality, separated it from passion, undermined the human motivation for procreation contained in Eros, and forced people into uncaring and indifferent attitudes toward each other.

The issues of good and evil occupied May at some length. He argued that human nature is a composite of both good and evil, and he wrote metaphorically about this composite in his conception of the *daimonic*, which is defined as any natural human function which can reach such intensity that the person is overcome by it. On the positive side, the daimonic is the force underlying creativity and self-affirmation. On the negative side, the daimonic can be destructive addiction to power or fascination with death.

May addressed the issues of freedom, responsibility, and determinism with his conception of destiny. In his view, destiny is a kind of dimension ranging from cosmic acts that affect us but over which we have no control to the inheritance of talents and handicaps, about which we may exert some choice. He argued that ultimately people are free in being, if not in action, because they can choose the meaning they will place on what reality provides. Intentionality, to be distinguished from intention, is a kind of subjective bridge between the passive and the active, between the subject and object in existence. Reality may provide its own input into our lives, but we make much of the reality that we interpret.

Our evaluation of May indicates that his blend of existential phenomenology and psychoanalysis focuses on broad, philosophical questions. As such, May's theory is largely, but not completely, untestable. It is strongly pushed toward the idiographic end of the idiographic-nomothetic spectrum, and it conceptualizes people as largely active agents with the freedom to act or to choose how they will permit fate or destiny to affect them.

FOR FURTHER READING

The clearest overview of existential phenomenology in psychology that May provides is found in an anthology he coedited entitled *Existence: A New Dimension in Psychiatry and Psychology* (R. May, E. Angel, & H. F. Ellenberger [Eds.], New York: Basic Books, 1958). A more recent presentation of much of the same theoretical material may be found in May's *The Discovery of Being: Writings in Existential Psychology* (New York: Norton, 1994). To round out the historical and philosophical picture, William Barrett's classic *Irrational Man: A Study in Existential Philosophy* (New York: Doubleday Anchor, 1962) remains a scholarly and readable approach. Existential phenomenological psychiatrist Medard Boss's *Existential Foundations of Medicine*

and Psychology (New York: Jason Aronson, 1995) is similar to May's approach in that it is another comprehensive existential phenomenological theory informed by psychoanalysis. Boss's discussion of the psychological issues surrounding perception of one's own mortality is especially clear and engaging.

May's earliest theoretical writing on anxiety, *The Meaning of Anxiety* (New York: Norton, 1996), gives some indication of the development of his thinking. For comparison purposes, the reader might want to consult May's later writings, which expand upon many of the fundamental issues with which he began. A good starting place is May's *Love and Will* (New York: Norton, 1989).

Glimpses into May's personal history can be most efficiently accomplished by examining May's *My Quest for Beauty* (Dallas: Saybrook, 1985). This book also includes a sample of May's paintings and drawings, which are well worth more than a casual glance.

Viktor E. Frankl's *The Unheard Cry for Meaning: Psychotherapy and Humanism* (New York: Simon & Schuster, 1997) gives a concise overview of yet another way to interpret existential phenomenological philosophy in personality psychology.

Further suggested readings on Rollo May and existential phenomenology may be found on the web site for Chapter 12 at www.wiley.com/college/sollod

GLOSSARY

Agapé: Caring. In May's theory, *caring* is more than a feeling; it is a state of being that is the source of love and will.

Angst: In German, the feeling of "losing being," anguish, dread. It is, in May's theory, the basic anxiety of a finite being about the threat of nonbeing.

Anxiety and nonbeing: Anxiety is the state of the person in the struggle against what would destroy his or her being. At a deep level, anxiety always involves a confrontation with the possibility of nonbeing.

Awareness: The subjective side of centeredness is awareness. For May, this term means vigilance. The person is wary of external threats and dangers.

Becoming: The process in which an individual is continually struggling to develop and discover what his or her potentialities are, and assume responsibility for their expression.

Circumstantial destiny: Human events over which we individually have no control, and which we cannot ignore, undo, or avoid.

Cosmic destiny: Unpredictable, natural events that affect our lives, but about which we can do nothing.

Cultural destiny: The family, society, and culture into which we are born. We do not choose those givens, but we may influence their effects to some extent.

Daimonic: Any natural function that has the power to take over the whole person. This force can be either creative or destructive.

Dasein: (German for "being there") Human being, being-in-the-world. The term *Dasein* indicates that a human being does not exist apart from his or her experience of the world at a particular time in a specific place.

Destiny: May uses the term *destiny* to describe the limits of freedom. These limits or "givens" have four levels: *Cosmic, genetic, cultural*, and *circumstantial*.

Eigenwelt: (German for "one's own world") One's experience of thoughts and feelings, involving self-awareness and self-relatedness.

Eros: The passionate desire to unite with another person. It leads people to search for a tender relationship within a sexual context and to seek wholeness with that partner.

Existentialism: A philosophical approach emphasizing that people have a responsibility for their actions, beliefs, and commitments. Søren Kierkegaard and Jean-Paul Sartre are two philosophers associated with this approach.

Existential phenomenological psychology: An approach to psychology that combines the emphases of existentialism and those of phenomenology.

Fear: The emotions accompanying the sense of a threat to the periphery of one's existence; the person can stand outside and look at it objectively.

Freedom: The capacity to make choices. May distinguished between *freedom of doing* and *freedom of being*.

Freedom of being: An essential freedom, the deeper origin of the freedom of doing. It is concerned with the context of acts and the ability to choose one's attitude toward events—whether one acts or not. It is an inner spiritual freedom.

Freedom of doing: May stated that it is "the capacity to pause in the face of stimuli, from many directions at once, and in this pause, to throw one's weight toward this response rather than that one. It represents the myriad of choices and decisions we make on a daily basis."

Genetic destiny: That which is embodied in our genetic makeup.

Intentionality: A person's ongoing application of meaning to objects and people in his or her world, and to the experience of the world itself.

Mitwelt: (German for "with-world") One's experiential world of interpersonal relationships and interrelatedness. It includes the meaning the individual attaches to those relationships.

Ontological anxiety: The emotion accompanying the sense of a threat to the core of a person's self-esteem and sense of value as a self.

Ontological guilt: The sense of guilt that arises because we might not have made the choices that were open to us, or that we might not have made the best choices. This is a non-neurotic form of guilt.

Ontological principles: Six principles or guidelines that May thought are necessary to understand human behavior: *phenomenal centeredness, self-affirmation and courage, participation in other beings, awareness, self-consciousness*, and *anxiety and non-being*.

Ontology: A branch of philosophy that seeks to understand the nature of being. It studies the processes of *being* and *nonbeing*, and the person's own view of reality.

Participation in other beings: All existing persons have the need and possibility of going out from their centeredness to participate in other beings.

Phenomenal centeredness: Every person is centered in self and therefore lives, loves, hates, is creative or destructive, flexible or rigid, blind or perceptive because of that center.

Phenomenology: The philosophical approach pioneered by Edmund Husserl and Martin Heidegger, which focuses on the description of human experience as it appears or unfolds, without the application of explanatory or theoretical concepts.

Philia: Friendship or "brotherly love." It is a love that accepts and enjoys the other person.

Self-affirmation and courage: Every existing person has the character of self-affirmation, which is the need to preserve his or her centeredness, and can mobilize courage to do so.

Self-consciousness: The uniquely human form of awareness is self-consciousness. Self-consciousness permits the person to transcend the immediate, concrete situation, to live in terms of the possible, and to use abstractions. The person is conscious of self both as an active subject and as a passive object.

Sex: One of the biological drives, the biological aspect of love. It is often described as libido or lustful love.

The unconscious: According to May, those potentialities for knowing and experiencing that the individual cannot or will not actualize.

Types of love: May distinguished between four types of love: *Agapé, Sex, Eros*, and *Philia*.

Umwelt: (German for "around-world") The experience of the physical aspects of the internal and external environments. The *umwelt* is that aspect of the experienced world that includes biological needs, drives, and instinct. It is one mode of being-in-the-world.

Welt: (German for "world") Indicates the experiential world of a person in phenomenological philosophy and psychology. It has three modes or components: the *Umwelt*, the *Mitwelt*, and the *Eigenwelt*.

Will: The application of meaning to objects and people, which allow individuals to make decisions willfully. The capacity to organize one's thoughts and movements toward a goal or person.

Chapter 13

Abraham Maslow
& Carl Rogers

Humanistic Self-Actualization Theory

These are potentialities, not final actualizations.

A. H. Maslow, *Towards a Psychology of Being*

Evaluation by others is not a guide for me.

Carl Rogers, *On Becoming a Person*

About Maslow and Rogers' Humanistic Psychologies

Abraham Maslow and Carl Rogers were both pioneers of the humanistic psychological approach to understanding personality, a major alternative to both psychoanalysis and behaviorism.

From his research with primate and human subjects and drawing upon his in-depth and broad knowledge of personality and motivational theories, Maslow developed these main themes:

- Personality health is not merely the absence of pathology. It consists of many positive qualities and can be a subject of study in its own right.
- His theory of the hierarchy of needs indicated that behavior is not motivated entirely by physiologically based drives for food or sex. Once these basics are satisfied, other needs such as those for security, belongingness, and self-esteem become prepotent. Eventually, what Maslow termed "metaneeds" may develop. These steer the person toward a search for beauty, knowledge, justice, and truth.
- Self-actualization is the full development of a person's positive potentials.

- Peak experiences are altered states of consciousness in which a person has a deeper grasp of the meaning of his or her life or of existence. They are often significant confirmatory experiences or turning points in a person's life history.

Carl Rogers' theory developed out of his life experiences, his knowledge of contemporary philosophical traditions, and developments in the field of psychotherapy and his psychotherapeutic work with troubled children and their parents. Rogers emphasized understanding individual experience and the importance of personal freedom and choice. Some of the main tenets of his approach are:

1. The core of personality is the phenomenal self, the private world of experience and personal meaning.
2. In the absence of empathic understanding and unconditional love, a person's sense of self is shaped by qualified or conditional love and acceptance. Trying to meet the conditions of value may alienate the developing individual from being aware of and acting on his or her deepest and most authentic promptings.
3. Psychotherapy from the Rogerian point of view requires the establishment of a relationship in which the therapist has unconditional positive regard for the client, attempts to see the world as the client sees it, and is able to provide genuine empathic warmth for the client. When these conditions are met, the person is able to access his or her deeper feelings and desires and can begin to act more autonomously.

Both Maslow and Rogers emphasize the importance of the experience of the individual and the process of personal growth.

Abraham Maslow   Born: April, 1908 New York, New York
Died: June, 1970 Menlo Park, California

WHAT ABOUT THE HEALTHY PERSONALITY
AND THE STRIVING FOR FULL SELF-REALIZATION?

Most people generally are psychologically healthy, even though at times they may have difficult adjustments to make. Yet, many personality theories have been about maladjustment, personality flaws, and psychopathological behavior. Knowledge derived from this nonrepresentative sample of behavior has often served to obtain a pool of principles, which are then applied universally. What can we learn from studying the healthy personality?

Abraham Maslow, the first theorist we consider in this chapter, focused his attention on those rare persons who are on the verge of, or who have already achieved, psychological health. Maslow preferred to think of this state of exemplary personality development as **self-actualization.** Maslow's concern with such individuals also established a nonrepresentative sample of personalities as the basis of psychological generalizations, but this sample may serve as a much-needed corrective to a long history of focusing on psychopathology. Only by including the psychologically healthy as a subject of study can a comprehensive personality theory be developed.

> Health is not simply the absence of disease or even the opposite of it. Any theory of motivation that is worthy of attention must deal with the highest capacities of the healthy and strong man as well as with the defensive maneuvers of crippled spirits. (1970, p. 33)

Maslow regarded the healthy personality as one that possesses sufficient personal fortitude and creativity to be spontaneous and innocent. **Innocence**, according to Maslow, refers to the healthy personality's capacity to live without pretense, to be selflessly focused on a creative goal. Creative, innocent, and healthy people are able to devote themselves completely to whatever task is at hand. They are able to free themselves from the distractions, fears, and petty influences imposed by other people, for they are in the process of becoming completely themselves, becoming more real, authentic, and less influenced by a need to placate others. Maslow used the metaphor of the actor, the mask, and the audience to portray these qualities:

> This [freedom from the influence of others] means dropping masks, dropping our efforts to influence, to impress, to please, to be lovable, to win applause. It could be said so: if we have no audience to play to, we cease to be actors. With no need to act we can devote ourselves, self-forgetfully, to the problem. (1971, p. 65)

In becoming more our real selves and less the persons we expect others want us to be, we approach closer to our potential.

THE ORIGIN OF MASLOW'S INTEREST IN PSYCHOLOGICAL HEALTH

Maslow's original training was in experimental psychology, and he completed his doctoral thesis under Harry Harlow at the University of Wisconsin. Harlow was then (circa 1933) just beginning to set up his primate laboratory for the study of monkey behavior. Maslow's research involved a great many observational investigations of animal interaction and group affiliations. In fact, his doctoral study was concerned with the establishment of dominance hierarchies in a colony of monkeys.

Maslow noted throughout his early researches (e.g., 1936a, 1936b, 1937, in Maslow, 1973) that dominance of one animal over others was only rarely established through overt physical aggression. To Maslow it seemed rather that the dominant animal exhibited a kind of internal confidence or **dominance-feeling** that communicated to less assertive cage-mates that he would prevail (1936b, p. 45). The more dominant monkeys displayed very different behaviors from those lower in the dominance hierarchy, and subsequent research has shown that they differ hormonally and physiologically from those lower down on the ladder of influence.

Dominance-Feeling in Humans

When Maslow later applied his animal research findings and methods to the investigation of human behavior, he again employed the notion of dominance-feeling: "If we were forced to choose a single synonym or definition for dominance-feeling, we should say that it was chiefly the evaluation of, or confidence in, the personality (self-confidence)" (1937, p. 53). Maslow also indicated that people often wish for psychological health and effectiveness:

> ...it is possible that the most parsimonious way of treating this concept is to think of it in specific, rather than general terms. It may be possible and even desirable to speak *not* of a craving for dominance, but of craving for health *per se*.... Or one may crave to be free of timidity, not because of an attempt to increase self-evaluation, but simply for vocational efficiency; e.g., in order to be a better teacher or a more efficient physician. (1937, p. 64; italics in original)

To study dominance-feeling, Maslow developed a method he termed **conversational probing**. Conversational probing is intensive interviewing of a subject after satisfactory rapport is established: "This meant mostly a frank, trusting, friendly relationship, resembling somewhat the transference of the psychoanalysts" (Maslow, 1939, p. 75). Maslow studied approximately 130 women and a few men in this fashion. Of these, the majority of subjects were college students between the ages of 20 and 28; 75 percent were Protestant, 20 percent were Jewish, and 5 percent were Catholic.

The interview data were organized around a basic premise: *What personality variables correlate with dominance-feeling?* Dominance-feeling was now redefined in human terms as a form of self-evaluation:

> High dominance-feeling empirically involves good self-confidence, self-assurance, high evaluation of the self, feelings of general capability or superiority, and lack of shyness, timidity, self-consciousness or embarrassment. (Maslow, 1939, p. 74)

In addition to the traits Maslow listed as characteristics of high-dominance individuals, he also found evidence they were unconventional, less religious, extroverted, and, surprisingly, more hypnotizable than low-dominance subjects (1942, pp. 108 ff.). Furthermore, Maslow discovered a number of variables that were rarely found in high-dominance persons. If a subject was high in dominance-feeling it was unlikely that she was anxious, jealous, or neurotic. The high-dominance subjects appeared to be very psychologically healthy.

Sexual Behavior and Attitudes of High-Dominance Women

In a later study, Maslow focused attention on the sexual behavior of his subjects. He reported a wide range of impressionistic and statistical data about his high-dominance subjects' sexual preferences, but one particular phenomenon is striking. When one considers the findings of Maslow today, they very much seem to be a reflection of American culture in the early 1940s rather than the discovery of enduring psychological characteristics. Certainly, our attitudes about sexuality and the respective roles of males and females have markedly changed in the past 60 years.

The women of high dominance-feeling that Maslow studied, according to him, had very specific ideas about the "ideal man" and about the "ideal lovemaking situation." For the high-dominance woman, only a high-dominance man is attractive. Preferably, he should be even more dominant than she is. This paragon of masculinity was described as "highly masculine, self-confident, fairly aggressive, sure of what he wants and able to get it, generally superior in most things" (Maslow, 1942, p. 126).

In contrast, women of medium to low dominance-feeling stressed qualities like kindness, amiability, and love for children, along with gentleness and faithfulness as desirable masculine traits.

In Maslow's view, ideal lovemaking for the high-dominance woman involved a preference for:

> ...straightforward, unsentimental, rather violent, animal, pagan, passionate, even sometimes brutal lovemaking. It must come quickly, rather than after a long period of wooing. She wishes to be suddenly swept off her feet, not courted. She wishes her favors to be taken, rather than asked for. In other words she must be dominated, must be forced into subordinate status. (Maslow, 1942, p. 127)

Maslow was also interested in the preferences of the middle- and low-dominance woman. He found that women lower in dominance-feeling were repelled by the kind of "ideal man" that attracted high-dominance subjects. Middle-dominance women preferred an "adequate" rather than a superior man, "a comfortable and 'homey' man rather than a man who might inspire slight fear and feelings of inferiority" (Maslow, 1942,

p. 126). In short, high-dominance women seek a good lover; middle- and low-dominance women are more interested in a good husband and father.

The Good Specimen Strategy: "Exceptional" Primates

Maslow conceptualized the distinction between high-dominance and low-dominance individuals as a difference between relatively secure and relatively insecure personalities (1942, p. 133). He later developed an interest in the extremely secure personality, an individual completely accepting of self. People in whom dominance-feeling has come to complete fruition he later conceptualized as "most fully human."

Maslow eventually came to develop a strategy of research with what he considered psychologically healthy personalities:

> I proposed for discussion and eventually for research the use of selected good specimens (superior specimens) as biological assays for studying the best capability that the human species has.... What I am frankly espousing here is what I have been calling "growing-tip statistics," ... taking my title from the fact that it is at the growing tip of a plant that the greatest genetic action takes place. (1971, pp. 5–7)

Thus Maslow initiated the study of what he considered the "best" that human nature has to offer, the most "saintly," the wisest, most actualized human personality. In order to do so, he turned to a group of selected historical and contemporary figures who seemed to embody the traits he associated with this "good specimen." We shall see that the observational data Maslow collected tended to be similar, in some cases identical to, his early findings on dominance-feeling.

PERSONAL SOURCES OF THE HYPOTHESIS: "IN PURSUIT OF ANGELS"

Maslow (1971) reported the personal sources of his interest in the self-actualizing (SA) personality. Devotion to and admiration of two of his teachers, Max Wertheimer, a founder of Gestalt psychology, and Ruth Benedict, the eminent cultural anthropologist, sparked the young Maslow's interest in the exceptional person. Maslow's teachers had impressed him with their calm acceptance of life and with their special capacity to take delight in intellectual and cultural pursuits. Yet, at the same time, Benedict and Wertheimer were something of an enigma to Maslow. In trying to ferret out the sources of Benedict and Wertheimer's approach to life and its people, Maslow embarked on a private and informal investigation of self-actualization:

> [My investigation on self-actualization] ... started out as the effort of a young intellectual to try to understand two of his teachers whom he loved, adored, and admired and who were very, very wonderful people. It was a kind of high-IQ devotion. I could not be content simply to adore, but sought to understand why these two people were so different from the run-of-the-mill people in the world. These two people were Ruth Benedict and Max Wertheimer. They were my teachers ... and they were most remarkable human beings. My training in psychology equipped me not at all for understanding them. It was as if they were not quite people but something more than people. My own investigation began as a prescientific or nonscientific activity. I made descriptions and notes on Max Wertheimer, and I made notes on Ruth Benedict. When I tried to understand them, think about them, and write about them in my journal and my notes, I realized in one wonderful moment that their two patterns could be generalized. I was talking about a kind of person, not about two noncomparable individuals.... I tried to see whether this pattern could be found elsewhere, and I did find it elsewhere, in one person after another. (1971, pp. 41–42)

Begun as a private and informal undertaking, Maslow's interest in psychologically healthy, self-actualized people soon became a serious professional interest. It is clear that this concern with the exceptional organism, "the good specimen," was an extension of Maslow's early work with dominant animals and then dominant people he had interviewed.

Subsequently, Maslow began to develop criteria of normality and psychological health. From his observations of personal acquaintances who might embody such qualities, Maslow was able to develop an impressionistic sketch of the exceptionally psychologically healthy person. With time, Maslow developed a definition of the self-actualizing person:

> ... [self-actualization] may be loosely described as the full use and exploitation of talents, capacities, potentialities, etc. Such people seem to be fulfilling themselves and to be doing the best that they are capable of doing, reminding us of Nietzsche's exhortation, "Become what thou art!" (Maslow, 1970, p. 150)

Using biographical information on historical figures, and on some contemporary public ones, Maslow discovered only nine living individuals in whom he was "fairly sure" that self-actualization was well under way. The historical figures he chose as self-actualized subjects were Abraham Lincoln in his last years and Thomas Jefferson. Additionally, Maslow discovered seven "highly probable" figures: Albert Einstein, Eleanor Roosevelt, Jane Addams, William James, Albert Schweitzer, Aldous Huxley, and the philosopher, Benedict de Spinoza. Ultimately, 37 public and historical figures were selected as possible cases of self-actualization. Among these figures were Adlai Stevenson, Ralph Waldo Emerson, George Washington, Walt Whitman, Martin Buber, and Johann Wolfgang von Goethe (Maslow, 1970, p. 152).

In the course of his work, Maslow interviewed and studied more than 3,000 individuals, of whom he considered only a "handful" to have the potential for self-actualization. In fact, only one individual who was self-actualized in the fullest sense was found. Maslow's analysis of those individuals with whom he was directly familiar was different from the usual clinical-experimental investigation. Because subjects tend to freeze up when informed they are being studied as examples of exceptional psychological health, most of Maslow's observations had to be surreptitious (1970, p. 152). Therefore, the data took the form of impressionistic analyses of informal conversations and easily observable behaviors.

From Dominant Monkeys to the Study of Self-Actualizing Persons: Exceptional Humans

Maslow's childhood, like that of so many personality theorists, had been lonely:

> With my childhood, it's a wonder I'm not psychotic. I was the little Jewish boy in the non-Jewish neighborhood [see Erik Erikson, Chapter 8]. It was a little like being the first Negro enrolled in the all-white school. I was isolated and unhappy. I grew up in libraries and among books, without friends. (Maslow, in Hall, 1968, p. 33)

As a student, Maslow not only sought out the most esteemed people in his chosen field, but he attached himself to them in the most personal ways:

> I was young Harry Harlow's first Ph.D. And they were angels, my professors. I've always had angels around. They helped me when I needed it; fed me; Bill Sheldon taught me how to buy a suit. I didn't know anything of amenities. Edward L. Thorndike was an angel to me. Clark Hull was another. (Maslow, in Hall, 1968, p. 33)

As with his relationship with Wertheimer and Benedict, Maslow chose idealizing words to describe his attachments to his professors. Maslow idealized his professors as superhuman in more than one way. Once, for example, having stood beside his philosophy professor at an adjoining urinal, Maslow was shocked at the realization that even professors needed to urinate from time to time: "... it stunned me so that it took hours, even weeks, for me to assimilate the fact that a professor was a human being and constructed with the plumbing that everybody else had" (Wilson, 1972, p. 138).

Maslow described his fantasy of participating in the greatest academic procession in the most astounding commencement exercise of all time:

> I was in a faculty procession here at Brandeis. I saw the line stretching off into a dim future. At its head was Socrates. And in the line were the ones I love most. Thomas Jefferson was there. And Spinoza. And Alfred North Whitehead. I was in that same line. Behind me that infinite line melted into the dimness. (Maslow, in Hall, 1968, p. 35)

In this ideation, Maslow saw himself among the company of the best minds in civilization.

The transition of interest from studying monkeys to focusing on self-actualized individuals thus now seems more understandable. Central in Maslow's life history was the clash between feelings of childhood isolation, inferiority, and powerlessness and yearnings for intellectual superiority and eminence (Maslow, 1979, pp. 101 ff.). His first goal, intellectual superiority, could be obtained by an academic career, whose prime research interest was focused on dominant "best specimens." While Maslow was among the academic behaviorists, monkeys were the best-specimen subjects. The second goal, personal eminence, could be had only vicariously, only through association with eminent teachers, who would presumably reveal the secret of their renown. While he was among the "angels," near-perfect-people were the best-specimen subjects (Maslow, 1979, p. 115).

Commenting on his techniques for handling critics of his life work, Maslow revealed this not-unexpected strategy:

> ... I have worked out a lot of tricks for fending off professional attacks.... I have a secret. I talk over the heads of the people in front of me to my own private audience. I talk to people I love and respect. To Socrates and Aristotle and Spinoza and Thomas Jefferson and Abraham Lincoln. And when I write, I write for them. This cuts out a lot of crap. (Maslow, in Hall, 1968, p. 36)

Upon the birth of his daughter, Maslow also had an intuitive insight that was related to his shift from behavioristic studies of monkeys to the exploration of human experience. He reports that he had a growing disaffection with behaviorism, which stemmed initially from his reading of philosophers and psychoanalytic psychology, and reached a crisis at the birth of his child:

> ... [W]hen my baby was born that was the thunderclap that settled things. I looked at this tiny, mysterious thing and felt so stupid. I was stunned by the mystery and by the sense of not really being in control. I felt small and weak and feeble before all this. I'd say that anyone who had a baby couldn't be a behaviorist. (Maslow, in Hall, 1968, p. 36)

CHARACTERISTICS OF SELF-ACTUALIZING PERSONS

From his observations, interviews, and research, Maslow developed a picture of the self-actualizing personality. The self-actualizing pattern consists of fifteen characteristics that are positive or favorable and five negative (from the viewpoint of other people) traits. All 20 items have been summarized in Table 13.1 with a brief description of

Table 13.1 Maslow's Self-Actualization (SA) Pattern

Self-actualization characteristic	Description
Reality (1) and Problem-centered (4)	More efficient and accurate perception of reality; unusual ability to detect the fake, phony, and dishonest; focus on problems external to self; invests energies in "causes."
Acceptance of self and others (2); Spontaneity and simplicity (3)	Accepts own nature in stoic style; accepts what cannot be changed; is spontaneous and always natural; prefers simplicity to pretense and artificiality in self and others; conventional on surface to avoid hurting others.
Need privacy (5); Independence of culture and environment (6); Resists enculturation (15)	Relies on own judgment; trusts in self; resists pressure from others and social norms; able to "weather hard knocks" with calm; resists identification with cultural stereotypes; has autonomous values carefully considered.
Freshness of appreciation (7); Creativeness (14)	Maintains constancy for awe and wonder; ability to marvel at and enjoy the good things of life: food, sex, sports, travel; thousandth baby seen is as wonderful as first; creative in daily tasks of living; inventive and original in childlike way.
Unhostile sense of humor (13); Democratic (11); Gemeinschaftsgefühl (9); Intimate personal relations (10)	Does not enjoy jokes at expense of others; prefers a philosophic humor that pokes fun at the human condition; enjoys company of all people regardless of social or racial origins; Adler's Gemeinschaftsgefühl means 'fellow-feeling" or social interest; strong interest in others' welfare; small number of intense and intimate friendships.
Peak (mystical) experiences (8); Discrimination between means and ends (12)	Has experienced mystic states characterized by feelings of limitless horizons opening, being more powerful and more helpless simultaneously, with loss of time sense; strong ethical-oral sense but not in conventional ways; discriminates between moral means and ends differently from average person; means can be ends.
Imperfections: Unexpected ruthlessness; occasional absentmindedness; overkindness; non-neurotic guilt and anxiety	"There are no perfect people"; SA individuals can display surgical coldness when called for in situations of betrayal; overkindliness gets them into trouble by letting others impose on them; uninterested in social "chatting" or party-going; anxiety and guilt present, but from realistic not neurotic sources; sometimes philosophical concerns cause loss of sense of humor.

Based on Maslow, 1970, pp. 153–176.

the meaning of each item. In addition, the 20 separate items have been grouped into seven classes where overlap and similarity permit such redistribution. To preserve the essence of continuity in Maslow's original list, the number of the item in that list is indicated in parentheses (see Maslow, 1970, Chapter 11).

From Table 13.1 it can be seen that self-actualizing people are generally characterized by independence and self-trust. They are accepting of others and self, and most important, accepting of what life holds in store for them. They are people in whom basic needs for food, shelter, and sexual intimacy have been satisfactorily met. Self-actualizers, consequently, are functioning in response to higher needs, needs for the classic "Goods" of the well-lived life. Beauty, Truth, Justice, and many other capitalized virtues are the very essence of the self-actualizer's existence. People therefore strived *for* meaningful existence. The question that now occupied Maslow was, *How do such higher motivations develop to engage the self-actualizer's being*?

LEARNING FROM CRITICAL MENTOR FIGURES

In the 1930s, Maslow was living in the New York City area as a professor of psychology at Brooklyn College. This location gave him a chance to meet many psychologists and engage in exchanges of ideas with them.

> I never met Freud or Jung, but I did meet with Adler in his home where he used to run Friday night seminars, and I had many conversations with him.... As for many of the others, I sought them out—people like Erich Fromm and Karen Horney and Ruth Benedict and Max Wertheimer and the like.... I think it's fair to say that I have had the best teachers, both formal and informal, of any person who ever lived, just because of the historical accident of being in New York City when the very cream of European intellect was migrating away.... There has been nothing like it since Athens. And I think I knew every one of them more or less well.... I cannot say that any one of them was any more important than any other. I was just learning from everybody and from anybody who had anything to teach... I learned from all of them. So I could not be said to be a Goldsteinian nor a Frommean nor an Adlerian or whatever.... I learned from all of them and refused to close any doors. (Maslow, 1968 in Goble, 1970)

Maslow's remarkable openness to such diverse creative thinkers enabled him to put different theories of motivation into a single conceptual framework in his development of the concept of the hierarchy of needs.

THE HIERARCHY OF NEEDS: FROM DEFICIENCY TO GROWTH MOTIVATION AND SELF-ACTUALIZATION

Maslow conceptualized a **hierarchy of needs**. Needs lowest in the scale are prepotent to needs lying above them. Such prepotency indicates that higher needs cannot emerge in full motivational force until lower ones have first been potentially satisfied. Thus, basic needs or what Maslow terms **deficiency needs** shape an individual's behavior *before* the higher needs, and continue to have a major impact until relatively gratified in full. The physiological needs, safety needs, love and belongingness needs, and esteem needs are included in the category of deficiency needs.

In some academic textbooks, Maslow's hierarchy of needs is geographically illustrated by a pyramid with the physiological needs located at the bottom and self-actualizing needs at the top. This representation suggests that a person must have full gratification of a lower need before a higher need emerges and effects behavior.

However, this is an incorrect representation of what Maslow wrote in his magnum opus, *Motivation and Personality*.

> At once [there is some need satisfaction] other (and higher) needs emerge and these, rather than the physiological hungers, dominate the organism. And when these in turn are satisfied, again new (and still higher) needs emerge, and so on. This is what we mean by a hierarchy of relative prepotency. (1970, p. 17)

Maslow specifically discusses the issue of how relative satisfaction of one set of needs relates dynamically to the other four basic needs.

> So far, our theoretical discussion may have given the impression that these five sets of needs are somehow in such terms as the following: If one need is satisfied, then another emerges. This statement might give the false impression that a need must be satisfied 100 percent before the next need emerges. In actual fact, most members of our society who are normal are partially satisfied in all their basic needs at the same time. A more realistic description of the hierarchy would be in terms of decreasing percentages of satisfaction as we go up the hierarchy of prepotency. For instance, if I may assign arbitrary figures for the sake of illustration, it is as if the average citizen is satisfied perhaps 85 percent in his physiological needs, 70 percent in his safety needs, 50 percent in his love needs, 40 percent in his self-esteem needs, and 10 percent in his self-actualization needs.
>
> As for the concept of emergence of a new need after satisfaction of the prepotent need, this emergence is not a sudden, salutatory phenomenon, but rather a gradual emergence by slow degrees from nothingness. For instance, if prepotent need A is satisfied only 10 percent, then need B may not be visible at all. However, as this need A becomes satisfied 25 percent, need B may emerge 5 percent, as need A becomes satisfied 75 percent, need B may emerge 50 percent, and so on. (1970, pp. 27–28)

This passage is a clear statement that the hierarchy of needs is not an "achievement step-ladder," but rather an indication that there are varying degrees of need satisfaction at any given point in time. Furthermore, since all five sets of needs characterize personality and motivation, they all play important roles in daily functioning. For example, students who receive superior grades on an examination may feel a boost in self-esteem and a lowering of insecurity and anxiety about test performance. On the other hand, a woman who learns that she has breast cancer may have strong needs for safety, security and reassurance as to her future. In a different way, children in genocidal warfare, as now exists in parts of Africa, may only have concern with having food, water, shelter and surviving threat and terror.

Thus, the concept of a hierarchy of needs is one of five sets of basic needs interacting with each other to propel motivation to select specific types of reinforcements for the external world.

> So far I have spoken only of the nature of the organism itself. It is now necessary to say at least a word about the situation or environment in which the organism finds itself. We must certainly grant at once human motivation rarely actualizes itself in behavior in relation to the situation and to other people. Any theory of motivation must, of course, take account of this fact, including not only in the environment but also in the organism itself, the role of cultural determination. (1970, p. 10)

This quote illustrates Maslow's view that there is a dynamic interaction between the person and their environment. Therefore, depending on the relative strength of the five basic needs, what the person seeks, in terms of motivated behavior, is determined by the principle of relative prepotency of any set of needs within an environmental (i.e., cultural) context. However, as the lower needs become more chronically gratified, they command less attention and the other needs emerge as more powerful determinants of behavior. In terms of the need for self-actualization, it becomes stronger each and

Figure 13.1 Maslow's hierarchy of needs.

every time that there is partial gratification of the lower needs (e.g., safety, love, belongingness, and esteem). If one were to make a graphic picture, it would look more like a bar graph indicating the strength of the five basic needs in relation to each other, rather than a pyramid with five levels.

In this view, for example, people whose every biological need is satisfied are capable of turning to poetry, photography, art, or music to have some meaningful way of spending their energies and occupying their time.

> It is quite true that man lives by bread alone when there is no bread. *But what happens to man's desires when there is bread and when his belly is chronically filled?* (Maslow, 1943, in 1973, p. 157; cf. 1970, p. 38; italics added)

The answer, of course, is that higher needs emerge to shape people's strivings. The cycle continues indefinitely, for once needs for Beauty, Truth, Justice, and so on are fulfilled, even "higher" needs emerge. The highest of the needs in the hierarchy are the **B-values** (**Being-values**), or **metaneeds** as Maslow termed them. The metaneeds will be considered shortly, but it is important to note that the 15 metaneeds are *not* hierarchically arranged. Having reached the self-actualization step in the hierarchy, the individual experiences needs for the B-values like Beauty, Truth, and Justice more or less simultaneously, though not necessarily with equal intensity. The basic hierarchy may be schematized as in Figure 13.1 (based on Maslow, 1970, pp. 35–46).

Hierarchy of Needs: Uses

Maslow's concept of the hierarchy of needs has had great value for a variety of purposes. Let us take the case of a college student who might be having some trouble with studying and getting good grades. A self-analysis of need satisfaction might quickly reveal that the student was not getting his or her needs for belongingness met, so the self-esteem related goal of achievement seemed irrelevant. In other words, getting good grades was not motivating for this lonely student. The answer would be not simply to study more but to take some steps to meet his or her social needs. Likewise, a manufacturing company might be having a problem with employee morale in spite of high wages. Institutional research might reveal that workers do not feel either a sense of pride or self-esteem in their work. Nor is there much of a sense of belongingness. Merely increasing the workers' pay will not solve these problems or meet these needs. Instead, efforts to enhance the sense of belongingness and to bolster a meaningful sense of achievement seem like a good idea.

PEAK EXPERIENCES AS MOMENTARILY INTENSE STATES OF INDIVIDUAL FULL POTENTIAL

In 1902, William James published his Gifford Lectures under the title *The Varieties of Religious Experience*. In a series of 20 lectures, James surveyed from a variety of poetic, theological, and biographical writings the diversity of ways in which individuals reported experiencing God. One particular subclass of such experiences called the "mystical state" occupied James at some length. From his researches, James was able to distinguish four characteristics of the mystical experience that separated it from states of normal consciousness. Maslow accepted James's descriptive criteria as adequate characterization of **peak experiences** undergone by self-actualizing people (see Maslow, 1964; 1970, p. 164). James listed the following characteristics of the mystical experience (1902, pp. 371–373):

1. **Ineffability:** "The subject of [a mystical experience] immediately says that it *defies expression*, that no adequate report of its content can be given in words. It follows from this that its quality must be directly experienced; it cannot be imparted or transferred to others."

2. **Noetic quality:** The word "noetic" is based on a Greek root meaning "mind" or "intellect." James employed the term to indicate the essentially intellectual, "truth-finding" quality of a mystic experience.

3. **Transiency:** "Mystical states cannot be sustained for long. Except in rare instances, half an hour, or at most an hour or two, seems to be the limit beyond which they fade into the light of common day."

4. **Passivity:** "... the mystic feels as if his own will were in abeyance, and indeed sometimes as if he were grasped and held by a superior power."

Maslow initially thought that only self-actualizing people underwent these peak experiences with any appreciable regularity (1964, p. 22). But as he became more skilled in interviewing subjects and in phrasing questions to elicit the information, Maslow discovered that most people have had some peak experiences.

When peak experiences are sought, actively induced, or otherwise treated as a commodity to be acquired, the value of the experience is lost. Maslow cautioned that drugs, meditation rituals, and shortcuts of all kinds cheapen the peak experience (1971, p. 345). Maslow suggested that people may approach even the deepest peak experiences with apathy or superficiality, a tendency to desanctify or *desacralize* life.

Dimensions of Peak Experience

What characterized the nature of integrative experiences in optimal states of functioning? Peak experiences are expressions of optimal states of integrated personality functioning and self-actualizing syndromes. Clinical research on peak experiences has identified the dimensions that define these optimal states: (1) perception; (2) memory; (3) levels of consciousness; (4) identity; (5) self-capacities; (6) motivational dispositions; (7) affect regulation; and (8) somatic/motor behavior (Maslow, 1968, 1970). In peak experiences these dimensions of psychic functioning are synergistic. They augment and intensify consciousness and capacity for performance.

In *Towards a Psychology of Being* (1968), Maslow analyzed the effects of peak experiences to optimal states of psychological functioning. Peak experiences serve as *acute identity experiences* (1968, pp. 103–115) and consequently enable individuals to experience more integrative and self-actualizing states of being. After the peak experience, mindful reflection empowers the individual to see self-actualizing potential "in the mirror," so to speak. As a form of optimal functioning, the peak experience is an inner glimpse of self-actualizing potentialities, like opening a door to a room full of hidden treasures that one did not know existed.

Acute identity episodes in peak experiences are a source of self-discovery. In a metaphorical sense, the organism is speaking to the person: "look, this is the real you and how you can be when functioning fully with your highest potential." In this way acute identity episodes are positive in nature and can mobilize growth and personality development in self-actualizing directions. To quote Maslow:

> . . . the person in the peak experiences feels more integrated (unified, whole, all of a piece) than at other times. He also looks (to the observer) more integrated in various ways, e.g., less split, dissociated, less fighting against himself, less split between experiencing self and observing self, more one-pointed, more harmoniously organized, more efficiently organized with all his parts functioning very nicely with each other, more synergistic with less internal friction, etc. (1968, p. 104)

Peak experiences are spontaneous, subjectively positive emotional experiences that occur without conscious intention, planning, or will. Individual accounts of peak experiences and optimal states of functioning are reported as effortless, fluid, natural, playful, egoless, and automatically taking place. During the peak experience, the individual is actively or passively involved in activities such as exercise, athletics, sexuality, listening to music, viewing inspiring artistic productions, reading literature, walking in nature, giving birth to a child, or participating in a celebration of an accomplishment. In a more basic way, peak experiences may occur while looking at a magnificent ocean sunset with its orange hue descending below the Earth's horizon or taking a stroll on a resplendent spring day with flowers in bloom and the smell of nitrogen-enriched earth and freshly cut grass.

Peak experiences are described as nonhabitual and effortless; being "in the flow," "natural," "just happening," and synchronous in multi-modal sensory-perceptual channels (Maslow, 1968). During peak experiences, perceptual processes are characterized as holistic, "the big picture" and unifying, seeing figure and ground as one. In terms of emotional states, peak experiences are described as exciting or serene. As subjectively experienced, they are replete with a sense of acceptance of self, nature, and life itself as natural occurrences, without blocks, fear, or judgment as to the moral goodness of the experience.

Maslow (1968) believed peak experiences are intrinsically valuable and growth promoting, facilitating psychological health and feelings of well-being. However, his research subjects report *distortions in time and space perception*; i.e., losing track of time by being fully absorbed in the peak experience. Some individuals describe how during a peak experience they feel like an external observer or experience an "out-of-body" phenomenon that is emotionally positive and psychically fluid in nature. Hence, the term "being in the flow" of one's event. Unlike dissociative experiences, the memory of peak experiences is lucid, accurate, detailed, and recollected as important, sometimes leading to changes in personal identity, values, world view, and systems of meaning. A few individuals describe peak experiences in mystical terms and as transcendent in nature. They report experiencing unity with the "great chain of humanity." They have a capacity to look "backward" in time at significant events, persons, and accomplishments and feel a kinship, identification, and sense of connection to the past and others' lives. At the same time, they may envision future goals and aspirations and project themselves forward in time with anticipated achievements or actions. Other subjects report physical and sensory qualities to their peak experiences, with heightened perceptual sensitivity and intense awareness of their internal states.

Peak experiences are universally reported in emotionally positive ways, a fact of great relevance to the transformation of psychic states. Individuals report states of heightened (positive) tension or extreme relaxation and peacefulness. Peak experiences are devoid of distress, anxiety, fear, and uncertainty. Maslow's subjects reported enhanced feelings of creativity during and after the peak experiences.

As optimal integrative experiences, the peak experience involves unifying cognitions of objects in-the-world in relation to self-as-processes. Maslow (1968, p. 71) characterized such perceptual qualities as metacognition or B-cognition, to describe functioning at "Being levels" of self-actualizing experience. Analysis reveals that peak experiences are *integrative, synergistic*, and *synchronous* in nature. Peak experiences reflect enriched, lucid sensory-perceptual experience, positive affective states, luminous memories, and recall. There are acute, intact bodily sensations and feelings of wholeness; a sense of self at optimal centeredness. Peak experiences are growth-promoting, identity-enhancing, and reveal actual and unrealized human potentials (Maslow, 1968).

In peak experiences, the subcomponents of the self fuse their functions in the service of optimal states. Peak experiences involve synergy in the structural components of the self: that is, autonomy, coherence, continuity, connection, vitality, and energy (Wilson, 2004). The usually integrative functions of consciousness and behavior combine in the service of maximizing adaptation. The synergistic functions of psychological processes were described by Maslow (1968) as an *altered psychological state* and a characteristic of B-motivation and cognition. Peak experiences salutogenically alter states of consciousness, memory, identity, and perception of the environment.

In terms of memory, peak experiences are lucidly recalled with brilliant and detailed accuracy. Memory for peak experiences is rich, fulgent, vitrified, transparent, and fully encoded. Peak experiences are recalled with precision, clarity, and accuracy because they are strong experiences with positive affective valence. The memory for peak experiences is continuous and without gaps, amnesia, distortion, or missing information. According to Maslow (1968), persons report unusual degrees of perceptual perspicuity and salience during the peak experience (i.e., unity, awe, wonder, deep absorption). Peak experiences are described in terms that emphasize perceptual luminosity and sharply heightened sensory experience involving touch, taste, smell, movement, and audition. It is as if extraneous noise in channels of sensory-perceptual experience is filtered out during the peak experience. The strength, clarity, and purity of the signal emanating from the peak experience is fully received in all modalities with similar frequency and amplitude and has maximal impact on consciousness. In a metaphorical sense, it is as if the peak experience emanates from the center of being, like light spreading outwards from its source, radiating a uniform energy pattern in all directions.

With regard to the stream of activity, peak experiences have continuity, flow, and naturalness in the stream of activities taking place. The synchronous flow in peak

Table 13.2   Basic Psychological Processes During Peak Experience

Psychological Dimensions	*Qualities of Peak Experiences*
Perception	Vivid, clear, in-the-moment, centered, holistic, lucid, accurate, ego-transcending, unity, B-cognition, fulgent, detached, synchronicity, figure-ground unity, perspicacious, richer, centered
Memory	Clear, total, continuous accurate recall, nondistorted, no amnesia, eidetic; intact, vivid, detailed
Consciousness/Awareness	Fluid, clear, resolute, acute, sharp, total attention, B-cognition, open to experience, oriented to person and place, disoriented to time and space, transcendent, mystical, ineffable
Identity	Integrative, egoless, acute identity experience, identity enhancing; peak experience may alter self- and world view, sense of meaning and sharpened sense of continuity and sameness; fully functioning; here-now awareness
Self-capacities	Unified, whole, spontaneous, aware of potential, integrated, coherent, autonomous, connected, high energy, sense of vitality, synergistic self-function, positive self-reference
Motivation	Effortless, intrinsic; self-directed, spontaneous, growth producing, need gratifying; releases and expresses creativity, sense of flow
Affect	Positive, synchronized affects; subjectively pleasurable; increased positive arousal; experience intrinsically valued; no fear, anxiety, inhibition or negative self-reference; awe, wonder
Somatic/Motor	Sensitive, aware of sensory modalities, feelings of wholeness, heightened states of proprioception, effortless motor control, high states of tension or relaxation, peacefulness

Source: Maslow, 1968.

experiences is described as automatic or effortless with a disorientation to time and space, including experiences of being an external observer that are characterized as emotionally positive in nature. Unlike dissociative states, peak experiences reflect higher levels of integrative functions in cognition, memory, and sensory-perceptual modalities. Table 13.2 summarizes the processes during peak experiences.

Peak experiences involve powerful, positive emotional states (Maslow, 1962, 1968, 1970, 1971). Peak experiences have a continuum of positive emotional arousal. At one extreme, are heightened states of positive arousal and expectations; at the other, are states of tranquility, calmness, quiescence, and passive contentment. These positive emotional states are expressions of increased sensory nervous system arousal. Subjects describe these states as rapture, ecstasy, joy, bliss, serenity, excitement, contentment, a sense of well-being, euphoria, transcendence, and free-flowing energy. There are reported states of relaxation, quiescence, and peacefulness.

The Growth Promoting Effects of Peak Experiences

Maslow (1968) suggested that peak experiences, as "mini self-actualizing" episodes, can have salutogenic effects. Table 13.3 summarizes the nature of alterations in psychological functioning for consciousness, memory, identity, perception of the environment and time and space perspectives. In terms of salutogenic effects, it may be seen that consciousness is increased in clear holistic ways but sometimes with disorientation to time and space. Similarly, memory for the peak experience is intact, lucid and accurate

Table 13.3   Cognition and Personal Identity During Peak Experience

Alteration in Psychological Functioning	Salutogenic Effects of Peak Experiences to Self-Actualization States
Consciousness	Increased, clear, heightened, unified, holistic; disoriented to time and space, mindfulness of self and the world
Memory	Intact, clear, accurate recall, continuity, nondistressed, positive recall
Identity	Integrated identity, identity-enhancing experience, acute identity episodes, sense of continuity and sameness
Perception of Environment	Holistic, clear, rich, lucid, unified, meta-cognition, synergistic in nature; here-now, freshness of appreciation, external observer of self
Time/Space Perception	Loss of time perception but lucid memory for events

Source: Maslow, 1968. Salutogenic alterations in the usually integrative functions of consciousness, memory, identity, and perception of the environment.

as to the subject nature of the experience itself. As noted by Maslow (1968), peak experiences can be acute identity crises as they may facilitate the person becoming aware of their potentials for growth and change. Moreover, during the peak experience, the person may have a mindful sense of 'here-now' being in the moment with a freshness of appreciation for life, persons, and the world.

The Psychological Defense of Desacralizing

Desacralizing, a term adopted from the philosopher, Mircea Eliade (1961; see also 1958), was used by Maslow to indicate the process of denying the awesome, marvelous, beautiful, and sublime aspects of people and the universe. In effect, the desacralizer has learned to "reduce the person to the concrete object and to refuse to see what he might be or to refuse to see him in his symbolic values or to refuse to see him or her eternally" (Maslow, 1971, p. 49). A 1970 popular song written by Joni Mitchell, "Big Yellow Taxi," included the sentence, "They paved paradise and put up a parking lot." This song mocked our society's desacralizing attitudes and materialistic values.

Along with the concept of desacralizing, Maslow introduced the notion of the **Jonah complex**. In this syndrome, a person, like the prophet Jonah in the Bible, avoids the deeper pursuits of which he or she is capable. It is a pattern of running away from one's calling. Such a person prefers to stay on the surface of life, and he or she pays a huge price in the sense of subsequent meaninglessness, unfulfillment, and guilt.

Maslow has suggested that one characteristic of the self-actualizing personality is the ability to *resacralize* people and things, to bring the sense of the sacred back into experience. The self-actualizing person has learned to be awe-inspired, to marvel at the beauty, mystery and infinite complexity of life, to include an appreciation of the cosmic and the spiritual as well as the material.

Extending his criticism of desacralization to the domain of the sciences, Maslow found the social sciences in particular to be wanting in their treatment of persons:

> Briefly put, it appears to me that science and everything scientific can be and often is used as a tool in the service of a distorted, narrowed, humorless, de-eroticized, de-emotionalized, desacralized, and de-sanctified *Weltanschauung* [philosophy of life]. This desacralization can be used as a defense against being flooded by emotion, especially the emotions of humility, reverence, mystery, wonder, and awe. (1966, p. 139)

Particularly for those who work in the fields of psychology, sociology, and anthropology, classical scientific method may serve the function of a defense mechanism. Maslow thought that, by abstracting, objectifying, and generally dehumanizing their human subjects, social scientists unknowingly seek to separate themselves from the all-too-human failings, emotions, anxieties, and confusion they investigate in others (Maslow, 1966, p. 33).

> More than any other kind of knowledge we fear knowledge of ourselves, knowledge that might transform our self-esteem and our self-image.... While human beings love knowledge and seek it, they are curious they also fear it. The closer to the personal it is, the more they fear it. So human knowledge is apt to be a kind of dialectic between this love and this fear. Thus knowledge includes the defenses against itself, the repressions, the sugar-coatings, the inattentions, and the forgettings. (Maslow, 1966, p. 16)

Maslow suggested that the acquisition of knowledge about the experience of others is fraught with anxiety and can amount to a "cognitive pathology." For example, when the need to know is based on a compulsive seeking after certainty rather than on enjoyment of discovery, it is pathological. Or, when individuals compulsively deny their doubts, ignorance, and mistakes from a fear of confessing human fallibility, their scientific skills and knowledge are serving pathological ends. Or, when individuals feel that knowledge makes them "tough-minded," "hard-nosed," and "scientifically rigorous," they may defensively close themselves off to the tender, romantic, poetic, and spiritual aspects of the people they study.

Maslow summarized his view of the desacralizing tendency by indicating the directions that a new and more humanistic scientific enterprise should pursue:

> If humanistic science may be said to have any goals beyond sheer fascination with the human mystery and enjoyment of it, these would be to release the person from external controls and to make him less predictable to the observer (to make him freer, more creative, more inner-determined) even though perhaps more predictable to himself. (1966, p. 40)

Hence, for Maslow, the sciences, and psychology in particular, are value-laden enterprises in which the psychological makeup and needs of the investigator become mingled with the virtue of the investigated.

The Issue of Safety versus Growth:
Existential Choices in Life-Course Development

In his book, *Towards a Psychology of Being* (1968) Maslow wrote about peak experiences, self-actualization and the nature of the hierarchy of needs. Among the many creative and intellectually stimulating aspects of this book, is his ability to make rather complex psychological phenomena, lucid and simple. Nowhere was this more evident in his characterization of personal life choices and fundamental existential choices: choose for safety, security and illusory comfort or choose for growth, change, self-realization and further differentiation of self to meet new and often uncertain life-choice changes. Maslow created a simple vector diagram to illustrate this existential dilemma.

Safety ⟵ Person ⟶ Growth

This simple diagram reflects Maslow's view that in everyday life, we are confronted with stressors, challenges and unexpected events, including traumas, that require "choice points" as to how we manage such difficult experiences. Towards the direction of further growth, development and self-actualization, persons endure the anxiety, uncertainty and risk to grow, to further explore their individual potentialities, abilities, and qualities of character. In the direction of safety-needs, the person tends to amplify the real or imagined dangers of their situation and to minimize the potential attractions for continued growth and self-development.

> I can put all this together in a schema, which though very simple, is also very powerful, both heuristically and theoretically. This basic dilemma or conflict between the defensive forces and the growth trends I conceive to be *existential*, embedded in the deepest nature of human beings, now and forever into the future. (1968 pp. 46–47, italics added)

The Higher Order Human Values

The B-values—Truth, Beauty, Goodness, Unity, and so on—that assume such significance for the self-actualized person are intensified in states of peak experience. The individual who has undergone such moments comes away from them feeling that the world "looks different." A peak experience may change the course of a person's life. Maslow isolated 16 aftereffects of the peak experience (Based on Maslow, 1962, pp. 97–107). The person who has undergone a peak experience feels

1. more integrated, whole, and unified;
2. more at one with the world;
3. as if he or she were at the peak of his or her powers, more fully her or himself;
4. graceful, without strain, effortless;
5. creative, active, responsible, self-controlled;
6. free of inhibitions, blocks, doubts, self-criticisms;
7. spontaneous, expressive, innocent;
8. creative, self-confident, flexible;
9. unique, individualistic;
10. free of past and future limits;
11. free of the world, free to be;
12. undriven, unmotivated, nonwishing, beyond needs;
13. rhapsodic, poetic;
14. consumed, finished, closed, complete, subjectively final;
15. playful, good-humored, childlike;
16. lucky, fortunate, grateful.

In short, the peak experience is evidence that

> Man has a higher and transcendent nature, and this is part of his essence, i.e., his biological nature as a member of a species which has evolved. (Maslow, 1971, p. 349)

BEYOND SELF-ACTUALIZATION: THE B-VALUES

Self-actualized people develop B-values and metaneeds. They have already successfully progressed through the hierarchy of basic needs. They now embark on the growth processes of living to *enhance their being, to expand their knowledge of self and others, and to operationalize their self-actualized personalities in* any activity that they undertake.

In this sense, Maslow proposed the further set of Being-needs that emerge at the point of self-actualization in the basic hierarchy. To these B-values, Maslow assigned the name *metamotives*. "Self-actualizing people are not primarily motivated by basic needs; they are primarily metamotivated, by metaneeds or B-values" (1971, p. 311).

With the B-values, Maslow proposed that individuals may satisfy all their basic needs through to the esteem levels in the hierarchy and yet not be self-actualized. To be fully self-actualized, one must be committed to long-reaching goals: the B-values. Thus, Maslow revised his definition of the self-actualizing personality:

> ...it may turn out to be useful to add to the definition of the self-actualizing person, not only [a] that he be sufficiently free of illness, [b] that he be sufficiently gratified in his basic needs, and [c] that he be positively using his capacities, but also [d] that he be motivated by some values which he strives for or gropes for and to which he is loyal. (1971, p. 301)

Originally, Maslow proposed a list of 14 B-values (1962, p. 78), only later to add one more (1971, pp. 318–319). The 15 B-values are listed in Table 13.4 along with the "deficiency diseases" or metapathologies that result when one of the B-values is unsatisfied.

Table 13.4   B-Values and Metapathologies

B-Value or metaneed	Pathogenic deprivation	Specific metapathologies (motivation disease)
1. Truth	Dishonesty	Disbelief; mistrust; cynicism
2. Goodness	Evil	Utter selfishness; hatred, reliance only on self; disgust, nihilism
3. Beauty	Ugliness	Vulgarity; loss of taste; tension; fatigue
4. Unity-Wholeness	Chaos, atomism	Disintegration; arbitrariness
4A. Dichotomy-Transcendence	Black/White dichotomies; forced choices	Either/or thinking; seeing everything as dualistic; a simplistic view of life
5. Aliveness; process	Deadness; mechanizing of life	Robotizing; feeling totally determined; loss of zest in life
6. Uniqueness	Sameness; uniformity	Loss of feeling of individuality or being needed
7. Perfection	Imperfection; sloppiness	Discouragement (?); hopelessness
7A. Necessity	Accident; occasionalism; inconsistency	Loss of safety; unpredictability
8. Completion; finality	Incompleteness	Cessation of striving; no use trying
9. Justice	Injustice	Insecurity; anger; cynicism; mistrust
9A. Order	Lawlessness, chaos	Insecurity; wariness; loss of safety
10. Simplicity	Confusing, complexity	Overcomplexity; confusion; loss of orientation
11. Richness; totality	Poverty	Depression; uneasiness; loss of interest
12. Effortlessness	Effortfulness	Fatigue; strain; clumsiness
13. Playfulness	Humorlessness	Grimness; depression; paranoid humorlessness
14. Self-sufficiency	Accident; occasionalism	Dependence upon the perceiver and others
15. Meaningfulness	Meaninglessness	Despair; senselessness of life

Condensed from Maslow, 1971, pp. 318–319.

The B-values in Table 13.4 overlap to some degree. In Maslow's opinion, the overlap is an essential characteristic of Being-values:

> It is my (uncertain) impression that any B-value is fully and adequately defined by the total of the other B-values. That is, truth, to be fully and completely defined, must be beautiful, good, perfect, just, simple, orderly, lawful, alive, comprehensive, unitary, dichotomy-transcending, effortless, and amusing.... It is as if all the B-values have some kind of unity, with each single value being something like a facet of this whole. (Maslow, 1971, p. 324)

HUMANISTIC PSYCHOLOGY: THE THIRD FORCE

Both Maslow and the second theorist we consider in this chapter, Carl Rogers, considered themselves to be *humanistic psychologists*. Humanistic psychology emphasizes human capacity for goodness, creativity, and freedom. Unlike the strictly deterministic and somewhat mechanistic views of humans to be found in Freud's psychoanalysis and in contemporary behaviorism, **humanistic psychology** construes the human being as rational, purposeful and autonomous, capable of creativity and able to experience deep insight into reality. Maslow, like Rogers (and Allport) emphasized wholeness; in particular, Maslow—much more than Rogers—emphasized the spiritual or transcendent aspects of the person:

> If I had to condense the thesis of this book into a single sentence, I would have said that *in addition* to what the psychologists of the time had to say about human nature, man also had a higher nature and that this was instinctoid, i.e., part of his essence. And if I could have had a second sentence, I would have stressed the profoundly holistic nature of human nature in contradiction to the analytic atomistic Newtonian approach of the behaviorisms and of Freudian psychoanalysis. (1970, p. ix; italics in original)

The work of Maslow and Rogers, and many others, has been called the **third force** of psychology to emphasize its stature as a viable viewpoint that is distinctive from both psychoanalysis and behaviorism. Toward the end of his life, Maslow emphasized that he had not intended to be either pro-Freudian or anti-Freudian, pro-behaviorist or anti-behaviorist:

> In my opinion all such loyalty-positions are silly. Our job is to integrate these various truths into the whole truth, which should be our only loyalty. (1971, p. 4)

One piece of evidence of his futuristic thinking was his vision of a psychological utopia in which healthy, self-actualized people would live and work in harmony. Called *Eupsychia*, this utopia would represent an attempt to blend what is godlike in our nature to what is most fully human, to actualize what Maslow saw as our inherently "good being." For Maslow, Eupsychia would attempt to provide the environment in which humans could become all that they could be (1970, p. 277).

TOWARD A TRANSPERSONAL VIEWPOINT

Maslow is considered one of the founders of the field of **transpersonal psychology**, an area that emphasizes the spiritual dimension of human experience (Vaugan & Walsh, 2000). He labeled transpersonal psychology as the "fourth force" of psychology. Psychodynamic approaches are generally considered the "first force," behaviorism the "second force," and humanistic psychology the "third force." This emphasis grew out of Maslow's interest in altered states of consciousness and self-actualization (Hoffman, 1988). One branch of transpersonal psychology focuses on research with altered states and another branch focuses on working out models of consciousness and personality associated with the highest levels of human functioning. In addition, some aspects of transpersonal psychology are involved with the normative processes of psychospiritual development. The connection of these efforts with Maslow's earlier work is evident.

Carl Rogers   Born: January, 1902 Oak Park, Illinois
Died: February, 1987 La Jolla, California

A HARBINGER OF THINGS TO COME

In 1961, Carl Rogers recounted an event that occurred while he was a student at Union Theological Seminary. At the time, Rogers was 22 years old, and he was in the first year of Divinity School. He and a number of other students formed a group to explore their own ideas. Rogers explained,

> A group of us felt that ideas were being fed to us, whereas we wished primarily to explore our own questions and doubts and find out where they led. We petitioned the administration that we be allowed to set up a seminar for credit, a seminar with no instructor, where the curriculum would be composed of our own questions.... The only restriction was that in the interests of the institution a young instructor was to sit in on the seminar, but would take no part in it unless we wished him to be active. (1961, p. 8)

Because of the discussions and soul-searching that occurred during this group, most of the members, including Rogers, decided to abandon the vocation of the ministry:

> The majority of the members of that group, in thinking their way through the questions they had raised, thought themselves right out of religious work. I was one. (1961, p. 8)

Rogers himself went on to study psychology at Teachers College, Columbia University, which was in the immediate neighborhood of the theological seminary.

His account indicates the importance of personal freedom in his choice of career:

> I felt that questions as to the meaning of life, and the possibility of the constructive improvement of life for individuals, would probably always interest me, but I could not work in a field where I would be required to believe in some specified religious doctrine. My beliefs had already changed tremendously, and might continue to change. It seemed to me it would be a horrible thing to have to profess a set of beliefs, in order to remain in one's profession. (1961, p. 8)

This incident reveals certain themes and emphases in Rogers' life that were established even before his graduate training in psychology had begun. In client-centered therapy, which Rogers would develop over a decade later, the authority figure was seen as someone whose role is to help and who does not act in a directive manner. Significant change in the life paths of the seminar members arose as a result of the free exploration and discussion (Sollod, 1978). Rogers demonstrated that he valued personal freedom and the possibility of exploring options and making choices. He distrusted authority, though the for-credit seminar he participated in was not a total repudiation of authority. Rather, authority was used to legitimize free discussion and choice.

In the ensuing years, Rogers would gradually realize that his approach to issues in his own life might also be helpful to others within a professional framework.

ROGERS' THEORY OF PERSONALITY AND BEHAVIOR

Carl R. Rogers is best known for his writings on client centered psychotherapy. Indeed, he wrote in detailed ways about the nature and process of non-directive psychotherapy, which ultimately earned him worldwide recognition for his innovative work. However, what is often ignored or absent from academic textbooks on theories of personality is his theory of personality. The over emphasis on his clinical theories and applications has overshadowed the brilliance of his conceptual thinking which, like Freud, was informed by his work with patients. Therefore, to be clear and historically correct, it is necessary to present Rogers' major propositions about personality and behavior. Table 13.5 lists his 19 propositions concerning his theory of personality and behaviors as originally presented in his 1951 book, *Client Centered Therapy* (Rogers, 1951).

To begin, it is important to understand that Rogers, much like those who preceded him with an existentialistic emphasis on self-actualization, was interested in how persons find ways to develop their potential to live healthy and creative lives. In terms of psychotherapy, he understood that among many critical principles that the patient needs to feel or experience a sense of unconditional respect and care from a genuine, nurturant psychotherapist. In this same way, normal persons need similar experiences in safe, nurturing environments in which to grow and release their potentialities for personal growth and the realization of innate talents, skills and qualities of self. In this regard, Rogers' theory of personality focuses on a few key concepts. First, the existential perspective that to appreciate personality in its complexity, it is pragmatically useful and necessary to view personality from a phenomenological perspective, that is, how does the person perceive and interpret their experiences in life. Second, Rogers places theoretical emphasis on the *self-actualizing tendency*, meaning that the organism will strive to maintain or establish optimal levels of integrative functioning. Third, Rogers believed that it was important to understand the disparity between individual experience and how the person viewed themselves as a person. Thus, when the individuals' sense of self-worth, esteem and integrity was congruent with life experiences, the self-actualizing tendency would flourish and manifest itself in behavior. On the other hand, when experience was incongruent with the structure and basis of the self, incongruity would lead to defensiveness, anxiety, tension, depression or other problems of living and adaptation. Thus, self-realization and psychopathology could easily be conceptualized as a continuum predicated on the degree of congruence or incongruence of the self-structure, beliefs, values and attitudinal dispositions to behavior within a cultural and social context. Fourth, Rogers believed that there was a kind of synergistic isomorphism between the psychological and organismic aspects of mental life. Thus, the conditions and social relationships that promoted psychological health and well being also promoted organismic well being, i.e., total health of personality and the person.

It was Rogers' view of human beings, much like that of Maslow, that persons have an inborn genetic tendency towards striving to actualize their potentials. By carefully examining Table 13.5, it can be seen that the first seven of his propositions embrace this idea from existential and phenomenological perspectives. To state this in simple language, what Rogers is proposing is that we all strive to master our lives in healthy ways, with minimal defensiveness to perceived threats, stresses and sources of anxiety. When this striving and innate ability goes well, we feel a sense of enhanced competence and self-esteem. However, when it does not go well in the way we wish, we tend to perceive threat, in varying ways and degrees, that leads to defensive self-protective efforts to preserve our sense of self and well being.

Table 13.5 Rogers' Theoretical Propositions about Personality and Behavior (1951)

1. Every individual exists in a continually changing world of experience
2. The organism reacts to the field as it is experienced and perceived. This perceptual field is, for the individual, reality.
3. The organism reacts as an organized whole to this phenomenal field.
4. The organism has one basic tendency and striving—to actualize, maintain and embrace the experiencing organism.
5. Behavior is basically the goal-directed attempt of the organism to satisfy its needs as experienced, in the field as perceived.
6. Emotion accompanies and in general facilitates such goal-directed behavior, the kind of emotion being related to the seeking versus the consummatory aspects of the behavior and the intensity of the emotion being related to the perceived significance of the behavior for the maintenance and enhancement of the organism.
7. The best vantage point for understanding behavior is from the internal frame of reference of the individual himself.
8. A portion of the total perceptual field gradually becomes differentiated as the self.
9. As a result of interaction with the environment, and particularly as a result of evaluational interaction with others, the structure of the self is formed—an organized, fluid, but consistent conceptual pattern of perceptions of characteristics and relationships of the "I" or the "me," together with values attached to these concepts.
10. The values attached to experiences, and the values which are part of the self-structure, in some instances are values experienced directly by the organism and in some instances are values introjected or taken over from others, but perceived in distorted fashion, as if they had been experienced directly.
11. As experiences occur in the life of the individual, they are either (a) symbolized, perceived and organized into some relationship to the self, (b) ignored because there is no perceived relationship to the self-structure, or (c) denied symbolization or given distorted symbolization because the experience is inconsistent with the structure of the self.
12. Most ways of behaving which are adopted by the organism are those which are consistent with the concept of self.
13. Behavior may, in some instances, be brought about by organic experiences and needs which have not been symbolized. Such behavior may be inconsistent with structure of the self, but in such instances the behavior is not "owned" by the individual.
14. Psychological maladjustment exists when the organism denies to awareness significant sensory and visceral experiences, which consequently are not symbolized and organized into the gestalt of the self-structure. When this situation exists, there is a basic or potential psychological tension.
15. Psychological adjustment exists when the concept of the self is such that all the sensory and visceral experiences of the organism are, or may be, assimilated on a symbolic level into a consistent relationship with the concept of self.
16. Any experience which is inconsistent with the organization or structure of the self may be perceived as a threat, and the more of these perceptions there are, the more rigidly the self-structure is organized to maintain self.
17. Under certain conditions, involving primarily complete absence of any threat to the self-structure, experiences which are inconsistent with it may be perceived, and examined, and the structure of self revised to assimilate and include such experiences.
18. When the individual perceives and accepts into one consistent and integrated system all his sensory and visceral experiences, then he is necessarily more understanding of others and is more accepting of others as separate individuals.
19. As the individual perceives and accepts into his self-structure more of his organic experiences, he finds that he is replacing his present value system—based so largely upon introjections which have been distorted symbolically—with a continuing organism valuing process.

Source: Rogers, 1951.

What is the nature of the self that guides healthy striving and needs to protect itself when threat is perceived? Table 13.5 shows that propositions 8–12 directly concern Rogers' ideas about the self. Consistent with his view that to understand personality is to understand it from the perspective of the person, i.e., how do they perceive and interpret their world? This proposition is critical and profound, as Rogers is suggesting that to truly "know" another person, one must try, through empathy and compassion, to "see the world as they see it," for if not, then, there will be distortions or misunderstanding in the social interaction process at all levels of communication. In other words, the failure of therapist and client to focus on critical "in-the-moment" presentations of self could result in a discordance in therapeutic communication and understanding.

Rogers' proposition about the saliency of understanding the existential phenomenological reality of another person, to understand what is "beneath the mask," is critical to his theory of personality. In other words, how can one understand the nature and process of self-actualization without some concrete knowledge of what the components of the self-structure are composed of? What Rogers proposed in 1951 is the following:

> The self-structure is an organized configuration of perceptions of the self which are admissible to awareness. It is composed of such elements as the perceptions of one's characteristics and abilities; the percepts and concepts of the self in relation to others and to the environment; the value qualities which are perceived as associated with experience and objects; and the goals and ideals which are perceived as having positive or negative values. (1951, p. 501)

Rogers' theory of personality embraces second and third levels of ideas as it pertains to self-realization. The second tier involves his concepts regarding interpersonal relationships. As reflected in propositions 11–18, he explicitly details how we come to differentiate ourselves from others in culture and sub-societies. In essence, he sees interpersonal relationships anchored in the degree to which we develop a solid sense of self-worth from feelings of being respected for who we are without conditions of self-worth that would impose a sanctum of requirements that must be met in order to receive love, approval and recognition from significant others. For example, a parent may say to a child, you are a "good person, but only when you achieve top academic or other honors," thus setting conditions of worth within the relationship. Thus, in Rogers' view, the formation of the self-structure and personal identity emerges from the quality of interpersonal relationships and the genuineness of emotions expressed in verbal and non-verbal communications. Therefore, the "purer" the sincerity and openness of good communication, the greater the potential for the self-actualizing tendency to express itself in behavior and developmentally age-appropriate growth (see propositions 12–14).

Life is not a continuous series of good or bad events. Rogers' theory of personality explicates that psychological maladjustment stems from a number of sources, but at the phenomenological level, anxiety, depression and maladjustment originate from distressing life events or experiences that are denied or inconsistent with the self-structure and values that the person holds dear to their heart. Thus, such discrepancies present challenges to the individual and activate defensive processes to thwart the tensions generated by such incongruities in experience (see Figure 13.2). Given this hypothesis or theoretical premise, Rogers' theory thus returns to the idea that psychological well being occurs when a person can assimilate a variety of potentially good and bad experiences into their sense of self and reality, i.e., within their self-structure and view of life (see proposition 15). In this way, Rogers sees psychological health and psychopathology on a fluid continuum of daily existence. Moreover, it was stated by Rogers that the more a person could internalize and accept themselves, without undue

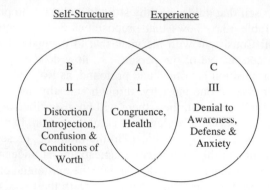

Key:

I: Experienced congruence between self-structure and experience

II: Experiences are distorted and/or introjected from others

III: Experience (sensory and visceral) denied to awareness due to inconsistency with self-structure

A: The greater the congruence, the greater possibility for self-esteem and self-realization

B: Distortion may lead to confusion in self and degrees of self-worth

C: Denial generates sources of defense and anxiety

Figure 13.2 Rogers' Representation of Personality: The Self-Structure and Individual Experience Total Personality

Source: Rogers, 1951.

constricting conditions of worth, the more they would be able to accept other people and life events without imposing "conditions of worth or acceptance." In this regard, Rogers' theory bears similarity to Buddhist emphases on mindfulness and compassion.

PSYCHOTHERAPIST AS SELF-ACTUALIZATION FACILITATOR

Unlike Maslow, Rogers began his study of human nature with troubled personalities. As a clinical psychologist, Rogers explored the potential for change in the therapeutic relationship. Rogers found that what is considered as psychopathology results when persons are prevented or do not have the chance to become who they truly are.

Rogers' personality theory emerged in part from his careful and exacting psychotherapeutic studies. He was among the first therapist-researchers to record psychotherapeutic sessions. Along with his willingness to commit the process of therapy to scientific scrutiny, Rogers pioneered a pervasive change in the way the clinical relationship could be used to induce personality change and in the ways personality data could be derived from the relationship.

Consider, in Table 13.6, fragments of two recorded counseling interviews with college students. They are printed side by side to facilitate direct comparisons. The left-hand transcript is of a client and a therapist who view the therapeutic situation as structured, problem-centered, and under the direct control of the therapist. The right-hand column contains the transcript of a client-therapist interview in a situation with a counselor who recognizes that therapeutic processes are very much person-centered.

Table 13.6 Directive versus Non-Directive Counseling Processes

Directive Counseling Transcript	Nondirective Counseling Transcript
COUNSELOR: I noticed that you stated you enrolled in Psychology 411 [study habits course] because you didn't know how to study well enough uh and then I checked over the problem list, and I saw that you went rather heavy on you worried about low grades and poor memory and so on. How well did you do in high school?	STUDENT: I haven't written to my parents about this at all. In the past they haven't been of any help to me in this respect, and if I can keep it away from them as much as possible, I'll do so. But there's a slight matter of grades to explain, and they're not good, and I don't know how I'm going to explain without telling them about this. Would you advise me to tell them about it?
STUDENT: Well, I was just an average student.	COUNSELOR: Suppose you tell me a little more about what you had thought about it.
COUNSELOR: And what major did you have there?	STUDENT: Well, I think I'm compelled to, because
STUDENT: Ah, you mean	COUNSELOR: It's a situation you've really got to face.
COUNSELOR: In high school, you took college preparatory or commercial?	STUDENT: Yes, there's not use getting around it, even if they can't take it the way they should, because I've already flunked my gym course, I just haven't come . . .
STUDENT: It was an academic course. I took languages and English and history.	COUNSELOR: It will be fairly hard for you to tell them.
COUNSELOR: What course did you like the best? [Student presumably answers; later in session counselor summarizes:]	STUDENT: Yes. Oh, I don't know if they're going to sort of condemn me. I think so, because that's what they've done in the past.
COUNSELOR: It seems to me that your problem is that you want to learn more about yourself. We'll be getting all these tests back, and there are those [study] projects, and the way we do, I see you each week at this time and you'll begin to get a little better picture and then I'll help you check it and I'll tell you if it's right (Laugh)	COUNSELOR: You feel that they'll be unsympathetic and they'll condemn you for your failures.
STUDENT: Mm-hm.	STUDENT: Well, I'm pretty sure my father will. My mother might not. He hasn't been he doesn't experience these things; he just doesn't know what it's like . . .
COUNSELOR: So we can work it out. I would suggest I would more or less work this project out because you say you are having difficulties concentrating. . . .	COUNSELOR: You feel that he could never understand you?
(From Rogers, 1942, pp. 135–136).	(From Rogers, 1942, pp. 116–117).

Focus on the Client's Feelings

There are significant and easily discernible differences between the two counseling interviews. The essence of the directive counselor's effort is information gathering and dispensing. The flow of communication between counselor and client tends to be one way: from counselor to client. Responsibility for the direction and outcome of the relationship implicitly lies with the authoritarian counselor. Restricted to the role of question answer, the client is led through a series of diagnostic queries and away from any confrontation with his or her feelings, confusions, and anxieties. To the degree that client feelings are mentioned at all, they are *talked about* rather than genuinely experienced or forthrightly made the focus of concern. The counselor goes so far as to summarize by assuming the "wise knower" role: "It seems to me that your problem is you want to learn more about yourself." It is a rational, perhaps even correct statement. But it is the counselor's statement, one not arrived at or formulated by the client.

The second counseling transcript has a different emotional flavor. Here, the client is encouraged to express a wealth of feelings. In all replies, the counselor responds to the emotional content of the client's statements, not to the cognitive aspects or the information provided. The nondirective counselor tried to respond to the troubled person by helping him or her to clarify his or her feelings: "It's a situation you've really got to face" or, "It'll be fairly hard for you to tell them." When the counselor is successful in detecting the emotional meaning of a client remark, rephrasing the client's statements allow the client to examine his or her feelings openly. When the counselor is unsuccessful at mirroring the emotional tone of the client's statements, the client sometimes feels that the counselor "does not understand" or is "putting words into my mouth." But even when mistaken, the counselor's attitude communicates to the client a genuine concern about the experience of the client.

These differences between these two counseling interviews are only a small sample of the insights about the counseling relationship systematized by Rogers. His develop-ment of a personality theory is so inextricably interwoven with his clinical therapeutic work that some consideration must be given to the slow development of what Rogers came eventually to call *client-centered counseling and theory* as a replacement for the original "nondirective" label.

DEVELOPMENT OF THE NONDIRECTIVE VIEWPOINT

In 1974, as part of his address to the American Psychological Association on the occasion of receiving its Distinguished Professional Contribution Award, Rogers traced his impact on psychology. In particular, he formulated from his perspective of nearly half a century of therapeutic work the kernel of the central hypothesis that had initiated and guided his theoretical development:

> ...the gradually formed and tested hypothesis [was] that the individual has within himself vast resources for self-understanding, for altering his self-concept, his attitudes, and his self-directed behavior and that these resources can be tapped if only a definable climate of facilitative psychological attitudes can be provided. (1974a, p. 116)

The similarity to Maslow's conception of human nature is obvious. Both theorists regard humans as inherently good, as self-directed, and as striving toward increased autonomy. Rogers' theory, then, can be understood as the attempt to discover the conditions that foster the individual's utilization of *his or her own powers* for health and understanding.

Early Pragmatism: "If It Works, Do It"

Rogers began his career as a clinical psychologist trained in empiricism. He was granted an internship at the newly founded Institute for Child Guidance while in doctoral training, and in the atmosphere of this clinic Rogers was exposed to a mul-tiplicity of theoretical viewpoints. Members of the staff at the guidance clinic were largely psychodynamic in their orientation, and a contrast to the statistical, objective atmosphere of graduate school. Rogers later recalled " . . . I was functioning in two completely different worlds, 'and never the twain shall meet' " (1961, p. 9; cf. 1974b, p. 7).

The conflict of intellectual traditions was an important learning experience for Rogers, opening him to the possibility that experts differ drastically in their interpretations. Before completion of his doctorate, Rogers obtained a position in the Child Study Department of the Society for the Prevention of Cruelty to Children in Rochester, New York (1961, p. 9). For the next 12 years, Rogers was engaged in the application of psychological services to delinquent and underprivileged children. Many of the staff at the Rochester facility were trained in the Philadelphia School of Social Work and operated from the neopsychoanalytic viewpoint developed by Otto Rank. Rank focused on the individual exploring and expressing his or her own inner experiences:

> I conceive of human help for the individual not as a planned method of psycho-therapeutic techniques with respect to a control of his stimuli and responses but as *his experiencing of the irrational forces within himself* which he has not heretofore dared to express spontaneously. (1941, p. 47; italics added)

Rogers later commented that his own early emphasis on responding to the feelings of the client sprang from the influence of Rank and his followers at the Rochester facility (Rogers, 1966, in Hart & Tomlinson, 1970, p. 515). Most important of all, however, was the lesson to be learned from his colleagues' attitude toward therapeutic technique: "There was only one criterion in regard to any method of dealing with these children and their parents, and that was, 'Does it work?'" (1961, p. 10).

This emphasis on effectiveness was reinforced for Rogers when his careful psychodynamic prodding and questioning to uncover the sexual conflicts of a young arsonist did not prevent the boy from repeating his illegal behaviors. On probation after therapy with Rogers, the boy continued to set fires (1961, p. 10).

Insight into the Dignity of the Individual Person: A "Failure"

Another influence that shaped Rogers' slowly developing theoretical formulations occurred during an interview with a client's mother. The boy was something of a "hellion," and Rogers could clearly see that the mother's early rejection of the boy was responsible. Despite repeated attempts at directing her flow of conversation toward the attainment of this insight, he could not accomplish a successful breakthrough. His report of the experience is particularly instructive:

> Finally I gave up. I told her that it seemed we had both tried, but we had failed. . . .
> She agreed. So we concluded the interview, shook hands, and she walked to the door
> of the office. Then she turned and asked, "Do you ever take adults for counseling here?"
> When I replied in the affirmative, she said, "Well then, I would like some help." She came
> to the chair she had left, and began to pour out her despair about her marriage, her troubled
> relationship with her husband, her sense of failure and confusion, all very different from the
> sterile "case history" she had given before. Real therapy began then. . . . (Rogers, 1961, p. 11)

From this experience Rogers learned an important lesson about the nature of the ideal psychotherapeutic experience and about the dignity of the person:

> " . . . it is the *client* who knows what hurts, what directions to go, what problems are crucial, what experiences have been deeply buried" (1961, pp. 11–12)

Thus Rogers slowly came to the viewpoint that authoritative, directive, and diagnostically oriented psychological service was far less important than allowing the client to speak freely, feel freely, and think freely.

PERSONAL SOURCES OF ROGERS' EMPHASIS ON FREEDOM AND SELF-WORTH

Rogers' theory of personality, like other humanistic approaches, such as those of Maslow or Allport (Chapter 11), stresses the dignity and worth of the individual. The accent is on the inherent capacity of the person to direct his or her own life when the interpersonal environment provides sufficient freedom from both subtle and overt coercion. In Rogers' view, the primary, indeed essential, ingredient of the well-lived life is, simply, *freedom* to be, to choose, and to act.

The core of Rogers' approach to personality is the belief that every individual requires freedom from coercion—from, as Karen Horney (Chapter 10) had written, internalized "shoulds" and "oughts." His own experience growing up in a strict family appears to be one source of his emphasis on personal freedom.

Rogers' Growing-up Years: Faith and Rebellion

Carl Rogers was born in 1902 in a Chicago suburb as the fourth of six children of parents he described as "highly practical, 'down to earth' individuals" (Rogers, 1967b, p. 344). His father was an engineer and his mother had finished two years of college. Despite their level of educational achievement, Rogers describes his parents as being "rather anti-intellectual, with some of the contempt of the practical person toward the long-haired egghead" (1967b, p. 344). Both parents were hard workers, convinced that there was no virtue higher than hard work and no problem that could not be solved by even harder work.

Rogers' mother, who wore her religion on her sleeve, shaped the family atmosphere. Among her frequently uttered biblical expressions according to Rogers, were "Come out from among them and be ye separate"; and, "All our righteousness is as filthy rags in thy sight, oh Lord."

> The first [saying] expressed her conviction of superiority, that we were of the "elect" and should not mingle with those who were not so favored; the second her conviction of inferiority, that at our best we were unspeakably sinful. (Rogers, 1967b, p. 344)

The main consequence of such convictions was a pervading sense in the Rogers family children that they were specially set apart from the children of other families, and that most typical enjoyments were faintly "sinful." For example, Rogers wrote, "I remember my slight feeling of wickedness when I had my first bottle of 'pop'" (1961, p. 5).

Rogers remembers both parents as extremely loving but subtly controlling:

> I do not remember ever being given a direct command on an important subject, yet such was the unity of our family that it was understood by all that we did not dance, play cards, attend movies, smoke, drink, or show any sexual interest. (1967b, p. 344)

One major result of this stringent upbringing was that Rogers had little social life. Rogers reports that he never had a "real" date until his junior year in high school, when he nervously asked a girl he had admired "from afar" to a school dinner-dance.

Rogers was a very good student. He took an active interest in doing research at a very young age. He became a "student of scientific agriculture" at the age of 14. His early research provided an early grounding in empirical scientific methodology. He learned,

> ...how experiments were conducted, how control groups were matched with experimental groups, how conditions were held constant by randomizing procedures...how difficult it is to test a hypothesis. (1961, p. 6)

During Christmas vacation of his college sophomore year, Rogers pursued his religious interests by attending a conference of student volunteers for evangelical work.

> I decided at this conference that I should change my life goal and go into Christian work.... Having made this decision, agriculture no longer seemed to be a very suitable field. I felt that I should shift to some subject which would prepare me for the ministry.... (1967b, p. 350)

In his junior year of college, Rogers was selected as one of ten students to travel to what was then called Peking, China, as a representative of the World Student Christian Federation. The other members of the group were mostly young intellectuals with far more liberal backgrounds than Rogers. The long voyage provided Rogers with much needed social interaction and intellectual exchange. Decades later, Rogers speculated that there might be an Eastern aspect to his thinking that traced back to this early trip:

> In more recent years, I have wondered about the possibility of the effect of my trip to China. Prior to that trip and on the ship going over, we held many discussions about China and its history and undoubtedly about its philosophy. I don't remember any of those. It is quite possible, however, that some of the ideas were taken in but did not seem real to me until I had experienced them myself.... So the Oriental influence on my thinking may go back to 1922. (Rogers, 1978)

The key element in the rift with his family centered on a fundamental theological tenet that separated more liberal from more conservative Christians. One evening, aboard ship, a traveling companion, Dr. Henry Sharman, a student of the sayings of Jesus, made some provocative remarks. Rogers later indicated that this event led him to doubt the divinity of Jesus. Rogers left behind his family's conservative religious views by coming to the conclusion that Jesus was a man. Rogers had freed himself from parental authority, and he attempted to minimize his experience of conflict at the time by asserting that the rift was accomplished with minimal pain.

Rogers kept a journal of his personal reactions to his new acquaintances and their ideas. He sent a copy to a girl he had been seeing and who was to become his fiancée upon his return. But he also, without realizing the upsetting impact his new ideas would have on his religiously conforming family, sent a copy home to his family:

> Since we did not have the benefit of airmail it took two months for a reply to arrive. Thus I kept pouring out on paper all my new feelings and ideas and thoughts with no notion of the consternation that this was causing in my family. By the time their reactions caught up with me, the rift in outlook was fully established. Thus, with a minimum of pain I broke the intellectual and religious ties with my home. (Rogers, 1967b, p. 351)

In 1924, Rogers set out to study for the ministry at Union Theological Seminary in New York. Union Theological Seminary had then, as it does now, a reputation for liberality, the kind of radical liberalism of which Rogers' father disapproved.

> Knowing my plan to go to Union, my father had made one offer that was very close to a bribe. I suspect he was not proud of himself afterward for this. Certainly I rejected it indignantly. He told me that he would pay all the expenses for both of us [Rogers and his wife] if I would go to Princeton Seminary, which was at that point a center of fundamentalist thinking. (Rogers, 1967b, p. 353)

During this period a child was born to Rogers and his wife, and they attempted to raise him by "the book of Watsonian behaviorism, strict scheduling and the like" (1967b, p. 356). Rogers' recent experience with freedom had not yet worked its way down to the second generation.

As we have seen, Rogers stayed only briefly at Union. He thought his way out and became a psychologist instead.

The Importance of the Intellectual Climate

In addition to personal and professional experiences, ideas were very important to Carl Rogers. He was affected by philosophical and ideological currents that emphasized personal responsibility and choice and evidenced a deep trust in the ability of individuals and free societies to solve their own problems. Such ideas were congruent with Rogers' own personal proclivities.

Rogers appears to have been influenced by the ideas of the American philosopher John Dewey, and the leader of the progressive education movement, William Kilpatrick. Dewey's functionalism and Kilpatrick's progressive education movement emphasized the importance of an individual's own experience in coming to grips with and solving problems in his or her own life. The ideal in progressive education was to work in accordance with a child's readiness rather than to impose tasks that did not interest him or her. This theme of working in accordance with a person's readiness was to be central in Rogers' subsequent development of therapeutic approaches (Sollod, 1978).

But Rogers did not apply these ideas in his early professional work. After graduate school at Columbia, Rogers worked at the Child Study Department of the Society for the Prevention of Cruelty to Children in Rochester, New York. He followed the conventional directive techniques he had been taught in his work with delinquent and underprivileged youngsters. He was unhappy with the results and with his approach and experienced, "disillusionment with authority, with materials, with myself (1951, p. 10). He continued, "There were mistakes in authoritative teachings and that there was still new knowledge to discover." At this point he began to rediscover the ideas of John Dewey and William H. Kilpatrick and to search for kindred spirits in the psychotherapeutic world.

It was also at this point he discovered the work of Jesse Taft, a social worker in Philadelphia who had developed what she termed a "controlled relationship" method. Rogers (1942) drew on her ideas liberally in his first book. Taft (1951) emphasized that there should be a lack of control or coercion in psychotherapy and that the patient should be allowed to express whatever thoughts or feelings he or she wished. Taft emphasized the importance of the patient focusing on the feelings he or she was experiencing at any given time. The therapist should do nothing more than facilitate such exploration.

A leading educator and psychologist, Goodwin Watson (1940), presented ideas at a 1940 conference, "Areas of Agreement in Psychotherapy," that Rogers took part in. Watson emphasized the expression of feelings in psychotherapy as well as the importance of rapport between the therapist and patient. He stressed the value of "a relationship in which the therapist tries not to let his own values influence the patient" (1940, p. 708). He said, "We do not believe that mere catharsis of feelings is therapeutic. We distrust advice and exhortation" (1940, p. 709). The influence of these ideas is apparent in Rogers' subsequent development of nondirective psychotherapy (Sollod, 1978).

In summary, some central themes of Rogers' formulation of a theory of personality stressing freedom to be self-actualized, and his theory of psychotherapy stressing the creation of an atmosphere of permissiveness and warmth, have deep and broad roots. Rogers' personal and professional experiences and his intellectual background were the foundations for the development of his emphasis on personal freedom and his creative contributions in personality theory and in the field of psychotherapy. His personal outlook and professional contributions are connected.

EARLY NONDIRECTIVE VIEW: TOO MUCH FREEDOM

In 1940 Rogers accepted a position with The Ohio State University to teach graduate students about counseling. As he taught, he was forced to focus his views more sharply, in the process forming a perspective of psychotherapy that was unique. Up to this point, Rogers thought that he was simply writing and teaching about clinical techniques that all clinicians were using (1959, p. 187). But when invited to deliver a lecture at the University of Minnesota chapter of the Psi Chi Society entitled "Newer Concepts in Psychotherapy," Rogers soon discovered from the furor and controversy the lecture aroused that he was indeed saying something new (1974b, p. 8).

It was from this Minnesota lecture that Rogers derived the second chapter of his book on **nondirective therapy.** In *Counseling and Psychotherapy* (1942), Rogers emphasized four important principles of the "new" psychotherapy:

1. The newer therapy "relies much more heavily on the individual drive toward growth, health, and adjustment. Therapy is not a matter of doing something *to* the individual, or of inducing him to do something about himself. It is instead a matter of freeing him for normal growth and development..." (1942, p. 29).

2. "...this newer therapy places greater stress upon the emotional elements, the feeling aspects of the situation, than upon the intellectual aspects" (1942, p. 29).

3. "...this newer therapy places greater stress upon the immediate situation than upon the individual's past" (1942, p. 29).

4. The newer approach "...lays great stress upon the therapeutic relationship itself as a growth experience.... Here the individual learns to understand himself; to make significant independent choices, to relate himself successfully to another person in a more adult fashion" (1942, p. 30).

Thus, the central concept in Rogers' first formulation of his views was that people have within themselves the capacity to solve their own problems, as previously pointed out. The task of the therapist is to establish the conditions that allow people to attain this insight themselves: *Attainment of insight* was, therefore, one of the key goals of nondirective therapy in the 1940s. To enable the client to achieve self-insight, the counselor's chief tool was the *clarification of feelings* through rephrasing the emotional content of the client's statements (cf. Hart, 1970, pp. 6 ff.). Rogers summarized his early view of the counselor's role in this way:

> *Effective counseling consists of a definitively structured, permissive relationship which allows the client to gain an understanding of himself to a degree which enables him to take positive steps in the light of his new orientation.* (Rogers, 1942, p. 18, italics in original)

Though controversial, Rogers' techniques and philosophy were widely adopted by practitioners. The problems that followed in the application of nondirective counseling and therapy were due in part to two crucial aspects of this early formulation:

1. Little or no *explicit* theory had been developed to guide the counselor's efforts;
2. In the hands of an unskilled or inadequately trained therapist, the permissive and accepting attitude was construed by his clients as a threatening "don't care" attitude or as a directionless, disorganized relationship.

Rogers believed that the difficulty lay in the tendency of some counselors to interpret his formulations too literally (1951, p. 26). In effect, some counselors supposed that their role was to be merely passive and to adopt a laissez-faire policy: "the passivity and seeming lack of interest . . . is experienced by the client as a rejection, since indifference is in no real way the same as acceptance" (Rogers, 1951, p. 27).

The criticisms of Rogers' nondirective psychotherapy as well as his own awareness of its shortcomings led to Rogers' modification and further development of his psychotherapeutic approach.

CLIENT-CENTERED THERAPY: EMPATHIC UNDERSTANDING

In 1951, Rogers published a second major work on counseling, carefully delineating his views on what he now termed **client-centered therapy.** The book's title, *Client-Centered Therapy*, was meant to emphasize the new rationale of his approach: "The client, as the term has acquired its meaning, is one who comes actively and voluntarily to gain help on a problem, but *without any notion of surrendering his own responsibility for the situation*" (Rogers, 1951, p. 7n.; italics added).

Thus the publication of *Client-Centered Therapy* marked the beginning of a second phase in Rogers' thinking (cf. Hart, 1970). The focus had shifted to the counselor's efforts to be *empathic* in understanding the client's world, and to the *communication* of that understanding to the client. The technique of reflection of feelings, though present from the first nondirective period, now assumed more importance. Reflection of feelings was not merely to be used to help the client attain insight and clarification of his or her emotions, but also to communicate the counselor's understanding of the client's inner world. In mirroring back the client's feelings, the counselor simultaneously transmits the desire to perceive the world as the client perceives it. In effect, the goal of the counselor is to achieve the *internal frame-of-reference* of the client:

> . . . it is the counselor's aim to perceive as sensitively and accurately as possible all of the perceptual field as it is being experienced by the client . . . and having thus perceived this internal frame of reference of the other as completely as possible, to indicate to the client the extent to which he is seeing through the client's eyes. (Rogers, 1951, p. 34)

This approach on accurate empathy goes along with Rogers' view of the individual's subjective experience, his or her **phenomenal world,** as the fundamental psychological reality. As Rogers stated this proposition, *"Every individual exists in a continually changing world of experience of which he is the center"* (1951, p. 483). The individual's experience is his or her reality (1959, p. 222). For this reason, the effort to empathically understand the experiential world of the client takes on central importance in Rogers' approach to psychotherapy.

Thus, by 1951, two of the three major elements that characterize Rogers' view of personality were present to his thinking. First was the necessity for the counselor to provide a warm and permissive relationship; second was the necessity for the counselor to assume the internal frame of reference of the client and to communicate empathic understanding of the client's world.

EXPERIENTIAL THERAPY:
THE CONDITIONS OF PERSONALITY CHANGE

The third element characteristic of Rogers' view of personality emerged during the third aspect of the development of client-centered theory. Joseph Hart (1970) and Eugene Gendlin (1964, 1968, 1970) have characterized this phase of Rogers' and their own work as the "experiencing" phase or as *experiential therapy*.

By 1957 the focus had again shifted to a *mutual expression of feelings* by both client and counselor. *Experiencing* became the technical term to describe the internal, directly experienced emotional processes that the client and counselor struggle to put into words. Because tangled and latent feelings are the core of psychological maladjustment in Rogers' view, the tasks of learning to experience one's own distorted and trapped emotions and of learning to communicate them to oneself and to the counselor became the central goals of experiential therapy.

One of the key causes of this shift in emphasis from pure verbal transactions to direct emotional experience can be found in a research effort undertaken by Rogers and his colleagues at the University of Wisconsin. Working with nonverbal, often uncooperative, schizophrenic patients in a state hospital required the radical shift in therapeutic strategy (see Rogers, 1967a; Gendlin, 1966). If psychotherapy from the client-centered framework had been a verbal interchange between a willing client and a warmly accepting therapist, it now had to be something more direct, less verbal, and increasingly experiential.

Along these lines Rogers had already provided a theoretical rationale for personality change in therapy, which implied that constructive alterations in personality could occur regardless of the specific verbal techniques employed by the counselor. If six operationally defined conditions of relationship were met, then any person-to-person contact embodying them could promote personality growth. The six conditions postulated by Rogers (1957) were:

1. *Two persons are in psychological contact* so that each of them is aware, even if in only the dimmest fashion, that the other's presence makes a difference.

2. *The first person, the client, is in a state of self-incongruence*, being vulnerable or anxious. **Self-incongruence** means that a discrepancy exists between the client's self-image and his or her ongoing experiences, between the actor and the mask. Any experience that threatens the self-picture will be defensively distorted.

3. *The second person, or therapist, is self-congruent* or integrated in the relationship. **Self-congruence** means that the therapist is genuinely him- or herself, totally free to express what he or she actually feels, positive or negative, in the situation with the client. Such spontaneity includes the ability to express feelings that are not particularly pleasing: "I am afraid of this client;" or "I am bored with this client."

4. *The therapist experiences unconditional positive regard for the client*. **Unconditional positive regard** means that the counselor warmly accepts the client. It is unconditional. The counselor prizes the person in a nonjudgmental way.

5. *The therapist experiences an empathic understanding of the client's internal frame of reference and endeavors to communicate this experience to the client*. The counselor tries to see the world as the client sees it and to communicate that he or she does so.

6. *The communication to the client of the therapist's empathic understanding and unconditional positive regard must be minimally achieved*. If the client does not perceive acceptance and understanding, they are not real for him or her.

When these six conditions are fulfilled in a relationship, intentionally therapeutic or otherwise, personality change in a positive, healthy direction will occur. Clients who experience these conditions will be more able to accept their feelings and perceptions freely as their own; they will grow in the direction of their idealized self-images; they will become more autonomous in their decision making. The emphasis is clearly not on the counselor's technique, nor on the specifics of verbal interchange. Crucial to personality change is the quality of the directly experienced relationship. Unlike directive approaches in which there is an effort to shape the client's behavior, the client-centered approach is one that facilitates change.

PERSONALITY CHANGES EVOKED BY THE THERAPEUTIC RELATIONSHIP

Rogers and his colleagues formulated a conceptualization of the specific process of personality change that occurs when these six conditions exist between two persons. From hundreds of recorded therapeutic sessions and from his own experiences, Rogers was able to discern the basic similarities of the client's progressive changes in experience within the therapeutic relationship. Rogers proposed that such personality changes might be thought of as a continuum of experience. One end of the continuum is personality or experiential rigidity; the opposite end is fluidity or psychological flow (Rogers 1958, 1961). Clients with differing degrees of personality difficulty may be conceptualized as initially occupying different positions between the two extremes. As therapy progresses, the client progresses toward the fluidity end of the spectrum.

In all, Rogers identified seven steps in the process. The first three phases through which clients pass involve their initial inability to see their difficulties, a gradual dim recognition that some problem exists, and a tendency once a problem is recognized to speak of themselves as objects without a real feeling. Thus, the first three stages of personality change in Rogerian psychotherapy are identified as:

1. *Rigidity of self-perception:* no recognition of need to change self
2. *Dim recognition of problem:* problem exists in others, not self
3. *Self treated as object:* does not own his or her feelings

In the fourth stage, there is some movement in the direction of greater flexibility. But clients continue to discuss emotions of their past rather than feelings they now experience. Some questioning of their own interpretations also occurs and consequently anxiety and distrust of their own perceptions begin to develop. This fourth or middle phase may be identified as:

4. *Partial recognition of feelings:* tendency to treat feelings as colorless objects

In the last three phases of the process of personality change, the client progressively approaches accurate recognition and ownership of feelings, acceptance of self, with reevaluation of personal interpretations, and finally, in the seventh phase, experiencing of feelings with richness and clarity. These last three phases of the process of personality change may be identified as:

5. *Improved recognition of feelings:* feelings of wanting to be the "real me"
6. *Acceptance of feelings with richness:* self is free to "own" feelings
7. *New feelings experienced freely:* self is totally flexible, trustworthy, and capable of change and growth

The seven phases outlined here provide an instructive scheme by which to understand Rogers' developing conception of personality. It is easy to see that Rogers views the psychologically maladjusted personality as one who is defensively rigidified, constricted in his or her experiencing of self, and conflicted in his or her willingness to "own" his or her feelings. To describe this phenomenon, Rogers, too, employed the metaphor of the actor and the mask, for the rigid, defensive person is adopting a series of false fronts or masks to deceive others and him- or herself. In the warm and accepting empathic relationship of psychotherapy, the person

> ... begins to drop the false fronts, or the masks, or the roles, with which he has faced life. He appears to be trying to discover something more basic, something more truly himself. (Rogers, 1961, p. 109)

The task that remains is to explore how Rogers systematized these discoveries into an explicit theory of personality.

THE FULLY FUNCTIONING PERSON: IDEAL MENTAL HEALTH

From his experience in psychotherapy, and from the consistency of the changes he observed as his clients grew toward more personal freedom, Rogers formulated a concept of the ideally free and self-accepting person. He first committed his ideas to paper during the winter of 1952–1953, but the journal editor to whom he submitted them rejected them. The paper was finally published in original form in 1964 (see also Rogers, 1961, Chapter 9), and it presented Rogers' view of what he called "the fully functioning person."

Rogers approached the problem of defining a **fully functioning person.** In order to do so, Rogers characterized the traits of a person who successfully completes psychotherapy and exhibits in his or her behavior the highest goals of the best and most effective psychotherapy available. Rogers distinguished three primary characteristics of the fully functioning person, who Rogers viewed as a person after successful therapy:

1. The fully functioning person is *more fully open to experience* (1964, p. 18). He or she has become freed of the need to distort defensively both inner and outer reality

---

BOX 13.1 *Only Connect . . .*

Rogers' concept of the fully functioning person is similar to Maslow's notion of the self-actualized (SA) personality. Maslow used a greater range of descriptive terms than Rogers does, and Maslow's SA person seems slightly more autonomous with a possibility of ruthlessness. Nevertheless, the two concepts can be compared as seen in the accompanying table.

Rogers' Fully Functioning Person and Maslow's Self-Actualized Person Compared

Rogers' Fully Functioning Person	Maslow's Self-Actualized Person

1. More fully open to experience
    Unafraid of own feelings
	1. Reality and problem-centered
	    Accepting of self
	    Unexpected ruthlessness

2. More existential living
    Nondetermined, independent
	2. Spontaneity and simplicity
	    Freshness of appreciation
	    Discrimination between means and ends
	    Need for privacy

3. Increased trust in own organism
    More creative, nonconformist
	3. Acceptance of others
	    Resistance to enculturation
	    Creative
	    Unhostile sense of humor
	    More intimate personal relations
	    Gemeinschaftsgefühl (social interest)
	    [cf. Alfred Adler, Chapter 4]

and is able to listen perceptively and unanxiously to the demands of his or her body and mind.

2. The fully functioning person has the capacity to experience life *in an existential fashion* (1964, p. 20). He or she lives each moment of life more spontaneously, enjoying the exuberance and the joy of seeing life as one new moment following another. The person realizes that "What I will be in the next moment, and what I will do, grows out of that moment, and cannot be predicted in advance either by me or by others" (1964, p. 20).

3. Fully functioning people experience an *increased trust in their own organisms* (1964, p. 20). They feel free to do what "feels right" at any given moment, fully expecting that they will prove competent to meet any challenge, judge accurately any obstacle, and regulate their behavior realistically as the situation demands.

Three secondary personality characteristics are connected with Rogers' concept of the fully functioning person:

1. Fully functioning people grow unafraid of their own feelings; emotions become important but not overwhelming personal experiences.
2. They are neither determined nor controlled by external influences.
3. With increased trust in their own cognitive and emotional processes, these people find themselves more creative in their relationships. They are able to harmonize themselves with the needs of others because they find themselves trusting human nature in general.

ROGERS' MODEL OF DEVELOPMENT

The most basic, innate tendency of the human infant is a drive toward "actualizing his organism." Instead of postulating a long list of needs or drives, Rogers chose to hypothesize that most biological functions and psychological urges could be subsumed under one major heading: a need to maintain and to enhance one's life (1951, p. 488):

> We are talking here about the tendency of the organism to maintain itself, to assimilate food, to behave defensively in the face of threat, to achieve the goal of self-maintenance even when the usual pathway to that goal is blocked. We are speaking of the tendency of the organism to move in the direction of maturation, as maturation is defined for each species.... [The organism] moves in the direction of limited expansion through growth, expansion through extending itself by means of its tools, and expansion through reproduction. It moves in the direction of greater independence or self-responsibility. (1951, p. 488)

As the infant develops biologically, its psychological maturation tends to keep pace through increasing self-awareness. Gradually, a part of the infant's phenomenal world becomes differentiated and recognized as "me," "I," or "myself." From the total global mass of perceptual stimuli, the infant learns slowly and cautiously to identify itself as an independent agent (Rogers, 1951, p. 497; 1959, p. 233).

THE IMPORTANCE OF APPROVAL

The infant develops its picture of "me" through its interactions with significant others. Much as Harry Stack Sullivan (Chapter 9) had described, Rogers indicated the importance of the child's sensitivity to the praise and blame of the adults in its world. These evaluations of its behavior are assimilated to the infant's self-structure, and as socialization continues, the infant's perceptual field continues to grow in complexity. Many behaviors consistent with its parents' conception of what it should be will be praised; a variety of behaviors that are disapproved of by its parents will be punished or responded to by them with emotionally abrasive communications.

> [The child]...experiences words and actions of his parents in regard to these satisfying behaviors, and the words and actions add up to the feeling "You are bad, the behavior is bad, and you are not loved or lovable when you behave in this way." This constitutes a deep threat to the nascent structure of the self. The child's dilemma might be schematized in these terms: "If I admit to awareness the satisfactions of these behaviors and values I apprehend in these experiences, then this is inconsistent with my self as being loved or lovable." (1951, p. 500)

Thus, to preserve the continuity of parental love in its world, the child must fend off threats of withdrawal of that affection. Rogers hypothesized that the infant must deal with those of its behaviors that arouse parental disapproval by removing both the threat and the motive for the behavior from its awareness. For example, the infant may distort its experience of the situation: "The accurate symbolization would be 'I perceive my parents as experiencing this behavior as unsatisfying to them.' The distorted symbolization, distorted to preserve the threatened concept of self, is '*I* perceive this behavior as unsatisfying'" (Rogers, 1951, p. 500).

In short, the child learns to experience reality secondhand. It adopts not its spontaneous feelings and perceptions as guides to its behavior, but the defensively safe feelings that maintain parental love and approval. Experience is thus distorted in the service of "self" survival. The **self-structure** becomes "an organized configuration of perceptions of self which are admissible to awareness" (Rogers, 1951, p. 501). Threatening self-perceptions are excluded.

As the self-structure develops, a need for approval, or what Rogers termed **positive self-regard**, grows in intensity. Positive regard is the experience of feeling accepted, loved, and "prized." The source of the infant's sense of positive regard is located in the approval of others.

People feel good when they realize that others are approving and prizing them: "when an individual discriminates himself as satisfying another's need for positive regard, he necessarily experiences satisfaction of his own need for positive regard" (1959, p. 223). Satisfying another's need for love and acceptance is in itself satisfying. Rogers' description of the infant's developing need for positive regard bears quoting:

> The infant learns to need love. Love is very satisfying, but to know whether he is receiving it or not he must observe his mother's face, gestures, and other ambiguous signs. He develops a total gestalt as to the way he is regarded by his mother and each new experience of love or rejection tends to alter the whole gestalt. Consequently, each behavior on his mother's part such as a specific disapproval of a specific behavior tends to be experienced as disapproval in general. So important is this to the infant that he comes to be guided in his behavior not by the degree to which an experience maintains or enhances the organism, but by the likelihood of receiving maternal love. (1959, p. 225)

The infant gradually acquires a knowledge of relevant **conditions of worth**. That is, the infant "understands," however dimly at first, that only under certain conditions is he or she positively esteemed by others, by self in response to others, and most important, by his or her parents. The infant realizes that certain behaviors are the conditions of worth that provide acceptance or provoke rejection.

How is it possible for any infant ever to develop a healthy, spontaneously natural, self-concept? Rogers suggested that three parental characteristics foster healthy self-structure formation: (1) ability to accept the child's feelings and strivings; (2) ability to accept one's own feelings that certain of the child's behaviors are undesirable; (3) and communication of acceptance of the child as a person (based on Rogers, 1951, p. 502). The child who experiences a relationship with its parents based on the three previously listed qualities experiences no threat to itself as a loved or lovable person.

INCONGRUENCE BETWEEN SELF AND EXPERIENCE

Rogers emphasized the importance of an individual protecting his or her sense of **self-regard** and developed the concept of self-incongruence.

> Because of the need for self-regard, the individual perceives his experience selectively, in terms of the conditions of worth that have come to exist in him.
>
> a. Experiences that are in accord with his conditions of worth are perceived and symbolized accurately in awareness.
>
> b. Experiences which run contrary to the conditions of worth are perceived selectively and distortedly as if in accord with the conditions of worth, or are in part or whole, denied to awareness. (1959, p. 226)

Rogers suggested that the conditions of worth by which the individual has learned to navigate his or her world serve as selective filters in screening new experiences. Those experiences that are denied access to awareness because they violate the self-structure form the foundation of potential psychological maladjustment. The resulting self-incongruence means that one's actual core of experience, which constitutes the **real self,** is discrepant with the self-picture or **perceived self** and denied to awareness. The individual is thus vulnerable to anxiety every time a fresh experience threatens to trigger perception of the discrepancy.

Experiences that are threatening to one's self-structure are said to be "subcepted." **Subception** means that the individual perceives the threat but does not admit it to full awareness in the higher cognitive brain centers (Rogers, 1959, p. 200; see also McLeary & Lazarus, 1949). Subception of threatening discrepancies between self-structure and new experiences begins the process of defensive personality disorganization.

PERSONALITY DISORGANIZATION

When the discrepancy between self-structure and experience becomes so great that subception no longer functions with complete success, the result for some people can be personality disorganization (Rogers, 1959, pp. 228–229). This may arise if the perception of a threatening experience occurs suddenly and so forcefully that further denial is impossible. Because the perception is accurately symbolized in awareness, the gestalt of the self-structure is broken by the intrusion of discrepant data (Rogers, 1959, p. 229). This Rogerian concept is reminiscent to Erik Erikson's discussion of the loss of a sense of ego identity among "shell-shocked" combatants of World War II (Chapter 8).

BOX 13.2   *Only Connect . . .*

Rogers' idea of filtering experiences so that one is aware only of those that protect one's self-regard is his version of a defense. This is not an ego defense as in Freudian psychology but a defense against one's often unrealistic sense of self. Thus the experiences not consistent with one's idea of self are warded off or, as Rogers terms it, subcepted.

Rogers offered an example of this kind of maladjustment:

> ...take the familiar picture of a mother whom the diagnostician would term rejecting. She has as part of her concept of self a whole constellation that may be summed up by saying, "I am a good and loving mother...." With this concept of self she can accept and assimilate those organic sensations of affection which she feels toward her child. But the organic experience of dislike, distaste, or hatred toward her child is something that is denied to her conscious self. The experience exists, but it is not permitted accurate symbolization.... Since the good mother could be aggressive toward her child only if he merited punishment, she perceives much of his behavior as being bad, deserving punishment, and therefore the aggressive acts can be carried through, without being contrary to the values organized in her picture of self. (1951, pp. 511–512)

At times of great provocation, such a mother might scream at her child, "I hate you." But almost in the same breath she would rush to explain that "she was not herself."

Sometimes the individual experiences psychological maladjustment when the total self-structure is founded on the evaluations of others. Since these alien values have no genuine connection with the person's own experiences, he or she may perceive him- or herself as a "nothing," as a "zero" (Rogers, 1951, p. 512).

SOME CRITICISMS OF ROGERS' APPROACH

Rogers' ideas have been criticized in terms of the values expressed by his theories. There is no doubt that Rogers asserts the quintessential importance for mental health of individual freedom and choice, but one can question whether this emphasis is empirically based or rather a reflection of his own values. Certainly, many mentally healthy and happy people have made commitments and stuck to them in spite of their own personal wishes (Sollod, 1978). Rogers and other humanistic psychologists have been criticized for promoting selfishness and egoism (Wallach & Wallach, 1983). What one feels like or wants to do, for most people, is only one aspect of their decision-making process. For religiously committed people, a question they might consider is what they believe is the correct course of action or, after prayerful consideration, what they feel God wants them to do. Rogers has been criticized for abandoning a God-centered approach to values and decision making in favor of an unqualified "selfist" or self-centered approach (Vitz, 1977).

OPERATIONALIZING THE CONCEPT OF SELF: Q-SORT METHODOLOGY

Rogers' reliance on the concepts of self, self-incongruence, and ideal self emerged from his experiences with patients in therapy. Often, when he had allowed clients to express their problems in their own fashion, without guidance or interpretation, they would refer to the *self* as the core of their experience: "I feel I'm not being my real self"; "I never had a chance to be myself"; or, "It feels good to let myself go and just be myself here" (1959, p. 201).

As a consequence of their therapeutic efforts, Rogers and several of his students and colleagues mounted an early research project to investigate the individual's changing conception of self in therapy (Rogers & Dymond, 1954). The process of psychotherapeutic change seemed to be directly expressible in terms of changes in the individual's perceived self and movement toward the **ideal self.**

At about the time that Rogers had begun to conceptualize the self as the key element in any description of the person's experience, a colleague at the University of

Chicago, William Stephenson, developed a rationale and a statistical method uniquely applicable to a study of the **phenomenal world,** or the individual's experienced world of perceptions and meanings. Called a *Q-sort* technique, Stephenson's procedures were applied to a variety of social and personal processes (1953). Rogers and his research team adopted Q-sort methods to operationalize the conception of self.

Essentially, the **Q-sort** technique involves providing a person with a large number of written statements and asking him or her to sort them into a deliberately determined number of piles. The array of categories into which the subject places his or her statements is purposefully constructed to approximate a statistically normal distribution. Printed on cards, the statements describe various aspects of a person's self. In the most widely used version, the subject is asked to sort 100 statements into nine piles ranging from "least like me" to "most like me." Other variations involve the inclusion of additional categories: "what I most would like to become," or "what I most dislike about me." A typical arrangement of a Q-sort distribution looks like this:

	Least Like Me			**Undecided**			**Most Like Me**		
Pile No.	0	1	2	3	4	5	6	7	8
No. of Cards (Total: 100)	1	4	11	21	26	21	11	4	1

(Based on Dymond, in Rogers & Dymond, 1954, p. 77.)

The criteria by which the self-statement cards may be sorted are nearly limitless. One very instructive example of a subject's card-sorting responses before and after therapy is provided in Table 13.7.

In the left-hand column of Table 13.7 is a small sample of "Mrs. Oak's" statements chosen as *most characteristic* of herself before therapy. In the right-hand column are her statements describing herself after therapy. The bottom half of the table contains an additional sample of Q-sort statements that were chosen before and after therapy by Mrs. Oak as least characteristic of herself.

Table 13.7   Mrs. Oak's Changes in Perceived Self in Terms of Q-Sort Statements

Before therapy	After therapy
"Most characteristic"	
I usually feel driven.	I express my emotions freely.
I am responsible for my troubles.	I feel emotionally mature.
I am really self-centered.	I am self-reliant.
I am liked by most people who know me.	I understand myself.
I am intelligent.	I feel adequate.
"Least characteristic"	
I feel comfortable while talking with someone.	I have few standards and values of my own.
I make strong demands on myself.	I feel helpless.
I am optimistic.	I often feel guilty.

From Rogers, in Rogers & Dymond, 1954, p. 275.

The items of Table 13.7 show that before therapy, Mrs. Oak regarded herself as driven, insecure, and disorganized. After therapy, by the time of the five-month follow-up interview, she viewed herself as more in control and more secure. The items that Mrs. Oak considered to be least characteristic of herself before therapy included an ability to be independent and comfortable with others. After therapy, Mrs. Oak perceived herself to be less helpless and less guilty.

The correlation between the perceived self before and after therapy was low: .30. In another Q-sort, Mrs. Oak was asked to sort the items in order of importance to her for the *person she would like to be*, thus providing an estimate of her ideal self. After therapy, Mrs. Oak again sorted the items in relation to her ideal self. The before self-ideal included "I feel emotionally mature"; "I can live comfortably with people around me"; "I am a rational person." The after self-ideal included the following items: "I understand myself"; "I express my emotions freely"; and, "I am poised" (Rogers, 1954, p. 274). The degree of similarity for Mrs. Oak's self-ideal before and after therapy was great: The correlation for before and after ideal selves was .72. The key question is whether Mrs. Oak perceived her actual self to have become more like her ideal self after therapy. The correlation between her perceived self and ideal self before therapy was .21, a very low degree of relationship. Thus before therapy Mrs. Oak perceived a large discrepancy between what she was and what she would like to be. After therapy, the correlation between her ideal self and her actual self, that is, the self she thought she had become was .69 at termination and .79 within several months after therapy (1954, p. 282). Thus the Q-sort method had shown that Mrs. Oak believed herself to be more like her ideal self after therapy than before.

Rogers and his colleagues used a variety of other assessment techniques; but in all cases the client's consistent movement in the direction of greater freedom, more independence, and more congruence between perceived self and ideal self was measurably real.

EVALUATING ABRAHAM MASLOW AND CARL ROGERS

Both Maslow and Rogers were independent thinkers, who in their different ways tilted at windmills. Both thinkers had their share of successes and failures as they struggled against established ideas drawn from behaviorism and psychoanalysis. Rogers, for example, was instrumental in the political fight for psychologists and social workers to practice psychotherapy alongside their medical colleagues. And Maslow struggled against depersonalizing educational institutions. We could say that both were committed to and lived the ideas they espoused.

Both Maslow and Rogers have left a major legacy in the way our society thinks about human nature and in the way psychotherapy is practiced. Maslow's idea of the hierarchy of needs and self-actualization has had a transformative impact on the workplace, and many of the therapeutic approaches that Rogers developed are now widely used in the mental health professions.

Refutability of Maslow and Rogers' Concepts

Maslow grew up in a largely empirical branch of psychology, and for a time, even practiced a kind of naturalistic behaviorism. Rogers was one of the first, if not the very first, clinicians to open the doors of the consulting room and expose psychotherapy to scientific scrutiny.

Maslow created a great wealth of ideas, most of which lack the rigor and empirical referents that would permit them to be tested. This chapter has noted some major flaws with two of his most important theoretical contributions: the concept of the self-actualized person and the hierarchy of needs. Some of Maslow's ideas, in principle, are highly testable, such as the hierarchy of motivational needs, at least up to, but not necessarily including, needs such as the need for beauty, truth, and self-actualization. But on the whole, Maslow's humanistic psychology has not attracted empirically minded psychologists to create empirical translations of his ideas.

Rogers opened the process of psychotherapy to research, and under his leadership, a whole program of empirically based research on the therapeutic process, the characteristics of the helping relationship, and the characteristics of the helping person was done. Studies of empathy, warmth, directiveness versus nondirectiveness, pre- and postmeasures of personality, and even attempts to use client-centered therapy to aid schizophrenic people have been researched. So, on the clinical side of the enterprise, Rogers gets high grades for stimulating hypothesis testing and for refutable therapeutic concepts.

On the downside, the theory that underlies Rogers' clinical practices is frequently vague, subjective, and not tied to empirical referents. Concepts such as the phenomenal self, conditions of worth, and "fully functioning" person are not easily testable in the precise form in which they exist in Rogers' theory. Some of these concepts could be translated into operations that lend themselves to measurement. The difficulty seems to be that few psychologists are willing to test Rogers' theories of personality although many have tested his clinical strategies.

Maslow and Rogers' Conception of Human Agency

Both Maslow and Rogers regard people as capable of active decision making. Rogers, early on, was even reluctant to take a clinical history with his clients or perform diagnostic testing because he believed that whatever information would be needed in treatment would emerge as the client decided to communicate it. Maslow argued that human motivation is more of a "pulling" *toward* goals than it is a "pushing" by human drives. People set their own standards and discover their own paths to achieving them. When life events intervene to block pursuit of self-chosen goals, the person is frustrated but no less free to make new decisions. In short, both Maslow and Rogers picture people as active determiners of their lives rather than as passive receptacles of reality.

The Idiographic/Nomothetic Nature of Humanistic Psychology

Rogers' theory is largely a phenomenological model of human personality, which is to say that its focus is on the subjective meanings a person lives by, although he indicates universal factors that are important for everyone. Rogers' emphasis can be characterized as largely idiographic. Maslow is less focused than Rogers on clinical work with individuals and more on abstract ideas such as the hierarchy of needs or the concept of self-actualization, so his approach is more nomothetic in its emphasis.

SUMMARY

Maslow's interests in psychological health followed his early work on dominance-feeling in infrahuman primates and from his interview research of domi-

nant women. Rogers developed his conceptualization of the self-actualizing nature of human motivation from his experiences in psychotherapy. The ideas of both converged in the direction of a humanist approach that emphasized the full development of the individual.

Maslow's central concept is the growth of the health-striving character of human personality. Proceeding through a hierarchy of basic needs, the individual progresses toward ultimate health and fully spontaneous expression of the self. At the lowest level of the hierarchy are the physiological needs such as hunger and thirst. These having been satisfied, the individual's behavior becomes directed by his or her needs for safety, then by needs for love and esteem. Finally, when these basic motives have been fulfilled, the need for self-actualization emerges.

Rogers discovered essentially the same rule of human growth from his observations of clients in therapy. In the earliest stages of his work, Rogers' central concern was to allow clients to feel warmly accepted and fully free to express themselves. Slowly, Rogers developed this nondirective orientation to include the necessity for the counselor to enter the client's phenomenal world or internal frame of reference. In order for constructive personality change to occur, the counselor must communicate an understanding of the client's internal frame of reference to the client.

Maslow's conceptualization of the self-actualizing person as independent, creative, and growth-motivated corresponds to Rogers' notion of the fully functioning person who emerges from a successful psychotherapeutic relationship. Maslow has gone further than Rogers in one respect. Specifically, Maslow has postulated that the self-actualizing person embarks on a further course of metamotives. These Being-values, or B-values as Maslow termed them, include the classic virtues like Beauty, Truth, Justice, Honesty, and Freedom. When denied or frustrated, these B-values show evidence of being innate, for the frustrated individual succumbs to metapathologies.

Maslow's development of the construct of peak experiences was closely connected with William James' exploration of spiritual experiences. James was one of the founders of the field of transpersonal psychology, which explores the psychology of spirituality, including transcendent and anomalous experiences.

In Maslow's theory, the motor of personality is the drive toward self-actualization, toward psychological health, toward fully accepted humanness. In Rogers' theory, the same innate striving toward enhancement and expression of one's spontaneous urges and feelings constitutes the fundamental layer of personality. In both theories, psychological maladjustments are the product of learned tendencies to subvert or block the spontaneous and natural expression of self.

Our evaluation of Maslow and Rogers indicates that both theorists constructed largely nonrefutable theories, although Rogers' clinical work did produce empirically testable therapeutic strategies. Human agency, from the viewpoint of both theorists, is active rather than passive. Rogers' theory, with its clinical emphasis, is more idiographic and Maslow's approach, with its emphasis on general constructs, is more nomothetic.

FOR FURTHER READING

Maslow's definitive statement of his position is located in *Motivation and Personality* (New York: Addison-Wesley, 1987). His early papers on dominance-feeling with primates have been collected into a single volume by J. Lowry and entitled *Dominance, Self-Esteem, Self-Actualization: Germinal Papers of A. H. Maslow* (Monterey, CA: Brooks/Cole, 1973). A collection of Maslow's later papers, including a semi-autobiographical account of the sources of his interest in self-actualization, is *The Farther Reaches of Human Nature* (New York: Arkana, 1993). Sometimes bitter, sometimes ironic, Maslow's criticism of classical scientific method in application to persons may be found in his *The Psychology of Science: A Reconnaissance* (New York: Harper & Row, 1966). The collection of papers in Chiang and Maslow's (Eds.) *The Healthy Personality* (New York: Van Nostrand, 1977) demonstrates the application of humanistic psychology to a wide variety of fields and provides accounts of some of the personal sources of Maslow's, Rogers', and Allport's humanistic leanings.

A fascinating book is *Abraham H. Maslow: A Memorial Volume*, compiled with the assistance of Bertha G. Maslow, his widow (Monterey, CA: Brooks/Cole 1972). It consists of some of his writings, reminiscences of those who knew him well, and many intimate photographs. Frank Goble's *The Third Force: The Psychology of Abraham Maslow* (New York: Grossman, 1970) was published shortly after Maslow's death and is an excellent review of the ideas that he was working on at that time, including his thoughts about mental health and more enlightened management practices. Edward Hoffman has written a largely adulatory biography of Maslow, now in paperback: *The Right to Be Human: A Biography of Abraham Maslow* (New York: McGraw-Hill, 1999). *Maslow on Management*, written by Deborah Stephens with Abraham Maslow (New York: John Wiley & Sons, 2000) contains a number of writings of Maslow that have to do with the transformation of management practices and the business world.

William James' lectures on mystical experience bear a strong similarity to Maslow's views on peak experiences. James' very readable lectures are located in *The Varieties of Religious Experience* (New York: MacMillan Publishing Company, 1997). For Maslow's own account of peak experiences, see *Religions, Values and Peak-Experiences* (New York: Viking, 1994).

Two of Rogers' early works set forth his initial strategy and philosophy: *Counseling and Psychotherapy* (Boston: Houghton Mifflin, 1942) and *Client-Centered Therapy* (Boston: Houghton Mifflin, 1951). To bring Rogers' perspective on theory and therapy up to date, two volumes should be consulted. The first of these is a collection of research and theory papers edited by J. T. Hart and T. M. Tomlinson under the title *New Directions in Client-Centered Therapy* (Boston: Houghton Mifflin, 1970) and is, perhaps, the better of the two. The second collection of papers is in David Wexler and Laura North Rice's (Eds.) *Innovations in Client-Centered Therapy* (New York: Wiley, 1974).

Rogers gives a definitive statement of his position in "A Theory of Therapy, Personality and InterPersonal Relationships as Developed in the Client-Centered Framework," in S. Koch (Ed.), *Psychology: A Study of a Science, Vol. III, Formulations of the Person in the Social Context* (New York: McGraw-Hill, 1959). A current survey of Rogerian method and philosophy is provided by Betty Meador in "Client-Centered Therapy," in Raymond Corsini (Ed.), *Current Psychotherapies* (Itasca, IL: Peacock, 2000). A personally revealing account of Rogers' early career is in *On Becoming a Person: A Therapist's View of Psychotherapy* (Boston: Houghton Mifflin, 1995). *Carl Rogers on Personal Power* (New York: Delacorte Press, 1977) contains Rogers'

updated views on the self-actualization motive and its political implications for personal knowledge. *A Way of Being* (Boston: Houghton Mifflin, 1995) by Rogers and Irvin Yalom is a personal and direct statement of Rogers' approach to human experience.

Rogers' own expansion of his ideas to the field of marriage and to other two-person intimate relationships is contained in his *Becoming Partners: Marriage and Its Alternatives* (New York: Dell, 1972). The efficacy and process of encounter groups are treated to a sympathetic examination by Rogers in *Carl Rogers on Encounter Groups* (New York: Harper & Row, 1970). An interview with Rogers, along with a reprint of his ongoing debate with B. F. Skinner and one of his previously unpublished papers, are located in R. I. Evans' *Carl Rogers: The Man and His Ideas* (New York: Dutton, 1975). The interview in condensed version may also be found in Evans' *The Making of Psychology* (New York: Knopf, 1976). Howard Kirschenbaum has written a biography of Carl Rogers with Rogers' and his wife's cooperation, but *On Becoming Carl Rogers* (New York: Delacorte Press, 1979) is marred by its uncritical, almost worshipful, appraisal. Rogers' autobiography (in E. G. Boring and Gardner Lindzey's *A History of Psychology in Autobiography*, *Vol. 5*, New York: Appleton-Century-Crafts, 1967) is far more revealing. Robert Sollod's "Carl Rogers and the Origins of Client-Centered Therapy" (*Professional Psychology*, 1978, 9, pp. 93–104) explores in depth the sources of Rogers' psychotherapeutic approach.

Psychology's Sanction for Selfishness: The Error of Egoism in Theory and Therapy by Wallach & Wallach (San Francisco, CA: W. H. Freeman, 1983) presents a critical view of the values expressed by humanistic psychologists. Paul Vitz's *Psychology as Religion: The Cult of Self Worship* (Grand Rapids, MI: William B. Eerdmans, 1994) critically evaluates what he terms Rogers' "selfism" from a religious perspective.

Further suggested readings related to Chapter 13 and its topics may be found on the web site for Chapter 13 at www.wiley.com/college/sollod

GLOSSARY

Abraham Maslow

B-values (Being-values)/metaneeds: Growth needs that deal with the quality and nature of beingness. They include striving for goodness toward others, seeking truth and justice, yearning for knowledge, and trying to create beauty and order.

Conversational probing: A qualitative research method Maslow developed that involves establishing rapport with a subject and engaging in an intensive interviewing process.

Deficiency needs: The physiological drives, safety needs, love and belongingness needs, and the esteem needs are comprised in this part of Maslow's hierarchy of needs.

Desacralizing: The denial of the awesome, marvelous, beautiful, sublime aspects of people and the universe. Leads to a tendency to be cynical and disrespectful, and steers the individual to focus on others' weaknesses and disregard of their strengths and virtues.

Dominance-feeling: A sense of oneself that involves good self-confidence, self-assurance, high evaluation of the self, feelings of general capability or superiority, and lack of shyness, timidity, self-consciousness, or embarrassment.

Hierarchy of needs: A scale in which the deficiency needs are prepotent to needs lying above them. It begins with basics such as physiological needs, survival, safety, and self-esteem and steers toward a search for beauty, knowledge, justice, and truth.

Humanistic psychology: An approach that emphasizes the dignity and worth of the person. It presumes that the individual advances creatively toward growth and psychological health.

Ineffability: A term indicating that something cannot be described, imparted, or transferred to others. It defies words—it defies expression.

Innocence: The healthy personality's capacity to live without pretense, to be genuinely spontaneous and free of guilt.

Jonah complex: Maslow's term for the pattern of avoiding challenges and of not fulfilling one's potential or one's calling. This term is an allusion to Jonah, the Bible's reluctant prophet.

Noetic quality: The word "noetic" is based on a Greek root meaning "mind" or" intellect." The term indicates an essentially meaningful, "truth-finding" quality. Maslow used this term to describe a peak experience.

Passivity: A term indicating that mystics feel as if their own wills were not active and that they were under the control of a superior power.

Peak experiences: Intense, mystical experiences in which a person exists momentarily in a state of joy, awe, and wonderment. The qualities of such experiences are their noetic quality, transiency, passivity, and ineffability.

Self-actualization: A state of exemplary personality integration; the full development of one's abilities and potentialities; the process of seeking one's essential nature.

Third force: A term that refers to the humanistic approach, as opposed to psychoanalysis, often referred to as the *first force*. Behaviorism is referred to as the *second force*.

Transiency: A term used, in this instance, to indicate that peak experiences are not usually sustained for long periods of time.

Transpersonal psychology: An approach to psychology that studies spirituality, higher states of consciousness, and ego transcendence. It is often referred to as the *fourth force*.

Carl Rogers

Client-centered therapy: An approach to counseling and psychotherapy that potentiates the client's own ability to discover and resolve problems. The therapist provides unconditional positive regard, accurate empathy, and a genuine relationship.

Conditions of worth: Conditions applied to a person to determine whether he or she receives approval or not. Parents and other people important in one's life may either give or withhold approval depending on one's behavior.

Fully functioning person: A person who is engaged in self-realization or self-actualization. Such a person is growth motivated, open to new experiences, and uses his or her potential maximally.

Ideal self: The individual's description or visualization of how he or she would like to be or become.

Nondirective therapy: An approach to counseling and therapy that relies on the individual's resources. The therapist uses techniques empathically to facilitate self-insight and clarification of feelings and refrains from unnecessary directness and advice.

Perceived self: The self, as perceived by an individual; how one perceives oneself.

Phenomenal world: The private world of experience and personal meaning, the individual's subjective reality.

Positive self-regard: The process of viewing oneself positively. A person with high self regard is open to the warmth and respect of others.

Q-sort: A technique used by Rogers to measure a person's self-concept. Rogers used it, for example, to assess the discrepancy between an individual's perceived self and ideal self.

Real self: A person's actual core of experience.

Self-congruence: The absence of any discrepancy between an individual's experiences and his or her self-concept.

Self-incongruence: The discrepancy between a person's experiences and his or her self-concept.

Self-regard: The personal estimation of self-worth that a person has for himself or herself.

Self-structure: Parental conditions of worth (praise or blame) become internalized. They eventually form the basis of a person's self-structure.

Subception: The process of keeping an experience inconsistent with one's self-structure outside of awareness.

Unconditional positive regard: A relationship involving prizing or valuing another person without reservations or conditions of worth.

Chapter 14

George A. Kelly

Personal Construct Theory

In this new way of thinking about psychology, there is no learning, no motivation, no emotion, no cognition, no stimulus, no response, no ego, no unconscious, no need, no reinforcement, no drive.

George A. Kelly, *Theory of Personality*

As a man thinketh in his heart, so he is.

King Solomon, *King James Bible*

George A. Kelly Born: 1905 not far from Perth, Kansas
Died: 1967 Waltham, Massachusetts

About George A. Kelly's Personal Construct Theory

Kelly emphasized the fact that persons anticipate the future on the basis of their experience. He elaborated the ways in which they try to understand events and the personalities of others. The approach to personality that emphasizes the ways people make sense of their experiences and develop new approaches to dealing with life is called constructivism. Kelly's major theory is called the personal construct theory.

A few major concepts are central to Kelly's work:

- It is necessary for persons to predict with some accuracy how others will behave and how events will proceed.

- People maintain or revise such predictions as their experience either does or does not confirm them. They develop bipolar categories (constructs) and construct systems in order to assess and predict events and the behaviors of others.

- A person's behavior and his or her own psychology can best be understood by learning about his or her own ways of categorizing people and events and making predictions.
- Personality concepts such as anxiety, guilt, and ego defenses can be understood in light of this process of developing bipolar categories (constructs) and systems of categorization (construct systems) and applying them.

UNCOVERING A PERSON'S CONSTRUCTS OF PERSONALITY

George A. Kelly thought of each individual as a theorist of human nature or as a personality scientist. In Kelly's view, each of us constructs conceptual models and tests predictions of others' behavior. In order to uncover the predictive models or constructs that people held, individuals who came to Kelly for counseling would be asked to indicate their own ways of conceptualizing others. The **Role Construct Repertory Test (REP Test)** that follows was a major method that Kelly developed for indicating and assessing such constructs. You are invited to participate in this test.

REP TEST PART A: ROLE TITLE LIST

Instructions:

Write the name of the persons indicated in the blanks provided. Do not repeat names. If any role appears to call for a duplicate name, substitute the name of another person whom the second role title suggests to you (based on Kelly, 1955).

1. Your mother or the person who has played the part of mother in your life.   1. _____
2. Your father or the person who has played the part of a father in your life.   2. _____
3. Your brother nearest your age. If you have no brother, the person who is most like one.   3. _____
4. Your sister nearest your age. If you have no sister, the person who is most like one.   4. _____
5. A teacher you liked or the teacher of a subject you liked.   5. _____
6. A teacher you disliked or the teacher of a subject you disliked.   6. _____
7. Your closest girl (boy) friend immediately before you started going with your wife (husband) or present closest girl (boy) friend [Ex-Flame].   7. _____
8. Your wife (husband) or closest present girl (boy) friend.   8. _____
9. An employer, supervisor, or officer under whom you served during a period of great stress [Boss].   9. _____
10. A person with whom you have been closely associated who, for some unexplainable reason, appears to dislike you [Rejecting Person].   10. _____
11. The person whom you have met within the past six months whom you would most like to know better [Sought Person].   11. _____
12. The person whom you would most like to be of help to, or the one whom you feel most sorry for [Pitied Person].   12. _____
13. The most intelligent person whom you know personally.   13. _____
14. The most successful person whom you know personally.   14. _____
15. The most interesting person whom you know personally.   15. _____

REP TEST PART B: CONSTRUCT SORTS

Instructions:

The sets of three numbers in the following sorts refer to the numbers 1 to 15, inclusive, in Part A.

In each of the following sorts, three numbers are listed. Look at your Part A sheet and consider the three people whom you have listed for these three numbers.

In what important way are two of these three people alike and at the same time, essentially different from the third?

After you have decided what the important way is, write it in the blank opposite the sort marked CONSTRUCT.

Next encircle the numbers corresponding to the two people who are alike.

Write down what you believe to be the opposite of the construct in the blank marked CONTRAST.

NUMBERS Sort Part A	CONSTRUCT (EMERGENT)	CONTRAST (IMPLICIT)
1. 9, 11, 14	_____	_____
2. 10, 12, 13	_____	_____
3. 2, 5, 12		
4. 1, 4, 8	_____	_____
5. 7, 8, 12	_____	_____
6. 3, 13, 6	_____	_____
7. 1, 2, 9	_____	_____
8. 3, 4, 10	_____	_____
9. 6, 7, 10	_____	_____
10. 5, 11, 14	_____	_____
11. 1, 7, 8	_____	_____ ✓
12. 2, 7, 8	_____	_____
13. 3, 6, 9	_____	_____
14. 4, 5, 10	_____	_____
15. 11, 13, 14	_____	_____

(The form of the test that appears here is a slightly modified and shortened version of an early form of the Group REP Test. Number combinations making up the 15 sorts are virtually unlimited. Subjects could be asked to repeat their constructs and contrast evaluations with a new set of sorts, depending on the judgment of the administering psychologist.)

The ways in which psychologists can choose to analyze the subject's sorts are varied. They may rely on an impressionistic analysis. In this approach, they may receive assistance from a subject's answers to questions about their responses as well as spontaneous comments. Another more objective approach is to analyze the themes revealed in the construct and contrast columns more objectively. This can be done by tabulating the frequency of key phrases and combinations such as Mother-Father, Teacher-Boss, Husband-Lover.

A sample REP protocol of a pseudonymous subject identified by Kelly as "Mildred Beal" appears in Table 14.1. Only five of her sorts need be reproduced for the sake of illustration (after Kelly, 1955, pp. 242 ff.).

A number of interesting personal meanings stand out from Mildred Beal's partial protocol. For example, in sorts numbers 3 and 11, the description "easygoing" was applied by Mildred to Father, Liked Teacher, and Boyfriend. In sorts numbers 4 and 11, she described Mother as "hypercritical of other people" and "socially maladjusted." It is clear that Mildred Beal construed her sister as different from her father and boyfriend

Table 14.1   Mildred Beal's Constructs

Sort number	Similar figures	Similarity construct	Dissimilar figures	Contrasting construct
2	Rejecting Person (10) Pitied Person (12)	Very unhappy persons	Intelligent Person (13)	Contented
3	Father (2) Liked Teacher (5)	Very quiet and easygoing	Pitied Person (12)	Nervous, hypertensive
4	Mother (1) Sister (4)	Look alike Both hypercritical of people in general	Boyfriend (8)	Friendliness
11	Mother (1) Ex-Flame (7)	Socially maladjusted	Boyfriend (8)	Easygoing, self-confident
13	Disliked Teacher (6) Boss (9)	Emotionally unpredictable	Brother (3)	Even temperament

in the same way that her mother is. Analyses like these yield insights about the way Mildred construed significant people in her world and her view of their relationship patterns.

GRID FORM OF THE REP TEST: A PERSON'S OWN PERSONALITY THEORY

Mildred's responses to the role constructs of the REP test may also be analyzed mathematically. Correlation coefficients and factor analysis can be applied to a grid form of the test. In the grid version, the subject is asked to make the sorts several times, applying each of his or her constructs developed in response to particular pairs of figures successively to all 15 roles. (The full form of the REP test may include 22 figures, of which the Self is one; it has been shortened in this presentation.) The first time around, the subject is presented with the standard sort-combinations in the form of a 15″ × 15″ grid, as illustrated in Figure 14.1. He or she is instructed to indicate which two of the figures in the first sort (9, 11, 14) are similar by placing an "X" in the appropriate circles of the grid. The circles are placed in each line only in the boxes corresponding to the three figures the subject is asked to compare.

Thus, for example, in Figure 14.1, Mildred has placed an "X" in the circles of numbers 9 and 14, Employer and Successful Person, indicating that she construes these two as similar (Emergent Pole). She has left number 11 unfilled, indicating that Sought Person is, in her view, different from the other two. On the first line of the emergent pole column, she then writes in her own words the way in which 9 and 14 are similar. Likewise, in the implicit pole column, she writes her ideas of what makes figure 11, Sought Person, different. Reading from Figure 14.1, Mildred regards Employer and Successful Person as similar because they are "related to me." "Sought Person" is different by being "unrelated."

The second time, after Mildred has completed all 15 sorts and listed her constructs, she is asked to make systematic comparisons of her 15 similar and different constructs to all of the remaining figures on each line. Mildred is thus instructed to start again with the constructs she listed for sort number one, namely, "related to me" versus

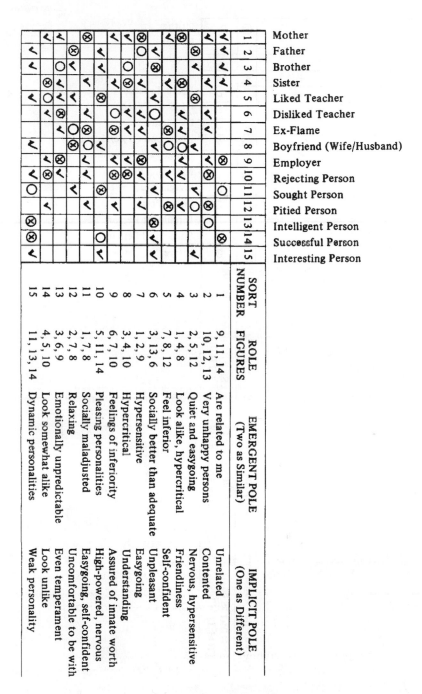

Figure 14.1 A grid analysis of Mildred Beal's role construct repertory test.

Constructed after Kelly, 1955, p. 242 ff.

⊗	1	Mother
	2	Father
	3	Brother
✓	4	Sister
	5	Liked Teacher
✓	6	Disliked Teacher
⊗	7	Ex-Flame
○✓	8	Boyfriend (Wife/Husband)
✓	9	Employer
✓	10	Rejecting Person
	11	Sought Person
✓	12	Pitied Person
	13	Intelligent Person
	14	Successful Person
	15	Interesting Person

SORT NUMBER	ROLE FIGURES	EMERGENT POLE (Two as Similar)	IMPLICIT POLE (One as Different)
11	1, 7, 8	Socially maladjusted	Easygoing, self-confident

Figure 14.2 A single construct from Mildred Beal's grid REP analysis.

Constructed after Kelly, 1955, p. 242 ff.

"unrelated," and systematically consider this dichotomous construct in relation to the 12 remaining figures on line one. For each figure to which the construct of Sort 1 applies, Mildred is asked to place a check mark in that figure's box on the Sort 1 line.

Mildred proceeds down the remaining 14 constructs, repeating her search for applicable figures for each of the constructs on that line. For the sake of simplicity, Sort 11 has been abstracted from the total grid and enlarged in Figure 14.2. The first time that Mildred sorted the figures of line 11, she chose Mother and Ex-Flame as similar by placing an "X" in the circles for those roles. Now Mildred is asked to take the remaining 12 roles and to indicate whether her construct "socially maladjusted versus easygoing, self-confident" applies to any of them. For the sake of illustration, figures 4, 6, 9, 10, and 11 have been checked to indicate that Mildred feels the similarity construct "socially maladjusted" applies to them. Those she has left blank indicate that the similarity (emergent pole) construct cannot be used to describe them.

The resulting grid pattern of checks and "X's" may be converted to a series of numbered coordinates without reference to Mildred's verbal labels. All that matters is the pattern of expressed similarity and difference indicated by the check marks, not the verbal labels that led Mildred to assign these marks. The procedures employed in mathematically analyzing the data are very complex and need not concern us here.

The grid or matrix of Mildred's REP test represents her own unique personality theory, the system of personal constructs or interpretations by which she conducts her life. Kelly frequently used the term **construe** to indicate the active process of trying to explain, interpret, and give meaning to our experiences. Reading across Mildred's grid we can answer questions about the figures she construes as similar on a particular dimension of her theory. Reading down the columns, we can ask questions about how Mildred construes each person on a whole series of dimensions. To illustrate, consider what is learned about the way Mildred construes the world when columns 1 (Mother) and 12 (Pitied Person) are read downward together, as shown in Table 14.2.

KELLY: THE INVENTIVE PSYCHOLOGICAL TINKERER

Kelly's theory is an original and idiosyncratic one; it could even be labeled a "home-brewed" theory. Looking back at Kelly's development of personal construct theory, we find him in the great tradition of American tinkerers and inventors. We might include the young Wright brothers, Thomas Alva Edison, and a score of others in many

Table 14.2   Constructs Compared

(1) Mother	*(12) Pitied person*
(1) Are related to me	(1)
(2) Very unhappy person	(2) Very unhappy person
(5) Feels inferior	(5) Feels inferior
(7) Hypersensitive	(7) Hypersensitive
(8) Hypercritical	(8)
(9) Feelings of inferiority	(9) Feelings of inferiority
(11) Socially maladjusted	(11) Socially maladjusted
(13) Emotionally unpredictable	(13)
(14) Looks like sister and rejecting person	(14) Looks like sister and rejecting person

fields at a time when Americans tended to be rather skeptical of traditional ways of doing things and often tried to start from scratch to solve problems that conventional wisdom proclaimed were unapproachable. Such resourceful optimism characterized George Kelly's work; it was also a keynote of the theories and methods he developed.

Writing in the 1960s, Kelly recounted his early disappointment with standard theories years earlier as a graduate student. One day his professor wrote on the blackboard an "S" with an arrow pointing to an "R." Anticipating that after several weeks of dull course work, the crux of psychology's explanation of humans was about to be discussed, Kelly listened attentively but was disappointed: "... [T]he most I could make of it was that the 'S' was what you have to have in order to account for the 'R' and the 'R' was put there so the 'S' would have something to account for. I never did find out what the arrow stood for—not to this day—and I have pretty well given up trying to figure it out" (Kelly, 1963, pp. 46–47). He therefore dismissed stimulus-response psychology.

Kelly graduated from the University of Iowa in 1931 with a doctor of philosophy degree. He ran headlong into the Great Depression and spent 12 years at a small college in western Kansas, an impoverished dust bowl region. He soon discovered that his background, which was in physiological psychology and speech pathology, was useless for helping often-despairing young people. He turned to Freudian theory even though he had dismissed it as preposterous when he was a student. "Through my Freudian interpretations, judiciously offered at those moments when clients seemed ready for them, a good many unfortunate persons seemed to be profoundly helped" (Kelly, 1963, p. 51).

His Freudianisms worked most of the time. His unsophisticated clients readily accepted them. Despite his success with his quasi-Freudian approach, he was not satisfied. Kelly began to change his approach:

> ... I began fabricating "insights." I deliberately offered "preposterous interpretations" to my clients. Some of them were about as un-Freudian as I could make them—first proposed somewhat cautiously, of course, and then, as I began to see what was happening, more boldly. My only criteria were that the explanation *account for the crucial facts as the client saw them, and that it carry implications for approaching the future in a different way*. (1963, p. 52; italics added)

Kelly might tell a client, for example, that his or her nervous stomach was "rebelling against nourishment of all kinds, parental, educational, and nutritional." His clients felt that even these interpretations were worth applying. They often successfully changed the direction of their lives by adopting new outlooks implied in Kelly's "preposterous" suggestions. In Kelly's terminology, they had developed alternative constructions. Evidence began to mount for Kelly's developing view that patients could change if they would attempt to see things differently. When, for instance, more clients than he could handle applied to him for treatment, he began giving them a few hints about what to do while on the waiting list. Months later, when their turn came, Kelly often found that they had solved or were well on the way to resolving their difficulties. His few hints about how to look at their problems differently resulted in positive changes. He later termed this process of changing one's view or interpretation of problems and events **constructive alternativism**.

Kelly therefore began to formulate a new clinical perspective—one emphasizing present activities. "... I began to pursue the notion that one's current acts and undertakings might have as much to do with the development of his personality as did the imprint of events with which he came in contact or the insights he was able to conjure up with the help of his therapist" (1963, p. 56).

Kelly founded a statewide traveling clinic with some of his graduate students to reach more people in crisis. Visiting schools and agencies, they found that teachers and staff did not often understand problem students or clients very well. Kelly introduced a personality test, the Maller Inventory, to provide insight into how people conceptualized their experience. This test consisted of cards containing self-descriptive statements that the subject was asked to sort. It was an early version of the Q-sort technique used by Stephenson and Rogers. The results of this test aided teachers and staff to understand those they were trying to help. Kelly used the results of this test to provide information for a role-playing technique. This technique was the basis for his later development of *fixed-role therapy*.

EACH PERSON IS A SCIENTIST

According to Kelly, a major human characteristic is the need to know and to control one's own universe:

> Might not the individual man, each in his own personal way, assume more of the stature of a scientist, ever seeking to predict and control the course of events with which he is involved? Would he not have his theories, test his hypotheses, and weigh his experimental evidence? (Kelly, 1955, p. 5)

A return look at Mildred Beal's REP protocol is an example of the idea of person as scientist. Mildred created explanatory hypotheses about the significant figures in her life. She predicted their behavior with more or less accuracy on the basis of her past experiences with them; she even discerned similarities and differences among subgroups. In short, she made sense of or construed her world by attempting to anticipate the behavior of the people in it.

Early on, Kelly noted the contradiction between the self-concepts of many psychologists and their erroneous views of research subjects: "I, being a psychologist, and therefore a scientist, am performing this experiment in order to improve the prediction and control of certain human phenomena; but my subject, being merely a human organism, is obviously propelled by inexorable drives welling up within him, or else he is in gluttonous pursuit of sustenance and shelter" (1955, p. 5).[1] He noted that psychologists do not expect those whom they study to seek understanding of themselves and others.

KELLY'S FUNDAMENTAL POSTULATE AND 11 COROLLARIES

The **fundamental postulate** relates the psychological processes of a person to the way he or she understands and predicts or anticipates events:

FUNDAMENTAL POSTULATE: *A person's processes are psychologically channelized* [this term was coined by Kelly; it simply means *directed* or *determined*] *by the ways in which he anticipates events* (1955, p. 46).

A key word in Kelly's fundamental postulate is *anticipates* because it is the need for prediction that Kelly sees as fundamental. Kelly presented eleven corollaries to the fundamental postulate. Together they comprise the overall framework for his theory of **personal constructs**.

---

[1]Kelly wrote his theory in an era when sensitivity to gender references in language did not prevail. In the interests of scholarly accuracy, Kelly's own words have been left unedited with respect to the use of the male pronoun and referents—even when Kelly was actually referring to *all humans*—not just males.

FUNDAMENTAL POSTULATE

1. Construction Corollary   3. Organization Corollary
2. Individuality Corollary   4. Dichotomy Corollary

5. Choice Corollary
6. Range Corollary
7. Experience Corollary

8. Modulation Corollary   10. Commonality Corollary
9. Fragmentation Corollary   11. Sociality Corollary

CONSTRUCTION AND INDIVIDUALITY COROLLARIES: THE PERSON AS A PROCESS

Over time, the individual is able to detect recurrent themes, repetitive events, and their onset and termination. "Once events have been given their beginnings and endings, and their similarities and contrasts construed, it becomes feasible to try to predict them, just as one predicts that tomorrow will follow today" (Kelly, 1955, p. 53). Kelly therefore formulated a first corollary to the fundamental postulate:

CONSTRUCTION COROLLARY: *A person anticipates events by construing their replications* (1955, p. 50).

The next assertion follows from Kelly's emphasis on the individuality of cognitive activity. Kelly called this proposition the

INDIVIDUALITY COROLLARY: *Persons differ from each other in their constructions of events* (1955, p. 55).

HIERARCHY OF EXPERIENCE: ORGANIZATION AND DICHOTOMY COROLLARIES

Kelly believed that people impose meaning on the events they experience using bipolar constructs. The person notes the similarities among various events, and groups them together under one construct; but that same construct derives some of its meaning from those events that were excluded by contrast. Hence, the construct *introvert* not only indicates all traits the person associates with introversion but also defines what introversion is not for that person.

A person's system of constructs is not static. Their interpretations change and are modified by new experience. Contradictions and conflicts between constructs often emerge. One way to resolve any such conflicts is to organize one's constructions of events into a hierarchy in which particular constructs may subsume many other constructs in the system. When one construct subsumes another, it is called a **superordinal construct**; conversely, the construct so subsumed is termed a **subordinal construct**.

It is possible for super- and subordinal constructs to change places in the hierarchy. For example, the construct good versus bad may include the two poles of the intelligent versus stupid dimension of experience. Good subsumes intelligent, and bad subsumes stupid. Good and bad may, of course, assimilate other constructs as well. Furthermore, good and bad may change ordinal position with intelligent and stupid:

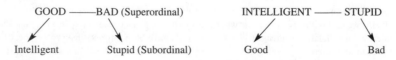

Another way in which constructs may be ordinally ranked is for one to create categories that subsume complete dimensions under one pole of a superordinal construct. For example, the good-bad construct might itself be subsumed under one pole of a broader superordinal construct: evaluative versus descriptive. Thus the pair, good bad, would be globally subsumed under evaluative, whereas other constructs like light versus dark would be subsumed under descriptive:

To make sense out of the world, people systematize their constructs into hierarchies for convenience in anticipating occurrences of events. This insight led to the

ORGANIZATION COROLLARY: *Each person characteristically evolves, for his convenience in anticipating events, a construction system embracing ordinal relationships between constructs* (1955, p. 56).

As we have seen, Kelly proposed that every personal construct is dichotomous and bipolar in structure. In order to derive meaning from a construct, it must indicate at least two elements as similar, and a third as contrasting. In this regard, you may recall the structure of the REP test, in which the subject is asked to find similarity between two figures and to determine how they differ from a third. Kelly's view that people think in terms of dichotomies does not accord with classical logic. In classical logic, a thing is either "A" or "not-A": masculine or not, feminine or not. But in Kelly's system, three elements are required to establish the identity of a thing: two similar and one contrasting.

To illustrate, suppose that there are three people, Alice, Betty, and Carl. Trying to find ways in which two might be similar to one another but different from the third, an individual might categorize them on the basis of the construct, "assertive-shy" Alice and Carl are viewed as similar because they are both seen as assertive, whereas Betty is shy. She is categorized under the opposite pole of this construct, assertive-shy. Kelly formulated these ideas in his fourth corollary:

DICHOTOMY COROLLARY: *A person's construction system is composed of a finite number of dichotomous constructs* (1955, p. 59).

CHOICE, RANGE, AND EXPERIENCE COROLLARIES: LIMITATIONS OF ANTICIPATION

People choose the pole of a dichotomized construct that provides the greater scope for secure activity and growth. Kelly formulated his fifth corollary around these ideas regarding individual choices:

CHOICE COROLLARY: *A person chooses for himself that alternative in a dichotomized construct through which he anticipates the greater possibility for extension and definition of his system* (1955, p. 64).

A sixth corollary stated the limits of constructs:

RANGE COROLLARY: *A construct is convenient for the anticipation of a finite range of events only* (1955, p. 68).

The range corollary implies that any construct is limited to a finite range of events. The limiting factor is relevance. What is outside the range of a given construct is not considered as contrasting or opposite; it is viewed as irrelevant.

One's categories and category systems are modified with changing experience:

EXPERIENCE COROLLARY: *A person as construction system varies as he successively construes the replications of events* (1955, p. 72).

When anticipations of events are violated and fail to conform to expectations, people are stimulated to modify their construct systems. They change their views and expectations. Individuals do not have to be merely inert onlookers. They are like scientists, who revise their hypotheses when they do not pan out experimentally.

> A person can be a witness to a tremendous parade of episodes and yet, if he fails to keep making something out of them, or if he waits until they have all occurred before he attempts to reconstrue them, he gains little in the way of experience from having been around when they happened. It is not what happens around him that makes a man experienced; it is the successive construing and reconstruing of what happens, as it happens, that enriches the experience of his life. (Kelly, 1955, p. 73)

Taken together, the choice, range, and experience corollaries can account for such classical psychological concepts as *motivation*, *anxiety*, and *learning*. Kelly did not abandon these concepts. Rather, he viewed them as inherent in the process of prediction. Motivation in Kelly's theory is related to the concept of the human need to predict; anxiety is construed as a consequence of faulty anticipations; and learning is inherent in a person's continuing process of the modification of constructs and construct systems.

MODULATION AND FRAGMENTATION COROLLARIES: VARIATION VERSUS STABILITY

People can be cognizant of the changes they make in their construction systems. Any change in construction may be placed in context and viewed in the light of its effect on the entire system. Just as scientists may use their existing theories as guides to making new observations, individuals employ their existing construction systems as guides for new constructions. And just as the scientist's theory may become a set of intellectual blinders, the individual's construction system may also be limiting.

Certain constructs are uniquely susceptible to change. Such constructs are said to be **permeable constructs**. "A construct is permeable if it will admit to its range of convenience new elements which are not yet construed within its framework" (Kelly, 1955, p. 79). Conversely, an **impermeable construct** is one that will admit of no new elements. Kelly coined the term, *range of convenience* to indicate that each construct is applicable only to a finite range of events or experiences and is not applicable to others. Kelly formulated the implications of permeable and impermeable constructs into an eighth proposition:

MODULATION COROLLARY: *The variation in a person's construction system is limited by the permeability of the constructs within whose range of convenience the variants lie* (1955, p. 77).

As a teenager, we might have divided people into the two classes of the construct "fear versus domination." There were, consequently, those whom we feared and those whom we dominated. With the passing of years, this dichotomy itself might be viewed as immature. The notion of "immaturity," itself a construct, has an opposite pole: "maturity." If this new construct, "immaturity versus maturity," is permeable, we may be able to subsume the previous construct, "fear versus domination," under "immaturity" as a rejected value. Under the pole of "maturity" we incorporate a new construct: "respect versus contempt." We are now, consequently, in a position to classify our acquaintances in what we perceive to be a more mature fashion: those whom we respect versus those whom we hold in contempt (1955, p. 82). The permeability of the superordinal construct, "immaturity versus maturity," thus allows for this modulation or "fine-tuning" of the construct system. The respect-contempt construct can be assimilated under the permeable "maturity versus immaturity" construct. Sometimes, however, an individual may use subsystems of constructs that are not logically consistent with one another. Kelly termed this theoretical assumption, his ninth, the

FRAGMENTATION COROLLARY: *A person may successively employ a variety of construction subsystems which are inferentially incompatible with each other* (1955, p. 83).

Kelly put the fragmentation corollary in context. He indicated that we should overlook the inconsistencies in construction subsystems to see the whole picture:

It should make even clearer the assumed necessity for seeking out the regnant construct system [that is, the larger whole system and its dominant themes] in order to explain the behavior of men, rather than seeking merely to explain each bit of behavior as a derivative of its immediately antecedent behavior. (1955, p. 83)

COMMONALITY AND SOCIALITY COROLLARIES: SHARED EXPERIENCE

In addition to an individuality corollary, in which people see things differently, a *commonality corollary* is a logical necessity:

COMMONALITY COROLLARY: *To the extent that one person employs a construction of experience which is similar to that employed by another, his psychological processes are similar to those of the other person* (1955, p. 90).

An example of the commonality corollary is that people with similar political views might experience an election outcome in similar ways. Kelly added some distinctions to clarify the commonality corollary:

It is important to make clear that we have not said that if one person has experienced the same events as another he will duplicate the other's psychological processes.... One of the advantages of this position is that it does not require us to assume that it would take identical events in the lives of two people to make them act alike. Two people can act alike even if they have each been exposed to quite different phenomenal stimuli. It is the similarity in the construction of events that we find the basis for similar action, not in the identity of the events themselves. (1955, pp. 90–91)

Kelly's next corollary, the *sociality corollary*, deals with how people understand the construct systems of others:

SOCIALITY COROLLARY: *To the extent that one person construes the construction processes of another, he may play a role in a social process involving the other person* (1955, p. 95).

Kelly emphasizes in this corollary that the basis of social interaction is interpersonal understanding, not simply shared experience. If one can anticipate (predict) another's behavior, one can modify one's own behavior in response.

In order to play a constructive role in relation to another person one must not only, in some measure, see eye to eye with him but must, in some measure, have an acceptance of him and his way of seeing things. We say it in another way: the person who is to play a constructive role in a social process with another person *need not so much construe things as the other person does as he must effectively construe the other person's outlook.* (1955, p. 95; italics added)

THE MASK METAPHOR AGAIN

An important part of the sociality corollary is its use of the concept of social role. Kelly defined roles as "psychological processes based upon the role player's construction of aspects of the construction systems of those with whom he attempts to join in a social enterprise" (1955, p. 97). Kelly's definition of role is consistent with the cognitive orientation of his theory. Kelly is yet another psychologist who presents the actor-mask metaphor of personality. In his version, there is the chance of merging the actor with the role:

> It may be helpful at this point to ask ourselves a question about children at Halloween. Is the little youngster who comes to your door on the night of October 31st, all dressed up in his costume and behind a mask, piping "trick or treat, trick or treat"—is that youngster *disguising* himself or is he *revealing* himself? Is he failing to be spontaneous? Is he *not* being himself? Which is the *real* child—the child behind the mask or the barefaced child who must stand up in front of adults and say "please" and "thank you"? I suspect costumes and masks worn at Halloween time, as well as uniforms worn by officers on duty, doctoral degrees, and the other devices we employ to avoid being seen as we are, are all ways we have of extricating ourselves from predicaments.... *But masks have a way of sticking to our faces when worn too long.* (Kelly, 1964, p. 158; last italics added)

Kelly used the mask analogy to illustrate how individuals may be trapped into believing they are the role that they portray. Such an insight has also been verified by the classical experiments of Stanley Milgram (1974) and Philip Zimbardo (Zimbardo et al., 1974), in which experimental subjects were found to identify with their assigned roles. It has also been noted that in reality television programs such as *Survivor,* people often quickly become very attached to the roles they play.

Change Through Fixed-Role Therapy

Kelly believed that persons are free to revise their view of themselves and of their relationships to others. **Fixed-role therapy** was one of Kelly's methods to aid his clients to construe themselves deliberately differently. You may recall that fixed-role therapy involves the clinician's writing a narrative sketch for the client that represents a change from the client's present personality. The therapist says, in effect, to the client: "Here is another way of construing yourself. Pretend for two weeks or so that you are this (fictional) person. Monitor your experience."

For Kelly, fixed-role therapy was a creative process mutually shaped by client and therapist. It was not to be understood as a "repair" technique to fix wounded personalities (Kelly, 1955, p. 380). Rather, Kelly's conception of the technique is most accurately described as a kind of personal experiment.

Kelly developed some simple rules for the writing of fixed-role sketches by clinicians (1955, pp. 368 ff.):

1. It should ideally be constructed by a panel of clinicians familiar with the client.
2. The sketch should develop a major theme rather than attempt to correct minor personality faults.
3. The sketch should sharply contrast with the client's real character, for it will be easier to pretend to be a person he or she believes is totally opposite from the one he or she presently is.

4. The sketch should attempt to engage the client's own personality growth processes and mobilize his or her own resources for change.

5. Testable hypotheses that the client can immediately check in his or her own life should be part of the sketch so that it is plausible and real to the client.

6. The client should be given the full protection of "make-believe," so that he or she can experiment with the role without making a permanent commitment. Kelly called this protective screening a "protective mask" (1955, p. 373).

Writing the Fixed-Role Sketch

One basis for constructing a new fictional personality consists of clients' self-characterization sketches. In addition to explicit content, the clinician considers the way clients have organized the sketch, emphasized certain phrases, and highlighted specific themes. Clinicians also incorporate personal constructs revealed by the REP test. The actual construction of a fixed-role sketch requires both clinical skills and creativity. Table 14.3 contains side-by-side excerpts from the self-characterization sketch of "Ronald Barrett," the pseudonym of a patient of Kelly's, and the fixed-role sketch written for him with the fictional name of "Kenneth Norton."

This client's self-characterization and Kelly's fixed-role sketch indicate the central theme. Ronald was invited to perceive the subtle feelings of other people rather than argue with them about the literal meanings of words (Kelly, 1955, p. 375). After the period of fixed-role therapy, Ronald Barrett was able to change his way of construing himself. He began selectively to adopt aspects of "Kenneth Norton" that he found worthwhile and congenial. He found himself capable of being more open and friendly with others.

THE CPC CYCLE: CIRCUMSPECTION, PREEMPTION, AND CONTROL/CHOICE

Kelly developed a model, the **CPC cycle**—*circumspection, preemption*, and *control/choice*—for indicating how a person's constructs and construct system could accommodate new realities. The first phase, **circumspection**, involves the development of propositional thinking. In propositional thinking, a person considers alternative ways of construing experience. A **propositional construct** is one that facilitates openness to seemingly contradictory experiences. Developing propositional constructs is a flexible mode of thinking that avoids black/white pigeonholing and "nothing but" thinking. Propositional constructs are the opposite of rigid, constellatory constructs.

The second phase, **preemption**, involves choosing the relevant elements from among various propositional alternatives. Having reduced the field to one dichotomous issue, the individual still has to make the choice between the opposing poles.

In the third phase, **control/choice**, the individual, who has already reduced the field to one dichotomous issue, finally chooses between the opposing poles.

Let us consider how these concepts would apply in a psychologically complex interpersonal scenario. Consider the predicament in which a hypothetical protagonist, young Jean-Mary, found that some of her key personal constructs had lost their usefulness. Note the process (CPC cycle) through which her thinking progressed as she dealt with a very challenging situation:

> Jean-Mary's eighth grade teacher precipitated a crisis in the relationship between Jean-Mary and her younger sister, Robin. Called to Robin's sixth-grade classroom by a note from

Table 14.3   Excerpts from Ronald Barrett's Self-Characterization and Fixed-Role Sketches

Self-characterization by "Ronald Barrett"	"Kenneth Norton": Fixed-role sketch
An overall appearance of Ronald Barrett would give one the impression that he has a rather quite [*sic*] and calm personality. Furthermore, he dislikes doing or saying anything that will draw unfavorable attention in public.... However, he has been known to flare up (not in public, though) very easily and often gets quite worked up or frustrated over something done or spoken by (usually not his friends or anyone with him) someone that he feels should know better.... He very rarely shows signs of anger toward his friends. On the other hand, he is apt to be inconsistent in that it sometimes takes a lot to get him worked up over some subject at hand, while at other times he will very easily get very worked up.... A feeling of guilt often comes over him if he thinks he has not been kindhearted enough.... His tendency to criticize and correct people, esp. in his family, on major as well as minor issues, shows some decrease outside his family, but not too much within. Proving his point, or arguing his point, and arguing against other people's points, seems to be one of his major "hobbies." ...He has some ideas concerning girls that seem odd or just plain crazy to most people. He completely refrains from calling a girl "beautiful." She may be cute, pretty, attractive...but he uses the word "beautiful" only [to] describe material things that have no "feeling" as humans have. Although he listens attentively to stories or general discussion about sex, he rarely enters into the conversation. One may say that he puts too much meaning and thought into kissing a girl.... He is usually lost for conversation when meeting someone new, or seeing a girl he knows, but if he once "breaks the ice," he can usually talk freely. From Kelly, 1955, pp. 326–328.	Kenneth Norton is the kind of man who, after a few minutes of conversation, somehow makes you feel that he must have known you intimately for a long time. This comes about, not by any particular questions that he asks, but by the understanding way in which he listens. It is as if he had a knack of seeing the world through your eyes. The things which you have come to see as being important he, too, soon seems to sense as similarly important. Thus, he catches not only your words but the punctuations of feeling with which they are formed and the little accents of meaning with which they are chosen. Kenneth Norton's complete absorption in the thoughts of the people with whom he holds conversations appears to leave no place for any feelings of self-consciousness regarding himself. If indeed he has such feelings at all, they obviously run a poor second to his eagerness to see the world through other people's eyes.... Girls he finds attractive for many reasons, not the least of which is the exciting opportunity they provide for his understanding the feminine point of view. Unlike some men, he does not "throw the ladies a line" but, so skillful a listener is he, soon he has them throwing him one—and he is thoroughly enjoying it. With his own parents...he is somewhat more expressive of his own ideas and feelings. Thus his parents are given an opportunity to share and supplement his new enthusiasms and accomplishments. From Kelly, 1955, pp. 374–375.

Robin's teacher, Jean-Mary was startled to find her sister tear-stained, flushed, and trembling at the blackboard. When Jean-Mary arrived, Robin was trying to endure a tirade from the teacher. The gist of the verbal assault was an unfavorable comparison of her math abilities to the teacher's former student, Jean-Mary.

Moreover, the teacher wanted Jean-Mary to complete a problem that her sister was not able to solve correctly. Jean-Mary was caught in a conflict between obedience to an adult authority figure and compassion for and loyalty to her own sister. Unable to decide between defiance and submission, Jean-Mary initially froze. She finally relented to the teacher's pressure and solved Robin's long division problem correctly in front of the whole class. In

Had George Kelly formulated his theory in the 1970s and 1980s, instead of in the 1950s and 1960s, it would have been hailed as a cognitive theory rather than as an eclectic one. Kelly's ideas are compatible with contemporary cognitive psychology in a way that is surprising for a theory whose origins preceded psychology's current willingness to focus on what people think. There was a time in our history as a science, especially during the 1960s, when the prevailing radical behaviorism made *thinking* a dirty word in psychology. Kelly was well ahead of his time in discussing thinking, decision making, and the cognitive activity of anticipating consequences.

that moment of hurt and humiliation for Robin, a wall had been built separating the two sisters in a way that neither of them could verbalize.

Jean-Mary was faced with an awful realization. Up to this time, teachers had always been objects of her respect and admiration. They were people to be obeyed without question. But clearly, as her experience had just painfully shown, a specific teacher was cruel and stupidly hurtful. Jean-Mary experienced three conflicts: She felt guilt for having participated against her own sister in a situation that required her to change her views quickly and decisively; she experienced anger at her own gullibility in having uncritically accepted teachers as paragons of virtue; she struggled against an emerging distaste for all teachers and for schoolwork in general.

Jean-Mary was belatedly able to reason that some teachers are less than perfect, and that sometimes being a teacher was no safeguard against cruelty and stupidity. Jean-Mary was even able to redefine her own self-image to admit that she had acted with less courage than her personal values had demanded. She resolved never again to be an unwitting pawn of her own preconceptions, and she apologized to her sister and re-affirmed her loyalty.

Jean-Mary's predicament and how she solved it illustrates the CPC cycle—a sequence of thought involving the revision of constructs and construct systems. Up to the time of her experience with the long division episode, her construction of teachers could be characterized as stereotypical: She thought that all teachers were necessarily good, kind, intelligent, and just. Kelly called such stereotypes **constellatory constructs** (1955, p. 155). Constellatory constructs are rigid "constellations" or configurations of qualities that are applied in an automatic manner to a person, object, or situation. Fortunately, Jean-Mary's constellatory construct of "teacher" also had the characteristic of permeability. Recall that a permeable construct is one that is susceptible to change through the addition of new elements to its range of convenience. Constellatory constructs, however, are not easy to modify.

When confronted with a violation of her expectancy in the form of a teacher who was capricious and hurtful, Jean-Mary was confused and anxious: "This teacher is not at all like teachers whose behaviors I thought I could anticipate." Such a discrepancy could be resolved only by eventually restructuring the construct of "teacher." It had to be changed into a more relativistic concept that admits variations to the stereotype of "good, just, and intelligent."

The series of changes in Jean-Mary's construct system involves each of the three phases—circumspection, preemption, and control/choice—of Kelly's CPC cycle.

Phase One: Circumspection

When confronted with a situation that required her to act in a way that violated several personal constructs, Jean-Mary was forced to view the elements that composed her "teacher" construct with circumspection. "A teacher is good, just, kind, and intelligent, but may sometimes also be cruel, stupid, and unjust—and a lot of other incompatible things." Unfortunately, Jean-Mary was not able, until after the fact, to enter the first phase of the CPC cycle, circumspection, and survey the situation and the persons involved for possible alternative constructions.

Phase Two: Preemption

The circumspection phase must come to an end if we are to be able to act on the propositions that have been developed. Circumspection finally enabled Jean-Mary to free herself from the rigidity of her constellatory construct of "teacher" and provided her with a more propositional version—that teachers were not necessarily considerate, kind, and intelligent. But only when Jean-Mary was able to leave the circumspection phase could she decide among the various possible options. Jean-Mary finally began thinking more preemptively. Kelly described the preemptive phase:

> The preemption of issues characterizes the "man of action." He is likely to see things in what may appear to his associates to be an oversimplified manner. He consolidates all the possible perspectives in terms of one dichotomous issue and then makes his choice between the only two alternatives he allows himself to perceive. (1955, p. 516)

Jean-Mary finally preempted the issues to one dichotomous theme: "defiance of a heretofore respected authority figure versus allegiance to my sister." Unfortunately, Jean-Mary had entered the preemption stage (and the earlier circumspection state) too late to keep from hurting her sister.

Phase Three: Control/Choice

In Jean-Mary's case, the final choice was for loyalty and trying to remedy any hurt she might have caused. Her apology and allegiance of loyalty to her sister are indicative of this choice. Unfortunately for her sister, Jean-Mary's entrance into and completion of the CPC cycle was too late to prevent harm. But real change has occurred. When confronted with similar situations in the future, Jean-Mary would not hesitate to act on her new constructions.

SOME TRADITIONAL PERSONALITY VARIABLES AS KELLY RECAST THEM

Kelly thought about some basic psychological concepts in a new way. Old concepts such as the unconscious, anxiety, hostility, and guilt were recast in his theory.

The Unconscious

The concept **unconscious** is partly subsumed under Kelly's notion of pre- and non-verbal constructs. In this sense, his idea is similar to that of Freud himself. Freud had proposed that repression proper consisted of the preconscious system's removal of language "cathexes" from threatening ideas that have a relationship with content already primally repressed into the unconscious (cf. Chapter 3). Kelly, however, suggests that lack of a word label alone is not sufficient to prevent a construct from entering awareness. For a personal construct to be truly removed from consciousness, it must be *submerged* along one of its two poles.

BOX 14.2   *Only Connect . . .*

What Kelly was clearly trying to do in his reformulations of concepts such as the unconscious, anxiety, guilt, and aggression was to create a thoroughly cognitive psychology that would provide an alternate explanation to Freudian psychodynamics for phenomena that Freudian theory emphasized. Kelly wanted his cognitive approach to account for far more than simply the way in which people construed their experiences.

Recall that each construct has a *similarity pole* by which two or more elements are construed as alike, and a *contrast pole* by which at least one other element is seen as different. One or the other pole of the construct may be submerged so that, for example, the similarity elements are kept out of awareness.

Submergence of one pole of a construct implies the *suspension* of whole categories of constructs from the total system. In contrast with some notions of repression, suspension implies that the idea or element is forgotten simply because the person cannot tolerate any structure within which the idea would have meaning. Once he or she can entertain such a structure, the idea may again become available within it (Kelly, 1955, p. 473).

Kelly has thus translated the idea of *unconscious* into the concepts of *nonverbal constructs, submergence*, and *suspension*.

Anxiety

Constructs that compose the central anticipations by which people set their life goals and construe themselves in relation to these outcomes are called **core constructs** (Kelly, 1955, p. 482). An individual can tolerate some incompatibility between expectancy and experience. As that discrepancy becomes greater, anxiety and confusion may result. Experiences that are incompatible with core constructs may threaten such constructs. According to Kelly (1955, p. 495), **anxiety** is the feeling that accompanies, *"the cognition that the events with which one is confronted lie outside the range of convenience of one's construct system."* Similar ideas to those of Kelly have emerged within cognitive dissonance theory (Festinger, 1957). Also, Erikson's notions of identity conflict, and his observation of the anxiety experienced from the loss of identity among combat soldiers (Chapter 8) are largely consistent with Kelly's formulations. Erikson's concept of *identity* would be considered a core construct in Kelly's theory.

Guilt

In Kelly's terms, **guilt** is defined as a *"Perception of one's apparent dislodgment from his core role structure"* (1955, p. 502). Core role structure can be thought of as one's fundamental identity in regard to others. One might see oneself as a nurturing caretaker, for example. Parents with a core role of being such caretakers would feel guilt if they started neglecting their children to handle other competing responsibilities.

Aggressiveness

Kelly defined **aggressiveness** in a way that is clearly different from the usual usage of the term. His use of the term seems to have little to do with expressions of anger but indicates being assertive or taking initiative on the basis of one's goals and views of reality. *"Aggressiveness is the active elaboration of one's perceptual field"* (1955, p. 508). For Kelly, the individual who actively seeks to construct a greater number of alternative choices is acting "aggressively": "They are always precipitating themselves and others into situations which require decision and action" (1955, p. 508).

EVALUATING KELLY'S PERSONAL CONSTRUCT THEORY

Kelly's theories about human nature have proven quite durable over the years. His notion of personal constructs was first quite popular and led to numerous speaking engagements and visiting appointments at many universities as well as an endowed chair at Brandeis University. During the 1960s and early 1970s, his ideas were eclipsed by the behavioral movement and some less elaborate cognitive approaches. Subsequently, a number of trends have led to a renewed appreciation of Kelly's work. A constructivist movement has taken form in many disciplines as has an emphasis on individual experience and narratives. There is now an active journal devoted to constructivist psychology, the REP test has been computerized so that its scoring is simpler, books based on Kelly's ideas continue to be published, and societies devoted to personal construct psychology have sprung up in the United States and internationally.

Refutability of Kelly's Ideas

In principle, much of personal construct theory is refutable (testable). Certainly the REP test grid approach lends itself to empirical studies (Bannister & Fransella, 1971, esp. Chapters 3 and 6). Other central concepts from Kelly's theory appear to be testable:

- Repression as a kind of "refiling," "mislabeling," or "redefining" threatening ideas could certainly be tested in the laboratory with a verbal learning design or with a recognition memory design drawn from signal detection theory.
- The efficacy of Kelly's fixed-role therapeutic technique, like other psychotherapeutic techniques, is capable of being assessed with empirical studies.
- The power of expectation or anticipation has already been tested in a variety of other research paradigms in psychology that range from social psychology studies to current social learning theory research (e.g., Bandura, 1986, reviews many of these studies on what he terms *expectancy effects*).
- Personality change in psychotherapy has been studied using Kelly's personal construct system (Martin, 1994).

Human Agency in Personal Construct Theory

Kelly developed a theory that emphasizes active human agency. In his view, it is the person who constructs meaning from reality. It is the person who tests personal hypotheses and confirms or disconfirms anticipations, much as a scientist does. The person is active in regard to challenges and to new circumstances, not reactive.

Personal Constructs are Idiographic

Kelly's theory is idiographically focused. It is primarily concerned with understanding the personal constructs of specific individuals. Idiographic theories tend to be *ipsative*, a term drawn from psychometrics and psychological testing. Ipsative tests (and theories, and constructs) compare the individual with his or her own past and future performances, but they do not permit comparison across individuals. There is also a nomothetic aspect to Kelly's theory for the fundamental postulate and the 11 corollaries apply universally and are viewed as indicative of human nature in general.

SUMMARY

George A. Kelly's theory of personal constructs is built upon his conviction that all persons behave "as if" they were scientists. Each of us, out of the fundamental human need to understand the world, creates and tests hypotheses about the behavior of significant others. Kelly formulated a fundamental postulate to embody this concept: *"A person's processes are psychologically channelized by the ways in which he anticipates events"* (1955, p. 46).

Eleven corollaries expand this basic theme:

1. *Construction Corollary:* A person anticipates events by construing their replications.

2. *Individuality Corollary:* Persons differ from each other in their construction of events.

3. *Organization Corollary:* Each person characteristically evolves, for his or her convenience in anticipating events, a construction system embracing ordinal relationships between constructs.

4. *Dichotomy Corollary:* A person's construction system is composed of a finite number of dichotomous constructs.

5. *Choice Corollary:* A person chooses that alternative in a dichotomized construct through which he or she anticipates the greater possibility for extension and definition of his or her system.

6. *Range Corollary:* A construct is convenient for the anticipation of a finite range of events only.

7. *Experience Corollary:* A person's construction system varies as he or she successively construes the replications of events.

8. *Modulation Corollary:* The variation in a person's construction system is limited by the permeability of the constructs within whose ranges of convenience the variants lie.

9. *Fragmentation Corollary:* A person may successively employ a variety of construction subsystems that are inferentially incompatible with each other.

10. *Commonality Corollary:* To the extent that one person employs a construction of experience which is similar to that employed by another, his or her psychological processes are similar to those of the other person.

11. *Sociality Corollary:* To the extent that one person construes the construction processes of another, he or she may play a role in a social process involving the other person.

Among other innovations, Kelly developed an assessment method, the Role Construct Repertory Test (REP), and a therapeutic technique called fixed-role therapy. The REP test requires the individual to compare systematically his or her personal interpretations of the roles of significant people. Such comparisons can then be analyzed impressionistically or objectively with the tools of correlation and factor analysis. Fixed-role therapy involves the psychologist writing a personality sketch that differs in significant ways from the client's usual roles. The client is then invited to enact the role for two or more weeks. The alternative construction of events embodied in the fixed-role sketch is often sufficient to aid the client in construing life differently.

Personal constructs may be thought of as a person's means of making sense of life. Changes in a person's constructions may be necessitated by the demands of reality. The circumspection-preemption-choice/control (CPC) cycle involves the person in a restructuring of his or her construct system in three phases: (1) the circumspection phase, which involves the development of propositional constructions of events; (2) the preemption phase, during which the individual must narrow constructions to one significant dichotomous construct; and (3) the control or *choice* phase, in which the individual decides to act on one or the other pole of the dichotomous construct that was chosen in phase two.

Kelly's system has led to new ways of thinking about basic personality constructs like the unconscious, anxiety, aggression, and guilt. Each of these variables can be viewed either in terms of the individual's capacity to modify and rearrange his or her system of constructs or the emotions that result when constructs fail to predict events reliably. Kelly's theory is refutable in principle and has led to empirical studies of personality and personality change. His theory emphasizes active agency and focuses largely on uncovering the idiographic or individual aspects of personality.

Initially, Kelly's ideas were first applauded and then largely ignored by other psychologists. In the last decade or so, however, Kelly's ideas have attracted increasing interest. Today, there is much theorizing and research as well as therapeutic activity that has been inspired and influenced by Kelly's work.

FOR FURTHER READING

Kelly's influence as a personality theorist has waxed and waned and waxed again. Kelly's own comprehensive masterwork (most recent edition) is the two-volume *Psychology of Personal Constructs* (New York: Routledge, 1992). The first three chapters of Vol. 1 of this work have been published as a self-contained paperback introduction to Kelly's theory under the title *A Theory of Personality: The Psychology of Personal Constructs* (New York: Norton, 1963).

Brendan Maher has compiled and organized many of Kelly's theoretical papers into a single volume, *Clinical Psychology and Personality: Selected Papers of George Kelly* (New York: Wiley, 1969). Of particular significance among the papers in this volume are "The Autobiography of a Theory" and the "Language of Hypothesis: Man's Psychological Instrument."

The collection of research papers contained in D. Bannister and J. M. Mair's (Eds.) *The Evaluation of Personal Constructs* (New York: Academic Press, 1968; especially Chapters 3, 4, and 10) will provide some indication of the investigations stimulated by Kelly's ideas. In a similar way, J. C. Bonarius's review, "Research in the Personal Construct Theory of George A. Kelly: Role Construct Repertory Test and Basic Theory," in Vol. 2 of B. A. Maher's (Ed.), *Progress in Experimental Personality Research* (New York: Academic Press, 1965), indicates the kinds of research questions that have been explored with Kelly's concepts.

Additional research efforts can be surveyed in D. Bannister's (Ed.) collection of papers entitled *Perspectives in Personal Construct Theory* (New York: Academic Press, 1970). Bannister and F. Fransella have put together a paperback book summarizing Kelly's theory and surveying their own and others' research efforts on its behalf: *Inquiring Man: The Theory of Personal Constructs* (Baltimore: Penguin, 1986).

J. Martin's book, *The Construction and Understanding of Psychotherapeutic Change: Conversations, Memories and Theories* (New York: Teachers College Press, 1994), utilizes Kelly's personal construct theory to investigate personality change in psychotherapy. F. Fransella's, *George Kelly* (London: Sage Publications, 1996), is a contemporary summary and evaluation of Kelly's influence on psychotherapeutic practice. Robert Neimeyer and Michael Mahoney have recently edited a comprehensive book, *Constructivism in Psychotherapy* (Washington, DC: American Psychological Association, 1999), describing a contemporary approach based in large measure on Kelly's original theorizing and therapeutic work.

The Journal of Contructivist Psychology publishes current articles in personal construct theory and constructivist thinking as well as related empirical and applied areas in psychology.

Further suggested readings related to Chapter 14 and its topics may be found on the web site for Chapter 14 at www.wiley.com/college/sollod

GLOSSARY

Aggressiveness: In Kelly's eyes, actively assimilating a greater range of experiences and constructing alternative choices.

Anxiety: In Kelly's theory, the feelings of threat when confronted with experiences discrepant with one's expectations and outside of one's construct system.

Circumspection: The first stage in the CPC cycle that involves the use of propositional constructs enabling one to reason relativistically. Propositional thinking is hypothetical, tentative, and relativistic.

Constellatory constructs: A construct in which the elements are applied automatically and rigidly to a person, object, or situation.

Constructive alternativism: The capacity of an individual to change his or her view or interpretation of problems and events. In Kelly's theory, such an ability was the key to successful adaptation.

Construe: An active effort to explain, interpret, and give meaning to experiences. We place interpretations on events, that is, we *construe* them.

Control/choice: The third stage of the CPC cycle, which involves deciding which pole of the dichotomous construct, selected in the preemptive phase, is most relevant to the situation.

Core constructs: Constructs, largely inflexible and resistant to change, on which we rely most heavily when explaining experience.

Corollaries: See the definitions for the eleven corollaries as given on pages 457–461.

CPC cycle: A problem-solving process in a construct system that involves three phases: *circumspection, preemption*, and *control/choice*.

Fixed-role therapy: A clinical technique that asks clients to act as if they were other people with different psychological characteristics.

Fundamental postulate: In Kelly's words, "A person's processes are psychologically channelized by the ways in which he anticipates events." This means that a person's psychological reactions are determined by the way he or she makes sense of or experiences different events.

Guilt: In Kelly's theory, feelings and thoughts that accompany a person's acting in a way that is outside or inconsistent of the person's core role or self-image.

Impermeable construct: A construct that does not admit new experiences or new elements to be included within its boundaries.

Permeable constructs: A construct that assimilates new experiences within its boundaries.

Personal constructs: An individual's implicit or explicit ways of looking at, explaining, and interpreting events in the world. Personal constructs are used to give meaning to, interpret, or predict experiences and events.

Preemption: The second stage in the CPC cycle, in which a person chooses the relevant elements from among his or her propositional alternatives and chooses the one construct that seems particularly relevant.

Propositional construct: A construct in which the elements are open to modification based on new experiences.

Role Construct Repertory Test (REP Test): A test Kelly devised to identify the constructs a person uses to construe the relevant people in his or her life.

Subordinal construct: A construct that is subsumed under a broader and more general construct.

Superordinal construct: In a hierarchical construct system, a construct that subsumes others.

Unconscious: In Kelly's view, constructs with a low level of cognitive awareness.

Chapter **15**

Albert Bandura

Social Cognitive Theory

. . . trying to shape auto driving skills through operant conditioning would unshape the driver and the surrounding environment!

Albert Bandura (2001c)

The theorizing that is currently in vogue attributes behavior to multilevel subpersonal neural networks devoid of any consciousness, subjectivity or self-identity. While this line of theorizing views humans as high-level automatons, I have been emphasizing the exercise of human agency.

Albert Bandura (2001c).

An old story illustrates the limitations of conditioning and the importance of expectations as an explanation for human behavior:

A shabbily dressed person went to a fancy hotel and was treated poorly by the concierge. The concierge was surprised when this man rewarded him with a large tip. The next day he provided great service.

At the end of the day, he received no tip at all.

The concierge asked the guest, "Why did you give me a good tip when I provided poor service but no tip after I provided excellent service?"

The guest replied, "Today's tip was for yesterday's service."

Anonymous

| Albert Bandura | Born: 1925 Mundare, Alberta, Canada |
| | At present: Professor Emeritus at Stanford University |

About Social Cognitive Theory

Social cognitive theory, as proposed by Bandura, sees people as both acting on the environment and affected by their understanding of it. They are proactive and self-regulating. Cognitive processes and self-reflection are central to human behavior. People are not reactive organisms or conditioned by the environment; they plan and predict the consequences of their actions. In a word, they are **agentic.**

Albert Bandura and Richard Walters, his first doctoral student (1963), took up the task of advancing our understanding of complex activities without taking on what they viewed as the limitations of psychoanalytic theory. Since Richard Walters's untimely death, Bandura and his colleagues at Stanford University have worked to develop the social cognitive theory with the methodological rigor of behaviorism, while neverthe-less taking account of the human capacity to think about and to plan for experiences and to deal with the varied situations faced in daily life.

MISCONSTRUED AS A BEHAVIORIST

From the very beginning of his graduate training, Bandura was interested in approach-ing psychology as an empirical discipline. However, even though he was surrounded by behaviorists and in an institution known for behaviorism, he did not become a behaviorist himself. In recent correspondence, he indicated:

> At the time of my graduate training, the entire field of psychology was behaviorally oriented with an almost exclusive focus on the phenomenon of learning. But I never really fit the behavioral orthodoxy. At the time virtually all of the theorizing and research centered on learning through the effects of reinforcing outcomes. In my first major program of research, I argued against the primacy of conditioning in favor of observation learning in which people neither emit responses nor receive reinforcements during the process of learning.... I conceptualized observational learning as mediated through perceptual and cognitive processes. (Bandura, 2001c)

He continued,

> I rejected Miller and Dollard's [cf., behavioristic researchers][1] view of imitation as merely a special case of instrumental [operant] conditioning. While behaviorists were plotting learning curves as a function of number of reinforced trials, I published a chapter on "No trial learning." (Bandura, 2001c)

Further, he expressed concern that he has often been mistakenly viewed as a behaviorist, even though he challenged the major tenets of behaviorism.

> In the early writings I acknowledged the phenomena encompassed under the labels of conditioning and reinforcement. But what text writers and those relying on secondary sources were missing is that I conceptualized these phenomena as operating through cognitive processes. (Bandura, 2001c)

How did this misattribution occur? One reason is that, like behaviorism, social cog-nitive theory largely relies on laboratory research and the results of experiments. The processes of imitation learning and vicarious reinforcement superficially seem to be behavioral processes because of the use of the words *learning* and *reinforcement*. As we shall see, however, imitation learning and vicarious reinforcement involve a cog-nitive change or a change in expectations that occurs as a result of observation; they are not conditioning processes involving shaping or direct reinforcement.

---

[1]Dollard and Miller, and other members of the Yale Group, were focused on making Freud's contributions more verifiable. They succeeded in translating key Freudian ideas into stimulus-response-almost-cognitive psychology. Anxiety was treated as a subjective cognitive-emotional cause of defensive behavior. Repression was translated into a functionally equivalent response that avoids painful thoughts as rats learn to avoid cues that signal electric shock.

Bandura endeavored to study some phenomena having to do with daily behavior as well as clinically relevant behavior with empirical methods and to explain those phenomena with concepts and language drawn from the psychology of learning and cognition. The body of research literature connected with Bandura's approach is now so vast that it would require a substantial handbook merely to survey it. We cannot undertake that survey here, but we can describe the main features of the paradigm.

Imitation Learning: Dealing with the Complexities of Learning in Daily Life

Complex human learning occurs with the help of reinforcement and association, but not exclusively in those ways. We also learn by imitating others or by watching them model behavior. We attend to the details of their actions, but we also observe the consequences of their actions and can learn the principles that guide their actions. In addition, sometimes we learn through exposure to the thinking of other people, as, for instance, when we read a textbook that conveys the written ideas of others.

The novice surgeon observes many surgical procedures before attempting to participate in small ways in a supervised operation. The beginning driver observes and listens to explanations of what to do before, under careful guidance, he or she is permitted to attempt controlling a car. And the neophyte clinical psychologist observes therapy and reads extensively about the process before conducting therapy under supervision.

In short, people learn by watching other people, and by encoding all kinds of information in symbolic form. Miller and Dollard (1941) introduced the concept of learning by imitation. Bandura understood the significance of Dollard and Miller's concept of imitation learning and its improvement over a conditioning model:

> I was very attracted to Miller and Dollard's book on social learning and imitation. It seemed to provide an alternative to the somewhat prevailing theory of learning which assumed that we acquire competencies and new patterns of behavior through response consequences. At that time, it seem to me that I couldn't imagine how a culture would transmit its language, its mores and all of the complex competencies that are required to function effectively through this tedious trial and error process. *You would need three or four lifetimes to acquire even some basic functioning.* (Bandura, in Evans, 1989, italics added)

Bandura more fully developed and elaborated the concepts of modeling: Modeling is more than imitation learning or a kind of mimicry. In modeling the learner must (1) attend to the model, (2) remember what is seen and extract the essential elements, (3) reproduce symbolically what has been learned, and (4) be motivated to perform the activity. Figure 15.1 summarizes these main steps and their components. What the information in Figure 15.1 emphasizes is that the processes involved in observational learning go far beyond mere mimicry or a rote kind of imitation. They involve the observer's development and utilization of a cognitive model based on observation. The behavior described in Bandura's model thus requires more cognitive activity unlike the reinforcement of chance responses as in operant conditioning.

Bandura's research has demonstrated that a wide range of learning is possible through **modeling** and **observational learning.** All manner of novel responses may be acquired through observational learning so that the learner is able to expand his or her behavioral repertoire.

Observational learning can include response facilitation effects whereby the presence of a model performing a particular action induces the observer to make a similar response in direct imitation. Fads in hairstyles, clothing, and diet are good examples of response facilitation effects. New dance steps are often quickly adopted through the means of response facilitation that occurs when the steps are observed.

Attentional Processes	Retention Processes	Production Processes	Motivational Processes
Modeled Events 　Salience 　Affective Valence 　Complexity 　Prevalence 　Functional Value	Symbolic Coding Cognitive Organization Cognitive Rehearsal Enactive Rehearsal	Cognitive Representation Observation of 　Enactments Feedback Information Conception Matching	External Incentives 　Sensory 　Tangible 　Social 　Control Vicarious Incentives Self-Incentives 　Tangible 　Self-Evaluative
Observer Attributes Perceptual Capabilities Perceptual Set Cognitive Capabilities Arousal Level Acquired Preferences	*Observer Attributes* Cognitive Skills Cognitive Structures	*Observer Attributes* Physical Capabilities Component Subskills	*Observer Attributes* Incentive Preferences Social Comparative 　Biases Internal Standards

Modeled Events →　　　　　　　　　　　　　　　　　　　　　　　　　　　→ Matching Pattern

Figure 15.1 Subprocesses governing observational learning.

Vicarious Reinforcement

Bandura ascertained that complex behavior could be acquired by watching another's performance and the ensuing consequences. Observing another person reinforced can affect the behavior of the observer. Being so affected by such reinforcement that is not part of one's own direct experience is termed **vicarious reinforcement.** In Bandura's view, the effect of the reinforcer is on the person's *expectations* for future responding. A reinforcer, in his theory, provides an incentive to act; unlike the view of radical behaviorism, it is not simply a reward for past action. Reinforcement serves as a source of information to the person about his or her environment and the requirements for successful behavior. Foresight can be acquired either by direct experience or by watching what happens to another person. Figure 15.2 compares behavioral and social cognitive views of reinforcement.

It is important to emphasize that Bandura did not dismiss the importance of direct reinforcement as a powerful determinant of learning (Bandura, 1969). Rather, his social cognitive theory required the traditional view of reinforcement to be expanded to include vicarious reinforcement, in which there was actually no reinforcement provided to the learner at all.

The Self-System and the Environment: Reciprocal Determinism

Bandura (1978a, 1986) proposed the existence of a cognitive-emotional set of processes regulating and regulated by environmental input. The **self-system,** as Bandura prefers to call these internal processes, is not an autonomous agent like Freud's ego. The self-system is not isolated and is not a "little person" inside the person. In Bandura's model, the self-system is a complex of processes interdependent with the person's social and physical environment (Bandura, 1977b, pp. 194ff.; 1978, 1986, pp. 369ff.).

Bandura calls his complex interactional viewpoint **triadic reciprocal determinism,** and it is the key to the puzzle of studying private events scientifically. Human behavior is regulated in a reciprocally determined way. Bandura pictures reciprocal determinism as an interactive triad (Bandura, 1978, p. 345). The three elements that interact are: (P) the person's awareness and thinking, (B) the person's ongoing behavior, and (E) the person's environment. In this triad, each of these three factors

Radical Behaviorism

Model's Behavior ⟶ Observer's Imitative Response ⟶ Reinforcement

Problem: reinforcement appears to act backward in time on a response that no longer exists.

Cognitive Social Learning Theory

C o g n i t i v e   P r o c e s s e s

Anticipations of reinforcement ⟶ Attention to model's behavior and its consequences ⟶ Retention Selection Organization Rehearsal ⟶ Reinforcement

Solution: reinforcement is conceptualized as an incentive, as a source of information, and as a facilitator of performance. Learning the response is a cognitive process that does not require direct reinforcement.

Figure 15.2 Behavioristic and social cognitive views of reinforcement.

Based on Bandura, 1977b, p. 38.

may both affect and in turn be affected by the other two factors. This process can continue. As the person's behavior affects his or her environment, the environment in turn affects the person's behavior, and the person's awareness and thinking about these interdependencies affects behavior, environment, and changed expectations.

A key point in the scheme in Figure 15.3 is that:

> By their actions, individuals contribute to the nature of their situations (Bandura, 1981). People are therefore at least partial *creators of their own history*. Moreover, memory representation of the past involves constructive rather than reproductive processes in which events are filtered through personal meanings and biases and cognitively transformed. People thus serve as partial authors not only of their past experiences but of their memory of them as well. (Bandura, 1982, p. 157, italics added)

There are three major classes of **self-regulatory processes in the self-system:** We will see that the common denominator connecting and underlying these processes is the theme of competence, mastery, or self-efficacy. These processes are represented in Figure 15.4.

Key:
P = the person's awareness and thinking
B = the person's ongoing behavior
E = the person's environment

Figure 15.3 Triadic reciprocal determinism.

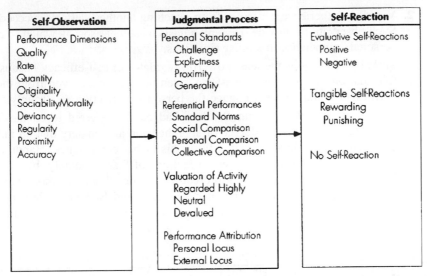

Self-Observation	Judgmental Process	Self-Reaction

Performance Dimensions
Quality
Rate
Quantity
Originality
Sociability/Morality
Deviancy
Regularity
Proximity
Accuracy
	Personal Standards
	   Challenge
	   Explictness
	   Proximity
	   Generality
	
	Referential Performances
	   Standard Norms
	   Social Comparison
	   Personal Comparison
	   Collective Comparison
	
	Valuation of Activity
	   Regarded Highly
	   Neutral
	   Devalued
	
	Performance Attribution
	   Personal Locus
	   External Locus
		Evaluative Self-Reactions
		   Positive
		   Negative
		
		Tangible Self-Reactions
		   Rewarding
		   Punishing
		
		No Self-Reaction

Figure 15.4 Processes involved in the self-regulation of behavior by internal standards and self-incentives.

From Bandura, 1986, p. 337.

1. The first class of self-regulatory processes involves the **self-observation of behavioral quality**. Concepts such as originality, authenticity, and ethicalness are applied as evaluative standards to one's own behavior.
2. The second set of self-regulatory processes that make up the self-system are the **judgments of excellence** and goodness of one's own behavior relative to the behavior of others and to one's own past performances.
   a. Included among these judgments is the individual style of attributing responsibility for action to self or to external causes.
   b. Blame for a failure attributed to self has remarkably different psychological effects from those of blame attributed to external causes.
3. The last processes in the self-system are those termed **self-reaction processes** but which would be better termed self-reward/punishment.

The Importance of a Sense of Self-Efficacy

Bandura (1977a, 1982, 1997) proposed that the sense of **self-efficacy** or personal competence underlies a great many behavioral phenomena, including the effectiveness of psychotherapy (e.g., Bandura, Adams, & Beyer, 1977), persistence in the face of obstacles (Bandura & Schunk, 1981), accuracy of the self-concept (e.g., Lazarus & Launier, 1978), and depression (e.g., Abramson, Seligman, & Teasdale, 1978).

In Bandura's analysis, the experience of self-efficacy or personal competence has four sources:

1. **Enactive attainments,** or what Bandura used to refer to as **performance accomplishments** (Bandura, 1986, p. 399) are the most powerful regulators of self-efficacy. A person's own efforts either succeed or fail, and the outcome is instructive in planning future efforts.

2. Vicarious experience is derived from watching another's efforts succeed or fail. Such observations provide one with a basis of comparison by which to estimate personal competence in similar situations.

3. Verbal persuasion is the least powerful regulator of self-efficacy because being told that one can or cannot master a given task is far removed from the actual performance and does not engage the person's conviction as strongly.

4. Physiological state, or what Bandura had earlier referred to as the level of emotional arousal, is the degree of apprehension and anxiety that an individual experiences in a situation that will test his or her competence (Bandura, 1986, p. 401). If a person concentrates on feelings of fear or anxiety, he or she may bring about the very failure that is dreaded. On the other hand, moderate degrees of arousal are likely to enhance performance. And Bandura (1986) points out that people are aware of and try to determine not only their anxiety levels, but their levels of physical fatigue and pain as well.

Bandura (1997, pp. 113 ff.) has also thought about how an individual might integrate the four components of self-efficacy—enactive attainment, vicarious experience, verbal persuasion, and physiological arousal. Each of the four sources may have different informational value for different people, who will weigh various components differently. For example, one person may more heavily weigh the experience of emotional arousal from past successes and failures—how good and bad such experiences felt. Another puts primary weight on past performance accomplishments. Yet another person may factor in the opinions of others.

Bandura also distinguishes between **efficacy expectations** and **outcome expectations,** an important difference for predicting effort and persistence. An efficacy expectation is an individual's belief that a given outcome can be accomplished because one possesses the requisite skills. By contrast, an outcome expectation is a person's belief that a certain course of action will result in a specific outcome, even if he or she is not the person to do it successfully.

One of the important features of Bandura's social cognitive theory is that it brought psychological concepts into understanding many complex phenomena important in daily life. In his development of the concept of self-efficacy, Bandura approaches questions that have to do with achievement, effort, goal-setting, and success and failure in daily life. Moreover, the processes that regulate our expectations are susceptible to scientific study by manipulating the variables of past performance, vicarious modeling, verbal instruction, and degree of emotional arousal.

Self-Efficacy: Its Impact in Daily Life

Bandura (1997) elevated the theoretical status of self-efficacy to the role of a nearly universal mediator of personality phenomena. His review of a wide range of research aimed to demonstrate how a person's belief in personal effectiveness and control shapes an extraordinary range of psychological phenomena extending from family interactions and general social transactions to the clinical phenomena of psychopathology. Three of the areas he considered were how a person copes with threat, how intellectual interests are developed, and the impact of self-efficacy appraisals on physical and psychological health. In all of this work, we see the further extension of his concepts to different areas of life.

The personality theorist, Robert W. White (1959), also developed a theory emphasizing the importance of the development of a sense of self-efficiency or what he termed competence. He indicated that people are motivated by what he termed, "effectance motivation." Bandura acknowledged White's contribution (1997, p. 13) but also criticized it in part as not being a "...particularized theory from which testable deductions can be made." In other words, Bandura viewed White's theory as nonrefutable.

Coping with Threat, Revisited

Bandura maintains his earlier conception of anxiety as "a state of anticipatory apprehension over possible deleterious happenings" (1997, p. 137). A threatening perception is related to the degree of threat experienced: the more the person believes he or she can cope with a potentially noxious experience,

- the less threatening that experience will seem,
- the less likely will the person scare self with anxiously unrealistic fantasies,
- the less likely will the person dwell on unpleasant bodily arousal, and
- the more likely will the person transform the meaning of the threat into one that he or she believes they can manage.

Motivating Intellectual Interests

The process by which people develop intrinsic interests in activities at which they initially possess little or no skill is regulated by self-efficacy beliefs.

> To mountaineers, the toilsome activity of crawling over slippery rocks in foul weather is not inherently joyful. It is the self-satisfaction derived from personal triumphs over lofty peaks that provides the exhilaration. Remove the personal challenges, and crawling over rocks becomes quite boring. (Bandura, 1997, p. 219)

Personal standards and the perceived meaning of the challenge contribute to the development of interests and satisfactions in three ways:

1. Challenging personal standards enlist sustained effort and involvement in activities needed to build personal competencies. Only a long-term investment can accomplish a worthy goal.
2. Mastering a challenge yields the feeling of satisfaction, a very reinforcing subjective state that enhances interest in the activity leading to mastery.
3. Personal standards of high caliber are also highly individualized markers, and, like pencil marks on the closet door indicating spurts in height over time, such self-set appraisals permit monitoring of one's progress in mastery.

> Most academic activities present ever-rising challenges. Whatever knowledge and cognitive skills are acquired, there is always more to learn. Past accomplishments are quickly outdistanced, and self-satisfactions are sought in higher accomplishments. Thus, in the pursuit of excellence, the higher the students' efficacy beliefs, the higher the academic challenges they set for themselves and the greater their intrinsic interest in scholastic matters.... (Bandura, 1997, p. 220)

Biological Effects of Self-Efficacy in Health and Psychopathology

Bandura (1997, pp. 262 ff.) reviews an extensive and developing literature showing that a person's self-efficacy beliefs and self-appraisals exert significant changes in physiological status for physical and psychological "health." For example, strong and realistic self-efficacy beliefs appear to protect people from the deleterious bodily effects of prolonged stress. People who believe they are in control and can master even ordinarily unpredictable events maintain lower levels of blood pressure, heart rates, and stress hormone levels.

In the psychological arena, catecholamine secretions—neurotransmitters regulating important brain activities—were shown to fundamentally mirror self-efficacy for phobic patients in the face of threat. High self-efficacy—belief that the threat is easily managed—was associated with low levels of catecholamine activity and stress hormones. Low self-efficacy beliefs were associated with elevated levels of catecholamines. When threats were altogether removed, the levels of catecholamines and other stress hormones dropped (Bandura, 1997, p. 265).

The central point emerging from these studies is that belief in personal control shapes a person's characteristic conduct and health status across a wide variety of situations. Bandura also reviews research showing similar positive effects of high self-efficacy belief in the areas of athletic achievement, vocational goal setting, political activism and effectiveness, and several psychopathologies, including eating disorders and substance abuse. Self-efficacy, in Bandura's view, is an important mediator of behavior.

WHAT ABOUT BANDURA'S OWN LIFE?

Bandura's life and theories are, as is the case in many other theorists we have studied, all of a piece. In Bandura's case, it is precisely the limitations in his environment that provided the occasion for him to develop the agentic approach to coping that he so thoroughly formulates and demonstrates in his scientific work. He was born in a small town in northern Alberta. In a personal communication, Bandura commented on his life:

> A limited educational system in my hometown promoted many of us to become self-directed learners. This and other life experiences fostered my interest in self-directedness and the exercise of human agency, i.e., people have a hand in shaping their life course. How does a kid from a small hamlet in northern Alberta end up with an endowed chair at Stanford University, the presidency of APA, etc? This calls for resilient agency. (Bandura, 2001a)

Bandura further stated,

> The limited resources in the small hamlet I grew up in and parental support for transcending those limitations got me on venturesome paths to the Yukon [where Bandura spent a summer after high school] and other places that provided a rich broad perspective on the human condition. (Bandura, 2001a)

In a later communication, Bandura pointed out the competitive atmosphere and the tough hardiness required in his boyhood,

> Competitive hockey is deeply ingrained in the Canadian human nature. We played it in 20 below zero in open-air rinks without any protective gear, including none for the goalie. As wee youngsters, we used the Eaton catalogues as shin pads. How's that for forging steely character? (Bandura, 2001b)

Bandura's early life history thus was an ideal background for his development of a strong personal sense of individual self-efficacy and personal agency. His own life experiences served as a background from which his theories, emphasizing just such self-efficacy and personal agency, emerged.

DEVELOPMENTAL PHASES OF SELF-EFFICACY

Bandura (1997) incorporated a developmental perspective into his theory of self-efficacy. He portrays the course of a person's life history as a series of interconnected phases, each of which requires specific types of mastery skills. Bandura (1997, p. 163) points out that people take control of their lives only in regard to the available opportunities. Occasionally even seemingly random events profoundly alter the life course. Bandura asserts that it is always the reciprocal interplay of personal qualities, such as the belief that one can control one's life, and the attributes of the social milieu that combine to launch a new life trajectory. Different kinds of interpersonal and personal competencies are required at each stage of living from birth to old age.

Infancy: Linking Action with Outcome

By observing repeatedly that events happen only when some action has been performed, infants learn that actions produce effects (Bandura, 1997). However, they must also learn to "self-observe" to make the crucial link: *my* actions produce effects. At first, effects produced by an infant have the character of pure trial and error. Infants flail about and generate all manner of outcomes, only some of which are intended and even fewer of which have desirable outcomes. Happenings unrelated to their behavior teach infants that they cannot completely control their world. If the infant's efforts appear to have little or no intended effect, the infant grows apathetic and loses interest in trying to exercise personal control. Under these overwhelming circumstances, a darker lesson is learned: There is no benefit in anticipating consequences when most things that happen in your world are unpredictable or unreliable.

Acquiring Social Competence

Competent infants, by contrast, learn that many, but not all, of their actions have intended, anticipated outcomes. Much of their earliest competency learning is linked to the physical environment during the early months because physical effects are immediate and clear. Months later, and continuing throughout childhood, the competent infant learns to produce intended effects on the important people in his or her world. Learning to control the social world and develop **social competence** is more difficult because so many intended effects are delayed or hidden from the weak attentional and discriminatory abilities of the very young child. Parents may skillfully promote mastery learning by reacting to their child's efforts. In this way, even a spontaneous game of peek-a-boo can be transformed into a pivotal social transaction that teaches the child that he or she can have an impact on the environment.

Recognition and Differentiation of the Self as Active Agent

Infants acquire a sense of personal agency when they realize that they are the *doers of action*. Acquisition of this sense of a personal "me as agent" is acquired through family interactions, the use of personal names, and the verbal labeling of personal possessions

---

BOX 15.2 *Only Connect...*

Erik Erikson's developmental theory would note the same phenomena and classify them under the areas of developing a basic sense of trust as well as initiative. Bandura's theory, like Erikson's (see Chapter 8), indicates the importance of learning that one has a reliable or trustable environment before being able to take initiative.

---

as "mine." By about 18 months, the typical infant has sufficient language skills to apply verbal labels to him- or herself, indicating at least a rudimentary awareness of *being* a self (Bandura, 1997, p. 167). By 20 months, children can spontaneously describe themselves as the agents or authors of intended actions, and quickly thereafter, they can describe aloud their thoughts and feelings while performing an action sequence. They are aware of personal agency at least enough to warily deny authorship of some deeds (Bart Simpson's strategic agency: "I didn't do it. No one saw me do it. You can't prove a thing.") To achieve any and all of these accomplishments, we must infer that the infant grasps the concept of self as active agent with the particular meaning of "self-as-one-who-intends-a-thing-to-happen."

Bandura emphasizes that all competency learning is possible only through the reciprocal interaction of the child and his or her environment, particularly interchanges with others. A family that enhances a child's mastery and learning is likely to be positively affected by having a bright and competent child in the family environment. A family that actively promotes the competence of younger members can usually be a family that communicates genuine enjoyment in the personal triumphs of its members (Bandura, 1997, pp. 169 ff.). As language acquisition proceeds apace, the child can use words to recall encouragement and prohibition, articulate success and failure, and actively and willfully engage the family's attention and admiration. The family's response can be supportive of the child's newfound sense of mastery or the family can discourage, humiliate, or simply ignore such efforts.

Childhood: Comparing One's Competence with Others

The earliest efficacy learning occurs almost exclusively within the family, but as the child matures, influences beyond that immediate circle take on increasing significance.

Sibling Comparisons

First born and only children are often enriched by extra attention from their parents, who initially have extra time and energy to invest in mutually satisfying mastery-enabling experiences. For second and subsequent children in larger families there is often less parental time available for parental enablement, but more time and opportunity for comparisons with siblings closest in age. Initially competition and interaction with age-close siblings are the second and middle child's most important source of self-knowledge about its capabilities compared to others like himself or herself.

Peer Comparisons and Validations

Eventually, however, peer interactions supplant the interactions of siblings as important sources of competition and comparison. The self-evaluative habits acquired in relation to brothers and sisters are extended now to comparisons with children outside the immediate family, and personal efficacy is judged against their less familiar accomplishments (Bandura, 1997, p. 170). However, children do not choose peers randomly. They tend to associate with children like themselves when they can. Thus, friendships are more likely to be formed with children of similar ages who share a child's interests, values, gender, and experiences. Such choices narrow the range of comparative experiences, but are not likely to obstruct the important avenue of learning about one's own competencies relative to others.

Beyond six years, the child's attention to comparisons becomes more focused on abstract social and psychological attributes of action and less on its immediate practical consequences. Thus, the seven- or eight-year-old child learns to compare self with similar children—sometimes preferring children who are just a *little* "better." Similarity of self to models grows increasingly important for the developing child in middle to late childhood and on into adolescence. Children are quick to imitate the admired models, quick to evaluate bluntly and loudly their own and their peers' performances, and sometimes quick to mimic dangerous performances outside the range of their current skills. Verbal instructions and evaluations, especially among a group of interactive peers, often serve as important sources of self-appraisal information.

School Age: Social Validation of Self-Efficacy

By the time the child enters school, an event that seemingly occurs earlier and earlier in our society, emphasis is placed on cognitive problem-solving skills as the chief age-appropriate competency.

Enabling Versus Discouraging Schools

The goal of attending school is to become an effective and productive member of one's culture. A child's acquired knowledge and thinking skills are tested. Institutionally sanctioned evaluations and personal comparisons with one's grademates are inherent to the educational enterprise. Schools and the classroom experiences they provide vary in the degree to which they promote self-efficacy learning or instill self-doubt and the expectation of failure.

Student Reputation

Lockstep educational programs that ignore individual differences in ability and motivation are prone to damage a child's sense of personal control and mastery. Programs that classify students into different ability groupings often communicate negative evaluations to those in the "lower" groupings, no matter how carefully the constituency of the group is disguised. Children assigned to the lowest reading level group may feel inferior to others. Classroom teaching style is also a powerful influence over the child's acquisition of realistic self-efficacy knowledge. Comparison of one child's performance with that of the others enhances only some children's sense of mastery at the inevitable motivational expense of the less successful children. Once a child's reputation among his classmates for good, average, or poor performance is established, it is difficult for the child to alter it, even when the attributes on which the reputation supposedly rests have changed. Other children's judgments, teachers' reactions and expectations, and parental evaluations all interact to solidify a child's reputation as a success or failure academically.

Social Consequences of School Efficacy Learning

The lessons the child learns about intellectual performance, competition, success, and failure are not limited to the intellectual domain as the child progresses through the grades. There are repercussions for social interaction that stem from the child's belief in his or her power to master academic challenges. A sense of poor control or cognitive inadequacy that some children acquire because of their school experience promotes aggressive acting out (Bandura, 1997, p. 176). A child who regards him- or herself as less able than peers is less likely to engage in prosocial activities, can become alienated, and is more likely to engage in antisocial behavior and substance abuse. Lack of confidence in one's cognitive abilities inhibits the child from routine learning about good health habits, grooming, exercise, nutritional eating, and disease prevention.

Adolescence: Risky but Proactive Transition to Adulthood

Adolescents are confronted with what seems to be an overwhelming number of changes. In rapid succession the adolescent experiences biological changes in the physical self at puberty, educational changes associated with the advancement to upper school grades, and the social stress of demands by parents and society for changes to behavior that is more adult-like.

Bandura points out that many of our theories of development overpredict the incidence of psychopathology under conditions of adversity. Adolescence has become a riskier developmental period in recent years because the threats loom larger and more frequently: unprotected sex, drugs, guns, fractured families, poverty, and social displacement (Bandura, 1997, p. 177).

Competence Enablement versus Vulnerability Protection

Self-efficacy, a sense of personal control and mastery, empowers the adolescent more successfully to navigate the transition from childhood to adulthood. Bandura distinguishes the concept of "enabling competent development" from that of "protection from psychopathology." Viewed as a means to empower the developing person to construct and pursue a productive life plan, self-efficacy is the tool of an active agent rather than the "shield" of a protected victim. Enablement through self-efficacy equips adolescents:

> ...to select and structure their environments in ways that set a successful course for their lives. This is the difference between proactive recruitment of sources of positive guidance and support and reactive adaptation to life circumstances. An agentic view of resilience also differs from the dualistic diathesis-stress model of psychopathology in which external stressors act upon personal vulnerabilities. Individuals play a proactive role in their adaptation rather than simply undergoing happenings in which environments act upon their personal endowments. The success with which the risks and challenges of adolescence are managed depends, in no small measure, on the strength of personal efficacy built up through prior mastery experiences. (Bandura, 1997, p. 178)

Biological and Social Changes at Puberty

Learning to deal with puberty often involves coping with emotionally invested partnerships. Biological maturation also has an impact on physical prowess and appearance, which in turn elicits the approval or disapproval of others. Self-efficacy is simultaneously linked to these social evaluations and is one major determinant of them.

Even the timing of pubertal changes can have an impact on the adolescent's sense of self-efficacy. In contrast to the enhanced social status usually enjoyed by early maturing boys, late-maturing boys are often the subject of peers' ridicule or deliberate indifference. Precociously developed adolescent girls may have to cope with bodily changes for which they are not ready and which may attract unwanted attention. On the whole, early maturers of both genders are more likely to be initiated prematurely by peer pressure into dating rituals, sexual conduct, drinking activities, and rule-breaking behaviors that have a negative impact on their educational and vocational progress.

Managing Adolescent Sexuality and Other High-Risk Behaviors

Teenagers are initiating sexual activity at younger ages than during previous generations. Exposure to media models and peer pressures that portray sexual conduct in the context of uncommitted relationships without consequences accelerates sexual acting out and enforces sexual ignorance, immaturity, and interpersonal blind spots. Precocious sexual activity is more closely linked with impoverished adolescents who have poor educational attainments than with middle-class, well-educated youth (Bandura, 1997, p. 179).

Bandura argues that sexual risk reduction depends on enhancing interpersonal self-efficacy to equip teenagers with the personal motivational and social skills to put protective sexual information into practice. Providing information alone is not sufficient. The adolescent should learn self-regulatory skills. Internalized standards and values play a bigger role than mere information, especially when those standards are associated with the experience of mastery that can generalize beyond sex to interpersonal relations.

In addition to sexuality, the adolescent has to learn to avoid illegal substances. Temptations range from tobacco and marijuana to alcohol, cocaine, and hallucinogens. Beginning substance abuse can lead to a vicious cycle: a weakened personal sense of control prompts further substance abuse in an effort to feel better by self-medication, and so on. Such drug involvement can often be ended by competent adult and peer guidance in concert with a network of adaptive social relationships from which the adolescent draws strength and confidence.

Adulthood: Vocation, Stable Partnerships, and Children

The demands of early adulthood bring the person face-to-face with the economic and social challenges of building a stable life.

Vocation

For those young people who pursue higher education, a structured life path usually awaits. Such continuing students often receive counseling, advice, and career information, and they may have clear-cut occupational goals that require clearly prescribed, tradition-bound steps.

Young people who do not continue their education often follow a more difficult, less structured path. According to Bandura, in addition to learning specific job-related skills, they most need preparation in self-management skills that promote adaptation to the world of work. The person's beliefs about self-capabilities are also a powerful predictor of vocational success. A high sense of personal efficacy is linked with more successful career choices, hireability, and sustained performance.

Middle Adulthood: Stability versus Crisis

By midlife, basic economic and interpersonal issues are usually resolved, freeing the individual to pursue new interests, retrench youthful aspirations, and sometimes reluctantly scale back or exuberantly fulfill lifelong dreams.

Declining Opportunities, New Dreams

For some, midlife may represent a period of diminishing vocational opportunities. Careers that involve physical strength or prowess are most vulnerable to decline, but certainly, other occupations are sometimes in jeopardy. The needs to restructure one's life and reconstrue what might have been overambitious goals are not unique to the middle years. Efficacious people are open to new opportunities, advance to new horizons, and can envision new dreams.

Advanced Age: Reappraisals, Regrets, and Reaffirmations

Even though there have been many advances in prolonging healthy life, old age is often a time of declining physical stamina, mental capabilities, and motivation.

Cognitive Changes

Some reduction in overall intellectual functioning ordinarily does not observably affect daily performance. Indeed, the person's expectations may play a stronger role in diminishing performance, enthusiasm, and energy than actual biological change (Bandura, 1997, p. 199). Capacities that depend on accumulated knowledge and experience—problem solving, reasoning, forecasting—may actually improve well into advanced age. Some folks call these enhanced cognitive capacities "wisdom."

Maintaining a Sense of Control

Maintaining social connectedness is an essential aspect of adaptive advance into advanced age. A low sense of self-efficacy, as we have seen, is associated with increases in a sense of vulnerability and social withdrawal. Efficacious people are much more likely to socialize, to maintain a personal network of friends and contacts, and to feel better about each day's tasks. The stereotypical view of older adults is that they invariably become increasingly dependent and dysfunctional. Physically and psychologically healthy older adults may conduct quite masterful and satisfying lives.

Realistic Social Comparisons

Aging does not take place in a vacuum. The person advancing in years does so in the context of the larger society and its views of older people, and in the context of family expectations for its older members. Older people can sustain a high level of experiencing oneself as efficacious despite declines in physical or psychological functioning. Because of their accumulated knowledge and life experience, comparisons with younger people are often quite favorable to them. And the more those comparisons yield favorable results, the more likely the person of advanced age will be able to keep up his or her skills, continuing to use them effectively and with satisfaction.

Table 15.1 summarizes the life demands on self-efficacy through the developmental cycle.

Table 15.1   Bandura's Developmental Analysis of Self-Efficacy

Life phase	*Typical demands*	*Role of self-efficacy*
Infancy	Learning: Actions produce effects. My actions produce effects.	Reliable link between action and outcome builds self-efficacy. Sustained caring by parents "enable" child's self-control. Self-efficacy learning is the core of infant's self.
Early childhood	Learning: Nature of family constellation Siblings' strengths and weaknesses Self-comparisons with siblings	Confidence in self permits attention to relevant models. Self-efficacious children resist risky behavior, view others' superior competence as a goal rather than as crushing competition.
School age	Knowledge and problem-solving skills Peer pressures, peer comparisons, peer competitions	Efficacious children establish "good" reputations that generalize across situations. Self-efficacy permits child to explore new interests in physical, social, and interpersonal areas without inhibition or aggression.
Adolescence	Transitions to adult-like performances in school, dating, friendships, and beginning of vocational identity explorations. Physiological changes of puberty. The temptations of risky sex, aggression, rule-breaking, and substance abuse.	Children who enter adolescence with strong self-efficacy are enabled, rather than protected, to equip themselves for a well-structured path in life. Sexual, vocational, and interpersonal issues are resolved adaptively by children who feel sufficiently in control to remain engaged in prosocial behavior.
Adulthood	Vocational identity crystallizes. Stable partnerships in world of changed families. Having and raising children.	Efficacy as "enabling," i.e., equipping adults to make realistic decisions, sustain intimate relationships, and develop good work habits, rather than as a "protector" from stress.
Advanced age	Physical, psychological, and mental capability decline; reduced vocational opportunities.	Efficacy aids person to see accumulated knowledge and skills as "wisdom" leading to favorable comparisons with others. Masterly older people seek new challenges, build new dreams.

Based on Bandura, 1997, Chapter 5.

Transitional Summary

As conceived by Bandura, self-efficacy is a central feature of personality. Bandura's analysis of the changing demands on self-efficacy with progress through the life course brings a developmental dimension to social cognitive theory. There are no startling insights in this life-course analysis that one could not encounter among other theories of personality. What typifies Bandura's approach is his consistent reliance on an active agent conception of personality functioning and his predilection for testing what are sometimes commonsense predictions with empirical data. Generally accepted psychological truisms and common sense are thus either validated or disproved. We again see in Bandura's work an expansion of cognitive behavioral concepts to a wide variety of situations and circumstances that people face in their lives.

SELECTIVE ACTIVATION OF SELF-CONTROLS

Bandura (1986, pp. 375ff.) has emphasized that self-controls are not automatic and unvarying. Theories such as Freud's that portray conscience, for example, as an "internalized" agency imply that the agency is an ever-present overseer, autonomously deciding when to act to pass judgment. Freud sometimes described the superego as if it were a "censor" ready to pounce at the first hint of a taboo wish or unacceptable impulse. Bandura, by contrast, pictures self-control as a process that the person is free to activate or deactivate. A given action will not be uniformly rewarded or punished because the circumstances may change sufficiently to deactivate or alter self-appraisal.

Bandura describes this flexibility as the **selective activation of internal control,** and he describes eight cognitive strategies through which a person can disengage self from condemnation during conduct he or she would ordinarily regard as worthy of self-punishment. These eight mechanisms are largely similar to defense mechanisms, but with major differences. The strategies Bandura is describing are largely conscious—unlike most of the psychoanalytic defense mechanisms. In formulating these strategies, Bandura focuses on the interaction of person and situation, not the control of internal impulses, as in Freud's defense mechanisms. The eight selective activation mechanisms are:

1. **Moral justification:** By providing what appears to be a moral explanation for conduct that would be seen by a person as reprehensible, the person may "restructure" the meaning of his or her behavior sufficiently to justify the conduct. For example, persuading soldiers that "killing the enemy" serves a higher moral purpose—such as preserving freedom—can turn reluctant recruits into skilled combatants. Moral restructuring can certainly be used for self-serving purposes, as for example when terrorists justify their random killing and maiming as serving a higher moral goal.

2. **Euphemistic labeling:** What something is called substantially affects the meaning we place upon it. Convoluted verbiage is a wonderful mask for unethical conduct. For example, when the military describes an invasion of a country with its attendant killing and destruction as an "incursion" rather than as an attack, the conduct is sanitized and euphemized. Bandura (1986, p. 378) offers the example of instructors who teach business students how to lie in competitive situations by calling it "strategic misrepresentation."

3. **Advantageous comparison:** If one chooses a sufficiently poor standard against which to compare one's own conduct, then much of the blame can be avoided.

BOX 15.3   *Only Connect . . .*

Bandura's *selective activation mechanisms* are very similar in function to Karen Horney's *secondary defenses*, which we considered in Chapter 10. Bandura's selective activation mechanisms and Horney's secondary defenses allow individuals to function relatively free of anxiety, guilt, and self-condemnation when they engage in behaviors that are damaging to others or to themselves.

For example, if an automobile salesperson overcharges customers, he or she can justify the deception by saying that the dealer down the street overcharges even more. Bandura provides the example of the promoters of the Vietnam War who excused the killing of thousands of people as a way of stopping their enslavement by Communism. Somehow, the fact that the intended beneficiaries were being killed was obscured by the dramatic comparison with "massive Communist enslavement."

4. **Displacement of responsibility:** If the personal sense of responsibility for an action is removed from one's own shoulders, usual self-regulatory controls can be rendered ineffective. For example, soldiers might fire upon civilians or commit atrocities when so ordered. Displacement of responsibility not only weakens personal restraints, but it also lessens concern for the well-being of others (Bandura, 1986, p. 379).

5. **Diffusion of responsibility:** Similar to the displacement of responsibility, the strategy here is to confuse or "lose" a precise locus of responsibility by resorting to a kind of division of labor. Group decision making can result in inhumane treatment for others, whereas any single member of the group taken alone would not condone such conduct. A person can even go so far as to tell self that it is the other group members who are responsible.

6. **Disregarding or distorting consequences:** One can avoid facing the harm one does to others, so that the action and the outcome are disassociated. In this way, the person can disregard consequences. For example, bomber pilots rarely see close-up the destruction and murderous effects of their efforts. The chain of command in organizations is another example. The person at the top of a very long hierarchy may be separated from observing the consequences of his or her decisions.

7. **Dehumanization:** One can disengage self-controls against mistreating people if one can find a way not to see them as people. Pejorative and stereotyping labels are one way to dehumanize another. The reverse, of course, is sometimes true. Some captors find it difficult to harm their hostages once they have gotten to know them (Bandura, 1986, p. 383).

8. **Attribution of blame:** If a person can justify mistreatment of another by saying that the person "deserved it" or was "just asking for it," then self-controls can be disengaged. This strategy is sometimes called "blaming the victim." Assaultive behavior toward women is sometimes "justified" in this way by men who subscribe to stereotyped beliefs and myths about their victims. One can also trivialize the consequences to the victim as another way of disengaging self-condemnation. Some rapists may believe that women secretly enjoy being raped (Bandura, 1986, p. 385).

Bandura points out that not one of these disengagement mechanisms by itself can turn a law-abiding or ethical person abruptly into a criminal. Rather, they tend to be cumulative and interactive, so that, combined and reinforced over an extended period, there can be a reduction of self-control in some people.

BANDURA'S MODEL OF ANXIETY AND REPRESSION

Bandura endeavored to fit together the signal function of anxiety, the accompanying feelings of helplessness, the causal status of anxious thoughts, and the resulting repressive-coping responses into a verifiable explanation.

Bandura's solution captures the clinical insight of Freud's description of the ego's helplessness and the empirical strength of behaviorism's focus on response consequences:

> ...A painful event has two arousal components to it—discomfort produced by the aversive stimulation and the thought-produced arousal. It is the thought component—the arousal generated by repetitive perturbing ideation—that accounts for much of human distress...people who judge themselves inefficacious dwell on their coping deficiencies and view trying situations as fraught with peril. They not only magnify the severity of possible threats but worry about perils that rarely, if ever, happen. As a result, they experience a high level of cognitively generated distress. Elevated arousal, in turn, heightens preoccupation with personal inefficacy and potential calamities. (Bandura, 1982, p. 137)

In Bandura's formulation, anxiety arousal and defensive behavior are co-effects rather than being causally related. The cause of defensive behavior, including repression, is not the emotional arousal of anxiety but the cause of the anxiety in the first place: expectation of injury or pain (Bandura, 1977b, p. 61).

Bandura (1969, pp. 426ff.) has reviewed research that shows autonomic nervous system arousal and defensive behavior are frequently unsynchronized or even disassociated. For example, Dollard and Miller's explanation of anxiety as resulting through "not thinking" the anxiety-arousing thought is based on the assumption that anxiety is an aversive stimulus with drive properties. Not thinking the thought associated with the anxiety stimulus is negatively reinforcing because it reduces the unpleasant drive state of anxiety.

A variety of research shows, however, that even when autonomic nervous system arousal is blocked chemically, defensive behavior can be triggered. In the same vein, when autonomic anxiety arousal is permitted to extinguish, defensive behavior persists (e.g., Black, 1958; see the review of much of this literature by Rescorla & Solomon, 1967).

Anxiety reduction and defensive behavior may occur together, but anxiety is not the sufficient cause of defensive behavior in the cognitive social paradigm. Rather, in Bandura's analysis, aversive events trigger avoidance behavior because they are signals of impending pain or injury; anxiety arousal is triggered simultaneously with this expectation through exposure to the threatening event. Nevertheless, it is the person's expectations of not being able to cope with the impending dangerous event that make both the event and any associated anxiety so distressing. The focus here is on the person's efficacy expectations—his or her thoughts about the meaning of anxiety stimuli and the self-evaluations of available coping skills:

> *Acquired threats activate defensive behavior because of their predictive rather than their aversive qualities.* They signal the likelihood of painful outcomes unless protective measures are taken. Defensive behavior, in turn, is maintained by its success in forestalling or reducing the occurrence of aversive events. Once established, defensive behavior is difficult to eliminate even when the hazard no longer exists. This is because consistent avoidance prevents the organism from learning that the real circumstances have changed. Hence, the failure of anticipated hazards to materialize reinforces the expectation that the defensive maneuvers forestalled them. This process of subjective confirmation is captured in the apocryphal case of a compulsive who, when asked by his therapist why he snapped his fingers ritualistically, replied that it kept ferocious lions away. When informed that obviously there were no lions in the vicinity to ward off, the compulsive replied, "See, it works!"(Bandura, 1977b, p. 62; italics added)

The defense of *repression*, in Bandura's theory, is therefore not an automatic response to anxiety. It is an avoidance response to the aversive thoughts that accompany the anxiety. Thoughts about potential failure or pain, the inability to cope with demands, and expectations that one will not meet challenges successfully can be inhibited by focusing on an incompatible thought or behavior (Bandura, 1969, p. 592).

Thus, in social cognitive theory, repression is conceptualized differently from the psychoanalytic version. Repressed ideas are not seen as having a life of their own in the unconscious; they are not held in check by an internal agency employing psychic energy; and repressed thoughts do not have independent drive properties that regulate and necessitate substitute forms of behavior to keep them perpetually restrained and out of awareness.

Rather, repressed thoughts are treated like any other behavior that lies inert until the appropriate stimulus activates it. If the person can arrange circumstances such that incompatible responses successfully compete with the inhibited ones, then those inhibited responses will not even reach the level of thought. If an anxiety-arousing thought or behavior cannot be inhibited by substitute thoughts and acts, it may emerge sufficiently strong in the person's awareness to create anxiety and conflict (Bandura, 1969, pp. 592–593).

In essence, social cognitive theory draws from the behavioristic, the cognitive, and psychodynamic formulations those elements supported by research and susceptible to laboratory testing. Anxiety is an emotional concomitant of aversive stimulation. However, the stimulation is aversive and defense-provoking because the person thinks about his or her capacities to master it. A low or inaccurate sense of self-efficacy is predictive of a person's response to threatening ideas and stimuli.

The response to repression, as in Dollard and Miller's formulation, is actually "not thinking" (or "not doing") those distressing thoughts, and/or substituting incompatible thoughts (and behaviors). The difference between Bandura's and Dollard and Miller's formulation is that Bandura does not conceptualize anxiety as a negative drive that impels the person to reduce the arousal. Instead, the person is impelled to avoid the feeling of helplessness implicit in his or her low self-efficacy expectations. It is not anxiety reduction itself that is reinforcing; it is the reduction of a sense of helplessness. Conversely, the more one can increase a person's sense of efficacy, the greater the reduction in his or her anxiety and fear (Bandura, 1982).

DOES CHANCE PLAY A ROLE IN LIFE?

In an interesting addition to the problems of synthesizing the many variables that regulate personality, Bandura (1986, p. 32) has devoted some attention to the effects of chance events on shaping a person's life. The idea is reminiscent of the existentialist's notion of destiny as circumstances that affect us but over which we have little control and even less foresight. Chance can provide an occasion for someone to enter a lifepath that he or she would not even have envisioned without the lucky accident. For example, the college student who has to meet a requirement in social science signs up for a sociology course but is placed in a psychology course when enrollments in sociology reach their ceilings. Because of the course, the student decides to become a psychology major. This opens the way toward an eventual choice of career in the counseling area.

Bandura's own life was marked by his response to chance occurrences. He recently wrote one of the authors of the present text, "The bio sketch describes the role of fortuity in my inauguration into psychology and choice of marital partner" (Bandura, 2001b).

As an undergraduate at the University of British Columbia, I commuted to the university with a group of pre-meds and a group of engineers, who tended to be very early risers. And so, I found myself filling a gap in an early schedule by taking a psychology course that was offered at that particular time. I became fascinated with the subject matter, particularly the clinical aspects. (Bandura, in Evans, 1988)

He met his wife while they both were playing golf. Again, we see that Bandura drew on aspects of his own life experience in developing his theories.

Bandura argues that fortuitous events are not foreseeable, but, once having occurred, personal factors, talents, and personal meanings then enter into the causal chain to shape behavior. Factors such as the prior skills of the person, whether the person likes or dislikes people, personal vulnerability and emotional state all influence the degree to which a chance event can influence a person's life (Bandura, 1986, p. 35). It is to the credit of social cognitive theory that even these unpredictable events, which can have a strong impact on personality, are recognized and considered objects of study.

BANDURA'S THEORIES AND TODAY'S WORLD

The development of mass media has been a major cultural development over the latter half of the twentieth century. One of the most important aspects of Bandura's theories is their ability to help us comprehend the important impact of the media on current behavior. Modeling of behaviors and observational learning can occur quite effectively through television and the movies. In fact, one could persuasively argue that the impact of the media is of the same order of magnitude as the effect of one's family and peers and their direct influences. In fact, one's family and peers are themselves also impacted by the media.

Bandura has stated,

I really became impressed with the growing power of the symbolic environment in shaping human thought, affect, and action. That we've had a 'communication revolution' in which television, combined with satellite transmission has greatly expanded the speed and scope of human influence, so that most of people's images of reality in which they base most of their actions are shaped by what they see and hear rather than by their direct experience. (Bandura, as told to Evans, 1988)

Major personality theorists of the past did not account for the burgeoning effects of the media. It is Bandura's social cognitive approach that best enables us to study these contemporary phenomena.

EVALUATING THE APPROACH OF BANDURA

Refutability

The model was based on differing degrees on empirical findings. It lends itself to testing, generates testable hypotheses, and has had its share of confirmations and disconfirmations.

Bandura's model is intimately tied to laboratory and field research; it is highly refutable, capable of generating new research ideas in many areas of life, and has been widely tested. Social cognitive theory is capable of being fine-tuned and adjusted as new data are collected. It should also be pointed out that Bandura's conception of vicarious reinforcement and observational learning give due weight to the sophistication of the human organism and the complexity of learning in real-life situations.

Human Agency

Bandura's model strongly emphasizes an active conception of human agency. Bandura (1989) put it this way:

> Social cognitive theory rejects the dichotomous conception of self as agent and self as object. Acting on the environment and acting on oneself entail shifting the perspective of the same agent rather than reifying different selves regulating each other or transforming the self from agent to object. In acting as agents over their environments, people draw on their knowledge and cognitive and behavioral skills to produce desired results. In acting as agents over themselves, people monitor their actions and enlist cognitive guides and self-incentives to produce desired personal changes. They are just as much agents influencing themselves as they are influencing their environment. (Bandura, 1989, p. 1181)

It is clear that Bandura rejects any simple split between object and subject or between passive and active. The person is seen as a whole entity or agent for whom previous learning history, expectations of mastery (efficacy), and current interpretation of the world all interact to regulate behavior. Bandura's conception of reciprocal determinism is a highly sophisticated active-reactive agency viewpoint.

Idiographic Versus Nomothetic

Again, we find that the most sophisticated approach lies with Bandura's model. Given its empirical basis, its vast research support, and its attention to the "rules" of self-control, the theory produces nomothetic (generalizable) principles. Yet, as we have seen, Bandura's principles of self-efficacy, self-monitoring or control, and his conception of triadic determinism clearly permit empirical statements about the individual. There is a genuine balance of the nomothetic and the idiographic in Bandura's model. He provides nomothetic or general principles that can be applied in individual cases.

SUMMARY

Bandura's approach is called the *social cognitive theory*. It emphasizes the findings of cognitive psychology and learning theory within the many contexts of daily life.

Beginning in the early 1960s, Albert Bandura and Richard Walters introduced the study of observational learning into psychology. Although Dollard and Miller had considered imitation learning as early as 1941, it was Bandura and his colleagues who drew out the implications of such learning, including:

- The internal cognitive processes of *attention, retention, reproduction*, and then *vicarious or direct reinforcement*. These have to exist for learning from a model's behavior to occur.

- The self-regulatory aspects of many behaviors, which demonstrate the person's capacity to reward and punish self for meeting or failing to meet self-standards.

- The significance of a person's efficacy expectations in regulating the process of learning and the application of self-reinforcement.

Bandura has argued cogently that even the most basic conception of reinforcement must be understood in cognitive terms. A person learns to expect, to anticipate, and to predict the consequences of his or her behavior; reinforcement does not act backward in time to stamp in a response already made. Thus reinforcement is more a matter of information and performance enhancement than it is automatic response strengthening.

Bandura developed a multicausal perspective called *reciprocal triadic determinism*, by which a person's behavior regulates and is regulated in turn by the environment, and the person's awareness of this interaction can also change the nature of the interaction. Psychopathology can be looked at through the lens of reciprocal determinism with a focus on the principles of direct and vicarious learning responsible for the acquisition of inappropriate and maladaptive behavior.

Bandura has added a welcome developmental dimension to his concept of *self-efficacy*, tracking the unique demands on personal mastery operating at the various phases of life from infancy to old age. From infancy through adolescence, successful mastery of living demands learning not only that one can be effective, but also that personal effectiveness often is linked with relationships to other people. By young adulthood, typical life demands include making vocational choices that will enhance one's sense of personal control and effectiveness and preparing for a stable intimate relationship with another to build a family. By the later years, a strong belief in personal efficacy enhances the quality of life so that the expected deterioration in cognitive and motor skills is not inevitable. The later years can also be a time of "wisdom," during which the older person passes along the wealth of experience and positive attitudes accumulated through a lifetime of efficacious living.

Our evaluation of these approaches led to the following conclusions:

- The social cognitive theory of Bandura is based on a great deal of empirical research. This theory is refutable, that is, it has led to numerous testable hypotheses.
- Psychodynamic social learning theory sees individuals as mostly reactive. Bandura's social cognitive theory embodies an active agent conception of the person.
- The ideas of Bandura are general concepts that can be applied in individual cases. Thus, they provide some balance between nomothetic and idiographic aspects.

FOR FURTHER READING

Albert Bandura's *Social Learning* (Englewood Cliffs, NJ: Prentice-Hall, 1977) is a concise statement of his formulation. His more recent *Social Foundations of Thought and Action: A Social Cognitive Theory* (Englewood Cliffs, NJ: Prentice-Hall, 1986) presents the empirical findings and theoretical framework for his concepts.

As part of his series of interviews with prominent psychologists, Richard Evans has contributed *Albert Bandura, the Man and His Ideas—A Dialogue* (New York: Praeger Press, 1989). An excellent biographical web site on Bandura can be found at http://www.emory.edu/EDUCATION/mfp/bandurabio.html

Bandura's latest restatement of a major portion of his theory refocused on self-efficacy as a near-universal mediating variable can be found in *Self-Efficacy: The Exercise of Control* (New York: Freeman, 1997). In this text, Bandura presents critical arguments against many other theoretical approaches. *In Self-Efficacy in Changing Societies* (New York: Cambridge University Press, 1995),

Bandura edited a companion volume of readings on self-efficacy that present a wide range of ideas and research. Chapter 3 of this book (pp. 69–113), "Developmental Analysis of Control Beliefs," by A. Flammer is particularly worthwhile reading for those interested in the parallels between object-relations theory and social cognition. Michael H. Kernis's (Ed.) *Efficacy, Agency, and Self-Esteem* (New York: Plenum, 1995) presents a broad spectrum of theoretical and research papers that extend the idea of personal competence into areas traditionally considered "self-esteem" variables.

A deep understanding of contemporary empirical work in social cognition and personality can be achieved by reading nearly any chapter in Susan T. Fiske and Shelly E. Taylor's second edition of *Social Cognition* (New York: McGraw-Hill, 1991).

Further suggested readings on Bandura and social cognitive theory may be found on the Wiley web site for Chapter 15 at www.wiley.com/college/sollod

GLOSSARY

Advantageous comparison: Choosing a sufficiently poor standard against which to compare one's own conduct, then much of the blame can be avoided.

Agentic: A term indicating a proactive rather than a reactive approach to life. Such an approach involves active problem solving, planning, action, and, at times, innovation.

Attribution of blame: Justifying mistreatment of another by saying that the person "deserved it" or

was "just asking for it;" this strategy is sometimes called "blaming the victim."

Dehumanization: Disengaging self-controls against mistreating people by finding ways not to see them as people; pejorative and stereotyping labels are one way to dehumanize another.

Diffusion of responsibility: The strategy of confusing or "losing" a precise locus of responsibility by resorting to the notion that no one in particular is accountable.

Displacement of responsibility: Hiding or distorting the relationship between a given action and its effects in order to disengage the usual self-regulatory controls; it weakens personal restraints, and lessens concern for the well-being of others.

Disregarding or distorting consequences: The strategy of dissociating the action and the outcome.

Efficacy expectations: A person's belief that given outcomes can be personally accomplished because one possesses the requisite skills.

Enactive attainments/performance accomplishments: The outcomes of a person's own efforts. A person's own efforts either succeed or fail, and the outcome can become an instructive guide to planning.

Euphemistic labeling: The idea that what something is called or labeled substantially affects the meaning we place upon it; convoluted verbiage is a wonderful mask for unethical conduct.

Judgments of excellence: Self-regulatory processes include judgments of the creativity, excellence, and goodness of one's own behavior.

Modeling: An efficient way of affecting behavior through demonstration; the steps in which a person learns through modeling are *attention, retention, symbolic reproduction* or *representation*, and finally receiving either *vicarious reinforcement* or *direct reinforcement*.

Moral justification: Providing what appears to be a moral explanation for conduct that would be seen by a person as reprehensible; a person may restructure the meaning of his or her behavior sufficiently to justify the conduct.

Observational learning: Learning by watching and imitating others engaging in behaviors. In Bandura's model, observational learning is mediated through perceptual and cognitive processes.

Outcome expectations: A person's estimate that particular outcomes will occur. They are usually based on the success or failure of similar efforts. Success is most likely to occur if the right situational and personal processes are brought to bear.

Selective activation of internal control: The processes by which a person is free to activate or deactivate self-control. They are: *moral justification, euphemistic labeling, advantageous comparison, displacement of responsibility, diffusion of responsibility, disregard or distortion of consequences, dehumanization,* and *attribution of blame.*

Self-efficacy: A person's expectancy that he or she will perform successfully in a given task or behavior, and meet the challenge competently.

Self-observation of behavioral quality: The awareness of qualities such as originality, authenticity, and ethicalness are applied as evaluative standards by the person to his or her own behavior to create incentives to act in a particular way.

Self-reaction processes: Rewards or punishments that an individual provides to his or her own behavior with feelings of competence or with feelings of self-devaluation.

Self-regulatory processes in the self-system: Processes in the self-system with the underlying themes of competence, mastery, and self-efficacy. These processes are *self-observation of behavioral quality, judgments of excellence,* and *self-reactions.*

Self-system: A complex of processes interdependent with the person's social and physical environment; the self-system is not a "little person" inside the person.

Social cognitive theory: Bandura's theory, in which cognitive processes and self-reflection are viewed as central to human behavior; people are seen as planning and predicting the consequences of their behaviors with an interpersonal context.

Social competence: The ability to have desired impacts interpersonally.

Triadic reciprocal determinism: An interactive triad that determines behavior; elements that interact are: (P) the person's awareness and thinking, (B) the person's ongoing behavior, and (E) the person's environment.

Vicarious reinforcement: A change in attitude and behavior that may ensue after a person watches another person being reinforced for engaging in a behavior; vicarious reinforcement is not actually direct reinforcement.

Chapter 16

Hans Eysenck

Hans Eysenck

Biologically Based Typology

Most people of course, whatever they may say, do not in fact want a scientific account of human nature and personality at all. . . . Hence they much prefer the great story-teller, S. Freud, or the brilliant myth-creator, C. G. Jung, to those who . . . study physiological details of the nervous system, and actually carry out experiments rather than rely on interesting anecdotes, sex-ridden case histories, and ingenious speculation.

Hans Eysenck, *Psychology Is About People*

. . . our belief is finally irrelevant. What matters—all that matters—is fact.

Hans Eysenck & D. K. B. Nias, *Astrology: Science or Superstition*

Hans Eysenck   Born: 1916 Berlin, Germany
                Died: 1997 London, England

About Eysenck's Biologically Based Typology

Hans Eysenck constructed a multileveled model of behavior that ranges from genetics to social psychology. Eysenck's work is broad and complete. His ideas include these major points:

- Central nervous system activity is the source of personality functioning.
- Research in learning, conditioning, perception, and drug effects shows that people can be reliably distinguished into introverts and extroverts. Introverts are considered stimulus shy, because they are acutely sensitive to incoming stimulation as if their brain arousal levels were chronically high. Extroverts are stimulus hungry because they seek and easily process intense stimulation as if their brain arousal levels were chronically low or inhibited.

- Introverts—with their high arousal levels—are prone to anxiety disorders. Extroverts—with their low arousal levels—are more likely to have dramatic, acting-out disorders such as hysterical disorder and antisocial personality disorder.

RESEARCH PSYCHOLOGIST AS SCIENTIST
AND A BIT OF A MAVERICK

When Hans Eysenck, a graduate of the University of London, obtained his first job during World War II as a research psychologist in the Mill Hill Emergency Hospital, he must have been professionally threatening to his immediate superiors. The hospital received mentally disturbed war casualties. Eysenck was not sure of the degree of reliability of the psychiatric diagnoses by which incoming airmen and soldiers were classified. If two or more physicians examined the same patient, would their diagnoses agree? Furthermore, if they did agree, would the prescribed treatments correspond? All a research psychologist had to do to find out was to collect information from a sample of cases and perform the necessary statistical calculations. Eysenck's account of what happened when he requested permission to carry out this piece of research reveals many of the personality traits that came to typify his approach to professional issues:

> [The Superintendent] received me in a fatherly fashion, and listened patiently to my plan. Then, to my surprise, he suggested that as there were so many more interesting things that I could be doing, it would be a pity to waste my time in this fashion. After all, did not everyone know that these psychiatrists had been well trained, had medical degrees, and could therefore (almost by definition) do no wrong? When I cheerfully suggested that even such supermen might welcome definitive proof of the reliability of their judgments he became more serious.... [H]e told me in no uncertain terms that I was at liberty to collect these data, but I was also at liberty to look for another job. This argument seemed a winner, and I acknowledged its superior force by withdrawing from the unequal contest. I did, to be sure, collect my data but kept rather quiet about it. (1972, pp. 357–358)

Eysenck's subsequent research did show that diagnostic conclusions had very little similarity from one psychiatrist to another—even when the second diagnostician already knew of the first diagnosis. Eysenck's suspicions about the lack of reliability of the diagnostic process were confirmed.

CHILDHOOD SOURCES OF EYSENCK'S
INTELLECTUAL INDEPENDENCE

In his autobiography, appropriately entitled *Rebel with a Cause,* Eysenck (1990) indicated that he was an angry, assertive person who collided early and frequently with established authority and with unexamined attitudes and beliefs, no matter how popular. He portrayed himself as a tough-minded intellectual with a tender heart. The finished autobiography also reveals that Eysenck had been a lonely child, largely ignored by his divorced parents (Eysenck, 1990).

Childhood: Neglectful Parents, Caring Grandmother

Eysenck was born during World War I in Berlin and grew up during Germany's period of defeat and ensuing economic crisis. His mother, Ruth Werner, had been born in the late 1800s in a small town in what is now Poland. Eysenck reports that his mother's ambition was not to become a physician like her father but rather to study law. Women, however, were largely excluded from a legal career at the turn of the century, so Ruth followed her mother's advice to pursue silent film acting. By age 15, she was already regarded as quite a beauty, and her success in an acting career seemed assured. She assumed the stage name of "Helga Molander" for screen roles in the silent films of the era.

The actress, Helga Molander, met actor Anton Eduard Eysenck during her first professional engagement. She was to be a rising starlet, and he was a star of stage and operettas (Eysenck, 1990, p. 153). They fell in love, married, and Hans was born shortly thereafter. They chose "Hans Jurgen" for their son's name because, in German, it "had the connotation of a simple, honest, none-too-bright youngster, reliable and trustworthy" (Eysenck, 1990, p. 10).

> ...that was roughly how I saw myself—a large good-natured dog, always ready to be friendly, but possibly dangerous when kicked in the teeth. I was to receive many such kicks in the course of my life—but then I suppose most people do. Rebels are particularly exposed to such extremities, of course, and a rebel I was to become, more through force of circumstances than predilection. (Eysenck, 1990, p. 10)

Although neither parent was especially religious, Eysenck's father, Anton Eysenck, had been raised in a Catholic family, whereas his mother's family was Protestant. Anton's unfaithfulness led to a quick divorce (Eysenck, 1990, p. 11). By the time Hans Jurgen was two, his parents' marriage was over (Eysenck, 1990, p. 153).

Relationship with Parents

Eysenck describes Anton Eysenck as an authoritarian man with racist views. During World War II, Anton Eysenck joined the Nazi Party, a fact that Hans recalls with bitter distaste. A successful actor for many years, Anton eventually switched professions from stage and film actor to stage entertainer, stand-up comic, political commentator, and master of ceremonies who traveled from one hotel, nightclub, or convention to another. He became very successful, and as one of the few such non-Jewish entertainers in Germany, members of the Nazi regime accepted and admired him. "My own hatred of the Nazis had led me by this time to leave Germany, and my father's hobnobbing with these people did nothing to increase my love for him" (Eysenck, 1990, p. 12).

In Eysenck's account of his childhood, he recalls both parents as neglectful and unconcerned with parenting. Neither parent had an interest in children and neither communicated warmly or effectively with Hans.

> Typical perhaps of my father's method of upbringing is the occasion when he bought me a bicycle, and promised to teach me how to ride it. He took me to the top of a hill, told me that I had to sit on the saddle and pump the pedals and make the wheels go round. He then went off to release some balloons and shoot them down with the rifle he still had from the war, leaving me to learn how to ride all by myself....A good training in independence, but perhaps not the behavior of a loving father. (Eysenck, 1990, p. 12)

Of his mother, Eysenck recalls:

> I don't think nature intended her to be a mother. I saw very little of her, except occasionally on holidays, and she never managed to treat me as a child, or show much interest in what I was doing. Conversation with her was always on strictly adult lines. (1990, p. 7)

Both parents found new spouses during Hans's childhood. His mother married an important figure in the movie industry, and his father married a considerably younger woman, who was also a stage entertainer.

Eysenck's Maternal Grandmother

Eysenck's warm, accepting, loving, and actively religious maternal grandmother largely raised him. He attributes to her his rescue from what might otherwise have been a lonely and unhappy childhood (1990, p. 14). During childhood, neither parent provided Hans's grandmother with money to support him. His maternal grandmother's poverty took its toll on Hans as well as on her. She eventually died in a Nazi concentration camp. In addition, Eysenck remembered that his parents were mean and stingy:

> If my parents were mean toward my grandmother, I felt they were equally mean toward me. I received very little pocket-money, and they seldom agreed to pay for what I considered reasonable expenses. (1990, p. 15)

He recalls how this stinginess prevented him from participating in tennis and swimming at a racquet club, where he could not pay the fees to use the facilities. In resilient and rebellious fashion, Hans found the silver lining in this cloud:

> However, all this meanness had one positive side-effect; I knew that all the girls I was friendly with loved me for myself! It couldn't have been the non-existing money that might have attracted them.... (1990, p. 15)

Eysenck characterized himself as unsatisfied with his family life, feeling unwanted and angry. In his seventies, he wrote, "I wish I had had brothers and sisters, and perhaps even a pair of loving parents; if I had, perhaps I would have been a nicer person!" (Eysenck, 1990, p. 278).

School Memories: Biting Hard and Holding on "Like a Bull Terrier"

When Eysenck was approximately eight years old, he encountered Herr Meier, the new music teacher in school. At the first class meeting, Herr Meier directed each student to sing aloud, whereupon the young Hans Jurgen informed his teacher that he could not sing a note, had no singing voice at all, and there was simply no point to it. Herr Meier insisted. Hans resisted. Meier shouted. Hans persisted in resistance. Meier responded aggressively:

> He ordered me to go up to the dais where he was sitting, grabbed my right hand with his left, and threatened to hit me with the ruler he had in his right hand. When he brought it down I drew back my hand, and he hit the table, which seemed to infuriate him even more. He again grabbed my hand, holding it very tight, and lifted the ruler, to hit my hand really hard.

> Without thinking I leaned forward and sank my teeth in the fleshy part of his hand, underneath his thumb. I have always been tall and strong, and I bit him very hard indeed.

BOX 16.1   *Only Connect...*

Karen Horney's concepts (Chapter 10) shed light on Hans Eysenck's personality development. Eysenck was raised in a neglectful family environment with an authoritarian father. Faced with basic anxieties that come from such an upbringing, in Horney's terms, he developed the neurotic trend of consistently *moving against* others. As a youth, he repudiated his pro-Nazi father by leaving Germany to try to enlist in the British Royal Air Force. His academic career was marked by his often brilliant, persistent, iconoclastic opposition to conventional wisdom, whether it was in the form of Freudian orthodoxy or in the popular position that cigarette smoking is damaging to health. Perhaps, if Eysenck had been brought up in a more loving family, he would not have become a highly original thinker.

> He dropped the ruler, blanched (I have never seen anybody's face go so white so quickly) and tried to withdraw his hand. I hung on like a bull terrier, and the class of course started erupting in a welter of shouts, screams and jumpings up and down. (Eysenck, 1990, p. 16)

Ultimately, it took the headmaster and several teachers to separate mouth from hand, or hand from mouth, depending on your viewpoint. In any event, as Eysenck recalls with relish, Herr Meier was gone from school for the next two weeks, and when he reappeared, he did not return to Hans's music class. Eysenck aptly points out the long-term, character-reflecting significance of the event:

> In many ways what I did then was prognostic of what I was to do later on, though in rather less physical fashion. You cannot let people get away with wrongdoing just because they are strong and powerful; whatever the cost, you have to stand up for yourself. (1990, p. 17)

In the episode with which we began this chapter, we noted another example of Eysenck's rebellious streak: Hans J. Eysenck, as a young experimental psychologist, doubted the psychiatric establishment at the Mill Hill Emergency Hospital, and conducted clandestine authority-defying studies of diagnostic reliability.

Eysenck's Rebellious, Iconoclastic Streak

Eysenck's autonomous mind and rebellious streak can be traced to his life history and his behavior before becoming a psychologist. As a boy and teenager, he was critical and skeptical about the tenets of Nazism. He was not swayed by the many methods the Nazis used to attract adherents. In spite of the fact that Nazi doctrines were widely held, Eysenck subjected one of them to a simple empirical test.

> On hearing that German Jews were supposed to have been cowardly during the First World War, the adolescent Eysenck promptly made his way to the public library, where he ascertained that Iron Crosses had in fact been awarded with greater relative frequency to Jewish than to non-Jewish soldiers.... [Later] Eysenck stood unmoved through a Hitler rally—only marveling at other's excitement and realizing that war with Britain and France must be inevitable. (Brand, 1997)

Eysenck's intellectual autonomy, rebellious streak, and personal courage were also evident when, as an 18-year-old son of a Nazi father in Hitler's Germany, he emigrated to Britain and then (unsuccessfully) attempted to join the British Royal Air Force (Brand, 1997; Eysenck, 1990).

Eysenck has frequently criticized what he considers to be nonempirical, less factual, and less scientific approaches to the study of personality. One of the chief targets of his criticism and, at times, scorn, has been Freudian psychoanalysis. He regarded psychoanalytic theory as, at worst, fictional, and at best, untestable (Eysenck, 1953a, 1957b, 1960, 1963b, 1965; Eysenck & Wilson, 1973; cf. Rachman, 1963, and Eysenck & Rachman, 1965).

Eysenck's intellectual battles often involved attacking whatever he perceived as unthinking fads or popular fallacies. Among his favorite targets, in addition to Freudian psychoanalysis, have been established psychiatry and clinical psychology, medical hierarchies, and traditional views of psychotherapy. He became a proponent of the importance of genetic and hereditary influences in personality throughout the 1960s, 1970s, and 1980s, when an emphasis on the primary importance of environmental factors prevailed in academic circles. He also criticized those who questioned the value or fairness of intelligence tests (1979). Among other targets were the prison system, the monarchy, the intellectual left, and radical feminism (Brand, 1997; Eysenck 1990). Eysenck took a fact-based, but nondebunking, attitude toward the ever-popular field of astrology (Eysenck & Nias, 1982), and encouraged an objective, empirically based approach to paranormal experiences, designed to please neither true believers nor doubters (Eysenck & Sargent, 1982).

He took the position that cigarette smoking was not proven to be a cause of lung cancer but only a correlate. He showed that both smoking and lung cancer were correlated with certain personality types, and speculated that personality type could well represent a genetic or hereditary cause of the development of such cancer (Eysenck, 1980). He was correct in his assertion that statistical analyses of the epidemiological data regarding smoking did not (and could not) strictly prove any cause. He stuck to this position, however, in spite of increasing evidence, including physiological findings, to the contrary over the years.

EARLY DESCRIPTIVE RESEARCHES:
INTROVERSION-EXTROVERSION AND NEUROTICISM

One of Eysenck's major areas of research, the description of personality types, began with his efforts to assess empirically prior typological models of personality.

Carl Jung had proposed a *typological model* of personality that included the concepts of introversion and extroversion. It will be helpful to refresh our memory of Jung's descriptions of these personality types (see also relevant sections of Chapter 5):

> The first [introvert] attitude is normally characterized by a hesitant, reflective, retiring nature that keeps to itself, shrinks from objects, is always slightly on the defensive and prefers to hide behind mistrustful scrutiny. The second [extrovert] is normally characterized by an outgoing, candid, and accommodating nature that adapts easily to a given situation, quickly forms attachments, and, setting aside any possible misgivings, will often venture forth with careless confidence into unknown situations. In the first case obviously the subject [i.e., the person himself], and in the second the object [i.e., external reality] is all-important. (1917, pp. 44–45)

It was thus Jung's opinion that extroverts focus on and are very responsive to external events and objects, and that they are very highly influenced by prevailing social opinion. **Introverts,** much to the contrary, give greatest weight to their own subjective reactions to external events; they devalue and deemphasize the significance of the objective world by focusing on their own emotions and personal reactions (Jung, 1921, p. 500). Consequently, those introverts who become neurotic are most likely to experience anxiety.

Extroverts, easily influenced by outside occurrences, are most likely to succumb to hysterical neuroses. In order to divest themselves of emotional pain they tend to repress unacceptable thoughts and to externalize or convert threatening impulses into objectified bodily symptoms. *Hysteric extroverts* often profit from the sympathy of others. The sympathy and concern of others is a positive reinforcer for the hysteric's impulsivity and demands for attention.

Partly Validating Jung's Typology

In an initial test of Jung's introversion/extroversion model (see Chapter 5), Eysenck and his colleagues selected a sample of 700 neurotically maladjusted patients at the Mill Hill Emergency Hospital for whom comprehensive case histories and clinical observational data were available. The psychiatrist in charge of each case prepared an item sheet on which the patient's familial and personal history, symptoms, diagnosis, treatment, and various social data were recorded. Eysenck selected 39 items from each of 700 such data sheets and factor-analyzed the results.

Factor analysis is a statistical method that looks at how individuals' scores on one measure correlate with their scores on other measures. Variables highly correlated with one another are highly related to a single factor. Factor analysis is therefore a method that reduces a large apparent number of original variables to fewer essential underlying variables or factors. In Eysenck's study, many correlations resulting from the data analysis yielded only two factors, each consisting of a number of traits.

Eysenck described one factor associated with a group of traits as "general **neuroticism.**" Specifically, the items in the psychiatrists' ratings that tended to be correlated on this factor included: badly organized personality, dependency, psychopathology before illness, narrow interests, dismissal from military service, parental psychopathology, unsatisfactory home, and poor muscular tone (Eysenck, 1947, p. 36).

Eysenck divided those scoring high in the general neuroticism factor into two groups. One group was neurotically maladjusted by virtue of possessing symptoms associated with high ratings on anxiety: obsessive tendencies, headache, tremor, and irritability, among others. The second group of individuals tended to have somewhat different symptoms characteristic of **hysterical disorder:** bodily symptoms with no organic basis, little energy, narrow interests, hypochondriasis, poor work history, and sexual difficulties.

In summary, Eysenck's analysis of the item sheet data thus demonstrated that a general factor or dimension of neuroticism versus normality could categorize psychologically disabled patients. Eysenck further subdivided the high neuroticism group into anxiety neurotics and hysterical neurotics.

Evidence for an Introversion-Extroversion Dimension

Starting from the premise that Jung's hypothesis of the two types of introversion and extroversion was correct, Eysenck surveyed the available experimental literature. He generally found support from a wide variety of sources that introversion was associated with anxiety, obsessive-compulsive symptoms, and reactive-depression neuroses. The extroverted personality type was associated with symptoms characteristic of hysterical neuroses (Eysenck, 1947, Chapters 2 and 7).

Eysenck found direct evidence in a sample of neurotic soldiers that a dimension of extroversion-introversion could distinguish between the two groups of neurotic illnesses. Eysenck (1947, p. 37n). coined a new term, **dysthymia,** for the first group of neurotic symptoms (anxiety, phobia, depression, and obsessive-compulsive disorders). Dysthymia corresponded to Jung's concept of **psychasthenia** and to his introvert personality type label. Eysenck retained Jung's label, *hysteric,* for the second group, and he found that hysterics tended to be extroverted in accordance with Jung's hypothesis. Eysenck concluded:

> . . . (neurotic) introverts show a tendency to develop anxiety and depression symptoms . . . they are characterized by obsessional tendencies, irritability, apathy . . . their feelings are easily hurt, they are self-conscious, nervous, given to feelings of inferiority, moody, day-dream easily, keep in the background on social occasions, and suffer from sleeplessness. . . . Withal, they are rather rigid, and show little interpersonal variability. (1947, pp. 246–247)

The 30 traits that cluster together into the pattern of the neurotic introvert, as stated here by Eysenck, are characteristic of his early descriptive research. More investigation into the causes underlying the clustering of traits for the neurotic introvert would eventually follow. At this stage of the research, however, Eysenck was limited to specification of descriptive traits. Thus, in contrast to the neurotic introvert, he found

... (neurotic) *extraverts*[1] show a tendency to develop hysterical conversion symptoms, and a hysterical attitude to their symptoms. Furthermore, they show little energy, narrow interests, have a bad work-history, and are hypochondriacal. According to their own statement, they are troubled by stammer or stutter, are accident prone, frequently off work through illness, disgruntled, and troubled by aches and pains.... They are not very rigid, and show great interpersonal variability. Their aesthetic preferences are towards the colorful, modern type of picture. They appreciate jokes, and are particularly fond of sex jokes. (Eysenck, 1947, p. 247)

Neurotic introverts and extroverts share some traits, but overall their patterns of responses to Eysenck's various tests and measurements are distinguishable. The pattern of measurements for neurotic introverts and neurotic extroverts resembles the hypothesized classes of dysthymic (anxiety) neuroticism and hysterical disorder.

HISTORICAL ANTECEDENTS OF INTROVERSION-EXTROVERSION DIMENSIONS

Eysenck went to great lengths to point out that Jung did not originate the concepts of introversion-extroversion, rather, these ideas had a 2,000-year history in philosophy, medicine, and psychology (1947, 1953a, 1967, 1970).

Two ancient Greek physicians, Hippocrates (about 460 to 377 B.C.) and Claudius Galen (about A.D. 130 to 200), devised a **temperament theory** of personality and human conduct. Galen systematized the previous notions of character types into a coherent typology. Galen related personality to four body fluids or humors: blood, black bile, yellow bile, and phlegm. He theorized that an excess of one of the four **humors** (bodily fluids) determined emotional temperament. A **sanguine temperament** (warmhearted, volatile, optimistic, easygoing) is seen to be caused by an excess of blood; a predominance of black bile results in a **melancholic temperament** (sad, depressed, anxious); yellow bile produces the **choleric temperament** (quick to action, angry, assertive); and, finally, when phlegm predominates, the resulting temperament is **phlegmatic** (slow to action, lethargic, calm) (cf. Allport, 1937; Eysenck, 1964, 1967, 1972; R. I. Watson, 1963, p. 80).

The German philosopher, Immanuel Kant (1724–1804), amplified the classical temperament theory by proposing separate trait descriptions for each of the four temperaments. For example, Kant described the sanguine personality as one who is carefree and full of hope, good natured and sociable, but capricious and given to pranks (Eysenck & S. B. G. Eysenck, 1969, p. 12.). Kant's labels indicated how various traits were associated together in a given type of temperament. Kant's was a categorical system with four categories. He did not consider the possible overlapping of types or different degrees of temperamental expression (Figure 16.1).

Most people, however, do not fall clearly into only one compartment. Personalities generally possess some unique combination of qualities from a broader spectrum of traits than merely four. Various nineteenth-century philosophers and psychologists thus sought to revamp temperament theory. They devised a series of scales that would represent each type as a continuum. This is the dimensional approach to personality classification (Figure 16.1).

Eysenck's own work on the introversion-extroversion and neuroticism-normality dimensions produced a comparable picture of human character types. Eysenck's two dimensions agreed quite closely with the dimensions introduced into classical

---

[1]Eysenck uses *extravert* rather than the more conventional spelling *extrovert*.

Figure 16.1 Dimensional and categorical personality classifications.

Adapted from Eysenck, 1953a, p. 17; 1967, p. 35.

temperament theory by the experimental psychologist, Wilhelm Wundt. However, Wundt based his views only on descriptions and did not validate them by any research. The explanation of different types of bodily fluids or humors causing the psychological types had no empirical basis. The tasks confronting Eysenck were to subject the concept of psychological types to empirical tests and then, if the theory was validated, to explain the results. To answer the question of why a particular personality's traits cluster together, or why an introvert differs from an extrovert would require looking beneath the readily observable aspects of personality for the sources of behavior.

Ideas that came from Pavlov's research with dogs provided the key to the explanation of personality types. In them, Eysenck discovered a possible physiological explanation for the classical temperaments. Moreover, it was not a confirmation of Galen's theory of four separate bodily fluids or humors, even though Pavlov came up with a similar typology, in which the magic number was four.

PAVLOV'S DOGS: EXCITATION-INHIBITION TEMPERAMENTS

At the start of the twentieth century, the Russian physiologist Ivan Petrovitch Pavlov (1849–1936) measured the secretion of digestive hormones in dogs in different conditions. Pavlov had the dog's salivary ducts surgically diverted so he could collect and measure the amount of saliva secreted. In addition, the upper portion of the digestive track was severed from the stomach and then rerouted to an external opening, or fistula. Food taken into the mouth, chewed and swallowed, never reached the stomachs of these dogs. Instead, it fell into a collection dish under the external opening.

Pavlov could then weigh the quantity of food that the dog had temporarily ingested. He discovered that, under such conditions, gastric secretions were still produced at a rate nearly half that of normal. Pavlov concluded that some unknown brain processes were responsible for triggering digestive activity, even in the absence of food in the stomach (Pavlov, 1927, 1928).

In order to investigate this phenomenon, Pavlov devised a standard experimental setup. Dogs were isolated from distracting visual and auditory stimuli by putting them into a sound-deadened chamber. The experimenter was able to present stimuli: a ticking metronome, flashing lights of controlled intensities, and bell or buzzer sounds. The experimenter could offer meat to the dog at any time.

The first experiments consisted of a number of steps. First, the experimenter presented an unfamiliar, or what was termed a "neutral," stimulus such as the sound of a buzzer (metronome or bell) to the dog. The dog's level of salivation was measured. In this initial condition, it was very low or nonexistent and did not increase with the presentation of the unlearned or unconditioned stimulus (the meat). In the next step, meat was given to the dog immediately after the neutral stimulus (the bell) was presented. The two stimuli (let's say, the sound and meat) were thus associated. The presentation of a sound came to signal the subsequent occurrence of the dog being "fed." You may recall that the food did not actually enter the dog's stomach, rather it dropped through a fistula into an outside container. During these times, the dog produced an increased level of saliva. After a suitable number of pairings of the sound and meat feedings, the experimenter began presenting the sound without providing any meat. Dogs again salivated, even though no food was given (Pavlov, 1927, Lectures II, III).

A daily life example of this type of conditioning would be a dog starting to salivate when its owner begins opening a dog food can or package. The sight of the owner taking a can or package out and beginning to open it has been paired many times with the dog's subsequent ingestion of food. People, too, will salivate when they see a can or package containing a tasty or even a not-so-tasty dish being opened.

Excitation and Inhibition Processes in the Cortex

To explain these findings, Pavlov theorized that the cortex of the brain is composed of two types of cells or neurons: those engaged in **excitatory processes** and those involved in **inhibitory processes.**

When the dog's sensory receptors detect incoming stimuli, the excitation of the nerves travels to the brain, where *excitatory* cortical cells begin firing in response. This cortical process would be evoked each time the same stimulus pattern is repeated, allowing the dog to show the benefit of its experience by being able to anticipate one stimulus from the presence of the other. In short, Pavlov theorized that excitatory cell firings are the basis of positive conditioned reflexes.

Pavlov also theorized the existence of *inhibitory* cortical cells. Inhibitory centers of the cortex would function to dampen or retard the activity of the excitatory cells. In some cases, inhibitory cells would even compete with excitatory processes.

Pavlov termed one kind of inhibition *external inhibition* (1927, p. 48). Being distracted or having attention diverted would be an example of such external inhibition. A dog conditioned to salivate at the sound of a buzzer ceases to salivate if a novel stimulus like a loud bang or an unfamiliar person is suddenly introduced. Pavlov theorized the unfamiliar distracting stimulus inhibited the conditioned reflex of salivation.

Pavlov also postulated a second type of inhibition—*internal inhibition.* This cortical process involves a slow or gradual development of a tendency to withhold the response (Pavlov, 1927, Lecture IV). For example, the continual presentation of the conditioned stimulus (the bell) without the unconditioned stimulus (the meat) ever again being presented leads to a gradual termination of the conditioned response (salivation). In more concrete terms, the experimenter continues to press the buzzer without ever following it with meat. The dog eventually ceases to salivate at the buzzer sound. The former conditioned response is now inhibited. This process is often considered as an instance of extinction of a conditioned reflex. Pavlov, however, explained it in a different way as stemming from learning a new inhibitory response (Pavlov, 1927, p. 48).

Differences in Excitation and Inhibition: A Typology

Pavlov developed a typology based on the dog's level of conditionability. He based this typology on his discovery that there was a correlation between a dog's temperament and its conditionability. Dogs that were most sociable and active proved to be the worst subjects when it came to developing conditioned reflexes. Strapped into a harness in an experimental chamber, such normally active dogs soon became drowsy and often even fell asleep. By contrast, dogs that were quiet outside the experimental situation were easily conditioned (1928, p. 306).

Pavlov initially thought that, in difficult-to-condition dogs, excitatory cortical processes predominated. Pavlov assumed that the excitatory cells of such dogs would be quickly exhausted. Inhibitory processes would then take over, causing drowsiness and sleep. For such a dog, the repetition of the same constant sequence of stimuli in conditioning rapidly depletes the easily aroused excitatory cells. Pavlov also found that such dogs were good conditioning subjects if the conditioning procedure was varied so that a constant succession of novel stimuli was available (Pavlov, 1927, pp. 287ff.).

The second type of nervous temperament is predominantly inhibitory in normal behavioral activities. Outwardly, this dog appears cowardly, cringing in corners and slinking along the floor as if afraid of everything and everyone. Even though this dog is easily conditioned with repetitive experimental stimuli, its positive conditioned reflexes are easily disrupted and extinguished. Only inhibitory reflexes (e.g., learning *not* to respond to one of a pair of stimuli that is not reinforced by meat) are stable and strongly established (Pavlov, 1927).

Between these two extremes of excitatory and inhibitory types, Pavlov found other dogs that were equilibrated or balanced in their degree of inhibition and excitation (1928, pp. 374ff.). This *balanced type* of dog is found in two distinct varieties. In the first type, the balance between excitation and inhibition is well established so that the dog conditions well in both positive and inhibitory reflexes. This first balanced type tends to *behaviorally* resemble the extreme excitatory dog in its lively, outgoing manner. In the second balanced type of nervous system, excitatory and inhibitory processes are in a tenuous or unstable balance. The balance can easily be disrupted at the slightest provocation or distraction (Pavlov, 1928, p. 375).

Based on his experimental results, Pavlov proposed four types of nervous systems, which turned out to be the same as the classical types of temperament.

Extreme Excitatory Type:	Choleric (poor conditionability)
Extreme Inhibitory Type:	Melancholic (good inhibitory conditionability)
Balanced (Excitatory) Type:	Sanguine (good conditionability)
Balanced (Inhibitory) Type:	Phlegmatic (good, but easily distracted)

Galen and Kant would have felt vindicated by this validation of their classifications. Pavlov also ended up with the number *four* to describe the types of temperament.

Experimental Neurosis: Breakdown of the Inhibition-Excitation Balance

One of the chief distinguishing features of Pavlov's nervous system types was the degree of susceptibility to experimentally induced neurotic behavior. Pavlov could induce such a neurosis, for example, with a conditioning procedure in which both excitatory and inhibitory cortical processes are made to alternate rapidly. They are then thought to "collide" in the dog's nervous system. Whatever the explanation, each of the extreme nervous types will then succumb to a different form of what might informally be termed a "nervous breakdown."

Using a mechanical vibrator applied to the dog's skin, Pavlov conditioned an extreme excitatory dog to salivate at 30 vibrations a minute. When the vibrator was set to oscillate at only 15 vibrations per minute, no food was presented. In this way, the dog learned to discriminate between 30 and 15 vibrations. It salivated to 30 vibrations, an excitatory response, and withheld salivation to 15 vibrations, an inhibitory response. When, however, Pavlov employed 15 and 30 vibrations in close succession, dogs of the *excitatory type* suffered an extreme disorganization of behavior. Their weak inhibitory processes completely failed to keep pace with the rapid alternation between 15 and 30 vibrations. Their stronger excitatory processes assumed dominance in this collision with inhibitory processes. The animal became uncontrollably excited, straining and struggling to escape the harness and bite the experimenter. In short order, the extreme excitatory type of dog showed every sign of an anxiety attack. The effect was long-lasting, often requiring months of treatment with tranquilizers to effect a cure.

The *inhibitory type* of dog succumbed to a different type of experimentally induced neurosis when exposed to the same alternation of excitatory and inhibitory stimuli. Inhibiting all response, these dogs became rigid and drowsy. Outside the conditioning chamber, they became withdrawn and easily frightened.

Dogs of the two central or balanced types did not succumb readily, if at all, to experimentally induced neuroses (Pavlov, 1928, p. 375). They could continue to respond to both excitatory and inhibitory stimuli.

Incompleteness of Pavlov's Model

Eysenck (1957a, pp. 111ff.) noted inadequacies in Pavlov's descriptions of the four nervous types. For example, Pavlov identified the extreme excitatory nervous type as a choleric personality. Presumably, in making this classification, Pavlov was focusing his attention on the dog's behavior in the conditioning situation, where the tedious experimental procedures made the animal drowsy and difficult to condition. However, the typical dog, when it is not confined or otherwise stressed, appears to be a sanguine type—outgoing, friendly, and emotionally expressive. Yet, in Pavlov's system, this dog would have been classified as a choleric type. Under appropriate conditions, furthermore, the choleric dog succumbs to anxiety that is more characteristic of the melancholic type.

So one might wonder, which type it really is. Is it to be labeled as a sanguine type of dog because it is normally outgoing and affable? Or is it fundamentally choleric because it becomes hard to handle in the conditioning situation? Or is it melancholic because it succumbs to anxiety neurosis?

Because of such incomplete explanations, Eysenck did not accept Pavlov's classification scheme without revision. Eysenck's first step in revising the Pavlovian model was to accept Pavlov's biological strategy: that differences in the four personality types have their source in inhibition-excitation processes of the nervous system. Eysenck applied this strategy to human temperaments in a much different way in his formulation of an **arousal theory.**

For Eysenck, the essence of melancholic and phlegmatic temperaments is their withdrawal from social and physical stimulation, as described by the ancients. Because both personality types have highly aroused cortical processes, the defining property of introversion in Eysenck's model, the melancholic and phlegmatic types, should form conditioned reflexes easily and strongly. In the phlegmatic type, high cortical excitation and sensitivity lead to withdrawal behaviors designed to escape overwhelming stimulation. Yet, the phlegmatic lacks the melancholic's high emotional reactivity, and thus remains free of neurotic anxiety and despair. Eysenck therefore classified both the melancholic and the phlegmatic as **stimulus shy** introverts but only the melancholic as neurotic.

At the other extreme, the essence of the choleric and sanguine personalities in Eysenck's view is their low cortical arousal level, which leads to responsivity and rapt attention to the social and physical environment. The sanguine personality is fundamentally outgoing, sociable, and emotionally tranquil. He or she delights in a constant succession of novel experiences. The choleric personality is also **stimulus hungry** and attentive to the social environment, but finds no delight in it. He or she is more emotional, more irritable, and more prone to become irascible. The choleric may even turn mean, taking delight in manipulating or hurting others.

Eysenck thus classified the choleric and sanguine personalities as extroverts but only the choleric as neurotic. He assumed that their cortical processes were far less sensitive, far less aroused, and considerably more inhibitory than those of introverts. Strong inhibitory processes cause the extrovert types to seek constant stimulation from the social environment to provide adequate stimulation. Because both personality types have strong inhibitory processes, the defining property of extroversion in Eysenck's scheme, the sanguine and choleric personalities should, in principle, form positive conditioned reflexes poorly or weakly.

Comparisons of Pavlov's and Eysenck's explanations of temperaments are displayed in Table 16.1.

Table 16.1   Pavlov's Types and Eysenck's Dimensions Contrasted

Classical temperaments	Pavlov's types	Eysenck's dimensions	Classical temperaments
Choleric	Extreme excitatory	Extreme emotional introvert	Melancholic
Melancholic	Extreme inhibitory		Choleric emotional extrovert
Sanguine	Balanced excitatory		Phlegmatic introvert
Phlegmatic	Balanced inhibitory	Stable extrovert	Sanguine

Note reversal of classical temperaments between Eysenck's and Pavlov's schemes.
Based on Pavlov, 1928, p. 377; Pavlov, 1927, p. 286; Eysenck, 1957a.

Eysenck was aware of limitations in Pavlov's work. He eventually found in Clark Hull's theory the relevant concept that not only are external conditions important but also that the level of the drive arousal state must be taken into consideration.

HULL'S DRIVE THEORY:
INDIVIDUAL DIFFERENCES IN PERFORMANCE

Clark L. Hull (1884–1952) developed a **drive theory** of learning and performance that incorporated basic concepts similar to excitation and inhibition. The advantage of Hull's formulation over Eysenck's point of view was its precision in describing the interaction of inhibition and excitation.

Hull's theory (1943, 1951, 1952) was formulated to account for a different kind of conditioning from that of Pavlov's work with dogs. Instead of involuntary reflex conditioning, Hull was more concerned with instrumental (respondent) conditioning, which deals with voluntary behavior.

The basic premise underlying Hull's formulation was that reinforcers are stimuli that reduce or satisfy an organism's biological drives. For instrumental learning to occur, an organism must first be in a state of high drive arousal, for example, very hungry. Then, those responses that the organism uses to obtain satisfaction for the drive will become associated with the stimuli connected with satisfaction of the drive. For example, if a hungry rat discovers through trial and error that turning right at a certain point in a maze brings it into contact with food, then a right turn at that point will become habitual whenever it is hungry in that maze.

To indicate the learned connection between the stimuli of the maze's choice points and the response of turning right, Hull employed a "habit" symbol: $_sH_R$. If the rat is not in a state of drive arousal (i.e., not hungry) when placed in the maze, then its habit of turning right at a particular choice point will have a low probability of being translated into actual behavior. As the hunger drive begins to mount in intensity, it will activate the previously reinforced habit of turning right at the appropriate choice point. Hull indicated this relationship between drive and habits with the following formula:

$$D \times {}_sH_R = {}_sE_R$$

In words, this formula states that observable performance ($_sE_R$), is evoked when the strength of the drive (D) is multiplied by the strength of previously learned stimulus-response connections or habits ($_sH_R$). To be accurate, this formula should be modified to take account of any additional variables that might add to or subtract from the organism's drive arousal and past habit strengths. Hull suggested two additional and competing variables: reactive inhibition (I_R) and conditioned inhibition ($_sI_R$).

Reactive and Conditioned Inhibition

Reactive inhibition (I_R) in Hull's formulation is similar to Pavlov's concept of internal inhibition. In Hull's theory, reactive inhibition is neural fatigue that develops when responses are repeated. As I_R, a negative drive state, continues to increase, it cancels the positive drive to respond. The organism suffers a general feeling of fatigue and discomfort associated with continued responding. When it finally stops responding the fatigue of this reactive inhibition state is allowed to dissipate. Dissipation of I_R is experienced as satisfying or rewarding.

But note what is now being reinforced: the act of not responding. Thus there develops a conditioned negative habit, a tendency to not respond. This second kind of inhibition is a learned inhibitory response reinforced by the reduction in I_R that rest produces. Hull referred to this kind of inhibition as learned or **conditioned inhibition** ($_SI_R$). Both of these two kinds of inhibition, internal inhibition and reactive inhibition, are subtracted from a drive's activation to obtain a net result.

Eysenck's Formulation of Drive, Habit, and Inhibition

Eysenck eventually adopted the general Hullian notion that drive multiplies habits and that inhibition reduces the effects of positive drive. Eysenck discussed the relation of performance, drive, habit, and inhibition in the activity of a person playing tennis.

> Clearly, the excellence of his [tennis] performance will depend upon two things. It will depend, in the first place, on his drive. . . . It also depends, of course, on his experience and on the amount of practice that he has previously put into the task, on the length of time he has been playing, and so on. In other words, it will depend on the system of bodily habits which he has built up during the past [$_SH_R$]. . . . His actual performance will be a function of both these variables; the stronger the drive, and the more highly developed the habits which are necessary for carrying out his task, the better his performance will be. Where does inhibition fit into this picture?
>
> The answer of course is this. If a person is carrying out a task, particularly under conditions of massed practice, then inhibition will continue to accumulate. Being a negative drive, it will subtract from the positive drive under which the organism is working. And, finally, when inhibition builds up to such an extent that it is equal to positive drive under which the person is working, he will simply cease to work altogether because now drive is equal to inhibition, and drive minus inhibition equals zero. . . . [A]nything multiplied by zero—is, of course, zero and, therefore, performance will cease. (1964a, p. 73)

The logical deduction to be made from this conceptualization of the effects of inhibition on drive is that continued performance leads ultimately to a cessation of activity. Such a cessation may be only momentary, but if the prediction is correct, the performer will experience a fleeting block to further action. A good deal of experimental evidence has verified that such blocks to performance actually do occur.

INDIVIDUAL DIFFERENCES AND EYSENCK'S TYPOLOGY

Eysenck formulated two personality postulates that would lead to a coherent, yet still tentative, experimental model of why introverts differ from extroverts. To span the distance between the theory of excitation-inhibition and personality types, Eysenck proposed the **postulate of individual differences:**

> *Human beings* differ with respect to the speed with which excitation and inhibition are produced, the strength of the excitation and inhibition produced, and the speed with which inhibition is dissipated. These differences are properties of the physical structures involved in making stimulus-response connections. (1957a, p. 114, italics added)

In this statement, Eysenck was proposing that personality psychologists and experimental psychologists join forces in investigating a variable that had often been interpreted as having interest only for the experimentalist. Excitation and inhibition were now to be conceptualized as fundamental to any understanding of personality differences.

To extend the logic of his position, Eysenck also proposed a relatively precise specification of these personality differences in relation to excitation and inhibition processes, his **typological postulate:**

Individuals in whom excitatory potential is generated slowly and in whom excitatory potentials so generated are relatively weak, are thereby predisposed to develop extraverted patterns of behavior and to develop hysterical-psychopathic disorders in case of neurotic breakdown; individuals in whom excitatory potential is generated quickly and in whom excitatory potentials so generated are strong, are thereby predisposed to develop introverted patterns of behavior and to develop dysthymic disorders [anxiety, phobias, obsessive-compulsive symptoms] in case of neurotic breakdown. Similarly, individuals in whom reactive inhibition is developed quickly, in whom strong reactive inhibitions are generated, and in whom reactive inhibition is dissipated slowly, are thereby predisposed to develop hysterical-psychopathic disorders in case of neurotic breakdown; conversely, individuals in whom reactive inhibition is developed slowly, in whom weak reactive inhibitions are generated, and in whom reactive inhibition is dissipated quickly, are thereby predisposed to develop introverted patterns of behavior and to develop dysthymic disorders in case of neurotic breakdown. (1957a, p. 114)

With the typological postulate, Eysenck laid the groundwork for a model of personality based on empirical evidence as well as a concept of underlying physiological processes. Introverts were conceptualized as having stronger and more easily aroused excitatory processes, coupled with their rapid dissipation of inhibition. Extroverts, on the other hand, were conceptualized as having relatively weak excitatory processes and slow dissipation of inhibition. Taking only the extreme extrovert and the extreme introvert as models, the typological postulate can be summarized in the form of a table. When reading Table 16.2, it must be remembered that Eysenck's typology is dimensional, allowing for degrees of expression of inhibition and excitation, whereas the summary in Table 16.2 is essentially categorical.

Based on the typological postulate, a number of hypotheses can be deduced about introverts' and extroverts' performance in laboratory situations. For example, if introverts have stronger excitatory cortical processes and relatively weak inhibitory effects, they should condition more quickly than extroverts in laboratory tasks like eye-blink conditioning. Other deductions can be made along these same lines. For any task that requires strong excitatory processes and the rapid dissipation of inhibition, introverts should evidence superior performance.

Eysenck's Modifications of Pavlov's Typology

Pavlov had developed a typology that connected observable behavioral traits to underlying nervous system processes of inhibition and excitation. He then further attempted to coordinate classical temperament theory with his results.

Eysenck began with Pavlov's findings but revised his classification system. He agreed with Pavlov that observable differences between personality types are based on the inhibition-excitation processes of the nervous system. And he also revised Pavlov's theory. He developed a typology based on the level of cortical arousal and the level of

Table 16.2   Summary of Typological Postulate as Extreme Types

	Excitation	*Inhibition*	*Neurotic predisposition*
Introverts	High (rapid)	Low (slow)	Dysthymia
Extroverts	Low (slow)	High (rapid)	Hysteria-psychopathy

Based on Eysenck, 1957a.

emotional reactivity. Those with high levels of cortical arousal withdrew from external stimuli and were considered introverts. Those with low levels of cortical arousal were stimulus hungry; they sought out external stimulation. In addition, individuals could be rated as to their level of emotional reactivity.

In the melancholic type, he theorized that extreme cortical arousal is coupled with high emotional reactivity. The melancholic person thus feels intellectually and emotionally overwhelmed by even mild social and physical stimulation. He or she thus tends to retreat from his or her surroundings.

In the phlegmatic personality, this same high cortical excitation and sensitivity leads to withdrawal in the form of an apathetic attitude. The phlegmatic person lacks the melancholic's high level of emotional reactivity, and thus remains free of neurotic anxiety and despair.

Eysenck classified both types as introverts but only the melancholic as neurotic. Because both the phlegmatic and melancholic personality types have highly aroused cortical processes, the defining property of introversion in Eysenck's scheme, they should be readily conditionable.

The choleric and sanguine personalities in Eysenck's view have low levels of cortical arousal. They are both characterized by their responsivity and rapt attention to the social and physical environment. The sanguine type of person has low emotional reactivity. He or she is emotionally tranquil. The choleric personality has high emotional reactivity. He or she is thus more emotional, more irritable, and more prone to become irritated and angry.

In Eysenck's theory, the strong inhibitory processes of both the extroverted types leads them to seek constant stimulation from the social environment in order to provide cortical stimulation. Both the sanguine and choleric personalities should thus be difficult to condition. Similarities and differences between Pavlov and Eysenck's explanations of temperaments are summarized in Table 16.1.

AROUSABILITY AND THE ASCENDING RETICULAR ACTIVATION SYSTEM (ARAS)

The clear implication of Eysenck's proposal that individuals differ in their excitation-inhibition balance is that this difference is mediated by something in the **central nervous system.** In 1967, Eysenck revised and extended his basic introversion-extroversion theory by postulating specific relationships between these personality dimensions and the **ascending reticular activating system (ARAS)** of the brain. He also rooted the dimension of normality-neuroticism in central nervous system structures. Eysenck's theory was based on earlier research. Three decades earlier, James Papez (1937) had already specified a group of subcortical structures, including the hypothalamus, the gyrus cinguli, the hippocampus, and their interconnections, as related to emotional arousal. He reviewed evidence that these structures are responsible for changes in heart rate, respiration, blood pressure, and other signs of emotional activation. Together, these structures are called the visceral brain or **limbic system.**

The relationships that Eysenck proposed can be summarized succinctly in two verbal equations:

Introversion − Extroversion = Difference in ARAS Arousal

Normality − Neuroticism = Differences in Visceral Brain Activation

ARAS and Cortical Arousal

The ARAS is a network of fibers extending from the spinal cord to the thalamus of the brain at a level below the cortex. Figure 16.2 illustrates the basic location and boundaries of the ARAS. Figure 16.2 also shows the general location of the visceral brain (VB) structures. The ascending arrows indicate the direction of influence of the ARAS on the cortex. Descending arrows, from the cortex toward the ARAS, indicate the reciprocal influence of the cortex on the ARAS. Generally, the ARAS serves to stimulate the cortex, to activate its cells to a state of excitability. The cortex may in turn provide feedback to the ARAS either to further increase its excitatory input or to dampen its activity.

Physiological interest in this arousal network or reticulum of fibers began in the 1930s when it was discovered that cutting through the brain stem at midbrain level caused cats to become almost permanently sleeping animals. The electrical activity of such cats' brains showed a characteristic sleeping wave on the **electroencephalograph (EEG).** In a normally sleeping cat, it is possible to induce an arousal EEG pattern by simply waking the animal or doing something to engage its attention. But in cats with transected brain stems it was possible to produce an arousal EEG pattern only for short periods lasting as long as the stimulus used to arouse the cat.

In 1949, Giuseppe Moruzzi and Horace W. Magoun, instead of shutting down the ARAS by cutting into the brain stem, set out to stimulate it electrically. EEG tracings from the cortex of stimulated cats showed that stimulation of the ARAS evokes cortical arousal. The ARAS seems also to be involved in states of attention and concentration. Joaquin M. Fuster (1958) was able to improve rhesus monkeys' performance on a visual discrimination task by stimulating their ARAS. Results of further studies indicated that the ARAS is responsible for cortical efficiency in learning, conditioning, wakefulness, and attention. The ARAS appears to mediate states of arousal, ranging from sleep to extreme behavioral excitation.

Another portion of the ARAS, however, seems to have an inhibitory effect on the cortex. Known as the recruiting system, this portion of the ARAS serves to damp down

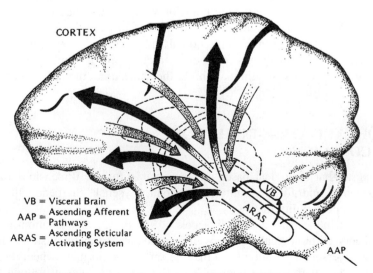

Figure 16.2 Anatomical locations of ARAS and VB.

Source: Eysenck, 1967, p. 231.

cortical excitation. Eysenck seems to have found the physiological causes of excitation and inhibition and, therefore, the basis of introversion-extroversion in the ARAS. He hypothesized that introverts are assumed to have higher levels of ARAS arousal (lower ARAS thresholds) than extroverts.

Visceral Brain and Emotional Activation

The second major personality dimension in Eysenck's theory is the dimension of normality-neuroticism. Eysenck assumes that this dimension consists largely of differences in emotional activation such that neurotics are more highly emotionally reactive than normal. The structures of the limbic system or visceral brain (VB) are conceptualized as the mediators of this reactivity. The hypothalamus and other parts of the VB impact the autonomic or involuntary nervous system, which in turn affects a wide range of end organs and functions. Glands, muscles, heart rate, respiration, and perspiration are among the many areas controlled, at least in part, by the **autonomic nervous system.** Individuals in whom the VB is most easily activated are thought to be most susceptible to neurotic disorder.

There is a complicating factor connected with the VB and neuroticism. In states of extreme emotional activation (e.g., intense rage, or profound sadness, or extreme fear), the normal independence of functioning between the ARAS's arousal of the cortex and the VB's emotional activation of the autonomic nervous system breaks down. (Eysenck, 1967, p. 232). Thus, although it is possible to be intellectually aroused without emotional activation, it is impossible to be emotionally activated without simultaneous intellectual or cortical arousal.

In the first case, that of cortical arousal without VB (emotional) activation, problem-solving activity dominates the individual. For example, Eysenck cites the case of a scientist who was sitting quite immobile and apparently fast asleep. But subjectively, his mind is hard at work tackling unsolved and intricate professional problems (Eysenck, 1967, p. 232). His cortex is aroused, but his emotions are not.

In cases where the level of emotional activation is intense, cortical arousal must also have occurred. Thus, in Eysenck's dimensional system, the separation of intellectual arousal from emotional activation holds only for normal individuals (Eysenck, 1967, p. 233; 1982; Eysenck & M. Eysenck, 1985). In more technical terms, the neurotic individual is reaching maximum cortical and emotional arousal nearly simultaneously because the hypothalamus and other structures in the limbic system (VB) are bombarding the ARAS with stimulation. At the same time, the ARAS is arousing the cortex.

TRANSLATION OF EXCITATION-INHIBITION INTO AROUSAL CONCEPTS

With his proposal that biological bases are responsible for the dimensions of introversion-extroversion and for normality-neuroticism, Eysenck sharpened the causal explanation in his personality theory.

To make clear the transition from Eysenck's 1957 theory of excitation-inhibition to his 1967 theory of biological functions, it is necessary to distinguish among four extreme types of personality. Individuals may be said to be normal or neurotic, introverted or extroverted, with various degrees between these absolutes. It follows that an individual may be a normal introvert or a neurotic introvert, just as he or she may be a normal extrovert or a neurotic extrovert. The hypothetical nervous system states

Table 16.3 Biological Basis of Personality

Dimensional position	Level of ARAS arousal	Level of VB activation
Normal introvert	High	Low
Normal extrovert	Low	Low
Neurotic introvert (dysthymic)	High	High
Neurotic extrovert (hysteric)	Low[a]	High

[a]Note that the neurotic extrovert's ARAS arousal is higher than the normal extrovert's ARAS arousal because of the breakdown of separation between ARAS and VB functioning in states of high (neurotic) emotion. But the extrovert's characteristic ARAS arousal level is always lower than the introvert's level and is, therefore, simply listed as "low." Based on Eysenck, 1967.

of ARAS arousal and VB activation that correspond to these four extreme types are indicated in Table 16.3.

The emphasis in this version of Eysenck's theory is on differences in arousal level (excitation) rather than on inhibition-level differences. Experimental tests of the biological (1967) theory usually spring from hypotheses specifically about the effects of the introvert's higher cortical ARAS arousal. With this shift in theoretical emphasis came several complications. The one of immediate interest in the present context concerns a general law of motivation proposed in 1908 by Yerkes and Dodson.

The Yerkes-Dodson Law: Inverted-U Hypothesis

Robert M. Yerkes and John D. Dodson proposed a principle of motivation and performance that, with few modifications, has been widely accepted. In briefest form, *Yerkes and Dodson's law* states that motivation, or arousal, may be conceptualized as a continuum ranging from very low levels through very high levels of excitation. At the low end of the continuum, the organism is so under-aroused that it actually falls asleep. At the high end, the organism is so aroused that its behavior is disorganized, fragmented, or frenzied. Yerkes and Dodson (1908) proposed that the optimal state of arousal lies between these two extremes. In this moderate level of arousal, the individual is sufficiently motivated to perform well, but not so aroused as to be disorganized or distracted. Subsequent theorists (e.g., Broadhurst, 1959; Hebb, 1955; Lindsley, 1951; Malmo, 1959) referred to this hypothesis as the "inverted-U hypothesis." The inverted, or upside-down, U can be seen in Figure 16.3.

Figure 16.3 shows the relationship between arousal level and quality of performance. As arousal increases, performance improves until it reaches a maximum at the height of the inverted-U curve. From that point onward, increases in arousal lead to decreases in performance.

What would happen when the task that the individual is performing varies in difficulty or complexity? Will tasks of different difficulty levels require different levels of optimal arousal? The answer is a definite "Yes." If we confine our consideration of task difficulty to three levels—low, medium, and high difficulty—then we can plot motivation-performance curves for each task level. Figure 16.4 illustrates the theoretical relationships among task-difficulty, performance, and arousal levels.

The three curves in Figure 16.4 are designed to indicate that the optimal level of arousal for best performance changes as task-difficulty level increases. For tasks of low difficulty, a somewhat higher level of arousal or motivation for tasks of moderate

AROUSAL LEVEL
Performance is optimal at moderate levels of arousal.

Figure 16.3 Inverted-U law of motivation and performance.

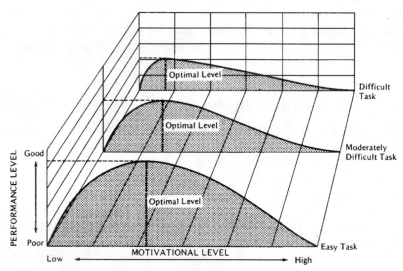

Figure 16.4 Yerkes-Dodson law for interaction of arousal level, performance, and task difficulty. As task difficulty increases, optimal level of arousal for best performance decreases.

Source: Eysenck, 1963a, p. 131.

difficulty is optimal. Tasks of greatest difficulty require the lowest level of arousal. The general rule is: *The more difficult the task, the lower the level of optimal arousal.*

Thus, with the Yerkes-Dodson law in mind, predictions from Eysenck's biological model of personality not only can be more precise, but also can take account of the interaction between cortical arousal and emotional activation.

We are now in a position to pose an interesting question. The four extreme types of individuals (normal and neurotic introverts, and normal and neurotic extroverts) should, in principle, possess differing levels of combined cortical and emotional arousal. Presumably, neurotic introverts, in whom ARAS and VB excitation are both chronically high, should be placed at the top rank of a hierarchy of arousal. Normal extroverts, having low ARAS arousal and low VB activation, should fall at the bottom of the hierarchy of arousal. In between these extremes, normal introverts and neurotic extroverts, each having one form of high arousal, should evidence moderate degrees of excitation. The theory, however, does not specify whether the normal introvert is more highly aroused than the neurotic extrovert.

One might predict that a very neurotic extrovert would surpass a normal introvert in absolute drive level because the neurotic extrovert's emotional reactivity acts as a multiplier of habits in Hull's sense of the term. Thus, our final hypothetical hierarchy of differential combined arousal for the personality types looks like this:

> Neurotic introvert   [*highest arousal*]
> Neurotic extrovert
> Normal introvert
> Normal extrovert   [*lowest arousal*]

But only an empirical investigation can provide actual rankings for these personality types (cf. Eysenck, 1953b, pp. 436ff., and 1967, pp. 182ff.). To illustrate this kind of experimental test of the theory, McLaughlin and Eysenck (1967) had the four different types of criterion personalities learn lists of paired nonsense syllables. One list was difficult to learn, and the other relatively easy. Results were tabulated by the number of errors a subject made in reaching a specified criterion of learning. In addition to determining the optimum level of arousal for learning, the experiment was also designed to test a hypothesis about a phenomenon called reminiscence.

Experimental psychologists had known for a long time that memory for a learned response improves if time intervenes between the acquisition of the response and its performance. Thus, when studying for an exam in psychology, recitation of what has been learned will be better the following day when compared to immediate recitation. During the period of rest, the memory is consolidated or made more permanent. However, while the process of consolidation is in progress, performance of the learned response is impeded.

Eysenck hypothesized that the process of consolidation is most facilitated in individuals having high initial cortical arousal, that is, in introverts. Thus introverts should show poorest performance on memory tasks that require immediate performance, whereas extroverts, who have low arousal and poor consolidation, will perform best immediately after acquisition (cf. McLaughlin & Eysenck, 1967, pp. 574ff.). In the experiment conducted by McLaughlin and Eysenck (1967), tests of memory for the learned lists were performed immediately after acquisition, and thus favored extroverts. But, as we already know, the Yerkes-Dodson law also governs performance on tasks of varying difficulty. It can thus be presumed that the difficult list of paired nonsense syllables would present a task requiring a moderately low level of arousal for optimal performance. Thus, taking the two effects together, the reminiscence evidence indicates that extroverts should perform better with immediate recall, whereas the Yerkes-Dodson law suggests that on the difficult list the low-arousal normal extroverts will show superior performance to neurotic extroverts, and to all highly aroused introvert personalities.

Conversely, learning the easy list should require a higher level of arousal than learning the difficult list to produce optimal performance. The prediction for the easy list thus must be that neurotic extroverts will evidence best performance because they have slightly higher arousal than normal extroverts. Neurotic introverts, having the highest level of combined ARAS and VB arousal, should, in principle, be too highly aroused to perform well on either list under conditions of immediate recall.

Figures 16.5 and 16.6 show the outcome of McLaughlin and Eysenck's investigation. The major predictions about the superiority of extroverts' performance were confirmed. Moreover, when a line is drawn through the plotted error scores for all subjects, the resulting curves resemble the inverted-U motivation-performance curve. As expected, the optimal level of arousal is shifted to the lcft (i.e., toward lower optimal arousal) for the difficult list.

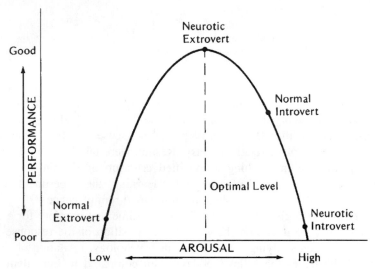

Figure 16.5 Easy list.

Based on McLaughlin & Eysenck, 1967, p. 131.

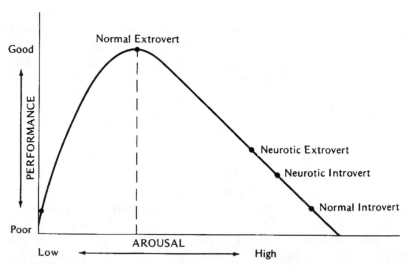

Relationship of error scores and arousal level for easy and difficult lists.

Figure 16.6 Difficult list.

Based on McLaughlin & Eysenck, 1967, p. 131.

A DIRECT TEST OF THE AROUSAL THEORY:
STIMULANT AND DEPRESSANT DRUGS

If ARAS bombardment of the cortex is really the basis of the introversion-extroversion dimension of personality, then stimulant and depressant drugs should produce behavioral effects similar to those produced by excitation and inhibition. Furthermore, stimulants and depressants were hypothesized to produce different effects in introverts and extroverts. "In general, the prediction would be that stimulant drugs lead to greater arousal and hence to more introverted behavior, while depressant drugs lead to greater inhibition and hence to more extroverted behavior" (Eysenck, 1967, p. 265).

The preexisting state of arousal in a particular experimental subject would have to be taken into account to allow for the fact that introverts begin any task with a higher arousal level than extroverts. Therefore, the general hypothesis can be refined: Introverts require less of a stimulant drug to reach a specified criterion of behavioral arousal than do extroverts. In a similar vein, it can be hypothesized that introverts require a larger dose of a depressant drug to reach a specified criterion of inhibition than do extroverts (Eysenck & M. Eysenck, 1985, p. 229).

Many research studies support these predictions (e.g., Claridge, 1967; Laverty, 1958; Shagass & Kerenyi, 1958). Such studies generally use a measurement of sedation threshold. A particular drug, for instance, a depressant, is injected intravenously at a known rate until slurred speech and specific EEG changes are noted. The amount of the drug required to reach this criterion is a measure of sedation threshold (Shagass & Kerenyi, 1958). Shagass and Kerenyi showed that subjects classified as introverts by psychiatric diagnosis and by paper-and-pencil measures had higher sedation thresholds (i.e., required a larger dosage) than extrovert subjects, thus confirming Eysenck's theory. Furthermore, subjects classified as obsessional (belonging to the dysthymic group in Eysenck's terminology) also had higher sedation thresholds than subjects classified as hysterics (see also Gupta, 1973).

ACQUISITION OF NEUROSIS: THE SOCIALIZATION
OF INTROVERTS AND EXTROVERTS

Dysthymic neurotic symptoms, such as phobias, obsessions and compulsions, and intense anxiety attacks are interpreted by Eysenck (1960, 1976) as conditioned maladaptive responses acquired by neurotic introverts in coping with the demands of life. Dysthymic disorders fundamentally are learned fears. The introvert who becomes dysthymic does so precisely because his or her high cortical and high emotional arousal facilitates rapid and strong anxiety conditioning.

Some research has suggested that scores on neuroticism and extroversion/introversion are not totally uncorrelated or statistically orthogonal (Claridge, 1967; Eysenck & S. B. G. Eysenck, 1969). Introversion is more closely related to neuroticism than

---

BOX 16.2   *Only Connect...*

The relation between cortical arousal and inhibition of behavior is applied in the current use and likely overuse of the stimulant Ritalin, for hyperactivity in youngsters (see Chapter 17). This medication has the superficially paradoxical effect of leading to some degree of inhibition of the behavior of these children. By causing a lower threshold for cortical arousal, it promotes withdrawal from stimuli and inhibits responsivity.

is extroversion. Eysenck has argued that this partial breakdown in orthogonality was a consequence of the early Maudsley Personality Inventory's overinclusion of certain biased items. To overcome the difficulty, a revision, the Eysenck Personality Inventory (Eysenck & S. B. G. Eysenck, 1968), was devised. Analysis of results with this instrument confirmed the statistical independence of the two dimensions.

Hysterical disorders result from failures to learn those anxiety-based responses that underlie normal socialization. The extrovert who becomes a hysteric (or a psychopathic personality) does so precisely because his or her cortical and emotional underarousal impedes the learning of anxiety-based self-restraint and moral or ethical inhibitions (Eysenck & Rachman, 1965, p. 40).

Some evidence suggests that extroverts may be of two types. In the first, sociability, or outgoing, stimulus-seeking behavior predominates. In the second type of extrovert, impulsivity and an inability to keep antisocial urges and behaviors in check predominate. The first type resembles the normal personality but may succumb to hysterical disorder. Criminal or psychopathic behavior is more characteristic of the second, impulsive type (Eysenck, 1964; Eysenck & S. B. G. Eysenck, 1969; Eysenck & Gudjonsson, 1989, pp. 118ff.). It is this second hysterical type who seems so opposite to the dysthymic personality, for the psychopath is one who has failed to acquire by conditioning the necessary socialization restraints that in the dysthymic become exaggerated into chronic anxiety symptoms (but see Sipprelle, Ascough, Detrio, & Horst, 1977).

Genetic and Environmental Interactions

Eysenck's early views stressed that dysthymic neuroses could be understood in terms of Pavlovian-like conditioning processes, just as the hysterical disorders could be thought of as failures of Pavlovian-like conditioning. Eysenck also regards differences in genetically determined central nervous system functioning as the foundation upon which life experiences lead to a healthy or unhealthy adaptation to reality. Put into its strongest form, Eysenck's theory asserts that the dimensions of normality-neuroticism and introversion-extroversion are genetically transmitted features of personality.

Eysenck has several times reviewed the evidence for the genetic basis of personality dimensions (1957a; 1967; for intelligence: 1973; 1979; for psychoticism: Eysenck & S. B. G. Eysenck, 1976; Eaves, Eysenck, & Martin, 1989). His underlying line of reasoning runs along the following lines: The introvert inherits a nervous system easily able to form conditioned responses, and if this personality type also inherits an emotionally reactive autonomic nervous system (high neuroticism), he or she will be in an ideal position to acquire strong anxiety responses. In effect, the introvert possesses a nervous system predisposition to be acutely sensitive to all forms of stimulation and therefore to become inhibited and withdrawing in the presence of a demanding social environment.

The extrovert, by contrast, inherits the type of nervous system that is not easily conditionable, not especially sensitive to stimulation, and not prone to withdrawal from a demanding environment. In fact, the extrovert is a stimulus-seeker because his or her relatively high levels of inhibitory cortical processes demand constant novel and potent input of external excitation to feed the resulting stimulus-hunger. Eysenck has summarized his position on the relative importance of biological and environmental factors in shaping personality as a **biosocial model:**

> Human behavior is rightly said to be bio-social in nature, i.e., to have both biological and social causes; it is time the pendulum started swinging back from an exclusive preoccupation with social causes to an appropriate appreciation and understanding of

biological causes. . . . Biological causes act in such a way as to predispose an individual in certain ways to stimulation; this stimulation may or may not occur, depending on circumstances which are entirely under environmental control. (Eysenck, 1967, pp. 221–222)

Eysenck's theory, therefore, may be understood as an attempt to bridge two very wide gulfs: the gulf between a study of individual differences in personality and the experimental investigation of conditioning, learning, and perceptual processes, the gulf between genetic or biological differences and environmental influences on behavior.

Explaining the Neurotic Paradox

Eysenck has asserted that a cardinal feature of human neurosis is the "neurotic paradox." The neurotic person's behavior typically has consequences that are unfavorable, painful, and self-defeating. The paradox is that the neurotic person nonetheless persists in that behavior. You would think that unfavorable consequences would cause any rational person to take stock of the problem and alter his or her actions.

According to Eysenck, a strict conditioning model drawn from Pavlovian theory or even from the operant model of the pioneering behavioral psychologist, Skinner, cannot explain why neurotic symptoms endure unchanged in the face of punishing consequences. Moreover, some forms of neurotic behavior are founded on irrational fears, fears so removed from actuality that the dreaded outcome never materializes. Yet, despite the continual failure of the fear to be reinforced, the fear-based symptoms never extinguish as they should, according to conditioning theory (Solomon, Kamin, & Wynne, 1953; Solomon & Wynne, 1954). Eysenck reviews evidence that will not be presented here which suggests that, under certain circumstances, unreinforced conditioned fears may even incubate with each unreinforced presentation of the conditioned stimulus.

Eysenck hypothesizes that an adequate learning model of neurosis must include the possibility that some neurotic anxieties and fears are based on innate sensitivity to certain noxious objects or events. A similar idea first proposed by Martin Seligman (1970, 1971, 1972; see also Rachman, 1978, 1990) suggests an evolutionary mechanism through which organisms are biologically "prepared" to respond to specific stimuli with fear. Thus, for example, there certainly would be survival value in the predisposition to be fearful of darkness, of poisonous snakes and insects, or of high places. Conditioned neurotic fears built upon any of these *prepared* survival phobias would not readily obey the ordinary laws of learning, including extinction. The concept of preparedness might also explain why neurotic phobias tend to be restricted to a relatively small class of stimuli when, in contrast, conditioning theory predicts that *any* stimulus can be made fearsome by proper association with a noxious event (see the discussion of preparedness in Chapter 17).

According to this theory, neurotics persist in self-defeating behavior because the negative consequences of their symptoms and the failure of dreaded outcomes to materialize cannot suppress or extinguish fears that have roots in evolutionary survival mechanisms. Evolutionary mechanisms persist in a species because they promote environmental adaptation, but the average contemporary neurotic remains neurotic because the results of natural selection have not caught up with our civilized existence (see Chapter 17, Evolutionary Psychology).

PSYCHOTICISM: PSYCHIATRIC DIAGNOSIS REVISITED

Eysenck's work, you recall, began with a rebellious investigation of psychiatric diagnostic reliability. One of the fundamental tenets of classical diagnostic systems is the qualitative distinction between neurotic and psychotic disorders (Eysenck & S. B. G. Eysenck, 1976, pp. 5, 157).

Eysenck proposed a dimensional model of personality, which suggests that what he termed "psychoticism" is not an all-or-none phenomenon. There are gradations of psychoticism, which range from normality at one extreme to full-blown psychotic separation from reality and thought disorder at the other extreme. Thus, in principle, it is possible for a normal person to possess some degree of those traits found in extreme form in the psychotic personality, just as it is possible for the neurotic person to possess *some* normal traits or *some* psychotic traits.

Psychoticism has entered Eysenck's theory as an additional dimension of disordered personality that, like neuroticism and introversion-extroversion, is genetically based. Eysenck views psychoticism as a *polygenic* personality trait. "Polygenic" means that a trait is determined by a large number of genes, each of whose individual effect is small (Eysenck & S. B. G. Eysenck, 1976, p. 29). Another group of genes, fewer in number than the first group, determines the probability that the person will not only evidence psychotic *traits* but will also suffer a fully developed psychosis. Eysenck's model of psychoticism also allows that a person with a high psychoticism (P) score who is *not* overtly psychotic may nevertheless possess traits that make him or her different from the norm but not necessarily disadvantaged socially. Some high P personalities may in fact evidence their unusualness as genius or artistic productivity.

Characteristics of the High-P Scorer

Eysenck and S. B. G. Eysenck (1975a, 1975b, 1976) developed a questionnaire, the **Eysenck Personality Questionnaire (EPQ),** which is a measure of neuroticism and introversion-extroversion, and also assesses the level of psychoticism. Factor-analytic studies were the basis on which questions were selected to measure the psychoticism dimension. A "high-P" person is one who answers affirmatively a selected pattern of questions that paints the following personality portrait:

> A high psychoticism scorer is a loner who cares very little for the company of other people. The high-P personality shows overt hostility to others, even to close relatives and tends to disregard dangers and social conventions. Making fools of other people is an enjoyable pastime, and this trait may be carried easily to an extreme of cruelty. The high-P scorer tends to enjoy "unusual things" and stands out as "peculiar" to his acquaintances. (Eysenck & S. B. G. Eysenck, 1975b, p. 5)

A person with a high score on the P dimension is not necessarily psychotic or schizophrenic, although a schizophrenic person would be expected to have a **high P score.** A high degree of psychoticism is independent of the person's degree of introversion or extroversion, as measured by the EPQ. Some neurotics *may* happen to have elevated P scores; but there is no correlation between the two traits (Eysenck & S. B. G. Eysenck, 1976, pp. 38ff.).

A person's P score should be interpreted in terms of the other Eysenck dimensions. A high P score will have very different meanings when embodied in high and low introverted personalities, and even more varied meaning when associated with high, as contrasted with low, intelligence or with high or low neuroticism.

PSYCHOTICISM, CRIME, AND GENETICS

Recall that Eysenck argued that the basic personality dimensions have a substantial degree of genetic loading that interacts with socialization experiences. When Eysenck added the psychoticism dimension to his theory, he reaffirmed this interactionist model and created several new hypotheses about the interaction of the three dimensions of extroversion, neuroticism, and psychoticism.

Eysenck at first concluded that a person who scores high in psychoticism had inherited a vulnerability to psychotic disorder but may not in fact succumb to a diagnosable illness. Instead, a person who embodies a large number of the traits associated with psychoticism and who is also high in neuroticism and extroversion may develop a pattern of antisocial or criminal behavior. Eysenck first proposed that criminal or antisocial behavior was linked to extreme extroversion. The link, however, has always been modest or inconsistently validated in research studies (Eysenck & Gudjonsson, 1989).

Eysenck, therefore, has modified his theory to conceptualize the criminal or antisocial personality as someone who is impulsive, extroverted, high in neuroticism, and who has a high P or psychoticism level. In other words, they are impulse-laden, outgoing, full of emotional problems, and have poor-reality testing. It is not hard to see how such people could come under the jurisdiction of the criminal justice system.

Eysenck's argument incorporates his arousal hypotheses, his measurements of the factors underlying the personality dimensions, and his interactionist model of socialization. His theory has three related parts—arousal and hedonic tone, extroversion, aggression, and testosterone, and psychoticism and criminality.

Arousal and Hedonic Tone

Eysenck's own work and his review of the literature on criminality (Eaves, Eysenck, & Martin, 1989; Eysenck & Gudjonsson, 1989) suggested to him that criminal behavior is associated with underarousal because a person with a relatively nonreactive nervous system does not condition or acquire anxiety-based restraints or controls as readily as people with more highly aroused nervous systems (Eysenck & Gudjonsson, 1989, p. 119). Figure 16.7 illustrates Eysenck's basic hypothesis.

Introverts, extroverts, and **ambiverts** have different levels of optimal arousal. Optimal arousal is the level of activation produced by the person's nervous system and the current level of stimulus input. The optimal level is the point at which a given personality type is most comfortable, most pleasantly activated, and most positively motivated.

Introverts, with the highest innate arousal levels, require less stimulation to achieve the optimal level than do extroverts. By contrast, the extrovert's chronic underarousal ensures that higher levels of stimulation will be required to reach optimal levels of arousal.

The curves in Figure 16.7 indicate that the **hedonic tone** (pleasure or pain) of stimulation is a function of personality type. What is massive overstimulation and pain for the introvert is exciting or pleasant for the extrovert. The indifference level indicated in Figure 16.7 represents a kind of boredom threshold, which differs for the two extreme personality types. Extroverts reach "indifferent hedonic tone" levels at much higher levels of stimulation than do introverts. Or, said another way, what an extrovert regards as boring understimulation, the introvert would find as peaceful, undemanding stimulation.

Eysenck suggests that the person destined to develop an antisocial personality is one whose arousal level is like that of the extreme extrovert in Figure 16.7. Specifically, the person would be excitement-seeking, easily distracted, and very resistant to levels of stimulation that would be regarded as unpleasant by others (Eysenck & Gudjonsson, 1989, p. 119).

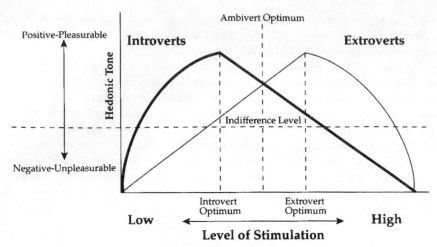

The optimal level of stimulation is higher for extroverts than for introverts both above and below the level of indifference. Eysenck predicts that levels of stimulation an introvert would find too intense would be "boring" for the extrovert. But levels of stimulation that the extrovert finds pleasurable or positively stimulating, the introvert experiences as overwhelming or painful. Most people, however, are ambiverts, and their optimal level of stimulation would fall theoretically between the optimal levels for the introvert and extrovert.

Figure 16.7 Positive and negative hedonic tone for introverts and extroverts.

Based on Eysenck & M. Eysenck, 1985, p. 249 and Eysenck & Gudjonsson, 1989, p. 118.

The second link in Eysenck's argument involves the effects of hormone levels on arousal.

Extroversion, Aggression, and Testosterone

Eysenck proposed that the extroversion dimension and aggressivity were mediated by the presence of male hormones or androgens. Eysenck and Gudjonsson (1989) reviewed literature that suggests a correlation between androgens (largely testosterone) and underarousal. Some of the evidence that Eysenck reviews indicates that high androgen levels have the effect of lowering the arousal levels in the brain's reticular system (Eysenck & Gudjonsson, 1989, pp. 130ff.). Because the pattern of androgen secretion is genetically based, a person with high androgen levels inherits a predisposition to underarousal, to masculinized appearance, and, at times, to aggressive behavior. Eysenck is thus proposing that criminality is mediated, in part, by the inheritance of an underaroused nervous system, which in turn is mediated by genetically regulated androgen levels.

Psychoticism and Criminality

Eysenck's initial formulation of the relationship between the main personality dimensions and criminality pictured the extreme extrovert as prone to hysterical disorders and to psychopathy or criminal behavior (Eysenck, 1964, 1976). But the criminal, long assumed to be an extreme extrovert and also high in neuroticism, appears with more recent evidence to fall into two different categories. The *primary psychopath* is the classical antisocial personality, who evidences little conscience, anxiety or guilt, poor judgment, and intense impulsivity. By contrast, the *secondary psychopath* may engage in antisocial behavior but is highly conflicted and anxious about his or her conduct.

Eysenck's later formulations show that criminals are high scorers on all three dimensions of extroversion, neuroticism, and psychoticism (Eysenck & M. Eysenck, 1985, pp. 330ff.). The addition of measurements for psychoticism has altered the interpretation placed on extroversion in mediating criminality. Eysenck concluded that the impulsivity component formerly associated with the extroversion dimension has to be understood as more strongly correlated to the psychoticism dimension. Thus, a person who scores highly on all three dimensions fits the role of criminal because:

1. as an extreme extrovert, the criminal is underaroused, sensation-seeking, poorly conditionable, and lacking in the restraints of conscience that are normally acquired through conditioning;

2. as a high scorer in neuroticism, the criminal evidences moody, irrational, and intensely emotional behavior;

3. as a high scorer in psychoticism, the criminal will lack empathy for other people, appear egocentric and impulsive, and act with poor judgment to gratify his or her needs.

The factors that determine whether the criminal will be a primary or secondary psychopath are to be found in the relationship between psychoticism and neuroticism. Generally, the theory predicts that the primary psychopath is one in whom the degree of psychoticism is higher than neuroticism; conversely, the secondary (anxious or guilty) criminal is a person who scores higher on the neuroticism dimension than on the psychoticism dimension. In both types, the person is an extreme underaroused extrovert (i.e., not readily conditioned). Figure 16.8 summarizes the key qualities associated with Eysenck's three main personality dimensions.

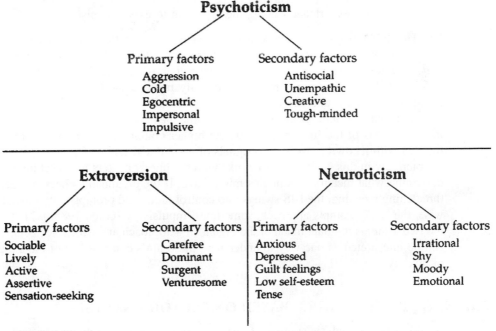

Figure 16.8 Eysenck's three main personality dimensions in descriptive terms.

Based on Eysenck & Gudjonsson, 1989, pp. 44–45.

Overview of the Psychoticism-Criminality Hypothesis

We can summarize the logic of Eysenck's **psychoticism-criminality hypothesis,** or hypotheses about psychoticism, arousal, and criminality as follows:

1. Inheritance of nervous system-associated hormonal regulators that establish chronic underarousal in the personality constitutes the predisposition to extreme extroversion and to antisocial behavior.

2. As the extreme underaroused extrovert matures socially, underarousal inhibits the acquisition of anxiety-based restraints and it promotes sensation-seeking behavior, resistance to pain, and aggressive action.

3. If the extreme extrovert also inherits a nervous system prone to neuroticism and high psychoticism, he or she is likely to develop criminal behavior. If psychoticism is higher than neuroticism, the orientation will be psychopathy or antisocial personality disorder. On the other hand, if neuroticism is stronger, the orientation is likely to be more in the direction of impulsivity.

Sensitivity to Reward and Punishment: Impulsivity and Anxiety

Jeffrey Gray (1985) reconceptualized how the limbic system and cortex of the brain function together as a kind of unified third biological system supplementing Eysenck's two systems of the visceral brain and ARAS-cortex. Gray proposed that the septum and hippocampus, and more recently, the amygdala, along with parts of the frontal cortex, constitute a *behavioral inhibition system* (BIS) that functions whenever the organism encounters one or more of three circumstances:

1. novel stimuli violating current expectations;
2. a naturally threatening stimulus engaging the organism's attention; or
3. previous experience leading the organism to expect punishment.

The BIS operates to arouse aversive states of fear that cause the organism to withdraw. Withdrawal, as Gray uses the term, consists of *inhibition* of action because particular responses provoke anxiety. Put another way, organisms differ in the sensitivity of their BIS: Some are constitutionally more prone to anxiety-inhibition and avoidance behavior than are others.

A second system proposed by Gray, the *behavioral approach system* (BAS), involves areas of the forebrain cortex, the higher cognitive centers, and complements the BIS with its own sensitivity to signals of reward and safety. The two systems work interactively in this way: The BIS works with the higher centers in "checking mode" to determine what meaning a stimulus might have. If the organism's checking registers a threatening meaning, the BIS swings into control mode and prompts withdrawal; otherwise, the BAS prompts approach, sometimes impulsively (Gray, 1985, p.7). Together, the two systems regulate much of the organism's approach and avoidance behavior and can be interpreted as one way to understand the brain's construction of the experience of anxiety.

THE "BIG FIVE": A MODEL BASED ON FACTOR ANALYSIS

A purely factor analysis approach to personality has led to five major personality traits or factors. This approach, unlike Eysenck's, did not focus on trying to understand the physiological underpinnings of the factors, but simply on factoring the terms people use to describe personality. Two of the factors that emerged, *neuroticism* and *extroversion,* were very similar to Eysenck's comparable dimensions. **The Big Five** model does not have a dimension comparable to Eysenck's *psychoticism* as it is largely derived from terms used to describe the general population rather than those who manifest great psychopathology.

Raymond Cattell began the factor analytic approach to personality. He originally determined that there were 16 underlying traits. Subsequently, researchers analyzed larger and larger numbers of correlations and generally found that five major personality traits or factors emerged. An individual may be precisely described by measuring his or her location on each of the five trait dimensions. These traits are conceptualized as lying on bipolar dimensions with persons at one end of the dimension exhibiting high degrees of the trait and persons at the other end exhibiting low degrees of the trait (or its opposite).

The Big Five are:

1. *Neuroticism*
2. *Extroversion*
3. *Openness*
4. *Conscientiousness*
5. *Agreeableness*

Each of these main dimensions is composed of several secondary traits or "facets." Thus, for example, the neuroticism (versus emotional stability) dimension has been shown to embody anxiety, depression, problems with intimacy, sensitivity to stimulation, impulsiveness, and narcissism, to name just a few (e.g., Schroeder, Wormworth, & Livesley, 1994; see also the application of the Big Five to the study of borderline personality disorder in the work of Clarkin, Hull, Cantor, & Sanderson, 1993; and Eysenck & M. Eysenck [e.g., 1985]). In similar fashion, the extroversion (versus introversion) dimension embodies facets of sociability, warmth, assertiveness, and excitement-seeking, among others. Thus a score of high or low on a particular trait of the Big Five is actually a cluster of scores on the subfacets, providing for the *uniqueness* of individual combinations, a fact that would bring an I-told-you-so-smile to Gordon Allport's lips (see Chapter 11).

The working clinician planning treatment for a patient might consider, for example, that the patient's high neuroticism score includes anxiety, hopelessness, and unrealistic expectations. This same patient's low openness score reveals a preoccupation with fantasy and daydreaming along with some eccentric thinking. And the patient's high agreeableness score is associated with gullibility and indiscriminate trust of others (McCrae, 1994, p. 306). Given this kind of psychological description of personality functioning and malfunctioning using three of the Big Five dimensions as an illustration, the clinician may very well be guided not only to better understanding of the patient's personality and personality disorder but also to better avenues of providing therapeutic educational and emotional interventions.

Although there is growing agreement about the utility of the five-factor model, skeptics and critics point out that factor analysis has certain limitations and weaknesses. For one thing, a surprising degree of creativity and subjectivity enters into organizing and naming clusters of correlations as factors (Eysenck, 1993; Shadel & Cervone, 1993; but see also Watson, Clark, & Harkness, 1994). As we have seen, there is much evidence for Eysenck's physiologically based three-factor solution to factor analytic data. On the other hand, an investigator can choose a more complex solution that includes many more than five dimensions (Cattell, 1993), or even choose a multilayered, two-tier approach to the factors (Guastello, 1993).

There is also the nagging notion that what the Big Five offer in precision measurement they lack in explanation power. As Eysenck (1993) has pointed out on numerous occasions, the most productive research begins from and is guided deductively by a theory that makes predictions that can be tested. The Big Five evolved more or less the other way around, inductively collating and synthesizing sometimes unrelated measurements until they more or less coalesced into meaningful dimensions.

EVALUATING EYSENCK'S TYPOLOGY

Eysenck's strategy for constructing his theory is based on scientific method. His conception of the three dimensions of neuroticism, introversion-extroversion, and psychoticism grew from empirical studies, was altered as more studies were done, and changed again when the research suggested new directions or disconfirmed his hypotheses.

Refutability of Eysenck's Model

Eysenck's model is, and was designed to be, eminently refutable. It is a research-based conception, or set of conceptions, and one of its prime goals is to provide predictions that may be tested in the laboratory. As various hypotheses were tested, Eysenck changed basic parts of the theory that were disconfirmed, strengthened those that received support, and deduced new hypotheses that begin the cycle again.

Eysenck has subsequently fine-tuned the model, qualifying the exact conditions under which generalizations are true and when they are false (e.g., Eaves, Eysenck, & Martin, 1989; Eysenck & Gudjonsson, 1989). However, by making many modifications to bring his theory into line with all of the exceptions it must account for, the theory runs the risk of no longer being intact or integral. It is in danger of becoming a collection of pieced-together, ad hoc explanations.

Eysenck's Conception of Human Agency

Eysenck consistently argued for a biosocial conception of humans. He thus affirmed that behavior is caused by a complex interaction between inherited nervous system predispositions and social reality. Even if a given choice may not seem predictable from the point of view of an outside observer, that choice is nonetheless lawful and determined.

Eysenck did not use the concepts of active and passive agency to describe people. But if we apply this evaluation scheme, we place Eysenck's model at the passive end of the spectrum and infer from his work that he does not view people as active agents.

The Nomothetic Nature of Eysenck's Theory

Eysenck's theory is definitely a nomothetic model of personality. It focuses on general principles. Study of the individual case is not part of Eysenck's interest or research methodology. It is possible to apply Eysenck's theory of types to specific individuals, but the vast bulk of the theory is derived from studying groups of people who are contrasted on the specific variables being studied. Eysenck commented on the question of the nomothetic versus idiographic nature of his theory:

Modern personality theory, with its types and traits and abilities, is situated somewhere between idiographic psychology stressing *uniqueness* and experimental psychology stressing the *identity* (i.e., similarity) of human beings. What one must say, essentially, is that although human beings clearly do differ from each other, they differ along certain dimensions and their differences and similarities can therefore be quantified and measured. Measurements of traits and abilities lead us to certain type constructs, such as extraversion-introversion; this simply means that for certain purposes we can point to groups of people similar with respect to a given trait or ability and contrast these with groups of other people not sharing this trait or ability or showing its opposite. (Eysenck & M. Eysenck, 1985, p. 8; italics in original)

SUMMARY

Eysenck's approach to the study of personality is at one with his own personality, which was ruggedly independent, skeptical, and in which he trusted his own observations and facts more than the views of other or popular beliefs.

Eysenck's theory of personality may best be described as a hierarchical model having three major levels.

At the first observable level, personality types of introversion and extroversion are described in terms of measurable traits like sociability, shyness, impulsiveness, and activity. These traits are usually measured with paper-and-pencil instruments such as the Eysenck Personality Inventory or the Eysenck Personality Questionnaire.

At the second level of the hierarchy, performance on laboratory tasks, such as motor move-

ments, conditioning, and vigilance, is used to define the dimensions of introversion and extroversion.

The third level is the fundamental, causal basis of the upper two divisions. Conceptualized as an excitation-inhibition balance (or ARAS arousal and inhibition of the cortex), this causal level may be classed as the genotypic basis of personality.

As an inheritable dimension, excitation-inhibition (or ARAS functioning) may be thought of as the biological root of personality. Figure 16.9 illustrates these levels of Eysenck's theory.

Eysenck's original factor analysis of personality performance and physiological data derived from a large group of subjects demonstrated that two independent dimensions could be used to describe their personalities. A dimension of introversion-extroversion and a dimension of

Figure 16.9 Three levels of Eysenck's theory.

Based on Eysenck, 1964 and 1967.

normality-neuroticism were conceptualized as independent and continuous variables. The extrovert type of person likes people, and is sociable, strongly attracted to novel and exciting stimuli, easygoing, and optimistic. He or she is often fond of practical jokes and may become aggressive and impulsive, unable to inhibit or control anger. The typical introvert, by contrast, may be characterized as shy, quiet, withdrawn, and somewhat detached from the social environment. He or she is usually a planner, looking ahead to anticipate problems before they arise. He or she avoids overt and intense stimulation and excitement and usually keeps emotions under strict control (Eysenck & S. B. G. Eysenck, 1975b). The typical individual who scores high in neuroticism may be characterized as emotionally reactive, anxious, moody, and depressed.

Following Carl Jung's clinical insights that introverts succumb to dysthymic (psychasthenic) or anxiety disorders, and that extroverts succumb to hysterical neuroses, Eysenck was able to show that a long tradition stemming from Hippocrates and Galen through Pavlov and Hull had confirmed and refined Jung's hunches. Pavlov's conditioning investigations established the existence of excitation and inhibition as fundamental cortical processes underlying types of temperament.

Clark L. Hull's concepts of drive and habit, along with his notions of reactive and conditioned inhibition, provided Eysenck with key conceptual tools to begin devising a biological and causal account of the introversion-extroversion dimension. Introverts are individuals in whom the excitation-inhibition balance is tipped in the direction of excitation, giving them weak or sensitive nervous systems. Thus they condition more easily than extroverts, are more easily pained by excessive stimulation, and generally perform in a superior way on laboratory tasks requiring sustained attentiveness. Extroverts, by contrast, are individuals in whom the balance is tipped in the direction of greater inhibitory cortical functioning. For this reason, extroverts are said to have a "strong" nervous system not easily aroused by excessive stimulation, but one that is easily overcome with boredom by repetitious or monotonous tasks that rapidly build inhibition.

Eysenck provided a biological translation and refinement of his excitation-inhibition theory. The ascending reticular activating system (ARAS) has been conceptualized as the basis of cortical arousal and inhibition. In this role, the ARAS is also the basis of introversion-extroversion. Introverts have more highly aroused ARAS functioning than extroverts. The dimension of neuroticism has been conceptualized as related to the functioning of the autonomic nervous system. Subcortical brain structures of the limbic system and the hypothalamus, known collectively as the visceral brain (VB), have been postulated by Eysenck to underlie the dimension of emotionality or neuroticism. Neurotics have a higher level of chronic VB activation than do stable or normal individuals.

In terms of socialization, Eysenck has postulated that introverts are more socialized (inhibited, ethical, anxious) than extroverts because of their greater ease of conditioning. Extroverts are less socialized and may be divided into two extreme groups. Some extroverts are characterized essentially by a trait of extreme sociability, and these individuals tend to resemble the normal personality on measures of neuroticism. On the other hand, some extroverts are characterized by a trait of extreme impulsiveness and by a lack of ethical and moral inhibitions. These individuals are generally described as criminal or psychopathic personalities.

An addition to Eysenck's personality dimensions is psychoticism, represented in some personalities as inheritable traits of social withdrawal, impulsivity, hostility, and a general quality of what Eysenck termed, "peculiarity." The dimension of psychoticism, as measured by Eysenck, is not identical to the use of the term in conventional diagnosis, but his is derived from his factor analysis of different traits. The psychoticism dimension, furthermore, implies that neurotic, normal, and psychotic personalities are not categorically different entities; rather, both normal and neurotic individuals may possess some degree of psychoticism without evidencing an overt psychosis.

Eysenck's theoretical strategy allows for concrete predictions and tests of its validity. Furthermore, Eysenck's theory may eventually provide the basis for more rational and scientifically precise diagnosis and treatment of disordered behavior. The possibility of altering an individual's position on the introversion-extroversion dimension by means of depressant and stimulant drugs to alter disordered behaviors may soon be feasible.

Evaluation of Eysenck's theory shows it clearly to be a highly testable, empirical, and scientific model of personality. Eysenck is fundamentally a biosocial type theorist who believes that patterns of behavior are determined by biological and psychological factors, so that human agency is essentially irrelevant. It follows that this theory is almost exclusively nomothetic.

Raymond Cattell and others, using factor analysis alone—without consideration of physiological underpinnings—arrived at five major factors of personality. These are labeled *neuroticism, extroversion, openness, conscientiousness,* and *agreeableness.* These factors have been confirmed by many empirical studies and comprise what is termed the "Big Five" model of personality. *Extroversion* and *neuroticism* are comparable to two of Eysenck's factors.

FOR FURTHER READING

Eysenck was a prolific writer with numerous empirical articles, scholarly books, and popular renditions of his theory to his credit. The development of Eysenck's continually more biological formulations may be gleaned from successive reading of three of his works: *The Scientific Study of Personality* (London: Routledge & Kegan Paul, 1952), which concerns his early descriptive measurements of introversion-extroversion; *The Dynamics of Anxiety and Hysteria* (London: Routledge & Kegan Paul, 1999), which presents his more causal inhibition theory; and *The Biological Basis of Personality* (Springfield, IL: Charles C. Thomas, 1967), which presents the definitive statement of his cortical hypotheses of arousal. Joseph LeDoux's *The Emotional Brain (New York: Simon & Schuster* [Touchstone], 1998) contains a very readable and comprehensive discussion of the limbic system and other brain structures involved in emotional arousal.

All four of the above-mentioned books are difficult reading. A reprinted key work of Eysenck is *Dimensions of Personality* (New Brunswick, NJ: Transaction Publishers, 1997). A more readable, though less comprehensive, overview of Eysenck's system is his *Crime and Personality* (London: Routledge & Kegan Paul, 1964). Related is a book he wrote with G. H. Gunderson, *The Causes and Cures of Criminality* (New York, Plenum Press 1989). At a popular level of presentation, *Eysenck's Psychology Is About People* (New York: Library Press, 1972) not only provides a short account of his introversion-extroversion concepts but also surveys some of his wartime research on humor and aesthetic preferences. Another aspect of Eysenck's theory may be observed in *The Inequality of Man* (London: Maurice Temple Smith, 1973), in which Eysenck enters the controversy surrounding the nature of IQ measurements. Eysenck's continued emphasis on genetic factors in personality reaches its strongest expression in the sophisticated arguments of *The Structure and Measurement of Intelligence* (New York: Springer, 1979). In a similar vein, *Eysenck and Eysenck's Psychoticism as a Dimension of Personality* (New York: Crane, Russak, 1976) discusses the statistical and experimental evidence in support of a genetic model of this new personality dimension. *Intelligence: A New Look* (New Brunswick, NJ: Transaction Publishers, 2000) is an updated version of Eysenck's defense of intelligence tests.

A three-volume collection of research papers connected to his theory was edited by Eysenck under the title *Readings in Extraversion-Introversion* (London: Staples, 1970–1971). Eysenck's low opinion of psychoanalytic theory and method may be sampled from his *Uses and Abuses of Psychology* (Baltimore: Penguin, 1953) and from his essay "Psychoanalysis: Myth or Science?" in Stanley Rachman's (Ed.) *Critical Essays on Psychoanalysis* (New York: Pergamon, 1960). Eysenck's controversial largely erroneous position that lung cancer is not caused by smoking itself but rather by personality types to which smoking is correlated is in *Smoking, Health and Personality* (New Brunswick, NJ: Transaction Publishers, 2000).

Eysenck's position on behavior therapy for neuroses is lucidly presented in *The Causes and Cures of Neurosis* (San Diego: Robert Knapp, 1965), co-authored with Stanley Rachman. Eysenck also edited a collection of research papers on various forms of conditioning therapy, published as *Behavior Therapy and the Neuroses* (New York: Pergamon, 1960).

An interview with Eysenck, in which he discusses the implications of his work for psychotherapy and for unifying the whole of psychology, is contained in R. I. Evans's *The Making of Psychology* (New York: Knopf, 1976).

For more readings on Eysenck, please see Chapter 16 at www.wiley.com/college/sollod

GLOSSARY

Ambivert: Someone who displays both introvert and extrovert behaviors.

Arousal theory: The theory that behavior is partially a function of the general state of arousal (excitation) or de-arousal (inhibition) of the cortex. This excitation-inhibition balance varies among individuals. People vary in how rapidly this cortical arousal occurs, and to what extent.

Ascending reticular activating system (ARAS): A system in the central nervous system that is responsible for patterns of excitation and inhibition of the cerebral cortex.

Autonomic nervous system (ANS): Part of the nervous system that governs the smooth muscles, the heart muscle, the glands, and the viscera and controls their functions, including physiological responses to emotion. It has two divisions, the sympathetic and the parasympathetic.

Biosocial model: A concept of personality that includes inherited biological tendencies and the influence of the interpersonal environment.

Central nervous system: The major part of the nervous system, which is made up of the brain and spinal cord. It contains inhibition-excitation processes.

Choleric temperament: (Galen) Personality type said to be quick to action, angry, assertive, and irascible; thought to be caused by an excess of yellow bile, one of the four bodily fluids or humors.

Conditioned inhibition: A learned inhibitory response.

Drive theory: A theory that states that a bodily tension is a strong internal stimulus, felt as a need or an urge, that impels the individual to take action to relieve this arousal or tension.

Dysthymia: A chronic mood disorder involving mild, persistent depression, often found in disordered introverted neurotics.

Electroencephalogram (EEG): Recording of electrical activity in the cerebral cortex acquired via electrodes placed on the surface of the skull. EEG recordings assess the pattern of waves.

Excitatory processes: The processes that occur when the excitatory cells in the cortex start firing.

Extrovert: A personality type characterized by an outgoing nature that adapts easily to any given situation. Such an individual seeks social and physical stimulation.

Eysenck Personality Questionnaire (EPQ): A personality questionnaire Eysenck developed, based on factor analysis, that measured the dimensions of introversion-extroversion, psychoticism, and neuroticism.

Factor analysis: A statistical method that looks at how individuals' scores on groups of measures correlate with their scores on other measures. Particular variables often group themselves to form a factor.

Hedonic tone: Positive or negative feelings and appraisals related to different levels of arousal.

High-P score: A score high on psychoticism on the Eysenck Personality Questionnaire(EPQ).

Humors: To Galen, the four vital fluids possessed by human beings: blood, phlegm, black bile, and yellow bile. The balance of these humors in each person was presumed to influence personality.

Hysterical disorder: The loss or impairment of some motor or sensory function for which there is no organic cause, often seen in disordered neurotic extroverts.

Inhibitory processes: The processes that act to dampen or retard the activation of the excitatory cortical cells. It hinders nervous system arousal.

Introvert: A personality type characterized by a hesitant, reflective, retiring nature. There is withdrawal from social and physical stimulation.

Limbic system: The visceral brain, which relates emotional feelings and expression, and influences the autonomic nervous system.

Melancholic temperament: (Galen) Personality type said to be sad, depressed, and anxious; thought to be caused by a predominance of black bile, one of the four bodily fluids or humors.

Neuroticism: A maladaptive personality pattern typified by negative emotionality. This condition includes traits of anxiety, depression, guilt, low self-esteem, and associated characteristics.

Phlegmatic temperament: (Galen) Personality type said to be slow to action, lethargic, and calm; thought to be caused by an excess of phlegm, one of the four bodily fluids or humors.

Postulate of individual differences: Human beings differ with respect to the speed with which excitation and inhibition are produced, and the speed with which inhibition is dissipated.

Psychasthenia: A disorder characterized by a lack of energy and low-level depression. This term, used by Jung, is similar to Eysenck's concept of dysthymia.

Psychoticism: A maladaptive personality pattern characterized by traits of aggression, hostility, aloofness and egocentricity, and impulsiveness and related attributes. It is related to nonconformity or social deviance and to criminality.

Psychoticism-criminality hypothesis: Eysenck's hypothesis that the extreme extrovert is prone to hysterical disorders and to psychopathy or criminal behavior.

Reactive inhibition: (Hull) Neural fatigue that develops when responses are repeated.

Sanguine temperament: (Galen) Personality type said to be warmhearted, volatile, optimistic, and easygoing; thought to be caused by an excess of blood, one of the four bodily fluids or humors.

Stimulus hungry: Weak cortical arousal causes the extrovert to seek social and physical stimulation. This type is stimulus hungry.

Stimulus shy: Strong cortical arousal causes the introvert to avoid social and physical stimulation. This type is stimulus shy.

Temperament theory: A theory that categorizes people according to their pervasive patterns of behavior, which are presumably caused by biological factors. Some behavioral patterns considered often include level of activity, emotionality, and sociability. Hippocrates, Galen, Pavlov, and Eysenck, among others, developed temperament theories, which they based on different assumptions.

The Big Five: This model of personality is derived from factor analysis of terms used to describe personality. The five traits that emerge from this analysis are *neuroticism, extroversion, openness, conscientiousness,* and *agreeableness.*

Typological postulate: Patterns of introversion and extroversion as well as predispositions to types of psychological symptoms are based on differences in excitatory potential and reactive inhibition.

Chapter 17

Edward O. Wilson

Evolutionary Psychology

Thinking of "Go to the ant, thou sluggard; consider her ways," *I knelt on the cobblestones to watch harvester ants carry seeds down holes to their subterranean granaries. . . . As I walked with my host back past the Temple Mount toward the Muslim Quarter, I made inner calculations of the number of ant species found within the city walls. There was a perfect logic to such eccentricity:* the million-year history of Jerusalem is at least as compelling as its past three thousand years.

Edward O. Wilson, *Biophilia* (emphasis added)

Grant for the moment that snake aversion does have a hereditary basis in at least some kinds of nonhuman primates. The possibility that immediately follows is that the trait evolved by natural selection.

E. O. Wilson, *Biophilia*

Edward O. Wilson	Born: 1929	Birmingham, Alabama
	At present:	Professor Emeritus, Harvard University, Cambridge, Massachusetts

About Evolutionary Psychology

Evolutionary psychology or human sociobiology is an approach to understanding behavior that views human behaviors (including cognitions and emotions) in terms of their presumed origins in the evolutionary process. It grew out of the more inclusive field of sociobiology, which refers to "the biological basis of all forms of social behavior in all kinds of organisms, including man" (Wilson, 1978).

Some of the major tenets of evolutionary psychology or human sociobiology are:

- The process of natural selection discovered by Charles Darwin applies not only to the physical features of organisms but also to the development of instincts, or proclivities to behave in certain ways in certain circumstances.
- Human beings, as well as members of other species, have such instincts.
- Many of our current patterns of behavior, thinking, and emotion thus exist because of their adaptive significance in our evolutionary history.
- Evolutionary psychologists have examined a number of specific types of behavior in light of theories of evolutionary psychology. These areas include altruistic behavior, patterns of bonding, incest taboos, aggression, mate selection, and attractiveness. Numerous other areas have been explored and can be investigated using this model.
- One of the important mechanisms of natural selection is sexual selection, which involves both competition for mates and mate selection. Sexual selection is a major factor determining the degree to which an organism passes its genes on to the next generation.
- In addition to the selection of the fittest organisms through natural selection, another means of selection is inclusive fitness or kin selection, the degree to which an organism enhances the survival of relatives, who have some identical genetic material.
- Many of our behaviors can be understood in terms of the environment of evolutionary adaptedness (EEA) in which our hominid ancestors lived for millions of years.
- The concept of mental modularity, in which the brain is seen as having numerous adaptive programs, is a new area of theory and research in evolutionary psychology.
- Evolutionary psychology provides a new perspective for considering types of psychopathology.

The past decade has shown a burgeoning increase of activity in this rapidly developing field, which promises to be a major integrative focus in the behavioral sciences.

The development of modern **evolutionary psychology** is best traced by following the life and thought of Edward O. Wilson. In addition, a number of other researchers and theorists have made contributions to the development of the field. These include William Hamilton, who originated the concept of inclusive fitness, Robert Trivers, who studied resource allotment and reciprocal altruism, John Tooby, Leda Cosmides, David Buss, David Barash, Randy Thornhill, and many others.

THE ROOTS OF A NATURALIST

Edward O. Wilson's parents were in the process of getting divorced when he was seven years old. They sent him, their only child, during the summer vacation to board with a family in Paradise Beach, Florida. He spent most days on the beach exploring life in the sea and on the seashore. In his autobiography, Wilson described his interactions with the natural world that summer in vivid language:

> Why do I tell you this little boy's [Wilson, himself] story of medusas, rays, and sea monsters, nearly sixty years after the fact? Because it illustrates, I think, how a naturalist is created. A child comes to the edge of deep water with a mind prepared for wonder. He is

like a primitive adult of long ago . . . the experience must have been repeated countless times over thousands of generations, and it was richly rewarded. (1994, p. 11)

Sounding much like a Jungian (see Chapter 5), he continues:

The sea, the lakes, and the broad rivers . . . were impervious, it seemed, to change of any kind. The waterland was always there, timeless, invulnerable, mostly beyond reach, and inexhaustible. The child is ready to grasp this archetype, to explore and learn, but he has few words to describe his guiding emotions. Instead, he is given a compelling image that will serve in later life as a talisman, transmitting a powerful energy that directs the growth of experience and knowledge. (1994, p. 11)

He continues in the story of his life:

Hands-on experience at the critical time, not systematic knowledge, is what counts in the making of a naturalist. Better to be an untutored savage for a while, not to know the names or anatomical detail. Better to spend long stretches of time just searching and longing. (1994, pp. 11–12)

During this summer, while fishing, young Wilson pulled a small fish out of the water too fast. It flew into his face and one of its spines pierced the pupil of his right eye. He became blind in that eye as a result. His vision in his left eye was 20/10, which meant that it was more acute at close range than that of most people. In addition, he was handicapped as a naturalist by hereditary partial deafness, which made it hard for him to hear birdsongs or identify frogs by their sounds (Wilson, 1994).

In spite of these handicaps, serious deficits for a budding naturalist, the young Wilson found that his remaining senses were ideal for the study of insects. Figure 17.1 shows him pursuing this interest in a field near his home.

I was destined to become an entomologist. . . . I would thereafter celebrate the little things of the world, the animals that can be picked up between thumb and forefinger and brought close for inspection. (Wilson, 1994, p. 15)

Figure 17.1 Edward O. Wilson at age 13 in a field near his home in Mobile, Alabama. In this photo, young Wilson evidences his already strong level of curiosity about the insect world.

Wilson's compensatory behavior in response to his partial blindness is consistent with Alfred Adler's (Chapter 4) early concept of organ inferiority as a motivating source of superiority strivings. In this view, the way individuals adapt to life is likely to be shaped by their reactions to their organ inferiorities. Wilson's compensatory behavior took the form of intense scientific curiosity regarding insect behavior and, eventually, a desire to understand and even protect the natural world. Whereas Adler's concept of *social interest* stressed a concern for the well-being of other people, Wilson emphasized the caring for and love of all life, *Biophilia* (Wilson, 1984). His efforts to make the world a better place for generations to come is also consistent with Erik Erikson's (Chapter 8) concept of *generativity*.

After his parents' divorce, Wilson eventually lived with his father and his new wife. He remained an only child. The family moved numerous times. Thus, young Edward had to transfer from one school to another until he finally graduated from high school in 1945. During his period of schooling, he formed a close bond with nature and the various plants and animals he found there. They provided reliable companionship. He loved nature and was fascinated by all the phenomena of life that he explored (Wilson, 1994).

Wilson majored in biology in college and received a bachelor's and a master's degree in this field. His mother offered to support him in medical school, but Edward's mind and heart were already set on becoming an entomologist. He first went to the University of Tennessee but transferred to the Harvard program, which attracted him in large part because it possessed the world's largest ant collection and had a distinguished reputation in the field of myrmecology—the study of ants (Wilson, 1994).

In 1953, as a very promising young scholar, Wilson was appointed a Junior Fellow in Harvard University's Society of Fellows. This was a three-year appointment that indicated recognition of a young scholar's promise and provided freedom and support for research. Wilson and the other young fellows stood as the initiatory statement was read to them:

> You have been selected . . . for your promise of notable contribution to knowledge and thought. That promise you must redeem with your whole intellectual and moral force. . . . You will seek not a near, but a distant, objective, and you will not be satisfied with what you have done. All that you may achieve or discover you will regard as a fragment of a larger pattern, which from his separate approach every true scholar is striving. . . . (Wilson, 1994, p. 145)

As a member of the Society of Fellows, Wilson was not only encouraged for his research as a young biologist but was able to have many discussions with leading scholars in a variety of fields. He heard the ideas of philosophers, sociologists, and leading scientists. This experience at Harvard broadened the perspectives of the young naturalist from Alabama. According to Wilson,

> The Society proceeded to transform my self-image and my career. Its greatest immediate impact was a sharp rise in my expectations. . . . I thought, I have three years to justify the confidence placed in me, the same amount of time it took to make Eagle Scout. No problem. The Society's alumni and Senior fellows were outstanding achievers; they included Nobel and Pulitzer winners, I thought. That's a reasonable standard to shoot for. (1994, p. 145)

So encouraged and stimulated, Wilson continued a career that eventually would have an impact on our thinking not only about insects but also about human behavior.

ENCOUNTERING LORENZ AND HIS IDEAS

In the fall of 1953, Niko Tinbergen and Konrad Lorenz, the founders of the field of ethology, arrived to present their work at Harvard University. Wilson attended the presentation and found himself intrigued by Lorenz and his ideas:

> He [Lorenz] was a prophet of the dais, passionate, angry, and importunate. He hammered us with phrases soon to become famous in the behavioral sciences: imprinting, ritualization, aggressive drive.... He had come to proclaim a new approach to the study of behavior. Instinct has been reinstated, he said; the role of learning was grossly overestimated by B. F. Skinner and other behaviorists; we must now pass on to a new direction. (Wilson, 1994, pp. 285–286)

Lorenz subsequently explained that he saw most animal behavior as preordained. He saw the elements of behavior as **fixed action patterns.** He defined such fixed action patterns as:

> ... sequences of movements programmed in the brain by heredity, which unfold through the life of an animal in response to particular signals in the natural environment.... (Wilson, 1994, p. 286)

Lorenz said that, when such fixed action patterns were:

> ... triggered at the right place and time, they lead the animal through a sequence of correct steps to find food, to avoid predators, and to reproduce. The animal does not require previous experience in order to survive. It has only to obey. (Wilson, 1994, p. 286)

Wilson quickly saw the relevance of the idea of fixed action patterns for his research into the social behavior of insects:

> It occurred to me immediately that the fixed-action patterns of ants and other social insects are triggered by chemicals.... The idea of fixed-action patterns and releases suggested to me a way to enter this unexplored world of ant communication. The method should, I reasoned, consist of a set of straightforward steps; break ant social behavior into fixed-action patterns; then by trial and error determine which secretions contain the releaser; finally, separate and identify the active chemicals in the secretions. (Wilson, 1994, p. 288).

In the late 1950s and the early 1960s, as a member of the Harvard faculty, Wilson became increasingly interested in population biology and the related field of **evolutionary biology,** which he believed could, along with the burgeoning field of molecular biology with its newly discovered DNA, serve to unify the field of biology. Wilson wrote an article (Wilson, 1959) based on his research, which indicated the evolution of a certain species of ant toward smaller and smaller varieties. The current form of this species of ant is much smaller than that of its evolutionary ancestors.

From the early 1950s through the early 1970s, Wilson, often working with other naturalists and students, made many interesting creative and theoretically important contributions to the study of ants, the workings of ant society, the evolution of species of ants and ant castes, and the use of chemical trails among ants. He even collaborated with a graduate student, Daniel Simberloff, to develop a method called "experimental zoogeography" (Wilson, 1994, pp. 260–281) in which very small islands of the Florida Keys were stripped of life by fumigation and then species were observed and counted as they reestablished themselves on the island. Simberloff and Wilson were able to arrive at the principle that a specific number of species exists for any island, based on its size and location. Such findings eventually had great significance for the conservation movement, because they implied that only large contiguous areas would allow large numbers of species to exist.

Before proceeding further with the development of Wilson's thinking, we can review the contributions of Charles Darwin and his theory of evolution by natural selection a century before. Darwin's theory of natural selection provided a unifying view of nature that was an integral and basic part of Wilson's thinking.

DARWIN'S (AND WALLACE'S) THEORY OF NATURAL SELECTION

Charles Darwin (1809–1882) is generally credited with originating the theory of biological evolution. As is the case with most other major theories in the history of science, he did not come up with these ideas in a vacuum. Alfred Russel Wallace, another English naturalist, engaged in almost identical reasoning at about the same time. After some correspondence between the two, excerpts from Darwin and Wallace's writings were presented to the Linnaean Society in London. The date was June 30, 1858. A year later, Darwin sent Wallace a copy of *On the Origin of Species by Means of Natural Selection* (Darwin, 1859). Indicating some awareness of the revolutionary significance his ideas would have, he included a note saying, "God knows what the public will think" (Darwin as quoted in Zimmer, 2001, p. 46).

There are many similarities between the lives of Charles Darwin and Edward O. Wilson. Like Wilson a century later, Darwin was a naturalist. He too was fascinated by the natural world and wanted to learn from it. He also rejected medicine as a career in favor of becoming a naturalist. Darwin and Wilson both engaged in worldwide travels to conduct their studies and explorations. Darwin sailed to the Galapagos as a young man, Wilson traveled to the Amazon, the South Pacific, and the Florida Keys. Darwin and Wilson were independent, very logical thinkers, and excellent writers. Like Wilson, Darwin was also aware of the intellectual currents of his time in fields outside of biology. In both cases, their thinking aroused a good deal of vehement opposition and controversy that did not cause either of them to waver in their thinking.

Darwin proposed and argued for the concept of natural selection as a mechanism for biological evolution in *On the Origin of Species by Means of Natural Selection* (1859). The proposal of the mechanism of **natural selection** accompanied by the examples Darwin provided comprised a very persuasive argument for the process of biological evolution. In addition, Darwin developed a well-articulated theory of **sexual selection** (1871).

Introductory biology courses generally cover the logical rationale of Darwin's theory of natural selection:

- There is natural variation among organisms.
- There is a struggle for survival as not all organisms can survive.
- Those with characteristics that lead to greater survivability and reproductive success are likely to have more descendants.
- These descendants in turn will more likely have those qualities that have led to greater survival.

Darwin, who was familiar with the mating of domestic animals, compared this process of natural selection to the process of **artificial selection,** in which breeders of animals and plants select those with the most desirable traits to breed. Over time, the animals and plants are likely to have the traits considered desirable by the breeder. For example, one of the authors of the present text has bred guppies. Using artificial selection, he has developed a strain with long, black flowing tails and largely black bodies. They do not breed one hundred percent true but are distinctive and far more striking than the typical guppy.

The idea of evolution had been around before Darwin, but no explanation in accordance with biological science had been proposed. Jean-Baptiste de Lamarck (1744–1829), a French biological theorist, had proposed the idea that characteristics acquired during an organism's lifetime are inherited. Lamarck's explanation of how giraffes came to have long necks, for example, was that generations of ancestors each stretched their necks a little bit. Unfortunately for the viability of Lamarck's theory, no biological mechanism for such a process could be found. Darwin's theory relied simply on the idea of natural variation and the selection of the fittest, in this case giraffes with longer necks. Darwin's theory did not accept the idea of such **inheritance of acquired characteristics.** Rather, his theory focused on the notion that the taller animals would have greater survivability and thus be more likely to pass the characteristic of a long neck than their shorter-neck giraffe peers would be to pass the characteristic of a shorter neck on to the next generation. They would be more likely to survive in times of drought and the next generation would thus tend toward higher necks. The discovery of genes as the material basis for inheritance was in accordance with Darwinian rather than Lamarckian principles.

Darwin also realized that some of the selective pressure on a species was based on sexual selection, that is, on the fact that some individual organisms were more able to compete with others, to attract mates and reproduce more successfully than others. Within species reproductive competition led to the selection of certain characteristics. Some of these characteristics were those that permitted individuals to gain an advantage over others. Among mammals, direct competition among males for females has led to the development of aggressivity, larger size, sharp teeth, horns, and antlers in some species, and a variety of other behaviors and physical traits designed to help their possessor win out over other males. In many species, competitive behaviors are at least partially ritualized. In both sexes, there has been an evolution of features and behaviors designed to attract the opposite sex. Good examples of the kinds of characteristics that are selected are the bright plumage of some male birds or many of the secondary sexual characteristics of human males and females (Darwin, 1871). Mate selection strategies as well as competition between potential mates are both behaviors of interest to contemporary evolutionary psychologists.

Regarding Darwin's theory, it is fascinating to note that he had knowledge neither of genes nor of DNA. He derived his theory from commonly observed phenomena, his own exploration of the variety of species, particularly in the Galapagos, and his deep thought and reflection about the processes that might be occurring in nature. His theory of evolution was based on thousands of observations, but it did not grow out of experimental laboratory research. If there was an experimenter, it was nature herself. Darwin was an observer of the results of the experiments of nature.

Robert M. Young (1996) has reviewed the various sources of ideas leading to Darwin's theory and commented that, to a large extent, Darwin extrapolated from the competitive no-holds-barred capitalism of the eighteenth century and social doctrines compatible with such an economic system to the entire biological world. In a sense, he was reasoning from his culturally embedded understanding of human society to that of all life. It was the reverse of what the naturalist Edward O. Wilson would do a century later when, getting ahead of our story, he applied ideas drawn from biology to human society.

Darwin is often overlooked in comparison with the more modern theorists of evolutionary psychology that this chapter will consider. In part, this is because Darwin's views about the evolution of human behavior were embedded in his overall theory. In addition to the theory of natural selection itself and the idea of sexual selection, some of Darwin's contributions most relevant to the eventual development of evolutionary psychology are:

- Darwin saw the biological makeup and form of an organism, whether it is a reptile or a human, as part of a single whole, and he recognized that organisms inherit not only their biological makeup but many instincts as well—that is, proclivities to behave in certain ways.
- Also, he focused explicitly on emotional expression (Darwin, 1872) and the similarity between human emotional expression and those of other primates, thus indicating the evolutionary origins of much of human expression of emotions.
- Finally, he focused on the development of a moral sense as part of his understanding of the evolutionary legacy of mankind (Darwin, 1859).

These subjects—particularly those of an evolutionary basis for human morality and altruistic behavior—were largely ignored for a century after Darwin and did not begin to surface again until after Hamilton's contribution of the theory of kin selection in 1964.

WILSON ENCOUNTERS HAMILTON'S IDEAS

During the early 1960s, London-based evolutionary biologist, William Hamilton, then a graduate student at Oxford, published groundbreaking articles (1964a, 1964b). These papers presented a new idea, **inclusive fitness,** that would be vital in the development of neo-Darwinism and eventually of evolutionary psychology. Hamilton proposed that biological selection operated not only in choosing the most fit individual, but that individuals might be selected because they enhanced the overall fitness of related individuals. Another term that was applied to the concept was kin selection. It took over a century for a major addition to Darwin's ideas to be proposed, and Hamilton was the person who did it. His articles have subsequently been cited thousands of times in scientific and scholarly publications.

Wilson, a leading scholar in evolutionary theory and insect behavior, read Hamilton's articles while traveling along the East Coast of the United States by train and quickly realized that Hamilton's ideas constituted a major paradigm shift in evolutionary theory. According to Wilson:

> What made Hamilton's idea immediately attractive was that it helped to resolve the classic problem in evolutionary theory of how self-sacrifice can become a genetically fixed trait. It might seem on first thought—without considering kin selection—that selfishness must reign complete in the living world, and that cooperation can never appear except to enhance selfish ends. But no, if an altruistic act helps relatives, it increases the survival of genes that are identical with those of the altruist, just as the case in parents and offspring. (Wilson, 1994, p. 317)

Wilson could see that Hamilton's ideas, as he proposed them, were immediately relevant to understanding the evolutionary rationale underlying the self-sacrificial behavior of the social insects. It was apparent to him that Hamilton's theory could explain such behavior in a way that Darwin's theory never could.

Hamilton's principle was **kin selection,** an inherent and inherited predisposition to act altruistically for relatives (kin or kinfolk). Most simply expressed, it works like this: an individual who is closely related to other individuals is likely to have many genes in common. That individual whose behavior enhances the survival of relatives, or *kin*, is thus likely also to promote the survival and reproduction of genes identical to those in his or her body.

Hamilton's proposal prompted a revolution in thought that led to contemporary evolutionary psychology. The switch was from focusing on differential survival of the fittest person to differential survival of the fittest gene. This gene-centered, or **selfish gene theory** (Dawkins, 1989), indicated that a gene might be selected not only if it enhanced the survivability of the individual organism in which it was found, but also if that organism acted in such a way as to enhance the survivability of other organisms with the same gene. With this shift in focus from the "fit individual" to the "selfish gene," evolutionary theory was able to accommodate not only nature "red in tooth and claw" but also the evolutionary value of prosocial and altruistic behaviors. It became a theory of much greater interest and relevance to psychologists.

Good examples of inclusive fitness, kin selection, or selfish genes can be found in an ant colony, one of Wilson's most familiar areas of study. Hamilton's theory provided a rationale for the "altruistic" behavior of a nonreproducing member of the colony such as a worker ant or, more dramatically, a soldier ant. In such cases, the activities of these ants, that do not reproduce themselves, engage in activities that enhance the survivability of the colony and, specifically the survivability of genes in the queen or males, genes which are identical to many genes in the soldier or worker ants.

David Barash drew attention to the example of a theorist, Ronald Fisher, who in the 1920s anticipated the evolutionary significance of altruism and even altruistic sacrifice. Fisher understood that a brightly colored, but bad-tasting caterpillar killed by a hungry bird would serve to make it less likely that the bird would attack other similarly colored caterpillars (Barash, 2001, p. 45). However, Fisher's ideas were that of sacrifice for the common good and did not include Hamilton's more precise and valid theory of kin selection.

A personal example of kin selection may be helpful as an illustration of the kin selection process. One of the authors' grandmothers had a sister who never married or had any children of her own. The unmarried sister devoted much of her life to helping rear her married sister's six children, her nieces and nephews. Her genes did not directly reproduce themselves, but the family members she helped nurture in infancy and childhood had many genes identical to her own. Her altruistic maternal nature thus promoted the survival of genetic material identical to her own, even though it was passed on from her sister to her children, the aunt's nieces and nephews.

One concept that evolutionary psychologists emphasize is the meaning of the term **altruism.** In relation to the concepts of kin selection, inclusive fitness, and the selfish gene, the meaning is somewhat different and more general than the usual usage of the term. The term *altruism*, as used in ordinary discourse, usually refers to behavior that is guided by an altruistic intent. From the point of view of modern evolutionary theory, *altruism* refers to behavior or activity that may occur with or without any conscious altruistic intent.

FROM INSECT SOCIETIES TO SOCIOBIOLOGY TO HUMAN NATURE

At the beginning of the 1970s, Wilson was writing a book on the behavior of the social insects. This book, *Insect Societies* (1971), applied the principles of sociobiology, which included natural selection, sexual selection, and Hamilton's new ideas of kin selection as a unifying construct in the structure and functioning of insect society. At that time, Wilson envisaged proceeding even further in the future. He was already thinking about applying the principles of **sociobiology** to other species, even including vertebrates. He wrote:

> In spite of the phylogenetic remoteness of vertebrates and insects and the basic distinction between their respective personal and impersonal systems of communication, these two groups of animals have evolved social behaviors that are similar in degree of complexity and convergent in many important details. This fact conveys a special promise that sociobiology can eventually be derived from the first principles of population and behavioral biology and developed into a single, mature science. (Wilson, 1971, p. 460)

In his next book, *Sociobiology: The New Synthesis* (1975), Wilson summarized his understanding of the principles of sociobiology to the whole array of social organisms, from colonies of bacteria, coral colonies, and social insects to social vertebrates, including the great apes. Finally, in the last chapter, he included in his analysis a sociobiological view of human behavior. He wrote that, if we were zoologists from outer space:

> ...the humanities and social science [would] shrink to specialized branches of biology—history, biography and fictions are the research protocols of human ethnology; and anthropology and sociology together constitute the sociobiology of a single primate species. (1975, p. 547)

Later, in response to criticism, Wilson said that he did not see anything wrong in including humans in *Sociobiology: The New Synthesis*. After all, he reasoned:

> [Human] history did not begin 10,000 years ago.... It spans the 2 million years of the life of the genus *Homo*. Deep history—by which I mean biological history—made us what we are, no less than culture. (1994, p. 328)

In 1978 Wilson published *On Human Nature*, which fully focused on the relevance of sociobiology for human behavior. This book brought together many observations and areas of understanding to form a basis for a human branch of sociobiology, *human sociobiology*. Some topics that Wilson examined from the point of view of sociobiology include: aggression, altruism, bonding, child development, culture, extroversion, familial behavior, gender differences, heroism, introversion, learning, love, prepared learning, rites of passage, reciprocal altruism, sex, the soul, and warfare. As a mature scholar, Wilson still maintained his interest in ant behavior (Figure 17.2).

Sociobiology: A New Synthesis and *On Human Nature* were controversial books because they persuasively challenged prevailing environmentalist theories in psychology and the social science with new insights (Wilson, 1994, pp. 330–353). Some prominent critics incorrectly believed that Wilson's ideas were racist. Environmental determinists disagreed with the idea of a fundamental human nature and wanted to think that people could be molded to behave in radically new ways. Alcock (2001) recounts an incident illustrating the controversial nature of sociobiology in the late 1970s:

> On 15 February, 1978, a young woman carefully poured a pitcher of ice water onto the head of Edward O. Wilson while he sat waiting to address an audience at the annual meeting of the American Association for the Advancement of Science. A band of accomplices joined their pitcher-pouring confederate on stage to wave placards chanting, "Wilson, you're all wet." (p. 3)

Today, much of this controversy has died down. The issue now for psychologists is to sort out the degree to which inherited behavioral proclivities play a role in our behavior and to what extent we are free to change.

Figure 17.2 Edward O. Wilson studying ants in Costa Rica in 1984. As a middle-aged man, Wilson still had an avid interest in ant behavior.

Many of the ideas that Wilson put forth in *Sociobiology: A New Synthesis* and *On Human Nature* can be viewed as the presentation of the reasoning underlying a new field and the generation of ideas, many of which would be explored in the future by generations of researchers. Wilson's book has served as a basic foundation for the now burgeoning evolutionary psychology movement.

In the last decade, the term **evolutionary psychology** has increasingly been used for that sub-area of sociobiology that focuses on human behavior, both individually and in groups. The term *evolutionary psychology* also emphasizes the relevance of evolutionary theory for the different fields of psychology (including abnormal psychology, cognitive psychology, developmental psychology, learning, neuropsychological personality theory, sensation and perception, and social psychology) just as the term **evolutionary medicine** indicates a field that explores diseases and their treatments from the point of view of sociobiology. The term **human sociobiology,** favored by Wilson (2001), emphasizes the connectedness of human studies with the study of other organisms.

Before considering further developments in the thinking of evolutionary psychologists, we can examine some of the evolutionary concepts in classical personality theories.

EVOLUTIONARY CONCEPTS IN CLASSICAL PERSONALITY THEORIES

Modern evolutionary psychologists are not the first to take evolutionary theory into account in their explorations of human behavior. Many of the classical personality theorists also considered the process of biological evolution as relevant to their work. They drew on various elements of evolutionary theory and applied it in different ways. Their efforts to base personality theory on evolutionary concepts were hampered, however, by their lack of expertise in evolutionary biology or by inadequacies in the theories that were available to them at the time of their theorizing. Most of them completed their theories before the development of Hamilton's concept of *inclusive fitness*.

Freud was familiar with Darwin's theory, referred to him often in his works, and had an extensive library of the writings of Darwin and related theorists (Ritvo, 1990). Freud's theorizing was very much concerned with the instinctual makeup of humans. His ideas of sexual and aggressive instincts were based as much or more on his reading of Darwin's idea of selection of the fittest as on clinical observation. Freud's *id* contained biological drives, which had evolved through the process of natural selection. He understood altruism and abstinence from behaviors hurtful to others as superego functions, which could be understood not as proclivities based on biology, but as learned forms of behavior. Today much altruistic behavior is seen as a biological proclivity based on the idea of inclusive fitness or kin selection.

In addition to Darwin's idea of natural selection, Freud referred to what he thought to be the early experiences of humanity in *Totem and Taboo* (1913b) in his derivation of many concepts (Freud, 1913b). Freud's resort to the inheritance of ancestral experiences was a throwback to discredited Lamarckian thinking, reviewed earlier in this chapter.

Does Pathology Recapitulate Phylogeny?

Freud specifically proposed that the transference and narcissistic neuroses form a chronology that parallels and recapitulates in individual development the evolutionary development of the human species (**phylogeny**). Specifically, he proposed that if the transference and narcissistic neuroses are arranged according to the developmental period in which they typically occur, a pattern emerges that parallels evolutionary development:

> ...anxiety hysteria, almost without precondition, is the earliest [neurosis], closely followed by conversion hysteria (from about the fourth year); somewhat later in prepuberty (9–10) obsessional neurosis appears in children. The narcissistic neuroses are absent in childhood. Of these, dementia praecox [schizophrenia] in classic form is [an] illness of the puberty years, paranoia approaches the mature years, and melancholia-mania the same time period, otherwise not specifiable. (Freud, 1915d, p. 12)

Freud was wrong about the absence of what he called "the narcissistic neuroses" (especially schizophrenia) in childhood, but that was the prevailing view in his day. Nevertheless, he argued that each characteristic neurosis represents a regression to:

> ...phases that the whole human race had to go through at some time from the beginning to the end of the Ice Age, so that at that time all human beings were the way only some of them are today, by virtue of hereditary tendency and by means of new acquisition. (Freud, 1915d, p. 13)

What can we make of Freud's speculations? They are of a piece with his speculations along evolutionary lines in such works as *Totem and Taboo* and *Beyond the Pleasure Principle*. They are fraught with biological, psychological, and anthropological errors and omissions. Nevertheless, they represent an imaginative attempt to bring order to a wealth of observations in a way that was consistent with Freud's central vision of metapsychology as the overarching theory of psychoanalysis as a science. Freud extended the biologist Ernst Haeckel's dictum ("**Ontogeny** recapitulates phylogeny"—development of the individual embryo parallels the stages of human evolution) with his own version: *pathology* recapitulates phylogeny. Today, Haeckel's concept is a historical curiosity no longer considered valid by biologists.

Jung's Lamarckian Views

Carl Jung (Chapter 5) also drew on ideas having to do with evolution in developing his theories. Jung did not believe that Darwin's ideas of selection of the fittest could adequately explain the collective unconscious and its contents. In Jung's view, all of the archetypes and their contents were derived from the repetitive experiences of our ancestors over thousands and thousands of generations. The collective unconscious was the sum total of such experiences, and the specific archetypes were, so to speak, crystallizations of experience. For example, the mother archetype was said to be the result of innumerable generations of human experiences with their mothers. Again, it should be pointed out that these Lamarckian ideas are now discredited. There is no biological mechanism to explain the inheritance of experiences.

So, Jung's view—similar to that of many contemporary evolutionary psychologists—was that humans inherit many proclivities to behave in different ways. But his idea of an explanatory mechanism was far different from that of contemporary biology or psychology. For the most part, his theories appear to be most consistent with the discredited Lamarckian view (i.e., the inheritance of acquired characteristics).

Nonetheless, many of Jung's conclusions, although without a valid biological basis, are often very similar to Wilson's views of human nature. Jung, like Wilson, wrote of deeply embedded proclivities to think, experience reality, and behave in specific ways. He spoke very clearly of the similarity of his concept of archetype with instincts in the animal world (Evans, 1964).

Adler, Erikson, and Evolutionary Theory

Alfred Adler (Chapter 4) drew conclusions based on evolutionary theory that were different from either Freud or Jung for understanding human behavior. In Adler's view, the prime motive of superiority was another way of referring to optimal adaptation. Adler believed that evolutionary factors motivated each individual to achieve maximal fitness ("superiority") in his or her environment and to overcome any inferiority feelings he or she might have. This emphasis on adaptive fitness was far different from Freud's view of our biological legacy as primarily consisting of sexual and aggressive drives.

Adler's notion of the ideal motive as an altruistic promotion of life wherever one found it is very similar to the importance of altruism in current evolutionary psychology. It did not seem to be based on any biological theory of the time.

Erik Erikson's concepts of *ritual* and *ritualization* (Chapter 8) were derived from the evolutionary views of ethologists. He thought people engaged in such patterns, as did many other vertebrates, but endowed them with human levels of meaning. This is consistent with Erikson's view of the biologically based psychosexual stages of Freud as replete with interpersonal significance.

Erikson's idea of the importance of generativity in midlife and beyond is consistent with the kin selection theory. Once a person is no longer able to reproduce, his or her evolutionary value lies only in the promotion of the viability of others. The healthy middle-aged person in Erikson's epigenetic theory moves toward helping the next generation.

Behaviorism and Evolutionary Theory

Ivan Pavlov and B. F. Skinner, in their studies of conditioning, tried to demonstrate how organisms had inherited mechanisms that enabled them flexibly to adapt to a variety of conditions in which they might find themselves. In their view, the possibility of being conditioned *itself* was adaptive.

Skinner, in fact, wrote a paper in which he indicated the parallels between operant conditioning and the survival of the fittest in evolution (1981). Just as Darwin indicated that natural selection depended upon choosing the most adaptive of many variations so, in conditioning, reinforcement of adaptive behavior through rewards or punishments shaped behavior (see Table 17.1).

Pavlov and Skinner originally assumed that all neutral stimuli could serve equally well as conditioning stimuli and that different behaviors could be equally conditioned. Findings contrary to these assumptions eventually surfaced. It is noteworthy that these contrary findings are along the lines of what might be expected if organisms had behavioral predispositions or instincts to act in certain ways that were adaptive from an evolutionary point of view.

In a landmark study, Jose Garcia and Kurt Koelling (1966) exposed rats to specific light, noise, and taste stimuli as they licked water from a drinking tube. Following drinking, the rats were exposed to radiation of sufficient dosage to induce nausea. If Pavlovian conditioning were automatic, then each of the stimuli preceding the unconditioned stimulus (irradiation-nausea) would become an effective avoidance cue in the future. But, in fact, the rats learned to avoid only the sweet taste of the water. Sweet, but not "bright" or "noisy" water became associated with illness. A second group of rats was subjected to the same procedure, but electric shock was used in place of the radiation. This electric shock group learned to avoid the "bright" and "noisy" water, but not the sweet water. Apparently, animals are more "prepared" to associate nausea with taste cues than with auditory or visual cues. Or, more generally, rats are biologically prepared to associate specific stimuli with particular effects while selectively ignoring other stimuli (see also Garcia, McGowan, Ervin, & Koelling, 1968).

Martin Seligman (1970, 1971, 1972) and Hans Eysenck (1976) have argued that organisms evolved to learn some stimulus relationships more effectively than others. An animal that rapidly learns to make associations, for example, between taste and subsequent illness is likely to survive by avoiding poisonous foods after only one taste. However, if all stimuli impinging on the animal at the time of the first poisoning were equally conditionable, its chances of repeatedly ingesting larger doses of the same noxious food increase.

In a similar way, human phobias reflect a limited number of feared stimuli rather than all possible objects in the neurotic person's world of dangers. Phobic people

Table 17.1 Comparing Natural Selection with Operant Conditioning

	Darwin's natural selection	*Skinner's operant conditioning*
Variation in:	Individuals of a species.	Behaviors of an individual organism.
Selective mechanism:	Survival of the fittest.	Reinforcement or punishment.
Consequence:	"Fit" organisms selected.	Reinforced behaviors of a single organism persist.

fear dangerous animals such as snakes and spiders; they fear high places, cramped places, and dark places; it is very rare they have phobias of cocktail tables, iPods, flowered wallpaper, or killer burritos. Our human forebears had legitimate survival needs reflected in their fears of snakes, spiders, and high and dark places, so an innate predisposition to be fearful of and to avoid certain classes of stimuli was favored by natural selection (Rachman, 1978). Such stimuli have been called "prepared" stimuli and the fears associated with them "prepared" fears on the assumption that evolution selection pressures have somehow selected nervous systems with special sensitivities (Seligman, 1970). By the same token, such "preparation" also limits the range of effective classically conditionable stimuli.

It is well to note that alternative explanations of why some stimuli are more easily conditionable than others have been offered (Bandura, 1977b, pp. 75 ff.). There is some evidence to suggest that instead of innate "preparedness" as the facilitator in some learning, it is rather the organism's capacity to discriminate selectively among stimuli and to be sensitive to the delay between the stimulus and its noxious effects (e.g., Krane & Wagner, 1975).

In the field of operant conditioning, similar biological and evolutionarily based limitations have been found. A husband and wife team of professional animal trainers, Keller and Marian Breland, reported an amusing and important set of limitations on the operant shaping techniques. Breland and Breland (1961) had, for a number of years, adopted the behavioristic spirit of the times: "If it moves, we can shape it." But they ran into trouble.

Working with a raccoon for a bank display, the Brelands tried to shape the animal to pick up coins one at a time and drop them into a container for positive reinforcement. Shaping worked well in getting the raccoon to pick up two coins, but he seemed not to be able to let go of them, despite the fact that reinforcement was available only when both coins had been dropped in the "bank." As the frustrated reinforcers reported:

> He would rub [the coin] up against the inside of the container, pull it back out, clutch it firmly for several seconds. However, he would finally turn it loose and receive his food reinforcement. Then the final contingency . . . that he pick up both coins and put them in the container.

> Now the raccoon really had problems (and so did we). Not only could he not let go of the coins, but he spent seconds, even minutes, rubbing them together (in a most miserly fashion), and dipping them into the container. He carried on this behavior to such an extent that the practical application we had in mind—a display featuring a raccoon putting money in a piggy bank—simply was not feasible. The rubbing behavior became worse and worse as time went on, in spite of nonreinforcement. (Breland & Breland, 1961, p. 682)

The recalcitrant raccoon was merely behaving instinctually, "washing" and rubbing clean his food—or anything else that found its way into his paws. Raccoons were not the only animals whose conditioning was affected by their instinctual behavioral proclivities:

> In a similarly frustrating fashion, attempts to train a pig to pick up a silver dollar, carry it to a "piggy bank" and deposit it were blocked by the pig's increasing slowness, his constantly dropping it to root it along the ground with his nose, toss it in the air, root it, and so on. (Breland & Breland, 1961, p. 683)

Like the raccoon's, the pig's behavior could be shaped only to the point at which its instinctual repertoire of behaviors took dominance.

"Instinctual drift," as the Brelands termed it, was responsible for the human frustration in these cases of well applied but futile operant conditioning techniques:

The general principle seems to be that whenever an animal has strong instinctive behaviors in the area of the conditioned response, after continued running the organism will drift toward the instinctive behavior even to the delay or preclusion of the reinforcement. In a very boiled-down, simplified form, it might be stated as "Learned behavior drifts toward instinctive behavior." (Breland & Breland, 1961, p. 684)

Even the most trainable animals are not the models of environmental plasticity envisioned by the early radical behaviorists. Biological limits, species-specific behaviors, and innate predispositions all place a ceiling on the effectiveness and reliability of operant conditioning (but see Skinner, 1975). It is worth mentioning in passing that in an updated account of the "misbehavior of organisms," Marian Breland-Bailey (formerly Marian Breland) and Robert Bailey (1993) have made clear that their experiences never caused them to dismiss reinforcement theory. Rather, in more sophisticated fashion, they had tried to understand the frustrating results they sometimes encountered as a window to understanding the limitations of operant theory.

FURTHER DEVELOPMENTS IN EVOLUTIONARY PSYCHOLOGICAL THINKING

We have already considered the importance of:

- the original Darwinian theory of evolution by natural selection,
- sexual selection, and
- the kin selection process

The insight that such processes have influenced the development of human as well as animal behavior has also been considered.

Some additional ideas that are central in the development of modern evolutionary psychology include: the importance of the environment of evolutionary adaptedness (EEA), reciprocal or "soft-core" altruism, the modularity of brain functioning, and the idea of the emergence of new behaviors through the process of exaptation. A timetable of developments in evolutionary psychology is presented in Table 17.2.

Table 17.2   Evolutionary Psychology Timetable

Theorist	Year	Discovery or publication
Charles Darwin, Alfred Wallace	1859	Evolution by natural selection
Charles Darwin	1871	Sexual selection
Konrad Lorenz & Niko Tinbergen	1951	Fixed action patterns
William Hamilton	1964	Inclusive fitness, kin selection
Robert Trivers	1972	Reciprocal altruism
Numerous authors	early 1970s	Early formulations of the impact of early human, hominid environments on current human behavior
Edward O. Wilson	1975	*Sociobiology: The New Synthesis* published
Edward O. Wilson	1978	Sociobiology applied to humans
Jerry Fodor	1988	Modularity of mind
John Tooby & Leda Cosmides	1990	More modules, EEA elaborated

Why the Environment of Evolutionary Adaptedness (EEA) Is So Important

A concept of great significance to many evolutionary psychologists is called, "the **environment of evolutionary adaptedness (EEA).**" This is the presumed environment in which our ancestors lived for about seven million years. The switch to agriculture as a source of food is thought to have occurred only in the last 10,000 years. Our early ancestors were hunter-gatherers and the selective pressures of their difficult environments for millions of years have shaped much of our genetically determined behavior. Consequently, many of the genes underlying our behavior may or may not be suited to our lives in a modern, industrialized world (Tooby & DeVore, 1987, Gaulin & McBurney, 2001, pp. 88–90).

An example of the impact of the EEA is our sweet tooth and love of sugar, as well as our love of fatty meats. In the EEA—and probably for millions of years among our prehominid ancestors—a sweet tooth and a craving for sweetness were very helpful in raising the caloric intake of our ancestors. Hominids with a sweet tooth and a craving for sugary items were more likely to find leaves, stems, flowers, and plants with higher caloric value. Love of fatty meats also helped provide adequate caloric intake in the EEA.

In today's society, with its processed foods and its plentiful food supply, the proclivity to eat sugary foods and fatty meats has contributed to obesity, illness, and death. Eating sugary foods and fatty meats are risk factors for a number of life-threatening diseases including heart disease (from arterial blockages) and diabetes. Most of us are outliving our hominid ancestors, but this knowledge is not comforting to a person in his or her fifties who develops heart failure.

It has been speculated that the EEA included a very competitive, politicized, social environment. A text on evolutionary psychology, in describing social aspects of the EEA, portrays a situation not unlike a contemporary academic department or part of a large corporation.

> ...hominids regularly associated with other members of their species. Their social groups were fairly small, consisting of fewer than one hundred individuals, and were semiclosed. As a result, hominids typically interacted with a limited set of associates whom they know as distinct individuals. (Gaulin & McBurney, 2001, p. 89)

And, perhaps more to the point:

> Within hominid groups, social interactions were complex. Members of the social group were potentially valuable allies whose favor was worth cultivating for the benefits they could provide in times of shortage or illness or when cooperative activities could increase foraging yields. However, as constant companions, other members of the groups were also often significant competitors for important resources. Gaining and keeping reliable allies without forfeiting too many key resources must have presented a constantly shifting set of social challenges. (Gaulin & McBurney, 2001, p. 89)

The more things change, the more they remain the same. We might consider human behavior to include not only altruistic behavior—as per the kin selection theory—but also tactics and strategies for dealing with others. Perhaps humans could properly be called, "the political animal."

In summary, the EEA can serve as a source of hypotheses for the genetic origins of behaviors that do not seem adaptive in the current environment.

Problems with the EEA Theory

The use of the EEA has a number of built-in problems. First, we have reason to doubt how accurate our knowledge of the EEA actually is. After all, we were not around seven million years ago to observe the behavior of our ancestors. We must extrapolate their behavior from the study of primates and from the findings of paleoanthropologists.

Also, the EEA is a rather long span of time. How do we account for the fact that our ancestors may have lived in different climatic periods, that they may have had different modes of adaptation at different times and in different eras? Are any of these periods of special importance? Any or all of these could have resulted in changes in our genomes. Perhaps, instead of EEA, we should refer to *environments* of evolutionary adaptedness, or EEA. Different behaviors could well have had their origins in different periods of evolutionary adaptation, some occurring before our hominid ancestors existed and others more recently.

The farming-civilization period, which occurred after the EEA, may have affected our genetic inheritance. Like domesticated animals, our genetically determined behavior may have been modified to a certain extent by our ancestors not living "in the wild" but living in relatively settled communities for 10,000 or more years. This appears to be the environment in which reading first appeared as an emergent function, not in the EEA.

Reciprocal, Soft-Core Altruism

Kin selection theory indicated that organisms, including people, would act in ways to promote the survival of relatives with many genes identical to their own. Wilson termed such altruism "hard-core" altruism in that it had a specific biological mechanism. The biologist Robert Trivers (1971) proposed another type of altruism that he termed **"reciprocal altruism,"** which Wilson would later call "soft-core altruism" (Wilson, 1978, p. 157).

Gaulin & McBurney (2001, pp. 75–76) have provided an example of reciprocal altruism, in which two hunter-gatherers share food. In this example, we assume that the two hunter-gatherers are strangers and not related. When "Zug" is successful in a hunt, he gives food to "Og," who otherwise might starve to death. Later Og returns the favor. Therefore, the result is that instead of becoming two dead hunter-gatherers, both Zug and Og survive to hunt again.

But, in Trivers's analysis, the important point is that, for altruism to be beneficial to the altruist, it must be reciprocal. That is, the person who is the recipient of help must be willing to provide it in the future if the quality of altruism is to be of selective value to the giver.

So, how can hard-core and soft-core altruism be distinguished? Helping kin who share your genes and can pass them on to future generations is hard-core altruism. Helping others in cooperative ventures in which you will likely benefit also is soft-core altruism. Occasionally hard-core and soft-core altruism might overlap, as in a family business or among a tribe of related hunters.

Modularity of Mind

A relative newcomer to the theories used by evolutionary psychologists is the notion of the **modularity of mind.** The modern version of the idea of mental faculties was proposed by Jerry Fodor (1983), who proposed that the mind also consisted of general-purpose central processes. Leta Cosmides and John Tooby (2003) have reduced

BOX 17.2 *Only Connect . . .*

The concept of mental modules is very similar to Gordon Allport's concept of trait. Allport's concept of trait does not, however, imply the necessary "hard-wiring" implied in the mental module concept. As indicated in Chapter 11, Allport defined trait as "a neuropsychic structure having the capacity to render many stimuli functionally equivalent and to initiate and guide equivalent (meaningfully consistent) forms of adaptive and expressive behavior (1961, p. 347). A mental module functions similarly. It, too, is a neuropsychic structure that identifies a variety of stimuli as having the same or similar meaning and leads to similar behavior. A predator detection module of a chick, for example, identifies the form of a hawk above it as a danger from which it must flee.

the emphasis of Fodor's central process and emphasized that the brain consists of many (hundreds or thousands) smaller sub-organs or modules, each of which evolved for specific purposes. They have alluded to their model as a Swiss Army knife model of the brain. Some of these modules, relatively unchanged, have an evolutionary history that is millions of years old.

We have traditionally viewed such behavioral proclivities without thinking of mental modules or neuronal wiring that underlies them. Even another way of looking at instincts is to think of them as a result of inherited parts of the genome that are responsible for the development of those brain patterns leading to specified mental activities.

According to the theory of the modularity of mind, the same sense of continuity and innovation applies to the workings of our brain. In the modular view of Cosmides and Tooby (1992), our brain consists of many such modules, some of which have been passed on with little variation from our reptilian and mammalian ancestors and others of which have developed anew or from small beginnings from our hominid or early human ancestors.

According to the modular theorists, there are inherited modules for any number of functions in animals and/or humans. Many animals have a **predator detection module,** which identifies dangerous predators. There are also mate selection modules and even language modules. One proposed module in humans is the **cheater detection module,** necessary if reciprocal altruism is to work (Barkow, Cosmides, & Tooby, 1992).

Exaptation: One Means of Evolution

One facet of current evolutionary theory is the idea of how new features or behaviors may emerge. In this process, a feature or behavior that was originally not selected may emerge (Wilson, 1978, pp. 71–97). The term **exaptation** indicates that characteristics that were selected in a given environment could prove valuable in a different environment, and for novel reasons. For example, birds' feathers are thought to have arisen for purposes of insulation from cold and only millions of years later developed for the purposes of gliding and then flying (Tattersall, 1998).

Some capacities, though initially not selected for, may thus become adaptive. A human example is that the complex human brain did not originally evolve to read or to do computer programming. Reading and computer programming are exaptations or emergent functions of a nervous system that did not evolve originally in order to be able to read or to do programming.

Facultative Adaptations

Many traits are facultative, that is, their expression depends on environmental conditions. In the area of physical characteristics, a person who uses tools frequently may develop calluses. The development of calluses is a **facultative adaptation,** a genetic potential that is expressed only with use. A person who never uses his or her hands to do heavy work will never develop calluses.

Likewise, a person who goes through intensive training to engage in special combat operations is likely to demonstrate a degree of alertness and readiness to spring into action not often seen among civilians. His or her level of alertness, readiness to fight, and associated hormonal activities are different from those of a sedentary civilian. In effect, the human species can provide a "soldier human" and a "worker human." Unlike an ant colony, these types do not represent separate fixed, biologically-determined castes but are facultative adjustments to different environmental requirements.

HUMAN NATURE DOES EXIST

In his book, *On Human Nature* (1978), Wilson indicated ways in which human nature was similar to that of the great apes and many monkey species:

- Our intimate social groupings contain on the order of ten to one hundred adults, never just two, as in most birds and marmosets or up to thousands, as in many kinds of fishes and insects.
- Males are larger than females.... ['I']he average number of females consorting with successful males closely corresponds to the size gap between males and females.... When the sexual size difference in human beings is plotted on the curve based on other kinds of mammals, the predicted average number of females per successful male turns out to be greater than one but less than three. The prediction is close to reality; we know we are a mildly polygynous species.
- The young are molded by a long period of social training, first by closest associations with the mother, then to an increasing degree with other children of the same age and sex.
- Social play is a strongly developed activity featuring role practice, mock aggression, sex practice, and exploration. (Wilson, 1978, pp. 20–21)

Wilson (1978) also noted commonalities among all human societies. He referred to the work of the anthropologist George Murdock (1945), who enumerated behavioral characteristics that have been noted in every culture that had been studied up to that time:

> Age grading, athletic sports, bodily adornment, calendar, cleanliness, training, community, organization, cooking, cooperative labor, cosmology, courtship, dancing, decorative art, eschatology, ethics, ethnobotany, etiquette, faith healing, family feasting, fire making, folklore, food taboos, funeral rites, games, gestures, gift giving, incest taboos, inheritance rules, joking, kin groups, kinship nomenclature, language, law, luck superstitions, magic, marriage, mealtimes, medicine, obstetrics, penal sanctions, personal names, population policy, postnatal care, pregnancy usages, property rights, propitiation of supernatural beings, puberty customs, religious ritual, residence rules, sexual restriction, soul concepts, status differentiation, surgery, tool making, trade, visiting, weaving, and weather control. (Murdock, 1945, pp. 124–142)

We could add music, dancing, and keeping rhythms.

Along the same, lines, David Barash commented,

...nowhere are there people among whom men are less violent than women, who consider eighty year olds more sexually attractive than twenty year olds, or who do not favor their relative over strangers. (Barash, 2001)

Wilson proposes that such qualities are among the basics of *human* nature and states, "It is easy to imagine nonhuman societies whose members are even more intelligent and complexly organized than ourselves, yet lack a majority of the qualities just listed" (1978, p. 22). Wilson, who had been immersed for many years in the study of ants, was well aware of the differences between ant and human societies and probably did not have much trouble imagining how different a more intelligent ant society would be from the human world.

One could argue that some of these characteristics listed by Murdock may have represented cultural innovations (without a genetic basis) that spread through prehistorical human societies; nonetheless, humans, by nature, had to have had the capacity to acquire and the proclivity to pass on such innovations. We might teach dogs or horses to dance in a rhythmic way, but they do not seem to continue to engage in such behaviors once outside of human influence.

The underlying ideas of sociobiology—*natural selection, sexual selection, kin selection, reciprocal altruism, exaptation, modularity of mind,* together with reference to our EEA—has led to examination of numerous behaviors and traits and could lead to the exploration of innumerable other characteristics of individuals and human groups and societies as well as interpersonal and intergroup behaviors. The purpose of this chapter is not to review all such areas but to demonstrate how the evolutionary psychological approach can proceed and to provide a number of examples.

EVOLUTIONARY PSYCHOLOGY FROM A BROADER, MORE OBJECTIVE PERSPECTIVE

In order to gain a little more objectivity, let us take the example, not of a human infant, but of a little puppy brought home from the pet store. One level of behavior has to do with experiences the little puppy might have had before you bought him. You might wonder or even ask, "How old was he when he was weaned? Was he treated with kindness or hit by people? Was he left alone and neglected? What was his position among the rest of the litter?" Accurate information about such areas might reveal something about his physical health and (depending on your preferred psychological theory) something about his ability to form ties or to bond and his general disposition or his conditioned patterns of behavior. The last part of the story has to do with the environment you provide, in terms of both the physical environment and the human and animal environment. Also, what new behaviors does the dog learn from you and your family? What pet tricks do you teach the puppy, and so on?

The part omitted from this analysis of your dog's behavior is its actual "dogginess." As a member of the dog species, your puppy is very likely to bond with you and other family members as its wolf ancestors would have done to the wolf pack. You or another family member might become your puppy's *alpha* male or female. Your dog will be territorial and, if given the opportunity, proceed to mark his territory. He may have a tendency to chase cars, to hunt squirrels, and to pile up newspapers at the front door.

So the full understanding of your dog's behavior requires knowing, not only about his early puppy experiences and his subsequent learning, but also about his instinctive behaviors and tendencies to act in certain ways, based on his legacy as a dog.

(We could even dig deeper and examine his instinctive behaviors that can be attributed to mammalian or even vertebrate legacies, which he shares with humans.) Regardless of his early and later influences, your dog is not going to behave like a cat, a ferret, a gerbil, or a pet lizard or a human. His genetic and evolutionary background is an overarching influence on his subsequent emotional development and environmental reinforcement.

Likewise, you, a human being, are shaped by your early experiences as an infant and a child, by your subsequent learning and development—as indicated by many of the theories in this text. What evolutionary psychology draws our attention to is the very fact that you are human and that it is not only your childhood and infancy that have an impact on you, but also those behaviors that evolved in your ancestors and enabled them to pass their genes on to you.

Unlike a Lamarckian or Jungian view (Chapter 5), this formulation does not indicate that your ancestors' experiences are reproduced in you or that their behaviors were in any way passed on to you. What it indicates is that, of the wide variety of humanoid beings that existed in the past, only those who had certain predispositions to behave (including thinking and feeling) in certain ways were able to continue to pass on their genes in the sequence of environments that they faced. And we current humans are *their* progeny.

An Aside: Comparing Kittens, Puppies, and Children

Concerning dog behavior, the evolutionary biologist David Barash points out a fact regarding toilet training that, using theories underlying evolutionary psychology, we can see with new eyes. He asks why it is that cats and dogs, which he terms "stupider" than humans, can be potty-trained in a few days or weeks, but human babies take years to learn the process. Answering his own question, Barash notes that the ground-dwelling ancestors of cats and dogs had to hide their fecal material or keep it away from their usual habitat in order to avoid attracting predators, while this factor was not present in tree-dwellers. But, he notes:

> By contrast [to dogs and cats], human beings, like other primates evolved in the trees. Tidy potty habits simply aren't an issue for arboreal creatures (although they can be a problem for those poor unfortunates down below!). This is almost certainly the reason why other primates, such as chimpanzees or monkeys, also resist toilet-training. It goes against a deep-seated inclination. (Barash, 2001, p. 208)

This example is a good illustration of the difference between the implications of Lamarck's theory of the inheritance of acquired characteristics and Darwin's theory of natural selection. If Lamarck's theory were correct, human infants by now would have gotten the hang of potty training because of the efforts of generations. This is clearly not the case. We might speculate that, unless facility at being toilet trained leads to a child's genes being more likely to be passed on to the next generation, human babies in the future will continue to have more trouble being toilet trained than cats and dogs.

The thinking of an evolutionary psychologist might also approach a very common phenomenon in a way different from the classical personality theories.

SOME MISCONCEPTIONS ABOUT EVOLUTIONARY PSYCHOLOGY

David M. Buss (1999) has summarized some frequent misunderstandings about evolutionary psychology. They include the following:

- Some falsely assume that evolutionary theory proposes genetic determinism without input from the environment. Buss points out that many evolutionarily determined behaviors are responses to specific environments. Such adaptations in response to specific conditions as we have noted, are termed facultative behaviors. A simple physical example of a facultative response is that calluses develop in response to use. A fight-flight response may occur in response to a physically threatening situation.
- Another false belief is that we humans cannot change our behavior, that it is entirely determined by evolution and by our genes. At the very least, our knowledge of evolutionary mechanisms can lead us to change our behavior. We might learn, for example, that we have an ingrained tendency to be afraid of closed-in places or nonvenomous snakes. We can often overcome such phobias through behavioral therapies, such as desensitization or implosion.
- A false assumption is that we have been optimally designed by evolution. Buss points to the time lag, that we in many cases are better adapted to earlier environments than to our current world. If we were better adapted to our current environment, then all of us would have as easy a time learning to read as we do to speak (cf. Cartwright, 2000, p. 40).
- Another assumption is that we are trying *consciously* to maximize our number of surviving genes in the next generation. We may exhibit genetically determined tendencies to pass on our genes to the next generation, but this is not necessarily our conscious goal.

Cartwright has added, as a false assumption, the notion of **Panglossism** (2000, p. 40). In Voltaire's classic book *Candide,* Dr. Pangloss referred to the present world as the best possible world and was such an optimist that no matter what happened, he thought it was for the best. The counterpart of Panglossism in evolutionary theory is that there must be an adaptive reason for everything, even the red color of blood. The fact is that many existing qualities and traits may have no particular adaptive significance.

In other words, unless we become clear about precisely what it is that evolutionary psychologists are saying, we can include ideas that are not part of current thinking in our view of evolutionary psychology. In many instances, people who believe that they are criticizing evolutionary psychology, are actually criticizing their own misconceptions of its field.

Individual Identity and Evolutionary Psychology

There are some paradoxes and ironies in the viewpoint of evolutionary psychology to individuality. Evolutionary psychology is, at its base, a nomothetic discipline. It is concerned with certain general principles and how they are manifested in human behavior. However, one of the most important aspects of human nature is our strong sense of individuality. Note the similarity of this idea to Jung's concept of *persona.* A persona is individually created and molded, but each person has an innate capacity for such a psychological reality. Erikson also emphasized the importance of each person to develop a sense of individual identity.

It is not difficult to speculate about the evolutionary basis for the importance of individuality among human beings. One area where individuality is important is bonding. In forming mating bonds and family groups, we form strong bonds with individual people, not people in general. It is true that one can be "in love with love" for a certain period of life, but such generalized temporary bonding does not lead to a settled life. People usually bond with specific others. A human face is usually unmistakably identifiable as is the human voice. In addition, humans have a certain amount of personal space. This differs among cultures but remains within certain limits.

Also, the kin selection theory indicates that we are most likely to help those individuals with whom we are closely related and most likely to form the strongest bonds.

We can say with assurance that one of the main general laws of human behavior is that we have a tendency to assume individual identities and that we experience one another as different, distinguishable individuals. Much thought and effort goes into how we relate to others in our personal and professional lives. So, the paradox becomes resolved. One of the most general or nomothetic laws of human nature is that we see others and ourselves as unique individuals.

A Common Criticism of Evolutionary Psychology

Evolutionary psychology has often been criticized for the fact that it does not lead to genuine predictions, as is the case of experimental disciplines. It has thus been accused of engaging in *post hoc* **predictions.** Evolutionary psychologists cannot proceed with human evolution in a laboratory setting. They are constrained to study only the effects of evolution, and those effects are already present.

> In response to a question that one of the authors of this text sent him, Wilson replied, ... evolutionary psychology has considerable importance for personality studies, both as a tool to trace adaptiveness and as a heuristic device for asking new solvable questions. (Wilson, 2001)

Evolutionary psychology thus aids in understanding the causes of *currently existing* patterns of behavior. It does not lead to predictions about the future but rather can guide hypotheses about as yet unexplored or unresearched situations. It can also offer *explanations* of personality patterns in terms of their evolutionary adaptive value.

HOW MIGHT AN EVOLUTIONARY PSYCHOLOGIST PROCEED?

Let us take a common behavior that most likely would have evolutionary roots. To our knowledge, this behavior has not yet been studied from this point of view, but it provides an interesting example for us to indicate how an evolutionary psychological approach might proceed. When we see someone with a spot of food, a bug, or some unknown piece of something on his or her face, most of us experience a strong urge to let this person know about it or a desire to wipe it off ourselves. Many of us can remember times when we were very uncomfortable in the presence of someone with a glob of something on his or her face, and we were not able to mention it. Is this tendency—to be uncomfortable around a person with a speck of something on his or her face and try to get the person to remove it or to remove it ourselves—an instinct or an evolutionarily determined behavioral proclivity?

We can locate a similar pattern in primates, social grooming, which has the beneficial effect of removing insects and dirt from the hair of the one groomed. It is also important in strengthening bonds between individual animals. To determine whether such a tendency is an instinct or an evolutionary adaptation, we might also check to see how common it is in different human cultures. We might look at this behavior developmentally, to see when it first develops, and to ascertain to what extent it is a learned behavior, involving imitation learning. We could even measure the subjective intensity of the wish of one person to engage in such behavior, and look for the heritability of this trait.

Perhaps studies of identical twins, fraternal twins, and people with different degrees of relatedness could establish the degree to which this trait is heritable. Also, analyzing the genome of those with or without this trait might lead to the discovery of a gene or set of genes that contribute to the development of this human type of social grooming. Such studies might well confirm the instinctive nature of such behavior, in which case it would join the array of human behaviors that have instinctive origins.

Regarding the tendency to engage in a human version of social grooming, there is a lesser degree of *post hoc* or after-the-fact thinking, but postdiction is still present. We start by knowing about our own tendency and that of people in our culture to engage in this behavior; we also know about social grooming in primates. We need to explore empirically the cross-cultural aspects as well as the genetic basis for such behavior before coming to any conclusions about its adaptiveness or its relation to our EEA.

AN ACTUAL EXAMPLE—NOT OF POSTDICTION, BUT OF PREDICTION—SORT OF

In the previous examples, the use of evolutionary psychology varies considerably from the experimental method, in which researchers predict the outcome of an experiment according to their hypotheses. In the case of toilet training, we are dealing, not with a prediction, but with a *post hoc* explanation, or what can be termed a **postdiction.** In other words, we are looking at behaviors of which we already have some knowledge, that is toilet training among humans and potty training among domestic cats and dogs, and attempting to come up with an explanation based on evolutionary theory.

The next example is a case of a prediction according to evolutionary psychological theory: starting with a theoretical premise, a prediction is made. Then empirical evidence is accumulated to see if the prediction is confirmed. In the field of evolutionary psychology, it is almost never possible to conduct an experiment in real time. Instead, what one has to do is to explore *currently existing evidence* that might be either consistent or inconsistent with the hypothesized outcomes.

Martin Daly and Margo Wilson (1985) published the unsettling results of a study they conducted. They had thought about the behavior of stepparents toward their biological children and toward stepchildren and speculated that, since the biological children contained more of their genetic material, that they would exhibit more caring toward such children. To test their hypothesis, they examined homicide data in the United States and Canada. It turned out that the percentage of children who were killed by a stepparent was about a factor of two, or one hundred times greater than the percentage of children killed by their biological parents. They did not claim that this difference was caused solely by evolutionary considerations, but certainly Daly and Wilson considered them a foundational cause. The results they studied were not really *post hoc*. The reality already existed, unlike the case in a genuine experimental model. However, the discovery of the corroborating data did occur after Daly and Wilson's generation of their hypotheses. As in a real laboratory experiment, they were not certain what their findings would be.

One does not have to look far to find a possible mechanism for the greater connectedness of biological parents and their children. One possibility is the mechanism of bonding, which occurs in the earliest part of life. Human infants and their biological parents develop strong bonds during this time. A stepparent is not often present during these early years and has less of a chance to develop such bonds.

One might argue for the presence of nonevolutionarily determined reasons for the greater danger in which stepchildren find themselves. Evolutionary psychology is open to the possibility that such nonhereditary factors may also play a role in determining such behavior. It also recognizes the fact that most stepparents do not kill or abuse their stepchildren and that many are kind and nurturing.

The Incest Taboo

One area that Wilson as well as other sociobiologists and evolutionary psychologists examined is the **incest taboo.** It is well known that, among humans, incest can lead to birth defects and reduced viability among offspring. The reasoning behind this phenomenon has to do with the fact that a defective gene often occurs twice in the chromosomes of the offspring of incestuous mating. A normal gene is not present to attenuate the phenotypic expression of the defective gene.

Over 100 years ago, the Scandinavian anthropologist Edward Westermarck (1891) ventured the hypothesis that individuals will not be interested in mating with individuals with whom they were associated as children. This phenomenon was confirmed in Israeli communes, in which children from different families spend much time together. In spite of their parents' wishes that they marry, such marriages appear to have been almost totally nonexistent. In one study, Joseph Shepher (1971) studied recorded marriages in Israel. He examined almost 2,800 marriage records and determined that not even one involved adults who were little children together before the age of six. The children reared together were like brothers and sisters and apparently experienced a type of bonding that precluded later sexual intimacy. According to Wilson, they must have experienced sexual aversion because of their proximity as children (Wilson, 1978).

To get a clear idea of how the thinking of evolutionary psychologists proceeds, it is helpful, in analyzing this example, to realize that the incest taboo occurred in spite of the fact that the children were, for the most part, *not related*. In other words, there was no increased likelihood that their offspring would have been defective. Yet they were affected by the same mechanism that human nature has provided, the purpose of which is to prevent incest. This mechanism, the product of tens of thousands of generations of evolutionary history, works against sexual involvement among children and people adjacent to them during rearing. This mechanism does not "see"; it is not able to identify kin *per se* and differentiate them from others.

Incest taboos were present before any knowledge of the biological dangers of incest was present. In other words, people do not need to make calculations about the evolutionarily most viable behavior in order to have motives in accordance with sociobiological principles.

Human culture and the law are very much in line with the biological incest taboo. The incest taboo thus stands on two legs—first, our genetic legacy, and second, cultural and legal restrictions. This should not be surprising. Both individual humans as well as human cultures of the past that did not have incest taboos were less viable than those that did. Wilson saw this phenomenon as an instance of the **leash principle,** that is, the close connection of human culture and laws with sociobiological principles. Wilson (as did Jung) thought that cultures and societies that departed too far from evolutionarily determined patterns of behavior were courting chaos and creating individual discomfort (Lumsden & Wilson, 1981). Such a thought definitely places Wilson, as well as Jung, in the position of being cultural conservatives, but evolutionary psychologists should also take into account the importance of the ability of individuals and societies to respond to change. In addition, we have inherited a brain that is capable of learning many behaviors not even imagined by our ancestors of 100 years ago.

Mate Selection

The area of sexual selection, that is the selection of mates and competition for them, as a major factor in natural selection has been well known for over a century—going back to Darwin's original theory. Evolutionary psychologists have carried out many studies in this area, as have evolutionary biologists. They have hypothesized that the purposes of sexual selection have to do with both the fertility of the mate, the number of offspring, and the likelihood that, with a specific mate, their offspring will themselves be cared for and, in turn, survive to reproduce.

All the ramifications that have to do with mate selection would take more than one volume to summarize. Here, we will touch on three areas: attractiveness in general, males' rating of the attractiveness of females, and the differential sexual choices of males and females.

Individuals with physical symmetry were found to be more attractive by both genders than others (Grammar & Thornhill, 1994). The evolutionary rationale for this behavior is that individuals with more symmetrical bodies and facial features are thought to have greater health and fewer genetic defects and thus would make better choices in the mate selection process. Subsequently, it has been found that males with the most symmetrical faces had first sexual intercourse younger than others and had more sex partners in general (Thornhill & Gangestad, 1994).

Males prefer the most physically attractive females as mates. This is a less important factor in the mate selection process of females. A survey of men from 37 countries throughout the world indicated that they emphasized physical attractiveness in mates more than their female compatriots did (Buss, 1989). Michael Wiederman (1993) actually looked at advertisements in personal sections of newspapers and found that American men were almost four times as likely as women to indicate that they were looking for a physically attractive partner.

But what features constitute attractiveness for men? A major aspect of such attractiveness, in addition to facial symmetry has turned out to be the ratio of the size of a person's waist to their hips. This is termed the waist-hip ratio. In a series of studies (Singh, 1993; Singh & Luis, 1995; Singh & Young, 1995), it was found that pictures of women with lower waist-hip ratios are rated most attractive and that, in particular, the 0.7 waist-hip ratio in women is rated as most attractive by men cross-culturally.

This ratio has been found to correspond with the highest level of fertility among young women. There is a close tie-in between physical health and the distribution of fat, as indicated by the waist-hip ratio. People at risk for diabetes, heart attack, vascular disease, and other disorders tend to have waist-hip ratios higher than 0.7 (Buss, 1999, p. 144). Thus, all other things being equal, women with the low waist-hip ratio of 0.7 are a better choice in terms of their reproductive potential and in terms of their ability to care for offspring in a vigorous manner.

Whereas men, in general, put their highest valuations on attractive women as sexual partners, the most important criterion for women is financial status and potential. This pattern reminds one of the words of reassurance to a baby in George Gershwin's "Summertime": "Your daddy's rich and your momma's good lookin." In a variety of studies, women have been found to rate financial status as twice as important as did men (Hill, 1945; McGinnis, 1958; Sprecher, Sullivan, & Hatfield, 1994). Michael Wiederman (1993) reviewed personal advertisements and found that, among heterosexuals in America, women were 11 times as likely to mention that somebody with a good financial status or prospects was desired. Buss (1989) corroborated such findings in surveying men and women in 37 countries.

Steven Gaulin and Donald McBurney have concluded that such choices did not necessarily represent a woman's lack of resources, for even well-to-do women or women with good financial prospects also were found to seek affluent men or those with excellent economic prospects (Weiderman and Allgeier, 1992). They point out, by way of explanation, that even though many women today are very well off financially, their mate-choice modules were shaped in the EEA, when women necessarily had to rely on the ability of men as hunters and providers (Gaulin & McBurney, 2001, p. 215).

EVOLUTIONARY PSYCHOLOGY AND PSYCHOPATHOLOGY

There are a number of ways of understanding psychopathology in terms of evolutionary psychology. Perhaps the simplest approach is to consider the EEA. This is clearly the case with many captive animals, particularly those with wide ranges in the wild. Kept in captive conditions, even with the best veterinary treatment, animals of many species may show signs of depression or become unable to reproduce. People in cities, which are often crowded and have high noise levels, may also show symptoms of anxiety and stress-related disorders.

In addition, some behaviors currently considered pathological might have been adaptive during the EEA. Paranoid alertness and a low threshold for arousal are two characteristics that might have been adaptive in a hunter-gatherer world, but not today. In the next section, we will look at the diagnosis of hyperactivity from this point of view.

Some traits that are adaptive when expressed to a moderate degree may be maladaptive when more extreme. In medicine, it is known that a moderate degree of the sickle cell anemia trait gives its possessor resistance to malaria. The full expression of the trait leads to an enfeebling form of anemia. An analogous process may exist in regard to the full expression of schizophrenia. It has been speculated that a more moderate expression of the schizophrenic characteristics leads to a high level of creativity. We have seen in the life history of Carl Jung (Chapter 5) the close connection between genius and psychosis.

A third area would be exemplified by dyslexia, a common disorder. In the EEA, people did not read. Individuals were not selected according to the ability to distinguish one letter from another. As indicated earlier in this chapter, the ability to read was an exaptation just as the ability to do calculus or to program computers. In other words, brain capacities that had developed for other purposes also enabled some people to be able to read. It should not be surprising, given the recent historical development of widespread literacy, that many people suffer from dyslexia.

An additional possibility is that a form of psychopathology is simply a result of an error of some sort: the psychopathology might result from a genetic defect or an environmental insult. In such cases, there might be no adaptive evolutionary basis involved.

Attention-Deficit Hyperactivity Disorder (ADHD) or Very Alert, Very Active Pattern (VAVAP)?

Attention-deficit hyperactivity disorder (ADHD) is a frequent diagnosis among school-age children in the United States. It refers to a maladaptive pattern of impulsive behavior, and difficulty paying attention, concentrating, and sitting still (APA, 2000, pp. 85–93). There is a large genetic or hereditary component to the disorder. In understanding this disorder, reference to the EEA is useful. Only in recent years have young humans been expected to devote a large portion of their day concentrating on their studies. In hominid as well as early human environments, a youngster with what today would be labeled as having ADHD might well have been as well or better adapted than a sedentary youngster. He or she might have been more alert to a predator's appearance or more likely to face a dangerous situation (Panskepp, 1998; Gaulin & McBurney, 2001). It would have thus been beneficial for the survival of groups of hominids and early humans to have some individuals with a very alert, very active pattern (VAVAP) of behavior.

From the standpoint of pre-evolutionary psychological theory, we might quickly draw the conclusion that an ADHD youngster's behavior is necessarily pathological. Taking the EEA into account, we can be open to the possibility that many hyperactive youngsters represent a normal, genetically determined variant, without any particular defects, family problems, or emotional issues. Along these lines, we might consider providing more physical activity in schools and more frequent breaks to accommodate the restlessness of the ADHD child who has to sit for hours on end.

Perhaps, in addition to the Axes in the DSM-IV, there should be one that indicates, "No emotional or situational cause for the behavior in question has been found in this case. The behavior appears to have been adaptive during the environment of evolutionary adaptedness or even more recently, but is not easily tolerated in today's society."

A FINAL WORD ON EVOLUTIONARY PSYCHOLOGY

The field of evolutionary psychology is a promising and rapidly expanding area of theory and research. New discoveries are made frequently, and many new articles and texts are being published. College and university courses on evolutionary psychology are becoming more prevalent. Evolutionary psychology is influencing thinking not only in the area of personality theory but also in other areas of psychology such as cognitive psychology, perception, sensation, social psychology, neuropsychology, and psychopathology. It is a unifying point of view that both helps explain many existing phenomena and leads to heuristic suggestions about other findings in the fields of psychology.

Because the field of evolutionary psychology is so much in the process of rapid development, it is not yet possible to predict the eventual status or to make a final evaluation of this point of view. The proponents may be overlooking or minimizing the vast cultural differences between groups of human beings or the plasticity or flexibility of individual behavior. It is not clear that a satisfactory system of ethics or morality can be based on evolutionary thinking. We can look forward, in the years ahead, to continuing dialogues between proponents of evolutionary psychology and other thoughtful advocates of a variety of different approaches to conceptualizing and understanding human behavior.

Refutability and Evolutionary Psychology

The question of refutability is an inherent problem for evolutionary psychology. One cannot conduct an experiment about events that have already happened. Given the theory as it is currently formulated, all existing behaviors must be in accordance with some evolutionary consequence, or at least *leashed* to it. If some societies have a great deal of aggression against females and rape, then there must be a reason; likewise, a reason can be found for behavior toward women that is kind and caring. Infanticide and cannibalism as well as taboos against these practices must be found to be in accordance with evolutionary psychology.

Therefore, the post hoc, after-the-fact quality of "predictions" in this field reveals that they are not predictions of the future as in experimental laboratory research. We should not, however, be too critical of the post hoc nature of much of evolutionary psychology, because such thinking is found in other areas as well. Could a behaviorist or a psychoanalyst come across evidence that counters his or her theory? Doubtful. Nor could an Adlerian ever discover a person without an inferiority complex.

One concept we might consider concerning the question of verifiability is the great variability of human behavior. If humans were like the giant panda, with a single species of bamboo that it can eat and a limited environmental range, then, perhaps predictions about our behavior would be more verifiable. What is revealed is that humans have an evolutionary history of many habitats and many conditions, many diets, and many climates. Just as we have many types of teeth to help us to eat and digest different foods, so we have an extensive repertoire of "prepared" behaviors. We are not a *tabula rasa* or blank slate but rather more like a Magic Slate, with evidence of many inherent patterns on the slate once you look beneath the surface layers. These do not represent past experiences as in Jung's theory but are our adaptive potentials, as carried in our genes and reflecting the varied environments in which our ancestors have existed, survived, and evolved.

Evolutionary Psychology and Human Agency

Evolutionary psychology can account for both human activity and passivity or, in other words, either for human choice and agency or for the idea that human behavior is determined. Some evolutionary psychologists see human behavior as a largely determined set of adaptations to situations presented in the course of evolution. Others view human agency itself as an evolutionary adaptation. Therefore, though evolutionary psychology refers human behaviors to a causal evolutionary process, it still can accommodate the model of an active, resourceful, and goal-oriented human being, at least in certain circumstances.

The Idiographic Versus Nomothetic in Evolutionary Psychology

In general, evolutionary psychology emphasizes the regularities of human behavior, not only between individuals but also between societies. From this point of view, the overwhelming similarity among individuals regarding their genetic inheritance (or what we now term their genomic makeup) is an overwhelming truth. Nonetheless, there is room in evolutionary psychology theory for an expression of individualism in every person. This apparent paradox is that our very capacity for individuality may be viewed as an evolutionarily determined quality.

SUMMARY

Evolutionary psychology is a new approach to understanding human behavior. It views patterns of behavior, thinking, and emotion in terms of their adaptive significance in our evolutionary history. Many classical personality theories included evolutionary concepts in their theories. They were handicapped, however, by using scientifically unsound ideas such as Lamarckian inheritance of acquired characteristics or unembellished Darwinian "nature red in tooth and claw" notions of evolution.

Edward O. Wilson is generally credited with spearheading the development of the modern field of evolutionary psychology, or what he prefers to call human sociobiology. His books, *Sociobiology: A New Synthesis* and *On Human Nature* have had a major impact on the creation of this field. Wilson is a leading biologist, who originally studied the social life of insects and gradually realized that some of the same factors explaining prosocial or "altruistic" behavior in insects also applied to vertebrates and, finally, to humans. He saw sociobiology as a theory that unified a wide array of findings regarding both animal and human behavior.

The development of contemporary evolutionary psychology is based on a number of contributions, starting with Charles Darwin's theory of evolution by natural selection. Darwin also proposed the importance of sexual selection and the evolution of emotional expression and a moral sense in his subsequent writings.

A necessary step in the development of modern evolutionary psychology was David Hamilton's idea of inclusive fitness or kin selection, in which he developed a broader view of the mechanism of natural selection. The kin selection theory proposed that evolution would favor behavior that increased the probability of survival of people carrying genes identical to one's own, even if these people were relatives or "kin," rather than one's own children. This development opened the way for psychologists to study the evolutionary origins of behaviors other than those merely associated with survival of the

fittest and sexual selection. The idea of "the selfish gene" was a popularization of Hamilton's view and indicated that evolution proceeds, not by selection of the fittest individual, but rather by selection of the "fittest" genes.

Other ideas important in the development of evolutionary psychology are the concept of the environment of evolutionary adaptedness (EEA), the environment in which our hominid ancestors lived for millions of years. Many of our behavioral traits, ranging from our sweet tooth to fear of snakes to patterns of social behavior, can be traced to our ancestors' adaptations to this environment. Another relevant concept is the modularity of mind. This concept indicates that the mind contains many programmed or partially programmed ("hard-wired") functions that have proven useful for survival.

One area that was investigated early was that of taboos on incest. It was found that nonrelated individuals reared with others as children developed a type of bonding that precluded later sexual intimacy. Wilson proposed the *leash principle,* to indicate that behavior might not be strictly determined biologically, but that it was leashed to biology and could not depart indefinitely from the vicissitudes of evolutionary adaptation. Sexual selection has led to attractiveness being linked to fertility and health, especially in the male's perception of the female. Women seem to be more focused on their mates' financial status, again a factor promoting survival of offspring.

Psychopathology can represent an atavistic adaptation to the EEA that is no longer adaptive. This appears to be the case with attention-deficit hyperactivity disorder (ADHD). Another possibility is that pathology represents "too much" or "not enough" of a quality or trait that is adaptive in a more moderate amount. A third possibility is that what is considered pathology is the absence of a trait or ability that has not been selected by evolution. An example is this is dyslexia, or the inability to discern letters and resulting difficulty or inability to read.

FOR FURTHER READING

Wilson's writings include a prize-winning account of his work as a naturalist and his development

of sociobiology and human sociobiology or what we term evolutionary psychology. *Sociobiology: The*

New Synthesis (Cambridge, MA: Harvard University Press, 1975) is his account of the tenets of sociobiology. *On Human Nature* (Cambridge MA: Harvard University Press, 1978) is Wilson's more fully developed view of the relevance of sociobiology for understanding human behavior. *Naturalist* (Washington, DC: Island Press, 1994) is Wilson's charming autobiographical account of his life and his intellectual and personal adventures in the interrelated worlds of scientific research and academic politics and ideas. John Alcock's *The Triumph of Sociobiology* (New York: Oxford University Press, 2001) is a sympathetic view of the sociobiological theory up to the present.

For those seeking to refresh their memory about the overall theory of evolution and its current status, a wonderfully accurate, readable, and well-illustrated volume is Carl Zimmer's *Evolution: The Triumph of an Idea* (New York: HarperCollins, 2001).

Some excellent textbooks on evolutionary psychology have become available in recent years. *Psychology: An Evolutionary Approach* (Upper Saddle River: NJ: Prentice-Hall, 2001) by Steven Gaulin and Donald McBurney is a clearly written exposition that covers the main concepts of evolutionary psychology and applies them to many areas of psychology. David Buss's *Evolutionary Psychology: The New Science of the Mind*. (Needham Heights, MA: Allyn and Bacon, 1999) includes the results of many studies on many aspects of human behavior. More textbooks on the subject can be expected in coming years.

David Barash's *Sociobiology and Behavior* (New York: Elsevier, 1977) was an early and accurate popularization of what, was then the novel concept of sociobiology. In *Revolutionary Biology* (New Brunswick, NJ: Transaction, 2001), he covers new thoughts on human behavior engendered by the new concepts of evolutionary biology.

A little paperback full of illustrations by Dylan Evans and Oscar Zarate, *Introducing Evolutionary Psychology* (New York: Totem Books, 2000), is excellent at conveying difficult concepts in the field of evolutionary psychology, especially those having to do with the idea of the modularity of mind.

Additional sources on Wilson and evolutionary psychology can be found on the Wiley web site at www.wiley.com/college/sollod

GLOSSARY

Altruism: Behavioral proclivities that benefit others, often at some cost to oneself. Altruistic behavior, in evolutionary theory, may or may not involve conscious altruistic intent.

Artificial selection: The process of selecting and breeding organisms of given species with desired characteristics.

Attention-deficit hyperactivity disorder (ADHD): A disorder characterized by poor attention span, distractibility, and impulsiveness. Some theorists have proposed that, even though no longer adaptive, it was an adaptation to the EEA.

Cheater detection module: A mental module that detects cheaters, those who benefit but do not contribute in the process of reciprocal altruism.

Environment of evolutionary adaptedness (EEA): The past environment, considered millions of years in duration, during which current human behaviors were selected. During this period, human ancestors were hunters and gatherers.

Evolutionary biology: A field that examines findings in biology through the lens of evolutionary theories. It serves as a unifying factor in the field of biology.

Evolutionary medicine: A field that considers diseases and their treatments from the point of view of their evolutionary adaptive significance.

Evolutionary psychology: The approach to understanding human psychology—including all of its basic areas such as learning, cognition, perception, personality and psychopathology—from the point of view of evolutionary theory.

Exaptation: A characteristic that evolved to serve a certain function but, once existing, was found to have other useful functions. For example, feathers are thought to have evolved to provide warmth, but later were found useful for flight.

Facultative adaptation: A trait or characteristic that is an adaptation to a specific environment. For example, calluses will develop when a person uses tools.

Fixed action patterns: Konrad Lorenz's concept of sequences of movements programmed in the brain by heredity, which unfold through the life of an animal in response to particular signals in the environment.

Human sociobiology: The application of the principles of sociobiology to all aspects of humans and their behavior. This term indicates the connectedness of human behavior with that of all organisms.

Incest taboo: The prohibition against sex with close relatives. There is a biological basis for this taboo, which is also embedded in law and culture.

Inclusive fitness: Concept that an organism's fitness is determined not only by its ability to leave descendants but also by its contribution to the overall fitness of organisms of the same species around it.

Inheritance of acquired characteristics: Lamarck's discredited idea that the acquired characteristics of an organism can be passed to its offspring. For example, a person who builds up his or her muscles will *per se* have muscular descendants.

Kin selection: William Hamilton's concept that an organism may be selected because it enhances the viability of related organisms, *kin,* with some identical genes.

Leash principle: The concept that human behavior and cultures cannot stray too far away from biologically based determinants.

Modularity of mind: The concept that the mind consists, in addition to a central processing unit, of many separate modules, each performing specific tasks.

Natural selection: Darwin's proposed means for evolution, the concept that better adapted organisms are able to pass on their genetic material to the next generation. They are thus said to be *selected* by nature.

Ontogeny: The development or course of development of an individual organism, often applied to embryological levels of development.

Panglossism: The false notion that there must be an adaptive reason for every trait.

Phylogeny: The evolutionary history of an organism.

***Post hoc* predictions/postdiction:** "Predictions" that are made about conditions that already exist but of which one does not currently have knowledge. For example, one researcher "predicted" that children reared together in a commune did not get married as adults. He subsequently analyzed marital records to confirm his hypothesis.

Predator detection module: A mental module that detects predators.

Reciprocal (soft-core) altruism: Robert Trivers's concept of a type of altruism involving giving and receiving help from others. He theorized that individuals demonstrating such behavior are selected in the process of natural selection.

Selfish gene theory: A gene-focused theory of evolution proposed by Dawkins: the idea that the organism is a means of perpetuating the survival of genes. The gene is not actually selfish, but evolution proceeds as if the gene were selfishly trying to perpetuate itself.

Sexual selection: The concept that some organisms are selected as part of the natural selection process as a result of their comparative success in mating.

Sociobiology: Edward Wilson's unifying concept of viewing organisms and their behaviors through the lens of evolutionary theories. He included human beings in his analysis.

Bibliography

Abramson, L. Y., Seligman, M. E. P., & Teasdale, J. (1978). Learned helplessness in humans: Critique and reformulation. *Journal of Abnormal Psychology*, *87*, 32–48.

Adler, A. (1907). The study of organ inferiority and its psychical compensation. In H. L. Ansbacher & R. R. Ansbacher (Eds.), *The individual psychology of Alfred Adler*. New York: Harper, 1956.

(1908). The aggression drive in life and neurosis. In H. L. Ansbacher & R. R. Ansbacher (Eds.), *The individual psychology of Alfred Adler*. New York: Harper, 1956.

(1910). The psychology of hermaphroditism in life and in neurosis. In H. L. Ansbacher & R. R. Ansbacher (Eds.), *The individual psychology of Alfred Adler*. New York: Harper, 1956.

(1913). The function of neurotic symptoms. In H. L. Ansbacher & R. R. Ansbacher (Eds.), *The individual psychology of Alfred Adler*. New York: Harper, 1956.

(1927). *Understanding human nature*. Greenwich, CT: Fawcett.

(1929a). *The science of living*. New York: Doubleday, 1969.

(1929b). *Problems of neurosis*. Philip Mairet (Ed.). New York: Harper, 1929.

(1930). *The education of children*. Chicago: Henry Regnery, 1970.

(1931). *What life should mean to you*. New York: Putnam.

(1932). The structure of neurosis. In H. L. Ansbacher & R. R. Ansbacher (Eds.), *Superiority and social interest: A collection of later writings*. New York: Viking Compass, 1973.

(1933). The meaning of life. In H. L. Ansbacher & R. R. Ansbacher (Eds.), *The individual psychology of Alfred Adler*. New York: Harper, 1956.

(1935). The fundamental views of individual psychology. In H. L. Ansbacher & R. R. Ansbacher (Eds.), *The individual psychology of Alfred Adler*. New York: Harper, 1956.

(1956). *The individual psychology of Alfred Adler: A systematic presentation in selections from his writings*. H. L. Ansbacher & R. R. Ansbacher (Eds.). New York: Harper.

(1959). *The practice and theory of individual psychology*. Totowa, N.J.: Littlefield-Adams.

(1964). *Social interest: A challenge to mankind*. New York: Putnam.

(1973). *Superiority and social interest: A collection of later writings*. H. L. Ansbacher & R. R. Ansbacher (Eds.). New York: Viking Compass.

Alcock, John. (2001). *The Triumph of Sociobiology*. New York: Oxford University Press.

Allport, Floyd. (1924). *Social psychology*. Boston: Houghton Mifflin.

Allport, G. (1937). *Personality: A psychological interpretation*. New York: Henry Holt.

(1942). *The use of personal documents in psychological science*. New York: Social Science Research Council Bulletin (No. 49).

(Ed.). (1946). Letters from Jenny (published anonymously in this edition). *Journal of Abnormal and Social Psychology*, *41*, 315–350 and 449–480.

(1950). *The individual and his religion*. New York: Macmillan.

(1955). *Becoming: Basic considerations for a psychology of personality*. New Haven: Yale University Press.

(1960). *Personality and social encounter: Selected essays*. Boston: Beacon Press.

(1961). *Pattern and growth in personality*. New York: Holt, Rinehart and Winston.

(1962). "My encounters with personality theory." Recorded and edited reminiscence at the Boston University School of Theology, October 12, 1962, transcribed by Douglas, W.

(1964). The fruits of eclecticism: Bitter or sweet? In G. Allport, *The person in psychology*. Boston: Beacon Press, 1968 (paper originally published in *Acta Psychological*, 1964, *23*, 27–44).

(Ed.). (1965). *Letters from Jenny*. New York: Harcourt, Brace & World.

(1966). Traits revisited. In G. Allport, *The person in psychology*. Boston: Beacon Press, 1968 (paper originally published in *American Psychologist*, 1966, *21*, 1–10).

(1967). Autobiography. In E. G. Boring & G. Lindzey (Eds.), *A history of psychology in autobiography*, Vol. 5. New York: Appleton.

Ansbacher, H. L., & Ansbacher, R. R. (1956). *The individual psychology of Alfred Adler: A systematic presentation in selections from his writings.* New York: Harper.

APA. (2000). *Diagnostic and statistical manual of mental disorders*: [DSM-IV-TRC], (4th ed., text revision). Washington, DC: The American Psychiatric Association.

Appignanesi, L., & Forrester, J. (1992). *Freud's women.* New York: Basic Books.

Atwood, G. E., & Stolorow, R. D. (1977). Metapsychology, reification and the representational world of C. G. Jung. *International Review of Psychoanalysis*, *4*, 197–214.

Atwood, G. E., & Tomkins, S. (1976). On the subjectivity of personality theory. *Journal of the History of the Behavioral Sciences*, *12*, 166–177.

Bandura, A. (1969). *Principles of behavior modification.* New York: Holt, Rinehart and Winston.

(1977a). Self-efficacy: Toward a unifying theory of behavioral change. *Psychological Review*, *84*, 191–215.

(1977b). *Social learning theory.* Englewood Cliffs, NJ: Prentice Hall.

(1978). The self-system in reciprocal determinism. *American Psychologist*, *33*, 344–358.

(1981). In search of pure unidirectional determinants. *Behavior Therapy*, *12*, 30–40.

(1982). Self-efficacy mechanism in human agency. *American Psychologist*, *37*, 122–147.

(1986). *Social foundations of thought and action.* Englewood Cliffs, NJ: Prentice Hall.

(1989). Human agency in social cognitive theory. *American Psychologist*, *44*, 9, 1175–1184.

(1997). *Self-efficacy: The exercise of control.* New York: Freeman.

(2001a) Personal communication. August 25, 2001.

(2001b) Personal communication. July 12, 2001.

(2001c) Personal communication. August 8, 2001.

Bandura, A., Adams, N. E., & Beyer, J. (1977). Cognitive processes mediating behavioral change. *Journal of Personality and Social Psychology*, *35*, 125–139.

Bandura, A., & Schunk, D. H. (1981). Cultivating competence, self-efficacy, and intrinsic interest through proximal self-motivation. *Journal of Personality and Social Psychology*, *41*, 586–598.

Bandura, A., & Walters, R. H. (1963). *Social learning and personality development.* New York: Holt, Rinehart and Winston.

Bannister, D., & Fransella, F. (1971). *Inquiring man. The theory of personality constructs.* New York: Penguin Books.

Barash, David P. (2001). *Revolutionary biology.* New Brunswick, NJ: Transaction Publishers.

Barkow, Jermone H., Cosmides, Leda & Tooby, John, eds. (1992). *The adapted mind: Evolutionary psychology and the generation of culture.* New York: Oxford University Press.

Berman, M. (1975). Review of *Life history and the historical moment* by Erik Erikson. In *New York Times Book Review*, March 30.

Bernstein, A. (1976). Freud and Oedipus: A new look at the Oedipus complex in the light of Freud's life. *The Psychoanalytic Review*, *63*, 393–407.

Bertocci, P. A. (1950). Critique of Gordon W. Allport's theory of motivation. *Psychological Review*, *47*, 501–532.

Black, A. H. (1958). The extinction of avoidance responses under curare. *Journal of Comparative and Psychological Psychology*, *51*, 519–524.

Blos, Peter. (1962). *On adolescence: A psychoanalytic interpretation.* New York: Free Press.

(1970). *The young adolescent: Clinical studies.* New York: Free Press.

Bottome, Phyllis. (1957). *Alfred Adler: A portrait from life.* New York: Vanguard.

Brand, C. (1997). Obituary of Hans Eysenck. In Upstream, an Internet publication: http://www.mugu.com/cgi-bin/Upstream/People/Eysenck/

Breland, K., & Breland, M. (1961). The misbehavior of organisms. *American Psychologist*, *16*, 681–684.

Breland-Bailey, M., & Bailey, R. E. (1993). "Misbehavior: A case history." *American Psychologist*, *48*, 1157–1158.

Breuer, J., & Freud, S. (1893–1895). *Studies on hysteria*, Vol. II of *The standard edition of the complete psychological works of Sigmund Freud.* London: Hogarth Press, 1955.

(1893). On the psychical mechanism of hysterical phenomena: A preliminary communication.

In J. Breuer & S. Freud, *Studies on hysteria*, Vol. II of *The standard edition of the complete psychological works of Sigmund Freud*. James Strachey (Ed.). London: Hogarth Press, 1955.

Brewster-Smith, M. (1971). Allport, Murray and Lewin on personality: Notes on a confrontation. *Journal of the History of the Behavioral Sciences*, *7*, 353–362.

Broadhurst, P. L. (1959). The interaction of task difficulty and motivation: The Yerkes-Dodson law revived. *Acta Psychologica*, *16*, 321–338.

Brown, Roger. (1965). *Social psychology*. New York: Free Press.

Buss, A. R. (1978). The structure of psychological revolutions. *Journal of the History of the Behavioral Sciences*, *14*, 57–64.

Buss, David M. (1989). Sex differences in human mate preferences: Evolutionary hypotheses tested in 37 cultures. *Behavioral and Brain Science*, *12*, 1–49.

(1999). *Evolutionary psychology: The new science of the mind*. Needham Heights, MA: Allyn and Bacon.

Cartwright, John (2000). *Evolution and human behavior: Darwinian perspectives on human nature*. Cambridge, MA: MIT Press.

Cattell, H. E. P. (1993). Comment on Goldberg. *American Psychologist*, *48*, 1302–1303.

Chapman, A. H. (1976). *Harry Stack Sullivan: The man and his work*. New York: Putnam.

Claridge, G. S. (1967). *Personality and arousal*. New York: Pergamon.

Clarkin, J. F., Hull, J. W., Cantor, J., & Sanderson, C. (1993). Borderline personality disorder and personality traits: A comparison of SCID-II BPD and NEO-PI. *Psychological Assessment*, *5*, 472–476.

Cosmides, Leda & Tooby, John. (2002). Unraveling the enigma of human intelligence: Evolutionary psychology and the multimodular mind. In Sternberg, R.J. & Kaufman, J.C. (Eds.), *The evolution of intelligence*. Mahway, NJ: Lawrence Erlbaum Associates, 145–198.

Crain, W. C. (1992). *Theories of development: Concepts and applications*, 3rd ed. Englewood Cliffs, NJ: Prentice Hall.

Daly, M., & Wilson, M. (1985). Child abuse and other risks of not living with both parents. *Ethology and Sociology*, *6*, 197–210.

Darwin, Charles R. (1859). *On the origin of species by means of natural selection*. London: John Murray.

(1871). *The descent of man and selection in relation to sex*. London, England: John Murray Publishers.

(1872). *The expression of emotion in man and animals*. New York: Appleton.

Dawkins, R. (1989). *The selfish gene*. New York: Oxford University Press.

Dyer, R. (1983). *The work of Anna Freud*. New York: Aronson.

Dymond, R. (1954). Adjustment changes over therapy from self-sorts. In C. R. Rogers & R. F. Dymond (Eds.), *Psychotherapy and personality change* (pp. 77–84). Chicago: University of Chicago Press.

Eaves, L. J., Eysenck, H. J. & Martin, N. G. (1989). *Genes, culture and personality: An empirical approach*. New York: Academic Press.

Eliade, M. (1958). *Rites and symbols of initiation*. New York: Harper (originally published as *Birth and Rebirth*).

(1961). *The sacred and the profane*. New York: Harper & Row.

Ellenberger, H. (1970). *The discovery of the unconscious*. New York: Basic Books.

(1972). The story of "Anna O.": A critical review with new data. *Journal of the History of the Behavioral Sciences*, *8*, 267–279.

Erikson, E. H. (1950). *Childhood and society* (2nd ed.). New York: Norton, 1963.

(1959). *Identity and the life cycle: Selected papers*. Psychological Issues, Monograph No. 1, Vol. 1. New York: International Universities Press.

(1962). *Young man Luther: A study in psychoanalysis and history*. New York: Norton.

(1963). Youth: Fidelity and diversity. In E. H. Erikson (Ed.), *The challenge of youth*. New York: Doubleday.

(1964). *Insight and responsibility*. New York: Norton.

(Ed.). (1968). *Identity: Youth and crisis*. New York: Norton.

(1969). *Gandhi's truth: On the origins of militant nonviolence*. New York: Norton.

(1974). *Dimensions of a new identity: Jefferson lectures, 1973*. New York: Norton.

(1975). *Life history and the historical moment*. New York: Norton.

(1977). *Toys and reasons*. New York: Norton.

(Ed.). (1978). *Adulthood*. New York: Norton.

(1982). *The life cycle completed.* New York: Norton.

Evans, R. I. (1964). *Conversations with Carl Jung and reactions from Ernest Jones.* New York: Van Nostrand Reinhold Co.

(1976). *Dialogue with R. D. Laing.* New York: Praeger.

(1976a). *The making of psychology: Discussion with creative contributors.* New York: Knopf.

(1989). *Albert Bandura, the man and his ideas—A dialogue.* New York: Pracger.

Evans, R. I. (1996). *Dialogue with Erik Erikson.* New York: Harper & Row.

Eysenck, Hans J. (1947). *Dimensions of personality.* London: Routledge & Kegan Paul.

(1953a). *Uses and abuses of psychology.* Baltimore: Penguin (Pelican ed.), 1953.

(1953b). *The structure of human personality* (rev. ed.). London: Methuen, 1970.

(1957a). *The dynamics of anxiety and hysteria: An experimental application of modern learning theory to psychiatry.* London: Routledge & Kegan Paul, 1957 (American edition: Praeger).

(1957b). *Sense and nonsense in psychology.* Baltimore: Penguin, 1957.

(1960). Learning theory and behavior therapy. In H. J. Eysenck (Ed.), *Behavior therapy and the neuroses.* New York: Pergamon.

(1963a). The measurement of motivation. *Scientific American*, May 1963, 130–140.

(1963b). Psychoanalysis: Myth or science? In Stanley Rachman (Ed.), *Critical essays on psychoanalysis.* New York: Macmillan, 1963.

(1964). *Crime and personality.* London: Routledge & Kegan Paul, 1964 (American edition: Houghton Mifflin).

(1967). *The biological basis of personality.* Springfield, IL: Charles C. Thomas.

(1970). Historical introduction. In H. J. Eysenck (Ed.), *Readings in extraversion-intraversion*, vol. 1: *Theoretical and methodological issues.* London: Staples.

(1972). *Psychology is about people.* New York: The Library Press.

(1973). *The inequality of man.* London: Temple Smith (American edition: Robert R. Knapp, San Diego, CA).

(1976). The learning theory model of neurosis—a new approach. *Behavior Research and Therapy*, *14*, 251–267.

(1979). *The structure and measurement of intelligence.* New York: Springer.

(1980). *The causes and effects of smoking.* London: Maurice Temple Smith.

(1982). *Personality, genetics, and behavior: Selected papers.* New York: Praeger.

(1990). *Rebel with a cause: The autobiography of Hans Eysenck.* London: W. H. Allen.

(1993). Comment on Goldberg. *American Psychologist*, *48*, 1299–1300.

Eysenck, H. J., & Eysenck, M. (1983). *Mindwatching: Why people behave the way they do.* New York: Garden Press/Doubleday.

(1985). *Personality and individual differences: A natural science approach.* New York: Plenum Press.

Eysenck, H. J., & Eysenck, S. B. G. (1968). *The Eysenck personality inventory.* San Diego, CA: Educational and Industrial Testing Service.

(1969). *Personality structure and measurement.* San Diego, CA: Robert R. Knapp.

(1975a). *Eysenck personality questionnaire.* San Diego, CA: Educational and Industrial Testing Service, 1975.

(1975b). *The manual of the Eysenck personality questionnaire.* San Diego, CA: Educational and Industrial Testing Service, 1975.

(1976). *Psychoticism as a dimension of personality.* New York: Crane, Russak.

Eysenck, H. J. & Gudjonsson, H. G. (1989). *The causes and cures of criminality.* New York: Plenum Press.

Eysenck, H. J., & Nias, D. K. (1982). *Astrology: Science or superstition?* New York: St. Martin's Press.

Eysenck, H. J. & Rachman, S. (1965). *The causes and cures of neurosis.* London: Routledge & Kegan Paul (American edition: Robert R. Knapp, San Diego, CA).

Eysenck, H. J. & Sargent, C. (1982). *Explaining the unexplained: Mysteries of the paranormal.* London: Prion.

Eysenck, H. J., & Wilson, G. D. (1973). *The experimental study of Freudian theories.* London: Methuen (American edition: Harper & Row).

Falk, J. L. (1956). Issues distinguishing idiographic from nomothetic approaches to personality. *Psychological Review*, *63*, 53–62.

Fenichel, O. (1945). *The psychoanalytic theory of neurosis.* New York: Norton.

Festinger, L. (1957). *A theory of cognitive dissonance*. New York: Row, Peterson.

Fischer, C. T. (1977). Historical relations of psychology as an object-science and subject-science: Toward psychology as a human science. *Journal of the History of the Behavioral Sciences, 13*, 369–378.

Fisher, S., & Greenberg, R. P. (1996). *Freud scientifically reappraised: Testing the theories and therapy*. New York: John Wiley & Sons.

Fodor, J.S. (1983). *The modularity of mind*. Cambridge, MA: MIT Press.

Freeman, L. (1972). *The story of Anna O.* New York: Walker Press.

Freud, A. (1922). Beating fantasies and daydreams. In Vol. 1 of *The writings of Anna Freud*. New York: International Universities Press, 1974.

(1927). Four lectures on Psychoanalysis. In Vol 1 of *The writings of Anna Freud*. New York: International Universities Press, 1974.

(1929). *Anna Freud's letters to Eva Rosenfeld*. Peter Heller (Ed.). New York: International Universities Press, 1992.

Freud, A. (1936). *The ego and the mechanisms of defense* (rev. ed.). In Vol. 2 of *The writings of Anna Freud*. New York: International Universities Press, 1966.

(1945). Indications for child analysis. In Vol. 4 of *The writings of Anna Freud*. New York: International Universities Press, 1968.

(1951a). The contributions of psychoanalysis to genetic psychology. In Vol. 4 of *The writings of Anna Freud*. New York: International Universities Press, 1968.

with Dann, Sophie. (1951b). An experiment in group upbringing. In Vol. 4 of *The writings of Anna Freud*. New York: International Universities Press, 1968.

(1952). The mutual influences in the development of ego and id. In Vol. 4 of *The writings of Anna Freud*. New York: International Universities Press, 1968.

(1952/1992). *The Harvard lectures*. J. Sandler (Ed.). Madison, CT: International Universities Press.

(1953). Instinctual drives and their bearing on human behavior. In Vol. 4 of *The writings of Anna Freud*. New York: International Universities Press, 1968.

(1958). Child observation and prediction of development: A memorial lecture in honor of

Ernst Kris. In Vol. 5 of *The writings of Anna Freud*. New York: International Universities Press, 1969.

(1962). Assessment of pathology in childhood. In Vol. 5 of *The writings of Anna Freud*. New York: International Universities Press, 1969.

(1965a). Metapsychological assessment of the adult personality: The adult profile. In Vol. 5 of *The writings of Anna Freud*. New York: International Universities Press, 1969.

(1965b). *Normality and pathology in childhood*. In Vol. 6 of *The writings of Anna Freud*. New York: International Universities Press, 1965.

(1967). Doctoral award address. In Vol. 5 of *The writings of Anna Freud*. New York: International Universities Press, 1969.

(1968). Indications and contraindications of child analysis. In Vol. 7 of *The writings of Anna Freud*. New York: International Universities Press, 1971.

(1969). Difficulties in the path of psychoanalysis: A confrontation of past with present viewpoints. In Vol. 7 of *The writings of Anna Freud*. New York: International Universities Press, 1971.

(1970a). Problems of termination in child analysis. In Vol. 7 of *The writings of Anna Freud*. New York: International Universities Press, 1971.

(1970b). The symptomatology of childhood: A preliminary attempt at classification. In Vol. 7 of *The writings of Anna Freud*. New York: International Universities Press, 1971.

(1972). The widening scope of psychoanalytic child psychology, normal and abnormal. In Volume 8 of *The writings of Anna Freud*. New York: International Universities Press, 1981.

(1978). The principal task of child analysis. In Volume 8 of *The writings of Anna Freud*. New York: International Universities Press, 1981.

Freud, A., & Burlingham, D. (1944). *Infants without families*. In Vol. 3 of *The writings of Anna Freud*. New York: International Universities Press, 1973.

Freud, A., Nagera, H., & Freud, W. E. (1965). Metapsychological assessment of The adult personality: The adult profile. *Psychoanalytic Study of The Child, 20*, 9–41.

Freud, S. (1894). The neuro-psychoses of defence. In Vol. III of *The standard edition of The complete psychological works of Sigmund Freud*. James Strachey (Ed.). London: Hogarth, 1962.

(1895). Project for a scientific psychology. In Vol. I of *The standard edition*. London: Hogarth, 1966.

(1896a). Heredity and the aetiology of the neuroses. In Vol. III of *The standard edition*. London: Hogarth, 1962.

(1896b). Further remarks on the neuro-psychoses of defence. In Vol. III of *The standard edition*. London: Hogarth, 1962.

(1896c). The aetiology of hysteria. In Vol. III of *The standard edition*. London: Hogarth, 1962.

(1897). Extracts from the Fliess papers. In Vol. I of *The standard edition*. London: Hogarth, 1966.

(1898). Sexuality in the aetiology of the neuroses. In Vol. III of *The standard edition*. London: Hogarth, 1962.

(1900). The interpretation of dreams. In Volumes IV and V of *The standard edition*. London: Hogarth, 1953.

(1901). The psychopathology of everyday life. In Vol. VI of *The standard edition*. London: Hogarth, 1960.

(1905). Three essays on the theory of sexuality. In Vol. VII of *The standard edition*. London: Hogarth, 1953.

(1908a). On the sexual theories of children. In Vol. IX of *The standard edition*. London: Hogarth, 1959.

(1908b). Character and anal eroticism. In Vol. IX of *The standard edition*. London: Hogarth, 1959.

(1910a). Five lectures on psychoanalysis. In Vol. XI of *The standard edition*. London: Hogarth, 1957.

(1910b). The psychoanalytic view of psychogenic disturbance of vision. In Vol. XI of *The standard edition*. London: Hogarth, 1957.

Freud, S. (1911). Formulations of the two principles of mental functioning. In Vol. XII of *The standard edition*. London: Hogarth, 1958.

(1912). A note on the unconscious in psychoanalysis. In Vol. XII of *The standard edition*. London: Hogarth, 1958.

(1913a). On beginning the treatment. In Vol. XII of *The standard edition*. London: Hogarth, 1958.

(1913b). Totem and taboo. In Vol. XIII of *The standard edition*. London: Hogarth, 1958.

(1914a). On narcissism: An introduction. In Vol. XIV of *The standard edition*. London: Hogarth, 1957.

(1914b). On the history of the psychoanalytic movement. In Vol. XIV of *The standard edition*. London: Hogarth, 1957.

(1915a). Instincts and their vicissitudes. In Vol. XIV of *The standard edition*. London: Hogarth, 1957.

(1915b). Repression. In Vol. XIV of *The standard edition*. London: Hogarth, 1957.

(1915c). The unconscious. In Vol XIV of *The standard edition*. London: Hogarth, 1957.

(1915d). A phylogenetic fantasy: An overview of the transference neuroses. Cambridge, MA: Harvard University Press, 1987.

(1916). Introductory lectures on psychoanalysis. Volumes XV and XVI of *The standard edition*. London: Hogarth, 1961 and 1963.

(1917a). A difficulty in the path of psychoanalysis. In Vol. XVII of *The standard edition*. London: Hogarth, 1955.

(1917b). Mourning and melancholia. In Vol. XIV of *The standard edition*. London: Hogarth, 1957.

(1918). From the history of an infantile neurosis. In J. Strachey (Ed. and Trans.), *The standard edition of the complete psychological works of Sigmund Freud* (Vol. 17). London: Hogarth, 1955.

(1919). "A child is being beaten": A contribution to the study of the origin of sexual perversions. In Vol. XVII of *The standard edition*. London: Hogarth, 1955.

(1920a). Beyond the pleasure principle. In Vol. XVIII of *The standard edition*. London: Hogarth, 1955.

(1920b). A note on the prehistory of the technique of analysis. In Vol. XVIII of *The standard edition*. London: Hogarth, 1955.

(1921). Group psychology and the analysis of the ego. In J. Strachey (Ed. and Trans.), *The standard edition of the complete psychological works of Sigmund Freud*. (Vol. 18). London: Hogarth, 1955.

(1923). The ego and the id. In Vol. XIX of *The standard edition*. London: Hogarth, 1961.

(1924). A note upon the mystic writing pad. In Vol. XIX of *The standard edition*. London: Hogarth, 1961.

(1925a). An autobiographical study. In Vol. XX of *The standard edition*. London: Hogarth, 1959.

(1925b). Some psychical consequences of the anatomical distinction between the sexes. In

Vol. XIX of *The standard edition*. London: Hogarth, 1961.

(1925c). Some additional notes on dream-interpretation as a whole. In Vol XIX of *The standard edition*. London: Hogarth, 1961.

(1926). Inhibitions, symptoms and anxiety. In Vol. XX of *The standard edition*. London: Hogarth, 1959.

(1930). Civilization and its discontents. In Vol. XXI of *The standard edition*. London: Hogarth, 1961.

(1931). Female sexuality. In Vol. XXI of *The standard edition*. London: Hogarth, 1961.

(1933). New introductory lectures. In Vol. XXII of *The standard edition*. London: Hogarth, 1964.

(1936). A disturbance of memory on the Acropolis. In Vol. XXII of *The standard edition*. London: Hogarth, 1964.

(1940). An outline of psychoanalysis. In Vol. XXIII of *The standard edition*. London: Hogarth, 1964.

(1954). *The origin of psychoanalysis: Letters to Wilhelm Fliess, drafts and notes, 1897–1902*. Marie Bonaparte, Anna Freud, & Ernst Kris (Eds.). New York: Basic Books.

(1960). *The letters of Sigmund Freud*. Ernst L. Freud (Ed.). New York: Basic Books.

Freud, S. and Jones, E. (1993). *The complete correspondence of Sigmund Freud and Ernest Jones; 1908–1939*. R. A. Paskauskas (Ed.). Cambridge, MA: Belknap-Harvard University Press.

Freud, S., & Jung, C. G. (1974). *The Freud/Jung letters*. William McGuire (Ed.). Princeton, NJ: Princeton University Press.

Freud, S., & Zweig, A. (1970). *The letters of Sigmund Freud and Arnold Zweig*. Ernst L. Freud (Ed.). New York: Harcourt.

Freud, W. E. (1972). The baby profile: Part II. *The Psychoanalytic Study of the Child*, 26, 172–194.

Friedman, L. J. (2000). *Identities architect*. Cambridge, MA: Harvard University Press.

Fromm, E. (1959). *Sigmund Freud's mission: An analysis of his personality and influence*. New York: Simon & Schuster, 1962.

(1973). *The anatomy of human destructiveness*. New York: Holt, Rinehart and Winston.

Furtmüller, C. (1973). Alfred Adler: A biographical essay. In H. L. Ansbacher & R. Ansbacher (Eds.), *Superiority and social interest*. New York: Viking.

Fuster, J. M. (1958). Effects of stimulation of brain stem on tachistoscopic perception. *Science*, *127*, 150.

Garcia, J., & Koelling, R. A. (1966). The relation of cue to consequence in avoidance learning. *Psychonomic Science*, *4*, 123–124.

Garcia, J., McGowan, B. K., Ervin, F. R., & Koelling, R. A. (1968). Cues: Their relative effectiveness as a function of reinforcer. *Science*, *160*, 794–795.

Gaulin, S. J., & McBurney, D. (2001). *Psychology: An evolutionary approach*. Upper Saddle River, NJ: Prentice Hall.

Gay, P. (1988). *Freud: A life for our time*. New York: Norton.

Gedo, J. E. (1976). Freud's self-analysis and his scientific ideas. In J. E. Gedo & G. H. Pollock (Eds.), *Freud: The fusion of science and humanism. Psychological Issues*, Monograph Nos. 34/35. New York: International Universities Press.

Gendlin, E. T. (1964). A theory of personality change. In P. Worschel & D. Byrne (Eds.), *Personality change*. New York: Wiley.

(1966). Research in psychotherapy with schizophrenic patients and the nature of that illness. In J. T. Hart & T. M. Tomlinson (Eds.), *New directions in client-centered therapy*. Boston: Houghton Mifflin, 1970 (paper originally published in *American Journal of Psychotherapy*, 1966, *20*, 4–16).

(1968). Focusing ability in psychotherapy, personality, and creativity. In J. M. Shlien (Ed.), *Research in psychotherapy*, Vol. III. Washington, DC: American Psychological Association.

(1970). Existentialism and experiential psychotherapy. In J. T. Hart & T. M. Tomlinson (Eds.), *New directions in client-centered therapy*. Boston: Houghton Mifflin.

Goble, F. (1970). *The third force: The psychology of Abraham Maslow*. New York: Grossman.

Goldman, D. (1993). *In search of the real: The origins and originality of D. W. Winnicott*. New York: Jason Aronson.

Grammar, K. & Thornhill, R. (1994). Human (Homo sapiens) facial attractiveness and sexual selection: The role of symmetry and averageness. *Journal of Comparative Psychology*, *108*, 233–242.

Gray, J. A. (1985). Issues in the neuropsychology of anxiety. In A. H. Tuma & Jack D. Masser (Eds.), *Anxiety and the anxiety disorders*, pp. 5–26. Hillsdale, NJ: Lawrence Erlbaum Associates.

Grigg, K. A. (1973). "All roads lead to Rome": The role of the nursemaid in Freud's dreams. *American Journal of Psychoanalysis*, *21*, 108–126.

Groddeck, Georg (1922). *The book of the it.* New York: New American Library, 1961.

Grosskurth, P. (1986). *Melanie Klein: Her world and her work.* Cambridge, MA: Harvard University Press.

Guastello, S. J. (1993). A two (and a half) tiered trait taxonomy. *American Psychologist*, *48*, 1298.

Gupta, B. S. (1973). The effects of stimulant and depressant drugs on verbal conditioning. *British Journal of Psychology*, *64*, 553–557.

Hall, M. H. (1968). A conversation with Abraham Maslow, In R. E. Schell (Ed.), *Readings in Developmental Psychology Today.* New York: CRM Books, 1977 (first published in *Psychology Today*, July, 1968).

Hamilton, William D. (1964a). The genetical evolution of social behavior. I. *Journal of Theoretical Biology*, *7*, 1–16.

(1964b). The genetical evolution of social behavior. II. *Journal of Theoretical Biology*, *7*, 17–52.

Hart, J. (1970). The development of client-centered therapy. In J. T. Hart & T. M. Tomlinson (Eds.), *New directions in client-centered therapy.* Boston: Houghton Mifflin.

Hart, J. T., & T. M. Tomlinson (Eds.). (1970). *New directions in client-centered therapy.* Boston: Houghton Mifflin.

Hartmann, H. (1939). *Ego psychology and the problem of adaptation.* New York: International Universities Press, 1958.

(1964). *Papers on psychoanalytic psychology. Psychological Issues*, Monograph No. 14. New York: International Universities Press.

Hebb, D. O. (1955). Drives and the C. N. S. (conceptual nervous system). *Psychological Review*, *62*, 243–254.

Hill, R. (1945). Campus values in mate selection. *Journal of Home Economics*, 37, 554–558.

Hoffman, Edward. (1988). *The right to be human: The biography of Abraham Maslow.* Los Angeles, CA: J. P. Tarcher, Inc.

Holt, R. R. (1962). Individuality and generalization in the psychology of personality. *Journal of Personality*, *30*, 377–402.

Horney, K. (1937). *The neurotic personality of our time.* New York: Norton.

(1939). *New ways in psychoanalysis.* New York: Norton.

(1942). *Self-analysis.* New York: Norton.

(1945). *Our inner conflicts.* New York: Norton.

(1946). *Are you considering psychoanalysis?* New York: Norton.

(1950). *Neurosis and human growth.* New York: Norton.

(1967). *Feminine psychology.* New York: Norton.

(1980). *The adolescent diaries of Karen Horney.* New York: Basic Books.

Hughes, J. M. (1989). *Reshaping the psychoanalytic domain: The work of Melanie Klein, W. R. D. Fairbairn, and D. W. Winnicott.* Berkeley, CA: University of California Press.

Hull, C. L. (1943). *Principles of behavior.* New York: Appleton.

(1951). *Essentials of behavior.* New Haven, CT: Yale University Press.

(1952). *A behavior system.* New Haven, CT: Yale University Press.

Jacobs, M. (1995). *D. W. Winnicott.* London, Great Britain: Sage.

James, W. (1902). *The varieties of religious experience.* New York: Modern Library.

Jones, Ernest. (1953). *The life and work of Sigmund Freud: The formative years and the great discoveries*, Vol. 1. New York: Basic Books.

(1955). *The life and work of Sigmund Freud: Years of maturity*, Vol. 2. New York: Basic Books.

(1957). *The life and work of Sigmund Freud: The last phase*, Vol. 3. New York: Basic Books.

Jung, C. G. (1905). The reaction time ratio in the association experiment. In Vol. 2 of *The collected works of C. G. Jung.* R. F. C. Hull (Trans.). Princeton, NJ: Princeton University Press, 1973.

(1909). The psychological diagnosis of evidence. In Vol. 2 of *The collected works of C. G. Jung.* Princeton, NJ: Princeton University Press, 1973.

(1912). Symbols of transformation (2nd ed.) In Vol. 5 of *The collected works of C. G. Jung.* Princeton, NJ: Princeton University Press, 1956.

(1913). On the doctrine of complexes. In Vol. 2 of *The collected works of C. G. Jung.* Princeton, NJ: Princeton University Press, 1973.

(1916). General aspects of dream psychology. In Vol. 8 of *The collected works of C. G. Jung.* Princeton, NJ: Princeton University Press, 1969.

(1917). Two essays on analytical psychology. In Vol. 7 of *The collected works of C. G. Jung.* Princeton, NJ: Princeton University Press, 1953 and 1966.

(1921). Psychological types. In Vol. 6 of *The collected works of C. G. Jung.* Princeton, NJ: Princeton University Press, 1971.

(1931). The structure of the psyche. In Vol. 8 of *The collected works of C. G. Jung.* Princeton, NJ: Princeton University Press, 1969.

(1936). The archetypes and the collective unconscious. In Vol. 9i of *The collected works of C. G. Jung.* Princeton, NJ: Princeton University Press, 1959 and 1969.

(1938). Psychological aspects of the mother archetype. In Vol. 9i of *The collected works of C. G. Jung.* Princeton, NJ: Princeton University Press, 1959 and 1969.

(1939). Conscious, unconscious and individuation. In Vol. 9i of *The collected works of C. G. Jung.* Princeton, NJ: Princeton University Press, 1959 and 1969.

(1948). On psychic energy. In Vol. 8 of *The collected works of C. G. Jung.* Princeton, NJ: Princeton University Press, 1959.

(1950a). On mandalas. In Vol. 9i of *The collected works of C. G. Jung.* Princeton, NJ: Princeton University Press, 1959 and 1969.

(1950b). Aion: Researches into the phenomenology of the self. Volume *9ii* of *The collected works of C. G. Jung.* Princeton, NJ: Princeton University Press, 1959 and 1969.

(1952). Synchronicity: An acausal connecting principle. In Vol. 8 of *The collected works of C. G. Jung.* Princeton, NJ: Princeton University Press, 1969.

(1959). Televised interview with John Freeman: *Face to Face: Carl Gustav Jung.* British Broadcasting Corporation, October 22, 1959.

(1961). *Memories, dreams, reflections.* A. Jaffé (Ed.). New York: Pantheon.

(1968). *Analytical psychology: Its theory and practice.* (The Tavistock Lectures.) New York: Pantheon.

(1972). The structure and dynamics of the psyche. *The collected works* (Bollingen series XX, 20 vols.). Trans. R. F. C. Hull. In H. Read, M. Fordham, & G. Adler (Eds.), *Psychological types* (CW 8). Princeton, NJ: Princeton University Press.

Kahr, B. (1996). *D. W. Winnicott: A biographical portrait.* New York: International Universities Press.

Kelly, G. A. (1955). *The psychology of personal constructs*, vols. 1 and 2. New York: Norton.

(1963). The autobiography of a theory. In B. Maher (Ed.), *Clinical psychology and personality: Selected papers of George Kelly.* New York: Wiley, 1969.

(1964). The language of hypothesis: Man's psychological instrument. In B. Maher (Ed.), *Clinical psychology and personality: Selected papers of George Kelly.* New York: Wiley, 1969 (paper originally published: *Journal of Individual Psychology*, 1964, *20*, 137–152).

Khan, M. (1975/1992). Introduction. In D. W. Winnicott, *Through paediatrics to psycho-analysis.* Collected papers. New York: Bruner-Mazel (Originally published: New York: Basic Books, 1958).

Klein, M. (1921/1975a). Development of a child. In R. E. Money-Kyrle (Ed.), *The writings of Melanie Klein* (Vol I, 1–53). New York: The Free Press (Macmillan).

(1926/1975a). The psychological principles of early analysis. In R. E. Money-Kyrle (Ed.), *The writings of Melanie Klein* (Vol I, 128–138). New York: The Free Press (Macmillan).

(1927/1975a). Symposium on child-analysis. In R. E. Money-Kyrle (Ed.), *The writings of Melanie Klein* (Vol I, 139–169). New York: The Free Press (Macmillan).

(1928/1975a). Early stages of the Oedipus conflict. In R. E. Money-Kyrle (Ed.), *The writings of Melanie Klein* (Vol I, 210–218). New York: The Free Press (Macmillan).

(1929/1975a). Infantile anxiety-situations reflected in a work of art and in the creative impulse. In R. E. Money-Kyrle (Ed.), *The writings of Melanie Klein* (Vol I, 210–218). New York: The Free Press.

Klein, M. (1931/1975a). A contribution to the theory of intellectual inhibition. In R. E. Money-Kyrle (Ed.), *The writings of Melanie Klein* (Vol I, 236–247). New York: The Free Press.

(1932/1975b). The psycho-analysis of children. In H. A. Thorner (Ed.) and Alix Strachey (Trans.), *The writings of Melanie Klein* (Vol II). New York: The Free Press (Macmillan).

(1933/1975a). The early development of conscience in the child. In R. E. Money-Kyrle (Ed.), *The writings of Melanie Klein* (Vol I, 248–257). New York: The Free Press (Macmillan).

(1935/1975a). A contribution to the psychogenesis of manic-depressive states. In R. E. Money-Kyrle (Ed.), *The writings of Melanie Klein* (Vol. I, 262–289). New York: The Free Press (Macmillan).

(1936/1975a). Weaning. In R. E. Money-Kyrle (Ed.), *The writings of Melanie Klein* (Vol. I, 290–305). New York: The Free Press (Macmillan).

(1937/1975a). Love, guilt and reparation. In R. E. Money-Kyrle (Ed.), *The writings of Melanie Klein* (Vol I, 306–343). New York: The Free Press (Macmillan).

(1940/1975a). Mourning and its relation to manic-depressive states. In R. E. Money-Kyrle (Ed.), *The writings of Melanie Klein* (Vol. I, 344–359). New York: The Free Press (Macmillan).

(1945/1975a). The Oedipus complex in the light of early anxieties. In R. E. Money-Kyrle (Ed.), *The writings of Melanie Klein* (Vol. I, 370–419). New York: The Free Press (Macmillan).

(1946/1975c). Notes on some schizoid mechanisms. In Roger Money-Kyrle (Ed.), *The writings of Melanie Klein* (Vol III, 1–24). New York: The Free Press (Macmillan).

(1952/1975c). The emotional life of the infant. In Roger Money-Kyrle (Ed.), *The writings of Melanie Klein* (Vol. III, 61–93). New York: The Free Press (Macmillan).

(1957/1975c). Envy and gratitude. In Roger Money-Kyrle (Ed.), *The writings of Melanie Klein* (Vol III, 176–235). New York: The Free Press (Macmillan).

(1958/1975c). On the development of mental functioning. In Roger Money-Kyrle (Ed.), *The writings of Melanie Klein* (Vol III, 236–246). New York: The Free Press (Macmillan).

(1961). Narrative of a child analysis. In Eliott Jacques (Ed.), *The writings of Melanie Klein* (Vol IV). New York: The Free Press (Macmillan).

Krane, R. V., & Wagner, A. R. (1975). Taste aversion learning with a delayed shock US: implications for the generality of the laws of learning. *Journal of Comparative and Physiological Psychology*, 88, 882–889.

Kris, E. (1954). Editor's introduction. In M. Bonaparte, E. Kris, & A. Freud (Eds.), *The origins of psychoanalysis: Letters of Sigmund Freud to Wilhelm Fliess, drafts and notes, 1897–1902*. New York, Basic Books.

Laufer, M. (1965). Assessment of adolescent disturbances: The application of Anna Freud's diagnostic profile. *The Psychoanalytic Study of the Child*, 20, 99–123.

Laverty, S. G. (1958). Sodium amytal and extraversion. In H. J. Eysenck (Ed.), *Readings in extraversion-intraversion*, vol. 3: *Bearings on basic psychological processes*. London: Staples, 1971 (paper originally published in *Journal of Neurology and Neurosurgery and Psychiatry*, 1958, *21*, 50–54).

Lazarus, R. S., & Launier, R. (1978). Stress-related transactions between person and environment. In L. A. Pervin & M. Lewis (Eds.), *Perspectives in interactional psychology*. New York: Plenum.

Lindsley, D. B. (1951). Emotion. In S. S. Stevens (Ed.), *Handbook of experimental psychology* (pp. 473–516). New York: Wiley.

Little, M. I. (1990). *Psychotic anxieties and containment: A personal record of an analysis with Winnicott*. New York: Jason Aronson.

Lumsden, C. J., & Wilson, E. O. (1981). *Genes, mind, and culture, the coevolutionary process*. Cambridge, MA: Harvard University Press.

Malmo, R. B. (1959). A neurophysiological dimension. *Psychological Review*, *66*, 367–386.

Marcia, J. (1966). Development and validation of ego-identity status. *Journal of Personality and Social Psychology*, *3*, 551–558.

(1993). The ego identity status approach to ego identity. In J. E. Marcia, A. S. Waterman, D. R. Matteson, S. L. Archer, & J. L. Orlofsky (Eds.), *Ego identity: A handbook for psychosocial research*. New York: Springer-Verlag.

Marcia, J., & Friedman, M. L. (1970). Ego identity status in college women, *Journal of Personality*, *38*, 249–263.

Martin, J. (1994). *The construction and understanding of psychotherapeutic change*. New York: Teachers College Press.

Maslow, A. H. (1936a). The role of dominance in the social and sexual behavior of infra-human primates: I. Observations at Vilas Park Zoo. In R. J. Lowry (Ed.), *Dominance, self-esteem, self-actualization: Germinal papers of A. H. Maslow*. Monterey, CA: Brooks-Cole, 1973 (paper originally published in *Journal of Genetic Psychology*, 1936, *48*, 261–277).

(1936b). The role of dominance in the social and sexual behavior of infra-human primates: II. An experimental determination of the behavior syndrome of dominance. In R. J. Lowry (Ed.), *Dominance, self-esteem, self-actualization: Germinal papers of A. H. Maslow*. Monterey, CA: Brooks-Cole, 1973 (paper originally published in *Journal of Genetic Psychology*, 1936, *48*, 278–309).

Maslow, A. H. (1937). Dominance-feeling, behavior and status. In R. J. Lowry (Ed.), *Dominance, self-esteem, self-actualization: Germinal papers of A. H. Maslow*. Monterey, CA: Brooks-Cole, 1973 (paper originally published in *Psychological Review*, 1937, *44*, 404–429).

(1939). Dominance, personality and social behavior In women. In R. J. Lowry (Ed.), *Dominance, self-esteem, self-actualization: Germinal papers of A. H. Maslow*. Monterey, CA: Brooks-Cole, 1973 (paper originally published in *Journal of Social Psychology*, 1939, *10*, 3–39).

(1942). Self-esteem (dominance-feeling) and sexuality in women. In R. J. Lowry (Ed.), *Dominance, self-esteem, self-actualization: Germinal papers of A. H. Maslow*. Monterey, CA: Brooks-Cole, 1973 (paper originally published in *Journal of Social Psychology*, 1942, *16*, 259–294).

(1943). A theory of human motivation. In R. J. Lowry (Ed.), *Dominance, self-esteem, self-actualization: Germinal papers of A. H. Maslow*. Monterey, CA: Brooks-Cole, 1973 (paper originally published in *Psychological Review*, 1943, *50*, 370–396).

(1962). *Toward a psychology of being*. New York: Van Nostrand.

(1964). *Religions, values and peak-experiences*. New York: Viking.

(1966). *The psychology of science: A reconnaissance*. New York: Harper & Row.

(1968). *Towards a psychology of being*. New York: Van Nostrand.

(1970). *Motivation and personality* (2nd ed.). New York: Harper & Row.

(1971). *The farther reaches of human nature*. New York: Viking.

(1979). *The journals of Abraham Maslow*. R. J. Lowry (Ed.). Lexington, MA: Lewis Publishing, 1982 (originally published as a two-volume work by Brooks-Cole Publishing, Monterey, CA, 1979).

Masson, J. M. (1984a). Freud and the seduction theory. *The Atlantic Monthly*, February, 33–60.

(1984b). *The assault on truth: Freud's suppression of the seduction theory*. New York: Farrar, Straus & Giroux.

(Ed.). (1985). *The complete letters of Sigmund Freud to Wilhelm Fliess: 1887–1904*. Cambridge, MA: Harvard University Press.

May, Rollo (1939/1967). *The art of counseling*. New York: Abingdon Press.

(1950/1970). *The meaning of anxiety*. New York: Ronald Press (paperback reissue) New York: Washington Square Press.

(1953). *Man's search for himself*. New York: Norton.

(1958a). The origins and significance of the existential movement in psychology. In R. May, E. Angel, and H. F. Ellenberger (Eds.), *Existence: A new dimension in psychiatry and psychology*. New York: Basic Books.

(1958b). Contributions of existential psychotherapy. In R. May, E. Angel, and H. F. Ellenberger (Eds.), *Existence: A new dimension in psychiatry and psychology*. New York: Basic Books.

(1960/1965). Existential bases of psychotherapy. In Ohmer Milton (Ed.), *Behavior disorders: Perspectives and trends*. New York: Lippincott (originally published in *Journal of OrthoPsychiatry*, 1960, *30*, 685–695; also anthologized in R. May [Ed.], *Existential psychology*. New York: Random House, 1961; see also May, 1983, Ch. 2).

(1961). The emergence of existential psychology. In R. May (Ed.), *Existential psychology*. New York: Random House.

(1967/1979). *Psychology and the human dilemma*. New York: Norton.

(1969). *Love and will*. New York: Norton (paperback: New York, Delta Books, 1969).

(1972). *Power and innocence: A search for the sources of violence*. New York: Norton.

(1973). *Paulus: A personal portrait of Paul Tillich*. New York: Harper & Row.

(1981). *Freedom and destiny*. New York: Norton.

(1983). *The discovery of being: Writings in existential psychology*. New York: Norton.

(1985). *My quest for beauty*. Dallas, TX: Saybrook Publishing.

(1986). The problem of evil. In *Politics and innocence*. Dallas, TX: Saybrook.

(1989). Rollo May: A man of meaning and myth. Interview with F. E. Rabinowitz, Glenn Good, and Liza Cozad. *Journal of Counseling and Development*, *67*, 436–441.

McCrae, R. R. (1994). A reformulation of Axis II: Personality and personality-related problems. In P. T. Costa, & T. A. Widiger (Eds.), *Personality disorders and the five-factor model of personality*. Washington, DC: American Psychological Association.

McGinnis, R. (1958). Campus values in mate selection. *Social Forces*, *35*, 368–373.

McLaughlin, R. J., & Eysenck, H. J. (1967). Extraversion, neuroticism and paired-associate learning. In H. J. Eysenck (Ed.), *Readings in extraversion-intraversion*, vol. 3: *Bearings on basic psychological processes*. London: Staples, 1971 (paper originally published in *Journal of Experimental Research in Personality*, 1967, *2*, 128–132).

McLeary, R. A., & Lazarus, R. S. (1949). Autonomic discrimination without awareness. *Journal of Personality*, *18*, 171–179.

McLynn, F. (1997). *Carl Gustav Jung*. New York: St. Martin's Press.

Milgram, S. (1974). *Obedience to authority*. New York: Harper & Row.

Miller, L. (1991). *Freud's brain: Neuropsychodynamic foundations of psychoanalysis*. New York: Guilford.

Miller, N., & Dollard, J. (1941). *Social learning and imitation*. New Haven, CT: Yale University Press.

Mitchell, Juliet (Ed.), (1986). *The selected Melanie Klein*. New York: The Free Press (Macmillan).

Monte, C. F. (1975). *Psychology's scientific endeavor*. New York: Praeger.

Moruzzi, G., and Magoun, H. W. (1949/1964). Brain stem reticular formation and activation of the EEG. In R. L. Isaacson (Ed.), *Basic readings in neuropsychology*. New York: Harper & Row. (paper originally published: *Electroencephalography and Clinical Neurophysiology*, 1949, *1*, 455–473).

Mosak, H. H., & Kopp, R. R. (1973). The early recollections of Adler, Freud, and Jung. *Journal of Individual Psychology*, 29, 157–166.

Mosak, H. M. & Maniacci, M. (1999). *A primer of Adlerian psychology: The analytic-behavioral-cognitive psychology of Alfred Adler*. Philadelphia: Brunner-Routledge.

Murphy, G., & Kovach, J. K. (1972). *Historical introduction to modern psychology* (3d ed.). New York: Harcourt.

Murray, H. A. (1938). *Explorations in personality*. New York: Oxford University Press.

Myers, I. B. (1972). *Myers-Briggs type indicator manual*. Palo Alto, CA: Consulting Psychologists Press.

Orgler, H. (1963). *Alfred Adler: The man and his work*. New York: Capricorn (Putnam).

Panskepp, J. (1988) Attention deficit hyperactivity disorders, psychostimulants and intolerance of childhood playfulness: A tragedy in the making? *Current Directions in Psychological Science*. *7*, 91–98.

Papez, J. W. (1937). A proposed mechanism of emotion. *Archives of Neurology and Psychiatry*, *38*, 725–744.

Parisi, T. (1987). Why Freud failed. *American Psychologist*, *42*(3), 235–245.

(1988). Freud's stance and mine. *American Psychologist*, *43*(8), 663–664.

Pavlov, I. P. (1927). *Conditioned reflexes: An investigation into the physiological activity of the cortex*. G. V. Anrep (Trans.). New York: Dover.

(1928). *Lectures on conditioned reflexes*, Vol. 1. W. Horsely Gantt (Trans.). New York: International Publishers.

Perry, W. G. (1970). *Forms of intellectual and ethical development in the college years: A scheme*. Fort Worth, TX: Harcourt, Brace Jovanovich.

Pettigrew, T. (1999). Gordon Willard Allport: A tribute. *Journal of Social Issues*, *55*(3), 415–427.

Phillips, A. (1988). *Winnicott*. Cambridge, MA: Harvard University Press.

Popper, K. (1959). *The logic of scientific discovery*. New York: Basic Books.

(1963). *Conjectures and refutations*. New York: Basic Books.

(1965). *Conjectures and refutations* (rev. ed). London: Routledge and Kegan Paul.

Postman, L. (1962). *Psychology in the making*. New York: Knopf.

Quinn, S. (1987). *A mind of her own: The life of Karen Horney*. New York: Summit Books (Simon & Schuster).

Rabinowitz, F. E., Good, G., & Cozad, L. (1989). Rollo May: A man of meaning and myth. *Journal of Counseling and Development*, 1989, *67*, 436–441.

Rachman, S. (Ed.). (1963). *Critical essays on psychoanalysis.* New York: Macmillan.

(1978). *Fear and courage.* San Francisco: Freeman.

(1990). *Fear and courage* (2nd ed.) San Francisco: Freeman.

Rank, O. (1929). *The trauma of birth.* New York: Harper & Row, 1973.

(1932). *The myth of the birth of the hero.* New York: Vintage, 1959.

(1941). *Beyond psychology.* New York: Dover.

Rescorla, R. A., & Solomon, R. (1967). Two-process learning theory: Relationships between Pavlovian conditioning and instrumental learning. *Psychological Review*, *74*, 151–182.

Ritvo, Lucille B. (1990). *Darwin's influence on Freud: A tale of two sciences.* New Haven: Yale University Press.

Roazen, P. (1968). *Freud: Political and social thought.* New York: Knopf.

(1969). *Brother animal: The story of Freud and Tausk.* New York: Knopf.

(1971). *Freud and his followers.* New York: Meridian Books.

Rogers, C. R. (1942). *Counseling and psychotherapy.* Boston: Houghton Mifflin.

(1951). *Client-centered therapy.* Boston: Houghton Mifflin.

(1954). The case of Mrs. Oak: A research analysis. In C. R. Rogers & R. F. Dymond (Eds.), *Psychotherapy and personality change* (pp. 259–348). Chicago: University of Chicago Press.

(1957). The necessary and sufficient conditions of therapeutic personality change. *Journal of Consulting Psychology*, *21*, 95–103.

Rogers, C. R. (1958). A tentative scale for the measurement of process in psychotherapy. In A. Rubenstein & M. B. Parloff (Eds.), *Research in psychotherapy*, Vol. 1. Washington, DC: American Psychological Association, 1962.

(1959). A theory of therapy, personality and interpersonal relationships as developed in the client-centered framework. In S. Koch (Ed.), *Psychology: A study of a science*, Vol. III, *Formulations of the person in the social context.* New York: McGraw-Hill.

(1961). *On becoming a person.* Boston: Houghton Mifflin.

(1964). The concept of the fully functioning person. *Psychotherapy: Theory, Research and Practice*, *1*, 17–26.

(Ed.) (1967a). *The therapeutic relationship and its impact: A study of psychotherapy with schizophrenics.* Madison: University of Wisconsin Press.

(1967b). Autobiography. In E. G. Boring & G. Lindzey (Eds.), *A history of psychology in autobiography*, Vol. 5. New York: Appleton, 1967.

(1974a). In retrospect: forty-six years. *American Psychologist*, *29*(2), 115–123.

(1974b). Remarks on the future of client-centered therapy. In D. A. Wexler & L. North Rice (Eds.), *Innovations in client-centered therapy.* New York: Wiley.

(1978). Personal communication, July 10, 1978. Sollod record, Archives of the History of American Psychology. University of Akron, Akron, OH.

Rogers, C. R., & R. F. Dymond. (1954). *Psychotherapy and personality change.* Chicago: University of Chicago Press.

Rowe, I., & Marcia, J. (1980). Ego identity status, formal operations, and moral development. *Journal of Youth and Adolescence*, *9*, 87–99.

Rubins, J. L. (1978). *Karen Horney: Gentle rebel of psychoanalysis.* New York: Dial.

Sandler, J. & Freud, A. (1985). *The analysis of defense: The ego and the mechanisms of defense revisited.* New York: International Universities Press.

Sanford, N. (1985). What have we learned about personality? In S. Koch & D. Leary (Eds.), *A century of psychology as a science.* New York: McGraw-Hill.

Sayers, J. (1991). *Mothers of psychoanalysis.* New York: Norton.

Schafer, R. (1976). *A new language for psychoanalysis.* New Haven, CT: Yale University Press.

(1983). *The analytic attitude.* New York: Basic Books.

Schorske, C. E. (1975). Politics and patricide. In *The annual of psychoanalysis*, Vol. 2. New York: International Universities Press.

Schroeder, M. L., Wormworth, J. A., & Livesley, W. J. (1994). Dimensions of personality disorder and the five-factor model of personality. In P. T. Costa & T. A. Widiger (Eds.), *Personality disorders and the five-factor model of personality.* Washington, DC: American Psychological Association.

Schulz, C. G. (1978). Sullivan's clinical contributions during the Sheppard Pratt era: 1923–1930. *Psychiatry*, *41*, 117–128.

Schur, M. (1972). *Freud, living and dying*. New York: International Universities Press.

Segal, J. (1992). *Melanie Klein*. London: Sage Publications.

Seligman, M. E. (1970). On the generality of the laws of learning. *Psychological Review*, *37*, 406–418.

(1971). Phobias and preparedness. *Behavior Therapy*, 2, 307–320.

(1972). *Biological boundaries of learning*. New York: Appleton-Century.

Shadel, W. G., & Cervone, D. (1993). Comment on Goldberg: The big five versus nobody? *American Psychologist*, *48*, 1300–1302.

Shagass, C., & Kerenyi, A. B. (1958). Neurophysiological studies of personality. In H. J. Eysenck (Ed.), *Reading in extraversion-intraversion*, vol. 3: *Bearings on basic psychological processes*. London: Staples, 1971 (paper originally published in *Journal of Nervous and Mental Diseases*, 1958, *126*, 141–147).

Shepher, J. (1971). Mate selection among second generation kibbutz adolescents and adults: Incest avoidance and negative imprinting. *Archives of Sexual Behavior*, *1*, 293–307.

Silverstein, B. (1985). Freud's psychology and its organic foundation: Sexuality and mind-body interactionism. *The Psychoanalytic Review*, *72*, 204–228.

(1988). Will the real Freud stand up, please? *American Psychologist*, *43*(8), 662–664.

(1989a). Oedipal politics and scientific creativity: Freud's 1915 phylogenetic fantasy. *The Psychoanalytic Review*, *76*(3), 403–424.

Silverstein, B. (1989b). Contributions to the history of psychology: LVIII. Freud's dualistic mind-body interactionism: Implications for the development of his psychology. *Psychological Reports*, *64*, 1091–1097.

Silverstein, S.M. & Silverstein, B.R. (1990) Freud and hypnosis: the development of an interactionist perspective. *The Annual of Psychoanalysis*, *18*, 175–194.

Singh, D. (1993). Adaptive significance of waist-to-hip ratio and female physical attractiveness. *Journal of Personality and Social Psychology*, *65*, 293–307.

Singh, D. & Luis, S. (1995). Ethnic and gender consensus for the effect of waist-to-hip ratio on judgments of women's attractiveness. *Human Nature*, *6*, 51–65.

Singh, D. & Young, R. K. (1995). Body weight, waist-to-hip ratio, breasts, and hips: Role in judgments of female attractiveness and desirability for relationships. *Ethology and Sociobiology*, *16*, 483–507.

Sipprelle, C. R., Ascough, J. C., Detrio, D. M., & Horst, P. A. (1977). Neuroticism, extroversion, and response to stress. *Behavior Research and Therapy*, *15*, 411–418.

Skinner, B. F. (1938). *The behavior of organisms*. New York: Appleton Century Crofts, 1966.

(1953). *Science and human behavior*. New York: Free Press.

(1975). The steep and thorny way to a science of behavior. *American Psychologist*, *30*, 42–49.

(1981). Selection by consequences. *Science*, *213*, 501–504.

Sollod, R. N. (1978). Carl Rogers and the origins of client-centered therapy. *Professional Psychology*, *9*(1) 93–104.

Solomon, R. L., & Wynne, L. C. (1954). Traumatic avoidance learning: The principles of anxiety conservation and partial irreversibility. *Psychological Review*, *61*, 353–385.

Solomon, R. L., Kamin, L. J., Wynne, L. C. (1953). Traumatic avoidance learning: The outcomes of several extinction procedures with dogs. *Journal of Abnormal and Social Psychology*, *48*, 291–302.

Sprecher, S. Sullivan, Q., & Hatfield, E. (1994). Mate selection preferences: Gender differences examined in a national sample. *Journal of Personality and Social Psychology*, *66*, 1074–1080.

Stepansky, P. E. (1983). *In Freud's shadow: Adler in context*. Hillsdale, NJ: The Analytic Press (Lawrence Erlbaum Associates).

(Ed.). (1988). Introduction in M. S. Mahler, *The memoirs of Margaret S. Mahler*. New York: The Free Press.

Stephenson, W. (1953). *The study of behavior: Q-technique and its methodology*. Chicago: University of Chicago Press.

Stolorow, R. D., & Atwood, G. E. (1976). An ego-psychological analysis of the work and life of Otto Rank in the light of modern conceptions of narcissism. *The International Review of Psychoanalysis*, *3*, 441–459.

(1978). A defensive-restitutive function of Freud's theory of psychosexual development. *The Psychoanalytic Review*, *65*, 217–238.

(1979). *Faces in a cloud: Subjectivity in personality theory.* New York: Aronson.

Sullivan, H. S. (1953a). *Conceptions of modern psychiatry.* New York: Norton.

(1953b). *The interpersonal theory of psychiatry.* New York: Norton.

(1956). *Clinical studies in psychiatry.* New York: Norton.

(1962). *Schizophrenia as a human process.* New York: Norton.

(1964). *The fusion of psychiatry and social science.* New York: Norton.

(1972). *Personal psychopathology.* New York: Norton.

Sulloway, F. J. (1979). *Freud: Biologist of the mind.* New York: Basic Books.

Swick-Perry, Helen. (1962). Editor's introduction to H. S. Sullivan, *Schizophrenia as a human process.* New York: Norton.

(1982). *Psychiatrist of America: The life of Harry Stack Sullivan.* Cambridge, MA: Belknap Press of Harvard University.

Taft, J. (1951). *The dynamics of therapy in a controlled relationship.* New York: Harper.

Tattersall, I. (1998). *Becoming human: Evolution and human uniqueness.* New York: Harcourt Brace.

Thompson, C. (1962). Harry Stack Sullivan, the man. In H. S. Sullivan, *Schizophrenia as a human process.* New York: Norton (first published in *Psychiatry*, 1949, *12*, 435–437).

Thornhill, R. & Gangestad, S (1994). Human fluctuating symmetry and sexual behavior. *Psychological Science*, *5*, 297–302.

Tillich, P. (1952). *The courage to be.* New Haven, CT: Yale University Press.

Tooby, J. & DeVore, I. (1987). The reconstruction of hominid behavioral evolution through strategic modeling. In W. Kinzey, (Ed.) *Primate models of the origin of human behavior* (pp. 183–237). New York: SUNY Press.

Trivers, R.L. (1971). The evolution of reciprocal altruism. *Quarterly Review of Biology*, *46*, pp. 35–37.

Vaihinger, H. (1911). *The philosophy of "as if."* New York: Harcourt, Brace and World, 1925.

Van den Berg, J.H. (1961). *The changing nature of man.* New York: Pantheon.

Vaugan, F., & Walsh, R. (2000). Transpersonal psychology. A. E. Kazdin (Ed.), *Encyclopedia of psychology*, *8*, 111–114.

Vitz, Paul (1977). *Psychology as religion: The cult of self worship.* Grand Rapids, MI: Eerdmans.

(1988). *Sigmund Freud's Christian unconscious.* New York: Guilford Press.

Wallace, E. R. (1976). Thanatos—A reevaluation. *Psychiatry*, *39*, 386–393.

Wallach, M. & Wallach, L. (1983). *Psychology's sanction for selfishness: The error of egoism in theory and therapy.* San Francisco, CA: W.H. Freeman.

Watson, D., Clark, L. A., & Harkness, A. R. (1994). Structures of personality and their relevance to psychopathology. *Journal of Abnormal Psychology*, *103*, 18–31.

Watson, G. (1940). Areas of agreement in psychotherapy. *American Journal of Orthopsychiatry*, *10*, 698–710.

Watson, R. I. (1963). *The great psychologists.* Philadelphia: Lippincott.

Westermarck, E. A. (1891). *The history of human marriage.* London: MacMillan.

White, M. J. (1977). Sullivan and treatment. *Contemporary Psychoanalysis*, *13*, 317–346.

White, R. W. (1959). Motivation reconsidered: The concept of competence. *Psychological Review*, *66*, 297–333.

(1981). Exploring personality the long way: The study of lives. In A. I. Rabin, J. Aronoff, A. M. Barclay, & R. A. Zucker (Eds.). *Further explorations in personality.* New York: Wiley-Interscience.

Wiederman, M. (1993). Evolved gender differences in mate selection: Evidence from personal advertisements. *Ethology and Sociology*, *14*, 331–352.

Wiederman, M. & Allgeier, E. (1992). Gender differences in mate selection criteria: Sociobiological or socioeconomic explanations? *Ethology and Sociobiology*, *13*, 115–124.

Wilson, C. (1972). *New pathways in psychology.* New York: Taplinger Publishing Co.

Wilson, Edward O. (1959). Adaptive shift and dispersal in a tropical ant fauna, *Evolution 13*(1), 122–144.

(1971). *The insect societies.* Cambridge MA: Harvard University Press.

(1975). *Sociobiology: The new synthesis.* Cambridge, MA: Harvard University Press.

(1978). *On human nature.* Cambridge, MA: Harvard University Press.

(1984). *Biophilia.* Cambridge, MA: Harvard University Press.

(1994). *Naturalist.* Washington, DC: Island Press.

(2001). Personal communication. May 25, 2001.

Wilson, J. P. (2004) Broken spirits. In J. P. Wilson & B. Drozdek (Eds.), *Broken spirits: The treatment of traumatized asylum seekers, refugees and war and torture victims* (pp. 141–173). New York: Brunner-Routledge.

Windelband, W. (1894). *History and natural science.* Strassburg, Germany: Heitz.

Winnicott, C. (1978). D. W. W.: A reflection. In S. A. Grolnick & L. Barkin (Eds.), *Between reality and fantasy: Transitional objects and phenomena* (15–33). New York: Jason Aronson.

(1983/1991). Interview with M. Neve. In P. L. Rudnytsky, *The psychoanalytic vocation: Rank, Winnicott and the legacy of Freud* (181–193). New Haven: Yale University Press.

(1989). D. W. W.: A reflection. In C. Winnicott, R. Shepherd, & M. Davis, *Psychoanalytic explorations.* Cambridge, MA: Harvard University Press. (For an earlier version, see C. Winnicott, 1978).

Winnicott, D. W. (1931a/1992). A note on normality and anxiety. In D. W. Winnicott, *Through paediatrics to psycho-analysis. Collected papers.* (3–21). New York: Bruner-Mazel.

(1931b/1992). Fidgetiness. In D. W. Winnicott, *Through paediatrics to psycho-analysis. Collected papers* (22–30). New York: Bruner-Mazel.

(1935/1992). The manic defence. In *Through paediatrics to psycho-analysis. Collected papers* (129–144). New York: Bruner-Mazel.

(1936/1992). Appetite and emotional disorder. In *Through paediatrics to psycho-analysis. Collected papers* (33–51). New York: Bruner-Mazel.

(1941/1992). The observation of infants in a set situation. In *Through paediatrics to psycho-analysis. Collected papers* (52–69). New York: Bruner-Mazel.

(1944/1992). Ocular psychoneuroses of childhood. In *Through paediatrics to psycho-analysis. Collected papers* (85–90). New York: Bruner-Mazel.

(1945a). Primitive emotional development. In *Through paediatrics to psycho-analysis. Collected papers* (145–156). New York: Bruner-Mazel (Collection originally published: New York: Basic Books, 1958).

(1945b/1996) Towards an objective study of human nature. In D. W. Winnicott, *Thinking about children* (3–12). R. Shepherd, J. Johns, & H. T. Robinson (Eds.). Reading, MA: Addison-Wesley.

(1948c/1992). Paediatrics and psychiatry. In *Through paediatrics to psycho-analysis. Collected papers* (157–173). New York: Bruner-Mazel.

(1948d/1992). Reparation in respect of mother's organized defence against depression. In *Through paediatrics to psycho-analysis. Collected papers.* (91–96). New York: Bruner-Mazel.

(1951/1992). Transitional objects and transitional phenomena. In *Through paediatrics to psycho-analysis. Collected papers.* (229–242). New York: Bruner-Mazel.

Winnicott, D. W. (1952). Anxiety associated with insecurity. In *Through paediatrics to psycho-analysis. Collected papers.* (97–100). New York: Bruner-Mazel.

(1954–55/1992). The depressive position in normal emotional development. In *Through paediatrics to psycho-analysis. Collected papers* (262–277). New York: Bruner-Mazel.

(1955/1989). Private practice. In D. W. Winnicott, R. Shepherd, and M. Davis (Eds.), *Psychoanalytic explorations* (291–298). Cambridge, MA: Harvard University Press.

(1956/1992). Primary maternal preoccupations. In *Through paediatrics to psycho-analysis.* Collected papers (300–305). New York: Bruner-Mazel (Collection originally published: New York: Basic Books, 1958).

(1957/1965c) Advising parents. In D. W. Winnicott, *The family and individual development* (114–120). Great Britain: Tavistock.

(1958/1965c) Theoretical statement of the field of child psychiatry. In *The family and individual development* (97–105). Great Britain: Tavistock.

(1959/1989). The fate of the transitional object. In *Psychoanalytic explorations* (53–58). C. Winnicott, R. Shepherd, & M. Davis (Eds.). Cambridge, MA: Harvard University Press.

(1960/1965a). Ego distortion in terms of true and false self. In D. W. Winnicott, *The maturational processes and the facilitating environment. Studies in the theory of emotional development* (140–152). New York: International Universities Press.

(1961/1990). Varieties of psychotherapy. In D. W. Winnicott, *Deprivation and delinquency*

(232–240). C. Winnicott, R. Shepherd, & M. Davis (Eds.). Great Britain: Tavistock/Routledge.

(1962a/1965a). The aims of psychoanalytical treatment. In D. W. Winnicott, *The maturational processes and the facilitating environment. Studies in the theory of emotional development* (166–170). New York: International Universities Press.

(1962b/1965a). A personal view of the Kleinian contribution. In *The maturational processes and the facilitating environment. Studies in the theory of emotional development* (171–178). New York: International Universities Press.

(1962c/1965a). Ego integration in child development. In *The maturational processes and the facilitating environment. Studies in the theory of emotional development* (56–63). New York: International Universities Press.

(1963/1965a). Training for child psychiatry. In *The maturational processes and the facilitating environment. Studies in the theory of emotional development* (193–202). New York: International Universities Press.   (Originally published: *Journal of Child Psychology and Psychiatry*, 1963, *4*, 85–89).

(1964a). *The child, the family, and the outside world.* Reading MA: Addison-Wesley (alternate edition: Pelican Books, 1964).

(1964d/1986). The concept of the false self. In D. W. Winnicott, *Home is where we start from.* C. W. Winnicott, R. Shepherd, & M. Davis (Eds.). New York: Norton.

(1965a). *The maturational processes and the facilitating environment. Studies in the theory of emotional development.* New York: International Universities Press.

(1965b/1989). A child psychiatry case illustrating delayed reaction to loss. In C. Winnicott, R. Shepherd, & M. Davis (Eds.), *Psychoanalytic explorations* (341–368). Cambridge, MA: Harvard University Press.

(1968a/1987). Communication between infant and mother, and mother and infant, compared and contrasted. In Winnicott, D. W. (1987). *Babies and their mothers* (89–103). C. Winnicott, R. Shepherd, & M. Davis (Eds.). Reading, MA: Addison-Wesley.

(1968b/1989). The use of an object and relating through identifications. In *Psychoanalytic explorations* (218–227). C. Winnicott, R. Shepherd,

& M. Davis (Eds.). Cambridge, MA: Harvard University Press.

(1969/1989). Development of the theme of the mother's unconscious as discovered in psychoanalytic practice. In C. Winnicott, R. Shepherd, & M. Davis (Eds.), *Psychoanalytic explorations* (247–250). Cambridge, MA: Harvard University Press.

(1971). *Playing and reality.* Great Britain: Penguin Books.

(1989). *Psychoanalytic explorations.* C. Winnicott, R. Shepherd, and M. Davis (Eds.). Cambridge, MA: Harvard University Press.

(1992). *Through paediatrics to psycho-analysis. Collected papers.* New York: Bruner-Mazel (Originally published: New York: Basic Books, 1958).

(1993). *Talking to parents.* Reading MA: Addison-Wesley.

(1996a/1996). The niffle. In D. W. Winnicott, *Thinking about children* (104–109). R. Shepherd, J. Johns, & H. T. Robinson (Eds.). Reading, MA: Addison-Wesley.

Yerkes, R. M., & Dodson, J. D. (1908). The relation of strength of stimulus to rapidity of habit formation. *Journal of Comparative and Physiological Psychology*, *18*, 459–482.

Young-Bruehl, E. (1988). *Anna Freud: A biography.* New York: Summit Books (Simon and Schuster).

Young, Robert M. (1996). Evolution, biology and psychology from a Marxist point of view. In Parker, I., & Spears, R. Eds. *Psychology and society: Radical theory and practice.* Chicago: Pluto Press, pp. 35–49.

Zeigarnik, B. (1927). On finished and unfinished tasks. In W. D. Ellis (Ed.), *A source book of Gestalt psychology.* New York: Humanities Press, 1967.

Zilboorg, G. (1941). *A history of medical psychology.* New York: Norton.

Zimbardo, P. G., Haney, C., Banks, W. C., & Jaffe, D. (1974). The psychology of imprisonment: Privation, power and pathology. In Z. Rubin (Ed.), *Doing unto others: Explorations in social behavior.* Englewood Cliffs, NJ: Prentice Hall. 61–73.

Zimmer, C. (2001). *Evolution: The triumph of an idea.* New York: Harper Collins.

Photo Credits

Chapter 2

Opener	© Hulton-Deutsch Collection/CORBIS
Figure 2.1	Sigmund Freud Copyrights
Figure 2.2	© University of Vienna Archive, Photo Collection # 106.I.1417
Figure 2.3	Courtesy Freud Museum, London
Figure 2.4	Courtesy Freud Museum, London
Figure 2.5	Mary Evans/Sigmund Freud Copyrights

Chapter 3

Opener	© Corbis-Bettmann
Figure 3.3	Courtesy Library of Congress

Chapter 4

Opener	© Corbis Bettmann
Figure 4.1	Erich Salomon/Magnum Photos, Inc.

Chapter 5

Opener	Courtesy National Library of Medicine
Figure 5.2	Courtesy Library of Congress
Figure 5.5	From *Concerning Mandala Symbolism,* C. G. Jung. trans. from "Uber Mandalasymbolik," *Gestaltungen des Unbewussten,* © 1950, Zurich: Rascher. Reprinted with permission.
Figure 5.6	From *Concerning Mandala Symbolism,* C. G. Jung. trans. from "Uber Mandalasymbolik," *Gestaltungen des Unbewussten,* © 1950, Zurich: Rascher. Reprinted with permission.

Chapter 6

Opener	© Corbis-Bettmann
Figure 6.1	Hulton/Archive/Getty Images
Figure 6.2	© Corbis-Bettmann
Figure 6.3	Courtesy Freud Museum, London/A.W. Freud, et al

Chapter 7

Opener	© The Wellcome Trust Medical Photographic Library, London (both photos)
Figure 7.1	© The Wellcome Trust Medical Photographic Library, London
Figure 7.2	From Max Schur (ed.), *Drives, Affects, Behavior.* Reproduced with permission of International Universities Press, Inc. © 1965 by International Universities Press, Inc.

Chapter 8

Opener	© Corbis-Bettmann

Chapter 9

Opener	Stock Montage
Figure 9.1	From Helen Swick Perry, Psychiatrists of America: *The Life of Harry Stack Sullivan,* The Belknap Press of Harvard University Press; © 1982 by Helen Swick Perry. Reprinted with permission.

Chapter 10

Opener	© Corbis-Bettmann

Chapter 11

Opener	© Corbis-Bettmann

Chapter 12

Opener   Photo by Bernard Gotfryd
Figure 12.1 From Rollo May, 1985, used by permission.

Chapter 13

Opener   © Corbis-Bettmann (both photos)

Chapter 14

Opener   Courtesy Ralph Norman

Chapter 15

Opener   Courtesy Albert Bandura

Chapter 16

Opener   Stock Montage

Chapter 17

Opener   Courtesy E. O. Wilson
Figure 17.1 Courtesy E. O. Wilson
Figure 17.2 Courtesy E. O. Wilson

Name Index

Page references followed by an n indicate material in footnotes. Italic page references refer to material in captions.

Rosenzweig, Saul, 67
Rowe, I., 292
Rubins, J. L., 327–331

S
Sanderson, C., 527
Sandler, J., 200, 201, 203
Sanford, N., 8
Sargent, C., 500
Sartre, Jean-Paul, 377, 400
Sayers, J., 186, 204, 210, 234, 235
Schafer, Roy, 115
Schopenhauer, Arthur, 160
Schorske, C. E., 78
Schroeder, M. L., 527
Schulz, Clarence, 308
Schunk, D. H., 477
Schur, M., 49, 50, 77–78, 103n.3, 108, 183
Schweitzer, Albert, 407
Segal, J., 210
Seligman, M., 477, 521, 547
Shadel, W. G., 527
Shagass, C., 519
Sharman, Henry, 431
Sheldon, Bill, 68
Shepher, Joseph, 559
Silberer, Herbert, 83
Silverstein, B., 16–18, 24, 25, 42, 44, 48, 70–71, 79, 108, 115, 117
Silverstein, S. M., 42, 71
Simerloff, Daniel, 538
Singh, D., 560
Sipprelle, C. R., 520
Skinner, B. F., 361–362, 446, 538, 547, 549
Socrates, 408
Sollod, R., 422, 432, 441, 446
Solomon, R., 490, 521
Sophie (Freud's daughter), 97, 180
Spinoza, Benedict de, 407, 408
Sprecher, S., 561
Stepansky, P. E., 142
Stephens, Deborah, 446
Stephenson, William, 442
Stevenson, Adlai, 407
Stolorow, R., 52, 80
Strachey, James, 19n.1, 70, 245

Sullivan, Ella, 304, *304*, 305, 438
Sullivan, Harry Stack, 298–321, *304*, 377, 392
Sullivan, Q., 561
Sullivan, Timothy, *304*, 305
Sulloway, F. J., 115
Summers, Frank, 265
Swick-Perry, Helen, 304–306, 308, 309, 320

T
Taft, Jesse, 432
Tattersall, I., 552
Taylor, Shelly E., 494
Teasdale, J., 477
Thompson, C., 304, 309
Thorndike, Edward L., 68
Thornhill, R., 535, 560
Tillich, Paul, 380, 384, 385, 387
Tinbergen, Niko, 538, 549
Tomkins, S., 351, 352
Tomlinson, T. M., 429, 446
Tooby, J., 535, 549–552
Trivers, Robert, 535, 549, 551, 566

U
Vaihinger, Hans, 129–131, 144, 145
Van Den Berg, J.H., 9
Van Gogh, Vincent, 155
Vaugan, F., 421
Vitz, Paul, 51, 441, 446
Voltaire, 556
Vygotsky, Lev, 298

W
Wagner, A. R., 547
Wagner, Jauregg, 182
Wallace, Alfred Russel, 539, 549
Wallace, B., 36
Wallace, E. R., 103n.3, 108
Wallach, L., 441, 446
Wallach, M., 441, 446
Walsh, R., 421
Walters, Richard, 473, 493
Washington, George, 407
Watson, D., 527
Watson, Goodwin, 432

Watson, John, 557
Watson, R. I., 27–28, 503
Weiss, Ilona (Fraülein Elisabeth von R.), 33–41, 44
Werner, Ruth, 497–498
Wertheimer, Max, 406
Westermarck, Edward, 559
Wexler, David, 446
White, M. J., 308
White, Robert, 8–9, 347, 479
White, William A., 298, 306
Whitehead, Alfred North, 408
Whitman, Walt, 407
Wiederman, Michael, 560, 561
Wilson, C., 408
Wilson, Edward O., 534–544, *536*, *544*, 546, 549, 551–554, 557, 559–560, 564–566
Wilson, G. D., 67, 500
Wilson, J. P., 277, 413
Wilson, Margo, 558–559
Windelband, Wilhelm, 11, 349
Winnicott, C., 242, 258, 259, 261
Winnicott, Donald W. (D. W.), 72, 208, 209, 237–240, 242–266
Winnicott, John Frederick, 258, 260–261
Wise, Nellie Edith, 351
Woods, Elizabeth Martha, 258, 259
Wormworth, J. A., 527
Wundt, Wilhelm, 504
Wynne, L. C., 521

Y
Yalom, Irvin, 446
Yerkes, Robert M., 515
Young, R. K., 560
Young, Robert M., 540
Young-Bruehl, E., 180–182, *183*, 206

Z
Zarate, Oscar, 565
Zeigarnik, Bluma, 366, 372
Zilboorg, G., 27–28
Zimbardo, Philip, 462
Zimmer, C., 539, 565
Zweig, Arnold, 184

Subject Index

Page references followed by an n indicate material in footnotes. Italic page references refer to material in captions.

in object relations theories, 247
during peak experiences, 415, 416
Integrative amalgam (individual psychology), 127, 145
Integrity (humanistic self-actualization theory), 423
Intellectual interests, motivating (social cognitive theory), 479
Intelligence agency psychologists, 12
Intentionality (existential phenomenology), 393–394, 400
Interests, development of (social cognitive theory), 479
Internal control, selective activation of (social cognitive theory), 488
Internal inhibition (brain), 505–506
Internalization (psychoanalysis):
defined, 118
in psychoanalysis, 107
Interpersonal theory (Sullivan), 298–321
concepts and themes of, 298–299
differentiation of self from universe, 302–303
epochs of development, 314–318
evaluation of, 318–319
me-you personifications, 313–314
modes of experience, 299–300
personality development, 301–302
personal sources of human relationships emphasis, 303–309
personifications of self, 309–311
selective inattention, 313
self-system, 311–312
The Interpretation of Dreams (S. Freud), 49, 76–77, 111
Intimacy vs. isolation stage (psychoanalytic ego psychology), 287–288, 295
Introductory Lectures (S. Freud), 82–83
Introjection, as classic ego defense (psychoanalysis), 203

Introversion:
in analytical psychology, 166–167, 170–171, 178
in biologically based typology, 501–504, 511–512, 519–520
defined, 178
genetic and environmental basis of, 520
and neuroticism, 519, 520
Introverts (biologically based typology), 501
arousal levels, 523
defined, 532
and inverted-U hypothesis, 516–518
melancholic and phlegmatic personalities as, 508
Intuition (analytical psychology):
defined, 178
as ectopsychic function, 167–169, 171
Intuitive extroverts, 160
Intuitive introverts, 171
Inverted simple negative Oedipus complex, 60
Inverted-U hypothesis, 515–518
Irrational functions (analytical psychology), 167, 178
Isolation:
as classic ego defense, 203
in existential phenomenology, 390
in interpersonal theory, 305–306, 318
intimacy vs., 287–288
during late adolescence, 318
overcoming through sex, 390
in psychoanalysis, 203
in psychoanalytic ego psychology, 287–288
and sexual adjustment of preadolescents, 305–306

Jealousy (object relations theories), 230, 265
"Jenny Gove Masterson" letters case, 358–361
Jonah complex, 417, 447
Judgments of excellence (social cognitive theory), 477, 495
Judicious ritualization (psychoanalytic ego psychology), 282, 296
Jungian psychology, *see* Analytical psychology
Justice, need for, 412. *See also* B-values (Being-values)

Kelly's theory, *see* Personal construct theory
Kin selection concept (evolutionary psychology), 289, 541, 566
Klein's theory, *see* Object relations theory (Klein)

Language development, 315
in interpersonal theory, 300, 315
and self as active agent, 482
in social cognitive theory, 482
in syntaxic mode, 300
Late adolescence epoch (interpersonal theory), 317–318
Latency stage (psychoanalysis), 64, 65
Latent content of dreams (psychoanalysis), 80–81
defined, 118
interpreting, 82–84
Learning:
corollaries accounting for, 460
drive theory of, 509–510
imitation, 473–475
observational, 474–475, 495
in personal construct theory, 460
in social cognitive theory, 473–475, 495
Leash principle, 560, 566
Legal interests of children, A. Freud's work for, 204
Legalism, 283, 296
Libido, 54, 152
in analytical psychology, 152, 178
anxiety from repression of, 110
defined, 72, 118, 178
ego and, 105–106
as energy of sexual/pleasure instincts, 94
fixation of, 64, 65, 72
instinctual dynamics based on, 96
in psychoanalysis, 54, 63–67, 72, 94, 96, 105–106, 110, 118, 152
regression of, 66–67
stages in development of, 63–67
Life-course development, existential choices in (humanistic self-actualization theory), 418–419

Self-punishment, symptoms as (psychoanalysis), 38–39
Self-reaction (social cognitive theory), 477, 495
Self-realization (humanistic self-actualization theory), 423–425
Self-regard (humanistic self-actualization theory), 439, 440, 448
Self-regulatory processes in self-system (social cognitive theory), 476, 477, 495
Self-structure (humanistic self-actualization theory), 439–440, 448
Self-system, 301, 311–312, 475–477
  defined, 321, 495
  in interpersonal theory, 301, 311–312, 321
  self-regulatory processes in, 476, 477, 495
  in social cognitive theory, 475–477, 495
Self-worth (humanistic self-actualization theory), 423, 430–433
Sensation (analytical psychology):
  defined, 178
  as ectopsychic function, 167–171
Sensation extroverts, 160
Sensation introverts, 170–171
Sex, as form of love (existential phenomenology), 390–391, 401
Sexual abuse, recovery of repressed memories of (psychoanalysis), 48
Sexual arousal:
  in early adolescence, 317
  in interpersonal theory, 317
  in psychoanalysis, 64
  sources of, 64
Sexual behavior:
  and dominance-feeling, 405–406
  in evolutionary psychology, 559–561
  healthy, criteria for, 287, 288
  incest taboo, 559–560
  mate selection, 560–561
  in psychoanalytic ego psychology, 287, 288
  and self-efficacy, 485
  in social cognitive theory, 485

Sexual development, *see* Psychosexual development
Sexual energy/drive, *see* Libido
Sexual hormones, neuroses caused by, 44
Sexual impulses in children (psychoanalysis), 50
Sexual instincts (psychoanalysis), 94–95, 101
Sexual motives (psychoanalysis):
  as basis of conflict, 44–47
  in dream interpretation, 85
Sexual selection, 539
  defined, 566
  mate selection, 560–561
Shadow archetype, 163–164
  Bad-Me and Not-Me personifications vs., 311
  defined, 178
Shallow living (psychoanalytic social psychology), 337
Shamans, 155–156
Shame, autonomy vs. doubt and (psychoanalytic ego psychology), 281–283
Sheppard and Enoch Pratt Hospital, 306–308
Siblings, relationships with:
  Adler's personal relationship, 122
  Allport's personal relationship, 352
  and birth order, 139–140
  competence comparisons in, 482
  in humanistic trait and self theory, 352
  in individual psychology, 122, 139–140
  in social cognitive theory, 482
Sickle cell anemia, 561
Significant others (interpersonal theory):
  defined, 321
  infants' dealings with, 311
  prototype for development of, 302
Similarity poles (constructs), 467
Simple positive Oedipus complex, 60
Social accommodation (interpersonal theory), 316, 321
Social cognitive theory (Bandura), 472–495
  anxiety and repression model, 489–491
  behaviorism vs., 473–474
  central ideas of, 472–473

chance events in life, 491–492
coping with threat, 479
defined, 495
developmental phases of self-efficacy, 481–488
evaluation of, 492–493
media's impact on current behavior, 492
modeling and observational learning, 474–475
motivating intellectual interests, 479
personal sources of theories, 480–481
reciprocal determinism, 475–476
selective activation of self-controls, 488–489
self-efficacy, 477–480
self-system, 475–477
vicarious reinforcement, 475
Social competence (social cognitive theory):
  defined, 495
  in infancy, 481
Social grooming (evolutionary psychology), 557–558
Social interest (individual psychology):
  and Adler's religious values, 129
  concept of, 136
  defined, 145–146
  individual psychology, 124–125
  in neurotics, 136
  and style of life, 129–130
Sociality corollary (personal construct theory), 461–462
Socially useful personality type (individual psychology), 138, 146
Social subordination (interpersonal theory), 316, 321
Social validation of self-efficacy (social cognitive theory), 483–484
Societal life tasks (individual psychology), 136
Society, impact on personality, 9–10
Society for the Prevention of Cruelty to Children, 432
Sociobiology, 542–543, 566. *See also* Evolutionary psychology

balance between
permissiveness and
authority, 190–192
in client-centered therapy,
436–437
maintaining and interpreting,
189–190
personality changes evoked by,
436–437
in preparatory period, 186–188
in psychoanalytic ego
psychology, 186–192
of S. and A. Freud, 181
Thinking. *See also* Thoughts
in analytical psychology,
167–170, 178
and behaviorist view, 465
defined, 178
as ectopsychic function,
167–170
Thinking extroverts, 160
Thinking introverts, 170
Third force of psychology, 421,
447
Thoughts:
"as if," 129–130
in individual psychology,
129–130
Oedipal repression of, 68
as omnipotent, in neurotic
personality, 52
primary process, 88
in psychoanalysis, 52, 68,
83–85, 99–90
secondary process, 88–89
verbal, origin of, 85
visual representation of, 83–84
Threat, coping with (social
cognitive theory), 479,
491
Thriftiness, in anal-erotic adults,
66
Thumb sucking (interpersonal
theory), 303
Time, erring sense of, 50
Time/space perception during
peak experiences
(humanistic self-
actualization theory), 416,
417
Toilet training:
and anal-erotic personality, 65,
66
of animals vs. humans, 555
in evolutionary psychology,
555
in interpersonal theory,
302–303
in object relations theories, 214
in psychoanalysis, 63, 65, 66

in psychoanalytic ego
psychology, 281
Topographic/systematic model
(psychoanalysis), 120,
193
Topographic viewpoint
(psychoanalysis), 90
Totalism (psychoanalytic ego
psychology), 287, 296
Totalitarian societies, 7
Totem and Taboo (S. Freud), 52,
108, 545
Towards a Psychology of Being
(A. Maslow), 414, 418
Traits, *see* Personality traits
Trait theory, 7. *See also*
Humanistic trait and self
theory (Allport)
Trance theory (hypnosis), 36
Transcendent function (analytical
psychology), 171, 178
Transference:
in child-analyst relationship,
189
defined, 120
and hypnotic suggestion, 42
in object relations theories, 216
in psychoanalysis, 42, 69, 73,
98
in psychoanalytic ego
psychology, 189, 216
Transiency (mystical
experiences), 413, 447
Transitional objects (object
relations theories),
255–257, 266
Transpersonal psychology,
421–422, 447
Transpersonal unconscious, 161.
See also Collective
unconscious
Traumatic neurosis
(psychoanalysis), 98
Traumatic situations
(psychoanalysis):
birth trauma, 110–111
Freud's chronology of,
112–113
Triadic reciprocal determinism
(Bandura), 475–476, 495
Trickster archetype, 163
Triumph (object relations
theories), 223–224
True Self (object relations
theories), 254–255, 266
Trust, in therapeutic alliance
(psychoanalytic ego
psychology), 192
Trust vs. mistrust stage
(psychoanalytic ego

psychology), 280–281,
297
Truth:
need for, 412. *See also*
B-values (Being-values)
Vaihinger's view of, 130
Tunnel vision, 19, 73
Turning against self, as classic
ego defense
(psychoanalysis), 202
Typological postulate
(biologically based
typology), 510–512, 533
Tyranny of the should
(psychoanalytic social
psychology), 333, 345

Umwelt, 377, 378, 385, 401
Unconditional positive regard
(humanistic self-
actualization theory), 435,
448
Unconscious, 161–162, 378–379,
466, 467
in analytical psychology,
148–149, 161–162
censorship system, 81
collective, 161–162. *See also*
Collective unconscious
defined, 120, 401, 471
dreams as revelation of, 75
dynamic, 40–41, 71
in existential phenomenology,
378–379, 401
instincts of, 93–96
in object relations theories, 227
personal, 161
in personal construct theory,
466, 467, 471
pleasure-unpleasure distinction
in, 88
primary process thinking in, 88
in psychoanalysis, 40–41, 71,
75, 81, 85–91, 93–96, 120
psychoanalytic meanings of
term, 89–91
and real vs. imaginary objects,
88
as repressed early memories,
89
response to pleasure principle
by, 89
revealed in dreams, 85–86
and splitting of ego, 227
as stored memories, 89
wish fulfillment in dreams, 87
word association test for
accessing, 148–149
Undoing, as classic ego defense
(psychoanalysis), 203